WEEKEND BREAKS

IN GREAT BRITAIN & IRELAND

timeout.com

Published by Time Out Guides Ltd, a wholly owned subsidiary of Time Out Group Ltd.
Time Out and the Time Out logo are trademarks of Time Out Group Ltd.

© Time Out Group Ltd 2005

10 9 8 7 6 5 4 3 2 1

This edition first published in Great Britain in 2005 by Ebury
Ebury is a division of The Random House Group Ltd,
20 Vauxhall Bridge Road, London SW1V 2SA

Random House Australia Pty Limited, 20 Alfred Street, Milsons Point, Sydney, New South Wales
2061, Australia
Random House New Zealand Limited, 18 Poland Road, Glenfield, Auckland 10, New Zealand
Random House South Africa (Pty) Limited, Endulini, 5A Jubilee Road, Parktown 2193, South Africa

Random House UK Limited Reg. No. 954009

Distributed in USA by Publishers Group West
1700 Fourth Street, Berkeley, California 94710

Distributed in Canada by Penguin Canada Ltd
10 Alcorn Avenue, Toronto, Ontario, Canada M4V 3B2

For further distribution details, see www.timeout.com

ISBN 1-904978-38-X

A CIP catalogue record for this book is available from the British Library

Colour reprographics by Icon, Crowne House, 56-58 Southwark Street, London SE1 1UN

Printed and bound in Germany by Appl. Papers used by Ebury Press are natural, recyclable
products made from wood grown in sustainable forests.

Time Out Guides Limited
Universal House
251 Tottenham Court Road
London W1T 7AB
Tel + 44 (0)20 7813 3000
Fax + 44 (0)20 7813 6001
Email guides@timeout.com
www.timeout.com

Editorial
Editor Sarah Guy
Deputy Editor Lisa Ritchie
Copy Editors Ros Sales, Peter Watts
Researchers Cathy Limb, Jill Emeny
Proofreader Adam Barnes
Indexer Anna Norman

Editorial/Managing Director Peter Fiennes
Series Editor Sarah Guy
Deputy Series Editor Cath Phillips
Business Manager Gareth Garner
Guides Co-ordinator Holly Pick
Accountant Kemi Olufuwa

Design
Art Director Scott Moore
Art Editor Tracey Ridgewell
Senior Designer Oliver Knight
Designer Chrissy Mouncey
Digital Imaging Dan Conway
Ad Make-up Charlotte Blythe

Picture Desk
Picture Editor Jael Marschner
Deputy Picture Editor Tracey Kerrigan
Picture Researcher Helen McFarland

Advertising
Sales Director Mark Phillips
Sales Manager Alison Gray
Advertisement Sales Simon Davies
Advertising Assistant Lucy Butler
Copy Controller Amy Nelson

Marketing
Marketing Director Mandy Martinez
Marketing & Publicity Manager, US Rosella Albanese

Production
Production Director Mark Lamond
Production Controller Samantha Furniss

Time Out Group
Chairman Tony Elliott
Managing Director Mike Hardwick
Group Financial Director Richard Waterlow
Group Commercial Director Lesley Gill
Group General Manager Nichola Coulthard
Group Circulation Director Jim Heinemann
Group Art Director John Oakey
Online Managing Director David Pepper
Group Production Director Steve Proctor
Group IT Director Simon Chappell

Contributors
London Sarah Guy, Simon Cropper; **Winchelsea to Dungeness & Romney Marsh** Yolanda Zappaterra; **Brighton** Peterjon Cresswell; **Chichester & Around** Will Fulford-Jones; **Isle of Wight** Lily Dunn; **Woodstock to Burford** Peter Watts; **Cirencester & Around** Lesley McCave; **Malmesbury & Tetbury** Jonathan Cox; **Bristol** Sophie Blacksell; **The Mendips** Charlie Godfrey-Fausset; **The South Hams** Portia Spooner; **Falmouth & the Roseland Peninsula** Helen Gilchrist; **Padstow & Rock** Hayley Lawrence; **The Isles of Scilly** Gareth Evans; **Orford to Southwold** Janice Fuscoe; **Bury St Edmunds to Lavenham** Angela Jameson Potts; **North Norfolk Coast** Phil Harriss; **The Brecon Beacons** Jessica Eveleigh; **Ludlow** Hugh Graham; **Manchester** David Lloyd; **Harrogate** Jill Turton; **Helmsley & Harome** Ruth Jarvis; **Seaham & the Durham Coast** Sarah Guy; **Windermere & Ambleside** Roopa Gulati; **Edinburgh** Keith Davidson; **Glasgow** Keith Davidson; **Mid Argyll & Bute** Keith Davidson; **Speyside** Keith Davidson; **Strangford Lough** Caroline Workman; **Mid Kerry** Keith Davidson; **Festivals & Events** Zoe Strimpel.

Additional reviews Peter Fiennes, Frances Paffard, Lisa Ritchie. **Thanks to** Simone Baird.

Maps JS Graphics (john@jsgraphics.co.uk)

Photography pages 9, 10, 207, 210, 211, 216, 217, 220, 221, 224, 225, 230, 231, 240, 241, 395 Sam Robbins; pages 16, 17, 169, 174, 175, 176, 179, 289, 372, 373, 377, 381 National Trust Photographic Library; pages 18, 19 Landmark Trust; page 27 Failte Ireland; pages 28, 29, 36, 42 Jonathan Perugia; pages 38, 39 Thomas Skovsende; pages 40, 206, 212, 213, 235, 238, 239 Heloise Bergman; pages 41, 322, 323, 330, 331, 332, 335 Muir Vidler; pages 46, 47, 51, 52, 54, 55, 90, 91, 94, 95, 97, 98, 99, 100, 101 Tove Breitstein; pages 60, 61, 67, 71, 76 Gordon Rainsford; pages 74, 75, 182, 192, 271, 350 Paul Carter; pages 102, 103, 260, 266, 305 Alamy; page 107 Britain on View; pages 112, 113, 116, 117 Alys Tomlinson; pages 134, 135, 139 Alys Tomlinson; pages 146, 147 Somerset Tourism; pages 156, 157, 161, 165 Simon Cooke; page 173 Cornwall Tourist Board; pages 188, 189, 195 Rick Stein; pages 197, 200 Isles of Scilly Tourist Board; pages 214, 219 Jonathan Cox; pages 242, 243, 249, 252, 255, 256, 259 BBMPA/Jon Dixon; pages 272, 273, 283 Nathan Cox; pages 272, 281, 316, 317 Phil Taylor; pages 285, 291, 296, 297, 299, 300 Roger Scruton; pages 302, 304, 307 Ian Stuart; pages 310, 311, 319 Ben Barden/Cumbria Tourist Board; pages 336, 337, 341, 342, 343, 346, 347, 349, 358 Sandy Young; pages 352, 353 Argyll, the Isles, Loch Lomond, Stirling & Trossachs Tourist Board; page 363 Highlands of Scotland Tourist Board; page 378 Kingdoms of Down Tourist Board; pages 384, 385, 389, 391 Irish Tourist Board.

The following images were provided by the featured establishments/artists: pages 3, 10, 12, 13, 35, 50, 51, 53, 58, 59, 68, 69, 78, 79, 84, 85, 86, 89, 108, 111, 115, 121, 122, 123, 140, 141, 142, 145, 150, 151, 155, 166, 168, 180, 181, 183, 186, 187, 196, 203, 204, 205, 252, 273, 278, 279, 284, 292, 293, 308, 309, 320, 321, 356, 361, 362, 367,369, 392, 393.

Contents

About the guide

This book is divided into 30 breaks, starting in London and moving out towards the further reaches of Great Britain and Ireland. (If you're looking for a particular hotel or restaurant, see the index *pp403-408*). Each of the breaks has something special about it, but absolutely central to each one are life-enhancing hotels, restaurants and pubs.

The details

Booking accommodation in advance is always recommended: most of the places we feature in this guide are very popular, and at least several weeks' (and often months') notice is required. We've tried to indicate where children, dogs and smokers are welcome (or not) – but it's always best to discuss this with the establishment in question. Unless otherwise stated, breakfast is included in room prices. Some hotels offer special rates for weekends, often including dinner. It's always worth asking about such deals when you book.

The maps featured in this book are intended (with the exception of the town plans) for general orientation, and you will need a road atlas or other detailed map to find your way around.

The listings

• Throughout this guide we have listed phone numbers as dialled from within the country in question, but outside the particular village, town or city.
• The times given for dining are those observed by the kitchen; in other words, the times within which one can order a meal. These can change according to the time of year and the whim of the owners. Booking is always a good idea, and essential on Fridays and Saturdays, or if you're travelling any distance.
• Main course prices are given as a range, from the cheapest to the most expensive – obviously these prices can and will change over the life of a guide.
• Where credit cards are accepted, the following abbreviations have been used: AmEx (American Express); DC (Diners Club); MC (MasterCard); V (Visa).

The reviews

The reviews in this guide are based solely on the experiences of *Time Out* reviewers. While every effort has been made to ensure the accuracy of the information contained in this guide, the publishers cannot accept any responsibility for errors it may contain. Opening times, owners, chefs, menus and other details can change at any time.

Let us know what you think

We hope you enjoy this book and welcome any comments or suggestions you might have. Email us at guides@timeout.com.

THESE BOOKS ARE MADE FOR WALKING

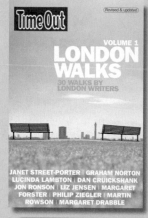

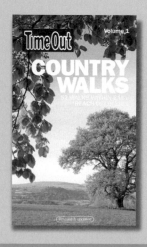

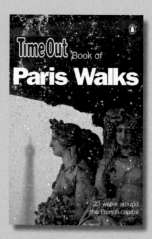

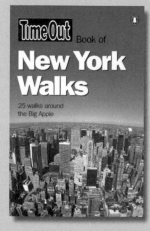

Available from all good bookshops
and £2 off at www.timeout.com/shop

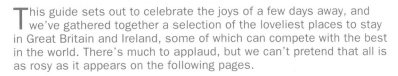

The state of the nation

Mind the gaps when you set off for your next weekend break.

By Sarah Guy

This guide sets out to celebrate the joys of a few days away, and we've gathered together a selection of the loveliest places to stay in Great Britain and Ireland, some of which can compete with the best in the world. There's much to applaud, but we can't pretend that all is as rosy as it appears on the following pages.

HAVE NO CAR, WON'T TRAVEL

In compiling the guide, we came across many obstacles to enjoying a break. Let's start with the fact that you can't really move around the countryside without a car. And our objection to this isn't just a green attitude – for many people a weekend can't be truly relaxing if it involves driving for hours on a traffic-clogged road. At weekends, public transport outside the major cities often seems to be little more than a poor joke.

Many services (bus and rail) don't even run on a Sunday (the day most people might want to don their hiking boots), even in some of the most scenic and well-trodden parts of the country (try catching a bus in and around North Yorkshire, for example). And even forgetting Sundays, transport systems never seem to be 'joined up': having caught a main-line train, it's not unusual to wait for an hour or more for a branch-line or bus connection. Different rail companies don't appear to talk to one another, and passengers fall into the timetabling gaps – in the course of researching this guide we spent a lot of time on station platforms.

And don't even think about taking your bicycle – unless you have a folding one (accepted without reservation and free of charge on every train company) or are able to book well in advance. Reservations are generally free, but most companies will only take two bicycles on any one train. First Great Western (covering Bristol, the Cotswolds, South Wales and the west of England) can carry up to six, but charges £1 a bike; GNER (covering the eastern side of England and Scotland), which recognises that 'many of our customers are keen cyclists', takes five (free of charge). For the full picture, see www.nationalrail.co.uk.

We've tried to include as many car-free breaks as possible, though the fact remains that too much of the countryside is inaccessible to anyone without a vehicle. But take comfort from the fact that once you've reached many of our most luxurious retreats, you won't want to wander too far from the grounds.

CLOSED FOR THE WINTER

We're also shut out from most of the nation's stately homes and historic houses for much of the winter – precisely the season when rainy-day activities are called for. The National Trust, being the owner of so many properties, bears the brunt of most complaints. We asked the Trust why the seasonal shutdown occurs, and were told it was 'to enable the important conservation work that needs to be carried out with often fragile historic houses'. Though we understand the need for conservation work, we can't believe that conservation requirements are the same throughout every single property, but the Trust says, 'Obviously each property is unique and the level of work does vary, but there is often more involved than people realise.' In order to give people some insight into this conservation work, the Trust runs a series of 'putting to bed' events – for details see www.

nationaltrust.org.uk/events or call 0870 458 4000. The few properties that are open in the off-season are the ones that are financially sustainable during this period, like the Red House, Bexleyheath. Otherwise, you're left with a range of gardens and parks for inclement-weather sightseeing trips.

English Heritage (different from the National Trust in that it is a public body partly funded by the government) has 303 properties and places of interest open during the winter (see www.english-heritage.org.uk for more details). Obviously some of these are ruins or other open-air sites, but many are houses or castles – Dartmouth Castle in Devon, Eltham Palace in London and Osborne House on the Isle of Wight, for example. As an organisation it is actively involved in trying to increase visitor numbers in the off-season, and so tries to balance conservation requirements with visitors' needs.

NO FOR AN ANSWER

The rest of what's wrong can really be summed up as a 'can't do' attitude. From the familiar story of the malicious glee with which pub and restaurant owners announce that the kitchen is shut at 2.01pm, to the fact that many places won't accept bookings for just one night at weekends, it all too often feels as though the answer to any request will be 'no'. 'Hospitality' can be hard to come by too – arriving at a hotel and being made to feel unwanted or inappropriate is a frequent occurrence. We've left several well-known places out of this guide on those grounds. And why is food and drink still the Achilles heel of so many establishments? Picture-postcard pubs with no real beer (or real food for that matter), hotels where the

in-room milk is UHT or the coffee instant, children's meals that are nothing but junk – all crop up with dismal regularity.

ON THE BRIGHT SIDE

Increasingly people are deciding where to go for the weekend on the basis of a special hotel, spa or restaurant – and when that (no doubt expensive) establishment doesn't deliver, then the weekend is no longer a treat. So praise is due to those establishments that get it right. For example, the Star Inn in Harome (see p301) runs Sunday lunch through until early evening; the Yorke Arms at Ramsgill (see p295) has a children's menu that lists smaller servings of what's on the main menu; the Fish Café in Rye (see p55) boasts a 'little people's menu' featuring char-grilled chicken with gravy and vegetables followed by chocolate pot; Calcot Manor (see p128) offers dedicated facilities that make families very welcome, but not at the expense of child-free guests; Cowley Manor (see p122) has service with a (genuine) smile down to a T – you really feel staff are glad to have you there and want to make your stay enjoyable.

And plaudits too to the new breed of boutique hotels – both chains such as Malmaison, Hotel du Vin and Alias (see p416 **Useful addresses**), and excellent one-offs like Hotel Tresanton (see p177) and the Place (see p53). Many of them have breathed new life into forgotten areas.

Another welcome development is the reinvention of the country-house hotel as an adult playground, with stuffiness removed – the roll-call includes Babington House (see p151), Barnsley House (see p116), Calcot Manor (see p128), Cowley Manor (see p122) and Whatley Manor Hotel (see p131). These places are so inviting that it really doesn't matter what the weather does – who cares if it's sleeting when you can hunker down in a screening room or sink into a hot tub?

It finally seems as though we're moving into a new age of tourism. The idea of the weekend break, all year round, has taken a firm hold, and a fresh generation of hoteliers is offering – as a matter of course – a beguiling mix of cool design, warm welcome, comfortable beds, good food and little luxuries, banishing the memory of unlovely B&Bs forever.

Zanzibar

Luxury for hire

Explore beyond the hotel room.
By Lily Dunn

For those who want a break from the usual hotel or B&B holiday, there are plenty of options available that incorporate as much luxury and charm, but with heaps more intimacy – and, in some places, breakfast and even dinner as well. From a romantic 16th-century folly to quirky modern seaside apartments, there's a plethora of interesting properties. And then there are the stunning mansions set in 20 acres of land, and castles that overlook the sea – many of these rely on holiday lets just to keep themselves going, so you'd be doing them a disservice not to hire one for your wedding or family reunion, or just to get all your friends together to play 'let's pretend' for the weekend. Most houses are associated with a holiday agent (*see p19*), but not all – here we've picked a few gems that are perfect for that special occasion, big or small, traditional or unique.

tony cragg

02/05/ 2005
—
30/04/ 2006

This will be the largest exhibition of Tony Cragg's outdoor sculptures in Britain to date and will include several sculptures commissioned specifically for the new outdoor exhibition space on the grounds of the Goodwood estate.

Advancing Twenty-First Century British Sculpture

Cass Sculpture Foundation Sculpture Estate

Goodwood
West Sussex PO18 OQP
Phone +44 (0)1243 538 449
Fax +44 (0)1243 531 853
Email info@sculpture.org.uk
www.sculpture.org.uk

Opening Times
Thursday—Saturday
10.30am—4.30pm

Cass Sculpture Foundation
Maquettes and Prints

3+4 Percy Street
London W1T 1DF
Phone +44 (0)20 7637 0129
Fax +44 (0)20 7631 1140
www.sculpture.org.uk

Opening Times
Tuesday—Saturday
11am—6pm

cass sculpture foundation

FOR COUPLES OR SMALL FAMILIES

Shaped like a wedding cake, West Usk Lighthouse (01633 810126, www.westusklighthouse.co.uk) is only two hours' drive from London, situated where the River Usk meets the Severn, between Newport and Cardiff. It is a B&B (its owners live on the property), but has enough privacy to have witnessed 20 marriage proposals over the years (a Rolls-Royce with chilled champagne can be arranged to take you to a local restaurant to celebrate). Other optional extras include a flotation tank, aromatherapy, reflexology and shiatsu (as well as a waterbed, a dalek and a red telephone box). This is one of the few lighthouse properties where guests can stay in the lighthouse itself, and the sound of the sea crashing against the side is sure to get even the most cynical down on one knee.

The Dovecote in Oxfordshire (01235 772809, www.the-dovecote.co.uk) started life in the 18th century, and has now been beautifully renovated and listed Grade II by English Heritage. It is an exceptional property with one double bedroom (from where you can see the exposed underside of the roof), under-floor heating, a sauna and all the mod cons needed for an intimate and peaceful break. Zanzibar (01841 521828, www.wave-scapes.com/zanzibar.htm) in Trevone, Cornwall, is the perfect quirky hideaway for the surfing or sea-worshipping couple. Guests are greeted with a complimentary bottle of wine, and food shopping can be arranged if needed. The flat is a wonderful contemporary mix of limestone and organic carved wood, and it's within diving distance of some of the UK's best beaches. Special features include a double jacuzzi, wet floor shower and open fire for the colder months.

Further afield, the Tower of Hallbar in the Clyde Valley, Scotland (0845 090 0194, www.vivat.org.uk) dates from the 16th century and has been beautifully preserved. It is set in five acres of orchard and meadow, and is perfect for a couple or family – it is intimate enough for two, but has enough bedrooms for five. There is also an adjacent cottage with facilities for a disabled person and their carer. For a luxury hideaway in the Outer Hebrides, try Blue Reef Cottages (01859 550370, www.stay-hebrides.com) – two turf-roofed cottages situated in a remote village but just a five-minute walk from an award-winning restaurant. Grocery starter packs and a pick-up service from the airport or ferry terminal are available. Fisher Gill Cottage (01697 476254, www.monkhousehill.co.uk) has views over Cumbria's Eden Valley. After a day's trekking, crack open the complimentary bottle of champagne and relax in the spa, before stretching out on the four-poster bed. Nestled in its own private valley and perfectly located for walks on Dartmoor, Tor Cottage in Devon (01822 860248, www.torcottage.co.uk) is a woodland oasis. For extra intimacy, book Laughing Waters, a cabin with a gypsy caravan in the garden, which is set apart from the other apartments down a woody path and just steps from a stream. Expect Shaker-style furniture, patchwork bedspreads and a pot-bellied stove. Luxury additions include bubbly, chocolate truffles and fruit. Picnic platters and breakfast hampers can be delivered to your door.

Luxury for hire

The Onion Store (01794 323227, www.theonionstore.co.uk) is an intimate B&B made up of three little 'stores', each big enough for a couple – Onion, Grain and Apple – set in eight acres of land near the New Forest. Each 'store' is quirkily decorated with rich woods and sensual fabrics, and has a private garden and use of an outdoor swimming pool (closed during the winter). Situated in a secluded corner of the Cawdor Estate in the Scottish Highlands, the decor in Achneim Cottage (01667 404666, www.cawdor.com), a converted gamekeeper's cottage, mixes the old and contemporary beautifully. It sleeps two and is the perfect romantic retreat, overlooking the fields towards the Moray Firth.

There are also a number of hotels that have apartments and cottages within the grounds, such as the Cotswold House Hotel (01386 840330, www.cotswoldhouse.com), which boasts a superior suite in a 17th-century grammar school where the massive school room is now a living room with a high-beamed ceiling and carved stone fireplaces (with a bust of the school's founder), plus plasma screen and stereo system.

SELF-CATERING HOUSES FOR LARGER GROUPS

Where to go for your hen do, university reunion, family party or just a weekend of indulgence and abandon? Think space, grandiosity and some of the finest architecture you've ever seen and you've got a beautiful country retreat. Of course it doesn't come cheap, but when you're saving on expensive drinks and meals, it'll work out cheaper than a hotel – and you get the whole place to yourselves.

Symondsbury Manor (www.symondsbury.com), a Tudor house situated in the pretty village of Symondsbury, very close to the Dorset coast, comfortably sleeps 22 in eight double and three twin bedrooms, but can be hired for 12 and above. It has an elegantly shabby interior with lots of Georgian features and eclectic furniture including a grand piano, roll-top baths and a pair of stuffed owls. It may not be the most luxurious of choices, but when the rate is only £90 per person per weekend (for a minimum of 12) plus £50 for fuel, you can't really go wrong.

If your party wants to be together but not on top of each other, Combermere Abbey in Shropshire (01948 662876, www.combermereabbey.co.uk) is a good option. Made up of 11 cottages clustered around a cobbled coachyard, with each one done out with fresh

National Trust

Luxury for hire

flowers and Penhaligon's goodies; hampers and comforting suppers (with dishes such as boozy beef pie) can be arranged at an extra cost. For a more cosy experience, Polhawn Fort in Cornwall (01752 822864, www.polhawnfort.com) has a cavernous feel with its bare brick-vaulted ceilings and thick walls. The place has panoramic views of Whitsand Bay, not to mention its very own drawbridge, private beach and tennis courts. The eight bedrooms are equipped with king-size beds and crisp linen, and rates start at £3,295 for a weekend, £5,890 for a week.

Tone Dale House in Wellington, Somerset (01823 662673, www.thebighouseco.com) is an elegant Palladian villa, built in 1797 and sympathetically updated. It sleeps 21 to 30 in 15 bedrooms (and nine bathrooms), one of which is a stunning suite in a converted laundry. There's a vast games room (with billiards table), grand hall, reception room and dining room. There is also pool and table tennis, and croquet, boules and badminton can be played on the (immaculate) lawn. Meals can be provided for an extra cost, as can aromatherapy massage.

For something completely different, try Cliff Barns in Norfolk (01366 328342, www.cliffbarns.com), a joint venture between interior designer Shaun Clarkson (of Atlantic Bar and Grill, Denim and the 10 Room) and set designer Russell Hall. Everything is thrown into the design mix here, including Aztec rugs, cowhide sofas and elegant chandeliers. There's also a hot tub and sauna, and complementary therapies can be arranged. Facilities include use of the owners' beach hut. Catering can be arranged, or home-made pies, quiches and puddings can be delivered to your door. The house sleeps 18 and prices start from £2,550 for three nights.

SERVICED HOUSES FOR LARGER GROUPS

There are times when you want to splash out and not only stay in a beautiful house surrounded by stunning countryside, but also be waited on hand and foot. The Samling in Cumbria (*see p316*) leads the pack in terms of luxury. The hotel, set in 67 acres, can be rented out in its entirety with full staff on hand and a Michelin-starred kitchen. There are 11 double suites, all with stunning views of Lake Windermere, and the rate of £5,500 for a weekend includes all food and alcohol (including unlimited champagne), but doesn't include nightly VAT.

Humewood Castle in Co Wicklow, Ireland (00 353 59 647 3215,

Luxury for hire

rent a fortified, 16th-century tower set in 20 acres in Scotland. Fenton Tower (01828 633383, www.scottscastles.com) has been stunningly restored to include a vaulted chamber dining hall, a stunning living room with double-height beamed ceiling, six bedrooms and unique antiques such as a silver-coloured bed and an original canopy bath.

And lastly, the most expensive property we found: St Catherine's Court (020 7947 3290, www.blandings.co.uk) is a Grade I-listed 14th-century house just outside Bath with four-poster beds, a grand Elizabethan dining room, and full staff who can organise a spot of horse-riding, polo or even a private watercolour lesson. Membership is also provided to the nearby Lucknam Park Club with an indoor swimming pool and gym. Prices start at £12,950 per week.

LETTING AGENTS

If using an agent, remember that the cottages they represent are all individually owned, so you won't get the same treatment from one house to the next; some may leave complimentary wine and chocolates, others may leave nothing at all (except when booking through Rural Retreats, where a food hamper and wine are left at all properties). Also note that some of the bigger agents are not always the best when it comes to finding that perfect little property in the Forest of Dean, for instance – you might be better off going to a local agent (*see p21*).

Among the big agencies are English Country Cottages (0870 078 1100, www.english-country-cottages.co.uk), a swish operation that covers the whole of the UK, with an accessible website offering virtual tours of its properties.

www.humewood.com) is set beneath the Wicklow mountains in 500 acres of land. The house sleeps 28 and can be hired in its entirety or per suite, with full staff and a kitchen that produces 'creative Irish cooking'. All bedrooms are themed – Vivaldi, Dynasty and so on – and the 'ballroom' accommodates up to 80 for dining and 120 for cocktails. Alternatively, you can

Classic Cottages (01326 555555, www.classic.co.uk) has nearly 600 properties throughout the West Country. Rural Retreats (01386 701177, www.ruralretreats.co.uk) has properties all over Britain and boasts a rigorous selection process. Premier Cottages (01271 336050, www.premier cottages.co.uk) has over 750 properties throughout Great Britain and Ireland, and all its cottages are graded four- or five-star. Hoseasons Country Cottages (01502 502588, www.hoseasons. co.uk) covers the whole of the UK and Ireland, and offers lodges and boat holidays as well as cottages on its website.

SPECIALISTS

Norfolk Country Cottages (01603 871872, www.norfolkcottages. co.uk) has a good range of personally selected cottages throughout Norfolk and north Suffolk. For Cornwall to the New Forest, check out West Country Cottages (01803 814000, www.westcountrycottages.co.uk). Powells Cottage Holidays (0870 514 3076, www.powells.co.uk) deals with the West Country, Cotswolds, Forest of Dean, Wye Valley and Wales. Cornish Cottage Holidays (01326 573808, www.cornishcottageholidays.co.uk) is based in the heart of the county and has over 300 holiday homes with a particularly good choice on the Lizard peninsula and in the far west. For a good selection in Devon and Cornwall, particularly between Torquay and Salcombe, visit Toad Hall Cottages (0870 077 7345, www.toadhallcottages.com). In the Lake District, try Heart of the Lakes (01539 432321, www.heartofthelakes.co.uk), a family-run business that has over 300 properties situated within the National Park; guests are offered free membership to a leisure club with a swimming pool. Cumbrian Cottages (01228 591555, www.cumbrian-cottages.co.uk) has over 500 properties in Cumbria and the Lake District, with regularly updated special offers. Scottish Country Cottages (0870 078 1100, www.scottish-country-cottages.co.uk) represents Scotland, as does Hamster Cottages (01764 685400, www.hamstercottages.co.uk), a family-run business. For properties in Wales, try Wales Holidays (01686 628200, www.wales-holidays.co.uk). Monkhouse Hill Cottages has nine properties in the North Lake Fells, with views across Cumbria's Eden Valley (016974 76254, www.monkhousehill.co.uk; *see p15*). Unique Home Stays (01637 881942, www.uniquehome stays.co.uk) offers luxury B&B accommodation and self-catering in the UK, particularly Cornwall. Harrogate Holiday Cottages (01423 523333, www.harrogate holidays.co.uk) offers cutting-edge apartments, townhouses, country cottages and barn conversions around Yorkshire.

PROPERTIES WITH DISABLED ACCESS

Holiday Care (0845 124 9971, www.holidaycare.org.uk) has details of accommodation that can be accessed with a wheelchair.

BIG PROPERTIES

The Big Domain (01326 240028, www.thebigdomain.com) is the first place to look for big properties for 12 people or more. Blandings has large luxury houses in the UK and abroad (020 7947 3290, www.blandings.co.uk; *see p19*). Scotts Castle Holidays (01828

633383, www.scottscastles.com) has an amazing array of Scottish castles to rent.

TRUSTS

The National, Landmark and Vivat Trusts are all charities that own unique, historically significant properties in beautiful situations. These are often properties that have been saved from dereliction and then decorated in accordance with the period in which they were built – for instance, a traditional Georgian workers' house in Birmingham or a stunning stone cottage on the edge of Murlough National Nature Reserve in County Down, Northern Ireland, which was built for the Marquess of Downshire in the 1870s. These two properties can be booked through National Trust Cottages (0870 458 4411, www.nationaltrustcottages.co.uk), which owns 320 holiday cottages in England, Wales and Northern Ireland. The Landmark Trust (01628 825925, www.landmark trust.org.uk) has 178 properties throughout Britain, with 23 on Lundy Island alone. You have to buy a handbook (£9.50) to view the properties, but the money is reimbursed with your first booking. The Vivat Trust (0845 090 0194, www.vivat. org.uk) has 12 properties available all year round, ranging from an 18th-century folly – perfect for a romantic hideaway – to a 16th-century tower set in five acres of orchard and meadow (*see p15*). All three trusts rely on donations and holiday lets to keep their charities going.

YOUTH HOSTELS

Yes, you often have to sleep in a dorm, but those who haven't holidayed in a youth hostel since their teenage days will be surprised at the accommodation that is now on offer. Over 200 places to stay in England, Wales and the Channel Islands include cottages, Victorian mansions, barns that can be hired out with friends (for just £5.50 per person per night) and even Native American tepees.

There is also a Rent-A-Hostel service where a group can have sole use of a hostel for a party or special occasion, with meal service. For more information log on to www.yha.org.uk.

LONDON APARTMENTS

If you're planning a trip to London but don't want to fork out for an expensive hotel, try the options below – but be aware that some companies have minimum stay requirements, making this an affordable option only if you're planning a relatively long trip. Typical daily rates on a reasonably central property are around £70-£90 a night for a studio or one-bed, up to £100 for a two-bed – though, as with any aspect of staying in London, the sky's the limit if you want to pay it.

Accommodation Outlet (020 7287 4244, www.outlet4holidays. com) is a lesbian and gay agency that has apartments in Soho (and also in Spain).

Recommended London all-rounders include Astons Apartments (020 7590 6000, www.astons-apartments.com), Holiday Serviced Apartments (0845 060 4477, www.holiday apartments.co.uk), Palace Court Holiday Apartments (020 7727 3467, www.palacecourt.co.uk) and Perfect Places (020 8748 6095, www.perfectplaces london.co.uk).

Luxury for hire

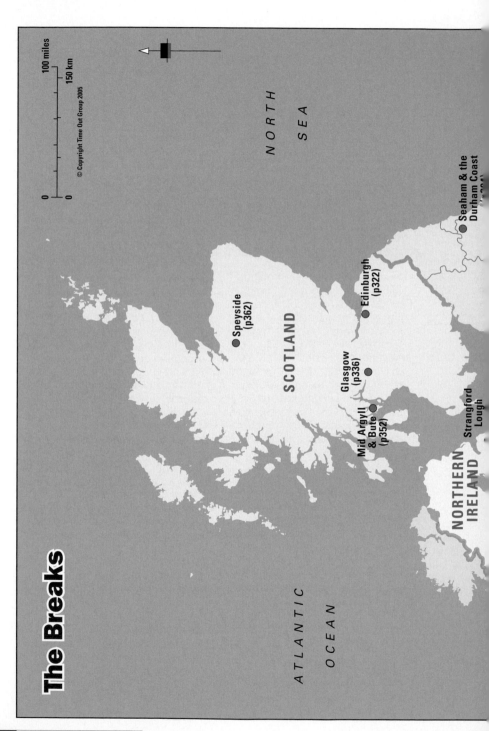

The Breaks

Speyside (p362)

Edinburgh (p322)

SCOTLAND

Glasgow (p336)

Mid Argyll & Bute (p352)

Strangford Lough

NORTHERN IRELAND

Seaham & the Durham Coast

NORTH SEA

ATLANTIC OCEAN

0 — 100 miles
0 — 150 km

© Copyright Time Out Group 2005

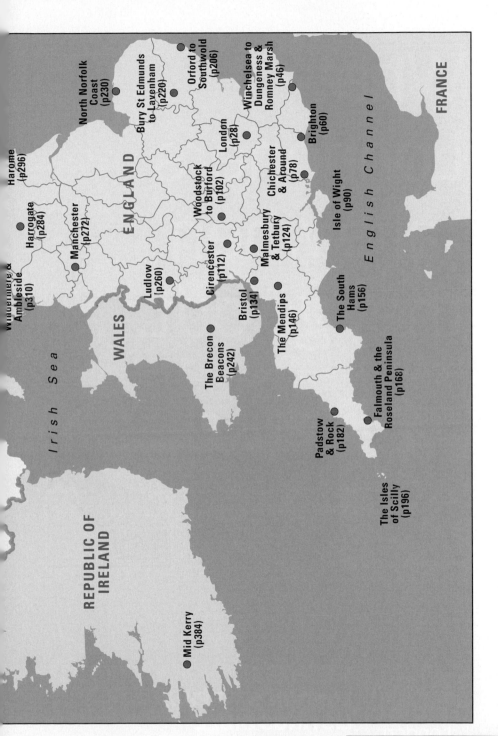

North Norfolk Coast (p230)

Bury St Edmunds to Lavenham (p220)

Orford to Southwold (p206)

Winchelsea to Dungeness & Romney Marsh (p46)

London (p28)

Brighton (p60)

Chichester & Around (p78)

Harome (p296)

Woodstock to Burford (p102)

Malmesbury & Tetbury (p124)

Isle of Wight (p90)

Harrogate (p284)

Manchester (p272)

ENGLAND

Cirencester (p112)

Windermere & Ambleside (p310)

Ludlow (p260)

Bristol (p134)

The Mendips (p146)

The South Hams (p156)

WALES

The Brecon Beacons (p242)

Falmouth & the Roseland Peninsula (p168)

Irish Sea

English Channel

Padstow & Rock (p182)

The Isles of Scilly (p196)

REPUBLIC OF IRELAND

FRANCE

Mid Kerry (p384)

What Londoners take when they go out.

The Breaks

London

The ultimate city break.

Given the dimensions of the place, it's unreasonable to imagine you can do more on a weekend visit than just scratch London's many-patterned surface. Fortunately, given the riches of the place, even a brief encounter is worth having. If you don't know where to start, take a look at **The concise capital** (*p44*). And if you fancy making a habit of weekend jaunts to London, or plan to return for a longer stay, you'll find the annual *Time Out London Guide* invaluable; for listings information while you're here, pick up a copy of the weekly *Time Out* magazine from any newsagent.

wagamama

positive eating + positive living

for menu and locations around the uk including manchester, nottingham, bristol, glasgow, birmingham, greater and central london visit **www.wagamama.com**

Accommodation	★★★★★
Food & drink	★★★★★
Nightlife	★★★★★
Shopping	★★★★★
Culture	★★★★★
Sights	★★★★★
Scenery	★★

WHERE TO STAY

London may be one of the world's top tourist destinations, but its hotels have a bad rep (tiny, overpriced, badly decorated rooms matched by inept service). However, since occupancy rates dropped to record lows in 2003, there have been signs of change. The luxury hotels have started offering special deals; the budget hotels are making an effort to smarten their decor; and there's a bumper crop of discount hotel websites. But the most encouraging trend is the appearance of designer hotels at prices mortals can afford; we list a selection here, alongside a few of London's admittedly expensive but unmissable gems.

Baglioni

60 Hyde Park Gate, SW7 5BB (7368 5700/ www.baglionihotellondon.com). High Street Kensington or South Kensington tube. **Rates** £300-£360 double; £500-£1,900 suite. **Credit** AmEx, DC, MC, V.
No tired minimalist aesthetic here. The Baglioni's fantastic lobby bar is part Baroque, part Donatella Versace, with spidery black chandeliers, burnished gold ceilings and vast vases filled with roses. The bedrooms are more masculine: dark wood floors, black lacquered tables and taupe walls, enlivened by brash striped sofas. Downstairs, the flashy Brunello restaurant serves pricey Italian food to ladies in sparkly tops. Ostentatious, yes – but when you're spending this kind of money, you want a good show.

Bentley Kempinski

27-33 Harrington Gardens, SW7 4JX (7244 5555/www.thebentley-hotel.com). Gloucester Road tube. **Rates** £440 double; £705-£3,525 suite. **Credit** AmEx, DC, MC, V.
Chandeliers are back in fashion, and there are plenty to swing from at London's most opulent new boutique hotel. They sparkle in the lobby and the bedrooms; you can even shave under one in the bathrooms. The Bentley's decorative template is Versailles: hence the profusion of Louis XV-style furniture, gilt mirrors and marble. Bedrooms have thick carpets, gold satin bedspreads and jacuzzi tubs; the spa features gold-laced mosaics and a Turkish hammam. Next to glitzy restaurant 1880, the Malachite Bar is a dim, decadent hideaway. But the real showpiece is the lobby's sweeping staircase – perfect for grand entrances.

Great Eastern Hotel

40 Liverpool Street, EC2M 7QN (7618 5000/ www.great-eastern-hotel.co.uk). Liverpool Street tube/rail. **Rates** £266-£675 double. **Credit** AmEx, DC, MC, V.
Once a faded railway hotel, the Great Eastern has been reborn. Thanks to a £70m overhaul by Sir Terence Conran, it's now a mammoth style mecca, though one sympathetic to its glorious Victorian structure. The six-storey atrium, overlooking a Zen rock garden lounge, is a show-stopper. The bedrooms wear the regulation style mag uniform: Eames chairs, chocolate shag-pile rugs and white Frette linens. There are four bars, including a swanky champagne bar and an atmospheric faux-Elizabethan pub; restaurants include the mandatory Japanese joint (Miyabi), a fish restaurant (Fishmarket) and the classy Aurora, with its elegant stained-glass dome.

Guesthouse West

163-165 Westbourne Grove, Notting Hill, W11 2RS (7792 9800/www.guesthousewest.com). Notting Hill tube. **Rates** £173-£202 double. **Credit** AmEx, MC, V.
Formerly the Westbourne Hotel, Guesthouse West looks the same as its predecessor: groovy retro lobby bar, minimalist bedrooms, arty photos. But now there are fewer frills – no room service, for example – and prices have been slashed. The rooms, though small, still have wireless internet access, air-conditioning and flat-screen TVs. The hotel's relaunch has been funded in part by a buy-to-let scheme: you can buy a room for £235,000, use it for 52 nights of the year – and, when you're not there, split the rental income with the hotel.

Malmaison

18-21 Charterhouse Square, EC1M 6AH (7012 3700/www.malmaison.com). Farringdon tube/rail. **Rates** £251 double; £329 suite. **Credit** AmEx, DC, MC, V.
When the first Malmaison opened in Edinburgh ten years ago, it made other hotels look backward. Despite providing facilities the market craved – handsome, thoughtfully equipped rooms, non-institutional public areas and restaurants that weren't just for guests – the 'Mal' nevertheless charged rates that seemed entirely reasonable. Now a small chain, Malmaison has brought the formula to a former nurses' home in Clerkenwell. You don't get costly luxuries, but stuff you need:

London

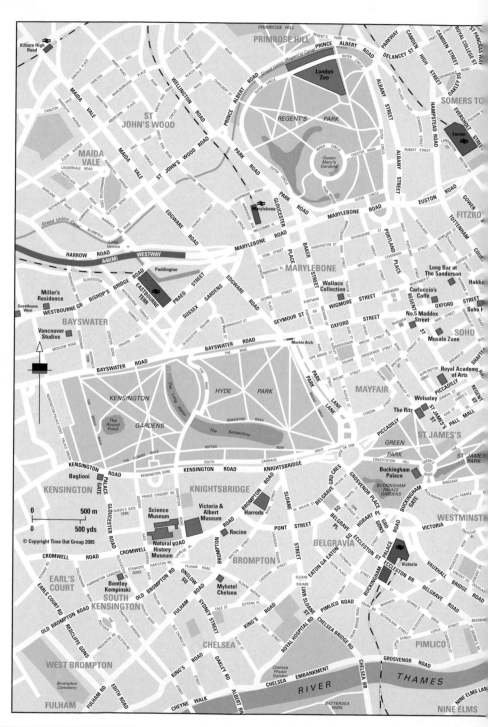

London

24-hour room service, CD players, ubiquitous free broadband access and enjoyable decor (with lovely London photos). There's even a gym.

Miller's Residence

111A Westbourne Grove, Notting Hill, W2 4UW (7243 1024/www.millersuk.com). Notting Hill Gate or Westbourne Park tube. **Rates** £176-£217 double; £270 suite. **Credit** AmEx, MC, V.

We're almost sorry to spill the beans, but this discreet little B&B is possibly London's most romantic hotel. The unmarked red door off Westbourne Grove doesn't look promising, but the interior is an Aladdin's Cave: rooms are dripping in gilt, chandeliers and ornate mirrors; 18th-century furniture straight out of a period drama; and shiny candelabra, baubles and gewgaws. Despite the antique treasures, it's not stuffy: there's a casual, Bohemian feel, with well-worn, comfy sofas, old Persian rugs and relaxed staff. In the salon, help yourself to whisky and curl up by the massive oak fireplace. Ordinary name, extraordinary place.

CLASSIC SWANK

Claridge's
55 Brook Street,
W1A 2JQ (7629 8860/
www.claridges.co.uk).
Rates £305-£552 double;
£717-£4,631 suite.
Dorchester
53 Park Lane, W1A
2HJ (7629 8888/
www.dorchesterhotel.com).
Rates £491-£527 double;
£726-£1,637 suite.
Ritz
150 Piccadilly, W1J
9BR (7493 8181/
www.theritzlondon.com).
Rates £495-£589 double;
£671-£2,704 suite.
Savoy
Strand, WC2R 0EU
(7836 4343/
www.savoygroup.com).
Rates £466-£519
double; £666-
£2,134 suite.

myhotel chelsea

35 Ixworth Place, SW3 3QX (7225 7500/ www.myhotels.com). South Kensington tube. **Rates** £294-£329 double; £423 suite. **Credit** AmEx, DC, MC, V.

This trendy boutique hotel is a rather gentler version of its Bloomsbury alter ego (11-13 Bayley Street, WC1B 3HD, 7667 6000). Like the original, it has lots of nice feng shui touches, an aquarium in the lobby, crystals and candles scattered just so. But the designers have chosen to tone down the oriental side and instead aimed for what they call 'traditional English meets *Sex And The City*': dusty pinks and purples, lush fabrics (cashmere throws) and velvet cushions. Rooms come with New Agey accessories – herbal wellness/hangover kits, say – and wireless internet access. Chill-out places include the spa, Cape Cod-influenced bar and conservatory-style lounge.

No.5 Maddox Street

5 Maddox Street, W1S 2QD (7647 0200/ www.living-rooms.co.uk). Oxford Circus tube. **Rates** £294 1-bed suite-£729 3-bed suite. **Credit** AmEx, DC, MC, V.

For a hip pad in the heart of swinging London, this boutique hotel is very discreet: blink and you'll miss the unassuming entrance. The smart lobby, with its huge aquarium, resembles a chic bank; the rooms themselves are actually trendy flats. The theme is East meets West: bamboo floors and Far Eastern furniture mixed with fake fur throws and the obligatory crisp white sheets. There's no bar, but Soho is nearby – and the kitchens are stocked with organic treats (room service will shop for you, too), so you could whip up dinner and throw your own party.

One Aldwych

1 Aldwych, WC2B 4RH (7300 1000/ www.onealdwych.com). Covent Garden or Temple tube/Charing Cross tube/rail. **Rates** £441-465 double; £670-£1217 suite. **Credit** AmEx, DC, MC, V.

A great deal has been written about this hotel, and once you see the lobby, with its sculpture of a hunched oarsman and sprays of flowers, you'll understand why. One Aldwych is a modern classic, an appealing mix of traditional and trendy with the attentive service of the Ritz; it's housed in an Edwardian bank building but the streamlined, minimalist rooms have up-to-date gadgetry (and original artworks). Londoners come for drinks in the elegant Lobby Bar; the restaurants are fine, the gym is well equipped and there's even a private cinema. But the highlight is the underground swimming pool, complete with subtle lighting and classical music piped into the water.

Portobello Hotel

22 Stanley Gardens, Notting Hill, W11 2NG (7727 2777/www.portobello-hotel.co.uk).

London

Holland Park or Notting Hill Gate tube. **Rates**
£160-£275 double. **Credit** AmEx, MC, V.
Bohemian chic reigns at the Portobello. The elegant rooms ooze colonial romance: potted palms,
ceiling fans, wooden shutters and oriental
antiques. Some are poky, some are spectacular:
Room 16, for instance, has a circular bed and a
clawfoot bathtub in the middle of the room –
Johnny Depp allegedly filled it with champagne
for Kate Moss. After a day of shopping locally,
you can drink in the hotel bar or soothe aching
muscles in one of the many jacuzzi tubs.

Rookery

*12 Peter's Lane, Cowcross Street, EC1M
6DS (7336 0931/www.rookeryhotel.com).
Farringdon tube/rail.* **Rates** £252 double;
£464 suite. **Credit** AmEx, DC, MC, V.
Squirrelled away down a Dickensian lane in
Clerkenwell, the Rookery is an irresistible period
piece. In a row of converted 18th-century houses,
it's stuffed with glorious antiques – Gothic oak
beds, plaster busts and clawfoot bathtubs – and
modern creature comforts (Egyptian cotton sheets
and plush towels on heated towel racks). The
wood-panelled public rooms resemble a decadent
gentleman's club; in contrast, staff are young and
relaxed. And the hotel's cosiness – curl up by the
fire in the library – makes it particularly appealing

Just across the
road from
Somerset House,
One Aldwych
Hotel has more
to offer than just
its fine location

St Paul's

London

in winter. Sister hotels Hazlitt's (6 Frith Street, W1D 3JA, 7434 1771, www.hazlittshotel.com) and the Gore (190 Queen's Gate, SW7 5EX, 7584 6601, www.gorehotel.com) are similiarly classy places.

Soho Hotel
4 Richmond Mews (off Dean Street), W1D 3DH (7559 3000/www.firmdalehotels.com). Leicester Square or Tottenham Court Road tube. **Rates** £303 double; £501-£566 suite. **Credit** AmEx, MC, V.
Kit Kemp is taking over London. The capital's hotel queen has unveiled her sixth property, and the Soho Hotel is her most edgy creation yet. Some say Kemp brings the country house to the city, but the aesthetic at the Soho Hotel is a long way from the shires. The new red-brick structure resembles a converted loft building; some of the public rooms feature colours like shocking pink or acid green. Refuel, the loungey bar and restaurant, has an open kitchen and a car-themed mural. And though the bedrooms are classic Kemp – soft neutrals, bold pinstripes and traditional florals – they've got a contemporary edge. They're also huge. Downstairs, there are two screening rooms for movie moguls and treatment rooms for stressed execs. For the other hotels, including the slightly more affordable Number Sixteen (16 Sumner Place, SW7 9EG, 7589 5232), see the website.

Vancouver Studios
30 Prince's Square, Bayswater, W2 4NJ (7243 1270/www.vancouverstudios.co.uk). Bayswater or Queensway tube. **Rates** £85-£95 double; £120 triple. **Credit** AmEx, DC, MC, V.
Vancouver Studios is almost a contradiction in terms: a good-looking budget hotel. The countrified sitting room is cosy and funky, with Mexican upholstery, cacti and a gramophone; it opens on to a lush, walled garden with a gurgling fountain. Studio rooms come equipped with kitchenettes. For the price, the bedrooms are surprisingly stylish. Being refurbished as we go to press (check the website or call for details of when the work is due to be completed), Vancouver Studios' proposed new aesthetics will include nautical, country-fresh gingham and Far Eastern chic. Staff are friendly and so is the resident cat. A great deal.

Zetter
86-88 Clerkenwell Road, EC1M 5RJ (7324 4444/ www.thezetter.com). Farringdon tube/rail. **Breakfast served** 7-10.30am Mon-Fri; 7.30-11am Sat, Sun. **Lunch served** noon-2.30pm Mon-Fri. **Brunchserved** 11am-3pm Sat, Sun. **Dinner served** 6-11pm Mon-Sat; 6-10.30pm Sun. **Main courses** £12-£17. **Set meal** £35-£45 for 3 courses. **Rates** £153-£305 double. **Credit** AmEx, DC, MC, V.
It was only a matter of time before Clerkenwell got a hip hotel. And the Zetter pushes all the right buttons: its snazzy Italian restaurant is buzzing; the lobby is decked out in a chic retro style; the

popular Match Bar is just across the road. In true Clerkenwell style, the hotel is housed in a converted warehouse, complete with a dazzling atrium. The bedrooms, all done up in creams and greys, are small but stylish. Their ecological credentials are impeccable: if you open a window, the air-con goes off; water comes from the hotel's own well. Instead of minibars, posh vending machines in the corridors dispense gin and tonics, champagne and cappuccinos. The roof-top suites have fantastic wooden decks (and, of course, the

SHOPPING: HOTSPOTS

Bond Street, W1 Great for designer labels; handy for Fenwicks.

Carnaby Street, W1 Great for funky fashion and gifts; handy for Liberty.

Covent Garden Piazza, WC2 Great for gifts and mainstream and street fashion; handy for Thomas Neal centre.

King's Road, SW3 Great for high-street fashion; handy for Peter Jones.

Knightsbridge, SW1 Great for designer and high-street fashion; handy for Harrods.

Marylebone High Street, W1 Great for food, designer homewares, books and one-off gifts; handy for the Conran Shop.

Spitalfields market, E1 Great for jewellery, gifts, cutting-edge fashion; handy for Brick Lane.

Tottenham Court Road, W1 Great for electronics, home accessories and furniture; handy for Heal's.

Westbourne Grove, W11 Great for classy homewares and upmarket-but-boho fashion; handy for Portobello Road.

London

best views in the house). Not quite the Sanderson, then, but almost as easy on the eye – and much easier on the wallet.

WHERE TO EAT

For an in-depth look at London's restaurant scene, see Time Out's *Eating & Drinking in London* or *Cheap Eats in London*.

Busaba Eathai

22 Store Street, WC1E 7DS (7299 7900). Goodge Street or Tottenham Court Road tube. **Meals served** noon-11pm Mon-Thur; noon-11.30pm Fri, Sat; noon-10pm Sun. **Dishes** £4.10-£8.80. **Credit** AmEx, JCB, MC, V.
Shared tables, bench seats, no smoking, no booking: this Thai canteen was created by Alan Yau, who created Wagamama's and now runs top Chinese spots Hakkasan (*see right*) and Yauatcha. Dark wood and walls evoke the Asia of opium dens. The excellent menu features ingredients such as wing beans, wood-ear mushrooms, morning glory and rose apple, and portions are generous. There's another branch at 106-110 Wardour Street in Soho, and a third is due to open in spring 2005 at 8 Bird Street, W1.

Carluccio's Caffè

8 Market Place, W1W 8AG (7636 2228/ www.carluccios.com). Oxford Circus tube. **Meals served** 7.30am-11pm Mon-Fri; 10am-11pm Sat; 10am-10pm Sun. **Main courses** £5.25-£10.95. **Credit** AmEx, MC, V.
This popular, friendly luncheonette – the original West End branch of what is now a widespread Italian chain – can be a little disorganised. But when food is this reasonably priced and delicious, such faults are easy to forgive. The specials board might list red wine risotto topped with zucchini fritte, or a hearty pasta dish of the day like penne with courgettes; the menu features some staples, such as a choice of tasty antipasto platters, but changes periodically. Carluccio's rich, dark and dense chocolate torta is perfectly judged and well worth saving room for – same goes for the coffees.

Hakkasan

8 Hanway Place, W1T 1HD (7907 1888). Tottenham Court Road tube. Bar **Open** noon-12.30am Mon-Wed; noon-1.30am Thur-Sat; noon-midnight Sun. *Restaurant* **Lunch served** noon-2.45pm Mon-Fri; noon-4pm Sat, Sun. **Dinner served** 6-11pm Mon-Wed, Sun; 6-11.45pm Thur-Sat. **Dim sum** £3-£18. **Main courses** £11-£55. **Credit** AmEx, MC, V.

Old-style opulence is the order of the day at The Wolseley.

Few London restaurants can match the thrill of descending the green slate staircase into Hakkasan. Incense smoke and outlandish flowers greet you as you enter a subtly lit space of dark latticed screens. Hakkasan breaks the Chinatown mould by offering fine, pricey Chinese food in a venue that satisfies both Western and oriental tastes. The dim sum is unrivalled in London. Come at lunchtime for crisp triangular pastries stuffed with venison; translucent, emerald green

BARS

London's hotels are always a good bet for a drink in a stylish setting: the Long Bar at the Sanderson (50 Berners Street, W1, 7300 1400/www.morgans hotelgroup.com) is a dreamy, Philippe Starck-designed oasis of silver, white and glass. Claridge's Bar (*see p34*) is the last word in Mayfair elegance: classy 1930s decor, immaculate cocktails and sophisticated service. The art deco American Bar at the Savoy (*p34*), where the Martini was invented, is a paean to the Golden Age of the silver shaker. The tasteful Lobby Bar at One Aldwych (*p34*), is notable for its arched windows and striking modern art. The Baglioni (*p31*) is a glitzy, black-and-gold affair; for a totally OTT South Pacific extravaganza, go to Trader Vic's at the Hilton (22 Park Lane, W1, 7208 4113/www.tradervics.com). Otherwise, try Hakkasan (*p38*) where the stunning bar combines warehouse chic with Chinese exoticism and LA glam. The kitsch Trailer Happiness (177 Portobello Road, W11, 7727 2700) is renowned for its killer cocktails. Shoreditch hotspot Loungelover (1 Whitby Street, E2, 7012 1234) is a rare breed: a camp straight bar, with flamboyant lighting and furniture. Young, loud and hip, Match Bar (37-38 Margaret Street, EC1, 7499 3443/ www.matchbar.com) is renowned for its gorgeous cocktails.

Hakkasan

333 Club

dumplings filled with prawn and fragrant Chinese chives; and light-as-a-feather deep-fried snacks – stick to tea and it'll cost around £25 a head. There's a fine wine list and enticing cocktails, and service is helpful. Booking is essential.

Inn The Park

St James's Park, SW1A 2BJ (7451 9999/ www.innthepark.co.uk). Green Park or Piccadilly Circus tube. **Breakfast served** 8-11am Mon-Fri; 9-11am Sat, Sun. **Lunch served** noon-3pm Mon-Fri; noon-4pm Sat, Sun. **Tea served** 3.30-5pm Mon-Fri. **Dinner served** 6-9.30pm daily. **Main courses** £8.50-£17.50. **Credit** AmEx, MC, V.

Oliver Peyton's striking new venture is a fine showcase for British talent. The wooden building, partly covered by a turf roof, was designed by Michael Hopkins, while the chic, sauna-like interior is by Tom Dixon. There's an all-day café menu – breakfast, self-service snacks, afternoon tea – but for lunch and dinner the place becomes a full-blown restaurant serving produce-led British dishes such as Bury black pudding, as a starter with beetroot, poached egg and watercress salad, or pollock deep-fried in beer batter, served with pea mash. Neal's Yard cheeses and a prawn cocktail are also hits. No smoking throughout.

J Sheekey

28-32 St Martin's Court, WC2N 4AL (7240 2565/www.caprice-holdings.co.uk). Leicester Square tube. **Lunch served** noon-3pm Mon-Sat; noon-3.30pm Sun. **Dinner served** 5.30pm-midnight Mon-Sat; 6pm-midnight Sun. **Main courses** £10.75-£30. **Set lunch** (Sat, Sun) £21.50 3 courses. **Credit** AmEx, DC, MC, V.

J Sheekey shares many wonderful things with its sister restaurant, the Ivy: elegant design, simple but sublime food and superior celebrities. It's become tough to get a booking, but this remains one of our favourite fish restaurants. Excellent main courses include delicate sea trout with steamed clams and samphire, or a robust lemon sole belle meunière with soft roes, shrimps and brown butter. Desserts are excellent: a raspberry trifle was rich and fruity. While it's easy to spend a lot of money here (watch those side dishes), it's possible to keep the bill down. The average main course is under £20 – great value with such superior cooking, especially on the weekend set lunch.

Masala Zone

9 Marshall Street, W1F 7ER (7287 9966/ www.realindianfood.com). Oxford Circus tube. **Lunch served** noon-3pm Mon-Fri; 12.30-

London

3.30pm Sun. **Dinner served** 5.30-11pm Mon-Fri; 6-10.30pm Sun. **Meals served** 12.30-11pm Sat. **Main courses** £5.50-£11.50. **Thalis** £6.50-£11.50. **Credit** MC, V.

A popular, modern dining spot for Indian food. Though there's a canteen vibe, fast throughput and (sometimes) queues, the authenticity survives. The mini chain is owned by the Chutney Mary group, and its great-value menu encompasses crisp Bombay beach snacks, meal-in-one plates, rare regional dishes (undhiyu or lentil khichdi – a mushy rice mix – for instance), well-made curries and satisfying thalis. For dinner, a combination thali is a good way to go, allowing a choice of any two pots of curry from the menu, plus a starter, two vegetable curries, raita, dahl, kuchumber (diced tomato and cucumber salad), popadoms and chutneys, a chapati and rice. The bustle of the open kitchen and attractive art murals make dining here a pleasure. No smoking throughout.

Moro

34-36 Exmouth Market, EC1R 4QE (7833 8336/www.moro.co.uk). Farringdon tube/rail. **Bar Open** 12.30-11.45pm Mon-Fri; 6.30-11.45pm Sat (last entry 10.30pm). *Restaurant* **Lunch served** 12.30-2.30pm Mon-Fri. **Dinner served** 7-10.30pm Mon-Sat. **Main courses** £13.50-£17.50. **Credit** AmEx, DC, MC, V.

With praise from all sides, a top-selling cookbook and near-permanently busy tables, Moro has set the standard for restaurants offering an imaginative English take on Mediterranean food traditions – in this case, those of Spain and North Africa. Since it opened in 1997, chef duo Sam and Sam Clark have kept quality impressively high, using prime-quality authentic ingredients. Moro's wood-fired oven and charcoal grill come into play with the mains, and while there are great fish choices, we're especially impressed by the superb meats: wood-roasted pork with potato, pepper and onion salad, and char-grilled lamb with leeks, yoghurt and mint. Service is as bright as the food, but the place is very noisy and there are few cheap wines.

Racine

239 Brompton Road, SW3 2EP (7584 4477). Knightsbridge or South Kensington tube. **Lunch served** noon-3pm Mon-Fri; noon-3.30pm Sat, Sun. **Dinner served** 6-10.30pm Mon-Sat; 6-10pm Sun. **Main courses** £12.50-£19.50. **Set meal** (lunch, 6-7.30pm) £15.50 2 courses; £17.50 3 courses. **Credit** AmEx, MC, V.

Racine looks and feels like a chic Paris brasserie. In a room lined with mirrors and deep-green banquettes, staff negotiate the mêlée of diners with impersonal efficiency. Chef Henry Harris's French bourgeois food has rustic leanings – take simple starters like tomatoes baked with basil and crème fraîche on toasted brioche – but the classics play a leading role. There are salty slices of bayonne ham offset by creamy celeriac remoulade; langoustines halved and grilled with lashings of garlic, butter and parsley; cod served with a spicy

crab butter sauce; and, of course, steak with plenty of excellent frites. Finish with a perfect petit pot au chocolat. Deservedly popular.

St John

26 St John Street, EC1M 4AY (7251 0848/ 4998/www.stjohnrestaurant.com). Farringdon tube/rail. **Bar Open/food served** 11am-11pm Mon-Fri; 6-11pm Sat. **Main courses** £3-£15. *Restaurant* **Lunch served** noon-3pm Mon-Fri. **Dinner served** 6-11pm Mon-Sat. **Main courses** £13-£19. **Credit** AmEx, DC, MC, V.

The take-no-prisoners British food served here has won St John many accolades. The whitewashed walls and steel kitchen counters are similarly no-nonsense. The daily menu doesn't bother with dish descriptions, but the friendly service team is happy to offer all the explanations you could need. A pan-fried bacon chop might come with prune chutney; sprouting broccoli salad with a lovely vinaigrette dressing. Puds – treacle tart with lemon-and-syrup-drenched breadcrumb filling – are to die for. Fans of full-on meaty flavours and fabulous nursery puddings will love St John. The Spitalfields branch at 94-96 Commercial Street, 7247 8724, is more casual and open all day.

Smiths of Smithfield

67-77 Charterhouse Street, EC1M 6HJ (7251 7950/www.smithsofsmithfield.co.uk). Farringdon tube/rail. Cocktail bar **Open** 5.30-11pm Mon-Wed, 5.30pm-1am Thur-Sat. **Snacks** £3-£6. *Dining room* **Lunch served** noon-3pm Mon-Fri. **Dinner served** 6-11pm Mon-Fri; 6-10.45pm Sat. **Main courses** £9.50-£11.50. *Ground-floor bar* 11am-11pm Mon-Wed; 11am-12.30am Thur-Sat; noon-10.30pm Sun. *Ground-floor café* **Meals served** 7am-5pm Mon-Fri; 10am-5pm Sat; 9.30am-5pm Sun. **Main courses** £3.50-£6. *Top-floor restaurant* **Lunch served** noon-3pm Mon-Fri; noon-3.45pm Sun. **Dinner served** 6.30-10.45pm Mon-Sat; 6.30-10.30pm Sun. **Main courses** £19-£28. **Set lunch** (Sun) £25 3 courses. **All Credit** AmEx, DC, MC, V.

Staying true to its roots as a former market store, Smiths retains an industrial, New York warehouse feel, with exposed bricks, reclaimed wood, metal tubing and raw concrete. Of the four storeys, the ground floor is the most laid-back, serving breakfast, brunch and other casual fare. The next level up is a cocktail and champagne bar, with plush red leather booths. The second-floor Dining Room (serving modern British dishes) is based around a central mesh gallery, overlooking the champers bar; it's noisy. Much more peaceful is the Top Floor restaurant on the third floor, which serves posh British food. Quality is high; organic or additive-free ingredients are used where possible.

The Wolseley

160 Piccadilly, W1J 9EB (7499 6996/www.the wolseley.com). Green Park tube. **Breakfast served** 7-11.30am Mon-Fri; 9-11.30am Sat, Sun.

THE CONCISE CAPITAL

Choose from our itineraries to enjoy the perfect weekend.

SATURDAY

Riverside: St Paul's – Tate Modern – Borough Market – Shad Thames – Design Museum

Start on the north side of the river (simply to see the beautiful, newly cleaned façade of St Paul's Cathedral), then walk across the no-longer-wobbly Millennium Bridge to Tate Modern. You won't be able to see everything there, as you have to be at foodies' favourite Borough Market before 4pm. To get there, walk eastwards along the riverside, passing Shakespeare's Globe and the Golden Hinde on your way. Have lunch in Borough Market: there are many options (grazing is half the fun), but the stall selling chorizo in a bun seems to attract the longest queue.

Once suitably fed, you can continue past Southwark Cathedral, sticking to the river, passing HMS Belfast the new City Hall and Tower Bridge, until you reach Shad Thames and the Design Museum. Even if you don't look at the exhibition, there's a good café, a stylish shop and a classy restaurant, all with great views over the Thames.

Shopping & culture: Somerset House – Covent Garden – British Museum

The collections at Somerset House are too large to do in one go – it includes the Courtauld gallery, Gilbert Collection and Hermitage Rooms – so choose your target carefully. Even museum phobics will be wowed by the courtyard fountains and the river terrace. Just across the Strand is pedestrian-friendly Covent Garden, packed with a something-for-everyone mix of chain stores and independents – as well as the covered Piazza; there are seemingly endless shop-lined streets to explore. So you may not make it as far the British Museum, just to the north – but you really should

try, if only for the sight of Norman Foster's covered Great Court.

Upmarket gawping: Buckingham Palace – Royal Academy – Bond Street

Some people really do live like this. Start with the Queen's pad, Buckingham Palace – then walk across Green Park to Piccadilly. If you stick to the eastern side of the park, you'll emerge near the Ritz hotel; stay on the south side of Piccadilly and walk east, passing the Wolseley (a possible brunch pit stop, but popular, so book; *see p45*) and Fortnum & Mason (savour the window displays). F&M's ground-floor food hall is worth a detour, and its Fountain café does a good line in very British savouries and cakes. Once fortified, cross the road to the Royal Academy for a blast of art. And then it's back down the north side of Piccadilly to Bond Street, home to all the designer labels you could ever wish for, and the last word in deluxe window shopping.

SUNDAY

A bit of everything: Wallace Collection – Marylebone – Regent's Park & the zoo

Follow the very manageable mix of paintings, porcelain and furniture that forms the Wallace Collection with a stroll down London's nicest 'village' street. Marylebone High Street has a near-perfect collection of shops, notably Daunt Books, Divertimenti, Skandium, Agnès B, the Conran Shop and a very good Oxfam (specialising in books and music), together with plenty of cafés and coffee shops. Linger here or wander north across Marylebone Road and head into Regent's Park. A handsome park (designed by architect John Nash) at any time of the year, it springs into life in summer, with sporting leagues, a boating lake and a café. At the northern end lies London Zoo. If the zoo has a particularly strong appeal for you, reverse the order and start the day here, as it closes at 5.30pm (4pm winter).

Go east: Docklands – National Maritime Museum – Greenwich Park – Greenwich Market
Start at Bank station and ride the Toytown-esque Docklands Light Railway through the brave new world that surrounds the Canary Wharf Tower. Get off and explore (the smart Canary Wharf shopping centre is open on Sundays and the tube station is an impressive sight), or carry on to Greenwich (Cutty Sark or Greenwich stops) for the National Maritime Museum, Royal Observatory and Greenwich Park. Or you could head straight to the centre of Greenwich for the antiques, bric-a-brac and crafts markets. Either way, Greenwich easily has enough to keep you occupied for the rest of the day – especially if you factor in a drink at the Trafalgar Tavern overlooking the river on Park Row.

Street markets and one-off shops: Columbia Road – Brick Lane – Spitalfields
Start at Columbia Road – the flower market opens from 8am every Sunday. The market remains true to its roots, selling plants and flowers, but chi-chi gift and homeware shops, galleries, bric-a-brac stalls and cafés have sprung up around it, making for beguiling browsing. It's a short walk to Brick Lane (to be sure you find it, take an A-Z) for an even more extreme contrast. Here and on the side streets you'll find design, jewellery and fashion shops alongside stalls selling batteries and fourth-hand stuff you can't imagine anyone ever buying. The best brunch spot is St John Bread & Wine (see p43) – you'll need to book. After sustenance there, you'll be ready for Spitalfields Market (see p37).

Lunch served noon-2.30pm Mon-Fri; noon-3pm Sat, Sun. **Tea served** 3-5.30pm Mon-Fri; 3.30-6pm Sat, Sun. **Dinner served** 5.30pm-midnight Mon-Sat; 5.30-11pm Sun. **Main courses** £8.75-£26. **Credit** AmEx, DC, MC, V.
Housed in a former car showroom, the Wolseley – the latest offspring of restaurateurs Chris Corbin and Jeremy King – is one of London's prized dining spots. The art deco interior recreates pre-war grandeur with vaulted ceilings, grand pillars, polished marble and weighty chandeliers. For all the opulence, the vibe is friendly. It's open from breakfast onwards, and the long menu has something for everyone. Afternoon tea ritual is memorable. Finger sandwiches, filled with smoked salmon, succulent chicken pieces and sliced cucumber are matched by scrumptious but dainty cakes, plus excellent macaroons and almond meringues.

NIGHTLIFE
No clubber can come to London and be disappointed. Prime weekend territories include Fabric (77A Charterhouse Street, EC1, 7336 8898, www.fabriclondon.com), which dishes out leftfield breaks, drum 'n' bass and electro on Fridays and housier techno stuff on Saturdays. You're guaranteed a fantastic time at the End (18 West Central Street, WC1, 7419 9199, www.endclub.com), which has rolling residencies each Friday and Saturday; Bugged Out!, Derrick Carter's Classic Records party, Layo & Bushwacka! All Night Long and more are here monthly. For a shot of übercool, try 333 (333 Old Street, EC1, 7739 5949, www.333mother.com). The nearby Legion pub (348 Old Street, EC1, 7729 4441) is owned by the lot who run the Heavenly Social, and has groovy DJs.

The cluster of clubs around King's Cross is more than a little happening: 3,000-capacity Canvas (King's Cross Goods Yard, off York Way, N1, 7833 8301, www.canvaslondon.net) does monster indie or breaks parties and the occasional enormous glam party; the Cross (Arches 27-31, York Way, N1, 7837 0828, www.the-cross.co.uk), a great brick arches space, is home to mainstream house parties like XPress 2's bi-monthly, the weekly Fiction, Renaissance, Space and more; and the Key (Lazer Road, off York Way, King's Cross, N1, 7837 1027, www.thekeylondon.com) is one of the best small clubs, with a kick-ass roster of leftfield clubs and a disco-lit dancefloor.

Turnmills (63 Clerkenwell Road, EC1, 7250 3409, www.turnmills.com) continues to be shockingly popular. Nights lean towards house, hard house and trance, with Friday's Gallery sold out nearly every time. The Chemical Brothers do New Year's Eve here every year, and it's a very odd mix of neo-classical bits and pieces and a big grotty warehouse with lasers.

London

Winchelsea to Dungeness & Romney Marsh

Quaint and quirky converge on this eerily beautiful coastline.

The combination of olde-worlde cobbled streets and ancient inns, miles of sandy beaches, a desolate promontory and, a few miles inland, as-far-as-the-eye-can-see marshland studded with tiny medieval churches makes this one of the most unusual coastlines in England. It's as if the natural strangeness of the place has inspired quirky, man-made additions; here is the world's smallest public railway, houses made of train carriages and upturned boats or clad in black rubber, and centuries of odd defensive constructions. It's a unique mix that gives this part of Kent a very individual charm, something filmmaker Derek Jarman was well aware of when he bought a little cabin here and unwittingly made the area famous.

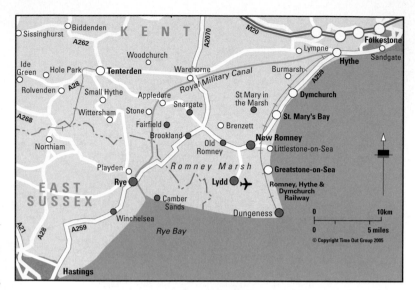

Winchelsea to Rye

Winchelsea was built on a never-completed medieval grid pattern (laid out by King Edward I) when the 'old' settlement was swept into the sea in the storms of 1287. The place is proud of its status as England's smallest town, but really it's a sleepy village of 400 residents with a wealth of medieval (and later) architecture, a very good pub, a tiny local museum stuffed with bits of broken pottery and old photos, and a tearoom. It's a pleasant place to while away a few hours. Pride of place goes to the church of St Thomas the Martyr, which rises up in the middle of town like a scaled-down cathedral (despite being merely the chancel of the 14th-century original). It boasts stunning 1920s stained-glass windows designed by Douglas Strachan along with some fine medieval carvings (including the head of Edward I) and tombs.

A further mile or so south-east of here (turn left into Dog's Hill Road) is pebbly Winchelsea beach, which at low tide reveals not just a sandy strip but also some beautiful, ancient, moss-covered wooden pillars, which are all that remain of old Winchelsea's eastern stone pier. Lined up like a petrified battalion presenting arms, their strangeness, combined with the silvery, mirror-like rock pools, makes a walk here a must.

Following the national trail that runs alongside the Royal Military Canal (built against the threat of invasion by Napoleon) in the direction of Rye brings you to Rye Harbour village (pick up a picnic at the Rye Harbour Stores, Rye Harbour Road, 01797

226444, which also has maps and walking leaflets for three circular walks) and the extensive Rye Harbour Nature Reserve. This rich and varied triangle of land features great natural pits that are a valuable habitat for wetland wildlife, as well as two farms, areas of peaceful woodland and Camber Castle (01797 223862, www.castlexplorer.co.uk). The crumbling edifice was built as part of England's coastal defences in the 16th century under Henry VIII, who obviously didn't count on the longshore drift and coastal erosion that make this coastline the world's largest area of shingle – the castle now lies two miles from the shore.

Bordering the nature reserve on the north side lies Rye, a town that's almost too quaint to be true. A gorgeous jumble of Norman, Tudor and Georgian architecture scrambles over one of the area's few hills; the narrow, cobbled streets are chock-full of antiques shops, tearooms and pubs, the best of which are undoubtedly the Mermaid Inn (see p56) and Ypres Castle Inn (see p59). The best antiques and curio shops are on High Street, where there's also a great old record shop in the Old Grammar School (built 1636) and the second-hand bookshop Chapter & Verse (105 High Street, 01797 222692). Apart from simply wandering the streets, it's worth taking a look at the medieval Landgate gateway (built in 1329) and the Castle Museum and 13th-century Ypres Tower (both Gun Garden, 3 East Rye Street, 01797 226728). Rye Art Gallery (107 High Street, 01797 222433) offers a changing series of exhibitions, mostly by locals and to a

Accommodation	★★★
Food & drink	★★★
Nightlife	
Shopping	★
Culture	★
Sights	
Scenery	★★★★

consistently high standard. Architecture fans shouldn't miss St Mary's church (Church Square), dating from 1150. It's capped with a delightfully over-the-top 16th-century clock decorated with a profusion of Baroque touches and two cherubic (and modestly attired) jacks, which curiously strike on the quarter-hour rather than the hour.

Rye to Romney Marsh & Camber

Heading east from Rye, you can go in two directions, two miles south-east to the coast or north-east into Romney Marsh. The latter is as flat as a pancake and criss-crossed with cycle paths – if you want to head out along the A259 to discover the 14 tiny medieval churches of the marsh, bikes can be hired from Rye Hire (1 Cyprus Place, Rye, 01797 223033). Among the most notable of these gems are St Augustine's at Brookland with its quite extraordinary detached wooden bell tower and All Saints (known as the 'Cathedral of the Marsh') at Lydd. North of here is St Thomas à Becket at Fairfield, which many consider to be the epitome of the isolated Romney Marsh church (look for the sign and approach via a causeway). St Clement in Old Romney has a particularly lovely interior, with a magnificent minstrels' gallery. And St Mary the Virgin at St Mary in the Marsh carries the understated gravestone of Edith Nesbit, author of *The Railway Children*, who loved the area and died in the village. Lydd is also home to a small airport (01797 322411, www.lydd-airport.co.uk, www.lydd air.com) and, while we wouldn't normally recommend an airport as an attraction, this is no ordinary airport. Hand-painted 1960s murals decorate the aviation-themed bar and restaurant (*see p56*), and there are scores of tiny planes to watch from a nice conservatory or outdoor terrace. If you feel inspired, you can even take a flying lesson or a low-level spin over the area. Walking on the Marsh offers rare pleasures too; the Romney Marsh Countryside Project (01797 367934, www.rmcp.co.uk) organises a good range of walks and events, most of which are free. They're weird enough to do justice to the mood of the area too, including evening walks, 'mini-beast' safaris, moth walks, pond-dipping for grown-ups and an introduction to the plants of Dungeness. Walks exploring the Marsh's listening ears are among the most interesting. They take place only a few times a year and it's well worth making

a special trip to take part. Built in the 1930s as part of an early warning system to detect enemy aircraft approaching from the Channel, these bizarre structures have been the subject of work by various artists, including Tacita Dean. Their presence is another piece of the jigsaw that makes the marsh the unique place it is.

Heading out of Rye along the coast road takes you to popular Camber Sands, a vast and glittering sandy beach that's a haven for kite-flying, riding, sand-yachting and invigorating walks. Backed with some crumbling outbuildings decorated with garishly Billy Childish-style murals, it has an undoubtedly faded charm, but, until last year's arrival of the Place (*see p53 & p57*) there was little reason to stay more than a few hours. It now makes arguably the best weekend base in the area.

Camber to Dungeness & Romney

It's hard to imagine a greater contrast to the tame pleasures of Rye than Dungeness, a few miles to the east. Clustered on the promontory are a lighthouse that offers wonderful views for those prepared to climb the 169 steps, a car park and a good café that does local fish and chips and a Sunday roast alongside the sandwiches. That's about it in an expanse of shingle and sea that creates an intense feeling of dislocation and disorientation best experienced by getting out of the car and walking the area – and there is plenty of wonderful walking to be done here (*see p56* **Dungeness: strange power**). The Dungeness RSPB Nature Reserve (Dungeness Road, Lydd, 01797 320588, www.rspb.org.uk/ reserves/dungeness), the oldest of the RSPB's reserves, is the best place to experience the fragile ecology of Dungeness Point. Hire binoculars at the visitors' centre, pick up a trail leaflet and head off to explore 2,000 acres housing a quarter of Britain's plant species and 1,550 species of invertebrates, some of which are unique to the area. This is an utterly magical place which, backed by the constant, pervasive hum of the Dungeness nuclear power station, makes you feel as if you're in an episode of *The Prisoner*. Then, when the miniature Romney, Hythe and Dymchurch Railway train barrels by, you *know* you're in an episode of *The Prisoner*. Proudly proclaiming to be the 'world's smallest public railway', it is fully functioning but one-third of the standard size. It was built by the millionaire racing driver Captain Howey in 1927 and even includes a buffet car. Sitting in one of the tiny carriages is a delightfully surreal experience as you meander from the wide-open shingle of the Point behind back gardens and caravan parks, through woodland and fields to arrive at Hythe, 13½ miles away.

Golf fans might want to stop off at New Romney though, where two courses alongside the Channel offer a great day for novices or keen amateurs. Littlestone Golf Club (01797 362310, www.littlestonegolfclub.org.uk) is the larger championship links course and accommodates a limited number of visitors, the smaller Romney Warren (01797 362231, www.romneywarrengolfclub.co.uk) next to it is a pay-and-play course with a practice putting and chipping green. Finally, a walk along the beach at Littlestone offers a changing landscape that takes in architectural curiosities such as a lovely 120-foot-high red-brick water tower; now a private residence, it was built in 1890 by local entrepreneur Henry T Tubbs, who hoped to turn the village into a major resort with a pier. Thankfully for fans of this quietly majestic coastline, it never happened.

WHERE TO STAY

Most of the good accommodation in the area is made up of small, independent hotels and award-winning guesthouses clustered around Rye. The smaller ones tend to get reserved weeks ahead, even in winter, so book as far in advance as possible. If the options we list are full, or you're looking for something on Romney Marsh proper, try the Olde Moat House (Ivychurch, 01797 344700/www.oldemoathouse.co.uk, doubles £70-£95), a medieval property surrounded by its own moat and set in more than three acres of land, or the pretty, three-bedroomed Terry House (Warehorne, Ashford, 01233 732443, doubles £70-£80). The Strand House (Tanyard's Lane, Winchelsea, 01797 226276/www.thestrandhouse.co.uk, doubles £60-£84) is a 15th-century house with ten rooms and a delightful garden.

Hope Anchor Hotel
Watchbell Street, Rye, East Sussex TN31 7HA (01797 222216/www.thehopeanchor.co.uk). **Rates** £95-£180 double; £130-£155 family room. **Credit** AmEx, DC, MC, V.

The wide open spaces of Camber Sands.

The Hope Anchor doesn't boast the cosy sweetness of some of Rye's smaller hotels, but as a decidedly above-par family hotel (thin on the ground in these parts) it's a godsend for parents with younger children. It boasts very individual rooms, all furnished and fitted to high standards, with lovely bed linen, and sherry on the welcome tea tray. All rooms have great views, and the log lounge is a great place to while away a rainy day. Children and dogs welcome. All rooms are no-smoking.

Jeake's House

Mermaid Street, Rye, East Sussex TN31 7ET (01797 222828/www.jeakeshouse.com). **Rates** £39 single; £70-£79 single occupancy; £94 double; £104-£118 four-poster. **Credit** MC, V. Wonderfully located in the heart of Rye, the atmospheric 17th-century Jeake's House is heavy on the mahogany and damask, but pale walls and white linen keep the decor the right side of chintzy. Each of the 11 rooms has been individually

decorated by proprietor Jenny Hadfield, daughter of Rye-born novelist John Burke. Service is attentive, the breakfast of devilled kidneys and succulent kippers is inspired, and an honesty bar completes the feeling of bonhomie. Children over-eight and dogs (£5 per night) welcome.

Little Orchard House

3 West Street, Rye, East Sussex TN31 7ES (01797 223831/www.littleorchardhouse.com). **Rates** £70-£100 double. **Credit** MC, V.
Staying in one of only two guest bedrooms in this delightful Georgian townhouse, replete with original artwork and personal touches throughout, could easily be more intimidating than intimate. But, to the credit of proprietor Sara Brinkhurst, the mood is one of welcoming informality, from the sitting room with its open fire to the book and games room for wet days. There's a large walled garden with an 18th-century smuggler's watch-tower and secluded corners for balmy summer days, and the generous breakfast makes good use of organic and free-range produce. No smoking throughout.

The Old Vicarage

66 Church Square, Rye, East Sussex TN31 7HF (01797 222119/www.oldvicaragerye.co.uk). **Rates** £90-£94 double; £132 family room (sleeps 4). **No credit cards**.
If the location in the gorgeous Church Square and lovingly decorated, updated-traditional rooms weren't enough, the attention to detail would make Julia and Paul Masters's B&B stand out from the crowd. On arrival at the 400-year-old house (largely rebuilt in the 18th century), you are treated to home-made cake and tea. It's the first of a series of perks: handmade fudge and biscuits on your in-room tea tray, sherry in the evening and

breakfasts that are fully deserving of the AA's award for Best Breakfast in England, bestowed a few years ago. Children over eight welcome. No smoking throughout.

The Place

New Lydd Road, Camber, Rye, East Sussex TN31 7RB (01797 225057/www.theplace cambersands.co.uk). **Rates** £75-£85 double; £95 triple; £120 family room (sleeps up to 5). **Credit** AmEx, MC, V.
Until last year, the stretch of coastline that connected Rye with Dungeness was a desert when it came to decent hotels, and no more so than at Camber Sands, where the stunning beach was backed by an empty road. Then ex-adman Matthew Wolfman and business partner Mike Ashton turned a small chalet-style holiday park opposite the beach into the Place; a stylish, mid-price, high-quality hotel featuring 18 small but wonderfully comfortable, modern rooms and a brasserie serving some of the best food in the region. Its child-friendly approach may not be to urbane singletons' tastes, particularly as its sprawling ranch-style openness makes it perfect for kids wanting to tear around while parents keep a watchful eye on them from the lovely outdoor terrace, but don't be put off; this is a relaxing haven in a great location that'll have you hooked from your first visit. No smoking in all rooms.

Romney Bay House Hotel

Coast Road, Littlestone-on-Sea, New Romney, Kent TN28 8QY (01797 364747). **Rates** £85-£150 double. **Credit** AmEx, MC, V.
The hotel's new young owners, Clinton and Lisa Lovell, have no plans to radically alter anything about the best place to stay on the Dungeness peninsula; this includes keeping the rooms ultra-

comfortable (down to a hot-water bottle) and individually styled and furnished, and the dinner menu a set four-course feast made from the best local produce and carefully sourced ingredients. The ten-bedroom house, originally designed for Hollywood gossip columnist Hedda Hopper by Sir Clough Williams-Ellis, who built *The Prisoner* village Portmeirion, is bang on a pebble beach at the end of a bumpy track, near the Littlestone Golf Club. The hotel also boasts a croquet lawn, tennis court and bicycles for hire. All of which make it an absolute idyll for gentle activity and luxuriant relaxation. Bedrooms are no-smoking. Children over 14 welcome.

White Vine House

24 High Street, Rye, East Sussex TN31 7JF (01797 224748/www.whitevinehouse.co.uk). **Rates** £115-£145 double; £145-£175 family room (sleeps 3-4). **Credit** MC, V.
From the outside, the 16th-century White Vine House looks rather like a vertical version of the Chelsea Flower Show, with greenery and blooms covering every inch of the Georgian façade. The

floral theme continues inside to the breakfast room, which features hand-painted sunflowers growing up the walls, but is thoughtfully dropped in the seven bedrooms, where plush red carpets and embroidered linens create an air of luxury and quiet calm. This mood is carried through into the beautiful mahogany-panelled residents' room and oak-panelled Elizabethan Room, which is licensed for civil weddings. Children and dogs (they can arrange for dogs to be boarded at a local kennel, not on site) welcome. All rooms are no-smoking.

WHERE TO EAT & DRINK

Really good places to eat used to be few and far between in an area that is reliant largely on atmospheric medieval pubs serving simply prepared Romney Marsh lamb and locally caught fish and shellfish, but in the last year two new additions to the food scene have brought the tally of excellent restaurants to four: the Landgate Bistro and the Fish Café in Rye, the Place at Camber Sands and Romney Bay House Hotel.

Winchelsea

The Fish Café

*17 Tower Street, Rye, East Sussex TN31 7AT
(01797 222210/www.thefishcafe.com).* **Lunch
served** noon-2.30pm, **dinner served** 6-9pm
daily. **Main courses** £6.50-£18. **Credit**
AmEx, MC, V.

This is a light and airy setting for what is some
of the best food in Rye. As you would expect from
the name, the majority of the Fish Café's menu
comprises a wide range of fish and seafood dishes, including an impressive seafood lunch platter
for two at £19, but there are also meat and vegetarian alternatives. An excellent plate of oysters,
char-grilled lobster, mussels in white wine and a
Thai beef salad were all satisfying dishes, but special praise goes to the delicious puddings, notably
a wonderful pear tatin with blueberry ice-cream
and a baked apple with dried fruits, pistachio
caramel and Calvados ice-cream. Staff are very
helpful and can suggest appropriate wines to go
with particular dishes. The café also offers a
good-quality children's menu (two courses and
a drink for £5) Options include real cod fingers,
tagliatelle, salmon fish cakes or chicken and
vegetables, followed by bananas and custard, a
chocolate pot or fruit fritters. The ground-floor
café is open for lunch only, but there is a more for
mal dining space upstairs offering a similar, but
extended, range of dishes during the evening
(when booking is essential).

Landgate Bistro

*5-6 Landgate, Rye, East Sussex TN31 7LH
(01797 222829/www.landgatebistro.co.uk).*
Dinner served 7-9.30pm Tue-Fri; 7-10pm Sat.
Main courses £9.90-£13.20. **Set dinner**
(Tue-Thur) £17.90 3 courses. **Credit** MC, V.

A small, unprepossessing and unpretentious place
that's as affordable as it is good, the Landgate
Bistro prides itself on its use of excellent, often
local, ingredients. It is very popular – with locals
and visitors alike – so booking is a good idea if
you want to guarantee a table, especially if you're
here at weekends. Culinary highlights include
salmon and smoked cod fish cakes, roast partridge, English asparagus with a tangy orange
hollandaise and a wonderfully garlicky squid.
Desserts were something of a mixed bag: cherries

with a bayleaf custard in a biscuit cup and hazelnut meringue with raspberries were much better than an indifferent crème caramel.

Lydd Airport

Lydd, Romney Marsh, Kent TN29 9QL (01797 322411/Fly'n'Dine reservations (Lyddair) 01797 320000). **Meals served** 9am-5.30pm Mon-Thur, Sun; 9am-7pm Fri, Sat. **Main courses** £5.25-£6.75. **Credit** (over £10) AmEx, MC, V.

One for those who value curious experience over the culinary arts is Lydd Airport's weekend Fly'n'Dine, which consists of drinks and canapés, a low-level flight over the Kent coast and a five-course candlelit dinner in the 1960s-style Biggles Bar and Restaurant. The quality of the food is on a par with local pub grub, but it's the flight that's the big attraction, enabling as it does a fantastic bird's-eye view over a bleakly beautiful area studded with strange concrete structures such as the listening ears and coastal defence buildings. At £59 we think it's a bit of a bargain. There's also a lunch option at £39.

The Mermaid Inn

Mermaid Street, Rye, East Sussex TN31 7EY (01797 223065/www.mermaidinn.com). **Lunch served** noon-2.30pm, **dinner served** 7-9.30pm daily. **Set meal** £36.50 4 courses. **Credit** AmEx, MC, V.

This 600-year-old pub and restaurant on Rye's most twee street oozes quiet confidence and classless good service, which may be why it attracts a BMW-driving clientele that includes everyone from ageing rockers to the country set. There's a compulsory minimum charge in the evening of £35 per head for the modern English menu

DUNGENESS: STRANGE POWER

A thousand years ago, Dungeness Point just didn't exist. Longshore drift has built up huge banks of flint shingle, some of them 57 feet deep, which stretch miles out into the sea in a unique promontory. The light on this remote, gloriously bleak patch of land is odd, reflected from the sea on both sides, and the surreal quality of the landscape is enhanced by the presence of the massive Dungeness nuclear power station that dominates the horizon; at night its lights make it look like the Pompidou Centre in Paris.

But while the power station is the biggest construction on the point, it's by no means the strangest. Perhaps inspired by the unusual landscape, here you'll find a wealth of constructed curios that make for a fascinating architectural exploration, beginning with director Derek Jarman's Prospect Cottage.

The pretty black-and-yellow building is typical of the fishermen's cottages that dot the area, but the garden sets it apart. Jarman's unification of this space with the wider area is inspired. Delicately beautiful, it combines plants straight out of a sci-fi film with driftwood and found materials to create a miniature sculpture park; it has obviously inspired many of the surrounding gardens.

Less aesthetically pleasing but equally worth exploring are shacks constructed of railway carriages dating back to the late 1800s, when the Southern Railway built a station to transport shingle extracted from the beach. When the line went, the carriages remained. The simplest homes retain the sleek, pneumatic shape of the carriage, others sport sundry outhouses and additions that make them look like relics from the Wild West.

The jewel in the crown, however, is the RIBA award-winning, rubber-clad weekend house Vista, designed by architect Simon Conder. The 990-square-foot house, built on the site of a 1930s fishing hut, is constructed of timber and plywood and covered in a skin similar to a wetsuit, making it reminiscent of an Anish Kapoor sculpture. The flat, matt material seems to form a black hole in this huge, light-filled space that contrasts wonderfully with the 1930s Airstream caravan serving as a spare bedroom outside. Conder's masterful use of rubber was no gimmick; picking up on the aesthetic of the traditional black pitch cottages surrounding it, it also does away with the need for exterior drainage and roof guttering.

(excluding drinks), but that gets you four courses of a small but varied set menu, or, if you opt for à la carte, dishes like lobster thermidor or Dover sole. Alternatively, a bar menu of baguettes, platters and sandwiches can be washed down with a fine selection of beers in the lovely bar or small, sunlit garden.

The New Inn

German Street, Winchelsea, East Sussex TN36 4EN (01797 226252). **Lunch served** noon-2.30pm, **dinner served** 6.30-9pm Mon-Sat. **Meals served** noon-9pm Sun. **Main courses** £5.95-£13.95. **Rates** £55-£70 double; £65 family (sleeps 4). **Credit** AmEx, MC, V.

Dante Gabriel Rossetti commented on Winchelsea's 'pleasant doziness' from this pub in 1866, and it's easy to see why. Stepping from the beautiful churchyard into the wonderfully cosy New Inn, one of just two surviving pubs in town, makes you feel as though you've wandered into *The Archers'* Bull pub (pre-computer). There's a louche, laid-back feeling that makes you want to sit and sup ale all day, the locals are as friendly and welcoming as the staff, good hearty bar snacks are there for the taking, and the wide-ranging menu includes traditional dishes such as roasts at £6.95, own-made pâtés and soups. Specials lean towards locally caught fish, including Rye Bay scallops with bacon, cream and wine (£12.95), and rooms are available should the doziness overwhelm you. There's also a lovely walled garden for outside dozing.

The Pilot

Battery Road, Lydd, Dungeness, Kent TN29 9NJ (01797 320314/www.thepilot.uk.com). **Lunch served** noon-2.30pm, **dinner served** 6-9pm Mon-Fri. **Meals served** noon-9pm Sat; noon-8pm Sun. **Main courses** £4.95-£9.50. **Credit** MC, V.

This down-to-earth pub serves some of the best fish and chips in Kent. Enormous portions of battered cod, huss, skate, plaice and haddock are as fresh as can be and cooked to order, but steak and kidney pie is popular too, with a proper baked-with-the-pie pastry crust. Give the starters and puddings a miss, drink beers from Greene King and lobby the landlord to stop serving plastic sachets of sauces – it's an insult to the fish.

The Place

New Lydd Road, Camber, Rye, East Sussex TN31 7RB (01797 225057/www.theplace cambersands.co.uk). **Lunch served** noon-2pm Mon-Fri; noon-2.30pm Sat, Sun. **Dinner served** 6.30-9pm Mon-Thur, Sun; 6.30-9.30pm Fri, Sat. **Main courses** £7.95-£14.95. **Credit** AmEx, MC, V.

The light-filled and expansive brasserie and terrace at the Place is a welcome addition to the area's restaurant scene, and not just for the laid-back atmosphere and friendly staff; the food is easily on a par with the best in the region. The excellent menu, which changes monthly, offers meat, game and fish in abundance. The extensive selection of starters included a celeriac and cinnamon soup that was delicate yet filling, and steamed Scottish scallops with garlic and ginger that were cooked to perfection, bringing out the intense flavour and meaty texture of the scallops. Mains and puds were equally delicious – and the portions generous, necessitating an eerie and wonderful midnight walk on the beach opposite before bedtime.

Red Lion Pub

Snargate, Romney Marsh, Kent TN29 9UQ (01797 344648). **Open** noon-3pm, 7-11pm Mon-Sat; noon-3pm, 7-10.30pm Sun. **No credit cards**.

The tiny, multi-award-winning Red Lion is something of a Romney Marsh institution, famed for its annual three-day beer festival (dates vary) and the fact that it doesn't do food; but, in a nice touch, you are welcome to bring your own. If you do, you can unpack your picnic lunch/supper in a pub that dates back to the early 17th century and has been run by the same family for a few years shy of a century. It's an absolute beauty as well: three tiny rooms featuring a wealth of intriguing memorabilia and photographs, an antique marble counter that makes it look more butcher's shop than bar, tongue-and-groove wall panelling, heaps of games (including nine men's morris and table skittles) and, of course, a range of beers and country wines wide enough to keep you sated and happy for a long time.

Romney Bay House Hotel

Coast Road, Littlestone-on-Sea, New Romney, Kent TN28 8QY (01797 364747). **Dinner served** 7.30pm Tue, Wed, Fri, Sat. **Four-course set dinner** £35 per person, excluding drinks (booking essential for non-residents). **Credit** AmEx, MC, V.

The Romney Bay House Hotel changed hands last year, and the new head of its kitchen is a chef whose approach to food and fine dining shares one key feature with former co-proprietor Jennifer: top-quality ingredients served over a four-course set menu. Arriving promptly at 7.30pm for an 8pm dinnertime, you'll be served delicious hors d'oeuvres and nibbles in the tiny drawing room as you and your fellow diners make your wine selection from what is undoubtedly the best list in the region. Then it's into the light, airy and very quiet dining room for a modern Anglo-French feast. While the food is undoubtedly excellent, there can be long silences as all diners are served at the same time, inducing a less than comfortable atmosphere. Also open for afternoon teas.

Tea Tree

12 High Street, Winchelsea, East Sussex TN36 4EA (Tel 01797 226102/www.the-tea-tree.co.uk). **Meals served** *Mar-Oct* 10am-5pm

It's the Place to stay and eat.

daily. *Nov-Feb* 10am-5pm Wed-Sun. **Main courses** £6.95-£7.95. **Set tea** £5.25 scones, tea for one. **Credit** (over £10) MC, V.

Housed in a 15th-century building that was once the town forge, the Tea Tree tearooms ooze olde-worlde charm. The food – a good range of sandwiches and baguettes through to lovely tea-time treats – is supplemented by a huge array of globally sourced teas and coffees. Particularly luscious are the specials, including the 'ultimate Tea Tree special for two' (£16.75): a choice of teas and sandwiches plus two home-made scones with butter, strawberry preserve and fresh dairy cream, rounded off with two pieces of cake (the carrot cake is particularly recommended).

Woolpack Inn

Beacon Lane, nr Brookland, Kent TN29 9TJ (01797 344321). **Lunch served** noon-2pm, **dinner served** 6-9pm Mon-Fri. **Meals served** noon-9pm Sat, Sun. **Main courses** £5.45-£19. **Credit** MC, V.

This lovely Romney Marsh pub, with its enormous, crackling log fire, low ceilings and original 15th-century beams sourced, rather enterprisingly, from local shipwrecks, is hugely popular with contented and clued-up locals, so get here early if you want some of the good-quality pub grub before they call last orders for food – or be prepared for a lengthy wait. The menu is extensive: the ploughman's – cheddar, pâté, stilton

or ham are generally on offer – comes piled high, and the dishes of the day on a recent visit included a platter of tender liver and bacon, steak and kidney pudding boiled in cloth and a range of local seafood dishes. A good range of fish dishes, salads and a kid's meal at £3 complete the menu. Accompany food with a strong selection of beers and wines, the latter starting at a very reasonable £8.50 a bottle.

Ypres Castle Inn

Gun Garden, Rye, East Sussex TN31 7HH (01797 223248). **Meals served** *July-Sept* noon-2.30pm, 7-9pm daily. *Oct-June* noon-2.30pm, 7-9pm Mon, Wed-Sat; noon-2.30pm Sun. **Main courses** £6.95-£12.50. **Credit** AmEx, MC, V.

Situated at the base of the 13th-century Ypres Tower overlooking the marsh and canal, the cosy Ypres Castle Inn serves an eclectic mix of superior pub food at moderate prices. There are locally produced steaks and lamb served with a choice of potatoes, whole grilled plaice, cod wrapped in prosciutto and a decent range of vegetarian dishes. Arriving late will entail a wait for your food, but a good selection of English ales and local publications – from newspapers to leaflets and guides – while away the time nicely, and the friendly staff make sure the wait is a relaxed, comfortable one.

Brighton

The seaside resort with urban style.

These are exciting times for naughty old Brighton. One of Britain's best-loved weekend seaside destinations, awarded city status in 2001, it's brimming with new architectural schemes. A new skating arena is being built next to Brighton Marina, Frank Gehry of Bilbao Guggenheim fame is behind a £220-million proposal for a sports complex, public gardens and flats on Hove seafront and every month a new designer bar or boutique hotel opens up. None of this has jaded Brighton's traditional sense of fun. A gay hub, a major international student town and child-friendly to boot – that stand-offish Antipodean taking his offspring to the free seafront play area will be latest resident Nick Cave – Brighton still welcomes weekend gaggles of hen parties, clubbers, nudists, discerning vegetarians, sunseekers, surfers and wastrels. It practically invented the dirty weekend.

Accommodation	★★★★
Food & drink	★★★
Nightlife	★★★★
Shopping	★★★
Culture	★★★
Sights	★★
Scenery	★★

Most visitors are happy to restrict themselves to the tumble downhill from the station to the seafront, calling at a couple of bars down Queen Street or West Street before plunging on to the pebbles or the pier and venturing little further beyond. Getting the best out of Brighton means discovering its unusual little pockets, perhaps in the gay quarter of Kemp Town, the savage drinking culture of Hanover, the airy terraces of Montpelier or the working-class chic of Hove. Although hilly, all is accessible by an award-winning bus network – with an all-night service on main lines, and some of which drop you off by South Downs footpaths – or by reasonably priced, readily available taxi. The list of renegades Brighton has accommodated and inspired would be too long to mention – each bus features the name of one – but suffice to say that every barfly has a tale to tell, and you're bound to bump into a bit player from *Z Cars* or an ex-*Blue Peter* presenter.

Rushing down to Brighton on a jolly is nothing new. Once the fishing village of Brighthelmstone had been transformed into a curative retreat by Dr Richard Russell and his seawater therapies in the mid 18th century, foppish Londoners flocked down in droves. Hotels were built and bathing machines wheeled out. In 1783 the future George IV rented a farmhouse here and eventually converted it into a faux-oriental pleasure palace – the Royal Pavilion, see it today and giggle – and invited the nation's creative, beautiful and ambitious young things to join him for a life of drinking, womanising and gambling. Suddenly fashionable, the town's population expanded from 3,500 in 1780 to 40,500 in 1831. The train line from London was opened ten years later, Queen Victoria stripped the Pavilion and snubbed the seaside resort, and Brighton has been a quirky, populist escape ever since.

Victorian Brighton saw a profusion of eccentric engineering projects including three piers, only one of which is still standing today. Brighton (or Palace) Pier is a messy clutter of hot dog stands, karaoke, candyfloss and fairground rides; this is the one Raymond Briggs's Snowman flies over in the Christmas cartoon. The superior West Pier was suspiciously firebombed while the funding of major restoration work

was being agreed in 2003. Today the West Pier sinks ever deeper into the sea while Palace Pier draws thousands of video-gaming, chip-chomping, rollercoaster-riding funsters. It's this tacky image, though, a vestige of the gangland lore of Greene's novel and bank holiday punch-ups enshrined by Townshend, that today's Brighton is trying to shed.

So much to do, so little time

With seven miles of coastline, Brighton is still first and foremost a seaside resort – but its role as an annexe of London means that the shopper, the foodie, the barhopper and the clubber are well catered for. As for the discerning sightseer – well, there's the Royal Pavilion (01273 292822, www.royalpavilion.org.uk). George IV's fantasy palace – Indian on the outside, dragon-festooned Chinese inside – is the city's only real cultural attraction, and a real wow at that. Its transformation from farmhouse to villa to extravagant party pad came about after George IV became Prince Regent in 1811. He had John Nash, create a no-expense-spared oriental fantasy, an opulent, camp and spectacular series of rooms recently restored in a £10-million refit. The banqueting room alone, with its extraordinary chandelier, is almost worth the £5.95 admission fee. The adjoining kitchen, like a set from Gosford Park, recreates the atmosphere behind the scenes with abundant pheasant, rabbit and fish. Elsewhere, tiny royal beds are embellished with lacquered dragon patterns, and the ballroom and music room exude style. Queen Vic would have none of it, though, and shipped much of the furniture to Kensington Palace. A 20-minute film tells the whole story.

In the gardens, the Brighton Museum and Art Gallery (01273 290900, www.brighton.virtualmuseum.info) offers an eclectic collection of 20th-century design, ethnic art and local social history; admission is free. The other attractions are child-friendly: the quaint, tatty Sea-Life Centre (Marine Parade, 01273 604234, www.sealife europe.com), its Ocean Tunnel below a rickety mock-up of Nemo's *Nautilus* letting you see sharks, rays and Lulu, the ailing giant turtle, swim overhead; and the Volks Electric Railway (285 Madeira Drive, 01273 292718, open Easter-mid Sept), a 12-minute ride along the beach from the Sea-Life Centre to the Marina. Free playparks line the seafront. More commercial leisure activities – bowling, a UGC multiplex, any number of chain eateries – can be found at the Brighton Marina (www.brighton marina.co.uk), just over a mile to the east of the Palace Pier. Fishing boats, diving trips and sailing excursions can be arranged at the little information hut next to the petrol station.

Brighton

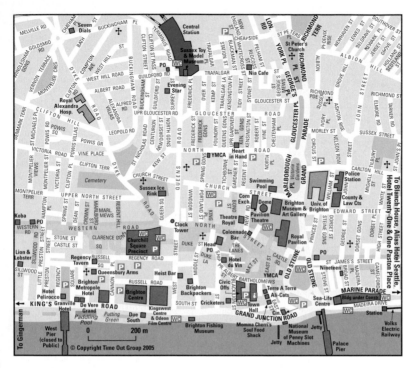

Brighton can offer the shopper any number of independent establishments. There's a high concentration of clothes, vinyl, gift and kitsch stores in and around North Laine, a short walk from the station, a slightly more haphazard collection of stalls and shops than you'll find in the network of narrow cobbled alleyways right in town known as the Lanes. Here bric-a-brac, jewellery and antiques shops abound. As well as equally excelling in kitsch, Kemp Town specialises in food stores and delicatessens.

Brighton's arts festival and carnival (www.brighton-festival.org.uk) in May, and simultaneous Fringe, are as punchy and prestigious as any in England. July's Beach Boutique party (currently under review), August's Pride rally and November's Brighton Film Festival (www.cine-city.co.uk) flood the town with visitors. The bar scene is booming, the clubs are packed and you'll need to book ahead for a bed at the key boutique hotels or a table at the signature restaurants. All Brighton needs now is a proper football ground.

WHERE TO STAY

Brighton now boasts some of England's coolest lodgings, with three or four establishments more worthy of Manhattan than a site a stone's throw from the tacky seafront. The upscale hotel stock has been further embellished with the opening of Drakes (43-44 Marine Parade, 01273 696934, www.drakesofbrighton.com), which has 20 bespoke, mainly seafront, rooms, and a branch of Gingerman (*p70*). Beware the fact that many local establishments, whether a trendy boutique hotel or a room above a pub, do not accept bookings for Saturday night only; and bear in mind that during the Brighton Festival in May, Pride weekend in August and for any party conference in September, hotels fill up fast. The Tourist Information Centre (*see p65*) can reserve on your behalf for £1 per person per reservation.

There are two main areas for hotels. On New Steine in Kemp Town, among the average three-star hotels and guesthouses, are the new, übercool Square Hotel (*see p66*) and the gay-friendly Elysian (19 New Steine, 01273 609632, www.hotel elysian.co.uk, doubles from £90). Around Regency Square, opposite the West Pier, there's more variety, the best of which are the Adelaide Hotel (51 Regency Square, 01273 205286, doubles £68-£92) and the Regency Hotel (28 Regency Square, 01273 202690, www.regencybrighton.co.uk, doubles £85-£110). Russell Square also has a host of guesthouses, and the seafront can turn up the odd bargain. For a clean, cheap and central chain option try Brighton Premier Lodge (144 North Street, 0870 990 6340, www.premierlodge.com, doubles £54). Brighton Backpackers (75-76 Middle Street, 01273 777717, www.brightonbackpackers.com, £13-£15 per person in four- to eight-bed dorms, doubles £30) is good for budget travellers.

Alias Hotel Seattle

Brighton Marina, BN2 5WA (01273 679799/ www.aliashotels.com). **Rates** £100-£155 double. **Credit** AmEx, DC, MC, V.

Hip, modern and high-tech, the Brighton branch of the Alias design-hotel chain makes full use of its marina backdrop. Flooded with natural light, cool, comfortable and quirky, its rooms have fabulous touches that will get you scouring the website for another hot deal: white leather headboards, monsoon showers, feather-and-down duvets and smart Italian furniture. Once the sun rises, forget tureens of lukewarm egg and beans for breakfast – indulge in Bento in Bed or a box of blueberry muffins and smoked salmon bagels. Seafood predominates at the Mediterranean-inspired Café Paradiso and superior cocktails are served in the candlelit Black and White bar, open only to hotel residents and their guests. Children welcome.

Blanch House

17 Atlingworth Street, BN2 1PL (01273 603504/www.blanchhouse.co.uk). **Rates** £125-£220 double. **Credit** AmEx, MC, V.

Hotel design at its best. That this unassuming Georgian terrace house should have its dozen rooms themed after snowstorms, roses, rococo decor and '70s disco is all well and good, but that's just for starters. Fogarty goose-and-duck down duvets and pillows, Relyon pocket-sprung beds, big plasma screens and numerous other thoughtful touches see Chris (Groucho Club) Edwardes and Amanda Blanch's boutique beauty showered in praise in broadsheets and style mags. Guests stumping up £125 for the most basic package at this chic retreat will not feel hard done by; those splashing out the full £220, jacuzzi and all, will be truly indulged. A full range of therapies and beauty pampering – Indian head massages, reflexology, Reiki treatments – is on offer, the cocktail bar cannot fail to hit the spot given the management pedigree, and the Modern European restaurant has diners dashing down from London and beyond. Children and pets welcome.

De Vere Grand

97 King's Road, BN1 2FW (01273 224300/ www.grandbrighton.co.uk). **Rates** £250-£360 double; £600-£1,500 suite. **Credit** AmEx, DC, MC, V.

The name fits the bill. This is, most certainly, Brighton's grandest hotel – from the outside at least. The ornate wedding-cake frontage, the

tinkling of piano ivories from the Victoria Lounge bar as you walk through reception, the superior spa facilities. Yet once past this façade, you may be in for something of a surprise (or even disappointment), particularly if you're in a rather bland (at best) inland room; although the sea view ones are fit for that special occasion. Note too that the 'leisure break' weekend tariff is a winner – book two nights in a double seaview for £130 per person per night; stay for a third night and the price drops by 50%. At these prices, impulsive love affairs can only blossom. Some local travel companies also offer bargain Sunday-night stays. There are high teas in the bar, fine dining at the King's Restaurant and a wild array of characters making bizarre chit-chat in both.

Granville Hotel

124 King's Road, BN1 2FY (01273 326302/ www.granvillehotel.co.uk). **Rates** £55-£185 double. **Credit** AmEx, DC, MC, V.

Billing itself as Brighton's 'original' boutique hotel, the seafront Granville has been somewhat left behind by the recent spate of all-singing, all-dancing boutique beauties opening up all around it. Still, the three-star Granville is handy if you're after a sea view but want something with more personality than the Grand or Metropole. The spacious front rooms have unrivalled views of what remains of the West Pier and are surprisingly quiet – all are individually themed. If you're feeling extravagant, opt for an elaborately carved four-poster with en suite jacuzzi; other themed rooms include the art deco Noel Coward Room and the romantic Brighton Rock Room, with muslin-draped Victorian four-poster. A Pacific Rim menu is offered in the basement restaurant, DaDu. All bedrooms are no-smoking. Children welcome.

Hotel du Vin

2-6 Ship Street, BN1 1AD (01273 718588/ www.hotelduvin.com). **Rates** £140-£165 double; £260-£360 suite. **Credit** AmEx, DC, MC, V.

This landmark hotel, wine bar and bistro is perfectly located between the shopping hub of the Lanes and the seafront. One of half-a-dozen classy, provincial venues in this beautifully appointed chain, the Brighton branch is set in a jumble of mock Tudor and Gothic revival buildings (note the gargoyles and inlaid staircase), within which three dozen rooms boast fine Egyptian linens on the beds and pounding showers next door. High-quality bistro food brings many non-guests to the restaurant, a carefully chosen cellar supplying an equally popular and talked-about wine bar on the first floor terrace. Staff are welcoming and very competent. Book well in advance.

TOURIST INFORMATION

Bartholomew Square, BN1 1JS (0906 711 2255/www.visitbrighton.com).

Hotel Pelirocco

10 Regency Square, BN1 2FG (01273 327055/ www.hotelpelirocco.co.uk). **Rates** £100-£140 double; £260 suite. **Credit** MC, V.

Is the joke wearing thin at the Pelirocco? Not yet, it seems: its 19 bedrooms with pop subculture themes are invariably all full at weekends. What better backdrop to a debauched two-dayer down at the seaside than the self-styled 'sauciest stopover' in Brighton? Crawl in to Modrophenia or Betty Page's Boudoir after a night on the razz and wake up to target bedspreads and scooter wing-mirrors, or fetish art and peepholes on the bathroom door. Once you stop giggling, though, you may remember you're spending over £100 (including an approximate £10 levy at weekends) on jokey decor you can brag to your mates about – apart from PlayStation consoles for post-clubbing insomniacs, the facilities are pretty standard. The bar, though, is a hoot, open till 4am, characterised by Jamie Reid's cut-and-paste Pistols artwork, also used for the lettering on all the literature. Real rock 'n' rollers can pay an extra £10 for a 2pm check-out. Now why doesn't that idea catch on?

Hotel Twenty-One

21 Charlotte Street, BN2 1AG (01273 686450/ www.smoothhound.co.uk/hotels/21.html). **Rates** £60-£80 double. **Credit** MC, V.

The accommodating couple who run this charming and unusual Kemp Town guesthouse, in a street lined with average ones, provide the friendliest welcome in Brighton – and then leave you well alone to do your own thing. Pick of the themed rooms is the Victorian one, the largest of the seven, and centrepieced by a relaxing four-poster bed. The other favourite is found in the basement, where (invariably hen) parties can be lodged in adjoining large rooms at an attractive rate per head. Four-posters also feature on other rooms, some of which get a slice of sea view. Breakfast is more than ample and the seafront as close as the bars of St James Street in the opposite direction. One word of warning to drivers – local parking regulations are set to change here in 2005, so ask advice when you book.

Neo Hotel

19 Oriental Place, BN1 2LL (01273 711104/ www.neohotel. com). **Rates** £85-£150 double. **Credit** MC, V.

Yet another townhouse reworked as a chic, designer pad, the Neo is big on mood and detail, even if its front door actually faces onto a grotty sidestreet parallel to the seafront. Each of the 11 rooms (numbered one to ten, and 12) is individually decorated in tasteful colours, though the management (interiors stylists, don't you know?) have been wise not to give them humourless themed names as well: room 12 is the attic, room one is ornate, and so on. As always, it's the little touches which earn repeat business – the luscious organic toiletries or the chandeliers in the breakfast room. Bathrooms glisten with chrome. The bar is unsurprisingly cool, with a well-informed wine list and proper cocktails. All that's missing is a restaurant, which is due to arrive in late 2005. Children welcome.

Nineteen

19 Broad Street, BN2 1TJ (01273 675529/ www.hotelnineteen.co.uk). **Rates** £70-£250 (min 2-night stay if incl Sat) double. **Credit** AmEx, MC, V.

Just eight rooms make this stylish townhouse hotel, which successfully mixes period features with contemporary works by local artists. Thanks to minimalist decor and light colours, even the smaller rooms feel bright and airy. Beds sit on bases of illuminated, coloured glass bricks, the linen and walls are fresh and white, and rooms have CD and video facilities and fresh flowers. Guests may help themselves to drinks and snacks from the kitchen, and borrow videos, CDs and magazines. Breakfast (everything is organic or free-range where possible) is served in a basement with small decked area, and there are plans for a roof-top suite and basement bar.

Square Hotel

4 New Steine, BN2 1PB (01273 691777/ www.squarebrighton.com). **Rates** £140-£190 double. **Credit** AmEx, DC, MC, V.

The newest hotel in town, talked about in hushed, reverent tones now that the dust has settled after its glitzy launch in October 2004. So cool it doesn't need to help out first-time visitors with so much as a sign above the door – look for the cube logo two-thirds of the way to the sea on the right-hand side as you walk down this guesthouse-fringed, quiet green square – Geoff Greenway's chic establishment is another step towards Stockholm for this once seedy resort renowned for its rickety B&Bs. Sophisticated would be the best way to describe the nine double and 'king' rooms, some offering glimpses of the sea – or, as the publicity material says, many have 'superb ocean views'. Similar bombast is also bandied about the admittedly neat basement area, which can be hired. This so-called 'reverse penthouse' provides pampering and privacy, and no designer hotel would be complete without its stylishly minimalist lounge bar. Only accessible to guests and friends, it opens late. The morning after, you can choose from a whole gamut of treatments and therapies, including a couples massage in your own room, reflexology and Indian head massage.

WHERE TO EAT & DRINK

Of the nearly 500 restaurants in Brighton alone, only a handful (Blanch House, One Paston Place, Gingerman, Seven Dials) are premier league. The rest comprise an attractive global mix, with plenty of seafood and imaginative choices for vegetarians; nearly every venue welcomes children.

Charismatic and fun, the Lanes are the centre of Brighton's shopping bustle.

Brighton

Idiosyncratic style at Blanch House.

For a sea view, you'll have to stick to chips or standard pizzas, with a couple of honourable exceptions: Café Paradiso (at Alias Hotel Seattle, *see p65*) and Due South (139 King's Road Arches, BN1 2NF, 01273 821218). Late-night dining is a rarity, although the reliable Buddies (*see p72* **Brighton by night**) can provide well-priced, staple meals and drinks – and a sea view – right round the clock.

Most local pubs worth their salt do food, and such is the competition, it shouldn't be shabby. Invariably it will be Thai, with meat and veggie roasts on Sunday. Traditional pubs, lower-league designer bars and chains dot the centre of town, but there's enough individuality – at least among the clientele – to subdue boredom. The Lanes are awash with bars – and hen parties and unruly weekenders. A better barhop is to be had in Kemp Town, on and off St James's Street, and in Hanover, on and around Southover Street.

The dearth of late-night licences means that post-midnight options fall between a nightclub (*see p72* **Brighton by night**) and the ever-increasing members' bars. Few offer temporary membership on the night.

Ali-Cats

80 East Street, BN1 1NF (01273 748103/ www.alicatsbar.com). **Open** 3-11pm Mon-Sat; 3-10.30pm Sun. **Credit** MC, V.

An independent basement bar underneath the Prodigal bar/restaurant just in from the seafront – look for the set of steps with cartoon fishbones carved into the concrete. This quite marvellous establishment, a dark cellar full of spiky characters, not only shows unusual and cult films (from French arthouse and local shorts to *Blue Velvet* and *Love Actually*) to coincide with happy hour, but gives local DJs a platform without thought for charging any entry fee (the music policy is particularly commendable: 'If there's anything with an ounce of funk in it, it'll be played'). It's Happy hour all night Monday, £2 pints on Sundays. Recommended.

Brighton Rocks

6 Rock Place, BN2 1TF (01273 601139). **Open** 11am-11pm Mon-Sat; noon-10.30pm Sun. **Meals served** noon-9pm Mon-Sat; noon-5pm Sun. **Credit** AmEx, MC, V.

Kemp Town's most talked-up bar, Brighton Rocks is modest in size, but makes up for it with a heated terrace, sparkling cocktails and superb organic cuisine. Oh, and friendly, switched-on staff who shake and spiel against an adventurous musical backdrop (DJs on Fridays), creating a constant buzz – whether last thing at night or during the popular Sunday lunch. Stylish yet cosy.

Colonnade Bar

10 New Road, BN1 1UF (01273 328728). **Open** noon-11pm Mon-Sat; noon-10.30pm Sun. **Credit** MC, V.

Although adjacent to the Theatre Royal (place your orders for interval drinks) and decked out in portraits of Penelope Keith, Leslie Phillips and a cast of hundreds, there is so much more to the classic Colonnade than the top hats, canes and white gloves adorning it. Excellent ales, for a start (Marston's Pedigree, John Smith's or Harvey's Sussex), plus a wine of the month at £8.75 a bottle – and a terrible urge to sip champagne. Most of all, this place scores for its civilised and civilising atmosphere and comfy alcoves of intense, arty banter, a world away from all the guzzling and groping going on around any nearby corner.

The Cricketers

15 Black Lion Street, BN1 1ND (01273 329472). **Open** 11am-11pm Mon-Sat; noon-10.30pm Sun. **Lunch served** noon-3pm Mon-Fri; noon-5pm Sat; noon-4pm Sun. **Credit** MC, V.

Cosy, historic and centrally located in the Lanes, the low-ceilinged Cricketers invariably accommodates gaggles of blokes, clusters of shoppers and local employees on their lunch breaks. As they stoop to scoff crisps or avoid clunking their head on some daft knick-knack, you might catch sight of the odd solitary, literary sole, attracted by mention of the place in *Brighton Rock* by former regular Graham Greene, and the chance of anonymity while seated in one of the many alcoves.

Ebony Room

1B Waterfront, Brighton Marina, BN2 5WA (01273 675007/www.ebonyroom.co.uk). **Open** noon-11pm Mon-Wed; noon-midnight Thur; noon-1am Fri, Sat; noon-10.30pm Sun. **Meals served** noon-9.30pm Mon-Wed, Sun; noon-10pm Thur; noon-10.30pm Fri, Sat. **Credit** AmEx, DC, MC, V.

Chic champagne and piano bar on the marina whose air of exclusivity is enhanced by the much-lauded private Two Ton Table, proudly raised in the middle of the main room to accommodate the eight people who are happy to shell out £200 for their own waitress and DVD player. The other guests, many of whom reserve of a weekend anyway, make do with 16 types of champagne, imaginatively subtle cocktails and jazzy tunes from a turquoise Roland keyboard. Sexy, curvaceous furniture and intimate booths concoct the perfect spot for a late date. If conversation drags, there's even a resident magician.

Evening Star

55-56 Surrey Street, BN1 3PB (01273 328931/www.eveningstarbrighton.co.uk). **Open** noon-11pm Mon-Sat; noon-10.30pm Sun. **Credit** MC, V.

A short walk down from the station, parallel to the main Queen's Road, this independent microbrewery is a rustic haven for real ale types. Ten hand pumps dispense house beers including some from Dark Star of Haywards Heath, whose Spiced Vice wheat beer is giving the Belgians a run for their money. A host of unpronounceable Flemish brews come by the bottle, including five by Cantillon, a rarity even in its native Brussels. Occasional pub quizzes and musicians offer blokey entertainment above the manly talk of unusual vintages.

Gingerman

21A Norfolk Square, BN1 2PD (01273 326688/www.gingermanrestaurant.com). **Lunch served** 12.30-1.45pm, **dinner served** 7-10pm Tue-Sat. **Set lunch** £9.95 1 course, £12.95 2 courses, £14.95 3 courses. **Set dinner** £22 2 courses, £25 3 courses. **Credit** AmEx, DC, MC, V.

Simplicity itself, Ben McKellar's Gingerman offers top quality continental – mainly French – cuisine at accessible prices. The weekly-changing lunch menu is an absolute winner. The main menu, available for lunch or dinner, shows style and imagination: starters include a crispy pig's trotter beignet with beetroot and tartare sauce, or warm bundles of asparagus with frisée, croûtons and pancetta; mains of monkfish and sweet potato red curry with jasmine rice or braised duck leg in red wine with spätzle and spring onions. Sauces are rich and meaty but once advised, the kitchen will cater each sauce to vegetarians' wishes. Equal care is taken over the desserts such as hot raspberry syrup poured into an erect soufflé. Coffee is served with delicate raspberry jam cakes, and an extensive choice of digestifs can be complemented by a seafront walk just three minutes away.

The Greys

105 Southover Street, BN2 9UA (01273 680734/www.greyspub.com). **Open** 5.30-11pm Mon; noon-11pm Tue-Sat; noon-10.30pm Sun. **Lunch served** noon-3pm Tue-Sun. **Dinner served** 6-9pm Tue-Thur, Sat. **Credit** MC, V.

In a street lined with good bars – check out the Geese Have Gone Over the Water opposite, or the Dover Castle and the Charles Napier a short walk up the incline – the Greys is the pick of the bunch. Homely and well run, this Hanover mainstay offers rare Belgian beer, imaginative food (a chicken dish from central Africa or cassoulet cooked in said Belgian beer), unplugged country or folk sessions, and a communal ambience enhanced by a wooden staircase and snugs, a fireplace and the tangible feeling that everyone, staff included, is enjoying themselves. The Belgian beer festival at Easter is a must.

Heist

57 West Street, BN1 2RA (01273 822555/ www.heistbar.com). **Open/meals served** noon-11pm Mon-Wed; noon-1am Thur-Sat; noon-12.30am Sun. **Credit** AmEx, DC, MC, V. The most palatable of the many venues lining the greyhound run from station to seafront, the rather tasty Heist is a dark lounge bar in which the glow of tealights reveals the casual interlocking of limbs by couples esconced in the intimate black seating. An original stained glass window, open fireplace and ancient furniture adds to the satisfyingly laid-back mood. Even the imbibers at the long, cool bar counter seem relaxed, although the atmosphere is upped a gear or two for late DJ sessions from Thursday through to open house on a Sunday. The private lounge downstairs is a popular option for local movers and shakers.

Heart In Hand

75 North Road, BN1 1YD (01273 683320). **Open** 11am-11pm Mon-Sat; noon-10.30pm Sun. **Meals served** noon-5pm daily. **Credit** MC, V. North Laine's classic rock 'n' roll bar, a green-tiled beauty propping up a street corner beside the commercial bustle of the North Laine. In fact, much of the custom either comes from street traders (not least from the two rare music shops in nearby Gardner Street) or local musicians talking shop

BRIGHTON BY NIGHT

Libertine, liberal Brighton is best appreciated by night. Mixed, irreverent and inventive, the local clubbing scene accommodates alcopoppers down West Street, undiscerning pleasure seekers on the seafront and diehard clubbers at little pockets around town. The key to this successful move away from seedy post-pub discotheques to quality, cosmopolitan nightspots has been a dynamic and influential gay community, marginalised in lesser seaside towns – coupled with the phenomenon known as Norman Cook. Fatboy Slim's free seafront clubfest, the Big Beach Boutique, launched in 2001, may have been temporarily postponed for a couple of years due to security concerns after a quarter of a million people swamped the city centre in 2002, but its success galvanised the local DJ community and put Brighton on the map as a music capital. What Glastonbury is to rock festivals, Brighton is to clubbing. When Rio adopted the Big Beach concept in 2003, it was Brighton's name that was evoked.

Still, none of this hides the fact that gangs of pissed-up hens in dog-eared devil horns invade the city centre every weekend. West Street at chucking out time is not a pleasant place to be of a Friday, with young shavers and squawky girlies heading for Event II (Kingswest, 01273 732627, www.event2night

club.co.uk) or Creation (No.78, 01273 321628, www.creationbrighton.com).

A more grown-up crowd is happier to cross King's Road and head down to the sea-level arches, for fun at Arc (No.160, 01273 770505, www.arcbrighton.co.uk), drum 'n' bass at the Beach (No.171, 01273 722272) – or, better yet, for the much-lauded and stylish Funky Buddha Lounge (No.169, 01273 725541, www.funkybuddha.co.uk), high-profile Honey Club (No.214, 01273 202807, www.thehoneyclub.co.uk) or long-established, reputable Zap Club (No.189, 01273 202407).

Nights out down here can be accompanied by all manner of stony romping on the beach followed by, when things get a little chilly, a late supper or early breakfast, with drinks, at 24-hour diner Buddies (46-48 King's Road, 01273 323600, www.buddies24 hour.net). Club admission prices being (generally) reasonable, you should still have enough in your purse to satisfy the munchies and, let's face it, there are worse starts to the day than sunrise over Brighton seafront with a beer and Buddie breakfast in front of you.

Most of the above clubs put on at least one gay night (look out for Wild Fruit and Vavavavoom!), but that's only the tip of the iceberg. Landmark Kemp Town funhouses such as the sleek Envy (8-9 Marine Parade, 01273 624091) and

Brighton

and trading drummers (or, failing that, jokes about traders). The rest of us can enjoy a small, vibrant, neighbourhood local, festooned with tatty flyers and posters for past and future gig information, and crowned by a tatty jukebox (playing proper old 45s!) by the back wall, out of which blast the MC5, Love, Gloria Jones and the 13th Floor Elevators. Draught Leffe and Gailes provide further attraction.

Koba

135 Western Road, BN1 2LA (01273 720059/ www.kobauk.com). **Open** 5pm-2am Mon-Sat; 5-midnight Sun. **Credit** AmEx, MC, V.

the trashier but mega popular Revenge (32 Old Steine, 01273 606064, www.revenge.co.uk) are the biggest gay clubs on the south coast. Such is Kemp Town's successful crossover mix, however, that key nightspots such as the Volks Tavern (Madeira Drive, 01273 682828), Audio (10 Marine Parade, 01273 606906, www.audiobrighton.com) in the former Escape Club, and Funky Fish Club (New Madeira Hotel, 19-23 Marine Parade, 01273 696961, www.funkyfish club.co.uk) attract music lovers across the board; note, though, that Marine Parade is now lined with trendy new gay bars, in particular Charles Street (Nos 8-9, 01273 624091), with the inventive Pool club upstairs. Every tranny in town – amiably accompanied by goths, drag queens, geezers and lezzers – turn the Danny LaRue-inspired Harlequin (behind Woolworths, 43 Providence Place, 01273 620630, www.harlequin-brighton.co.uk) into the living embodiment of what might loosely be termed the Brighton ethic: live it up and let live.

Finally, mention must be made of the keynote, award-winning Ocean Rooms (1 Morley Street, 01273 699069, www.oceanrooms.co.uk), a venue that was entirely and excellently revamped in January 2005 and whose fabulous sound system and cool upstairs cocktail bar attract world-class DJs into town on regular occasions.

The city's key late-night cocktail and members' bar sits incongruously above Waitrose on the main road out to Hove, five minutes from Brighton city centre. For all the talk around town it generates, Koba at first appears disappointingly tiny, a small brown box dotted with cube seats and a candlelit view of local buses ferrying punters from Churchill Square. But it's cosy, each of the 85 cocktails is expertly prepared, and the vibe is that everyone's enjoying the privilege of being in a very special place indeed. This, however, is the tip of the iceberg, for the members' bar (access is only bequeathed to registered brethren, though unofficially you can get in for a small fee on the night) through a secret passage is a peach: a champagne suite with a roaring fire/air-conditioning, and the Gods, a gleaming altar to decadent drinking.

Lion & Lobster

24 Sillwood Street, BN1 2PS (01273 327299). **Open** 11am-11pm Mon-Wed; 11am-midnight Thur-Sat; noon-11pm Sun. **Meals served** noon-3pm, 5-7pm Mon-Wed; noon-8pm Thur-Sun. **Credit** MC, V.

What a wonderful, wonderful little pub this is. Tucked away behind Regency Square a ten-minute walk from the city centre, this lovely, lived-in corner boozer, Irish in provenance, international in outlook, boasts superb beers and ales (Warsteiner, Abbot, Timothy Taylor), fine food (the best Sunday roast in Brighton for £6.50), occasional live music, inconspicuous Sky Sports – but most of all a fine vibe, cool and communal. Roaring fires, seats outside in summer, stills from *Blowup* over the bar, jazz cuttings over the walls, a cosy back room for diners all combine to create a wholesome local. There's even rooms upstairs if you get stuck into a real session.

Momma Cherri's Soul Food Shack

11 Little East Street, BN1 1HT (01273 774545/www.mommacherri.co.uk) **Dinner served** 5-11pm Tue-Thur; 5pm-midnight Fri; 11am-midnight Sat; 11am-5pm Sun. **Main courses** £8-£11.50. **Set dinner** £20 3 courses. **Credit** AmEx, MC, V.

Authentic, filling and fun, dining out at Momma Cherri's is everything that mid-range dining out should be. Run out of a modest, one-level terraced house amid higgledy-piggledy buildings, Momma's is down-home and dandy. A suitable soundtrack of soul, R&B and, on Sundays, gospel, glides out of the speakers, as smooth as the staff flitting between the narrow gaps allowed by ten tables squeezed in. Summer and special occasions (4 July, Thanksgiving and the like) bring diners out on to the adjoining slab of pavement. And the food? Heaps of hearty goodness, grits 'n' all, typified by hulking plates of jambalaya (meat, fish or veg varieties) heavy enough to sink a paddle steamer. Other mains are categorised according to chicken, fish, pork or vegetarian staples. The three courses should come to £20 and, thereafter, you shouldn't need to eat for a week. There's

No fakes at the Real Eating Company on the Hove border.

breakfasts and brunches too, a menu for the children (celebrated rather than merely accommodated), and Dixie, Lone Star, Cave Creek and Mexican beers. Book at weekends.

Nia Café

87-88 Trafalgar Street, BN1 4EB (01273 671371). **Meals served** 9am-10pm Mon-Sat; 9am-6pm Sun. **Main courses** £7.50-£14. **Credit** AmEx, MC, V.

By day a busy pit stop offering all-day breakfasts to market browsers, after dark the Nia dims the industrial lights hanging over its dozen wooden tables and becomes a fully fledged restaurant –

without losing any of the funky chic native to the North Laines. The à la carte main menu is changed fortnightly and always features vegetarian, fish and lamb options. Twenty well-priced wines come by the bottle, five by the large glass. A handy short walk from the station.

One Paston Place

1 Paston Place, Brighton, BN2 1HA (01273 606933/www.onepastonplace.co.uk). **Lunch served** noon-2pm, **dinner served** 7-9.30pm Tue-Sat. **Set lunch** £16.50 2 courses, £19 3 courses. **Set dinner** £32.50 2 courses, £39 3 courses. **Credit** AmEx, MC, V.

Refurbished and now under the considerable expertise of Neapolitan chef and owner Francesco Furriello, Brighton's premier restaurant (arguably) has lost its upmarket French formality but gained a metropolitan buzz. The food is exquisite and presented by experienced, unstuffy staff eager to advise. The set lunch, for which many regulars happily don jacket and tie, is a delightful way to relieve yourself of £20 and step out into the trendy vibe of Kemp Town perfectly satisfied. The three main options invariably feature a fish and a lamb dish, from a lighter menu than Furriello's predecessors would have opted for, and one that is changed monthly. A somewhat

formal interior of chandeliers, mirrors and a strange pastoral mural may be a hangover from the old days, but already they're warming the espresso cups and more changes might be on the way. No smoking throughout.

Queensbury Arms

Queensbury Mews, BN1 2FE (01273 328159).
Open noon-11pm Mon-Sat; noon-10.30pm Sun.
Credit MC, V.
Otherwise known as the Hole in the Wall – there's a blue plaque outside to prove it – this tiny pub is one of Brighton's little jewels. Set opposite the

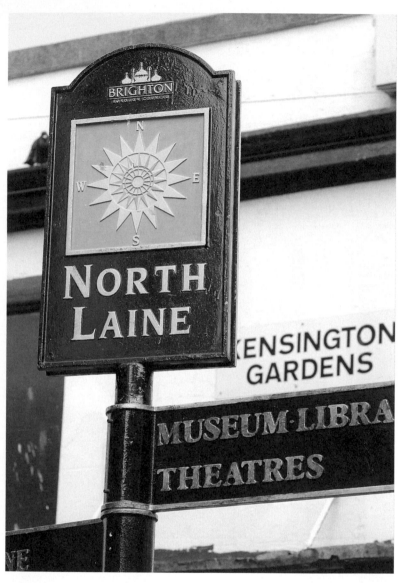

French Protestant church down a narrow mews beside the Hotel Metropole, this altar to Dora Bryan and the London Palladium is frequented by an older, gay clientele, bitching, bragging and waxing lyrical about Brighton's good old days. Two intimate bar spaces are provided for this entertaining sport, and spectators need only prop up the bar counter to appreciate the razor-sharp banter that is batted back and forth. A fine slice of life, indeed, buzzing beneath the bland commerce of a chain hotel.

Real Eating Company

86-87 Western Road, Hove, BN3 1JB (01273 221444/www.real-eating.co.uk). **Meals served** 9am-5pm Mon, Tue; 9am-9.30pm Wed-Sat; 10am-4pm Sun. **Main courses** £7.50-£15.95. **Credit** MC, V.

Opened in January 2004 as the flagship eaterie of a retail business specialising in quality foodstuffs, many sourced from local producers and/or organic, the plain and simple Real Eating Company provides all-day salads, soups and sandwiches headlined by a three-hour lunch period from noon. Seated either around the deli counter or at one of six tables in a tidy, skylighted back room, diners are treated to a daily-changing, seasonal choice of half-a-dozen eclectic starters – foie gras parfait, beetroot chutney and poilane toast – and eight mains – organic pork chop, quinces and curly kale, seared scallops with sautéed black pudding and new potatoes. Puddings (rhubarb and champagne sorbet), beers from microbreweries (Nyewood Gold from Ballards, £3) and hand-pressed apple and rhubarb juices from the Chegworth Valley stress the British influence. Yet to find its feet as a main lunchtime destination, but a welcome option on the otherwise bland Hove-Brighton border. No smoking throughout.

Regency Tavern
32-34 Russell Square, BN1 2EF (01273 325652). **Open** 11am-3pm, 6-11pm Mon-Fri; 11am-3pm, 6.30-11pm Sat; noon-3pm, 7-10.30pm Sun. **Lunch served** noon-2pm daily. **No credit cards.**
If Bet Lynch were a pub, this would be it. Behind a grand exterior on a corner of Russell Square right behind the city's main shopping centre hides an interior resembling an explosion in a tinsel factory. Although the staff serve as if performing at a post-war holiday camp, the place is run as a serious business. The commendable pub food is a main draw, so much so that bookings are taken for Sunday lunches. By the evening, staff and punters might team up for a spot of impromptu singing, arms linked, smiles wide. Unmissable.

Seven Dials
1-3 Buckingham Place, BN1 3TD (01273 885555/www.sevendialsrestaurant.co.uk). **Lunch served** noon-3pm Sun. **Dinner served** 7-10.30pm Tue-Fri; 6.30-10.30pm Sat; 7-9.30pm Sun. **Set lunch** (Tue-Sat) £10 2 courses, £15 3 courses. **Set dinner** £21.50 2 courses, £26.50 3 courses. **Credit** AmEx, MC, V.
Award-winning chef Sam Metcalfe has given this former bank some homely touches, decking out the staircase with arty black-and-white family photos, and providing his praiseworthy restaurant with hospitable staff. Most of all, Sam has lent imaginative touches to a capable kitchen – rump of lamb on aubergine caviar with sautéed wild garlic and a tomato, olive and rosemary sauce – that is visibly active from the summer terrace bordered by a row of box trees. Traffic noise and the constant bleep of the pedestrian crossing can infiltrate quiet moments, but bonhomie overcomes all and you will soon be contentedly digesting the appetiser of tomato and basil soup while awaiting one of half-a-dozen starters. Rich, classy desserts include a rather splendid pear and walnut tart with apricot glaze. Two- and three-course deals are a snip considering the quality of fare on offer.

Sidewinder
65 Upper St James's Street, BN2 1RF (01273 679927). **Open** noon-11pm Mon-Sat; noon-10.30pm Sun. **Meals served** noon-8.30pm Mon-Thur; noon-5.30pm Fri, Sat; noon-5pm Sun. **Credit** AmEx, MC, V.
This cool, crossover bar in the heart of Kemp Town is consistently popular thanks to its adventurous music policy (DJs spinning hip hop, jazz and points in between), high-quality food (plenty of mezze, subtle takes on standard meaty and veggie mains) and overall ambience. Parents with kids in tow feel as at home here as grungy students with an axe to grind. It's spacious enough to be both communal and intimate, and in summer its ample garden comes into its own.

Terre à Terre
71 East Street, Brighton, (01273 729051/www.terreaterre.co.uk). **Lunch served** noon-3pm Thur, Fri. **Dinner served** 6-10.30pm Tue-Fri. **Meals served** noon-10.30pm Sat, Sun. **Main courses** £11.50-£13.50. **Credit** AmEx, DC, MC, V.
Brighton's reliably inventive flagship vegetarian restaurant enjoys a reputation that attracts hordes of weekending pan-fried weary Londoners to its simple space. Friendly, child-welcoming and with homely jars of tangy oils and preserves on sale out front, Terre à Terre spreads a fine tapestry of meat-free delights. Each of the half-dozen starter and main dishes seems to require a four-line description, which may triumphantly culminate with show-stoppers like 'dusted with caraway seed and finished with wheat berry emulsion and celeriac straw'. The result is invariably tasty, and quite often delicious but sometimes it can verge on the needlessly fussy. The Kibbi Our Soles of spiced, soaked cane wrapped in kesthery kibbi aubergine soles, served with (for the sake of brevity) cinnamon soft onions, dry cranberry couscous and billy can escabeche, was blander than it was brilliant – although somehow you were pleased that somebody had concocted it anyway. With the addition of side salads and organic wine, prices can mount. There's also a splendid back terrace to be enjoed in the summer. No smoking throughout.

Victory
6 Duke Street, BN1 1AH (01273 326555). **Open** noon-11pm Mon-Sat; noon-10.30pm Sun. **Meals served** noon-8.30pm daily. **Credit** MC, V.
A cracking corner local in the heart of the Lanes, this historic tiled pub (rebuilt in 1824) is deceptive. You walk in expecting – and finding – a handful of rare Tamplin and guest ales in traditional surroudings, and end up in the classy upstairs lounge bar tucking into tasty Thai food and gawping at unusual art. Either way, the commendable Victory is a treat for sore arches, shoppers plonking themselves down gratefully over a fine pint and hearty pub lunch. There are seats outside in summer.

Brighton

Chichester & Around

Pub-crawl your way across the beautiful
South Downs.

East of Portsmouth and west of Worthing, southern England is at its
most handsome and easygoing. A few fairly substantial towns dot
the area, Chichester being by far the most notable, but the landscape
remains largely unsullied by development. If you've ever wondered
exactly what rolling hills look like, this is the place to visit: the
South Downs dominate and define this part of the world, the tiny
villages scattered across them barely disturbing their ebb and flow.

West Sussex is one of the most heavily wooded counties in England
and more than half of it, including Chichester Harbour, the Sussex
Downs and the High Weald, is designated an Area of Outstanding
Natural Beauty. With more than 2,500 miles of public footpaths,
including part of the South Downs Way, it is also a walker's paradise.
The area around Chichester Harbour and Bosham is great for sailing,
while further south the sea at Selsey is a popular place for divers
– under the waves here you can explore a submerged Roman road,
a World War II landing craft and a jagged outcrop of limestone that
is rich in marine life.

Accommodation	★★★
Food & drink	★★★
Nightlife	
Shopping	★
Culture	★★
Sights	★★★
Scenery	★★★★

Chichester

In many ways, Chichester is the archetypal English market town (even if it is a city), but it comes with one crucial difference: as the mournful cry of seagulls will remind you, the water is not far away. It was founded in AD 70 by the Romans, who laid out the main street plan and built the original city walls, which were subsequently rebuilt in flint in medieval times. The main streets of the city – called, with unimpeachable logic, North, South, East and West Streets – slice it neatly into four areas. The cathedral dominates the south-west sector, while the finest of the Georgian buildings are in the south-east, in the streets known as the Pallants.

The cathedral is still the centre of the city. Visible from miles away and immortalised by Turner in his painting of the Chichester Canal, it's a striking structure, best known for its spire and a Marc Chagall stained-glass window. There are concerts here regularly; visit www.chichestercathedral.org.uk or call 01243 782595 for details. The other main attraction is the Pallant House Gallery (9 North Pallant, 01243 774557, www.pallant.org.uk), hosting an outstanding selection of 20th-century British art that takes in works by Henry Moore, Peter Blake, Bridget Riley, Lucian Freud and Barbara Hepworth.

South & west from Chichester

The sweet village of Bosham (pronounced 'Bozzum'), two miles west of Chichester, extends right down to the water's edge. The road here is only passable at low tide; many of the houses have a high stoop at the front door, evidence of past floods. Bosham's history as a fishing port dates back to Roman times (the Emperor Vespasian allegedly had a residence here); today, traces of this history can be found in the exquisitely simple Saxon church, which includes stones from the original Roman basilica along with a truly beautiful arched chapel in the crypt, lit only by a shaft of natural light from a small window. A stone coffin discovered in the church in the 19th century contained a child's body, thought to be a daughter of Canute. This, legend dictates, is the spot where he tried to turn back the tide.

From Bosham, you can walk around the coast to Bosham Hoe, where a short ferry ride has, for centuries, saved travellers a 13-mile walk around the coast to the pretty village of West Itchenor. South of here are the twin villages of East and West Wittering. While pleasant in their own rights, the latter is still most famous as the long-time home of Rolling Stone Keith Richards (and, thus, the site of the infamous 1967 drugs bust, and its accompanying Mars Bar-related apocrypha).

The villages north and west of Bosham, meanwhile, are notable mainly for the pubs and pub-restaurants that dot them. Emsworth, a larger-than-expected town just over the border in Hampshire, boasts a pretty little waterfront; stop by on Sunday mornings to watch the locals race their remote-controlled boats across the calm, wide waters.

North & east from Chichester

As the flat coastal plain rises gently into the South Downs, a handful of attractions reveal themselves. But the main draw is the countryside. The 100-mile South Downs Way, the oldest long-distance footpath in Britain, passes through the area as it runs from Winchester to Seven Sisters near Dover. Most of the ancient trading route is also a bridleway, and as such is accessible to horse and mountain-bike riders. The 30-mile section that passes through West Sussex from South Harting to south of Storrington might be a bit much for a weekend, but there are plenty of shorter walks that give a taste of its sweeping views and enchanted woodlands.

Bisecting the footpath as it crosses the county are several skinny roads, which spool out in all directions from Chichester and connect it to other major towns in the area: on the south coast, Bognor Regis and Littlehampton; to the north, Petersfield and the agreeable little market town of Midhurst. In between are numerous villages scattered with pub-restaurants and other attractions. Singleton houses the Weald & Downland Open Air Museum (01243 811348, www.wealddown.co.uk), a highly unusual collection of 40 historic buildings that have been rescued, rebuilt and restored over a 50-acre site to offer a

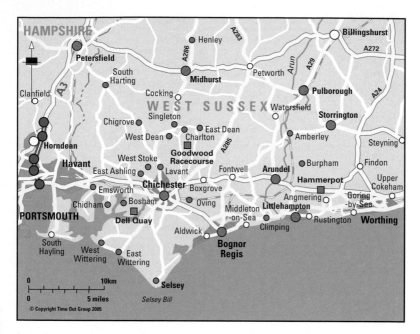

fascinating historical journey through the region's architecture over the past 500 years. Among the structures are a Tudor farmstead, a 17th-century water mill and some Victorian labourers' cottages.

Nearby are the West Dean Gardens (01243 818210, www.westdean.org.uk/site/gardens, closed Nov-Feb), inspirational for those of a horticultural bent. The working kitchen garden includes Victorian greenhouses with fig and peach trees and grape vines; there's also a 300-foot pergola, 35 acres of ornamental grounds with walks around an arboretum, a licensed restaurant and a very upmarket gift shop. Summer events include a garden show and outdoor theatre. Further north, Pulborough is home to Parham House (01903 742021, information 01903 744888, www.parhamin sussex.co.uk), a rare example of mid 20th-century restoration ideas in a large Elizabethan manor, highlighted by a fine panelled Long Gallery and Great Hall and set in 11 acres of gardens.

However, the largest draw remains Goodwood House (01243 755048, recorded information 01243 755040, www.goodwood.co.uk, closed Nov-Feb), a beautifully restored Regency mansion in the heart of the countryside. The house is still home to the Earl and Countess of March, but is also open to the public; exhibits include paintings by Canaletto, Stubbs and Van Dyck, as well as Napoleon Bonaparte's campaign chair. Surrounding the house is an immense estate, containing everything from a sculpture garden (01243 538449, www.sculpture.org.uk, closed Nov-Feb) to a racetrack.

Arundel & Amberley

Seen from across the river, Arundel, with its castle and church at the top of the hill and the water at the bottom, looks more like a stage set than a real town. It's easy to understand why tourists in search of Olde Englande are so drawn to it. Still, despite the prevalence of coach parties and weekenders, it has a pleasing sense of being very much at ease with itself, its tiny streets lined with antique shops, tearooms and homely places selling country jams. It's hard to imagine that as late as the 1920s it was still a working port, with big ships coming up the river.

The imposing Arundel Castle (01903 882173, www.arundelcastle.org, closed Nov-Mar) was built in the 11th century by Roger de Montgomery but extensively remodelled in the 18th and 19th centuries. Now the seat of the Dukes of Norfolk and Earls of Arundel, it's well worth exploring for its fine collections of paintings (by Van Dyck, Gainsborough and Reynolds, among others), tapestries and furniture, and the gorgeous Fitzalan Chapel.

The Catholic Arundel Cathedral (01903 882297, www.arundelcathedral.org) was built in 1873. It's Joseph Hansom's take on French Gothic. Its exterior is best viewed from a distance, but if you do decide to get close up, there's a fine rose window over the west door and, inside, the shrine of St Philip Howard, who converted to Catholicism after his father was beheaded by Elizabeth I for his part in Mary Queen of Scots' intrigues. The other notable attraction is the Arundel Wildfowl & Wetlands Trust (01903 883355, www.wwt.org.uk), which extends over 60 acres of parkland and lakes and is visited by thousands of migratory birds. It's lovely for a wander.

From Arundel, it's only a short drive around to Amberley, also accessible via the river courtesy of Arun Cruises (Arundel Boat Yard or the Town Quay, 01903 882609). The village is home to Amberley Working Museum (01798 831370, www.amberley museum.co.uk), a fascinating spot that traces the working heritage of the region with numerous craftsmen demonstrating everything from blacksmithery to clay pipe manufacture.

WHERE TO STAY

There's a huge range of accommodation in Chichester and, especially, the towns and villages surrounding it: a few ineffably posh country retreats are supplemented by several mid-range hotels and a good deal of more affordable B&B accommodation. No matter the grade, however, prices throughout the area soar during the Festival of Speed and Glorious Goodwood (*see p84* **Good sports**); book months ahead or avoid them entirely.

In addition to the establishments given detailed reviews below, several pubs listed in the Where to Eat & Drink section on *p85* also offer B&B accommodation; the better bets in this category include the Fox Goes Free (*see p87*), the White Horse Inn (*see p89*) at Chilgrove, the Royal Oak (*see p87*) in East Lavant and the Star & Garter (*see p88*) over in East Dean. On the edge of Midhurst, meanwhile, sits York House (Easebourne Street, 01730 814090, www.yorkhouserooms.co.uk, £90-£130 per suite), a handsome new B&B that differs from the norm in several ways. For one thing, each of the two suites is in a small cottage adjacent to the main house and is split over two floors (bed upstairs, lounge at street level); for another, decor is crisp and style-mag modern, with power showers and skinny-screen TVs.

Amberley Castle

Amberley, West Sussex BN18 9ND (01798 831992/www.amberleycastle.co.uk). **Lunch served** noon-2pm, **dinner served** 7-9pm daily. **Set meal** £43 2 courses, £50 3 courses incl coffee. **Set lunch** (Mon-Sat) £20 2 courses, £25 3 courses. (Sun) £30 3 courses incl coffee. **Rates** £155-£335 double/twin; £285-£375 suite. **Credit** AmEx, DC, MC, V.

Here for over 900 years but open to paying guests for less than two decades, this is perhaps the most extraordinary hotel property in Sussex. Scattered over numerous buildings behind 60-foot curtain walls, Amberley Castle isn't shy about playing up its history. And why should it be? The tale is fascinating: built as a hunting lodge in 1103, it was fortified in the 14th century before falling to Cromwell in the 1640s. Martin and Joy Cummings bought the property in 1988; since then, it's been run as an exclusive hotel, picking up numerous awards and just last year being admitted into the prestigious Relais & Châteaux group. The rooms are all decorated individually, but in a similarly plush and tastefully opulent fashion. The grounds include a treehouse by the main gates, a tennis court, an 18-hole putting green and strolling peacocks; to add to the effect, a portcullis is ceremonially raised and lowered each day. There's even a helicopter pad. The restaurant serves lunch and dinner daily; if you land a reservation, be sure to dress for the occasion (no jeans and trainers).

Bailiffscourt Hotel & Health Spa

Climping Street, Climping, nr Littlehampton, West Sussex BN17 5RW (01903 723511/ www.hshotels.co.uk). **Lunch served** noon-1.45pm, **dinner served** 7-9.30pm daily. **Set lunch** £11 2 courses, £16 3 courses. **Set dinner** £43.50 3 courses incl coffee. **Rates** £195-£305 double; £355-£460 suite. **Credit** AmEx, DC, MC, V.

Although this isolated retreat might look ancient, it's a grand illusion: Bailiffscourt is actually a faux-medieval structure that dates only to 1927, when it was built by Amyas Phillips for Lord and Lady Moyne (the former then just plain Walter Guinness, part of the brewing clan and MP for the Suffolk town of Bury St Edmunds). The deception is rendered highly convincing not just by the salvaged materials Phillips used in constructing the estate (the oak door dates back to the 15th century), but by the way in which the place is now maintained by Historic Sussex Hotels, which runs it as a high-end but pleasingly unsnooty hotel. The majority of guest rooms, done out with old-world ostentation and comfort, are both enormously handsome and terrific fun; some come with four-poster beds, while a number even have open fires, primed and ready for torching on chilly winter nights. A new purpose-built block houses eight rooms that are larger and more modern, but do lack character compared to the original bedrooms. Other perks include a well-regarded restaurant, a handsome new health spa (with indoor and outdoor pools, hot tub, steam room, sauna and nicely equipped gym) and a location that is a five-minute walk from the beach.

Spread Eagle

South Street, Midhurst, West Sussex GU29 9NH (01730 816911/www.hshotels.co.uk). **Lunch served** 12.30-2pm, **dinner served** 7-9.30pm daily. **Main courses** £20-£25.50.

GOOD SPORTS

The most famous of all West Sussex's sporting events is Glorious Goodwood. This five-day race meeting (2005's dates are 26-30 July) is both a sporting tradition – there's been racing here for two centuries – and a staple of the social calendar for certain sections of British society. The views across Sussex from the elevated and immaculately maintained course are almost spectacular enough to make you forget the £50 you just lost on Quicksand Spatula in the 3.30. And if the sheer occasion of it all is a little off-putting, worry not: there are less highfalutin meetings throughout the summer (01243 755022, www.goodwood.co.uk).

The other main draw at Goodwood is a little noisier, but also upholds a fine tradition. Goodwood boasted one of Britain's key motor-racing circuits in the 1950s and '60s, before the demands of the modern Formula One era overtook it. These days, though, it hosts a couple of highly enjoyable and immensely popular events. The Festival of Speed (24-26 June) grows in popularity every year, its mix of races drawing a crowd that's equal parts high society and hard-core fans, while the Goodwood Revival (16-18 September) is like a trip back in time to the circuit's glory days – all the cars date from the 1950s and '60s and many punters even dress to suit the occasion. For tickets, call 01243 755055 or see www.goodwood.co.uk.

There's further horsey action directly north and south of Goodwood, albeit of a very different stripe. Cowdray Park (01730 813257, www.cowdray polo.co.uk) hosts polo fixtures almost every weekend during the summer

months, and lives up to its high-class reputation. On the other side of the coin, Fontwell Park racecourse (01243 543335, www.fontwellpark.co.uk) can be a bleak place during winter meetings, the stands offering little shelter from the spiteful winds that whip in across the South Downs. But the facilities here are decent enough, the crowds are never overwhelming and you won't need a second mortgage to stand your round at the bar. Like what you see and fancy having a go yourself? A curious sign on the A27, on which the course sits, warns: 'No racing by horse-drawn vehicles'. That'll learn ya.

However, perhaps West Sussex's most delightful sporting spot is also its least heralded. Of all England's first-class grounds, perhaps only Worcester offers as gorgeous a backdrop to a lazy afternoon spent watching cricket as the field at Arundel (www.sussex cricket.co.uk). The ground, in the shadow of the castle itself, is used throughout the summer; its most notable fixtures are a five-day visit by Sussex CCC and an annual visit made by whichever national side happens to be touring England.

Set lunch £15 2 courses, £18.50 3 courses. Set dinner £35 4 courses. Rates £99-£228 double; £228 suite. Credit AmEx, DC, MC, V.
While the Bailiffscourt (*see p83*) boasts a thoroughly rural location, the other property in the area operated by Historic Sussex Hotels is in the heart of Midhurst. But the Spread Eagle has the advantage when it comes to history: there's been a hotel here for the better part of six centuries, accommodating the likes of Queen Elizabeth I, William Shakespeare and Hilaire Belloc down the years. Some sections of the hotel date back to the 15th century, but the place now holds 39 rooms in a labyrinthine and charmingly crooked series of corridors and stairwells. Decor, while consistently old-world English, does vary from room to room, and is most handsome in the older parts of the building: Egremont is one of several rooms featuring a vintage claw-foot bathtub, while the glorious Queen's Room can be expanded into the residents' lounge if you're travelling as a family. The hotel's restaurant offers a forward-thinking take on British cuisine; the on-site Aquila spa has a pool, sauna, steam room and various treatments.

West Stoke House

Downs Road, West Stoke, Chichester, West Sussex PO18 9BN (01243 575226/www.west stokehouse.co.uk). **Lunch served** 12.30-2.30pm Wed-Sun. **Dinner served** 7.30-9pm Wed-Sat. **Set lunch** (Wed-Sat) £17.50 2 courses. (Sun) £27.50 3 courses. **Set dinner** £35 3 courses. **Rates** £120-£150 double; £150 suite. **Credit** AmEx, DC, MC, V
Rowland and Mary Leach's conversion of this handsome mansion in the village of West Stoke is a textbook example of how to bring a historic property gently into the 21st century. Those seeking evidence of the building's history won't have to look far: the imprint of this country retreat is elegantly Georgian. But the crisp, cool decor with which the couple have updated its five guest rooms owes a little more to the 21st century: calming colours, super-comfortable beds, classic portraiture on the walls (supplemented by more contemporary works downstairs) and Philippe Starck fittings in the bathrooms. The unfussy mix of ancient and modern is impeccably rendered; this is certainly the most stylish hotel in the area, but also among the most relaxing. 'Bed, breakfast and bliss' is the Leaches' tag-line, though this rather underplays the sterling work undertaken in the evenings (Wed-Sun) in the dining room. The adventurous, modern British three-course menu is a steal at £22.50, as is almost everything on the wine list; repair to the reception room afterwards for a post-prandial coffee or something stronger. A brisk morning stroll through the expansive grounds will work off a few of the calories.

WHERE TO EAT & DRINK
Arundel and Chichester both have a decent spread of pubs and restaurants, but the best food is to be had out in the country.

Phillipe Starck fittings in a Georgian setting at the classy and comfortable West Stoke House.

You can eat pretty well at several of the traditional country pubs in the area. The Crown & Anchor at Dell Quay, near Bosham (Dell Quay Road, 01243 781712), is the perfect place for a pint or a meal watching the comings and goings of the little boats and the sun setting over Chichester Harbour. Real ale aficionados should seek out the Black Horse at Amberley (High Street, 01798 831700), handy for the South Downs Way and walks along the banks of the River Arun.

Also recommended are the Old House at Home in Chidham (Cots Lane, 01243 572477), Donnington's Blacksmiths Arms (Selsey Road, 01243 783999), the 16th-century Woodmans Arms in Hammerpot (01903 871240), where the landlord can provide a map of a local walk, or the Spotted Cow (1 High Street, 01903 783919) in Angmering, a former meeting place for smugglers, with a boules pitch and an obscure wheel game mounted on the ceiling. The Gribble Inn (Gribble Lane, 01243 786893, www.thegribble.co.uk), east of Chichester in Oving, brews its own ales, including Fursty Ferret, Plucking Pheasant and Pig's Ear. More restrained are the Horse and Groom in East Ashling (01243 575339, www.thehorseandgroom chichester.com), and the historic Partridge Inn in Singleton (01243 811251, www.the partridgeinn.co.uk). This 16th-century pub was recently given a sympathetic extension, whereupon it ditched its original name (Fox and Hounds) and relaunched itself. The menu is hearty pub grub.

In addition to the establishments reviewed below, West Stoke House (*see p85*) merits special mention for its excellent evening menu, while Amberley Castle (*see p83*) also offers high-class dining and both the Bailiffscourt (*see p83*) and the Spread Eagle (*see p83*) have well-regarded restaurants on site.

Duke of Cumberland

Henley Village, West Sussex GU27 3HQ (01428 652280). **Lunch served** noon-2.30pm daily. **Dinner served** 7-9.30pm Tue-Sat. **Main courses** £8.50-£15.95. **Credit** MC, V.
This wonderfully isolated pub is best known for its fresh fish and pints of prawns, but the menu has become more ambitious. Cauliflower and watercress eclairs being sold out, we opted for pan-fried salmon in a dill sauce and stuffed cabbage parcels. The garden menu (bar snacks) has a choice of five Caesar salads and seven varieties of ploughman's, including own-made pork and egg pie. Interesting puddings included Drambuie and oatmeal bavarois, and strawberry, elderflower and champagne terrine. From an eclectic wine list, the locally produced Nyetimber Classic Cuvée 1996 (a favourite of the Queen, apparently) exemplifies the new direction this tiny hostelry

has taken. However, it has by no means neglected its old clientele: with a roaring fire in winter and innumerable ales poured direct from their barrels, this is still a lovely pub in which to idle away an afternoon with a pint or three.

Fox Goes Free

Charlton, West Sussex PO18 0HU (01243 811461/www.thefoxgoesfree.com). **Lunch served** noon-2.30pm, **dinner served** 6.30-10pm Mon-Fri. **Meals served** noon-10pm Sat, Sun. **Main courses** £7.50-£16.50. **Rates** £70-£120 double. **Credit** MC, V.
William III used to drop in at this 300-year-old country inn on breaks from hunting. These days, though, the low, dark-timbered nooks host a much more mixed crowd, who pile in for a wide-ranging menu. The adventurousness leads far beyond traditional pub grub: pasta comes with blue cheese and red chard, and the roast birds are pigeon rather than chicken. Fish options, such as bream with mushroom velouté or monkfish with wild rice and chilli jam, sell out quickly. You can, of course, still comfort yourself with classic roasts, washed down with excellent beers such as the pub's own bitter or something from a short but well-chosen wine list. Lovely views across the Downs from the apple tree-filled garden are another plus. Upstairs are five B&B rooms.

George & Dragon

Burpham, West Sussex BN18 9RR (01903 883131). **Lunch served** noon-1.45pm daily. **Dinner served** 7-8.45pm Mon-Sat. **Main courses** £7.95-£15.95. **Credit** AmEx, MC, V.
It's a long and winding road that leads to the door of this sweet little English pub, opposite the rose-clad lychgate of a 12th-century flint church. Choosing from a menu full of modern European fare (from game terrine with celeriac remoulade to freshly baked tartlet of crab and tiger prawn with a sweet chilli dressing), both pan-fried scallops and crevette in garlic butter with a lemon risotto and caper dressing, and caramelised goat's cheese on croûton with chilli chutney were a delight to see and savour. Main courses included slow-cooked lamb shank on a chive mash, confit of duck leg, and fillet steak with Portobello mushrooms, as well as plenty of fresh fish. The only disappointment was the pudding: dark chocolate and hazelnut terrine didn't rise beyond its constituent parts. The same menu is available in the pub or in the more elegant dining area, frequented by a slightly older clientele.

Royal Oak

East Lavant, West Sussex PO18 0AX (01243 527434/www.sussexlive.co.uk/royaloakinn). **Lunch served** noon-2.15pm, **dinner served** 6.15-9.15pm daily. **Main courses** £5-£16. **Rates** £90-£130 double. **Credit** AmEx, MC, V.
Another fine old pub poshed up for the modern age. There's a small, cosy drinking area by the

door, and a good deal of outdoor space in the summer, but the Royal Oak is rather more of a restaurant these days, its handsome main room supplemented by a relatively sympathetic extension. The food is similarly modern, and, while laudably inventive, isn't wholly successful. The menu changes regularly, but as a rule, if a dish looks like it might be a little big for its boots, it almost certainly is. When we last visited, a starter of pan-fried pigeon breast was a less than perfect match for its vinaigrette and chocolate dressing, while cinnamon rice pudding was just plain bizarre. Happily, when the menu stays on slightly more familiar ground, it comes up trumps: a seared marlin steak with a chilli glaze and asparagus was particularly good. A half-dozen bedrooms are accessible via the rear of the building

St Martin's Tearooms

3 St Martin's Street, Chichester, West Sussex PO19 1NP (01243 786715/www.organic tearooms.co.uk). **Meals served** 10am-6pm Mon-Sat. **Main courses** £3.95-£7.95. **No credit cards.**
The java chains have descended on Chichester just as they have everywhere else in Britain, but they haven't managed to knock this delightful campaigner off its perch. Housed in an old terraced house sympathetically renovated in the 1970s, it's a charming labyrinth of nooks and crannies, as quiet and restful as the day is long. However, the real surprise is the menu: all-organic, mostly vegetarian (there's occasionally fish on offer) and largely excellent. Menus on the table offer a checklist of the various dishes (soups to chunky cakes, salads to risottos), including all the ingredients used in them (along with a calorie/fat count, for those who care about that sort of thing). Not everything is available at once: a blackboard at the counter details what's on offer. Service comes from an assortment of pretty young things who seem to take rare pride in their Saturday jobs.

Sawyards

Manleys Hill, Storrington, West Sussex RH20 4BT (01903 742331). **Lunch served** noon-1.30pm Tue-Fri, Sun. **Dinner served** 7-9pm Tue-Sat. **Set lunch** (Wed-Sun) £14.50 2 courses, £21.95 3 courses. **Set meal** £34.50 2 courses, £46.50 3 courses. **Credit** MC, V.
Michelin-starred Michel Perraud's decision to retire home to France has given his former No.2 Julien Ligouri the chance to take centre stage at the former Fleur de Sel, now sporting a rustic English name despite the Scottish nationality of its new owner. The theme, however, remains: excellent French-influenced food served in chintzy English surroundings. A cucumber gazpacho amuse-bouche came delicately spiked with chilli, quickly followed by excellent starters such as scallops with cauliflower purée and red wine dressing, and beautifully balanced smoked duck terrine with sweet potato, foie gras and salsify. Braised pork belly in spices showed a firm hand with

robust tastes, complemented by a lighter touch for a provençal-style halibut. Vegetarian options included butternut squash tortellini with cep and hazelnut sauce. Desserts reveal a willingness to play with classics. Expect it to be busy: though the restaurant name and chef changed in 2004, it's kept its Michelin star.

Star & Garter

East Dean, West Sussex PO18 0JG (01243 811318). **Lunch served** noon-2.30pm, **dinner served** 6.30-10pm Mon-Fri. **Meals served** noon-10pm Sat; noon-9.30pm Sun. **Main courses** £5-£18. **Rates** £80-£100 double. **Credit** MC, V.
The team that turned the Fox Goes Free (*see p87*) into a top-class foodie pub in the 1990s moved a few miles down the road in 2003, and are currently attempting to bless this old pub, formerly known as the Hurdlemakers, with a similar reputation. They're doing a very fine job, too: the airy, rustic decor has been immaculately rendered, the beers are extremely well kept, the welcome is warm and genuine, and, last but hardly least, the cooking is top-notch. While the menu is both varied and changing, it's highlighted by the selections of terrific seafood: we followed a daisy-fresh half-pint of prawns with a papillote of fish, which included salmon and some succulent cod. A fillet of pork came with a moreish wholegrain mustard sauce; happily, we still had room for a Bailey's bread and butter pudding. The tidy little garden has a seafood bar in the summer; there are sporadic musical performances all year round. Three small B&B rooms upstairs complete the picture.

36 on the Quay

47 South Street, Emsworth, Hampshire PO10 7EG (01243 375592, www.36onthequay.co.uk). **Lunch served** noon-1.45pm Tue-Fri. **Dinner served** 7-9.45pm Mon-Sat. **Set lunch** £17.95 2 courses, £22.95 3 courses. **Set meal** £42.95 3 courses, £55 10-course tasting menu. **Rates** £90 double; £115 suite. **Credit** AmEx, DC, MC, V.
Housed in a building dating from the 17th century, 36 on the Quay stands right on the quayside overlooking Emsworth harbour. It's a true South Coast gem. Chef Ramon Farthing and wife Karen moved here in 1996 and brought with them a reputation for outstanding and memorable modern British food. The setting is a pretty and pastel-coloured dining room with a large bay window that makes the most of the views. The set lunch is good value, though the choice is limited to two dishes per course; spend an extra £20 for the full run of the carte at lunch or dinner. Honey-spiced duck breast and crisp confit leg with pineapple tatin and spring onion noodles with a sherry vinegar reduction, or medallion of veal with a calf's liver and spinach lasagne, roasted butternut squash and Madeira and truffle sauce are typical mains. Alternatively, the sensational ten-course evening tasting menu (available by request at lunchtime) is surprisingly uncomplicated and beautifully bal-

anced. Accommodation includes a room with a view over the water, three smaller B&B rooms and a cutesy wee cottage.

White Horse Inn

1 High Street, Chilgrove, West Sussex PO18 9HX (01243 535219/www.whitehorse chilgrove.co.uk). **Lunch served** noon-2pm Tue-Sun. **Dinner served** 7-10pm Tue-Sat. **Main courses** £12.95-£16.95. **Set meal** (Oct-Apr only) £24.50 3 courses. **Rates** £95-£120 double. **Credit** MC, V.

The energy of both proprietor and chef guarantee that dining at this pub-restaurant-B&B – no-smoking throughout – is an occasion. While the former plays host extraordinaire, the chef busies himself with freshly roasted nuts and salmon and cream cheese tartlets as accompaniments to the aperitifs. Fresh fish is a speciality: a starter of fresh Selsey crab and avocado was exquisite. Slow-roasted half Gressingham duck on a bed of minted pea purée with rich cassis sauce was a superb mix; so were seared scallops served with seafood risotto and bacon. After the richness of the meal, the puddings (citrus tart and lemon souf-flé on a biscuit base with Cornish ice-cream and strawberries) were tempting but beyond us, so the chef obligingly provided a plate of fresh English berries. There are eight B&B rooms here, too.

Isle of Wight

A green and pleasant land.

It may be an island – separated from the mainland by 39 miles – but there's something quintessentially English about the Isle of Wight. An England of the past, perhaps; some accuse the island of being stuck in a time warp. But changes have been trickling through its crevices during the past couple of years, and they're not just of the music fest variety. Hotels have been upgraded and excellent restaurants have opened, to allow the Isle of Wight to compete happily with the likes of Cornwall and Devon for London's holidaying families, but with about three hours less journey time. Throw into the mix the crumbling chalk cliffs, downs, creeks, groynes, landslips and opportunities for stunning outdoor pursuits on land and water, and you have the perfect British getaway. From Tennyson Down, named in honour of the poet who lived nearby and described the air as being 'worth sixpence a pint', the Isle of Wight lies before you like a child's fantasy island. To the north-west, the River Yar flows out to the Solent past the castle guarding Yarmouth harbour; at the far western tip of the island, the jagged chalk line of the Needles, jutting from the sea, ends with a red-and-white lighthouse; to the south is the great crumbling sweep of Compton Bay, while further south the sheer cliffs of Blackgang Chine fall dramatically (and literally) into the Channel.

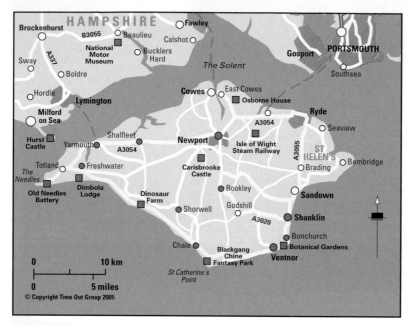

© Copyright Time Out Group 2005

Little England

Often described as recreating the whole of southern England in miniature, the island's 147 square miles contain rolling farmland, marshy estuaries, castles, cliffs, vineyards, beaches, steam trains, Roman villas, dinosaur fossils, red squirrels and a whole clutch of manor houses. During the 1800s visitors poured in from all over Europe to enjoy the water, the sea air and the balmy climate. Tennyson made his home, Farringford, at Freshwater (it is now a hotel) and the poet Swinburne was born (and buried) in Bonchurch, which is also where Dickens wrote *David Copperfield*; and the Russian writer Turgenev conceived his most famous novel, *Fathers and Sons*, while visiting Ventnor for the bathing. Meanwhile at Dimbola Lodge, Tennyson's neighbour, the Victorian photographer Julia Margaret Cameron, was taking pictures of whoever she could persuade to sit still long enough and developing the results in the coal shed. Charles I was held in the hill-top Norman Carisbroke Castle (near Newport, 01983 522107, www.english-heritage.org.uk) before being taken back to London to be executed. And, of course, Queen Victoria spent summers with her family at Osborne House (York Avenue, East Cowes, 01983 200022, www.english-heritage.org.uk), built in the style of an Italian villa and beautifully maintained since her death in 1901. Today, the most popular areas for tourists are Sandown and Shanklin. The rest of the island is blissfully free of visitors, even at the height of summer. And for unrivalled peace and quiet, visit in the winter when most of the attractions are closed, and the footpaths stretch out empty for miles and miles. There is one drawback, though. The south-west of the island is disappearing into the sea, not inch by inch, but acre by acre. Every winter more cliffs collapse like a soufflé on to the beaches below, leaving fences and steps suspended precariously in mid-air.

The free pocket guide (available on ferries and at tourist offices) is crammed with 'attractions', but unless it's raining stair rods and blowing a gale, give them a miss and explore the cliff paths, downs, woods, creeks and beaches instead. This is the best way to discover the island, a paradise for walkers, cyclists and horse riders. It boasts more footpaths per square mile than anywhere else in Britain – all meticulously signposted and maintained. The 77-mile coastal path around the island might be a bit much for a weekend, but to get a flavour of it take the train to Shanklin. Here you can join the path as it climbs up from the sea, before descending again through the mysterious ferny depths of the Landslip (so-called because much of it fell into the sea in 1810) to the pretty beach at Bonchurch. From there you can walk around Ventnor and, if you still have the energy, on to Steephill Cove and the Botanical Gardens and its Museum of Smuggling History, housed in the underground vaults

Accommodation	★★★
Food & drink	★★★
Nightlife	★
Shopping	★
Culture	★★
Sights	★★
Scenery	★★★★

(01983 855397, www.botanic.co.uk). Another lovely walk is along the north-west coast from Shalfleet to Yarmouth.

For beach fans, Sandown, Shanklin and Ryde offer all the traditional delights of miniature golf, amusement arcades and fish and chips. If that is your idea of hell, head for Compton Bay, a beautiful sweep of sand beneath collapsing cliffs, without a kiss-me-quick hat in sight. Here, surfers brave the waves, fossil hunters admire the casts of dinosaurs' footprints at low tide, kitesurfers leap and soar across the sea and paragliders hurl themselves off the cliffs. Totland Bay, with good sand, clean water and views across the Solent to Hurst Castle, is a lovely place to watch the sun go down. It's also where you'll find the Victorian fort, Needles Old Battery (01983 754772, www.nationaltrust.org.uk), which also has spectacular views. At high tide the beach all but disappears and the bay becomes a surfers' playground. Meanwhile, sailors weigh anchor in the natural harbours of Yarmouth, Cowes and Bembridge.

Many attractions are closed between the end of October and Easter, so phone ahead to check what's open when planning a visit. There are many seasonal events, including Britain's biggest walking festival in May, an international kite festival in July, a cycling season in September and White Air, a festival of extreme sports, at the end of October. For information on cycling and walking, call Rights of Way (01983 823741/www.iwight.com) or get a map from a Tourist Information Centre (see right).

For boat fans there is the Yarmouth Old Gaffers Classic Boat Festival during the May bank holiday weekend, the Round the Island Yacht Race in June and, of course, Cowes Week in August. Those looking for a quiet weekend might want to avoid Cowes in August as the place gets rammed. Also worth noting is the Isle of Wight Music Festival, which takes place in Newport in June (www.isleofwightfestival.com).

WHERE TO STAY

George Hotel

Quay Street, Yarmouth, PO41 0PE (01983 760331/www.thegeorge.co.uk). **Rates** £180-£242.50 double. **Credit** MC, V.

The George is easily the best hotel on the island. Not only is it an anchor's throw from Yarmouth harbour, but it is also a hotbed of luxury, and therefore the perfect place for an indulgent weekend away. Set in the 17th-century former home of the island's governor, the building and its decor breathe understated elegance, from the wood-panelled walls and cotton-wool soft beds, to the confident food served in the brasserie and restaurant (see p96) by charming staff. In summer, guests can take their gin and tonic into the lovely garden, which stretches all the way down to the sea; in winter, a massive roaring fire warms the bar area. And to top it all, a visit here doesn't even depend upon having a car. Assuming you can bring yourself to leave the hotel, there's plenty to see in 13th-century Yarmouth – it's the island's oldest town, complete with castle and charming winding streets dotted with lots of quirky shops and warm, welcoming pubs.

Old House

Gotten Manor, Gotten Lane, Chale, PO38 2HQ (01983 551368/www.gottenmanor. co.uk). **Rates** £60-£80 double; £250-£1,100/wk self-catering cottage (sleeps 4-10). **No credit cards**.
There is no mistaking the ancient charm of this B&B, situated in the 14th-century annexe to Gotten Manor in the south of the island. Perfect for a romantic weekend, there is the choice of two beautifully decorated rooms (with limewashed walls, quality textiles and wooden floors), both with double bed, sofa and cast-iron bath, and a shared living room, breakfast room and walled garden. Breakfast is made from local and organic produce, with own-made jams and smoothies to accompany, and even the house's water supply comes from the local stream. For bigger groups or families, there are also three attractive self-catering cottages in converted barns. Highly recommended for a unique, discreet hideaway. No smoking throughout.

Priory Bay Hotel

Priory Drive, Seaview, PO34 5BU (01983 613146/www.priorybay.co.uk). **Rates** £110-£258 double; £200 family suite (sleeps 4); £90-£110 cottage suite (sleeps 4); £300-£750 3-4 nights self-catering cottage (sleeps 4). **Credit** AmEx, MC, V.

TOURIST INFORMATION

Ryde
Isle of Wight Tourism, Westridge Centre, Brading Road, Ryde, PO33 1QS (01983 813818/ www.islandbreaks.co.uk).
Ventnor
Coastal Path Visitors' Centre, Dudley Road, Ventnor, PO38 1EJ (01983 857220/www.coastalwight.gov.uk)

Isle of Wight

Situated just south of Seaview, Priory Bay is a fascinating mix of old and new, traditional and quirky. Part of the building dates back to medieval times. Built by monks, the older part of the building has thick stone walls, large fireplaces and miniature windows. The hotel's facilities are perhaps best enjoyed in the summer, when guests can use the beach at the end of the garden, the nine-hole golf course, and eat seafood at the Oyster Bar, overlooking the sea. In winter, the grand drawing room and wood-panelled bar glow with warmth. The stunning restaurant (*see p100*) has spectacular views of the Solent. Rooms in the old part of the hotel have a lush, exotic feel, with oriental furniture, dark red bedspreads and cast-iron baths. But be sure to listen out for the 'Blue Lady', who sometimes can be heard skittering through the corridors or calling after her beloved dog.

Royal Hotel

Belgrave Road, Ventnor, PO38 1JJ (01983 852186/www.royalhoteliow.co.uk). **Rates** £120-£140 double; £126-£171 family room (sleeps 4). **Credit** AmEx, DC, MC, V.

While the George oozes luxury and the Priory Bay intrigue, the Royal Hotel, near Ventnor in the south of the island, is simply grand and efficient in equal measure. If you're not first struck by its large and imposing Victorian building, then it'll be the perfectly tended gardens that surround it (and the unheated outdoor swimming pool). There are plenty of places for guests to sit and drink tea or an aperitif, from the conservatory at the front of the hotel to the cosier bar and lounges. The hotel has few surprises – from the traditional menu in the restaurant to the 55 rooms, all classically decorated, some with terrific

views of the sea or hotel gardens. But guests come back for the reliable and friendly service and the perfect situation, moments from the sea. All bedrooms are no smoking and there are also three meeting rooms with conference facilities, including secretarial support.

Seaview Hotel

High Street, Seaview, PO34 5EX (01983 612711/www.seaviewhotel.co.uk). **Rates** £95-£165 double; £180-£235 family room (sleeps 6); £320-£700/wk 2-bed self-catering cottage; £600-£2,000/wk self-catering cottage (sleeps 10). **Credit** AmEx, DC, MC, V.

There's something very 1950s seaside resort about this hotel, on a steep street just moments from the sea. The house was built far earlier, of course (in about 1800 in fact), and has grand bay windows and a small conservatory at the front, with a dark and carpeted interior. The multitude of staff bustle around with purpose and professionalism. It's surprisingly large, with two restaurants and two bars, as well as 16 bedrooms. The Seaview gets booked up for long stays in the summer; it's geared towards families, with baby listening in all the rooms and children's menus. Dogs are welcome too. If there's no room in the hotel, two self-catering houses (one of which is a former bank and sleeps up to ten; the other a fisherman's cottage with space for a family of four) are available. At the time of writing, plans are afoot to expand the kitchen and dining room and add another restaurant, as part of a complete refurbishment. Let's hope the changes don't strip away the nostalgic charm.

Isle of Wight

WHERE TO EAT AND DRINK

Baywatch Beach Restaurant

The Duver, St Helens, PO33 1RP (01983 873259/www.bay-watch.co.uk). **Open** *Mar-Oct.* **Breakfast served** 10.30am-noon, **lunch served** noon-3pm, **dinner served** 6.15-9pm daily. **Main courses** £6.90-£19. **Credit** MC, V.

On a summer's day this is possibly the perfect spot to get the most out of sun, sea, sand and satisfyingly filling food. Located right on the beach, with tables outside for early birds, the Baywatch Beach operates as an all-purpose café during the day and in the evening becomes an informal restaurant. The extensive daytime menus have something for everyone, from own-made local crab soup with garlic bread baguette to sandwiches, burgers, pasta and pizzas. There's also a selection of simple seafood dishes: cod, haddock, scampi, shell-on prawns, whitebait and so on, but it's after 6.15pm when the quality stuff really kicks in. From a menu that's mainly devoted to seafood try a deliciously retro prawn cocktail, followed perhaps by spicy Cajun cod with baby leaf spinach and tomato salsa.

Buddle Inn

St Catherine's Road, Niton, Ventnor, PO38 2NE (01983 730243). **Open** 11am-11pm Mon-Sat; noon-10.30pm Sun. **Lunch served** noon-2.30pm, **dinner served** 6-9pm daily. **Main courses** £6.95-£13.95. **Credit** MC, V.

Close to St Catherine's lighthouse at the southern tip of the island, the Buddle Inn has been a popular haunt for both smugglers and customs men for the 150 years it has been in business. Steeped in history, it was built in the 16th century as a farmhouse, and manages to retain that homey feel thanks to an extraordinary inglenook fireplace, ancient beams and worn flagstone flooring. Pub grub is served and there are always good real ales on tap, including local brews Godnams and Duck's Folly. An adjoining bar in a converted barn, the scene of tea dances in World War II, is now a family room, with a pool table and games. This is the perfect place to take a break while walking the cliffs, or just to enjoy the stunning sea views from the garden.

Chequer's Inn

Niton Road, Rookley, PO38 3NZ (01983 840314/www.chequersinn-iow.co.uk). **Open** 11am-11pm Mon-Sat; noon-10.30pm Sun. **Meals served** noon-10pm Mon-Sat; noon-9.30pm Sun. **Credit** MC, V.

The different worlds of families and shooting parties sit comfortably together at this award-winning boozer. This is partly because of its size, which allows the men in their plus fours to occupy one side of the bar and the kids to run around in the other. There's a family area with more toys than most kids could dream of, not to mention an 'adventure playground' in the garden. Then there are shotguns and multicoloured cartridge cases, and endless sentimental watercolours of men on horses with little red foxes running for their lives. But everyone is happy: for ale drinkers there are five ales on tap, including two guest ales, such as the local Goddard's; and, for those who are hungry, there's an extensive menu majoring on fish and roasts. Its position, in the heart of the island, makes it a convenient and pleasant place to stop off while walking.

Crab Inn

94 High Street, Shanklin, PO36 6NS (01983 862363). **Open** 11am-11pm Mon-Sat; noon-10.30pm Sun. **Meals served** noon-9.30pm Mon-Sat; noon-9pm Sun. **Main courses** £4.95-£12.95. **Credit** MC, V.

The Crab Inn is reportedly one of the most photographed pubs in the UK, and it's easy to see why. It's a beautiful thatched building that sits on the curve of the road that runs through Shanklin old village at the top of the Chine, right next to the sea. It's a chain pub (recently taken over by the Greene King brewery), and the glare of shiny wood and gleaming surfaces slightly compromises the general air of romantic charm, but it tends to win people over with its overall smartness. The pub has two levels, with a bar, dartboard and pool table upstairs and a dining area downstairs where food (including plenty of crab) is served all day in a family-friendly environment. There's a quiz night on Tuesdays and musicians on Friday evenings.

Crown Inn

Walker's Lane, Shorwell, PO30 3JZ (01983 740293). **Open** 10.30am-3pm, 6-11pm Mon-Sat; noon-3pm, 6-10.30pm Sun. **Lunch served** noon-2.30pm daily. **Dinner served** 6-9pm Mon-Thur, Sun; 6-9.30pm Fri, Sat. **Main courses** £4.95-£12.95. **Credit** MC, V.

The Crown Inn, in the leafy village of Shorwell, has an island-wide following, and it's easy to see why. It's a handsome, cavernous, low-ceilinged pub, probably as old as the thatched cottages that surround it, with decent ales on tap (John Smith, Flowers, Wadworth 6X and Tanglefoot), superior pub grub (local produce, like roasted partridge) and a very welcoming atmosphere. Management goes to lengths to keep all regulars happy, with a family-friendly and no-smoking policy (smoking is allowed in one room only). In the winter there is a roaring fire, and the lovely big garden is a hit in summer, with its mini playground (slide and swing), trout stream and dovecote. The crown is in prime walking country, which makes it the perfect pub to plan into your route.

George Hotel

Quay Street, Yarmouth, PO41 0PE (01983 760331/www.thegeorge.co.uk). **Brasserie** **Breakfast served** 8-10am, **lunch served**

noon-3pm, **dinner served** 7-10pm daily.
Main courses £11.95-£19.95. **Set lunch**
(Sun) £19.50 2 courses, £23.50 3 courses.
Restaurant **Dinner served** 7-9.30pm Tue-Sat.
Set dinner £45 5 courses incl coffee, petit
fours. **Credit** MC, V.

The talent of chef Kevin Mangeolles ensures that
an evening meal at this stunning 17th-century
townhouse hotel is worth crossing the island for.
Mangeolles specialises in modern British cooking
with a French influence and the informal
brasserie, a bright room with a sunny decor, has
a menu that features starters like a fresh-tasting
ceviche of mackerel with crab salad and equally
excellent lamb cutlets with asparagus, spinach
and potato purée. But the real treat is to be had in
the elegant main restaurant, open for dinner only.
Don't be put off by the elaborately annotated
menu. It may seem to tell you everything, but a
meal here will be full of surprises: extraordinary
in presentation, extraordinary on the palate, from
the delicacy of tomato water or beetroot and

liquorice soup, to robust dishes such as exquisite
rib-eye steak, mashed potato and braised beef garnish. There is also a range of great-value house
wines on a serious list of great vintages. Worth
every penny.

Lugley's

*33 Lugley Street, Newport, PO30 5ET (01983
822994).* **Lunch served** noon-2pm, **dinner
served** 7-9.30pm daily. **Main courses** £10.95-
£15.95. **Set lunch** (Sun) £12.95 2 courses,
£15.95 3 courses. **Rates** £75-£95 double.
Credit MC, V.

If you are passing through Newport, this reasonably priced brasserie is a good place to stop for
lunch. The menu may be dominated by ciabatta
sandwiches, but these are sandwiches at their best
(smoked mackerel and horseradish ciabatta, say, or
houmous and sun-blushed tomatoes on flatbread),
served with excellent salt and pepper fries. There
are also a number of pasta and salad-based dishes,

Built by monks, Priory Bay Hotel can now be enjoyed by those of all denominations.

all lovingly prepared, such as deep-fried haloumi with shredded beetroot, and salmon-packed Thai fish cakes, served with shredded cucumber and an excellent own-made mint and chilli mayonnaise. The dinner menu is less café-like, and booking is recommended in the evening. The atmosphere is mellow. No smoking throughout.

New Inn

Mill Road, Shalfleet, PO30 4NS (01983 531314/www.thenew-inn.co.uk). **Open** noon-3pm, 6-11pm daily. **Lunch served** noon-2.30pm, **dinner served** 6-9.30pm daily. **Main courses** £6.95-£25.95. **Credit** AmEx, MC, V.

With its inglenook fireplaces, flagstone floors and original, low-beamed ceilings, this 18th-century pub close to Newtown estuary is about as traditional as they come. The nautical theme of the decor is reflected in a menu that majors on tried and tested seafood dishes, with the occa-sional innovative touch. Local crab and prawn cocktail vies for attention with grilled sardines and moules marinière among the starters. Mains range from whole grilled local plaice to a magnificent seafood platter. There's also a smattering of old-fashioned pub favourites: cod, chips and peas; ham, egg and chips; steak and ale pie. Desserts include sticky toffee pudding, crème brûlée and tarte tatin.

Pond Café

Bonchurch Village Road, Bonchurch PO38 1RG (01983 855666/www.pondcafe.com). **Meals served** noon-10.30pm daily. **Main courses** £9.50-£18. **Set lunch** (Sun) £20 3 courses. **Set dinner** £25 3-course tasting menu. **Credit** MC, V.

Just north of Ventnor is green and foresty Bonchurch, the perfect spot to park your car and do some rambling – but not before having a meal at one of the island's newest and best restaurants.

The Pond was opened in June 2003 by chef David Thomson, and has become the name on every islander's lips – even the proprietors of some of the best restaurants. The secret is a minimal white on wood decor, and a creative, daily-changing menu with an emphasis on seasonal food. On a recent visit, a rich and buttery celeriac and honey soup and soft and tender pork belly with apple purée were both beautifully presented. They were followed by salmon niçoise, with lemony mayonnaise and a perfectly cooked boiled egg, and a superior Sunday roast, which combined quail, chicken and beef surprisingly successfully. Dessert of mango tart took a while – as, we were informed, the pastry was made to order – but it was well worth the wait: light and flaky, and sweetened just a tad by the mango and a dollop of own-made vanilla ice cream. To top it all, melt-on-the-fingers chocolate truffles were served with our coffee, and service came with a smile. At the time of writing a hotel – the Hambrough – is planned in Bonchurch; it will also boast a brasserie and a seafood restaurant.

Priory Bay

Priory Drive, Seaview, PO34 5BU (01983 613146/www.priorybay.co.uk). **Lunch served** 12.30-2.15pm, **dinner served** 7-9.15pm daily. **Main lunch** £15.50 2 courses, £18.50 3 courses. **Set dinner** £21 2 courses, £27 3 courses. **Credit** MC, V.

The dining room at the island's most unique hotel is a truly stunning affair, with azure and gold walls and ceiling echoing the magical sea views. Food is stunning too; people travel across the island to enjoy it. For just £21 for two courses diners enjoy local produce, skilfully cooked. Starters are the likes of delicately smoked beetroot salmon with Bembridge crab salad, or perhaps tomato soup with a large piece of asparagus ravioli. A palate cleanser (watercress soup on a recent visit) is followed by mains such as perfectly cooked beef fillet with wild mushrooms, and tender pieces of lamb with caramelised apple. For an extra £6.50 comes dessert, often traditional with a twist (spiced quince soufflé and creamy rice pudding),

or a baby cheese-board with a mix of French and local cheeses, accompanied by a glass of fine port – to be enjoyed in the grand drawing room.

Red Lion

Church Place, Freshwater, PO40 9BP (01983 754925/www.redlion-wight.co.uk). **Open** 11.30am-3pm, 5.30-11pm Mon-Sat; noon-3pm, 7-10.30pm Sun. **Lunch served** noon-2pm daily. **Dinner served** 6.30-9pm Mon-Sat; 7-9pm Sun. **Main courses** £8.50-£13. **Credit** MC, V.

This Freshwater pub dates back to the 11th century, though the current building is not that ancient. The large garden at the rear is one attraction, the extensive menu, which features seafood prominently, though not exclusively, is another. Starters can include duck and port terrine, smoked haddock pâté, or herring roe on toast, while mains might be fish pie, Welsh rarebit-topped haddock, fish cakes, whole lemon sole, duck breast with black cherry sauce or ribeye steak with sautéed potatoes and peppercorn butter. Comfort puddings like rhubarb crumble, treacle sponge, spotted dick and apple pie make a fine finish.

Spyglass Inn

The Esplanade, Ventnor, PO38 1JX (01983 855338). **Open** 10.30am-11pm Mon-Sat; 10.30am-10.30pm Sun. **Lunch served** noon-9.30pm Mon-Sat; noon-9pm Sun. **Main courses** £6.95-£9. **Rates** £60 double. **Credit** MC, V.

This is a special pub, not only for its fabulous situation above the sea at Ventnor, but also for its cavernous interior. People of all ages and backgrounds huddle around the rickety tables and enjoy seafood, burgers and local brews. And if this isn't enough, the place feels like a shipwreck; there's a huge anchor at the bar and sailing and fishing memorabilia hanging from every wall and ceiling. A huge patio overlooking the sea is popular in summer and there are window bays for the colder months. overlooks the sea, and window bays for the colder months.

Woodstock to Burford

Impossibly perfect villages and an
awe-inspiring palace.

The Cotswolds are terribly nice. They never used to be – unless you
were a sheep – but these days the tranche of land north of Oxford
and south of Chipping Norton that roughly makes up the southern
Cotswolds is one of the prettiest and most photogenic parts of the
English countryside. It's also one of the poshest. The two main tourist
towns – Burford and Woodstock – are both attractive representations
of a certain English rural ideal (the kind that John Nettles scours for
psychos in *Midsomer Murders*), while outside these centres of tourism,
tiny, honey-coloured villages cluster round impressive churches and
stately piles. Throughout the area, shops sell expensive bric-a-brac to
well-heeled weekend breakers.

THE ONLY GUIDES YOU'LL NEED

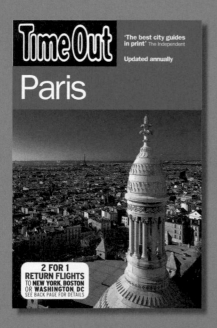

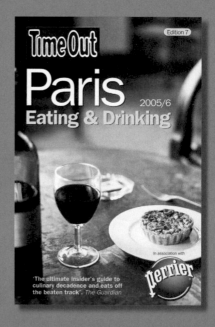

Accommodation	★★★
Food & drink	★★★
Nightlife	
Shopping	★★
Culture	★★
Sights	★★★
Scenery	★★★★

The Romans were responsible for the area's original wealth; they introduced the long-woolled breed of sheep, the Cotswold Lion, to these parts. Cotswold wool quickly gained an international reputation, flourishing between 1300 and 1500, and the money it brought to the area paid for the churches and grand houses that still dominate. In the Middle Ages, grazing sheep took precedent over human residents, occupying great tracts of land; in some cases, people were even evacuated from villages to give the sheep more room.

Nowadays, especially post foot-and-mouth, the Cotswolds' main industry is tourism, a fact that's reflected in some steep prices and a slew of themed attractions. Yet the real draw – the rich countryside dotted with ruins and historical houses – is free. There are attractive walks between most of the small villages – and pubs en route to ease the effort. The Thames Path (www.thames-path.co.uk) passes this way prettily; the river becomes navigable at Lechlade, with plenty of tour boats around to prove it.

Eight miles north of Oxford lies the historic market town of Woodstock, well placed for those who wish to visit the twin monuments to extravagance, Blenheim Palace (*see p108* **People's palace**) and Bicester Village. The former is the country seat of the Duke of Marlborough and birthplace of Sir Winston Churchill, and is one of the most extraordinary buildings in the country; the luxury and splendour of Sir John Vanbrugh's design is breathtaking and its sheer size will stop first-time visitors in their tracks. The same could be said of Bicester Village (50 Pingle Drive, 01869 323200/www.bicester-village.co.uk), a massive outdoor shopping mall that sells name brands at large discounts. The crowds at both must be seen to be believed.

Woodstock itself is best known for two trades – glove-making and decorative steel work. You can follow the area's heritage at the new, wide-ranging Oxfordshire Museum (Park Street, 01993 811456/www.oxfordshire.gov.uk/the_oxfordshire_museum), but you won't see many signs of the artisan life in the streets, which are filled with cars bringing custom to the classy pubs and restaurants. These attract Oxonians (often embarrassed

student-parent pairings) on evenings out of town. Like all the places featured in this chapter, Woodstock makes an excellent base for those who don't want to stay in Oxford itself.

Garden groupies should head north to Rousham House (01869 347110/www.rousham.org), near Steeple Aston. The rather gloomy, imposing Jacobean mansion was remodelled in Tudor Gothic style by William Kent, a predecessor of Capability Brown, in the 18th century. But the real point here is his outstanding garden, inspired by Italian landscape painting, with grouped trees, winding paths, glades and waterfalls dotted with statues and temples – which has remained pretty much unchanged. Inside, Rousham is determinedly uncommercialised, with no shop or tearoom; you're encouraged to bring a picnic and wander the grounds (but not if you are accompanied by children under 15 or a dog – neither are welcome).

Woodstock to Burford

Minster Lovell (on the road heading west from Woodstock to Burford) rewards a stop and a stroll. One of the quietest and most unspoiled villages in the area, it boasts a gorgeous 15th-century church and the dramatic ruins of Minster Lovell Hall. Dating from the 1440s, the Hall and its restored medieval dovecote make an imposing sight on the banks of the River Windrush, and the thatched cottages are some of the prettiest around. It's worth taking further detours for Swinbrook, where Nancy Mitford is buried, picturesque Asthall and the Roman ruins at North Leigh, which include some wonderful mosaics now kept under shelter. Also between Woodstock and Burford is Witney; although it's one of the largest towns in the Cotswolds, it offers fewer tourist attractions than its neighbours. Famous for manufacturing blankets, it boasts the first medieval market place in England, attractive almshouses and the magnificent St Mary's church. The charming Cogges Manor Farm Museum (Church Lane, 01993 772602/www.westoxon.gov.uk/culture/cogges.cfm)

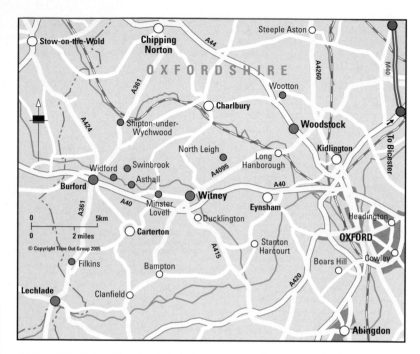

aims to recreate rural Victorian Oxfordshire with costumed guides and a 20-acre working farm, complete with traditional breeds of livestock. In the manor house, you can chat to the kitchen maids about its history, sample fresh baking from the range, and explore a variety of period displays. There's also an activities room in which children can try on Victorian clothes and play with replica toys.

Burford is the jewel of the Cotswolds. This elegant and historic coaching town makes a good, if pricey, base from which to explore the surrounding countryside (leaflets suggesting good local walks can be found at the tourist office). The broad main street comprises a welter of pretty buildings clinging to the slope leading down to the River Windrush; it's smattered with plenty of middle-England gift and antique shops, as well as England's oldest pharmacy, an excellent delicatessen and a few beauty salons for those vital post-walk pedicures. For much of the year the town is chock-full of traffic; aim to visit in early spring or winter to get the best out of it. One of the attractions is Burford Garden Company (Shilton Road, 01993 823117), a mammoth garden centre that stocks 30,000 plants and is a huge draw all year round. Cotswold Wildlife Park (01993 823006/www.cotswoldwildlife park.co.uk) houses lions, leopards, zebras, pandas, monkeys and other exotic and/or endangered species in spacious paddocks around a listed Victorian manor. There are separate houses for reptiles and insects, a penguin pool and a bat house, a mini railway and an adventure playground. It's a good place to bring a picnic as the grounds are extensive and the gardens beautiful.

Burford has one or two less commercial claims to fame. Nell Gwynn visited a number of times and the fruit of her liaisons with Charles II, Charles Beauclerk, was made Earl of Burford. The town's Norman church, remodelled in the 1400s, was the scene of Cromwell's dramatic siege against the Levellers in 1649. Insights into Burford's history are found in the Tolsey Museum (126 High Street, 01993 823196). If you want to explore the area on two wheels, you can hire bicycles at Burford Bike Hire (Woollands, Barns Lane, 01993 823326).

Around Burford

To the north, there are paintings and fragments of Roman mosaics in the tiny church at Widford. The petite village of Shipton-under-Wychwood boasts a pretty church, which has a stained-glass window designed by the William Morris company and some pre-Raphaelite archangels.

If you want to see how the Cotswolds made their money before the tourists came along, visit Cotswold Woollen

Weavers (01367 860491), a few miles south of Burford, in Filkins. At this working mill and museum, you can watch fleece being woven into fabric, then purchase a wide range of clothes, rugs and cushions from its shop.

Near Lechlade (about eight miles south of Burford) is Kelmscott Manor (01367 252486/www.kelmscottmanor.co.uk), the country home of poet and founder of the Arts and Crafts movement, William Morris, for the last 25 years of his life. The house is large but not ostentatious and is primarily a showcase for the work of Morris – tapestries, fabrics and wallpapers, plus examples of his printing, painting and writing – and his wife Janey, who helped revive traditional embroidery techniques. Morris, who died in 1896, is buried in the nearby churchyard.

WHERE TO STAY

Accommodation is also offered at Jonathan's at the Angel, the King's Head and the Lamb in Shipton-under-Wychwood (*see p109* **Where to eat & drink**). Our recommendations concentrate on Burford and Woodstock, but off the beaten track there's the Old Post Office (01367 850231), a good B&B (with cottage to rent) in Southrop, and Court Farm (01993 831515), a converted 17th-century farmhouse in Shipton-under-Wychwood.

Bay Tree Hotel

Sheep Street, Burford, Oxfordshire OX18 4LW (01993 822791/www.cotswold-inns-hotels.co.uk). **Rates** £165-£175 double; £240-£250 suite. **Credit** AmEx, DC, MC, V.

Located just off the top of the high street, the Bay Tree is typical of the excellent accommodation Burford has to offer. From a deceptively small front it sprawls out over a number of buildings, which between them offer 21 rooms of differing character – all well-sized, clean and with good facilities, some with great views of the garden, others with the homely feel of a small cottage – as well as a pleasantly laid-back bar and an excellent restaurant (*see p109*). Popular for weddings and conferences, it nevertheless retains an independent, personal air.

Bear

Park Street, Woodstock, Oxfordshire OX20 1SZ (0870 400 8202/www.bearhotel woodstock.co.uk). **Rates** £138-£188 double; £238-£288 suite. **Credit** AmEx, DC, MC, V.

Macdonald Hotels now owns this huge, ancient building in the centre of Woodstock, and while it may have lost a little of its individuality as a result, it is still every bit as appealing as the vaunted Feathers Hotel (*see p109*) down the road. Once a hideaway for Richard Burton and Elizabeth Taylor, it now has 54 rooms – making it the largest hotel in Woodstock – as well as conference facilities and a restaurant.

Burford

PEOPLE'S PALACE

The only non-royal residence in the country grand enough to go by the title 'palace', Blenheim (0870 060 2080, www.blenheimpalace.com) was the lavish reward bestowed on John Churchill, first Duke of Marlborough, by Queen Anne for defeating the French at the crucial battle of Blenheim in 1704. Designed by Sir John Vanbrugh with the assistance of Nicholas Hawksmoor and set in nearly 2,000 acres of grounds landscaped by 'Capability' Brown, this Baroque masterpiece is, quite simply, awe-inspiring. Only part of the palace is open to the public and at weekends crowds ensure it's a bit of a production-line trudge. But it's worth it to see the remarkable long library, gilded state rooms, some distinguished paintings and tapestries and an exhibition of

Churchilliana (Sir Winston was born here and is buried at nearby Bladon), and to gain an insight into the power and self-importance of nobility. The park is also a sumptuous manifestation of ego, with its artificial bridged lake, waterfall and temple. There is plenty to keep visitors busy: marked walks, boats to rent and plenty of idyllic picnic spots such as the Secret Garden, which opened in May 2004 after being allowed to grow wild for 30 years. The Pleasure Gardens, linked to the house by a mini railway and containing the world's largest maze, is a modern addition designed to keep families – and ticket revenues – rolling in. The Palace also holds frequent special events, such as concerts, crafts fairs – even a jousting tournament. In fine weather, plan to spend most of the day here.

Burford House Hotel

99 High Street, Burford, Oxfordshire OX18 4QA (01993 823151/www.burfordhouse.co.uk). **Rates** £125-£155 double; £235 2-bed suite. **Credit** AmEx, MC, V.

This 17th-century listed building in the centre of Burford High Street is the perfect townhouse hotel; the owners manage to strike a great balance between making the guest feel at home and providing top-quality service. The eight bedrooms are well sized and clean, there are a couple of pleasant living rooms (one of which contains an interestingly stocked honour bar), a dining room, a cute courtyard and a lovely hotel cat. Breakfast, lunch and afternoon tea are served (residents only Sun, Mon) with lots of freshly baked goods; for dinner you'll need to eat out, but staff are happy to make recommendations and reservations. They'll also make up picnics, should you wish to explore the local countryside.

Feathers Hotel

16-20 Market Street, Woodstock, Oxfordshire OX20 1SX (01993 812291/www.feathers. co.uk). **Rates** £135-£185 double; £200-£275 suite. **Credit** AmEx, DC, MC, V.

The formal (and floral) Feathers is Woodstock's most prominent hotel. It's a large, warren-like building, made up of seven 17th-century houses. The bar area has had a recent refurbishment and the bedrooms are also being renovated. There are 20 of them, the best of which comes with its own private steam room. The TV is tastefully hidden in a cabinet – it's that kind of place. There's also a beauty salon, Preen, on the premises (book in advance for any treatments), while a well-thought-of fine-dining restaurant (*see below*) completes the picture.

King's Arms Hotel

19 Market Street, Woodstock, Oxfordshire OX20 1SU (01993 813636/www.kings-hotel-woodstock.co.uk). **Rates** £130-£150 double. **Credit** AmEx, MC, V.

Right opposite the Feathers Hotel (*see above*), the King's Arms offers a completely different experience, with a more contemporary appearance and a complete absence of floral prints. The Georgian building's 15 recently refurbished bedrooms are decked out in slick off-whites, with striking bedspreads. The fresh-looking restaurant serves decent modern-bistro food, while the bar is popular with Woodstock's youth, so expect a bit of noise on your way to bed.

Lamb Inn & Restaurant

Sheep Street, Burford, Oxfordshire OX18 4LR (01993 823155/www.lambinn-burford.co.uk). **Rates** £130-£225 double. **Credit** MC, V.

Practically next door to the Bay Tree Hotel (*see p107*), the Lamb makes an equally appealing place to stay, offering a friendly welcome and fine

service. The 15 rooms are well equipped with leaf tea-making facilities, own-made biscuits and a flat-screen telly, and many of them overlook a sheltered courtyard. Decent bars and a well-regarded restaurant (*see p110*) round off a very pleasant, laid-back but on-the-ball operation.

WHERE TO EAT & DRINK

The area is full of attractive country pubs and restaurants, but this is moneyed land, and while standards are high, so are prices, and tastes tend to the conservative. Don't be surprised to see people in black tie in your hotel dining room.

On Burford High Street, the Golden Pheasant (01993 823223, www.golden pheasant-burford.co.uk) and the Old Bull (01993 822220) both serve reasonable food. Off the main drag, the tankard-bedecked Royal Oak (26 Witney Street, 01993 823278) is popular for its pies and other own-made staples.

Away from the Burford hordes, the Swan Inn (01993 822165) in Swinbrook is an unspoiled, down-to-earth old bar by the river serving decent pub-style food. In Woodstock, there is a highly regarded Chinese restaurant, Chef Imperial (22 High Street, 01993 813591). Brothertons Brasserie (1 High Street, 01993 811114) is good for a light meal.

Bay Tree Hotel

Sheep Street, Burford, Oxfordshire OX18 4LW (01993 822791/www.cotswold-inns-hotels.co.uk). **Lunch served** noon-2pm daily. **Dinner served** 7-9pm Mon-Fri, Sun; 7-9.30pm Sat. **Set lunch** £16.95 2 courses, £18.95 3 courses. **Set dinner** £24.95 3 courses, £27.95 3 courses. **Credit** AmEx, DC, MC, V.

The airy dining room overlooks the lovely gardens at this excellent hotel, and the food is equally impressive. As ever in Burford, nothing strays too far from the traditional, but when the Sunday roast comes with a Yorkshire pudding this impressive – a golden-brown tower of batter – who's complaining? Both beef and pork were perfectly cooked, and portions were hearty. We still found room for cheese and were promised local varieties, so were a little disappointed to get celtic promise and mull of kintyre, but soothed by the generous accompaniment of apple, celery, grapes and decent biscuits. *See also p107.*

Feathers Hotel

16-20 Market Street, Woodstock, Oxfordshire OX20 1SX (01993 812291/www.feathers. co.uk). **Lunch served** 12.30-2pm, **dinner served** 7-9pm daily. **Set lunch** £17 2 courses, £21 3 courses. **Set dinner** £30 2 courses, £39 3 courses. **Credit** AmEx, DC, MC, V.

The seriously swanky Feathers Hotel offers food that is a country mile ahead of its competitors. Dinner in the beautiful oak-panelled dining room includes starters such as wild mushrooms and duck confit and generous mains such as roast fillet of sea bass served with crushed potatoes, sauce vierge and caviar aubergine, or the gorgeous duo of lamb – a miniature rump and shank. The two well-priced 'Market Menus' – one vegetarian – are just as lavish and a tad more inventive. They come with amuse-bouches such as oysters with horseradish and cucumber jelly and foie gras cream. A more informal menu is available in the bar. Note that the rule is no smoking throughout. *See also p109.*

Fleece

11 Church Green, Witney, Oxfordshire OX28 4AZ (01993 892270/www.peach pubs.com). **Lunch served** noon-2.30pm Mon-Sat; noon-3pm Sun. **Dinner served** 6.30-10pm Mon-Sat; 6.30-9.30pm Sun. **Main courses** £8.50-£13.50. **Credit** AmEx, MC, V.
Modern, vibrant and stylish, the Fleece is an unexpected find in the Cotswolds. Avoid the melee at the bar and head to the back, where there's a much more congenial restaurant area. A deli board is piled with a vast array of cheese, charcuterie, antipasti and bread, while bigger eaters can tuck into pizzas, vegetable and goat's cheese parcels or duck breast with potato and carrot rösti in oriental juice. The portions are generous and the prices reasonable.

King's Head

Chapel Hill, Wootton, Oxfordshire OX20 1DX (01993 811340/www.kings-head.co.uk). **Lunch served** noon-2pm daily. **Dinner served** 7-8.30pm Mon-Fri; 7-9pm Sat. **Main courses** £9.95-£16.95. **Rates** £75-£100 double. **Credit** MC, V.
This pleasant old pub in a serene village features a reasonably ambitious restaurant, where you can sample the likes of Sichuan seared pigeon breast on shallots with black bean and oyster sauce, or a very good olive pâté with artichoke hearts and bramble dressing. Top marks to the closing dish, a sticky toffee pudding. The King's Head also offers accommodation.

Jonathan's at the Angel

14 Witney Street, Burford, Oxfordshire OX18 4SN (01993 822714). **Lunch served** noon-2pm Tue-Sat; 12.30-3.30pm Sun. **Dinner served** 7-9.30pm Tue-Sat. **Main courses** £13.95-£18.50. **Rates** £75-£100 double. **Credit** MC, V.
If the pubs or hotel restaurants of Burford don't appeal, this 16th-century coaching inn – down a side road just off Burford High Street – has a mellow, welcoming, personal feel. Customers order food at the bar and are then shown through to one

of various cosy nooks. Food is interesting – Gressingham duck with poached pear and pecorino; monkfish roasted in smoked bacon with a citrus salsa – and expertly cooked. In summer, there's a back terrace with an awning. There's also accommodation available.

Lamb Inn & Restaurant

Sheep Street, Burford, Oxfordshire OX18 4LR (01993 823155/www.lambinn-burford. co.uk). **Lunch served** noon-2.30pm Mon-Fri; noon-3pm Sat, Sun. **Dinner served** 7-9.30pm daily. **Main courses** £8.50-£14. **Set lunch** (Sun) £27.50 3 courses. **Set dinner** £32.50 3 courses. **Credit** MC, V.
The Lamb's large, square restaurant is down a corridor from the cosy pub. While formal, it isn't oppressive – in keeping with the generally friendly tone of the excellent hotel it is housed in. The menu is uncomplicated, hearty, seasonal and drawn from local produce where possible: whole Bibury trout, for instance, grilled and topped with lemon, tarragon and almond butter, or local asparagus and pecorino ravioli set on a sweet tomato and basil sauce. No smoking throughout.

Lamb Inn

Simons Lane, Shipton-under-Wychwood, Oxfordshire OX7 6DQ (01993 830465). **Lunch served** noon-2.30pm, **dinner served** 6.30-9.30pm Mon-Sat. **Meals served** noon-9pm Sun. **Main courses** £8.95-£16.95. **Set lunch** (Mon-Sat) £10 2 courses, £15 3 courses. **Credit** MC, V.
Charming but not chocolate box, this cute Cotswold-stone inn has been given a sleek update. The menu offers good old-fashioned pub meals like beer-battered fish, hearty pies and roasts, but also boldly flavoured, internationally influenced dishes like grilled scallops with cucumber noodles and tomato and herb consommé. If you just want a pint and a snack, there's a formidable array of filled baguettes. If you don't fancy booking a table in the tiny restaurant area, there's also the bar or an attractive garden.

Red Lion

South Side, Steeple Aston, Oxfordshire OX25 4RY (01869 340225). **Lunch served** noon-2pm Tue-Fri; noon-2.30pm Sat, Sun. **Dinner served** 7-9pm Tue-Thur; 7-9.30pm Fri, Sat. **Main courses** £11.50-£18.50. **Set lunch** (Sun) £14.95 2 courses, £17.95 3 courses. **Credit** MC, V.
This small, handsome country pub features a tiny, wonky-walled dining room that makes you feel a bit like Alice after she took the magic pill. Food is fairly traditional, but the local aged steak gets top marks. A popular place, the Red Lion has a good range of wines and excellent ales. A newly built conservatory extends the options of where to dine, and suggests that business is booming.

The very English charms of Burford House Hotel.

Cirencester & Around

Beautiful countryside and special retreats.

This area of Gloucestershire, bordering Oxfordshire to the east and Wiltshire to the south, is refreshingly free from the tourist hordes that are to be found in other parts of the Cotswolds. Perhaps that's why so many celebs have chosen to make it their home (there are rumoured to be more stars per square metre in the Cirencester branch of Waitrose than in the one in Notting Hill).

The scarcity of tourists doesn't mean there's nothing to do. On the contrary, this is England at its stereotypical best: gorgeous scenery, pretty roads, hearty country walks and plenty of decent gastropubs and quaint watering holes. The only downside is that you'll need to dig a bit deeper into your pocket when it comes to accommodation. But it can be worth it – there are a couple of standout hotels in the area.

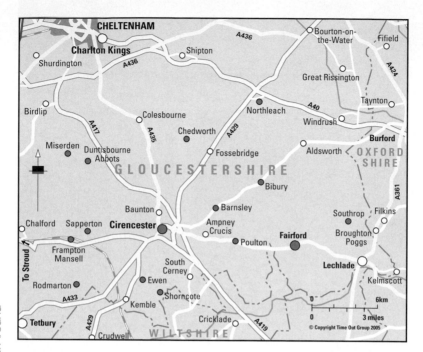

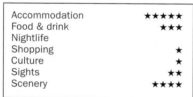

Accommodation	★★★★★
Food & drink	★★★
Nightlife	
Shopping	★
Culture	★
Sights	★★
Scenery	★★★★

On the eastern edge of the area, at the gorgeous but busy village of Bibury (*see p118 **England's prettiest village?***), the marked increase in tourist numbers is a hint that you're not too far away from more heavily visited Cotswold towns such as Burford and Woodstock. Visit Bibury at the right time of year, though, and you can have the place more or less to yourself.

You'll also discover some lovely driving (and walking) country to be found in the area between Bibury and Northleach, to the north, but history buffs will be better off heading north-west to Chedworth, where you can locate the remains of one of the largest Roman villas to be yet found in Britain (01242 890256, www.national trust.org.uk). The site, which was originally excavated in 1864, includes more than a mile of walls, mosaics, two bathhouses and hypocausts (the Romans' pretty effective version of central heating). A video introduction puts the ruins in context

and offers an insight into daily life in Roman Britain. (The Romans also settled Cirencester, now home to an overrated, lottery-funded museum on the subject.)

Garden lovers are well served in this part of the country. In addition to charming Cerney House Gardens (Cerney House, North Cerney, 01285 831205, www.cerney gardens.com), there is the impressive Miserden Park Gardens at Miserden near Stroud (01285 821303, closed Oct-Mar), where the 17th-century, 12-acre gardens are at 700 feet above sea level and overlook the Golden Valley. The site contains a walled garden, an arboretum, a yew walk and topiary, including some designed by Edward Lutyens. The small roads leading south to the A419 are again a scenic delight for drivers.

TOURIST INFORMATION

Cirencester
Cotswold Tourism Office, Cotswold District Council, Trinity Road, Cirencester, Gloucestershire GL7 1PX (01285 623006).
Cirencester Tourist Office, Cornhall Market Place, Cirencester, Gloucestershire GL7 2NW (01285 654180).
www.cirencester.gov.uk/tourism
www.cotswold.gov.uk

Cirencester & Around

The Falcon
Inn in Poulton.

BARNSLEY HOUSE

When Tim Haigh and Rupert Pendered first envisaged opening a country hotel, they wanted it to be a place where people could 'escape, relax and breathe'. All three criteria are amply fulfilled at this gorgeous country retreat in the village of Barnsley. The house was built in 1697 by Brereton Bouchier, squire of Barnsley (it's his initials you see carved in stone above the garden door), and ultimately came into possession of the Verey family. In the 1950s celebrated gardener Rosemary Verey began redesigning the garden, transforming it into its present layout of lovingly tended flowers and plants, plus kitchen garden.

The hotel opened in September 2003 and quickly gained the attention of the cognoscenti; as well as notching up awards from *Tatler*, *Condé Nast Traveller* (both UK and US) and the *Telegraph*, many a famous face has been spotted here (management are coy about naming names, but they will say that local celebs – known to include Liz Hurley and Kate Winslet – have been very supportive).

So has the project been a success? On the whole, yes. Bedrooms are the height of luxury, with Bose sound systems, plasma-screen and LCD TVs (including one in the bathroom), huge beds with Egyptian cotton sheets, artworks individually chosen for the room, and spare-no-expense bathrooms (the free-standing baths are a forte). It helps that the owners have, thankfully, chosen to keep many of the house's original features in place; exposed beams and original staircases remind the visitor that this is a 17th-century building at heart. This mix of old and new is continued throughout the hotel – so much so that the modern public spaces can come as a shock: this is especially true of the tiny bar on the ground floor. With its black and red decor (including red leather

seats), it's no exaggeration to say that it wouldn't look out of place in a swanky New York hotel. Still, at least it makes a refreshing change from the rule of chintz that typifies so many hotels of this standard. In any case, the long list of cocktails will soon be the only thing on

your mind. Other public areas include a modern reading room – again, no fusty, dusty library here.

Downsides? Well, the gardens are lovely but surprisingly small (the grounds cover 11 acres but this includes the fields beyond). Rooms don't have minibars, but rather mini fridges that are only stocked with fresh orange juice, water and champagne if you're paying rack rates. This is apparently to keep the service personal, so you can enjoy the pleasure of having a waiter bring drinks up. The restaurant is a little on the stuffy side: on a recent visit guests were conversing in hushed whispers. But these are minor points, and you'll be too busy lolling around in your room or ambling through the grounds to care.

And the plans don't stop there: in-room massages are already available, but a spa and heated outdoor pool are due for completion by the end of the summer 2005. There are currently ten rooms (including a garden suite with private garden and hot tub), but new ones are being added by converting existing buildings. Broadband internet access is now available – this, along with the existing meeting facilities, is bound to please the City crowd. And impatient film fans take note: a private screening room is on its way, which will be able to première films before they are shown in Leicester Square.

If your budget won't stretch to Barnsley House itself, note that the owners also run the Village Pub down the road (*see p121*), a much more low-key affair. The rooms are small and far less spectacular than Barnsley House, but also far cheaper (from £90 for a double room). *See also p120.*

Barnsley, nr Cirencester, Gloucestershire GL7 5EE (01285 740000/www.barnsley house.com). **Rates** £270-£385 double; £325-£475 suite. **Credit** AmEx, MC, V.

ENGLAND'S PRETTIEST VILLAGE?

If the tiny village of Bibury had a slogan, it would probably be William Morris's claim that it was 'the most beautiful village in England'. It crops up so frequently in literature about the place that you start to wonder whether its inclusion is some kind of legal requirement. That said, you can see what Morris was on about. Bibury, about ten miles west of Burford and the same distance north-east of Cirencester, is spread over a surprisingly large area around the trout-filled River Coln.

Driving down from Burford, when you reach the bottom of the hill you will see a small cluster of houses around the imposingly peaceful St Mary's church, just left of the road. Saxon in origin, this large church was added to many times over the centuries. Adjacent is the Bibury Court Hotel (*see p120*), whose extensive grounds, nestling against the wetland wildfowl reserve of Rack Isle, make delightful walking.

Just along the river from here, by the stone bridge that forms the centrepiece of the village, is the Swan Hotel (*see below*), a former manor, jail and now Bibury's second big hotel. Both are full during the summer, when the whole world seems to descend on the village, but visit out of season and, although its beauty is somewhat dimmed, you'll have the place more to yourself.

Across the bridge from the Swan are the two paying attractions of the village – Bibury Trout Farm (01285 740215), where kids can have fun making the water boil with fish at feeding time; and Arlington Mill (01285 740368), a museum, tearoom and shop, the last selling real oddities including a wide range of vintage Beatles memorabilia. Here, too, you'll find Arlington Row, an almost perfect example of typical Cotswold cottages now owned by the National Trust. When Henry Ford visited in the 1920s he liked them so much he tried to take them back to America with him, but was stopped. And that's it, bar enjoyment of the Cotswolds' greatest attraction – scenic strolling. The walk from here along the river to Coln St Aldwyns is particularly recommended.

Near Shorncote, more than 130 lakes over an area of 40 square miles make up Cotswold Water Park (Keynes Country Park, Spratsgate Lane, Shorncote, 01285 861816, www.waterpark.org). On the main sports lakes visitors can indulge in sailing, canoeing, waterskiing, windsurfing and jetskiing, and hire watercraft (from £5 per half-hour) or stick to land-based activities such as cycling (from £4 per hour) and horse riding. Elsewhere nature has the upper hand, with two country parks (one with a children's beach) offering fine walking (including guided wildlife walks) and birding. A programme of children's activities is run in the school holidays. To quote David Bellamy: 'It's a blooming marvellous place!'

WHERE TO STAY

The area has its fair share of mediocre accommodation, especially when it comes to twee rooms above pubs that masquerade as 'charming inns'. There are two shining stars, however: Barnsley House (*see p116*) and Cowley Manor (*see p122*). They're at the luxury end of the market, but both are worthy recipients of your hard-earned cash. Otherwise, there are a number of decent B&Bs; our pick of the bunch is the Old Rectory in Meysey Hampton (Rodmarton, 01285 841246, www.rodmarton.com, £70 double), parts of which date from the 1600s.

Swan Hotel

Bibury, Cirencester, Gloucestershire GL7 5NW (01285 740695/www.cotswold-inns-hotels.co.uk). **Rates** £140-£260 double. **Credit** AmEx, DC, MC, V.

Although it is owned by the same small group as the Bay Tree in Burford (*see p107*), the Swan is far more formal in its approach to accommodation. Its superb location is the main draw, alongside the River Coln and right next to Bibury's beautiful old bridge. A former manor, the building dates from the 16th century – the coal shed was used to hold local prisoners before they were transported to larger jails in the area. The 20 bedrooms are floral-heavy but perfectly comfortable and all have great bathrooms – five with jacuzzis. The hotel bottles its own spring water, which you'll also find in the starched-to-the-hilt restaurant, and has a spa offering a full range of treatments (book these in advance).

WHERE TO EAT & DRINK

The area has no shortage of cosy drinking pubs, many of which have also earned praise for the quality of their food (though London prices are the norm).

Allium

1 London Street, Market Place, Fairford, Gloucestershire GL7 4AH (01285 712200/ www.allium.uk.net). **Lunch served** noon-2pm Wed-Sat; noon-3pm Sun. **Dinner served** 7-10pm Wed-Sat; 7-9pm Sun. **Set lunch** £15 2 courses, £17.50 3 courses. **Set dinner** £28.50 2 courses, £32.50 3 courses; £45 10-course tasting menu. **Credit** MC, V.

An ambitious restaurant: stark white interiors, proactive service and discreet local art mark Allium out as a very different entity from the wealth of successful gastropubs in the area. Both poached breast of pigeon with tatin of endive, and confit shoulder of lamb with sweetbread and tongue were creatively executed, yet some dishes (a gazpacho of crab in jelly form, for instance) could be a step too far. Prices are reasonable and the wine list is interesting.

Barnsley House

Barnsley, nr Cirencester, Gloucestershire GL7 5EE (01285 740000/www.barnsleyhouse.com). **Lunch served** noon-2.30pm, **dinner served** 7-9.30pm daily. **Set lunch** £19.50 2 courses, £25.50 3 courses. **Set dinner** £39.50 3 courses, £46 4 courses. **Credit** AmEx, MC, V.

The hotel is an absolute stunner, and while the restaurant feels a bit on the stuffy side compared with the rest of the hotel, the food itself excels. The kitchen uses produce that's fresh from the extensive gardens. Breakfast means warm pastries and muffins, endless quantities of super-fresh orange juice and coffee and a top-notch fry-up. Dinner saw ballotine of foie gras with onion marmalade and brioche, each distinct flavour complementing the others; spaghetti with prawns, garlic, tomato and rosemary was OK, if slightly undercooked; mains of organic loin of pork with lentils, confit of fennel and salsa verde and rack of lamb with potato rösti were better, both featuring perfectly cooked, juicy meat. Puddings are the likes of raspberry and mascarpone brûlée – thick, with fresh fruit, and tart yet creamy. Portions could be a bit bigger, especially at these prices (to avoid complete wallet meltdown, go for the excellent lunch instead). *See also p116.*

Bell at Sapperton

Sapperton, Gloucestershire GL7 6LE (01285 760298/www.foodatthebell.co.uk). **Lunch served** noon-2pm daily. **Dinner served** 7-9.30pm Mon-Sat; 7-9pm Sun. **Main courses** £9.50-£16. **Credit** MC, V.

Outside, the Bell is a typical Cotswold stone hostelry; inside, pine furniture and contemporary prints decorate a series of interlinking rooms, and tables are well placed. The menu relies heavily on fish from Cornwall, complemented by local produce. There's a strong Mediterranean influence in the likes of goat's cheese panna cotta with roast pimentos, or duck breast and confit leg with pickled endive and curried lentils.

Bibury Court Hotel

Bibury, Cirencester, Gloucestershire GL7 5NT (01285 740337/www.biburycourt.com). **Lunch served** noon-2pm, **dinner served** 7-9pm daily. **Main courses** (lunch) £12.95-£14.95. **Set dinner** £27 2 courses, £32.50 3 courses. **Rates** £135-£155 double; £180-£220 suite. **Credit** AmEx, DC, MC, V.

The Bibury Court has a choice of dining rooms – a formal restaurant, the smaller study and, best of the three, the sunny, natural-wood conservatory. Food has a mix of influences, resulting in dishes such as salmon with crab and truffle-scented linguine, or Gressingham duck with stir-fried pak choi. As at the even more staid Swan Hotel (*see p118*), trout from Bibury Trout Farm is a speciality. The Bibury Court is also a good hotel: rooms are attractively furnished and comfortable.

Carpenters Arms

Miserden, nr Stroud, Gloucestershire GL6 7JA (01285 821283). **Lunch served** 11.30am-2.30pm daily. **Dinner served** 6.30-9.30pm Mon-Sat; 7-9.30pm Sun. **Main courses** £7.25-£14. **Credit** AmEx, MC, V.

This gem of a pub is located on the Miserden Estate overlooking the Golden Valley. Food is fine, if not outstanding, and features adventurous fare such as shark alongside baguettes and Sunday roasts. But the main attractions are the setting, the friendly atmosphere and the drinking – there's a good selection of well-kept ales and fruit wines. The open-plan room features low beams, wooden tables, storm lanterns, horse brasses and benches with name plates commemorating regulars. In the summer you can eat and drink in the garden, while in the winter attention turns to the huge fire that dominates the room. Afterwards, walk it off in Miserden Park Gardens (*see p114*).

Falcon Inn

London Road, Poulton, Gloucestershire GL7 5HN (01285 850844/www.thefalcon poulton.co.uk). **Lunch served** noon-2.30pm, **dinner served** 7-9pm daily. **Main courses** £8-£16. **Set lunch** (Sun) £15 2 courses, £20 3 courses. **Credit** MC, V.

Cirencester & Around

Decorated in aubergine and sage, and with plenty of simple wooden furniture, the Falcon looks the part of the contemporary pub/restaurant (though there's a comfortable bar area too). A heavenly starter of spiced prawn soup was followed by succulent duck breast with sauce jerez, and char-grilled rib-eye steak with roasted garlic butter and superb chips.

pers and shellfish ragoût was no more than the sum of its parts, and so lacked depth. Desserts of the comfort food variety lifted the standard once again – excellent apple and sultana crumble with custard, and a seriously good rice pudding with mixed berry compôte. We waddled out in hazy contentment. The interesting wine list is also worth a look.

Five Mile House

Duntisbourne Abbots, Gloucestershire GL7 7JR (01285 821432). **Lunch served** noon-2.30pm daily. **Dinner served** 6-9.30pm Mon-Sat; 7-9pm Sun. **Main courses** £9-£15. **Credit** MC, V.
A former coaching inn built in the 17th century to serve passing carriage trade on the historically important Ermine Street, this charming pub now sits in a virtual cul-de-sac, bypassed by the A417, but it's worth tracking down. The layout is a wonderful hotchpotch of rooms and periods, testament to piecemeal expansion over the centuries. There's a pleasant garden with great views. The food merits attention too; it's served gastropub style (in other words, get your own drinks from the bar). A starter of deep fried goat's cheese with chilli jam was an old favourite, done well. Mains were also excellent: faggots fantastically moist, spicy, oniony, with fresh mushy peas on the side; neck of lamb was chewy but very flavourful. A luxurious dessert of sticky toffee pudding with fresh custard also hit the spot. Five Mile House is a popular place, so it's wise to book at weekends and evenings.

Seven Tuns

Queen's Street, Chedworth, Gloucestershire GL54 4AE (01285 720242). **Lunch served** noon-2.30pm daily. **Dinner served** 6.30-9.30pm Mon-Sat; 7-9pm Sun. **Main courses** £7-£15. **Credit** MC, V.
You're spoilt for choice at this large, friendly old pub near Chedworth Roman villa. The small bar area, with log fire, wooden booths and tables, also has an interesting bar menu (baguettes, plus the likes of Cotswold pork and sage sausages, and Seven Tuns salad of warm chicken, bacon and avocado). Out back is a modern restaurant, and there's another, more up-to-date bar too. Ales include Youngs Special and Waggle Dance.

Swan

Southrop, Gloucestershire GL7 3NU (01367 850205). **Lunch served** noon-2.30pm daily. **Dinner served** 7-9pm Mon-Sat. **Main courses** £8.50-£14. **Credit** MC, V.
Quality of food and service is high at the Swan. And so it should be for these prices (starters are around £8). Thai pork salad with sour fruits, shallots, mint and coriander perfectly blended sweet with sour; it was a hard act to follow but grilled entrecôte with béarnaise sauce, frites and green salad – simple yet spot-on – was up to the task. On the other hand, seabass with courgette, pep-

The Village Pub

High Street, Barnsley, Gloucestershire GL7 5EF (01285 740421/www.thevillagepub.co.uk). **Lunch served** noon-2.30pm Mon-Fri; noon-3pm Sat, Sun. **Dinner served** 7-9.30pm Mon-Thur, Sun; 7-10pm Fri, Sat. **Main courses** £9.50-£15.50. **Rates** £90-£125 double. **Credit** MC, V.
From the preliminary pints of local beer to the exquisitely bitter chocolates with the coffee, the Village Pub barely puts a foot wrong. Diners have a choice of five rooms, each decorated in a different style; subtle paint effects, wood panelling and flagstones are a common theme. The menu – now presided over by Jonathan Lane-Robinson – makes a virtue of simplicity in flavour and presentation. A steaming bowl of sautéed scallops, clams and mussels with gremoulata was a generous starter; next, chicken breast with tomato, olives and rosemary was impressive.

White Horse

Cirencester Road, Frampton Mansell, Gloucestershire GL6 8HZ (01285 760960/ www.cotswoldwhitehorse.com). **Lunch served** noon-2.30pm Mon-Sat; noon-3pm Sun. **Dinner served** 7-9.45pm Mon-Sat. **Main courses** £9.95-£14.95. **Credit** MC, V.
Contemporary local art hangs on the walls and furniture is sleek and stylish, but behind the makeover there's still the warm glow of an exemplary English country pub. The food has a Mediterranean aspect – an antipasto of bresaola, milano salami and a delicious goose salami might be followed by whole grilled lemon sole with sun-dried tomato and saffron cream, though the menu changes daily. There's a good selection of wines.

Wild Duck Inn

Drakes Island, Ewen, Gloucestershire GL7 6BY (01285 770310/www.thewildduckinn.co.uk). **Lunch served** noon-2pm, **dinner served** 6.30-10pm Mon-Fri. **Meals served** noon-10pm Sat; noon-9.30pm Sun. **Main courses** £8-£18. **Rates** £95-£150 double. **Credit** AmEx, MC, V.
Moody dark reds, low beams and dried flowers give this busy pub a certain charm – enhanced by the loud music and occasionally raucous atmosphere of the bar. Diners spill through a series of interconnecting rooms with ample nooks and crannies. The menu runs from favourites such as beer-battered cod and roast belly pork to more adventurous offerings – whole red snapper with mango salsa, for example.

Cirencester & Around

Cowley Manor

Jessica Sainsbury and her husband Peter Frankopan opened Cowley Manor in 2002, having transformed the place with the help of a dedicated roster of designers and architects. The tone is stylish but unfussy – the staff's winter uniform is a variation on jeans and a jumper – but absolutely professional. The views of the surrounding Gloucestershire countryside are lovely; the manor house is stately on a manageable scale; the grounds are attractively landscaped and Grade II*-listed; the spa (C-side) is ultra modern but blends in beautifully with the older buildings. The 30 rooms are excellent – decorated in strong but appealing splashes of colour, with striking pieces of furniture, many of them bespoke.

Bathrooms are tranquil havens in neutral shades, boasting deep baths and huge showers. There are C-side lotions and potions, plenty of white towels and robes, and underfloor heating. Over at the spa the robes and towels are blue; there's a steam room (which smells amazing), a sauna, a gym and two pools.

Cirencester & Around

The outdoor pool is something special – even in winter it's possible to swim under the stars. Treatments run from pedicures, manicures and facials to aromatherapy massages. Attention to detail is impressive; from the moment you see the higgledy-piggledy line of wellington boots at the entrance, you feel they've probably thought of everything. We were particularly impressed by the fact that guests don't have to make dinner reservations – they can turn up whenever they want and a table will be waiting for them, or they can eat in the bar. The food is enjoyable, modern European stuff (cheese and herb omelette, big bowls of chips, blueberry cheesecake), but does a good job, and there's a very tempting room service menu.

Contemporary, luxurious and fun too – and there aren't very many country-house hotels you can say that about. Cowley, Gloucestershire GL53 9NL (01242 870 900/www.cowlcy manor.com). **Rates** £220-£445. **Credit** AmEx, DC, MC, V.

Malmesbury & Tetbury

Get away from it all in considerable style.

You'd be forgiven for thinking that the unremarkable chunk of northern Wiltshire squashed between the M4 and the southern reaches of Gloucestershire's Cotswold Hills holds few draws for weekend breakers. Scenically, it's a fairly half-hearted landscape of gently undulating farmland, broken by spindly hedges and scattered stands of trees. Just about the only high ground is occupied by the area's main settlements of Malmesbury and Tetbury (the latter just over the Gloucestershire border), which, while certainly charming, don't make for particularly thrilling destinations in themselves.

However, what you will find here are a couple of seriously fabulous spa hotels (Calcot Manor and Whatley Manor, plus the nearby stylish Barnsley House – *see p116*), which provide sufficient distractions to occupy an indulgent weekend. The other thing that's not in short supply is toffs. Prince Charles's Highgrove, Princess Anne's Gatcombe Park, Prince and Princess Michael of Kent's Nether Lypiatt Manor and Badminton Park (home of the horse trials) all lie within a few miles of each other, and it's entirely possible that the tweedy chap next to you, downing his pint of Badger and bemoaning the fox-hunting ban, is eighth in line to the throne.

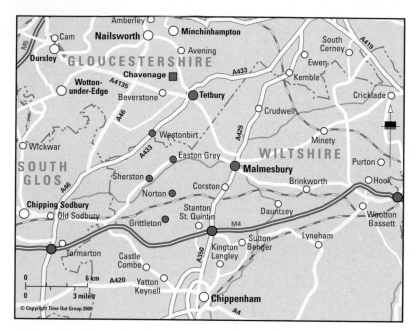

Flying monks, river rambles and a truncated abbey

In 1010 a whimsical monk called Eilmer built himself a pair of wings and jumped from the steeple of the old Minster Church in Malmesbury; he reputedly 'flew' an estimated 650 feet before hitting the ground with a wallop and breaking both his legs. One wonders whether anything quite so exciting has happened in Malmesbury since. This is a town where nothing happens – slowly. As a guilt-free destination for the perennially lazy, Malmesbury, and its surrounding countryside, is an ancient, cobbled dream of excellent food, antiques, walks and idle, boozy contemplation.

Perhaps that's not entirely fair. Eilmer aside, Malmesbury has managed to rack up some other claims to fame in its 1,300-odd years. Philosopher Thomas Hobbes was born in these parts, proving that boozy contemplation brings its own rewards, and it was home to 12th-century chronicler William of Malmesbury. The town is also the site of Malmesbury Abbey (01666 826666, www.malmesburyabbey.com), which once stood three times its still-impressive size. That such a commanding church was built here is no surprise. Because of its superb natural defences, the hill has been occupied since earliest recorded times. In 880 King Alfred was impressed enough to name Malmesbury a borough, making it the oldest in England. The Abbey was founded by Aldhelm in

676, though the basic structure you see today dates from the 12th century. Some of its earliest notable features are the south porch, containing a superb Norman arch, while later additions included an immense spire, taller than that of Salisbury Cathedral, which collapsed during a storm in the early 16th century. On Henry VIII's dissolution of the monasteries in 1539 it became a parish church, but then suffered centuries of neglect (by the 18th century it was being used as a barn and animal shed). It wasn't until the 20th century, when significant restoration work was undertaken, that the situation began to be reversed. In the north aisle is the tomb of King Athelstan.

Next to the Abbey are the lovely Abbey House Gardens (Market Cross, 01666 822212, www.abbeyhousegardens.co.uk, closed Nov-Feb). A decade ago Ian Pollard bought 16th-century Abbey House and started to develop its gardens to reflect the long history of the site. Within them you'll find a Saxon arch, a Celtic cross garden, a herb garden, an ornamental pond and 130 varieties of apple cordon and 2,000 of rose. (Guided tours of the garden with Ian can be pre-booked.)

And that's about the extent of Malmesbury's attractions. The tourist office (in the Town Hall) can supply an interesting town guide and a booklet detailing a must-do river walk that snakes around the foot of the old town.

Malmesbury Abbey; it dominates the town and can be seen for miles around, despite being a third of its original size.

Accommodation	★★★★★
Food & drink	★★★
Nightlife	
Shopping	★★
Culture	
Sights	★
Scenery	★★

A classic Cotswold wool town and antiques galore

Just five miles north-west of Malmesbury lies Tetbury. The animosity between the two towns in Saxon times was considerable (Malmesbury was in Wessex, Tetbury in Mercia). These days, that rivalry is more concerned with which town has better hotels, finer restaurants and more interesting shops. On one count Tetbury certainly wins: antiques shops. There are so many that, as one resident confided, 'You can't even find anywhere that sells underwear anymore.' Tetbury's other main feature is the sheltered Market House built on stilts in 1655 (Wednesday is market day). The Georgian Gothic church of St Mary the Virgin is also worth a look.

A monastery was built at Tetbury in 681, and during the Middle Ages the town grew in importance, becoming famed for one of the country's best wool and yarn markets. The Industrial Revolution bypassed Tetbury, leaving it economically impoverished but architecturally preserved, and gently pottering along its ancient streets (such as Gumstool Hill, site of the annual Woolsack Races) remains the number-one leisure activity today.

For an unusually personal country house experience, head to Elizabethan Chavenage House (01666 502329, www.chavenage.com, closed Oct-Apr), just outside Tetbury, where owner David Lowsley-Williams is often on hand to show guests around. The handsome house, built over a medieval original, has its own ghost. During the Civil War, its Parliamentarian owner, Nathaniel Stephens, was cursed by his own daughter for (reluctantly) acquiescing in the execution of Charles I. He died shortly afterwards, and legend has it that the headless king arrived in a hearse to carry his body away – a phenomenon repeated after the death of every patriarch in the line.

Another popular local spot is Trull House Gardens (01285 841255, www.trullhouse.co.uk, closed Nov-Easter), an intimate, eight-acre garden set in rolling country between Tetbury and Cirencester. It features a large lily pond,

TOURIST INFORMATION

Malmesbury
Town Hall, Market Lane, Cross Hayes, Malmesbury, Wiltshire SN16 9BZ (01666 823748/ www.malmesbury.gov.uk).
Tetbury
33 Church Street, Tetbury, Gloucestershire GL8 8JG (01666 503552/www.tetbury.org).

terraced gardens, a sunken garden leading to a summer house and a wilderness area that is alive with bulbs in spring and grasses and wild flowers in summer.

The only attraction of national importance in the area, however, is the superlative Westonbirt National Arboretum (01666 880220, www.forestry.gov.uk/westonbirt), located a few miles south-west of Tetbury. Westonbirt is world-famed for its stunning collection of over 18,000 specimens spread over 600 acres of Grade I-listed landscape and interlaced with 18 miles of marked trails. Started by Robert Holford in the 1830s, and run by the Forestry Commission since 1956, the Arboretum now pulls in around a third of a million visitors annually and offers year-round interest. Spring sees the spectacular flowering of camellias, magnolias and rhododendrons, and huge swathes of bluebells carpeting the woods; in summer grassland flowers come into their own, and the handkerchief and umbrella trees are in blossom; the blaze of autumn colour (at its best in the last two weeks of October), particularly from the Japanese maples, makes a trip to New England redundant; and, even in winter, willows, witch hazels and bright-stemmed dogwoods provide colour. Of the many annual events held at Westonbirt, highlights are the summer open-air classical concerts with fireworks as part of the Festival of Wood, and the Enchanted Wood illuminated trail in December. For information on free guided walks, call 01666 881222.

WHERE TO STAY

Calcot Manor Hotel

Junction of the A46 & A4135, 3 miles from Tetbury, Gloucestershire GL8 8YJ (01666 890391/www.calcotmanor.co.uk). **Rates** £185-£225 double; £240-£360 suite. **Credit** AmEx, DC, MC, V.

Though it started off as a fairly traditional, small country-house hotel in the early 1980s, Calcot Manor has metamorphosed over the years into one of the UK's finest, friendliest, most stylish and most enjoyable places to stay. Its secret lies in its inclusiveness. Calcot Manor is justly famed for its family-friendliness – a converted barn houses a series of dedicated family rooms and suites, while another holds the Playzone (open 9am-5.30pm daily), a superbly equipped, supervised crèche and play area catering to a wide age range, from babies to teenagers (computers, PlayStations, Xboxes and a mini cinema keep the latter happy). Other services include baby listening, a children's video library, an outdoor play area and a kids-only high tea (5.30-6.30pm). The clever part is that by keeping the family facilities largely separate from the main building, the hotel never feels overwhelmed by children and so appeals equally to couples.

For the child-free, one of Calcot's major draws is its impressive spa. Opened in 2003, it offers a broad spectrum of treatments, and features indoor and outdoor pools, a hammam massage table, dry flotation bed and, best of all, an outdoor hot tub facing a log fire. (Note that children are only allowed in the spa at certain times.) Further outdoor facilities include tennis courts and a footpath/cycle track (bikes can be borrowed) that winds its way through the estate's 220 acres.

Only nine of the 30 bedrooms are within the main house, and these have deliberately been given a more traditional (though far from fusty) look than those located in various buildings around the grounds. All are individually decorated and display a restrained modernity, muted colours, sleek bathrooms and facilities that include CD systems and swish TVs. Calcot offers two eating options, the informal Gumstool Inn (where families can eat together) and the posher Conservatory (where small children are 'discouraged'); *see p131.*

Close Hotel

Long Street, Tetbury, Gloucestershire GL8 8AQ (01666 502272/www.oldenglish inns.co.uk). **Rates** £100-£150 double. **Credit** AmEx, DC, MC, V.

In contrast to the contemporary country-house appeal of Calcot Manor (*see above*), the 15-room Close Hotel in the centre of Tetbury is very much of the old school. Housed within a splendid 16th-century townhouse, this is a place of swagged curtains, rich, multi-hued decor and antiquey furniture. The best three bedrooms have four-posters and views over the gardens. Attractions include a notable restaurant (*see p131*) and very friendly staff.

Old Bell

Abbey Row, Malmesbury, Wiltshire SN16 0BW (01666 822344/www.oldbellhotel.com). **Rates** £125-£175 double; £225 suite. **Credit** AmEx, MC, V.

In 1220, a building was erected next to Malmesbury Abbey that has been used as a place of entertainment until the present day; it's on that

Westonbirt National Arboretum

premise that the Old Bell claims to be the oldest hotel in England. Yet a couple of years ago this venerable 31-room hostelry was in a sorry state. It has taken a new owner and a complete revamp of the interior to bring back its warmth and vitality. Nothing too radical has been attempted – there are flashes of modernity in some of the artworks, but the overall style is an easy-on-the-eye, mix-and-match, comfy country-house one that has pleased both the local regulars and out-of-town guests. Bedrooms are quite simply decorated; it's worth paying more for one of the superior rooms, some of which have views of the Abbey. All have TVs with integral DVD players. The patio area and small gardens at the rear are a summer haven, while log fires burn in the lounges and bar in cold weather. A further draw is the superb restaurant (*see p132*).

Whatley Manor Hotel – the most luxurious opening of 2004.

Snooty Fox

Market Place, Tetbury, Gloucestershire, GL8 8DD (01666 502436/www.snooty-fox.co.uk). **Rates** £95-£199 double. **Credit** AmEx, MC, V.

The main alternative to the Close Hotel in Tetbury is this similarly decorated, traditional coaching inn right on the old Market Place in the centre of town. The vibe is warm and welcoming in the public rooms, while all 12 bedrooms (two with four-posters) have DVD players, and some have whirlpool baths.

Whatley Manor Hotel

Easton Grey, Malmesbury, Wiltshire SN16 0RB (01666 822888/www.whatleymanor.com). **Rates** £275-£450 double; £650-£850 suite. **Credit** AmEx, MC, V.

If Calcot Manor prides itself on its inclusivity, its near neighbour Whatley Manor shamelessly aims for the reverse. Converted at vast expense by Swiss owner Christian Landholt and opened in 2004, Whatley is the 'rarefied bubble of low-key luxury, peace and total privacy' that its brochure asserts. This is the sort of place where, even when all 23 rooms (8 suites and 15 doubles) are occupied, guests rarely glimpse each other. So if you want buzz, look elsewhere; but if you crave ultimate escapism (and your pockets are deep), this is the place for you.

Quality is apparent in everything, from the Cotswold stone walls lining the hotel drive (which took two workmen two years to build) to the hand-made French wallpaper, acres of oak panelling and Bang & Olufsen TVs in the bedrooms. The interior design is the work of the owner's mother, which gives it a certain quirky individualism rarely found in posh hotels.

Undoubtedly one of Whatley's major draws is its superlative Aquarias Spa (use of which is included in the room prices), whose centrepiece is one of the biggest and best hydrotherapy pools in the country. As well as a wide range of treatments (by La Prairie, at extra cost), the spa includes four thermal cabins, a gym and a 'VIP suite', where couples can indulge in a private, tailored package of pampering for two.

Perhaps an equal attraction is Martin Burge's cooking at the hotel's two restaurants: Le Mazot and the Dining Room (*see p132*).

Surrounding the house are 12 acres of stunning terraced gardens (made up of 26 distinct sub-gardens) leading down to a wild flower meadow bordering a tributary of the Avon. Created by head gardener Barry Holman from an essentially blank canvas, and remarkably mature considering there was nothing but grass here a couple of years ago, they have a tranquillity that is only disturbed by the occasional helicopter landing on the lawn.

The staff are attentive and efficient, but thankfully not afraid to crack a smile. Note that children under the age of 12 aren't accommodated at Whatley. The hotel is located between Easton Grey and Malmesbury, off the B4040.

WHERE TO EAT & DRINK

Among the best drinking pubs in the area are the Vine Tree in Norton (*see p133*) and the Neeld Arms in Grittleton (The Street, 01249 782470), just north of the M4.

Close Hotel

Long Street, Tetbury, Gloucestershire GL8 8AQ (01666 502272/www.oldenglish inns.co.uk). **Lunch served** noon-2pm, **dinner served** 7-9.30pm daily. **Main courses** £22.50. **Set lunch** £9.50 1 course, £13.50 2 courses, £17.50 3 courses. **Set dinner** £28.50 3 courses. **Credit** AmEx, DC, MC, V.

The setting might be country-house traditional, but the Close Hotel's kitchen is anything but. There is invention aplenty, which only occasionally descends into pretension. A typical meal might start with an appetiser of asparagus cappuccino, before heading into inventive starters like assiette of smoked salmon (with the fish in myriad forms: tortellini, tartare and a deliciously moist bundled sausage). Mains could be a 'study of Cotswold lamb' – a medley of mini kidney pie, loin, sweetbreads and faggots – or pan-fried cod with seafood foam, while desserts might include a cute trio of apple desserts. The selection of British cheeses is not to be sniffed at (literally, in the case of the stinking bishop). Excellent service too, despite the slightly formal surroundings.

The Conservatory, Gumstool Inn & Champagne Bar at Calcot Manor

Near Tetbury, Gloucestershire GL8 8YJ (01666 890391/www.calcotmanor.co.uk). Conservatory **Lunch served** noon-2pm daily. **Dinner served** 7-9.30pm Mon-Sat; 7-9pm Sun. **Main courses** £12-£30. *Gumstool Inn* **Lunch served** noon-2pm Mon-Fri. **Meals served** 7-9.30pm Mon Sat; noon-9pm Sun. **Main courses** £7-£15. **Credit** AmEx, DC, MC, V.

Calcot Manor's top-end dining option is the light, airy Conservatory. It's a smart but unimposing space, clad in soft, neutral tones with a recurring reed design. All eyes are drawn to the open kitchen and its crackling wood-burning oven, from which emerge many of the restaurant's most popular dishes, such as a superb, slightly smoky fillet of beef on the bone with garlic, ginger and caramelised shallots, and partridge with brussels sprout purée, potato pancake, maple-glazed turnips, prunes and bacon. Starters might be braised rabbit pappardelle with black olive tapenade and sage, or crab and avocado salad with confit tomato and lemon oil dressing, while baked chocolate fondant with rosemary ice-cream is a winning dessert. It's all good, classy, essentially simple cooking, though perhaps priced a little on the steep side.

A cheaper option is the neighbouring, pub-like Gumstool Inn. The atmosphere is casual (families often eat here) and somewhat echoey, and the menu is eclectic, tempting and cooked with flair.

For a twist on a classic, try venison bourguignon or char-grilled yellowfin tuna with spicy Asian slaw, or hearty classics like devilled lamb's kidneys (in a crisp pastry case) and fish and chips. Finish off with marbled fudge brownie with chocolate sauce and praline ice-cream. For a pre- or post-meal drink, Calcot's Champagne Bar is a sophisticated, clubby space, decked out in walnut and dark leather.

The Dining Room & Le Mazot at Whatley Manor

Easton Grey, Wiltshire SN16 0RB (01666 822888/www.whatleymanor.com). Le Mazot **Lunch served** noon-2pm, **dinner served** 7-10pm daily. *Dining Room* **Dinner served** 7-10pm Wed-Sun. **Main courses** *Le Mazot* £11.50-£14. *Dining Room* £15-£21. **Set dinner** *Dining Room* £60 3 courses, £75 7-course tasting menu. **Credit** AmEx, MC, V.

There have been few more ambitious hotel openings in recent years than Whatley Manor (*see p131*), and the presence of two fully fledged restaurants in a 23-room establishment indicates that food is taken as seriously as accommodation. The kitchen (shared by both the top-end Dining Room and more affordable Le Mazot) is headed by Martin Burge, a hugely talented chef who earned his culinary spurs working for the likes of Raymond Blanc and John Burton Race. Impeccable classical principles underlie the beautifully conceived and executed Dining Room menu, and, if prices are high, they are more than justified. Go for the tasting menu if you can stretch to it, and feast on the likes of roast breast of mallard with braised salsify and port wine sauce infused with juniper and orange, and possibly the largest scallop you'll ever see, roasted and served with spiced pumpkin purée and a light curry oil infusion. Le Mazot, though designated a brasserie, serves up dishes that would grace most first-rate restaurants – perhaps ravioli of smoked ham hock with pak choi and a gribiche sauce, or roast local pheasant with onion cream, wild mushrooms and a red wine sauce infused with thyme. The only discordant notes are the surroundings. The Dining Room is three anonymous little rooms devoid of atmosphere, while Le Mazot is housed within a weirdly incongruous mock Swiss chalet (the hotel owner is Swiss). Strange, but don't let it put you off; the food is fabulous. No smoking throughout.

Old Bell

Abbey Row, Malmesbury, Wiltshire SN16 0AG (01666 822344/www.oldbellhotel.com). **Lunch served** noon-2.30pm daily. **Dinner served** 7-9pm Mon-Thur, Sun; 7-9.30pm Fri, Sat. **Set lunch** (Mon-Sat) £11.50 2 courses, £14.50 3 courses; (Sun) £17.50 3 courses. **Main courses** £12.50-£19.50. **Credit** AmEx, MC, V.

The historic Old Bell's recent revamp has not only restored the hotel to its former glory but propelled its restaurant back into the first rank. Prices that wouldn't be out of place in an expensive London

eaterie indicate that executive chef Tom Rains is aiming high, and his assured and artfully measured cooking doesn't raise false expectations. Among his signature dishes are poached scallops, Dublin Bay prawns, saffron and aromatic vegetables, and roasted rack and slow-cooked shoulder of lamb with savoy cabbage, creamed potato and rosemary jus. For dessert, you won't better his classic bread and butter pudding. If you can stretch to it, go for the seven-course taster menu. The stately yet stylish dining room is presided over with great charm and efficiency by restaurant manager Saverio Buchicchio.

Rattlebone

Church Street, Shearston, Wiltshire SN16 0LR (01666 840871). **Lunch served** noon-3pm, **dinner served** 6pm-10pm daily. **Main courses** £6.95-£12.95. **Credit** MC, V.

Grab a table close to the log fire at this agreeable old village inn (there's also a less atmospheric room at the back and a handful of outdoor tables). It's a Young's house, so the beer's quality can be taken as read, and the food is solid and satisfying. The snack menu lists various paninis, ploughman's and baked potatoes, while the main menu (supplemented by blackboard specials) stretches from a classic honey-roast ham, egg and own-made chips to more ambitious dishes like pan-fried duck breast on tarragon rösti with cider brandy jus. Active minds will appreciate the countless games on offer (Connect Four, shove-ha'penny, cribbage). Come for the second Saturday of July to watch the pub's annual boules tournament. The Rattlebone's a child-friendly place, with high chairs available.

Smoking Dog

62 High Street, Malmesbury, Wiltshire SN16 9AT (01666 825823). **Lunch served** noon-2pm daily. **Dinner served** 7-9.30pm Mon-Sat. **Main courses** £9.25-£13.25. **Credit** MC, V.

Perennially rammed, the Smoking Dog is a good, simple, chatty pub at the lower end of Malmesbury's short High Street. As well as a fairly standard snacks menu of ciabattas, burgers, sausages and mash and the like, there is a dinner menu that might include stilton-stuffed chicken breast wrapped in smoked bacon with black pudding mash and port wine sauce, or roast duck breast on spring onion mash with plum and ginger sauce. The beers are good and, if you time your visit correctly, you could arrive for the annual sausage and ale festival – the ideal marriage of meat and mead. A back garden offers lovely views over the picturesque town.

Trouble House

nr Tetbury, Gloucestershire GL8 8SG (01666 502206/www.troublehouse.co.uk). **Lunch served** noon-2pm, **dinner served** 7-9.30pm Tue-Sat. **Main courses** £13-£16. **Credit** AmEx, DC, MC, V.

This modest, whitewashed former pub earned its curious name (according to one story) when it became a hotbed of rural agitation during the Luddite rebellion. These days it's the way-above-average food, served in the simple rustic interior, that is making waves locally. Chef-proprietor Michael Bedford, formerly a head chef for Gary Rhodes, offers an unfussy modern menu of solid yet polished stomach-pleasers. Start, perhaps, with haddock and whisky soup or crab risotto, then move on to roast cod with haricot beans, lentils and bacon, or seared black bream with braised red cabbage, and finish with glazed Basque tart or orange and rosemary syrup cake. The wines, like the food, are well balanced and kindly priced.

Vine Tree

Foxley Road, Norton, near Malmesbury, Wiltshire SN16 0JP (01666 837654). **Lunch served** noon-2pm Mon-Fri; noon-2.30pm Sat; noon-3pm Sun. **Dinner served** 7-9.30pm daily. **Main courses** £8.95-£15.50. **Credit** AmEx, MC, V. Well off the beaten track, this tiny and welcoming 18th-century mill house knocks out food of a quality you wouldn't necessarily expect from such a pint-sized pub. The menu offers the likes of classic moules marinière, smoked haddock fish cakes wrapped in parma ham with watercress mayonnaise, and char-grilled Cotswold pork fillet with haricot bean and chorizo cassoulet. Snacks, such as superb filled baguettes, are also available. It's as good for a pint as for a meal, and you might find yourself quaffing a jug of Butcombe Ale with anyone from the local landowner to the recently resident Hamiltons (surprisingly agreeable folk, according to the landlady). A gem.

Malmesbury & Tetbury

Bristol

A vibrant modern city that hasn't forgotten its roots.

For many years, Bristol had a reputation as a hard-working merchant city with little time for the trappings of tourism. What's more, since the 18th century, the city has lived in the shadow of her elegant little sister upriver. Bath has always been the tourist honeypot in this area, leaving Bristol's charms to go largely unnoticed – even by its own residents. In the last few years, though, Bristol has been redressing the balance and asserting itself as an ideal weekend break destination. Thanks to its proximity to both coast and countryside, the city combines a contemporary urban vibe with the promise of more rural pleasures on its doorstep. Bristol's fascinating past is brought to life by a number of engrossing historical sites and museums, while stylish restaurants and cafés provide welcome refuelling stops between photo opportunities.

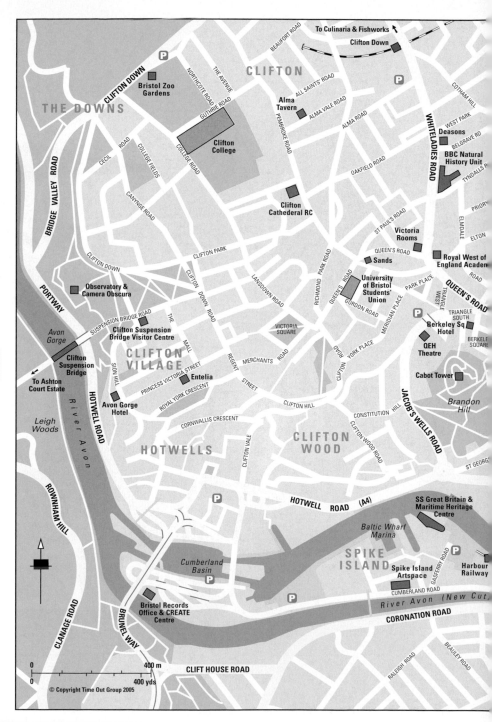

To Culinaria & Fishworks
Clifton Down

BEAUFORT ROAD

CLIFTON

CLIFTON DOWN

Bristol Zoo
Gardens

NORTHCOTE ROAD

THE AVENUE

ALL SAINTS' ROAD

Alma
Tavern

ALMA VALE ROAD

ALMA ROAD

WHITELADIES ROAD

COTHAM HILL

WEST PARK

Deasons

BELGRAVE RD

THE DOWNS

GUTHRIE ROAD

PEMBROKE ROAD

BBC Natural
History Unit

OAKFIELD ROAD

TYNDALL'S

CECIL ROAD

COLLEGE FIELDS

COLLEGE ROAD

Clifton
College

PRIORY

ELMDALE

ELTON

CANYAGE ROAD

Clifton
Cathederal RC

ST PAUL'S ROAD

Victoria
Rooms

QUEEN'S ROAD

Royal West of
England Academ

BRIDGE VALLEY ROAD

CLIFTON DOWN

CLIFTON PARK

LANSDOWN ROAD

RICHMOND PARK ROAD

QUEEN'S ROAD

Sands

University
of Bristol
Students'
Union

GORDON ROAD

PARK PLACE

QUEEN'S ROAD

TRIANGLE WEST

ROAD

PORTWAY

Observatory &
Camera Obscura

CLIFTON DOWN ROAD

VICTORIA
SQUARE

MERIDIAN PLACE

TRIANGLE
SOUTH

Berkeley Sq
Hotel

BERKELE
SQUARE

Avon
Gorge

SUSPENSION BRIDGE ROAD

Clifton Suspension
Bridge Visitor Centre

THE MALL

SION HILL

CLIFTON VILLAGE

PRINCESS VICTORIA STREET

Entelia

REGENT STREET

MERCHANTS ROAD

CLIFTON YORK PLACE

QEH
Theatre

Cabot Tower

Brandon
Hill

Clifton
Suspension
Bridge

To Ashton
Court Estate

Avon Gorge
Hotel

ROYAL YORK CRESCENT

CLIFTON HILL

CONSTITUTION HILL

JACOB'S WELLS ROAD

Leigh
Woods

HOTWELL ROAD

River Avon

CORNWALLIS CRESCENT

CLIFTON VALE

CLIFTON WOOD

CLIFTON WOOD ROAD

ST GEORG'

HOTWELLS

ROWNHAM HILL

HOTWELL ROAD (A4)

Baltic Wharf
Marina

SS Great Britain &
Maritime Heritage
Centre

Cumberland
Basin

SPIKE
ISLAND

Spike Island
Artspace

GASFERRY ROAD

Harbour
Railway

CLANAGE ROAD

BRUNEL WAY

Bristol Records
Office & CREATE
Centre

CUMBERLAND ROAD

River Avon (New Cut)

CORONATION ROAD

RALEIGH ROAD

BEAULEY ROAD

0   400 m
0   400 yds

CLIFT HOUSE ROAD

© Copyright Time Out Group 2005

Bristol

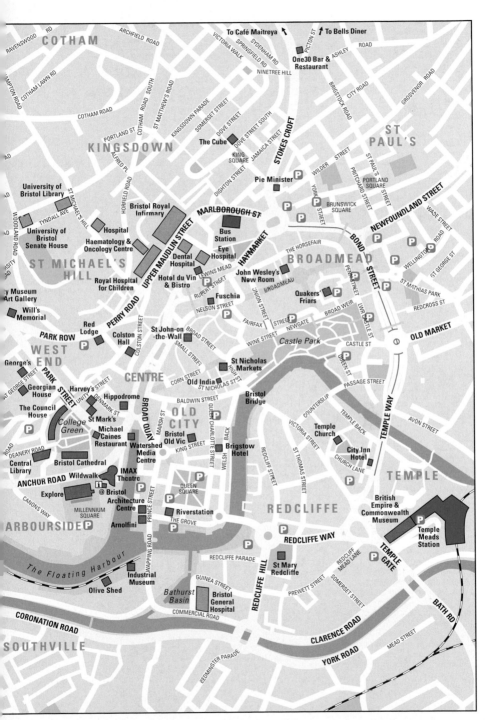

COTHAM

To Café Maitreya ↖   ↑ To Bells Diner

One30 Bar &
Restaurant

NINETREE HILL

ST
PAUL'S

KINGSDOWN

The Cube

KING
SQUARE

Pie Minister

STOKES CROFT

BRUNSWICK
SQUARE

PORTLAND
SQUARE

NEWFOUNDLAND STREET

University of
Bristol Library

Bristol Royal
Infirmary

MARLBOROUGH ST

University of
Bristol
Senate House

Hospital

Haematology &
Oncology Centre

Bus
Station

Eye
Hospital

UPPER MAUDLIN STREET

HAYMARKET

BOND STREET

BROADMEAD

ST MICHAEL'S
HILL

Royal Hospital
for Children

Dental
Hospital

Hotel du Vin
& Bistro

John Wesley's
New Room

BROADMEAD

y Museum
Art Gallery

Fuschia

Quakers'
Friars

Will's
Memorial

Red
Lodge

Colston
Hall

St John-on
-the-Wall

BROAD STREET

NEWGATE

OLD MARKET

PARK ROW

PERRY ROAD

Castle Park

WEST
END

George's

St Nicholas
Markets

CENTRE

Old India

Bristol
Bridge

Georgian
House

Harvey's

Hippodrome

St Mark's

Michael
Caines
Restaurant

BROAD QUAY

OLD
CITY

Temple
Church

AVON STREET

The Council
House

College
Green

Bristol
Old Vic

Brigstow
Hotel

City Inn
Hotel

TEMPLE

Central
Library

Bristol Cathedral

Watershed
Media
Centre

IMAX
Theatre

TEMPLE WAY

ANCHOR ROAD

Wildwalk

Explore
@ Bristol

Architecture
Centre

QUEEN
SQUARE

British
Empire &
Commonwealth
Museum

Temple
Meads
Station

MILLENNIUM
SQUARE

Riverstation

THE GROVE

REDCLIFFE

REDCLIFFE WAY

TEMPLE
GATE

ARBOURSIDE

Arnolfini

The Floating Harbour

REDCLIFFE PARADE

St Mary
Redcliffe

Industrial
Museum

Olive Shed

Bathurst
Basin

Bristol
General
Hospital

REDCLIFFE HILL

BATH RD

CORONATION ROAD

COMMERCIAL ROAD

CLARENCE ROAD

SOUTHVILLE

YORK ROAD

Bristol

Accommodation	★★
Food & drink	★★★
Nightlife	★★★★
Shopping	★★★
Culture	★★★
Sights	★★★
Scenery	★★

In autumn 2002 the former engine shed at Temple Meads station became the clumsily named but thoughtfully compiled British Empire & Commonwealth Museum (Station Approach, Temple Meads, 0117 925 4980, www.empiremuseum.co.uk). Tracing the history of the empire and commonwealth from the early explorers to the multiracial communities of today, it offers an international perspective on the motives, achievements, exploitation and impact of British imperialism. The museum handles this controversial subject with a laudable degree of imagination, using interactive displays, artefacts sourced from other major museum collections and some fascinating early photos, films and oral history exhibits.

In summer, make the most of Bristol's wide open spaces and outdoor festivals and, after dark, head for the city's critically acclaimed music, clubbing and theatre venues. Culturally, ethnically and economically diverse, it's a city where the maritime and industrial achievements of the past provide a context for present-day artistic and cultural success. And where ambitious self-promotion is tempered by a laid-back, easy-living attitude.

Clifton

This desirable residential suburb was developed during the late 18th and early 19th centuries with grand crescents and elegant Georgian architecture. Clifton did not become part of the city until 1835 and has managed to retain its exclusive (not to say snobbish) character to this day, looking down on the rest of Bristol from its imperious perch to the north-west. Royal York Crescent stretches in a wide arc for a quarter of a mile, making it the longest Georgian crescent in the UK. At the heart of the district, picturesque Clifton Village is an amalgam of bijou boutiques, traditional shops, cafés, restaurants and pastel-coloured terraces – perfect for Saturday-afternoon pottering.

Close by is Brunel's Suspension Bridge, which spans the chasm of the Avon Gorge. Despite the best efforts of quarry companies and road-builders, the gorge retains much of its wild, romantic scenery and the bridge is truly majestic. It measures 702 feet across and spans the gorge 245 feet above the river. The best

views are either from the large terrace of the Avon Gorge Hotel to the south or from the edge of Clifton and Durdham Downs to the north. Stretching for 400 acres east from the Avon Gorge, the Downs provide a vast, grassy, breezy playground for scores of dog-walkers, Sunday footballers, joggers and kite-flyers. Award-winning Bristol Zoo is nearby.

Theatre

Bristol has more than its fair share of excellent theatres. The Edwardian Bristol Hippodrome (St Augustine's Parade, 0870 607 7500, www.getlive.co.uk/bristol) is one of the largest provincial stages in the country and host to a steady stream of West End musicals, celebrity-festooned pantomimes and other crowd-pleasers. Cary Grant was a call-boy here before making his fortune in Hollywood.

However, it's the Bristol Old Vic at the Theatre Royal (King Street, Old City, 0117 987 7877, www.bristol-old-vic.co.uk, closed mid July-end Aug) that's the jewel in the city's theatre crown and esteemed as the foremost production company in the south-west. Also at the Theatre Royal is the New Vic, which stages in-house work and touring productions, and the excellent Basement Theatre, a forum for new writers. The Old Vic does not, however, hold the monopoly on quality theatre or imaginative use of space. The Tobacco Factory (Raleigh Road, Southville, 0117 902 0344, www.tobaccofactory.com), a studio theatre housed in a former warehouse, is the scene of some of the city's most innovative productions, including the award-winning 'Shakespeare at the Tobacco Factory' series. Less well known, the QEH (Jacob's Wells Road, Hotwells, 0117 930 3082) offers a nicely judged selection of fringe drama, dance shows and improv work.

Harbourside

A stroll and ferry trip around Bristol's harbourside is a great way to get a feel for the city's maritime past. First, make your way to the Arnolfini, a leading arts centre undergoing extensive redevelopment until autumn 2005. Outside is a pensive-looking statue of the Genoese explorer John Cabot, who set out from Bristol in 1497 and discovered Newfoundland. Cross the narrow swing bridge to the red and white hulk of the Bristol Industrial Museum (Princes Wharf, Wapping Road, 0117 925 1470, www.bristol-city.gov.uk/museums), fronted by sentinel-like electric cranes, which has displays on the city's engineering heritage and its association with the slave trade. In summer the museum's vintage boats tour the harbour and a steam railway carries passengers along the docks. You can follow the tracks on foot, past new designer apartment complexes, to the Maritime Heritage Centre

Bristol

The Annexe, Wildscreen Walk, Harbourside, BS1 5DB (0906 711 2191/www.visitbristol.co.uk).

(Great Western Dockyard, Gas Ferry Road, 0117 926 0680, www.ss-great-britain.com), which tells the story of ship-building in Bristol. Just outside is the *SS Great Britain*, designed by Isambard Kingdom Brunel as the first ocean-going ship to be constructed of iron and driven by a propeller (rather than paddles). Despite the ignominy of sitting high and dry in a dock, she still exudes an air of former grandeur. Moored next to the *SS Great Britain* is the touchingly small and fragile-looking *Matthew*, a life-size working replica of the boat sailed by John Cabot to Newfoundland, built to commemorate the 500-year anniversary of his Atlantic crossing.

Unaccompanied adults may find the super-abundance of levers, buttons, screens and pulleys at Explore@tBristol (Anchor Road, Harbourside, 0845 345 1235, www.at-bristol.org.uk) somewhat overwhelming, but for families this place is a rainy-day godsend. In-yer-face corporate sponsorship detracts from the appeal of some exhibits, but there's serious science here among all the gadgetry. Across the piazza is Wildwalk@tBristol, an impressive exhibition devoted to the natural world. Interactive screens and film footage are complemented by live exhibits – fish, insects, spiders, reptiles and two walk-through botanical habitats – to create an informative and thought-provoking attraction. An IMAX cinema is housed in the same building. Afterwards spend some time relaxing among the water features, skateboarders and statues in Millennium Square.

When you've finished, catch a ferry with the Bristol Ferry Boat Company (0117 927 3416, www.bristolferryboat.co.uk) to one of the harbourside pubs: Cottage Inn, Baltic Wharf, Cumberland Road, Hotwells, 0117 921 5256; the Mardyke, Hotwell Road, 0117 907 7499; or the Ostrich, Lower Guinea Street, 0117 927 3774, .

WHERE TO STAY

For a city this size, Bristol suffers from a dearth of good, stylish accommodation options. The chains are represented in abundance – the Marriott Royal (College Green, BS1 5TA, 0117 925 5100, www.marriotthotels.com) is the most luxurious, while Premier Travel Inn (Llandoger Trow, King Street, BS1 4ER, 0870 990 6424) is cheap and central – but there are few independent ventures offering rooms and services beyond the ordinary. Boutique-style guesthouses and B&Bs are also conspicuous by their absence.

Berkeley Square Hotel

15 Berkeley Square, BS8 1HB (0117 925 4000/www.cliftonhotels.com). **Rates** £95-£145 double. **Credit** AmEx, DC, MC, V.
The flagship of the Bristol hotel mini-chain enjoys an enviable position on a Georgian square with fine views over Bristol from the upper floors. The ground floor was extensively refurbished in 2004 to create an appealing, open-plan reception area and lounge. Although the eccentric fittings look as though they've been pilfered from a West End prop cupboard – stuffed peacock, leopard-print cushions, chaises longues and customised projection of swaying trees – the overall effect is bright and good-humoured. Adjoining is the more restrained Square restaurant (£7-£14 mains), which is open to the public for lunch but is reserved for hotel guests and members in the evening. The same exclusivity applies to the basement bar. The executive suites are smallish, considering the price, but have a contemporary vibe, with clean lines, bright colours, CD players and minibars – the complimentary decanter of sherry is a nice touch. Standard rooms – currently tired and dated, with unreconstructed floral prints on fabrics and wallpaper – are to be refurbished dur-

The Matthew

Bristol

ing 2005. Other hotels in the group are cheaper but in desperate need of a makeover.

Brigstow Hotel

Welsh Back, BS1 4SP (0117 929 1030/ www.brigstowhotel.com). **Rates** £95-£169 double; £175-£250 suite. **Credit** AmEx, DC, MC, V.

Perfectly situated for the centre of town and the docks, the harbourside Brigstow is both practical and good-looking. It has 115 rooms – you'll pay extra for a river view – kitted out in a subtle palette of beige, red and green, and sporting up-to-the-minute facilities, including air-conditioning, internet access and even a plasma TV screen in the bathroom – the perfect place to watch your favourite soap, perhaps. Shiny wooden floors and overhanging mezzanine balconies impart a hint of cruise-ship styling to the large, sleek reception area and the open-plan Ellipse bar and restaurant on the ground floor. Other facilities include a business centre, conference rooms and 24-hour room service. Weekend B&B is good value.

City Inn Hotel

Temple Way, BS1 6BF (0117 925 1001/ www.cityinn.com). **Rates** £65-£129 double. **Credit** AmEx, DC, MC, V.

This sleek urban hotel is close to Temple Meads station but backs on to the leafier surroundings of Temple churchyard. Very much a corporate hotel during the week, the City Inn's attention to detail and guest-focused ethos mean it's a good option for weekend leisure visitors too. The contemporary rooms are all identical, but they avoid the anonymity of the larger chains, with bright decor, large windows and excellent facilities: 24-hour room service, air-conditioning, CD player, satellite TV, internet and ISDN access all come as standard. They're also thankfully well soundproofed against noise from the busy main road. Classy modern British cuisine is served in the City Café (set menu £17.50, three courses).

Hotel du Vin & Bistro

The Sugar House, Narrow Lewins Mead, BS1 2NU (0117 925 5577/www.hotelduvin.com). **Rates** £130-£135 double/twin; £180-£330 suite. **Credit** AmEx, DC, MC, V.

Converted from an 18th-century sugar warehouse, this is a welcome change from the city's usual identikit accommodation. A sheltered courtyard leads from the busy, concrete-lined main road into a haven of sensitive restoration, thoughtful styling and good taste. Exposed brickwork, wooden floors and metal joists provide a soft industrial-chic setting for spacious bedrooms and loft suites in chocolate brown, beige and cream, with Egyptian linen bedclothes, stand-alone baths and enormous walk-in showers. On the ground floor, the comfortable lounge bar has a gentlemen's-club vibe, with carefully distressed leather sofas, low lights and its own cigar humidor. Beyond is a for-

Modern times at the central Brigstow Hotel.

mal dining room where excellent French and modern British bistro-style cuisine is accompanied by an exemplary wine list. Regular tastings and wine masterclasses are held throughout the year.

WHERE TO EAT & DRINK

Bristol benefits from a huge variety of high-class, mid-range restaurants and some very special neighbourhood eateries. The more appealing bars and pubs tend to be outside the city centre, although there are some notable exceptions, such as the unmissable Mr Wolf's (35 St Stephen's Street, 0117 927 3221, www.mrwolfs.com), a noodle, cocktail and music bar where the inimitable friendly atmosphere ensures a loyal local following. Another good bet for music while you eat is the Tantric Jazz Café (39-41 St Nicholas Street, 0117 940 2304, www.tantric-jazz.co.uk), a mellow venue serving Lebanese food to a jazz soundtrack.

On Bristol's dockside, a converted red-brick Victorian wine warehouse shelters the much-loved Watershed media centre (1 Canons Road, 0117 927 5100, www.watershed.co.uk), which has an airy bar-cum-café. Nearby is The River (1 Canons Road, 0117 930 0498, www.the riverbristol.com), a popular, spacious bar that serves cocktails for the boozers and a sausage-and-mash menu for the gorgers. On the other side of the harbour, just off Queen's Square, is the Mud Dock Café (40 The Grove, 0117 934 9734, www. mud-dock.com); it bizarrely but successfully combines a mountain bike shop with an atmospheric bistro. It now even provides bike lock-ups and showers for pedalling customers. Also here is the Severnshed (The Grove, 0117 925 1212, www.severn shed.co.uk), a spacious former boat shed, designed by Isambard Kingdom Brunel. Its

waterside terrace is perfect for summer lunch, while inside a sleek mobile bar separates the formal dining room from the ultra funky drinking area. Another good spot in the centre is the summer-only Spyglass Barbecue & Grill (Welsh Back, 0117 927 2800, www.spyglassbristol.co.uk), located on a converted barge. And don't miss the food stalls at St Nicholas Markets (Corn Street, 0117 922 4017) for a global range of lunchtime snacks.

Heading towards Clifton, there are noodles at Budokan (31 Colston Street, 0117 914 1488, www.budokan.co.uk) and Wagamama (63 Queen's Road, 0117 922 1188, www.wagamama.com); good coffee, light bites and dozens of workshy students at the Boston Tea Party (75 Park Street, 0117 929 8601) and some fab American-style burgers and steaks at Tootsies (74 Park Street, 0117 9254 811, www.tootsies restaurants.co.uk). In Clifton Village, The Mall (The Mall, 0117 974 5318) is just the place to relax after a yomp across the Downs; kick back into the comfort-worn seating to enjoy a coffee, a pint or some decent bar food. Nearby is Bar Chocolat (19 The Mall, 0117 974 7000, www.bar-chocolat.com), a café devoted entirely to the sweet stuff: artful piles of sweets, cake and biscuits plus mugs of wickedly decadent hot chocolate. Also visit tiny, funky Amoeba (10 Kings Road, off Boyces Avenue, 0117 946 6461), where you can buy designer furniture and artwork as well as drinks. There are dozens of bars and restaurants lining the Whiteladies Strip; many become unbearably crowded at the weekends, but offer a good time during the week. Try Bar Humbug (89 Whiteladies Road, 0117 904 0061) for top-quality cocktails and a relaxed atmosphere, or the Picture House Bar (44 Whiteladies Road, 0117 973 9302), where part of a

long-derelict cinema has been transformed into an opulent cocktail venue.

North of the centre, the Hare on the Hill (41 Thomas Street North, Kingsdown, 0117 908 1982), serves delicious local Bath Ales and simple food to a mix of regulars. Beyond, Gloucester Road is the Bohemian alternative to the brashness of the Whiteladies Road, with a range of hip, appealing restaurants, bars and cafés. Head to the Tinto Lounge (344 Gloucester Road, 0117 942 0526) for all-day, post-hangover lounging with newspapers, board games and restorative brekkies, or the Prince of Wales (5 Gloucester Road, 0117 924 5552) for good real ales, a friendly mixed clientele and excellent organic pub grub. The North (187 Gloucester Road, 0117 944 4717) is a galley-shaped bar and bistro with a faultlessly funky vibe; communal benches encourage a convivial atmosphere and the beautifully prepared food is excellent value.

The City Café at the City Inn (*see p140*) and the restaurant at Hotel du Vin (*see p140*) are also worth remembering.

Bell's Diner

1-3 York Road, BS6 5QB (0117 924 0357/ www.bellsdiner.co.uk). **Lunch served** noon-2pm Tue-Fri. **Dinner served** 7-10pm Mon-Sat. **Main courses** £13-£19.50. **Tasting menu** £45 for 7 courses Mon-Thur (max 6 people). **Credit** AmEx, MC, V.

This long-running restaurant remains at the forefront of Bristol's dining scene. Housed in a converted grocer's shop, it makes good use of the quirky space. There's a small reception at the entrance, with a log fire in winter, and two dining rooms: one rustic and atmospheric, the other modern and sleek. The menu of contemporary British food, with Mediterranean influences, changes daily. Among the starters is a sublime dish of scallops with a rich broad bean and pea soup and a parmesan crisp; and a beetroot terrine with goat's cheese ice-cream. Roast turbot comes with smooth artichoke purée, baby artichokes and basil oil, while saddle of rabbit, black pudding and spinach is served with rabbit ravioli and tarragon foam. The wine list includes good-value regional bottles, and there are surprising versions of favourite desserts for those with waistbands to spare.

Café Maitreya

89 St Mark's Road, BS5 6HY (0117 951 0100/ www.cafemaitreya.co.uk). **Lunch served** 11am-3pm Fri; 11am-4pm Sat; 11am-5.30pm Sun. **Dinner served** 6.45-9.45pm Tue-Sat. **Main courses** (lunch) £4.95-£7.25. **Set dinner** £13.45 2 courses, £16.95 3 courses. **Credit** MC, V.

Rated the UK's top gourmet vegetarian restaurant by the Vegetarian Society in 2004, Café Maitreya's food is 100% vegetarian and strives to use only organic, environmentally friendly and fair-trade

Bristol

ingredients. The result is fresh, tasty and highly accomplished. Maitreya's soft, lavender-coloured frontage occupies a corner site on busy, buzzy St Mark's Road, welcoming customers into a light open-plan dining room. By day, you can tuck into the thumpingly good 'mega maitreya' brunch, imaginative ciabatta sandwiches and energising juices. In the evening, a more sophisticated menu takes over: steamed mooli cannelloni, stuffed with parsnip and cumin, is served with rocket and radish sprouts, sweet red chilli and peanut dressing. This can be followed by a cockle-warming winter filo parcel, filled with truffle potato, kohlrabi, leek, cider and sage. A range of organic wines provides the accompaniment. Art exhibitions and events take place throughout the year. The name 'maitreya' comes from the Sanskrit for universal love – feel the vibe in person at this special place.

Culinaria

1 Chandos Road, BS6 6PG (0117 973 7999). **Lunch served** noon-2pm Fri, Sat. **Dinner served** 6.30-9.30pm Wed-Sat. **Main courses** £11.50-£14. **Credit** MC, V.
Following their retirement from Markwick's (now Lord's) in the centre, Stephen and Judy Markwick have opened a small, sassy neighbourhood bistro to fill the hole left by the much-loved Red Snapper restaurant, which shut up shop in early 2004. The modest dining room is decorated in a clean, subtle palette of cream and blue with wooden floors and plenty of space for 30 diners, while the rest of the space is devoted to a counter of luscious dinner-party food to go. There are echoes of Elizabeth David on the pared-down menu, which offers French, British and Mediterranean dishes that are low on fuss but high on flavour. Fusion cooking is cast aside in favour of classics cooked with integrity and aplomb: provençal fish soup, ham hock terrine, shank of lamb, cassoulet, grilled whole lemon sole with cockles and the like are followed by utterly familiar desserts like summer pudding, gooseberry fool, walnut and treacle tart. There's a small courtyard for alfresco drinking.

Michael Caines
Restaurant

Deason's

43 Whiteladies Road, BS8 2LS (0117 973 6230/ www.deasons.co.uk). **Lunch served** noon-2.30pm Tue-Fri. **Dinner served** 7-10pm Tue-Thur; 7-10.30pm Fri, Sat. **Main courses** (lunch) £12.90-£16. **Set dinner** £23.50 2 courses, £29.50 3 courses. **Credit** AmEx, DC, MC, V.
One of Bristol's most accomplished restaurants. Faultless French service and arresting flower arrangements can't dispel the slightly stilted atmosphere, but the unfussy interior allows the food to take centre stage. Jason Deason's extensive travels and his culinary finesse are both in evidence throughout the contemporary menu of British and fusion dishes. Mix and match from the carte and set menu: a delicate glass noodle salad with scallops and duck breast, perhaps, followed by a rich leek and blue cheese risotto, or a tender fillet steak lying seductively on an aromatic bed

Bristol

of wild mushrooms. Be sure to leave room for the show- and heart-stopping assiette of desserts – white chocolate and honeycomb-filled profiterole, tiramisu and rich chocolate samosa. The French and international wine list is supported by a selection of Emilio Lustau sherries.

Entelia

34 Princess Victoria Street, BS8 4BZ (0117 946 6793). **Lunch served** noon-2.30pm Tue-Sun. **Dinner served** 6-11pm Mon-Sat; 6-10.30pm Sun. **Main courses** £12-£13.95. **Set meal** (6-7pm) £10 2 courses. **Credit** AmEx, DC, MC, V.
This smart Greek restaurant is a buzzing, popular choice in Clifton Village. Despite tightly packed tables, the open-plan dining room is simple and stylish, with wooden floors and large picture windows looking on to the street. The menu features classic dishes, prepared and presented with a modern sensibility. Start with fish cake polpettes accompanied by a vibrant sun-dried tomato salsa, or sensuous spanakopita: crisp, warm layers of filo pastry filled with creamy feta and spinach. Follow this with one of the fresh fish specials – bass, bream, red mullet, red snapper and lemon sole are regular feature. The souvlaki are less successful, with a tendency for dryness that is unrelieved by unimaginative sides of rice and salad, but the portions are generous and an extensive range of Greek and international wines, plus some Greek beers, make good accompaniments.

FishWorks Seafood Café

128 Whiteladies Road, BS8 2RS (0117 974 4433/www.fishworks.co.uk). **Lunch served** noon-2.30pm, **dinner served** 6-10pm Tue-Sat. **Main courses** £8-£16. **Credit** AmEx, DC, MC, V.
FishWorks serves arguably the freshest fish and seafood in town, shipped in daily from around the British coast to ensure a specials board full of variety. Alongside the specials are 'classic' dishes that exemplify a simple and respectful attitude to fish cooking. Try the vat of steamed River Fowey mussels, dripping with wine and parsley; or heaps of steamed fruits de mer served on ice. A deep blue colour scheme, a hint of nautical paraphernalia and a buzzy atmosphere provide the perfect setting. You can buy some piscine goodies to take home from the fishmonger's counter or learn culinary tips from FishWorks' acclaimed cookery school.

Fuchsia

Nelson House, Nelson Street, BS1 2JT (0117 945 0505/www.fuchsia-bristol.com). **Lunch served** noon-3.30pm Mon, Tue, Sun; noon-3pm Wed-Sat. **Dinner served** 6-11.30pm Fri, Sat; 6-11pm Wed, Thur; 6.30-11pm Mon, Tue, Sun. **Main courses** £8-£15. **Credit** AmEx, MC, V.
Millennial sophistication meets 1970s kitsch at this stylish oriental restaurant, where polished lacquer surfaces and Chinese fretwork are offset by neon pink lighting and flamboyant murals. There are classy cocktails to enjoy in the glam bar before moving on to contemplate the large menu that appeals both to urban trendies and the city's Chinese community. Choices range from Szechuan king prawn and Singapore beef to stir-fried Mongolian venison or jasmine tea-smoked ribs, all served with faultless efficiency. The smooth and sexy lounge club upstairs features funky beats and a VIP bar, but you'll have to pay to get in, even if you've racked up an impressive bill in the restaurant.

Olive Shed

Princess Wharf, BS1 4RN (0117 929 1960/ www.therealolivecompany.co.uk). **Lunch served** noon-3pm Tue-Sun. **Dinner served** 7-10pm Tue-Sat. **Main courses** £10.50-£15. **Credit** MC, V.
The ground floor of this delightful restaurant comprises the kitchen and an open-fronted delicatessen, while upstairs is a single dining room with picture windows, terracotta decor and a heart-warming atmosphere. The menu is dominated by vegetarian and seafood dishes made from seasonal organic ingredients. A plate of mixed tapas is an excellent way to sample the goodies on show on the ground floor – Spanish tortilla, barbecued prawns, gravadlax, fresh anchovies, carrot and caraway salad and, of course, the company's superlative olives – so it's a shame that over-chilling steals some of the flavour. A more adventurous starter of gorgonzola and walnut ravioli is beautifully textured and complemented by watercress sauce and peppered pears. Best of the main courses is arguably the sea bass sandwich: courgette and sweet potato mousse served between two delicate fillets of bass with a leek and hazelnut sauce. Less successful is a rather dense pudding, made from panettone, apricots and walnuts. Poised on the edge of Bristol docks, the Olive Shed comes into its own in the summer months, when you can sit outside to enjoy the Mediterranean tapas and organic wine, as the sun sets on an industrial-lite backdrop.

One30 Bar & Restaurant

130 Cheltenham Road, BS6 5RW (0117 944 2442/www.one30.com). **Brunch/lunch served** 11am-3pm daily. **Dinner served** 6pm-midnight Mon-Sat. **Main courses** £8.50-£14.50. **Tapas** £2.50-£6.50. **Credit** MC, V.
A fantastic gastrobar. Exposed brick walls, shiny wooden floors and inviting leather sofas create a familiar but unpretentious setting for Sunday afternoon lounging, Friday evening drinks or informal dining on any day of the week. Hang about in the bar area for accomplished signature cocktails, including the One30 – rum infused with vanilla and fig – and a cutting-edge tapas menu that includes unmissable morcilla risotto with deep-fried sage. The restaurant offers serious bistro food, cooked with disarming flair. If you can tear yourself away from the irresistible tapas, then

Bristol

start with a meltingly rich onion tart made with Mrs Kirkham's Lancashire. Main dishes might include hake with potatoes and puy lentils or hearty winter warmers such as braised lamb shank with mash. Portions are not over-large but, then, neither are the prices and you can always fill up with a platter of Spanish cheese or a wickedly delicious praline semifreddo. Great stuff.

Michael Caines Restaurant and Vintage Champagne & Cocktail Bar

Bristol Marriott Royal, College Green, BS1 5TA (0117 910 5309/www.michaelcaine.com). **Lunch served** noon-2.30pm Tue-Fri. **Dinner served** 7-10pm Mon-Sat. **Main courses** £18.50-£26. **Set lunch** £17.50 2 courses, £21.50 3 courses, £57.50 tasting menu. **Credit** AmEx, DC, MC, V.

The UK's youngest two-starred Michelin chef has brought an unprecedented touch of formal glamour and prestige to Bristol's dining scene. Sip a champagne cocktail on the terrace before heading to the splendid 19th-century dining room, complete with stained-glass ceiling, Greco-Roman statues and imposing oil paintings. Such opulence might upstage less assured cooking, but here the food is the star of the show from first to last and will make up for the hushed and slightly stuffy atmosphere. You can opt for head chef Shane Goodway's hugely popular seven-course tasting menu, which showcases the kitchen's flair and spontaneity with the freshest ingredients. Or allow the exemplary staff to guide you through the à la carte and the serious wine list. Pan-fried scallops in pancetta with aubergine truffle purée and lemon thyme jus combined depth of flavour with an exquisite lightness of touch, while a main course of ruby red fillet of beef with celeriac remoulade, roasted shallots, lardons and a rich red wine sauce was meltingly tender and oozing with intense aromas.

Old India

Old Stock Exchange, 34 St Nicholas Street, BS1 1TL (0117 922 1136/www.oldindia.co.uk). **Lunch served** noon-2pm, **dinner served** 6-11.30pm Mon-Sat. **Main courses** £6.50-£14. **Set lunch** (Mon-Thur) £6.95 2 courses, £8 3 courses, incl soft drink. **Set dinner** (6-7pm) £12 2 courses incl tea/coffee. **Credit** MC, V.

Housed in Bristol's former Stock Exchange and making full use of the building's innate grandeur, this Indian restaurant is a real eye-opener. The beautiful mahogany-panelled dining room and colonial club atmosphere provide a conducive setting in which to try high-class, modern Indian cooking that has been modelled on the cuisine of Moghul princes. Traditional dishes are given an avant-garde makeover to create delicious contemporary flavours that are a far cry from chicken tikka masala. Start, say, with machli purée: an aromatic fish masala chat served between wafer-thin layered purée bread; or hariyali bortha: spinach and mashed potato patties with cheese

and ripe melon seeds. Main courses include moist anari lamb chops, tenderised with pomegranate juice, or an intensely spicy murga aloo: chicken and new potatoes cooked in a hot sauce. Partner these with fluffy, fresh naan and a delicious stir-fried courgette side dish. International wines or Indian beers provide the perfect liquid accompaniment. Take a look at the original Victorian-tiled bathrooms before you leave.

Pie Minister

Stokes Croft, BS1 3PR (0117 942 9500/ www.pieminister.co.uk). **Meals served** 11am-7pm Mon-Sat; noon-4pm Sun. **Main courses** £2.95-£4. **Credit** (over £5) MC, V.

Who ate all the pies? Well, since the arrival of this pastry-baking, meat-marinading, potato-mashing, gravy-serving outlet, the answer has been Bristolians – in their droves. With some pleasant café-style seating out front and a vast pie-producing kitchen out back, Pie Minister has already become a Bristol institution. Pies are made by hand, using top-notch ingredients, including free-range meat and local seasonal vegetables. Among the favourites are humble pie (British beef, shallots, real ale and rosemary); the Spanish-themed matador (beef, chorizo, olives, tomatoes, sherry and butter beans) and a wonderful vegetarian option featuring wild mushrooms, asparagus, shallots, white wine and black pepper. The very hungry (or very greedy) can opt for a tummy-filler, which includes fluffy, buttery mash and a rich veggie gravy, and even round off the pie-fest with a sweetie pie – seasonal fruits in sugar-coated pastry. Pie Minister's deserved success means its pies are also available in selected pubs around town, and they go down very well with a decent pint of beer.

Riverstation

The Grove, BS1 4RB (0117 914 4434/ www.riverstation.co.uk). Café **Meals served** noon-10pm Mon-Sat; noon-9pm Sun. **Main courses** £2.50-£7. *Restaurant* **Lunch served** noon-2.30pm Mon-Fri, Sun; 10am-2.30pm Sat. **Dinner served** 6-10pm Mon-Thur, Sun; 6-10.30pm Fri; 6-11pm Sat. **Main courses** £11-£16.50. *Both* **Credit** MC, V.

One of Bristol's most stylish restaurants. The converted former HQ of the river police is an architectural fusion of stone, hardwoods and acres of glass. On the ground floor (deck one), a deli, bar and outside terrace provide the perfect pit stop for light lunches, while upstairs a second deck opens out into a 120-seater restaurant. The Modern European food is as uplifting as the surroundings. Seared Scottish scallops are given a Middle Eastern twist with lemon couscous and pistachio sauce, while Mediterranean fish soup with rouille and gruyère has all the intense flavours you could wish for. On the right night you might enjoy rack of lamb with gratin dauphinoise, cherry tomatoes and green sauce or faultless fillet brill with baby leeks, thyme and cream. The global wine list has been thoughtfully put together and the dessert menu sticks to favourites. A class act.

Sands

95 Queen's Road, Clifton, BS8 1LW (0117 973 9734/www.sandsrestaurant.co.uk). **Lunch served** noon-2.30pm, **dinner served** 6-11pm daily. **Main courses** £8.95-£13.95. **Set mezze** £15.95-£17.50 2 courses (minimum 2). **Credit** AmEx, MC, V.

This spacious, low-lit basement is atmospheric enough to whisk you away from the humdrum of Queen's Road yet, thankfully, it steers well clear of any tired Arabian Nights theming. In the entrance a few cushions provide a chilled-out setting in which to sample a shisha or a sweet Arabic coffee, while, beyond, creamy, plaster walls with organic alcoves are softly illuminated by lanterns. Nibble on fragrant olives while you contemplate the Lebanese menu. Those in agonies of indecision should opt for the special mezze (£17.50), which delivers a vast quantity of irresistible flavours. Start with sultry, smoky baba ghanoush, silky houmous, kibbeh and fattoush, served with feather-light pitta breads. Follow this with a mixed grill that encompasses Armenian spicy sausages, lamb koftas and lemon chicken wings. Finish with saffron, pistachio and rosewater ice-cream to cool down your over-stimulated taste-buds. Service is smiling and efficient; the ambience romantic and unrushed.

NIGHTLIFE

On Park Row, Dojo Bar (12-16 Park Row, 0117 925 1177) is an intimate party den, thanks to a music policy that incorporates everything from soul to funk to hip hop. On the same stretch, the Level (24 Park Row, 0117 373 0473, www.levelnightclub.co.uk) is a favourite on Bristol's drum 'n' bass scene but is equally adept at R&B, funky electronica and UK hip hop. It also offers a great night view of Bristol from its groovy, airport-style upstairs lounge.

On Park Street, the Elbow Room (64 Park Street, 0117 930 0242, www.theelbow room.co.uk) combines full-size pool tables with a small and sweaty dancefloor, while further down, Bar Three (9 Park Street, 0117 930 4561, www.barthree.com) is a glammed-up bar, club and restaurant empire, with original wood panelling and a dress-to-kill clientele. Nearby is the New York-groovy Soda Bar (Frogmore Lane, 0117 922 5005) and the Queenshilling (9 Frogmore Street, 0117 926 4342, www.queenshilling.com, usually free), the city's most popular gay club.

The Bristol Academy (Frogmore Street, 0117 927 9227, www.bristol-academy.co.uk) is the city's largest live venue, hosting nationally touring rock, indie and dance acts that haven't quite graduated to the arena circuit. It also features big-name house DJs and funky breakbeats from local supremos, Blowpop.

Watershed

The Mendips

Take to these lovely, laid-back hills.

More than just a pretty name, Somerset is as magical as it sounds. And that's not just along the romantic wooded coast of Exmoor, on the heathery tops of the Quantocks or down by the watery Levels. In north-east Somerset, rising up gently between stately Bath and sanctified Glastonbury, the Mendip hills form an exceptionally charming corner of the county. Estate agents jump at the chance to compare this area to the Cotswolds. Sure there are plenty of rolling limestone hills, sheep-nibbled grass, drystone walling, old stone-built towns and villages, but the atmosphere is very different. More laid-back and welcoming, less precious and considerably less clogged with coach parties, the Mendips have a particular congeniality. They're about bridle paths and ponies, happy dogs, ancient holy places, bracing strolls, wide views, astounding scrumpy and old holes in the ground. Overlooking Glastonbury Tor and the miniature cathedral city of Wells, they're green and pleasant in the way Blake might have been picturing when he penned *Jerusalem*.

The Mendips

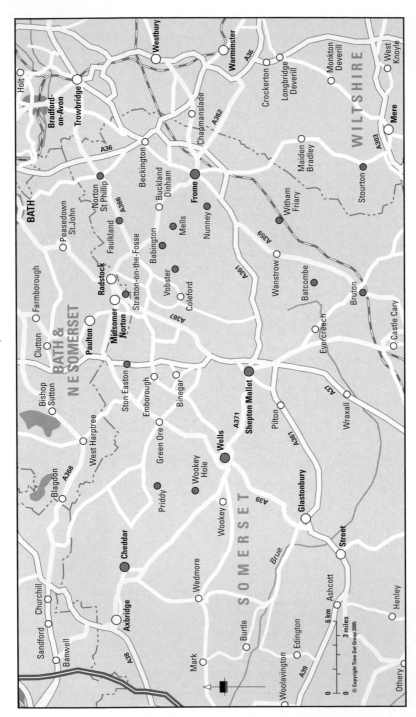

Accommodation	★★★★
Food & drink	★★★
Nightlife	
Shopping	★
Culture	
Sights	★★
Scenery	★★★★

Snuggled under the range to the south, Wells is the smallest cathedral city in England. And the cathedral is possibly the most beautiful in Britain, the niches in its west front retaining 300 medieval figure sculptures. Kings, bishops, angels and apostles survey a greensward close that keeps the proper little city at a respectable distance. Inside, the unique 'scissor arches' of the nave look like they might have been designed yesterday. In fact they've been holding up the tower for almost 700 years. Keeping track of time since the 14th century is the amazing clock invented by Brother Lightfoot. Knights joust while the sun, moon and stars revolve on the stroke of every quarter. Elsewhere in the city, it's worth leaving time to see the swans ring a bell for their supper – they can't sing for it, you see – in the moat of the Bishop's Palace; to browse around the ancient market place; to hear the water trickling down the High Street as it has done for a very long time.

When the Middle Ages begin to pall, head a couple of miles west to Wookey Hole, where HG Wells taught at the local school. The caves here (www.wookey.co.uk) are now run as an effective tourist magnet by circus supremo Gerry Cottle, including old-fashioned fairground attractions, a museum and a paper mill, which still produces fine handmade vellum. Wookey Hole has been drawing in illustrious visitors for centuries. Daniel Defoe wasn't impressed; Alexander

TOURIST INFORMATION

Cheddar
The Cliffs, Cheddar, Somerset
BS27 3QE (01934 744071/
www.somerset.gov.uk).
Frome
The Round Tower, 2 Bridge Street,
Frome, Somerset BA11 1BB (01373
467271/www.somerset.gov.uk).
Glastonbury
The Tribunal, 9 High Street,
Glastonbury, Somerset BA6
9DP (01458 832954/
www.glastonburytic.co.uk).
Shepton Mallet
70 High Street, Shepton Mallet,
Somerset BA4 5AS (01749
345258/www.shepton-mallet.org.uk).

Pope had the stalactites shot down for his grotto at Twickenham; Coleridge, who was probably on something, was put in mind of Xanadu. The site is dramatic enough to hold its own against the not-exactly-psychedelic sound-and-light effects that have been installed. After all, it's a hole in the ground with a river running through it, not a pleasuredome. Escape the queues and crowds by visiting out of season.

Natural wonders never cease on the south-facing flanks of the Mendips, reaching their commercialised apotheosis in Cheddar. Much smaller and less cheesy, just beyond Wookey, is the Ebbor Gorge, a wooded National Nature Reserve surrounding a craggy limestone gulch, home to the lesser horseshoe bat. Several well-signposted routes are recommended, none likely to be very busy at any time of year, while stunning views open up over the vale of Glastonbury from the start. Further up the same road, Priddy is an old agricultural village on the tops, laced about by wonderful drystone walls, with a couple of unreconstructed local boozers near an expansive green in the middle.

If anything, things get even more fanciful towards the eastern end of the region. Here winding roads run between high hedges and earthen banks, through hidden valleys and across fast-flowing fords. It's one of those secret Catholic enclaves of the countryside that have preserved a different pace of life. By way of examples, seek out the neo-Gothic glory of Downside Abbey and the Benedictines near Stratton-on-the-Fosse; check out the moated ruin of a Frenchified 14th-century castle in sleepy Nunney; or amble into the gorgeous old village of Mells. A medieval street leads up to a churchyard where Siegfried Sassoon, Ronald Knox and Violet Bonham Carter are buried. The church itself contains memorials by Eric Gill, Edwin Lutyens and Edward Burne-Jones as well as an unusual equine sculpture by Sir Alfred Munnings commemorating Edward Horner, who was killed in World War I. One of his ancestors was probably (not) Little Jack Horner, who sat in a corner pulling a plum (the deeds to the Manor of Mells at the Dissolution, supposedly) out of a pie with his thumb. In Mells there are plenty of thumbs in pies, as well as games, terrier races, market stalls and much jollity on the village's annual Daffodil Day in early April. Nursery rhymes crop up again for no apparent reason a short way to the north in Kilmersdon, where Jack and Jill went up the hill.

Frome is the major market town in the east, once busy enough making cloth to be described by William Cobbett in the early 19th century as 'a sort of little Manchester'. It may come as some surprise that this part of the country has never been a stranger to heavy industry. Quarries, mines and breweries are still responsible for some of its character, though ever less of its workforce, in towns like Shepton Mallet, Midsomer Norton and Radstock. Evidence of the Mendips' very earliest communities can be found on a quiet spur of a hill near the village of Wellow. Stoney Littleton Long Barrow is a remarkable chambered tomb constructed some 5,000 years ago. Unusually enough, you can clamber inside the four-foot entrance, decorated with an ammonite, and ponder upon the lives led by the occupants of this impressive burial site. Children may get spooked. If that's not your thing, try the highly rated Wellow Trekking Centre (01225 834376) for a spot of pony hacking, carriage hire or kiddie quad biking.

Further south, some ten miles east of Shepton Mallet across the valley of the Frome, Stourhead (01747 841152, www.nationaltrust.org.uk) is a Palladian mansion with one of the most beautiful landscaped gardens in all England. It was designed by the banker Henry Hoare in the 18th century – follies surrounding the lake include a grotto, a Tuscan Temple of Flora, an obelisk, a pantheon and a Temple of Apollo. The most dramatic of them all can be found a couple of miles' walk west through the woods: King Alfred's

Tower, a 160-foot triangular brick structure, was erected in 1772 to commemorate a nearby Saxon victory more than 900 years earlier. It gives tremendous views westwards towards the mellow contours of the Mendips.

WHERE TO STAY

Babington House

Babington, nr Frome, Somerset BA11 3RW (01373 812266/www.babingtonhouse.co.uk). **Rates** £215-£315 double (non-members); £180-£275 double (members). **Credit** AmEx, DC, MC, V.

The country home of Soho House, the media-orientated members' club in London, Babington House believes in showing its guests a good time. An 18th-century manor house at the end of a tree-lined drive, with a charming pepper pot of a chapel and sloping lakeside lawns, it brings a breezy confidence to the sometimes over-complicated business of hospitality. Young families and sybaritic professionals descend from town and the local area throughout the year to enjoy the Cowshed health club, with its two swimming pools (one in the barn and a wonderful open-air one by the riverbank), grass tennis courts, Lulu Anderson's select little fashion boutique and a wide variety of spa treatments (also available in the Mongolian yurt or Native American tepees). Couples could be equally

Babington House, where the rigours of the countryside never intrude.

happy never straying too far from their rooms, many complete with massive beds and baths, superb showers, funky furniture and fittings – suspended bubble chairs, oversized anglepoises and very deep-pile rugs – as well as wide flat-screen TVs with DVD players. In the attic, room six even has a hot tub on its balcony giving panoramic views over the lake towards the hills. The bar and restaurants are only open to residents and members. The terrace has recently been fitted with warm-air ducts, making it a pleasant place to enjoy the kitchen's adventurous and accomplished modern British cuisine year round. During the summer, the lawn by the lake comes into its own for light and reasonably priced lunches.

Charlton House

Charlton Road, Shepton Mallet, nr Bath, Somerset BA4 4PR (01749 342008/www. charltonhouse.com). **Rates** £165-£325; £425 2-bed suite. **Credit** AmEx, DC, MC, V.
This 17th-century manor-house hotel has been going from strength to strength since being bought in 1996 by Roger and Monty Saul, founders of the Mulberry fashion label. Long famous for its restaurant (*see p153*), it has a recently opened wing of luxurious rooms around a state-of-the-art spa. Bijou in scale, very intimate and beautifully designed, Monty's Spa features a health-food café overlooked by a saucy portrait of Salome, an indoor-outdoor, ozone-treated hydrotherapy pool, a laconium, sauna and steam room as well as light-infused Experience showers. Two of the bedrooms, Hayloft and Chesterblade, have been kitted out to enable couples to enjoy simultaneous treatments. This indulgent sanctuary is further inducement to sample the hotel's well-established atmosphere of courtly nostalgia with a comfortable, contemporary twist.

George Inn

High Street, Norton St Philip, nr Bath, Somerset BA2 7LH (01373 834224/www.the georgeinn-nsp.co.uk). **Rates** £80-£110 double. **Open** *Bar* 11am-2.30pm, 5.30-11pm Mon-Sat; noon-2.30pm, 7-10.30pm Sun. **Lunch served** noon-2pm, **dinner served** 7-9pm daily. **Main courses** £7.25-£15.95. **Credit** MC, V.
A true survivor from another era, the George is a magnificent Grade I-listed, stone-built, galleried coaching inn at the centre of doughty little Norton St Philip. Built in 1322, it once had at least 20 stabling rooms. Now it has eight, three with handmade repro four-posters and the rest doubles, all with uneven wooden floors, furniture in keeping with the antiquity of the place and surprisingly decent bathrooms. Used as a location for films like *Remains of the Day* and *Tom Jones*, the pub has a back garden overlooking the church and cricket pitch: a delightful place to while away a summer afternoon. The Monmouth Bar is warmed in winter by a huge real fire and a loyal local following. Owned by Wadworth's brewery of Devizes, it's family-run and something of a her-

itage treat. And you could always combine a stay here with a fitting at St Crispian Shoes, Bell Hill, Norton St Philip, BA2 7LT (01373 834639), where handmade shoes are a snip at £110-£450.

Spreadeagle Inn

Church Lawn, Stourton, Stourhead, nr Warminster, Wiltshire BA12 6QE (01747 840587). **Lunch served** noon-3pm, **dinner served** 6-9pm daily. **Main courses** £6-£15. **Rates** £90 double. **Credit** MC, V.
The pub in the estate village at Stourhead has the considerable advantage over many others of being surrounded by one of the most enchanting landscape gardens in Britain. Although it's mobbed on summer days, once the hordes have gone home you're likely to have the place almost to yourself. There are five bedrooms, all perfectly presentable and decorated in an old-fashioned but comfortable way. Downstairs, the bar also provides hearty pub fare such as chicken and sweetcorn pie.

Ston Easton Park

Ston Easton, nr Bath, Somerset BA3 4DF (01761 241631/www.stoneaston.co.uk). **Rates** £175-£195 double; £365-£395 suite. **Credit** AmEx, DC, MC, V.
Ston Easton Park is a stately and austere 18th-century country house, built on the profits of lead and coal mining in nearby Midsomer Norton. It is now run as a comfortable and surprisingly homely hotel by the burgeoning Von Essen group, which also operates Cliveden and the Royal Crescent in Bath. Some details of the interior are original – extraordinary plasterwork, for example – and the cheerful and easy-going atmosphere is considerably enhanced by the resident springer and cocker spaniels, Sorrel and Sweep. They're likely to be found in the back gardens (there are 30 acres of parkland), bounding about in the lakes and long grass. The Master Bedroom has a great view over the park to the east, while most of the rooms are beautifully proportioned, with large bathrooms and new handmade beds. Down by the river, the fully serviced Gardener's Cottage is a dinky little hideaway near the extensive kitchen garden and greenhouses.

The Wookey Hole Inn

Wookey Hole Road, Wookey Hole, nr Wells, Somerset BA5 1BP (01749 676677/www. wookeyholeinn.com). **Open** *Bar* noon-3pm, 6-11.30pm Mon-Sat. **Lunch served** noon-3pm daily. **Dinner served** 7-9.30pm Mon-Sat. **Main courses** £9.50-£16.50. **Rates** £70-£90 double. **Credit** AmEx, DC, MC, V.
This pub with rooms could be described as kooky. Manager Sarah Cunningham confesses that she sometimes likes to call it the Wonky Hole. Colourful, informal and laid-back, with wicker chairs in the dining area, board games littered around the tables in the bar, weird sculpture in the garden and a real fire, the Wookey Hole Inn has

The Mendips

been popular with weekenders from Bristol and London for some time. There are only five rooms, also quirkily decorated; the best is room two with its view of the churchyard and garden, but all have decent handmade beds and either shower or bath. Booking ahead is essential and only continental breakfasts are served. For lunch and supper, the restaurant rustles up freshly prepared wholesome recipes at fairly reasonable prices. The bar boasts a wide selection of Belgian beers as well as real ales, and often the enthusiastic participation of Fergus the labradoodle.

WHERE TO EAT & DRINK

Blostin's

29 Waterloo Road, Shepton Mallet, Somerset BA4 5HH (01749 343648/www.blostins.co.uk). **Dinner served** 7-9.30pm Tue-Sat. **Main courses** £15.95 2 courses, £17.95 3 courses. **Credit** MC, V.

A short climb out of Shepton Mallet up Waterloo Road brings you to Blostin's, a long-standing local restaurant with a loyal following. Right on the road, but quiet, clean and bright inside, it serves up largely traditional dinner combinations: seasonal mains might be loin of venison with braised red cabbage and game sauce, or escalope of veal with mushrooms and Marsala, along with marginally more adventurous vegetarian options and starters (portobello mushrooms stuffed with garlic and mozzarella, sun-dried tomatoes and olives, Cornish crab pastry cases with cucumber salad and sauce grelette). The capably handled menu is backed up by a serious wine list. For the price, you might reasonably expect a slightly more sophisticated ambience and more imagination in the kitchen, but the place has a steady, seemingly unchanging charm of its own.

Boxer's

1 St Thomas Street, Wells, Somerset BA5 2UU (01749 672317/www.fountaininn.co.uk). **Open** *Bar* noon-3pm, 6-11pm Mon-Sat; noon-2.30pm, 7-10.30pm Sun. **Lunch served** noon-2pm daily. **Dinner served** 7-9.30pm Mon-Sat. **Main courses** £8-£13.50. **Credit** AmEx, MC, V.

The front first-floor room of the old Fountain Inn, just east of the cathedral, has been home to Boxer's for a couple of decades. Woody and light, it has a congenial atmosphere even at the busiest times, when diners tuck into the wide range of hearty and defiantly unfashionable options on the menu, backed up by some excellent Spanish wines. For lunch, expect the likes of deep-fried brie followed, perhaps, by cod and chips or speciality sausages and mash. The supper menu is more adventurous. Sample starters might be pan-fried squid strips with a lentil salad or marinated chicken brochettes; mains roast monkfish wrapped in parma ham or a bocuf en daube. The recipes may not be cool, but they're professionally prepared and served in a cheerful, easy-going atmosphere.

Goodfellows

5 Sadler Street, Wells, Somerset BA5 2RR (01749 673866). **Lunch served** noon-3.30pm Tue-Sat. **Dinner served** 6.30-9.30pm Thur-Sat. **Main courses** £8-£18. **Set lunch** £12.50 2 courses, £15 3 courses. **Set dinner** £24 2 courses, £29 3 courses. **Credit** AmEx, MC, V.

Adam Fellows, for six years the chef at Charlton House, opened this seafish restaurant, complete with wet fish counter, just as we went to press. He promised the likes of sea trout with dried mushrooms, white wine and mustard, oak-smoked salmon with capers and red wine, and fillet of mackerel escabeche. Given his track record, you can expect something special. With plenty of purple, stainless steel and funky mood lighting, Goodfellows looks set to give Wells the seafood restaurant it deserves.

The Griffin

25 Milk Street, Frome, Somerset BA11 3DB (01373 467766). **Open** *Bar* 5-11pm Mon-Fri; 1-10.30pm Sat, Sun. **No credit cards.**

Quite hard to find (and don't count on those opening times), but one of the more happening pubs in Frome, the Griffin stages a variety of poetry and music events in a room upstairs, and displays interesting artwork on the walls. There are four of those and no more: it's one shabby-chic room with a small bar dispensing beers from their own microbrewery (the Milk Street Brewery), guest ales (landlord Nick Branwell refuses to sell lager), groovy sounds and a welcoming vibe.

The Restaurant at Charlton House

Charlton Road, Shepton Mallet, nr Bath, Somerset BA4 4PR (01749 342008/www.charltonhouse.com). **Lunch served** 12.30-2pm, **dinner served** 7.30-9.30pm daily. **Set lunch** £16.50 2 courses, £20 3 courses. **Set dinner** £49.50 3 courses. **Credit** AmEx, DC, MC, V.

The Restaurant at Charlton House has been one of the most expensive and sophisticated operations in the area for some time. Well-kept back lawns slope down from a young apple orchard to the conservatory dining room. Here the largely French menu, service and decor elevate the enjoyment of fresh seasonal produce, at lunch or dinner, to an elegant and theatrical treat. Carnivores and piscivores are particularly well catered for: delicious starters might include poached salmon with fennel, artichoke and olive salad, a smoked haddock and potato cake with pea purée, asparagus and red wine vinaigrette. Seared tuna with char-grilled courgette and fennel, blackened aubergine and tapenade arrived perfectly cooked, while the breast of duck with parsnip purée and duck confit with fig chutney and a port and star anise reduction was superbly sharp and succulent. With a legendary wine list and richly sweet desserts, this is a restaurant that all but guarantees a meal that's memorable for all the right reasons – although at a price.

Seymour Arms

*Witham Friary, Frome, Somerset BA11 5HF
(01749 850742).* **Open** *Bar* 11am-2.30pm,
6-11pm Mon-Sat; noon-3pm, 7-10.30pm Sun.
No credit cards.

A proper mid 19th-century estate pub, attached to
farm buildings of a similar period and seemingly
unaltered for decades, this is the kind of place you
have to travel far to find these days. Surviving
almost entirely on local custom, it offers bar billiards, pale green fixed benches round the wall of
one of its two large rooms and not much else.
Beers are served through a glass partition. There's
also a delightful and quiet little garden beside the
railway embankment. No food. Only sweets,
snacks and tobacco.

Ston Easton Park

*Ston Easton, nr Bath, Somerset BA3 4DF
(01761 241631/www.stoneaston.co.uk).* **Lunch
served** noon-2pm, **dinner served** 7-9.30pm
daily. **Main courses** £19-£22. **Set lunch**
£22.50 3 courses. **Set dinner** £34.50 3 courses.
Credit AmEx, DC, MC, V.

The dining room here is surprisingly small but the
kitchen has garnered quite a reputation in the area
and produces a reliable, locally sourced menu
(including herbs and vegetables from its own garden) that majors on French cuisine with significant
nods east and west. Chicken and wild mushroom
boudin proved an imaginative take on the legendary Louisiana sausage, while honey-and-
sesame-glazed duck breast with stir-fried veg was
a delicate and delicious treat. On our most recent
visit, the venison was the best we'd ever tasted.

The Talbot

*High Street, Mells, Frome, Somerset BA11
3PN (01373 812254/www.talbotinn.com).*
Open *Bar* noon-2pm, 6.30-10.30pm daily.
Lunch served noon-2pm, **dinner served**
7-9pm daily. **Main courses** £10-£18.
Rates £85-£135 double. **Credit** MC, V.

A jolly old coaching inn – the sociable heart of a
honey-coloured stone village – that has developed
quite a reputation for its food. The fish comes fresh
from Brixham; you might find lemon sole simply
grilled with fresh herbs, or a whole sea bass baked
with spring onions, ginger and garlic. Fresh scallops, grilled with coriander, are a speciality. Less
expensive options include standard pub grub,
ploughman's, omelettes or ham and eggs. There's
a sunny garden with a petanque pitch beneath old
stone walls round the back. You can also stay here
– several of the guest rooms are well proportioned
and look out towards old the manor house.

Three Horseshoes Inn

*Batcombe, Shepton Mallet, Somerset BA4 6HE
(01749 850359).* **Open** *Bar* noon-3pm, 6.30-
11pm daily. **Lunch served** noon-2pm Mon-Sat;
noon-3pm Sun. **Dinner served** 7-9.30pm daily.
Main courses £7.95-£14.95. **Credit** MC, V.

A snug old stone pub with a large garden, kids'
play area and probably some fairly flash motors
parked round the back. Their owners are likely to
be found in one of the variety of eating areas, tucking into a quite expensive menu that offers a
choice of about seven starters and eight mains.
The pub is equally popular with walkers.

Truffles

*95 High Street, Bruton, Somerset BA10 0AR
(01749 812255/www.trufflesbruton.co.uk).*
Lunch served noon-2pm Thur-Sun. **Dinner
served** 7-9pm Tue-Sat. **Set lunch** £10
2 courses, £15 3 courses. **Set dinner** £16.95
3 courses. **Credit** MC, V.

Truffles still tops the list for culinary finesse in
this solid old town. It's a tiny, rose-clad place, with
pansies in the window boxes, headroom best
described as cosy, starched linen tablecloths, and
a superb monthly-changing menu that keeps
locals and anyone else in the know coming back
regularly for more. Booking is essential. Dishes
are immaculately presented: duo of smoked
salmon and smoked haddock mousse with a
cucumber and dill salad and saffron sauce for
example. Slices of pork fillet served on
caramelised apple and thyme with a Calvados
sauce lifted an old favourite to new heights.

Tucker's Grave

*Faulkland, Radstock, Somerset BA3 5XF (01373
834230).* **Open** *Bar* noon-3pm, 6-11pm Mon-Sat;
noon-3pm, 7-10.30pm Sun. **No credit cards.**

On the main road between Faulkland and Norton
St Philip, this is another pub that's the real deal.
The mid 18th-century stone-built cottage is on the
site of a local suicide from that period, but it's far
from gloomy – you're likely to be greeted by a
friendly dog called Lucy, handed real ale direct
from the barrel (there being no bar as such) or a
pint of proper cider, then given a chance to enjoy
the two completely unspoiled little rooms, one
with a real fire, and the company of the locals.

Vobster Inn

*Lower Vobster, nr Radstock, Somerset BA3
5RJ (01373 812920).* **Lunch served** noon-
2pm daily. **Dinner served** 7-9pm Mon-Thur;
7-9.30pm Fri, Sat. **Main courses** £9-£16.
Credit MC, V.

With typical West Country wit, the Vobster is a
pub that specialises in seafood. And if lobster is
ever on the menu, you can rest assured that, funny
spellings aside, it will be expertly cooked. The
Vobster's simple way with fish has won national
accolades. Starters might include moules marinière
or scallops, followed by mains of monkfish or
Torbay sole, or a delicious local game pie. The fish
and chips are legendary. Main courses cost about
£13, starters £6. It's also a drinkers' pub, with
proper real ales like Buxton's and Marley's Ghost
as well as a fairly extensive wine list. The non-
smoking tables get booked up quickly.

The Mendips

Charlton House

The South Hams

Lush, fertile and just a little retro.

West of Torbay and stretching from Dartmoor's rocky foot to the English Channel, the South Hams is, frankly, the posh bit of Devon with its thriving market towns and chocolate-box scenery. The area's lush valleys and snaking rivers are a magnet for golfers, water sports enthusiasts and retirees, as well as a growing number of urban downshifters who are setting up smallholdings, making the most of broadband internet connections and working from home. As a result, property prices have shot up in the past five years.

It's obvious what attracts them. Devon has some of the most spectacular coastlines in the country. In summer it's all sparkling seas and silver sands; in winter, windswept cliffs and roaring waves. Beautiful, wild flower-strewn hedgerows frame every lane in the spring, and the autumn sees glorious sunsets and balmy afternoons.

There are some fine beaches (many of which are great for swimming, snorkelling, surfing, windsurfing and kite-surfing), secluded coves and wonderful coast paths. This is also good sailing country, particularly around the Yealm estuary, Salcombe and Dartmouth.

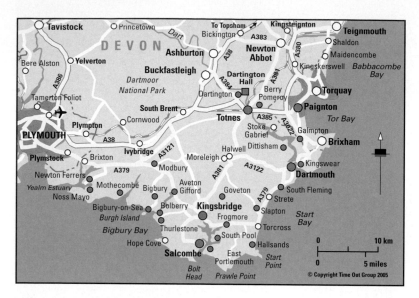

Totnes, Kingsbridge, Dartmouth and the smaller Modbury are the area's significant towns. All four serve the local population year round and are by no means merely tourist destinations; Kingsbridge has little in the way of tourist attractions, although there are some interesting shops and a famers' market. Many of the South Hams' pretty inland villages lie along its rivers – the Dart, Erme, Yealm and Avon. To the west of the area around the Yealm estuary are some of the most picturesque villages imaginable. Noss Mayo and Newton Ferrers are havens for yachtie types and admirers of picture-postcard scenery. The villages enter into a little friendly rivalry as to which one is superior; the truth is that each has its pros and cons. Noss Mayo is on the South West Coast Path and you can take a wonderful stroll through the village and wood that run along the river out to the sea. Here the path takes you along the cliffs and the Eddystone lighthouse in the far distance. You can take a circular walk from the National Trust car park at Worswell, with a lunch stop at the refurbished Ship Inn (see p165).

At low tide you can cross the voss, the path between the two villages; at high tide you will need to take the longer walk or short drive through the lanes. As well as some delightful cottages, Newton Ferrers has a few small food shops and a good pub, the Dolphin Inn (1 Riverside Road East, 01752 872007), with a beer garden at the front overlooking the river. In Noss Mayo, the sweet Swan Inn (Pillory

Hill, 01752 872392, www.swaninn.co.uk) offers outdoor seating, overlooking the public quay with fabulous views.

Heading west en route to Kingsbridge, Modbury is worth a brief visit; the Georgian market town stretches the length of the hill that forms its main street. There are some interesting antique shops, a couple of good eating and drinking pubs (Modbury Inn, Brownstone Street, 01548 830275 and the Exeter Inn, Church Street, 01548 830239), while the Stocks Café (Poundwell Street, 01548 831494) is a good place for a coffee, light lunch or cream tea.

The River Erme reaches the sea at Mothecombe and the vast expanse of sand at low tide is a favourite with walkers and horse riders. There is a car park which is privately owned by the estate (charges apply from Easter to end of September), with a rather steep hill down to the beach – but the walk is well worth it. The beach is overlooked by the Flete Estate (01752 830253, www.flete.co.uk), the location for the film adaptation of Jane Austen's Sense and Sensibility.

Further around the coast are the wonderful beaches of Bigbury and Bantham, on either side of the Avon estuary; both are favoured spots for surfers along this stretch of coast. There are also growing numbers of kite-surfers, who make interesting viewing from the beach, café or pub. You can undertake the eight-mile walk along both banks of the river via the 15th-century bridge at Aveton Gifford. Parking is available at both beaches and there is a good beach café at Bigbury. Just off the coast is Burgh Island with its splendid

Accommodation	★★
Food & drink	★★★
Nightlife	
Shopping	★★★
Culture	★★
Sights	★
Scenery	★★★★★

1920s hotel (*see p163*), accessible at low tide by foot, or on a bizarre sea tractor. The hotel grounds are off-limits to day trippers, but you can have a pint or a meal in the 14th-century smugglers' pub, the Pilchard Inn, and enjoy the views.

Further down the coast, Hope Cove is a pretty crab- and lobster-fishing village offering bracing walks and a welcome watering hole in the form of the Hope & Anchor. Just beyond, Bolt Tail juts into the sea, offering a fabulous view back to Bigbury Bay. This is the start of a breathtaking five-mile walk, across Bolberry Down, where the coastal path winds its way to Bolt Head, the rocky promontory that guards the mouth of the estuary. Heading east, you reach Salcombe, one of the most southerly towns in England. In the summer, it's heaving with second-homeowners, expensive yachts and the odd celebrity, earning it the sobriquet 'England's St Tropez' – much to the chagrin of the locals, who complain that the prices of property and eating out have spiralled out of control in recent years. In the winter, Salcombe is something of a ghost town, with many shops and restaurants closed until at least the school half-term in February. Having said all that, the place has good reason to be popular. Its position overlooking the water, the white sandy beaches and quaint fishermen's cottages, stylish nautical shops and a good choice of pubs and restaurants are all powerful enticements.

Near Bolt Head, in the village of Sharpitor, is the cliff-top Overbeck's Museum & Garden (01548 842893, www.nationaltrust.org.uk), an imposing Edwardian house owned until 1937 by the eccentric scientist Otto Overbeck. The upper floors are given over to a youth hostel (01548 842856), but downstairs you'll find a fascinating display of taxidermy, shipbuilding exhibits and a number of the scientist's bizarre inventions – look out for the Rejuvenator, a machine intended to extend human life expectancy. The terraced, subtropical gardens cover six acres and boast incredible views towards Salcombe.

From Salcombe's Ferry Steps, regular boats (01548 842364) will take you to the scenic village of East Portlemouth, from where you can walk along the craggy cliffs to Gara Rock and Prawle Point. Look out for seals around Mattiscombe Beach,

a secluded, sandy cove with plenty of rock pools to explore. Otherwise, there is little besides rugged coastline until you round the bend of Start Point, where the treacherous waters are littered with shipwrecks. There's a bracing walk downhill from the car park to Start Point Lighthouse (01803 770606, tours available in summer).

From here you can take the coast path to 'new' Hallsands, a rather desolate hamlet at the end of a shingle beach, which replaced the original village after a local (and man-made) disaster. Controversial dredging along the beach at the turn of the last century undermined the natural shingle breakwater, and a heavy storm in 1917 destroyed the once-thriving fishing village. All that remain are some crumbling ruins clinging to the cliffs. Beyond Hallsands, you'll pass the hamlet of Beesands before arriving at Torcross, where you can get a cream tea, ice-cream or something a little more substantial at the beachside Start Bay Inn (01548 580553), a 14th-century thatched pub renowned for its fish and chips.

Heading up the coast towards Dartmouth you will pass Slapton Sands. This dramatic three-mile stretch of shingle beach is where allied troops practised manoeuvres for the D-Day landings. In 1944, during a surprise German attack, 946 men lost their lives; a Sherman tank recovered from the water serves as a memorial. On the other side of the road is Slapton Ley Nature Reserve – the West Country's largest natural freshwater lake and home to some of the rarest birds in Britain. Just inland from the beach is the quaint little village of Slapton which has a friendly pub, the Tower Inn (01548 580216, www.thetowerinn.com),

TOURIST INFORMATION

Dartmouth
The Engine House, Mayor's Avenue, Dartmouth, Devon TQ6 9YY (01803 834224/www.discoverdartmouth.com).
Kingsbridge
The Quay, Kingsbridge, Devon TQ7 1HS (01548 853195/www.kingsbridge info.co.uk).
Modbury
5 Modbury Court, Modbury, Devon PL21 0QR (01548 830159/www.modbury devon.co.uk).
Salcombe
Council Hall, Market Street, Salcombe, Devon TQ8 8DE (01548 843927/ www.salcombeinformation.co.uk).
Totnes
The Town Mill, Coronation Road, Totnes, Devon TQ9 5DF (01803 863168/ www.totnesinformation.co.uk).
www.discoverdevon.com
www.south-hams.co.uk

The South Hams

offering good food, board games and a cosy fire. Outside is a large and attractive beer garden, overlooking the eponymous tower. Further along the coast road, as Start Bay opens up ahead, the scenery is so awesome that traffic slows as drivers take in the view. About three miles south of Dartmouth along the scenic coast road is the village of Stoke Fleming, where there are breathtaking cliff walks. Just beyond is the beautiful, golden shingle beach – with a pine forest backdrop – known as Blackpool Sands; it's clean, dog-free year round and has good facilities. Various water sports are available here: enquire in the shop for details of tuition and equipment hire. In addition, the Venus beachfront café dispenses everything from ice-creams and beers to organic sandwiches and salads.

The South Hams' western coastline ends around Dartmouth. The steep drive into the town reveals the picturesque estuary and the pretty village of Kingswear across the water. In summer, Dartmouth's narrow streets – lined with cafés and boutiques, galleries and yachting emporia – are packed, and there is no denying the parking chaos. The Regatta in late August (always including the last Friday in the month) sees the town reach gridlock. Conversely, much of Dartmouth shuts down in January, when major redecoration is undertaken. It can be pleasantly quiet out of season, but obviously, places to eat and stay are more limited.

Dartmouth has a long and interesting history: it was the departure point for the second crusade in 1147, the Pilgrim Fathers had their leaking boats repaired here en route to America (faulty ships necessitated another stop at Plymouth), and during World War II, US warships set off for the Normandy beaches from here.

Dartmouth castle, completed in 1403, was the first in Britain to be purpose-built for artillery warfare. Perched on the cliffs near the mouth of the estuary, it is best reached in the summer by ferry from Dartmouth's South Embankment.

In the centre of town, the 'boat float', an attractive harbour for small craft, is overlooked by the Royal Castle Hotel (see p164). Beyond the boat float is the Promenade, which stretches the length of the waterfront along the Embankment and is a great place to take in some sea air or eat fish and chips – just beware of the greedy seagulls. There is also a wide choice of more sophisticated eateries and some superior pubs.

Should you feel the need to get out of town – and you probably will in high season – there are some fabulous beaches and villages nearby. A short ferry trip across the river Dart, Kingswear is a sweet *Balamory*-esque village, with pastel-painted cottages tightly packed on the hillside. On a

headland to the east is the National Trust-owned Coleton Fishacre (01803 752466, www.nationaltrust.org.uk), an Arts and Crafts-style house with an art deco interior, built in the 1920s for Rupert D'Oyly Carte, son of impresario Richard. The grounds are a gardener's delight, incorporating woodland and rare rainforest species and a myriad of paths leading out to the cliff edge.

Dittisham (pronounced by locals 'Ditsum') is a beautiful village on the banks of the Dart with a couple of friendly pubs and a riverside café. There are some wonderful walks along the river. For a fabulous place to stay try the Fingals Hotel (see p164).

If you want to leave the car behind, there is a small Dartmouth to Dittisham ferry running March to October. Once in Dittisham, you can ring the bell outside the Ferry Inn and summon a ferry across to the magical woodland Greenway Gardens (Galmpton, Churston Ferrers, 01803 842382, www.nationaltrust.org.uk), the former home of Agatha Christie. While the house is owned and occupied by her daughter and closed to the public, the National Trust is responsible for the garden (visitors by car must prebook a parking space).

About 12 miles from Dartmouth, via the A3122 and A381, is Totnes, a bustling, ancient market town which has become a bit of a New Age centre. Herbalists, healers and alternative therapists have set up shop here, as well as artists in every discipline. There is a lively market every Friday and Saturday, where you can pick up anything from second-hand furniture and vintage clothes to fresh fish and handmade breads. There is also a monthly farmers' market in the Civic Hall, selling a wide range of local produce. Numerous buskers, hair-braiders and artists enliven the market area and the main strip, Fore Street. On Tuesdays during the summer months there is also an Elizabethan market, when locals in period garb sell handmade and second-hand goods and clothing for charity.

The history of the town stretches back to Saxon times when a fortified settlement was built to protect the upper reaches of the River Dart from Viking invasion. During the 16th century, Totnes was among the 20 richest towns in England, due largely to the Dartmoor tin and cloth trade. Fore Street runs up the steep hill from the Dart to the castle at the top of the town. It contains at least 60 examples of 16th-century buildings, so it's worth looking above shop-window level. Don't miss the Brutus stone (set into the pavement outside No.51); legend claims it's the stepping stone used by the founding king of Britain to reach the shore in 1170 BC. Amid the wide range of shops, selling

High Cross House

everything from organic vegetables to incense, is the fine period building housing the Elizabethan Museum (70 Fore Street, 01803 863821, www.devonmuseums.net). It houses displays charting the town's history and a room dedicated to its best-known former residents, including Charles Babbage (1791-1871), inventor of the early precursor to the computer.

It's worth stopping off at the beautiful 15th-century red sandstone church of St Mary. Behind the church is the colonnaded Guildhall (01803 862147, www.totnestown council.gov.uk), built around 1533 on the site of the former 11th-century priory. The council chamber, former magistrates' court and town gaol are all open to the public. In the Civil War, both sides used the town as a base, and you can still see the table where Oliver Cromwell planned his local campaigns in 1646.

Totnes has some great eateries and food shops, including the fabulous Ticklemore Cheese Shop (1 Ticklemore Street, 01803 865926). If you are planning a picnic, make a beeline for award-winning Effings (50 Fore Street, 01803 863435), a foodie's paradise stocked with wonderful cheeses, charcuterie, breads and takeaway dishes prepared by the on-site chef. There are a few tables at the back of the shop where you can enjoy a light lunch or a coffee and croissant.

Totnes Castle (01803 864406, www.english-heritage.org.uk/totnes, open April to October) sits perched on top of its grassy knoll giving uninterrupted 360-degree views over the town and surrounding countryside. Built shortly after the Norman conquest, it was one of the first stone forts to be constructed in Devon and it is an excellent example of a motte-

TAKE ACTION

BOATING

DART SAILING SCHOOL & CHARTERS
The Loft, 26 Foss Street, Dartmouth TQ6 9DR (01803 833973/ www.dartsailing.co.uk).

DEVON SAILING
11 Smith Street, Dartmouth TQ6 9QR (01803 833399/ www.devonsailing.com).

DITTISHAM SAILING CLUB
The Boathouse, The Ham, Dittisham, Dartmouth TQ6 0JH (01803 722365).

SALCOMBE BOAT HIRE
11 Clifton Place, Salcombe TQ8 8BX (01548 844475/ www.salcombe-online.co.uk/ boathire).

CANOEING

CANOE ADVENTURES
1 Church Court, Harberton, Totnes TQ9 7UG (01803 865301/ www.canoeadventures.co.uk).

HELICOPTER TOURS

HELICOPTERS UK
Longfield, Bantham, Kingsbridge TQ7 3AR (0870 046 0470/ www.helicopters-uk.co.uk).

HORSE RIDING

SORLEY RIDING SCHOOL
Loddiswell Road, Kingsbridge TQ7 4EH (01548 855035/www.sorley ridingschool.co.uk).

SURFING

MARTIN CONNOLLY
79 Newnham Road, Plympton, Plymouth PL7 4AT (07813 639622/ www.discoverysurf.com).

WATER SPORTS
on Blackpool Sands (01803 770606/ www.blackpoolsands.co.uk).

SEABREEZE SPORTS
Torcross, Kingsbridge TQ7 2TQ (01548 581247/www.seabreeze breaks.com).

and-bailey design. During the summer months the castle is a venue for special events; local theatre companies perform here, and there are medieval pageants, archery displays and court jesters. At the bottom of town lies the area known as the Plains and over the bridge is Bridgetown. A short walk from here, Steamer Quay, with its riverside café and wooden playship, is the departure point for riverboat cruises to Dartmouth (Riverlink, 01803 834488, www.riverlink. co.uk). If you'd rather travel up towards Dartmoor, South Devon Railway steam trains (0845 345 1427, www.southdevon railway.org, closed November-March), depart from the beautifully preserved station a short walk from the Totnes main line station (follow the brown signs). The picturesque journey (about an hour and a half) along the river takes you to Buckfastleigh on the edge of Dartmoor.

Dartington Hall (01803 847100, www.dartingtonhall.com), just outside Totnes, is a world-renowned arts education centre and valuable cultural resource for Totnes and the south west region. The medieval hall is magnificent – built in the late 1300s by the Earl of Huntingdon, it was saved from dereliction in 1925 when it was purchased by Dorothy and Leonard Elmhirst. The Elmhirsts turned the hall into a progressive school with creative, anti-authoritarian values (it closed in 1987). The Dartington Hall Trust now runs the estate – which is home to a number of organisations, including Dartington College of Arts – and promotes education and the arts. There is a year-round programme of cultural events, concerts, open-air theatre and film screenings and workshops. For details of what's on, including the Barn Cinema, which largely shows art-house and foreign films, visit www.dartington arts.org.uk (box office 01803 847070). There is also a good pub at the hall, the White Hart (01803 847111). The public is free to wander around the beautiful grounds and admire the ancient trees, plants and topiary and discover the number of sculptures hidden around the gardens. Also on the estate is the former headmaster's home, High Cross House, a fine example of 1930s architecture. It is now a gallery showcasing the Elmhirsts' own art collection. On the edge of the estate, a walk down the drive will lead you to the Dartington Cider Press Centre at Shinners Bridge (01803 847500, www.dartingtonciderpress.co.uk), where Dartington glass can be viewed and bought as well as work by local artists, clothing and jewellery. There are also a couple of cafés and gift, book and toy shops.

On the Paignton side of Totnes is the village of Berry Pomeroy, which also has a magnificent ruined castle (01803 866618, www.english-heritage.org.uk, open April to October) reputed to be the most haunted place in Britain; the wooded site certainly feels a bit eerie. The outer walls still stand and encircle the remains of a magnificent residence started by the Duke of Somerset but never completed. Excellent audio tours are available for a small charge and there is a café offering refreshments and surprisingly good Sunday lunches.

WHERE TO STAY

The Hope Cove Hotel (Hope Cove, near Kingsbridge, 01548 560909, www.the hopecovehotel.co.uk), perched on a 400-foot cliff, was being completed at the time of writing but should be open by spring 2005. Most rooms will have balconies with exhilarating views of Bigbury Bay.

Buckland-Tout-Saints Hotel & Restaurant

Goveton, nr Kingsbridge, Devon TQ7 2DS (01548 853055/www.tout-saints.co.uk). **Lunch served** noon-1.30pm, **dinner served** 7-9pm daily. **Set lunch** £19 3 courses. **Set dinner** £37.50 3 courses. **Rates** £150 double; £300 suite. **Credit** AmEx, MC, V.

Off the beaten track a few miles outside Kingsbridge, this beautiful country house is over 300 years old and sits in a stunning location in rolling countryside. The public rooms have an air of panelled opulence; the restaurant has won many accolades over the years and is well regarded locally. Each of the 11 rooms is unique and individually furnished with antiques. All have en suite facilities and some have four-posters and fireplaces. Golfing breaks are a speciality and transport is arranged to one of the three local courses. Dogs are welcome.

Burgh Island Hotel

Bigbury-on-Sea, Devon TQ7 4BG (01548 810514/www.burghisland.com). **Set lunch** £30 3 courses. **Set dinner** £45 3 courses. **Rates** £275-£420 double (incl dinner). **Credit** MC, V.

Reached by sea tractor, over the sand on foot or by hotel-run taxi, depending on the state of the tide, this island is a one-off (GMTV viewers will recognise it as the setting for its *Inch-Loss Island* series). The splendid hotel started life as a high-society hideaway in the late 1920s and '30s, for the likes of Noel Coward and Agatha Christie (the Mountbatten Room was a key location in TV's *Evil Under the Sun* in 2001) – Edward VIII even brought Wallis Simpson here. Since then, the hotel has had its ups and downs, but it has been painstakingly restored to all its art deco glory, complete with many original pieces of furniture

The South Hams

and classic bathrooms equipped with thoroughly modern REN toiletries. It's a glamorous and discreet place, not quite of this century. Televisions are out, cocktails are most definitely in. Dances are held in the ballroom and guests are encouraged to dress up. The Australian chef is well respected for his fish cookery and the food is of a high quality and sourced from local farms. The island's ancient pub, the Pilchard Inn, serves great beer and food cooked in the hotel kitchen (mains £5-£8.50, puddings £4.75).

Browns Hotel & Bar

27-29 Victoria Road, Dartmouth, Devon TQ6 9RT (01803 832572/www.brownshotel dartmouth.co.uk). **Rates** £80-£155 double. **Credit** AmEx, MC, V.

Formerly the Little Admiral Hotel, this has been revamped to become a stylish and modern addition to Dartmouth's hotels. The modern decor is in stark contrast to the traditional charm of the Royal Castle, the rooms are decorated in earthy tones, many with attractive wooden beds, and there are animal prints and textured finishes everywhere. The bar contains large comfortable sofas where you can relax with a coffee or enjoy a selection of tapas and a glass of wine.

Fingals Hotel

Coombe, Dittisham, Devon TQ6 0JA (01803 722398/www.fingals.co.uk). **Dinner served** 7.30-9.30pm Tue-Sat. **Set meal** £27.50 2 courses. **Rates** £75-£160 double. **Credit** AmEx, MC, V.

An extremely relaxed, fabulously quirky place to stay, this carefully restored and extended 17th-century farmhouse is like a mini resort, equipped with heated conservatory pool, sauna, jacuzzi and masseuse, plus croquet and lawn tennis courts. Rooms are predominantly of the English country mould, but in the best possible taste, and given a stylish twist with original modern artworks. Families may want to opt for the stunning, self-catering barn, while the two-floor 'folly', a tiny old mill house with a four-poster bed and an upstairs balcony overlooking the stream, offers privacy for couples. There are roaring fires and antique carpets in the sitting room, books and comfy sofas in the library, and dinner is served in the panelled dining room with convivial host Richard Johnston and the other guests (unless you choose to dine alone). Closed January and February.

Henley Hotel

Folly Hill, Bigbury-on-Sea, Devon TQ7 4AR (01548 810240/www.thehenleyhotel.co.uk). **Set dinner** £26 3 courses (advance booking essential). **Rates** £96-£110 double. **Credit** MC, V.

This small and unpretentious hotel has garnered glowing praise. The dining room and lounge have expansive views of the Avon estuary and the hotel's own lush gardens, and there are steps winding down to a sandy beach. The decor tends towards the trad, but tastefully so, and the proprietors are extremely friendly. Five of the six rooms have views of the sea. No smoking throughout.

Royal Castle Hotel

11 The Quay, Dartmouth, Devon TQ6 9PS (01803 833033/www.royalcastle.co.uk). **Lunch served** noon-2.30pm, **dinner served** 7-9.30pm daily. **Set meal** £25 3 courses. **Rates** £115-£195 double. **Credit** AmEx, MC, V.

This rather old-fashioned hotel in the centre of Dartmouth has plenty of charm. The rooms at the front of the building have wonderful views over the boat float (an attractive harbour for small craft), Royal Avenue gardens, the estuary and sea beyond. The rooms are all individual – with none of the bulk-bought fixtures and fittings of large hotel chains – and many of the rooms boast brass or four-poster beds and spa baths. The communal areas of the hotel are all comfortably furnished and there is a choice of bars, from the traditional pub-style Galleon, to the trendy, if rather stark, Harbour Bar. The restaurant is on the first floor and offers great views as well as locally sourced food. Special mini-break deals are available, including dinner and B&B.

Thurlestone Hotel

Thurlestone, nr Kingsbridge, Devon TQ7 3NN (01548 560382/www.Thurlestone.co.uk). **Lunch served** 12.30-1.45pm Sun. **Dinner served** 7.30-9pm daily. **Set menu** £32 5 courses; (Sun) £17 3 courses incl coffee. **Rates** £168-£224 double. **Credit** AmEx, MC, V.

This well-regarded four-star in the quaint seaside village of Thurlestone has recently been updated, so that most rooms have palatial, glass-fronted balconies with views out to sea. The interior of the hotel is very comfortable and facilities include indoor and outdoor pool, gym, plus a hair and beauty salon. If golf is your thing, the hotel offers discounts at both Bigbury and Dartmouth courses, and the Thurlestone links course is only five minutes away. In fine weather, lunch and drinks can be taken on the attractive terrace commanding expansive views of the bay. The restaurant makes good use of Devon produce and fresh fish.

WHERE TO EAT & DRINK

Diners are spoiled for choice in upmarket Salcombe. In addition to the places listed below, also recommended by locals is Dusters (50 Fore Street, Salcombe, 01548 842634) an unpretentious, light and uncluttered bistro which has jazz on Sundays; booking is advisable. Ripples Restaurant (84 Fore Street, Salcombe, 01548 844534) at the other end of the street offers surf and turf, Devon-reared steak and the sort of local fish and shellfish you would expect here.

River Dart

Totnes has some great eateries. In the Plains, as well as Wills (*see p167*), the Waterside Bistro (10 Symons Passage, 01803 864069) is popular with locals. It comprises a café and bistro serving locally sourced dishes in a friendly atmosphere. Fat Lemons Café (1 Ticklemore Court, 01803 866888), with its brightly covered rickshaw outside and pretty courtyard, offers literally hundreds of types of tea and coffee, delicious cakes and a meze menu as well as wholesome vegetarian main courses in an informal, unhurried setting. Pigoutz Café (26 High Street, 01803 868828) is a totally child-friendly place offering good soups and sandwiches based on local – and largely organic – produce.

The refurbished Ship Inn (Noss Mayo, 01752 872387, www.nossmayo.com), conveniently placed along the circular walk from Worswell (*see p158*), serves local and regional beers and a daily menu focused on local, seasonal produce. In the winter, log fires and newspapers are laid on.

There are two notable pubs in Dartmouth: the Windjammer (Victoria Road, 01803 832228), a family-run freehouse featured in the CAMRA *Good Beer Guide*, is a great place for a quiet pint and offers a seasonal menu. The atmospheric Cherub Inn (13 Higher Street, 01803 832571, www.the-cherub.co.uk), in Dartmouth's oldest building, is also CAMRA-recommended. Over the water in Kingswear, the Ship Inn (Highstreet, 01803 752348) offers scrumpy and the last of the evening sun.

Alf Resco

Lower Street, Dartmouth, Devon TQ6 9JB (01803 835880/www.cafealfresco.co.uk). **Food served** 7am-2pm Wed-Sun. **Dinner**

Kickstart the day at Alf Resco.

served *Summer* 6.30-9.30pm daily. **Main courses** £5-£10. **Set dinner** (Fri-Sun) £21.50 3 courses incl coffee. **Rates** £75 double. **No credit cards**.

There are few better places to eat breakfast in Devon. Alf Resco has punters queuing up for bacon sandwiches or a monumental full English. The front courtyard is a splendid place for people-watching, while the interior has the intimacy of a bustling ship's cabin. In the summer, managers Pete and Kate launch their weekend 'rustic suppers', which could feature anything from authentic Mexican to an evening of sea shanties and locally caught seafood.

New Angel

2 South Embankment, Dartmouth, Devon TQ6 9BH (01803 839425/www.thenew angel.co.uk). **Breakfast served** 8.30-11.30am,

lunch served noon-2.30pm Tue-Sun. **Dinner served** 6.30-10.30pm Tue-Sat. **Main courses** £14-£25. **Credit** AmEx, MC, V.

Despite its well established reputation and the magnificent location overlooking the Dart estuary, what was the Carved Angel had long been trading on past glories – that is until TV chef John Burton Race, fresh from his French adventures, undertook a timely revamp. Now resurrected as the New Angel, there's a vigour and energy about the place that's long been absent. Completely gone are the stuffiness, pretensions and wilful old-fashionedness, newly replaced by a thoroughly urban bustle; accessible, uncomplicated food (for example, chicken terrine with spiced pear chutney or sea bass with oyster broth) and an attention to detail. Devon needs more places like this. Note that the New Angel is closed for the whole of January.

Pig Finca

The Old Bakery, The Promenade, Kingsbridge, Devon TQ7 1JD (01548 855777). **Open/meals served** 10am-10pm Wed-Sat. **Main courses** £5.50-£10.95. **Credit** MC, V.

Apparently Pig Finca means something like pigsty in Spanish. The Iberian rather than porcine influence is in the ascendance at this buzzing café-bistro – although the informal, tapas style of dining definitely encourages troughing. The Gaudi-on-a-budget decor, attractive staff and cool music are all big factors in the popularity of the place – as is the well-priced food, which makes the most of limited ingredients. Expect uncomplicated but satisfying dishes such as mashtak lamb (a north African kofte-style meal), a zesty tuna with coconut and lemon, or some richly spiced chorizo chicken. Regulars swear by the pizzas. No smoking.

Oyster Shack

Milburn Orchard Farm, Stakes Hill, Bigbury, Devon TQ7 4BE (01548 810876/www.oystershack.co.uk). **Meals served** 9am-4pm daily. **Dinner served** 7.30-9pm Sat. **Main courses** £6.95-£16.95. **Credit** MC, V.

The Oyster Shack goes a long way to providing what people actually want from a restaurant, as opposed to what restaurateurs think their customers want. As many country-house hotels around the county face empty tables most weekday lunchtimes, the Oyster Shack is stuffed with punters – you must book here, regardless of the day. Not bad for a bring-your-own place that's little more than a shack with a tarpaulin out front. Of course, the setting's part of the fun, but the main draw at the Oyster Shack is the ultra-fresh seafood: own-farmed mussels and oysters, pan-fried sardines, potted shrimp, shell-on prawns or whatever the catch of the day might be. Note that the restaurant can be accessed from the tidal road at low tide from Aveton Gifford; it is posted from the A379 travelling in the direction of Kingsbridge.

Rumour Wine Bar

30 High Street, Totnes, Devon TQ9 5RY (01803 864682/www.eiaddio.com). **Lunch served** noon-3pm Mon-Sat. **Dinner served** 6-10pm daily. **Main courses** £9.50-£14.95. **Credit** AmEx, MC, V.

Rumour has something for everyone – a vibey bar with a well-priced wine list, a daytime hangout for late breakfasts and king-size cappuccinos, and a restaurant with two eating options. The pizza menu is the stuff of local legend – substantial, generously topped and affordable. The blackboard menu promises fancier offerings but nothing to break the bank – a grilled lemon chicken with slow-roast tomatoes and asparagus and rocket pesto, for example. Quality bistro food and a great atmosphere.

Willow

87 High Street, Totnes, Devon TQ9 5PB (01803 862605). **Meals served** 10am-5pm Mon-Thur, Sat; 9am-5pm Fri. **Dinner served** 7-9.30pm Wed, Fri, Sat; Thur during school summer hols. **Main courses** £6.50-£7.95. **No credit cards.**

Given the proliferation of alternative types in the area, it's surprising how few vegetarian restaurants there are in Totnes. Willow makes up for it in spades – it's a hub for food-related issues and is particularly active in highlighting concerns over GM crops. Yet the cheerful decor (with a pretty courtyard at the back), helpful staff and a back room with a pile of toys for kids are anything but po-faced. The self-service counter offers salads, wheat-free quiches and caffeine-free alternatives to tea and coffee (as well as full-strength, fair trade versions of the latter). Curry nights on Wednesday and music sessions on Friday are always busy, so it's worth booking. No smoking.

Wills

2-3 The Plains, Totnes, Devon TQ9 5DR (0800 056 3006/www.eiaddio.com). **Lunch served** noon-2.30pm daily. **Dinner served** 7-9.30pm Tue-Sat. **Main courses** *Café* £9.95-£14.95. *Restaurant* £11.95-£18.95. **Credit** AmEx, MC, V.

Until recently Wills was known as the posher sister to Rumour. Changes in the menu have brought the two much closer in style. Upstairs in this Georgian townhouse, the formal restaurant offers a modern British-style menu with plenty of interesting choice – mussel mousse with scallop carpaccio, or roast pheasant with stuffed wing and leg. The bistro-like downstairs is more informal, great for lunches such as fried halloumi with rocket or duck breast with port sauce. If you squint you could conceivably imagine you were in Vienna or Paris.

Winking Prawn

Main Road, North Sands, Salcombe, Devon TQ8 8JW (01548 842326/www.winkingprawn.com). **Lunch served** 10.30am-4.30pm, **dinner served** 7-9.30pm daily. **Main courses** £9.75-£14.95. **Set meal** (summer) £14.95 steak & king prawn barbecue. **Closed** weekdays during Nov-Easter. **Credit** AmEx, DC, MC, V.

This uncontrived, beach hut-style restaurant is reminiscent of the sort of seafront café you might find in Australia. It manages to be both functional and hip, with whitewashed floorboards and furniture, large windows dressed with canvas blinds, and a front garden with tables overlooking the beach. Unsurprisingly, prawns – and seafood in general – feature fairly heavily on the menu. During the day, you can have anything from a sandwich or ice-cream to a plate of fruits de mer, and more sophisticated dishes such as whole cracked crab with aïoli in the evening. There's even a nostalgic, on-site bucket-and-spade shop. Booking is recommended.

Falmouth & the Roseland Peninsula

The cream of Cornwall.

Forget the bucket-and-spade, windbreak, Cornish pasty and floral eiderdown memories of childhood holidays in Cornwall; the area around Falmouth and the Roseland Peninsula blows this image out of the water once and for all. Famously favoured by surrealist artists (Lee Miller, Roland Penrose and Man Ray, among others) in the 1930s, the glamorous yachting set in the 1950s and 1960s, and a string of A-listers including Pierce Brosnan, the Prince of Wales, Kate Winslet and Claudia Schiffer in recent years, this waterside haven could not ask for a more impressive string of endorsements.

The area is dominated by the Carrick Roads, a large flooded river valley (or ria), fed by the Fal and numerous tributary rivers and flowing into Falmouth Bay. After Rio de Janeiro and Sydney, it ranks as the world's third-largest natural harbour. Protected from the relentless Atlantic swell by the vast granite bulk of the Lizard Peninsula to the south and west, the rolling green hills that dip gently into the calm sea on both sides of the estuary are a far cry from the rugged cliffs and pounding surf of Cornwall's north coast.

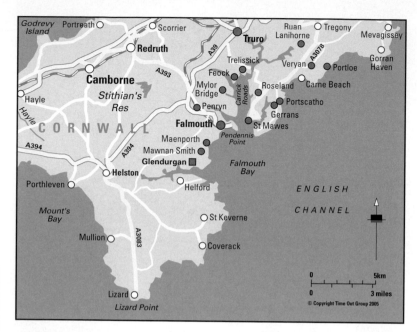

Map labels: Godrevy Island, Portreath, Scorrier, Ruan Lanihorne, Tregony, Mevagissey, Truro, Redruth, A39, Trelissick, Veryan, A3078, Portloe, Gorran Haven, Feock, Camborne, A393, Mylor Bridge, Carrick Roads, Roseland, Carne Beach, Hayle, Stithian's Res, Penryn, Portscatho, Hayle, C O R N W A L L, Falmouth, Gerrans, St Mawes, A394, A394, Maenporth, Pendennis Point, Mawnan Smith, Glendurgan, Falmouth Bay, Helston, Porthleven, Helford, ENGLISH CHANNEL, Mount's Bay, St Keverne, Mullion, A3083, Coverack, 0 5km, 0 3 miles, © Copyright Time Out Group 2005, Lizard, Lizard Point

The vestiges of a long and prosperous maritime history live on through the countless ships and smaller craft, while the rich crop of high-quality restaurants, pubs and hotels are evidence of the burgeoning upmarket tourist trade.

The Carrick Roads divides the area into two distinct parts. The Roseland Peninsula is quiet and sparsely populated – even in the busy summer months, it somehow seems to escape the hordes of holidaymakers that take over the north coast. Tucked below the high open fields that form the peninsula's broad back, narrow lanes weave through dense woodland and skirt around the idyllic creeks that penetrate miles inland. On the peninsula's eastern flank sit beautiful, often empty, stretches of beach, looking out over sheltered bays and translucent blue seas.

A short ferry ride across the estuary gives you a completely different atmosphere. A bustling town put on the map by its historic docks, colourful maritime history and highly acclaimed College of Art, pretty Falmouth combines its continuing working heritage with the kind of Bohemian charm you find north-west in St Ives and a moderate yachtie vibe (from the visiting cruisers and smart waterside developments).

The mild, year-round climate created by the Gulf Stream (it's not uncommon to see daffodils in November) makes the area a perfect habitat for subtropical plants. Lush testament to the zeal of the Victorian plant-hunters who brought back specimens from all over the world, the plentiful gardens contain plants from the Himalayas, Japan, China, Indonesia, Bermuda and the Andes, to name a few. Outside the magnificent gardens, dracaena palms and bright blue agapanthus punctuate many a front garden and suburban avenue.

At high tide, the river is navigable all the way to Truro, with regular passenger ferries making the trip every day (Easter to end October, call 01326 313234 for details).

St Mawes

Running 15 long miles from the A390 between Truro and St Austell, the A3078's sharp bends wind across the spine of the Roseland, sweeping across open fields framed with pretty Cornish hedges – panoramic vistas of the sea flitting by from time to time – and dipping down through wooded valleys. Attractive as it may be, a couple of return trips along this road from Falmouth to Truro is enough to make you swear to take the King Harry ferry next time (it shortens the journey by at least 40 minutes). The only vehicular crossing of the Fal, King Harry (01872 862312, www.kingharry-info.co.uk, £6.50 return with car, 20p per foot passenger) is one of only five remaining chain ferries in the country. Linking Feock near Truro and Philleigh on the Roseland in a mere five minutes, it's short but sweet – it was recently hailed as 'one of the most beautiful ferry crossings in the world' by the *Independent on Sunday*.

Accommodation	★★★★
Food & drink	★★★
Nightlife	★
Shopping	★
Culture	★
Sights	★
Scenery	★★★★★

At the end of the A3078, stunning St Mawes has been a swanky holiday destination since Edwardian times. Neat, whitewashed cottages and smart townhouses cling to the hillside above the small, sheltered harbour, with the dramatic shapes of dark Monterey pines framing the skyline on the brow of the hill behind. Across the clear, sheltered mouth of the Percuil River, the views of St Anthony Head Lighthouse, again framed by Monterey pines, have graced the covers of many a glossy holiday magazine citing comparisons with the south of France. The Riviera-style gloss of this exclusive retreat was given further polish in 1999 by the renovation of the Hotel Tresanton by celebrated interior designer Olga Polizzi.

St Mawes has two town beaches: both are thin strips of sand revealed at low tide, with sheltered bathing water and sunny, south-facing aspects. A short walk along the narrow road up to the headland leads to St Mawes Castle. Like its larger sister across the water, Pendennis Castle, it was built between 1539 and 1543 to defend against attacks from the French and Spanish that never came. When the castle was finally threatened with some serious action in the Civil War, its occupants quickly surrendered it to Parliamentarian forces, hence preserving its immaculate state (it is one of the finest, most complete examples of Henry VIII's South Coast chain forts to be seen).

St Mawes Castle has the same clover-leaf design as Pendennis, but the three semicircular bastions that surround the four-storey central tower make it the more architecturally distinguished of the two. This castle also benefits from its remote location; where Pendennis Point (below the castle on the Falmouth side) sees ice-cream vans, day trippers and canoodling teenagers crowding the car park day and night, St Mawes enjoys nothing but pure, exposed rocks and fresh, panoramic seascapes.

Back in town, there's a limited selection of shops and art galleries to browse, although Falmouth is by far the better option for a full day's shopping. In St Mawes, your best bet is Onda (also owned by the Polizzis), up the 'ope', or narrow alleyway, by the Victory Inn (Victory Steps, Victory Hill, 01326 270456). This boutique offers a stylish selection of clothes and accessories by both renowned and local designers. Just down the road, Chalmers & Short (1 The Quay, 01326 270998) is an upmarket deli offering divine food and drink in a stylish café/deli/wine bar setting. It's a great spot to enjoy a coffee and pain au chocolat while perusing the papers, or simply gazing out over the harbour.

To the lighthouse

The striking St Anthony Head Lighthouse (open to visitors Easter to October) was built in 1834, although a coal beacon burned at this crucial location for hundreds of years beforehand. Playing a critical part in guiding ships to safety both in the Carrick Roads and on the perilous Manacles Reef to the south, this lighthouse was also the set for the television series, *Fraggle Rock*. The many defensive batteries around this point demonstrate its strategic importance throughout World War I and World War II. These days, it's a delightful spot to potter around and take in the sweeping coastal views to either side of this narrow finger of land, with benches conveniently placed at peaceful points along the path.

In the summer (1 April to 30 October), take the five-minute St Mawes to Place ferry (07791 283884, every 30 minutes from 10am to 4.30pm daily) across the Percuil River, then follow the pretty coast path around to the lighthouse. Alternatively, the journey takes around 20 minutes from St Mawes by road.

Just above the lighthouse, the South West Coast Path (www.swcp.org.uk) skirts along the top of the cliffs towards the old pilchard port of Portscatho, commanding great views over the broad sweep of Gerrans Bay all the way. Pilchards, which dominated the Cornish fishing industry in the 19th century and brought relative wealth to these tiny coastal communities, were not just used for food and trade; their oil also fuelled local lamps. Along the coast path just past Portscatho is Porthcurnick Beach, a sheltered and delightfully undeveloped sweep of sand; a mile or so further is the larger stretch of the lovely Pendower Beach, which extends a couple of miles, backed by dunes and low cliffs.

TOURIST INFORMATION

Falmouth
28 Killigrew Street, Falmouth, Cornwall TR11 3PN (01326 312300/www.go cornwall.com).
St Mawes
Roseland Visitor Centre, Millennium Rooms, St Mawes, Cornwall TR2 5AG (01326 270440/ www.roselandinfo.com).

Falmouth & the Roseland Peninsula

Around the Roseland Peninsula

There are plenty of beautiful spots to explore just a stone's throw from St Mawes. If you take the coastal path around from the castle and head inland/north up the shore, the views west across the Carrick Roads towards Mylor, Feock and Trelissick are superb. Wind slightly eastwards up St Just Creek to reach St Just-in-Roseland church, set in steep, subtropical gardens on the side of the creek, with its sandbar and moored yachts. The granite church was consecrated in 1261, but evidence suggests there was a building here as far back as AD 500. It is a breathtaking spot – 'to many people the most beautiful on earth', as John Betjeman gushed.

Further north, the Carrick Roads splits into the Fal and Truro Rivers, the latter being the wider and deeper of the two (navigable all the way to Truro at high tide). At Tolverne, a 500-yard walk from the King Harry ferry at Philleigh, is Smuggler's Cottage (01872 580309, open May to October), a beautiful thatched cottage in a picturesque location on a small, grassy promontory, backed by woods. These days it's a regular stop for the boat trips chugging up the river to Truro – thanks in no small part to the cottage's excellent cream teas – but 60 years ago it played an important role in World War II, when it was requisitioned by the Admiralty in the build-up to the D-Day landings.

The River Fal, with its muddy flood plains of tufty grass, meanders through woods and fields (a bird-lover's paradise) up to the tranquil village of Ruan Lanihorne. This area grew rich on the pilchard boom and naval patronage in the 19th century, although it's hard to imagine it as anything other than the beautiful, sleepy backwater it is today. The King's Head (Ruan Lanihorne, 01872 501263) is a popular gastropub that comes with plenty of glowing local recommendations.

It's worth taking the time to pay a brief visit to Veryan, a pretty village made famous by its curious thatched and crucifix-topped round houses, built in the 19th century by a local minister for his five daughters. Constructed without any corners, these houses apparently meant that the devil would have nowhere to hide. There are also a couple of good local craft shops and galleries in the village.

A few miles on, follow the signs for Portloe and take the narrow lane down to this pristine fishing village, with its whitewashed and pastel-painted granite cottages tightly packed around a steep rocky inlet and harbour. Although the local fishermen still sell the day's catch on the small pebbly beach here, the smart four-wheel drive and Mercedes cars parked up the hill tell a very different story of the village's full- and part-time inhabitants. The coastal path heading westwards from here gives yet more stunning coastal views back towards the Roseland and nearby Gul Rock; poking dramatically out of the sea, this is the nesting ground for an array of seabirds.

Falmouth

The ferry crossing between St Mawes and Falmouth takes around 25 minutes. St Mawes Ferry Company (01872 862312) runs a daily service all year round.

Thriving Falmouth has many more accommodation, eating and drinking options than the peninsula opposite. It may not have the miles of glorious, unspoiled countryside, but it's a convenient base if you want more than to simply hole up and chill out in luxury for the weekend. Its buzzing arts scene, which has grown up around the highly acclaimed Falmouth College of Art, pushes the boundaries further than Cornwall's mainstream watercolour-seascapes genre and lends the town a more cosmopolitan, progressive edge. It still has some way to go, but Falmouth is witnessing the beginnings of a café culture, which, mixed up with the countless traditional purveyors of cream teas, fish-and-chips, pasties and souvenirs, gives the place a colourful yet slightly confused personality.

To the south of Pendennis Point, a string of sandy beaches – interspersed with classic rock-pooling territory at low tide – faces out over calm blue waters, often dotted with the white sails of yachts, or large tankers taking shelter in the bay. Backed by a number of hotels (including the grand, imposing Falmouth Hotel, which was the town's first purpose-built tourist accommodation when it opened in 1865), Falmouth's beaches may lack the rugged natural beauty of the Roseland, but are a pleasant counterpoint to the busy town. The water is surprisingly clear (Gyllyngvase Beach boasts a European Blue Flag), and the light in the bay can be superb.

Until the 17th century, Falmouth was no more than a fishing village – Penryn was the main town, with Pendennis Castle proudly protecting the mouth of the river. Established as the chief base for the packet ships in 1689, which took the first international mail to the Continent and the colonies, Falmouth developed quickly. Its massive natural harbour – the last/first stop before heading out/back across the Atlantic, and a safe haven to ride out bad weather – ensured the town's fortunes.

Carrick Roads is the last remaining oyster fishery in Europe still dredged under sail and oar, with over 15 traditional working boats on duty between October and March. The beginning of the season is celebrated

every October with the Falmouth Oyster Festival (01872 224367, www.falmouth oysterfestival.co.uk). Three days of lavish culinary celebrations are held in the impressive Events Square outside the National Maritime Museum, including cookery shows by celebrity chefs, local craft and produce markets, Falmouth Working Boat races, and champagne- and oyster-tasting aplenty.

The aforementioned museum is housed in a stunning teaked wooden building (Discovery Quay, 01326 313388, www.nmmc.co.uk) and features a huge collection of small boats suspended from the ceiling in the main hall, as well as hands-on interactive displays, audio-visuals, talks and special exhibitions, covering all aspects of maritime life, from boat design to fascinating tales of survival at sea. One highlight is the natural underwater viewing location (one of only three in the world, apparently); another is the 360-degree views over the harbour and town from the top of the 95-foot tower, or the stylish glass-fronted café on the first floor (which also serves an imaginative and tasty menu). Outside, a path leads around the quay to give more great views over the harbour and a close-up of the exclusive yachts moored up outside. During the summer months, Events Square and Discovery Quay feel a little like the waterfront area of Barcelona.

Framing the square, the Shed (6-7 Tidemill House, Discovery Quay, 01326 318502) is a kooky tapas bar, café and restaurant with lusciously kitsch decor and highly recommended by Falmouth's trendier locals. Next door, the Quay Deli (3 Tidemill House, 01326 210808) stocks a great variety of local cheeses, chutneys, meats and other delicacies, including dainty miniature pasties.

Heading into town from Discovery Quay, the road narrows into charming Arwenack Street, with its attractive pastel-coloured Georgian façades and a number of funky shops, cafés and restaurants. At the dog-leg corner by the attractive granite Church of King Charles the Martyr (whose palm tree-framed square tower overlooking the harbour features on many a postcard), Arwenack becomes Church Street. Along this cobbled street, again flanked by attractive Georgian façades, is the Falmouth Arts Centre (24 Church Street, 01326 314566, www.falmoutharts.org) – a buzzing hub of creativity comprising three

exhibition spaces, an art-house cinema, and a theatre, dance and live music venue attracting international performers. A little further along, the impressive art deco façade of the St George's Arcade marks the location of Falmouth's first custom-built cinema, opened in 1912. These days, it contains a hotchpotch of second-hand and curiosity shops.

At the far end of town, after the inevitable chain stores, mobile phone shops and estate agents, is the charismatic old High Street. Here you can delve through the galleries, antiques and second-hand shops, grab a coffee and catch some folk, roots, soul, funk and jazz rhythms at Jam (32 High Street, 01326 219123, www.jamrecords.co.uk), or head for the Old Brewery Yard a little further up, where a couple of great cafés sit alongside a regular outdoor second-hand book fair. Near the top of the High Street stands the old town hall, originally a Congregational chapel presented to the town by Martin Lister Killigrew in 1725. It was also used as the

courthouse and, as such, was the scene of an infamous trial in 1884 when two sailors were acquitted of a charge of cannibalism, having eaten the cabin boy while adrift in the Atlantic after their ship had sunk.

On the Moor, an attractive, large, continental-style square that serves as both marketplace and bus terminal, is another testament to the town's solid artistic identity: the award-winning Falmouth Art Gallery (Municipal Buildings, the Moor, 01326 313863, www.falmouthart gallery.com, open Monday to Saturday 10am-5pm, free entry). This is far beyond your average twee town gallery. Containing original works by major 19th- and 20th-century artists – including Alfred Mannings, HS Tuke, JM Waterhouse and Henry Moore – it also features upbeat and unusual contemporary art exhibitions. Its automata, papier mâché show and kids' workshops make it family friendly.

Leading sharply up off the Moor are the 111 steps of Jacob's Ladder, which ascend the large hill that sits above the town. The

steps have no real biblical association – they were installed by Jacob Hamblen, a builder, tallow chandler and property owner, to facilitate access between his business (at the bottom) and some of his property (at the top). Once you get your breath back, follow the road around the brow of the hill for a fabulous panorama over the town's roofs, palm trees, church tower, docks and castle, and out across the bay. The Seaview pub is a good place to take it in with a quiet pint.

Pendennis Castle (01326 316594, open daily 10am to 4pm) was built at the same time (1543) as its twin, St Mawes, around a mile across the estuary. A crucial defensive garrison from Tudor times to World War II, Pendennis is somewhat larger than St Mawes, having been extended by Elizabeth I at the end of the 16th century. During the Civil War, the young Prince Charles (who later became Charles II) hid here before escaping to the Continent – only just avoiding a siege of the castle by Parliamentarian forces. Visitors can explore the castle's fascinating history at the Discovery Centre, which also contains interactive displays and an exhibit on Tudor battles. In summer, battle re-enactments take place on the gun deck, and a number of open-air concerts and plays are held on the lawn (see www.seencornwall.com for performance listings).

Just below the castle, a road runs all around the point, taking in the mighty docks on the way. After the introduction of the electric telegraph, Falmouth became one of the few places where ships could call in to receive their cargo-delivery orders. In 1860, the foundation of Falmouth Docks created a focus for maritime-related industries, and an extensive ship-repair and maintenance industry developed. An observation platform on the Pendennis road provides fascinating viewing. Beneath the road that leads around the point, a number of narrow paths weave between the rocks, trees and remains of defensive batteries. At low tide, you can clamber across the rocks and search the rock pools. At high tide, stroll around the well-kept path and gardens parallel to the road, ending up at the town's three sandy beaches.

The Helford River

No visit to Falmouth is complete without a boat trip up the enchanting Helford River, a few miles south of the town. Home to many a millionaire and rock star, the stunning landscape of gentle hills, dense woods, sandy beaches, clear waters and chocolate-box villages makes it an obvious choice for an idyllic retreat.

Two excellent National Trust Gardens, Trebah and Glendurgan, overlook the river from the north bank (01872 322917, www.gardensincornwall.com,

www.nationaltrust.org.uk, call or see website for opening times). Trebah is a dramatic ravine garden tumbling down to a sheltered beach. Containing all manner of subtropical and native plants, it's said to be one of the top 80 gardens in the world. Glendurgan is also impressive, and has a recently restored laurel maze that is great fun for kids.

At Helford Passage, the Ferry Boat Inn (01326 250625, www.staustellbrewery.co.uk) sits right on the water's edge, and is a lovely spot for a beer and pub grub in the sunshine. Across the water on the south bank, Helford village, with its granite thatched cottages (mostly converted into luxurious second homes), is twee but makes for a pleasant amble, rounded off

by a pint in the Shipwright's Arms – which also has a prime waterside location and terraced gardens stretching down to just above water level. Boat trips depart from Falmouth's Prince of Wales Pier (timetable information on 01872 862312, www.falriverlinks.co.uk).

WHERE TO STAY

Budock Vean Hotel

Helford Passage, Mawnan Smith, Falmouth, Cornwall TR11 5LG (01326 252100/ www.budockvean.co.uk). **Lunch served** 12.30-2.30pm, **dinner served** 7.30-9pm daily. **Main courses** (lunch) £5-£10. **Set dinner**

£24.50 (residents)-£29.50 (non-residents)
5 courses. **Rates** £136-£224 double. **Credit** DC, MC, V.

Sitting proudly on the beautiful and affluent north bank of the Helford River, a short drive from nearby Falmouth, the Budock Vean is a lavish four-star boasting its own restaurant, golf course, tennis courts, pool and spa, and extensive gardens leading down to a private foreshore on the river, complete with conservatory sun lounge. From the jetty, guests can go fishing, take the ferry across to the Ferry Boat Inn, or explore the sheltered, wooded creeks by boat. It's all about luxury here, although the emphasis is less on innovative interior design and more on the traditional values of an exclusive hotel.

Hotel Tresanton

Lower Castle Road, St Mawes, Cornwall TR2 5DR (01326 270055/www.tresanton.com). **Rates** £130-£250 double; £265-£400 family. **Credit** AmEx, MC, V.

Undoubtedly the jewel in St Mawes's crown, Olga Polizzi's Hotel Tresanton has played no small part in putting the town on the map for the outside world. Originally created in the 1940s as a yachtsman's club, the hotel became a popular and well-known haunt for yachties and tourists from London in the 1950s and 1960s. Olga, a renowned interior designer and sister of Sir Rocco Forte, bought the place in 1997 and spent two years and a cool £2 million renovating and restoring it, before opening to much acclaim in 1999. It's made up of a cluster of houses built into the hillside on different levels, and 27 out of the Tresanton's 29 rooms look out over the sea and St Anthony Head Lighthouse.

The place has a sophisticated, airy minimalism: understated creams, beiges and natural materials are complemented by nautical blues and a mix of both antique and contemporary furniture, alongside original works of art from the likes of Terry Frost, Barbara Hepworth and acclaimed St Mawes sculptor Julian Dyson. Polizzi's personal touches create the illusion that you're staying in someone's home. Wellies are provided for guests, and a private cinema is available for those wild winter days. In fair weather (Easter to end of October), you can board the hotel's private yacht Pinucca and enjoy an invigorating day trip across the bay. There are also yoga weekends in January, bridge and poker weekends in November, and special Christmas and Valentine packages. Sarah Key, a physiotherapist who treats the Royal Family, also hosts the 'Back in a Week' spinal-therapy programmes in November and March. *See also p178.*

Lugger Hotel

Portloe, Cornwall TR2 5RD (01872 501322/ www.luggerhotel.com). **Rates** £150-£350 double. **Credit** AmEx, MC, V.

Giving the Hotel Tresanton a few miles up the road a healthy run for its money, the sophisticated Lugger Hotel offers weary urbanites a luxurious weekend retreat. Literally clinging to the cliffs over Portloe's picturesque natural harbour, the hotel combines the character of the building's traditional features with fresh, contemporary interior design – lots of creams, chocolates, wood, stone, hessian and leather. Huge, sumptuous sofas and open fireplaces give it a cosy country charm, while the smart, recently refurbished restaurant has echoes of a slick Soho affair.

St Mawes Hotel

The Sea Front, St Mawes, Cornwall TR2 5DW (01326 270266/www.stmaweshotel.co.uk). **Lunch served** noon-2.30pm Tue-Sun. **Dinner served** 6-9pm Tue-Sat. **Main courses** £3.95-£6.50. **Rates** £62-£112 double. **Credit** MC, V.

Recently refurbished, this friendly establishment right on the waterfront in the centre of town has five simple but attractively decorated rooms. Warm yellows, natural wood – plus superb sea views from the three upstairs rooms – are the order of the day, all for an incredibly reasonable price in this well-heeled town. The ground-floor brasserie and bar are popular with locals and visitors alike, so be warned that this may not be the most peaceful of retreats during the busy summer months.

St Michael's Hotel

Gyllyngvase Beach, The Seafront, Falmouth, Cornwall TR11 4NB (01326 312707/ www.stmichaels-hotel.co.uk). **Lunch served** noon-2pm, **dinner served** 6.30-9pm daily. **Main courses** £6.50-£12.95. **Rates** £36-£64 double. **Credit** AmEx, MC, V.

It may not command quite such a perfect beachfront location as the Best Western Falmouth Beach Resort Hotel next door, but St Michael's makes up for it with its crisp, modern, maritime interior, exceptional service and award-winning subtropical gardens. In addition to pleasant, comfortable and generally spacious rooms, the hotel has a host of facilities including a luxurious pool, spa and jacuzzi, and two highly recommended eateries; one pleasantly informal (the Flying Fish, with a great sun terrace outside) and the other pulling out all the stops with its table d'hôte and à la carte menus. Only ten minutes' walk from the Maritime Museum and the railway station, St Michael's is well situated for chilling out, but accessible for exploration if and when you feel the urge.

WHERE TO EAT & DRINK

Boathouse

Trevethan Hill, Falmouth, Cornwall TR11 2AG (01326 315425). **Lunch served** noon-3pm daily. **Dinner served** 6.30-9.30pm Mon-Sat. **Main courses** £6.50-£9.50. **Credit** AmEx, MC, V.

Winter or summer, this modern boozer is a great

place for food or drink. Perched on a hill just above the old High Street, the Boathouse commands unbeatable views over the river to Flushing – best enjoyed from the sail-covered decking area outside. This is the site of many a barbecue in the summer months, although the heated lights make it possible to sit outside even after the clocks have gone back. In winter, it's a case of enjoying the log fire and supping from a range of locally brewed Skinner's ales. Although there isn't a huge choice of food on offer, dishes are well executed; smoked haddock with parsnip, sweet potato and Thai green curry sauce, for example, was superb.

Cove

Maenporth Beach, Maenporth, Falmouth, Cornwall TR11 5HN (01326 251136). **Lunch served** noon-3pm, **dinner served** 6-9.30pm daily (closed Mon in winter). **Main courses** £10.50-£15.50. **Credit** MC, V.
Set well back from a beautiful view, which can only be glimpsed at a distance, this understated venue has a stylish new mint-and-aubergine interior and friendly, informal service. A detailed list of specials adds to a varied menu; South American music and jazz complement the bistro setting. Char-grilled Falmouth Bay scallops with bacon, sweet baby peppers, grapes, cos lettuce and a light mustard vinaigrette was a descriptive but satisfying starter. English venison on sweet potato mash with port wine sauce was a full-bodied pairing of indigenous and international ingredients. The dessert menu offers standard ice-cream, but also citrus cheesecake topped with crème fraîche, garnished with fresh berries and raspberry coulis.

Hotel Tresanton

Lower Castle Road, St Mawes, Cornwall TR2 5DR (01326 270055/www.tresanton.com). **Lunch served** 12.30-2.30pm, **dinner served** 7-9.30pm daily. **Set lunch** £20 2 courses, £26 3 courses. **Set dinner** £36 3 courses. **Rates** £165-£280 double; £265-£400 suites. **Credit** AmEx, MC, V.
Of the growing number of exclusive, stylish Cornish hotel restaurants, the Tresanton has to be one of the best looking. This beautiful dining room has spectacular views of the Fal estuary, best enjoyed from the outdoor terrace. The fish-based menu – roast monkfish with steamed clams; grilled langoustines with fennel mayonnaise – has an air of class about it, but the results, while usually good, don't quite warrant the elevated prices. On our last visit, the place swarmed with Londoners but few locals. Staff strike a comfortable balance between slick service and informal friendliness.

Hunkydory

46 Arwenack Street, Falmouth, Cornwall TR11 3JH (01326 212997). **Dinner served** 6-10pm daily. **Main courses** £11.75-£17.95. **Credit** MC, V.
Hunkydory joined the throng of nightspots in the Trago Mills end of Falmouth in 2001. The pleasing curve of its bar welcomes you, and from there you can choose either the cosy, wooden-beamed front room or the brighter and less charismatic back room with its big booths. To start there's a stellar array of seafood, with crab, squid, mussels and king prawns all present, and chorizo, chillies, ginger, lime and pumpkin seeds among the supporting flavours. Hunkydory bills itself as a fish restaurant (the name refers to John Dory by way of David Bowie), but only three main courses feature fish – cod, skate and bass, and the skate was bland. However, the five-spice roast duck, moreish crème brûlée tasters and effervescent service more than compensated.

Lugger

Portloe, Cornwall TR2 5RD (01872 501322/ www.luggerhotel.com). **Lunch served** noon-2pm, **dinner served** 7-9pm daily. **Set lunch** £15 2 courses, £20 3 courses. **Set dinner** £37.50 3 courses. **Credit** AmEx, MC, V.
On the water's edge in a beautiful fishing village, this 17th-century inn has a rich history. One landlord was hanged for smuggling in the 1890s; these days the proprietors are better behaved. The Lugger is a bastion of sophistication, frequented by wealthy weekenders. The set menu features local catches and classic meat dishes: say, pan-fried hand-dived scallops on pea purée with chardonnay, followed by Angus beef fillet wellington with Hermitage red wine jus. There's always plenty for vegetarians too. Another option is to come for lunch, when the tables on the beautiful cliff terrace come into their own.

Pandora Inn

Restronguet, Mylor Creek, Cornwall TR11 5ST (01326 372678). **Lunch served** 12.30-3pm daily. **Dinner served** 6.30-9pm Mon-Thur; 6.30-9.30pm Fri-Sun. **Main courses** £7.50-£11.50. **Credit** MC, V.
As any local will tell you, this beautiful 13th-century thatched pub is one of the best known in the area. Inside, it's a warren of interconnecting rooms with low beams, dark wooden panels, benches and fireside tables; the restaurant upstairs serves the same food but in a more upmarket environment. It's a little pricey, but usually well worth it, with dishes like venison, fresh sea bass, and roast pork bellies cooked to a turn. With an excellent selection of wines alongside hearty real ales, and a great atmosphere, the Pandora is also a good option for a drink on the jetty as the sun goes down, whether you fancy splashing out on food or not.

Seafood Bar

Lower Quay Street, Falmouth, Cornwall TR11 3HM (01326 315129). **Dinner served** July-Oct 7-10.30pm daily. Dec-June 7-10.30pm Mon-Sat. **Main courses** £14.25-£14.95. **Credit** DC, MC, V.
The long-established Seafood Bar remains huge-

ly popular with locals. The old rope fishing nets and glass balls hanging from the ceiling have been removed, giving the place a crisper, candlelit bistro feel. Despite the occasional exotic sauce or fresh tomato and coriander salsa, the emphasis is on fantastic fresh local seafood. Tiger prawns in garlic butter were just as described on the menu (messy but good), and portions are generous. Specials depend on what the fishermen bring in that day, but you won't be disappointed.

Three Mackerel

Swanpool, Falmouth, Cornwall TR11 5BG (01326 311886). **Open** *Bar* noon-11pm Mon-Sat; noon-10.30pm Sun. **Lunch served** noon-2.30pm Mon-Sat; noon-3pm Sun. **Dinner served** 6.30-9.30pm daily. **Main courses** £10.95-£15.95. **Credit** MC, V.

The spectacular location – perched on the edge of a cliff with a lovely wooden deck overlooking clear blue waters – means people would probably come here whatever was served. The fact that the menu is an alluring mix of modern British and fusion cuisines, blending local meat and fish with Mediterranean and oriental influences to great effect, only adds to the appeal. The solid choice of

European and New World wines and a funky atmosphere don't hurt either. Unsurprisingly, it can be difficult to get a table; although you can reserve one inside, you can't book the tables on the deck, so it's best to turn up early. There's an early evening terrace menu at weekends.

Victory Inn

Victory Hill, St Mawes, Cornwall TR2 5DQ (01326 270324). **Lunch served** noon-2pm; **dinner served** 6.30-9pm daily. **Main courses** £4.50-£14. **Credit** MC, V.

Whitewashed with an explosion of floral window boxes, this former fishermen's haunt is more likely to see chinos and blazers than yellow wellies and overalls. The beamed interior retains an intimate old-world vibe, while the restaurant upstairs (which serves the same food) is fresh, airy and modern. Offering a number of real ales and lagers, as well as an innovative pub menu that includes lots of seafood and as much local and organic produce as possible, this is a great place to while away those carefree holiday hours, be it in front of a roaring log fire in winter or at an outside table peeking out over the harbour in summer.

Southerly sophistication at Hotel Tresanton.

Falmouth & the Roseland Peninsula

Padstow & Rock

Where the views and the seafood vie for attention.

First and foremost, this is not a weekend destination for anyone even toying with the idea of shedding a few pounds. But who cares about a trim waistline when this divine corner of the world boasts romantic beaches, wild cliffs, sweeping countryside and fine food? And there are always adrenalin-fuelled activities if you're that way inclined.

Whereas farming, fishing and mining were once the stalwarts of Cornish industry, now tourism keeps the economy thriving. The craggy bays and tortuous inlets that stalled development around the Camel estuary are now attractions in themselves. The looming, buckled slate cliffs are walloped by thundering Atlantic waves that break on to some of the finest beaches in the UK. And thanks to some prime-quality local produce, talented chefs and the Rick Stein phenomenon, this area in particular has attracted a colossal wave of gastronomic tourism (*see p194* **Padstein**). So, if it's mouth-watering food and scenery you're after, you won't be disappointed.

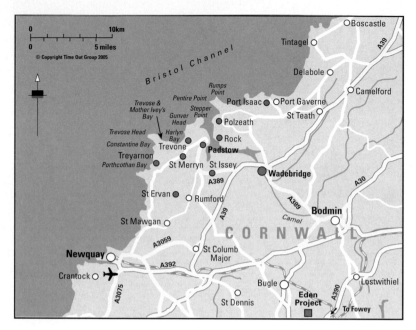

The approach to Padstow along the A389 is immediately soothing as you wind through low hills and sloping fields, past farm shops and a smattering of homesteads offering fresh eggs and organic produce. Once you've passed St Issey and St Petroc's, the road plunges and takes a looping detour, exposing a swipe of yellow sand that lines the blazing blue of the Camel estuary. Then before you know it you've arrived at the harbour: an animated marine shambles of crabbers, netters, yachts and pleasure cruisers. Surrounding the harbour, slate-hung, red-brick and grey-stone cottages accommodate pasty shops, boutiques, chippies and cavernous bars. Evidence suggests that Padstow has been used as a port since the 16th century, though the demise of shipping here is down to the 'doom bar' – shallow sandbanks at the mouth of the estuary on which many ships have foundered.

If you can't attend the May Day event of Obby Oss (see p187 **Rite of spring**), you can learn all about it in the Padstow Museum (the Institute, Market Place, 01841 532752, www.padstowmuseum.co.uk). The volunteer-staffed museum is a little the worse for wear, and opening times vary, but it's a good spot to delve into Padstow's history. The Cinedrome (Lanadwell Street, 01841 532344, www.wtwcinemas.co.uk), which opened in 1919 as a music hall and theatre, also has a deceptively tired-looking exterior. Walking through the doors feels like stepping back in time, but the cinema shows recent releases on an enlarged screen, with Dolby digital sound systems and luxury seats.

Another spot to uncover some of the area's past is St Petroc's church. This was dedicated to the monk who gave the town its name ('Petrock's Stow'). The church's most eye-catching features include a font with 12 apostles carved from Catacleuse stone and a medieval bench showing a fox preaching to a congregation of geese. Linking the town to the church is the beginning of the Saints Way, an ancient 30-mile trail across the peninsula which joins Padstow to Fowey on the south coast. The dark slate parish church houses the tombs of the Prideaux family, whose manor, Prideaux Place (01841 532411), sits imperiously in its own deer park above the harbour. The building dates from 1592 and is stuffed full of porcelain, antique glass, memorabilia and portraits by John Opie. There are other more unusual details too, including an art nouveau light switch, an ingenious early hi-fi system and a glorious 16th-century ceiling in the Great Chamber.

Back in town, as an utter contrast, visit the fascinating National Lobster Hatchery (South Quay, 01841 533877, www.national lobsterhatchery.com) where you'll learn that lobsters taste with their feet, have three stomachs and can live to be about 100. If you want an overview of the town's location, head up past the lower beach ferry-landing point, and through the Chapel Stile field to a war memorial.

Accommodation	★★★
Food & drink	★★★★
Nightlife	
Shopping	★★★
Culture	★
Sights	★
Scenery	★★★★★

Retail therapy

Cornwall's not short of an artist or two, and if you fancy snooping around a few creative corners, Padstow is a pretty good place to do it. At the expense of more practical retail outlets for residents, tourism has paved the way for a crop of galleries where you can select your own seascape to take home. Have a browse in the Padstow Contemporary Art Gallery (3A Parnell Court, 01841 532242, www.padstowgallery.com), which features 20th-century art and ceramics, as well as current work. At the Middle Street Gallery you can find paintings by Jane Darke among a selection from local artists (Middle Street, 01841 520393, www.jane darke.co.uk), but head to the Blue Wing Gallery (Hornabrook Place, 01841 533999, www.blue-wing.co.uk) if you're hunting for something more contemporary. The Drawing Room (Trevone, near Padstow, 01841 520409) is worth a trip for ocean-inspired paintings by Ian Reynolds, while tucked away at Car Space Studio (2 Fentonluna Lane, 01841 533546) is Grace Pattinson's studio, where the artist produces unique and colourful local landscapes on canvas.

If you fancy a bit of retail therapy beyond the sailing- and surf-brand heaven, Padstow can offer some unusual finds. Visit Avant Garde (Duke Street, 01841 533544, www.avantgardejewellery.co.uk), for contemporary designer jewellery that emphasises the work of Cornish jewellery-makers, or for wooden crafts, unusual gift ideas and unique teak root furniture try Dukeswood (Duke Street, 01841 533442, www.dukeswood.net).

The town is the epitome of fishing-village chic, but what you're really here for is its backdrop of stupendous scenery and golden beaches. Heading west, the estuary is lined with sweeping, dune-backed sands, which stop short of the climb up to the imposing headland of Stepper Point. From here the coast path continues along blustery cliff tops until it reaches the Edwardian holiday suburb of Trevone and then Harlyn Bay – a popular surfing beach sheltered by Trevose Head and Cataclews Point (for coastal walks, *see p188* **Best foot forward**).

Beyond Trevose Head, Booby's Bay has the skeletal remnants of a German World War I ship preserved in the sand, while Polventor – or Mother Ivey's Bay – gets its name from a farmer's widow who claimed the rights to all the shipwreck pickings along this part of the coast. Big breakers come bulldozing into Constantine Bay, making it a surfers' favourite, but beginners and bathers should be aware of the hazardous rip tides. It is named after the chapel of St Constantine, which is now standing in ruins in Trevose Golf Course. A stone's throw to the south of Constantine, Treyarnon Bay is another good spot for surfing, although caravans, an open-air tide pool and ample car parking make it a crowded family spot in peak season.

Continue down the coast and there are endless scenic beaches and coves, each with its own characteristics and appeal. The sandy funnel of Porthcothan boasts dramatic cliffs, caves and blowholes, and at Bedruthan Steps a steep descent leads down to one of the wildest beaches of the West Country.

To the north of Padstow, across the Camel estuary, lie the twin resorts of Rock and Polzeath. It's a short ride on the ferry (£3 return, every 20 minutes, from 7.50am to 4.30pm in winter or 7.30pm in summer, no Sunday service in winter; see www.padstowlive.com for details), during which you can catch a panoramic view of the Camel Valley countryside, the mouth of the estuary and the horizon beyond the striking headlands of Stepper and Pentire points. Slightly less accessible than the Padstow side, this is swimming, surfing, waterskiing and sailing country par excellence.

On approaching the Victorian-style houses and well-manicured driveways housing shiny 4WD chariots, it's not difficult to understand why Rock has been dubbed 'Kensington-on-Sea'. This is a haven for second-homers, and it's the monied West Londoners who flock here and bring it to life every summer. It's hard to put a finger on any distinctive features of the community, and the absence of local amenities is indicated by the hordes of Rockites to-ing and fro-ing on the ferry to Padstow. It's an appealing location if you want to be removed from the bustle of Padstow, and with late-running water-taxis in summer, there is no need to miss out on the town's gastronomic superiority at dinner time.

While Rock fails to embody any trace of an authentic Cornish environment, the dramatic landscape on its doorstep

TOURIST INFORMATION

The Red Brick Building, North Quay, Padstow, Cornwall PL28 8AF (01841 533449/www.padstowlive.com).

St Enodoc – away from the hurly burly.

does the exact opposite. In fact the jaw-dropping scenery serves up some of the best that Cornwall beholds – rolling greens contrasting with golden sands, topped off with a zillion hues of blue that streak the ocean and sky. The sweeping sands and dunes of Daymer Bay, beloved of kids, sun-worshippers and windsurfers, are backed by St Enodoc Golf Course – possibly one of the UK's most beautiful spots if you are inclined to spoil a good walk with the swing of a club. The perfectly rounded grassy knoll of Brea Hill makes a great place for a picnic, with a view over the rippled expanse of sand, decorated with the colourful specks of windbreaks, kites and sails.

To the right sits the 13th-century church of St Enodoc – once known as 'Sinking Neddy' as it was all but buried in sand – its wonky steeple now rising from where it sits serenely amid the grass-bound dunes. A stroll will lead you to the tranquillity of the parish where the late poet laureate Sir John Betjeman is buried. Betjeman spent many holidays in this area, based in the hamlet of Trebetherick and exploring the edge of Polzeath and its surrounds by bicycle.

Rock's family-friendly reputation has driven couples and more mature escapees to Polzeath. And while Rock is for sailing,

RITE OF SPRING

Arguably one of the UK's most vibrant community festivals is Obby Oss – Padstow's May Day celebration. Two Osses – monstrous effigies made out of hoop-work, tarpaulin and sprays of horsehair – are paraded through the streets to the accompaniment of song, accordions and drums. Attended by teams of Padstonians sporting red and blue sashes, each Oss is led by a Teazer who thrusts a phallic club around the beast's body. The ritual has ancient roots in what is generally believed to be some kind of fertility rite – the death and rebirth of the Oss represents the death and rebirth of the seasons – and therefore it becomes a celebration of the onset of summer. The festival's insistent, pulsing rhythms go on until midnight, and it marks the continuation of a tradition going back about 900 years, and the resilience of a community in the face of tourism.

Polzeath is for surfing. It has another alluring beach of fine sand and gentle surf that's perfect for beginners when the conditions prevail, while beyond the breakers loom the two National Trust headlands of Pentire and Rumps Point. The latter is home to the remains of an Iron Age fort, and a walk out to the promontories on a blustery day promises to blow the cobwebs away and leave you feeling inspired and exhilarated (for coastal walks, *see p188* **Best foot forward**).

WHERE TO STAY

There's no shortage of accommodation to choose from, but as peak season sees the whole area bursting at the seams, make sure you book in advance. The following offer one thing Padstow and Rock do incredibly well: something a little bit special.

No.6 Café & Rooms

6 Middle Street, Padstow, Cornwall PL28 8AP (01841 532093/www.number6inpadstow. co.uk). **Rates** £130 double. **Credit** MC, V. You need to book far in advance to get into this exclusive hideaway, and although the food (set dinner £28 3 courses) is rumoured to be top-notch, it's off-limits to non-residents.

Padstow & Rock

Padstow to Gunver Head circuit
Distance 5 miles.
Time approx 2hrs 30mins.
A spectacular and diverse circuit which covers sweeping countryside, wild cliffs and the banks of the Camel estuary. From the quayside, follow the path up past the low-tide ferry point, through Chapel Stile field and turn left just through the gates of the war memorial. Keep the boundary of the deer park to your left and extensive views to the estuary on your right, until you reach the road and Prideaux Place (*see p184*). Turn right and keep walking until you reach a stile marked with a public footpath sign on the left (about 500 yards). Follow the stiles diagonally across the farmland until you reach a cluster of farm buildings and a road, on which you head right until you cross a stile on your left-hand side, leading out to the coast path. With Gunver Head on your left, head right along the dramatic cliff tops, past the hollow Butter Hole and the collapsed sea cave of the Pepper Hole. Keep an eye out for hawks, buzzards, seals and dolphins. Beyond the coastguard lookout, follow the coast as it veers back around the estuary, past Hawker's Cove and down on to the beach of Harbour Cove. At low tide you can follow the sand all the way back to the low-tide ferry point, or climb back on to the path over Gun Point and St George's Well.

Trevone to Padstow circuit
Distance 7 miles.
Time approx 3hrs 30mins.
Slightly more demanding and time-consuming than the above option, this circuit can be started in either Padstow or Trevone. Facing the sea, a footpath leads up the right-hand side of Trevone Bay to the Round Hole, a collapsed coastal cave and ominous funnel through which the sea surges.

Follow the path to the natural arch of Porthmissen Bridge and on to Tregudda Gorge, an eerie chasm where, years ago, an old man is said to have heard mermaids singing to him. Offshore, Gulland Rock and the jagged grouping called King Phillip can be seen. Carry on for less than a mile to Gunver Head and beyond, along an exhilarating stretch that eventually reaches the huge hollow of the Butter Hole and the steep inlet of Pepper Hole, which takes its name from the cargo washed in from shipwrecked vessels.

The daymark tower at Stepper Point is now fenced off, but follow the coastal path to the manned coastguard lookout, then down into Hawker's Cove. Keep on the upper path that winds along the estuary to St George's Cove and the war memorial, from where you can continue into Padstow for a snack, or take a sharp right around the edge of the fields, culminating at Prideaux Place. Here turn right, then veer left when you reach a stile marked with a public footpath sign, and continue for just over a mile to the hamlet of Crugmeer. Go through the cluster of buildings and then turn off the lane to the right; the track leads downhill to Porthmissen Farm and back to Trevone.

Polzeath, Pentire & Rumps Point circuit

Distance 3½miles.
Time approx 2hrs.
Facing the sea at Polzeath, follow the coast path right, around the cove of Pentireglaze Haven (stay on the lower route along the ocean's edge). From the rocky outcrop of Pentire point, to your left, are Stepper Point and Trevose Head. Keep rambling along the obvious coast path, and where this divides as you near Rumps Point, again keep to the lower route, bearing left. A path created in the Iron Age takes you to the twin peaks of the headland, then turn back across the neck of the peninsula, taking the broad path straight ahead to a gate. Continue with the wall to your right until you reach a sign for Pentire Farm, which you follow to the yard of the farm where, opposite the farmhouse, you turn right, back to the coastal path and towards Polzeath.

Padstow to Polzeath

Distance 3 miles.
Time approx 2hrs.
You can start this easy walk at either end, and it includes the ferry ride as well as some mesmerising views from Brea Hill. From Padstow take the ferry across the estuary and, facing Rock, veer left along the coastal path, keeping the estuary on your left and the dunes and St Enedoc Golf Course on your right. When you reach the steep, grassy slope of Brea Hill, climb its back to take in the view that inspired Betjeman and many souls since. From the peak, head right, towards the sweeping sands of Daymer Bay and the leaning steeple of the tiny St Enedoc church where Betjeman is buried. Carry on past the church and follow the coast path back over the cliffs towards Polzeath bay, which sweeps into view ahead.

Old Custom House Inn

*South Quay, Padstow, Cornwall PL28 8BL
(01841 532359/www.smallandfriendly.co.uk).*
Rates £90-£155 double; £155-£170 suite.
Credit AmEx, MC, V.

The Old Custom House, now a listed building, has recently been refurbished; the result is an intimate and stylish hotel. Most of the rooms have harbour views, so you can wake up to the early-morning light rising over the estuary. We were nicely surprised by simple, elegant and spacious suites; the design isn't cutting-edge, but sand-coloured furniture and framed drawings of shells create a soft, beach-side feel. The downside to being smack in the middle of town is the late-night revellers being turned out of the pub below the window. For an extra-luxurious experience, you can indulge in spa and pampering packages in the hotel's Lavender Room beauty suite. Pescadou (*see p193*) serves fabulous fresh fish. Bedrooms are no-smoking.

St Edmund's House

*Riverside, Padstow, Cornwall PL28 8BY
(01841 532700/www.rickstein.com).*
Rates £235 double. **Credit** MC, V.

Although there are some atmospheric rooms above the Seafood Restaurant and at St Petroc's, the best accommodation in the Stein empire is at St Edmund's House, set in private gardens overlooking the Camel estuary. The six minimalist yet luxurious rooms are kitted out with en suite marble bathrooms, oak flooring and French doors; those on the ground floor also have a private deck area for sunbathing. Guests get an automatic reservation at the Seafood Restaurant (*see p194*).

St Enodoc

*Rock, Cornwall PL27 6LA (01208 863394/
www.enodoc-hotel.co.uk).* **Closed** Dec-1st week of Feb. **Lunch served** noon-2.30pm, **dinner served** 7-9.30pm daily. **Main courses** £15.25-£19.50. **Rates** £90-£210 double; £185-£345 suite; £130-£290 family suite (sleeps 4).
Credit AmEx, DC, MC, V.

Even among the elegant houses of Rock, St Enodoc sits a notch above the rest – boasting a superior view over the Camel estuary to the lush countryside. The chic interiors by Emily Todhunter work with the clear coastal light, and the walls are sparingly adorned with paintings by local artists. The modern cuisine takes full advantage of regional produce (including the hotel's own-grown herbs), Cornish seafood and locally reared meat. The dining-room terrace is the perfect place on a summer's day, but on a cooler evening squirrel away by a crackling log fire in the drawing room. Facilities include a heated outdoor swimming pool, a newly refurbished gym, plus a children's playroom.

St Ervan Manor

*The Old Rectory, St Ervan, Cornwall PL27 7TA
(01841 540255/www.stervanmanor.co.uk).* **Rates**
£110-£160 double; £200 suite. **Credit** MC, V.

Built in 1856, this Grade II-listed Victorian rectory is hidden away in tranquil grounds just four miles from the bustle of Padstow. Stumbled across by Betjeman, the rectory is in far from the primitive state which he refers to in 'Summoned by Bells'. It has been luxuriously refurbished in an exquisite mix of traditional and modern styles; the carpet is so thick you'll want to go barefoot to appreciate it, and the walls are adorned with vibrant, contemporary works from local galleries. One of the five unique suites bears Betjeman's name and boasts a luxurious sleigh bed, lavish long-drop curtains and double sinks in the bathroom. The Barton, named after the clergyman who built the rectory, houses a four-poster bed, and then there's the Ervan, the Rumford and the Penrose, each named after local hamlets. Being outside Padstow can be a blessing – even in peak season it's so quiet you can hear a pin drop. Plus it has its own fine-dining restaurant (*see p193*). No smoking throughout.

WHERE TO EAT & DRINK

Local produce, a handful of master chefs and more top-notch eateries than you can poke a fork at. If you like food, you can't go wrong in and around Padstow. In addition to the best of a good bunch that are reviewed below, there are cafés, restaurants, pasty shops and pubs aplenty to be discovered from Porthcothan to Port Isaac. *See also p194* **Padstein**.

Black Pig

*Rock Road, Rock, Wadebridge, Cornwall PL27
6JS (01208 862622/www.blackpigrestaurant.
co.uk).* **Lunch served** *Easter-Sept* 12.30-2pm Mon-Sat. **Dinner served** *Oct-Easter* 7-9pm Tue-Sat. *Easter-Sept* 7-9.30pm Mon-Sat. **Main courses** £21.50-£22.50. **Set lunch** £17.50 2 courses, £22.50 3 courses. **Set dinner** £60 6-course tasting menu. **Credit** AmEx, MC, V.

Since its spring 2003 opening, the Black Pig has become Cornwall's most applauded restaurant. For all the team's youth (none over 30) led by chef Nathan Outlaw, it's an impressively mature place. Ingredients are British and seasonal; there's an à la carte menu, but at dinner the tasting menu is the best way to assess Outlaw's skills, with such dishes as squab pigeon with bitter chocolate and rocket, or beef fillet with onion, beer, green beans and hazelnuts. For a smaller sampling, the set lunch is top value. Dinner reservations are essential in the summer, but at other times, and at lunch particularly, it's worth phoning on the off chance. No smoking throughout.

The Ebb

*1A The Strand, Padstow, Cornwall PL28 8BS
(01841 532565).* **Dinner served** *Oct-mid Nov* 7-9.30pm Mon, Wed-Sun. *July-Sept* 6-10pm Mon, Wed-Sun. **Closed** *mid Nov-Easter*.
Main courses £13.50-£17.50. **Credit** MC, V.

From an unassuming back alley, the Ebb challenges Stein's Padstow monopoly. Starting with the detail: good bread and olive oil, sparkling table settings, and just-so service in a modern room (beige, nicely lit, slightly disconcerting Schiele-esque art). Food and mood are contemporary, with an emphasis on local and organic. A short menu combines fish with Asian and Mediterranean borrowings: while a Thai-influenced Cornish crab salad hit the spot, fish bhaji with tomato and tamarind jam, and a fish and shrimp curry went a little astray. More appreciated were the baked sea bream with sea salt, rosemary, pesto and roast tomatoes; the pine nut and herb-crusted cod with a cannellini bean salad; and, from a varied dessert list, a mint and cardamom meringue. Not revolutionary, but personal, smartly done and popular for it.

Harbour Inn

South Quay, Padstow, Cornwall PL28 8BL (01841 533148). **Meals served** noon-9.30pm daily. **Main courses** £5.95-£6.75. **Credit** AmEx, DC, MC, V.

Tucked just behind the quay, this is a refreshingly local spot for a Cornish ale or a stiff gin and tonic well away from the foodie trail. A rustic, nautical theme oozes from place. There are dark-wood floorboards, low-beamed ceilings, a log fire, and fat leather sofas just begging to be sat on, amid bits of boating paraphernalia that subtly adorn the walls. If you find yourself in need of a snack, make a beeline for the handwritten menus behind the windows-in-the-wall – they offer hearty pub grub standards, without a hefty price tag attached.

TAKE ACTION

CYCLING

The Camel Trail follows a disused railway line along the estuary from Padstow to Wadebridge (6 miles); another 8 miles takes you through wooded river valleys to Bodmin and the western fringe of the moor. Bikes can be hired at **Padstow Cycle Hire** (South Quay, 01841 533533), and there are pubs and tea shops en route for refuelling.

FISHING

Sports and Leisure Shop (5 North Quay, 01841 532639) and the **Padstow Angling Centre** (Strand House, South Quay, 01841 532762) both offer deep-sea and mackerel fishing trips from Padstow.

GOLF

St Enodoc Golf Club in Rock (01208 863216, www.st-enodoc.co.uk) incorporates two beautifully sited courses on the edge of the estuary, one of which allows unrestricted access for visiting players. Enjoying a spectacular position over Constantine Bay is **Trevose Golf Club** (01841 520208, www.trevose-gc.co.uk), which has extensive country club facilities.

SAILING & WATERSKIING

The Camel School of Seamanship (The Pontoon, Rock, 01208 862881) offers two-hour lessons in dinghy sailing, as well as powerboating and other courses. Equipment is also available for hire. Or try **Sailing at Rock** (01208 841246) for tuition on traditional Drascombe Luggers and Cornish Shrimpers. If you want a bit more welly on the water, the **Camel Ski School** (Rock, 01208 862727) offers waterskiing.

SURFING

Rebound Surf (Constantine Bay, 01841 521185, closed Oct-Easter) offers one-to-one tuition, while **Harlyn Surf School** (16 Boyd Avenue, Padstow, 01841 533076, www.harlynsurf.co.uk, closed Nov-Apr) can combine tuition with accommodation and full board. On the other side of the estuary, **Surf's Up!** (Polzeath Beach, 01208 862003, www.surfsupsurfschool.com) offers short or full-day surfing lessons, plus wetsuit and board hire, as does **Animal Surf** (Polzeath Beach, 0870 242 2856, www.animalsurfacademy.com). If you're already ripping and just want a board or wetsuit, you can hire all equipment from **Anne's Cottage Surf Shop** (Polzeath Beach, 01208 863317).

Padstow & Rock

Margot's Bistro

11 Duke Street, Padstow, Cornwall PL28 8AB (01841 533441/www.margots.co.uk). **Lunch served** 12.30-2pm Wed-Sat. **Dinner served** 7-9pm Tue-Sat. **Main courses** (lunch) £12.50-£16.50. **Set dinner** £21.95 2 courses, £25.95 3 courses. **Credit** AmEx, MC, V.

Margot's may not have the celebrity status of a Rick Stein joint, but it's almost as difficult to get a table (we had to book a month in advance for late June). Admirably there's only one sitting per night, but the pace is slow; we were left staring at our dirty plates for a little too long. This small, quirky place has a sky- and sand-coloured interior and an intimate atmosphere. Staff are warm and chatty. We enjoyed ample servings of good food: fluffy warm goat's cheese set off nicely by sweet roasted peppers; scallops as tender as butter, served with lardons and a rich, grainy pistachio dressing; succulent lamb with rosemary jus; and a large meaty skate wing, flavoured with garlic and anchovies on herby mash. No smoking throughout.

Oyster Catcher

Polzeath, Cornwall PL27 6TG (01208 862371/ www.smallandfriendly.co.uk). **Sept-Apr Open** 11am-3pm, 6-11pm Mon-Fri; 11am-11pm Sat; 11am-10.30pm Sun. **Lunch served** noon-2.30pm, **dinner served** 6-9pm daily. *May-Aug* **Open** 11am-11pm Mon-Sat; 11am-10.30pm Sun. **Meals served** noon-9pm daily. **Main courses** £6.95-£12.95. **Credit** MC, V.

With a modern sanded-wood interior, this is a pleasant pint-stop with a view over the beach – especially if you've done a bit of leg work over to Padstow, St Enedoc and Daymer Bay *(see p188* **Best foot forward)**. There's a friendly and relaxed atmosphere (musicians play on Saturdays), a fabulous patio for surf-spotting on sunny days and snug sofas for a blustery afternoon. And if you fancy stopping over after one too many, upstairs there are also self-catering apartments for hire.

Pescadou

South Quay, Padstow, Cornwall PL28 8BL (01841 532359/www.pescadou.co.uk). **Lunch served** noon-2pm, **dinner served** 7-9pm daily. **Closed** Suns in winter. **Main courses** £12.75-£14.95. **Rates** £90-£155 double; £155-£170 suite. **Credit** AmEx, MC, V.

As the name suggests, the emphasis is on fish at the harbourside restaurant of the Old Custom House Inn *(see p190).* Pescadou tailors its menu around the best of what is caught on the doorstep. And what isn't – such as the succulent Fal River rope-grown mussels – doesn't have to travel far. While the selection attempts to cater outside of its seafood speciality, the lamb shank was disappointing next to the exceptional cod and crab pie: a succulent, generous fillet of cod, doused in a creamy wine and parsley sauce, dressed in hearty chunks of fresh crab and laid over fluffy Cornish yarg mash. In short – indulge in what the restaurant knows best – or give the place a miss.

Ripley's

St Merryn, Padstow, Cornwall PL28 8NQ (01841 520179). **Lunch served** noon-2pm, **dinner served** 6.30-9.30pm Tue-Sat. **Main courses** £12.95-£19. **Credit** MC, V.

Set up by a former head chef from the Seafood Restaurant, Ripley's bears all the marks of a top-quality establishment. It is housed in a beautiful whitewashed cottage, with tasteful and understated decor (wooden beams, stylish furniture). From complimentary nibbles of mussels in hazelnut pesto, to the cod in a delicate, mild and creamy curry sauce, and side dish of beautiful seasonal vegetables, the delivery was flawless. The small menu of local seafood and meat changes daily; vegetarians should order in advance. Desserts are innovative and light; passion fruit and nougatine parfait was outstanding. No surprise that Ripley's is usually fully booked.

Rock Inn

Rock Road, Rock, Cornwall PL27 6LD (01208 863498). **Open** 11am-11pm Mon-Sat; noon-10.30pm Sun. **Lunch served** noon-2.30pm, **dinner served** 7-10pm daily. **Main courses** £6.95-£12.95. **Credit** MC, V.

If you want to mix with the sailing crowd, there's nowhere better to catch them than over a sundowner on the balcony of the Rock Inn. And if you can't keep up with the yachtie talk, just focus on the stunning view back over the estuary.

St Ervan Manor

The Old Rectory, St Ervan, Cornwall PL27 7TA (01841 540255/www.stervanmanor.co.uk). **Dinner served** 7-9pm Wed-Sun. **Set dinner** £35 5 courses, £45 6 courses. **Credit** MC, V.

This award-winning guesthouse *(see p190).* has introduced an intimate dining experience set to rival the efforts of the Black Pig and Ripley's. It's too early to predict its success, but it's hard to fault its exquisite attention to detail and taste. Each platter is a feast for the eyes. It's a tantalising journey through six courses of skilfully blended flavours and textures. From Penryn smoked salmon with a twist, through cep risotto, to the Cornish cheeses, only one dish of monkfish was lost to an overpowering base of braised oxtails. The wine list has an extensive, French-biased choice.

Shipwrights

North Quay, Padstow, Cornwall PL28 8AF (01841 532451). **Open** 11am-11pm Mon-Sat; noon-10.30pm Sun. **Meals served** noon-9pm daily. **Main courses** £4.95-£8.95. **Credit** MC, V.

Right beside the ferry departure slip, this popular bar can be heaving in the summer, but it's a great spot to sit outside and watch quayside life. Downstairs is cosy and atmospheric, whereas upstairs the garish decor makes for a less intimate ambience, unless you score the corner booth with a view over the harbour.

Piscatorial magnate Rick Stein has left his mark everywhere in this town, his Padstow business having grown from a single harbourside bistro to encompass three restaurants, a chippie, a seafood delicatessen (South Quay, 01841 533466 ext 432), a pâtisserie, a gift shop (8 Middle Street, 01841 532221), accommodation and a master-chef school (01841 533466, www.rickstein.com). Under his tutelage, Padstow has shed its fishing jersey for a natty white dinner jacket to become one of the most popular dining destinations in the south west.

But while many businesses are thriving from the attention he has drawn to the area by putting North Cornwall in the foodie spotlight, the question is whether his empire has begun to steal a little too much of that limelight. As a visitor, the Stein theme park can become infuriating as you have to look harder to avoid his stamp on everything from your T-shirt to your wine bottle. Many local food businesses may be reaping the rewards of his 'source local' manifesto, but it is one that has noticeably stopped short of supporting the superb local Camel Valley vintages in preference to the Stein's Seafood White or Stein's Australian Red (plucked from his vineyards down under). And while some locals are grateful to launch their own reputations off the back of the Stein phenomenon, others are less impressed as the town gets busier and more expensive, squeezing them out of the centre.

There's no doubt Stein's food lives up to its flawless reputation, but it's worth noting that it's not the sum total of what's available in the area.

Rick Stein's Café

10 Middle Street, Padstow, Cornwall PL28 8AP (01841 532700/www.rickstein.com). **Lunch served** 9am-3pm, **dinner served** 7-9.30pm daily. **Main courses** £8.50-£15.95. **Credit** MC, V.

Expectations of a pretentious 'café' were pleasantly dashed by a setting in which you might be just as happy slurping coffee behind a newspaper as dressed up for Sunday lunch. A nautical theme befits its location: stripy cushions, watercolours adorning wood-panelled walls, and a glass-roofed courtyard. It was refreshing to find the seafood rubbing shoulders with such firm favourites as burgers and chicken, but, that said, the salt-and-pepper prawns were finger-licking spot-on. Providing much-needed light relief from Padstow's culinary onslaught, the Vietnamese pho was fresh and zingy, in accordance with Rick's declaration that it's 'possibly the best diet dish I've ever tasted'. For the mains, we reverted to a classic burger. Generously garnished with crunchy pickled gherkins and own-made tomato relish, it was mouth-watering. Although the style is simpler and the prices lower than at Stein's more formal establishments, the place delivers.

St Petroc's Bistro

4 New Street, Padstow, Cornwall PL28 8EA (01841 532700/www.rickstein.com). **Lunch served** noon-2pm, **dinner served** 7-9.30pm daily. **Main courses** £12.50-£16.50. **Credit** MC, V.

Here, a slimmer version of Stein's menu comes with a more affordable price tag than at his signature Seafood Restaurant (*see below*), yet the intimate setting didn't extend to a friendly greeting. Having been told on the previous day that we did not require a booking, we were curtly turned away as a large party arrived at our heels. A shame, as the menu promised an interesting range of posh nosh – frisée with poached egg, bacon lardons and croûtons, brandade de morue (cod) – or was it just a few simple flavours wrapped in a bit of hoity-toity language? Moules marinière and coq au vin sounded like a perfect Sunday lunch with a twist, but be warned and book ahead if you want to find out.

Seafood Restaurant

Riverside, Padstow, Cornwall PL28 8BY (01841 532700/www.rickstein.com). **Lunch served** noon-2.30pm, **dinner served** 7-10pm daily. **Main courses** £17.50-£38. **Set dinner** £50 5 courses. **Credit** AmEx, MC, V.

You can't avoid the Rick Stein presence in Padstow. It seems a fairly benevolent hegemony, fostering a food-aware micro-climate with custom to spare for other businesses. But we have had mixed experiences here. Seafood has been beyond reproach, the stuff of pilgrimage: a vast, impeccably sourced variety, from the au naturel (a veritable menagerie of fruits de mer, £15.50 and £39.50; whole boiled crab, £17.50) to the sensitively and imaginatively prepared (soup, ceviche, curried, simply fried and grilled). Cod and chips was as good as could be imagined. Hake with sauce verte and Spanish butter beans was flat-out superb. But outside its specialism the restaurant has stumbled when judged against others of this (hefty) price band. The conservatory decor is a little dated, and £8.50 is a lot to pay for a dessert, however fine.

Stein's Fish & Chips

South Quay, Padstow, Cornwall PL28 8LB (01841 532700/ www.rickstein.com). **Lunch served** noon-2.30pm, **dinner served** 5-9pm Mon-Sat; noon-6pm Sun. **Main courses** from £5.25. **Credit** MC, V.
The impressive choice of fish varieties on offer here blows your average fish-and-chip shop out of the water. Stein's boasts a menu that changes according to the day's catch, and an impressive supply of local shellfish to boot. It was a shame, then, that the experience was let down by sluggish, unfriendly service. Don't expect a plate or cutlery if you choose to eat in – while the neat presentation in chip boxes may save the washing-up, it doesn't save the trees. Still, you can get a beer in a glass, and the pebbled counters, shell-framed mirrors and clean interior create a comfortable atmosphere. Ultimately it's the food that matters, and the quality of the fish and its presentation can't be faulted. That 'something extra' you expect from Stein comes in an over-generous portion of plump, juicy fillets encased in a perfect golden batter, served with steaming-hot, crispy-shelled chips, a slice of fresh lemon and garnish for detail.

Stein's Patisserie

Lanadwell Street, Padstow, Cornwall PL28 8AN (01841 533901/www.rickstein.com). **Open** Summer 10am-4pm Mon-Sat; 10am-3pm Sun. Winter times may vary. **Credit** (minimum £10) MC, V.
Handcrafted cakes, chocolates, truffles and luscious pastries will have you salivating at the window display – this is a shop it's almost impossible to walk past.

The Isles of Scilly

Sun, sand, splendid isolation –
and no passport required.

People tend to look blank when you say you've been to the Isles of Scilly. Many would be hard-pressed to find them on a map, and know very little beyond the name – which makes them feel they're not missing much. Well, the urge to keep it that way is a powerful one, because this immaculate archipelago is one of Britain's most distinctive and beguiling locations. Just 28 miles from Cornwall's Land's End, it's both unmistakably English and magically 'other' in mood, not least because of its association with King Arthur. According to legend, the Scillies are the remains of the Lost Land of Lyonesse, to which his men retreated after their leader's last fatal battle. Basking in the warmth of the Gulf Stream, the five inhabited islands – St Mary's, St Martin's, St Agnes, Tresco and Bryher – have been settled for at least 4,000 years, but are also surrounded by hundreds of unoccupied islets, rock formations, outcrops and ledges. Hardly surprising, then, that the surrounding waters are the watery graveyard of hundreds of shipwrecks.

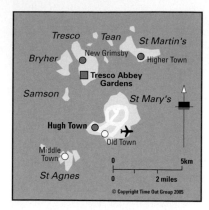

Tresco Tean St Martin's

Bryher New Grimsby Higher Town

Tresco Abbey Gardens

Samson St Mary's

Hugh Town

Old Town

Middle Town 0   5km

St Agnes 0   2 miles

© Copyright Time Out Group 2005

But it's not all treacherous seas and crashing foam. Within the ring of larger islands run channels that are positively Mediterranean in their brightness and hue. Once part of the Cornish mainland, and now home to a population of fewer than 3,000 (with the vast majority on St Mary's), the granite-bedded Scillies sit in clear and shallow waters, fringed by genuinely golden, even, white-sand beaches and heather-covered headlands. They regularly take the lion's share of British summertime sun (indeed, their name comes from the Roman appellation, *Sillinae Insulae*, or Sun Isles) and the temperate climate nurtures a fecundity of wild flowers and subtropical vegetation. However, the sea temperature remains bracing even in August. As sanctuary to seals, puffins, shearwaters and many migratory birds (see www.scilly birding.co.uk), it's not hard to see why, back in 1975, they were designated an Area of Outstanding Natural Beauty.

Today, carefully managed tourism dominates the economy, alongside fishing, low-impact farming, flower cultivation and small-scale family businesses – a far cry from the shipwreck-looting and smuggling inhabitants had to rely on in previous centuries. There is an abiding sense of the continuity of life here, evident in numerous prehistoric burial chambers, standing stones and settlements, as well as Roman and early Christian sites. And it's compounded by the fact that, except on St Mary's, there are practically no cars.

This creates a fundamentally different pace of life. There are no theme parks or nightclubs – you come to the Scillies because you want to do very little in quantifiable terms (walk, read, talk and, dare one say, reflect). Sure, there's great food, water sports (fabulous diving, especially) and atmospheric pubs, but the islands' main appeal are their beauty, stunning views and glorious isolation. They are also a great destination for children.

By any definition, these are small islands, so it's very hard to get lost. You can, however, still drift very pleasurably. All have general store provision and are entirely accessible on foot. St Mary's Boatmen's Association (01720 423999) runs a daily connecting service in high season (limited in winter) from St Mary's Quay to the 'off-islands', as the others are known, at 10.15am (10am for Tresco), and many independent launches operate between the islands – enquire at the tourist office.

St Mary's

Although it's only two and a half miles across at its widest point, St Mary's is the largest of the Isles. This, together with its full road system, makes it closer in feel to the mainland. Its centre, the bustling Hugh Town, is located on a narrow isthmus on the island's south-western side, flanked to the south by Porthcressa Beach, a pretty, sheltered bay, and to the north by the less appealing beach where the *Scillonian III* ferry from Penzance (Isles of Scilly Travel, 0845 710 5555, www.ios-travel.co.uk) and other passenger boats come and go.

The Isles of Scilly Museum (Church Street, Hugh Town, 01720 422337, www.iosmuseum.org) is an informative first stop, providing archaeological, cultural and historical insight. There's no escaping the thread of disaster and loss, primarily from shipwrecks, reflected in the museum's collections (at least 700 ships still slumber beneath the sea around the Scillies). Boating of another kind, however, now dominates the islands' waters. Gig racing, contrary to urban supposition, is not some kind of hard-run dash between concerts, but indigenous competitive rowing. This is the main sport in the islands, with races taking place on Wednesday (women) and Friday (men) evenings in summer from the uninhabited island of Samson to the quay at Hugh Town. The Scillies also host the annual World Pilot Gig Championships (www.pilotgigs.co.uk) over the first May bank holiday weekend, when you can cheer the crews on from passenger boats that follow each race.

Garrison Hill rises up at the end of the promontory west of Hugh Town, offering a perfect vantage point from which to view the archipelago. The hill is named after the fortifications built here in the 18th century, but the dominant structure is the 16th-century, eight-pointed Star Castle, built as a defence against the Spanish Armada, but now a hotel (*see p205*).

In the other direction, Telegraph Road leads from Hugh Town towards the island's interior; passing Carreg Dhu (pronounced 'Crake Dew', meaning Black Rocks; 01720 422404), a volunteer-run community garden whose one and a half acres house subtropical plants, shrubs and trees. It's

Accommodation	★★★
Food & drink	★★★
Nightlife	
Shopping	
Culture	
Sights	★
Scenery	★★★★★

open all year round, but call first if visiting off-season. Here also begins a pleasant trail around the island's dozen galleries, open studios and craft shops, making a comfortable circuit south to the Old Town (pick up the widely available leaflet map for details). A little further on is the Longstone Heritage Centre (01720 423770, closed mid Nov-early Mar), a local history museum, with restaurant and gift shop.

Heading east from Porthcressa Beach, a path loops south round the jagged rocks of Peninnis Head, passing intriguing geological formations such as the 'Kettle and Pans' close to Peninnis Lighthouse. Beyond is a sheltered beach at Old Town Bay; the straggling settlement here was the island's main port until the 17th century.

East of Old Town, near the airport, the small bay at Porth Hellick is overlooked by a monument to Rear Admiral Sir Cloudesley Shovell, who steered his fleet into the rocks off the island during a storm in 1707, resulting in the deaths of 2,000 men. A hoard of Spanish treasure was recovered from the wreck in the 1960s. Shovell's body was washed ashore the following day, and later buried at Westminster Abbey in London. A mile to the north, Pelistry Bay is one of the island's most secluded and picturesque beaches, which at low tide features a sand bar to Toll's Island. This is an idyllic spot, but on no account be tempted to take a swim at high tide, when the sand bar can cause dangerous rip tides.

Meanwhile, also near the airport, the last few years have seen the popular Camel Rock music festival plug in its amp over the August bank holiday. Local and mainland bands join forces against a spectacular marine backdrop.

Heading north-west round the coast you'll come to the most impressive prehistoric remains on the archipelago at Halangy Down, with stone huts, a burial chamber and a standing stone that are thought to date back to 2,000 BC.

Tresco

For some, visiting the Scillies' privately run and closely managed island estate will have echoes of *The Prisoner*. Others will appreciate the archipelago's unassailable selling point, therenowned subtropical Abbey Gardens (01720 424105, www.tresco.co.uk/the_abbey_garden,

gardens open daily; full facilities mid Feb-early Nov). Either way, there's no denying the unique atmosphere and ambience of this singular experiment in horticulture. When Augustus Smith arrived in 1834 to take on the lease of the islands (bringing much-needed educational and agricultural reforms), Tresco was, like the others in the group, exposed to fierce winds and far from sympathetic to the kind of vegetation now growing. To overcome this, Smith built tall windbreaks around the remains of the 12th-century Benedictine priory to shelter sloping terraces of varying warmth. Systematically laid out and then developed by generations of the family (who still lease Tresco from the Duchy of Cornwall), the gardens now boast over 20,000 plants from 80 countries, including stunning succulents, palms, cacti and eucalyptus. Italianate landscaping adds vistas and perspective, enhanced by sculptures, arbours and ornamentation. Shakespeare productions and concerts are staged here in summer. There's an on-site visitors' centre and included in the £8.50 admission price is access to Valhalla, a small collection of salvaged ships' figureheads.

But Tresco offers much more. At two miles by one, it's the largest off-island, and the only isle apart from St Mary's with a helicopter service. It has a varied topography, from the exquisite, and barely populated, beaches (Appletree and Pentle Bays) lining the eastern and western shores, peaceful lakes (the Abbey and Great Pools) and a secluded woodland interior to the north, and the heathered headland. It's here that the remains of two significant defensive fortifications can be found. The 1651 Cromwell's Castle at sea level, and the earlier King Charles's Castle above both look out on to the strait between Tresco and Bryher, which contains Hangman's Island, where 500 Royalists were said to have been executed in a single day during the Civil War.

Most settlement on Tresco runs across the island between Old and New Grimsby, the latter home to Gallery Tresco (01720 424925, www.tresco.co.uk/gallery), showcasing work by Cornish and Scillonian artists. Many of the attractive stone cottages are now part of the estate's expensive time-share scheme, meaning that there is little accommodation available

TOURIST INFORMATION

St Mary's
St Mary's Tourism, Hugh Town, St Mary's, Isles of Scilly TR21 0LL (01720 422536/www.simplyscilly.co.uk).
www.scillyonline.co.uk
www.tresco.co.uk
www.bryher-ios.co.uk

Great Bay Beach (above) on St Martin's and Cromwell's Castle on Tresco.

more spontaneously beyond the two impressively situated hotels. The New Inn (*see p204*) is the social heart of the island for visitors. Its bar, crafted from wreck-reclaimed timber, is the site of the biannual Real Ale festival in May and September.

Tresco has the most impressive general store (01720 422806) in the Scillies (stocking many deli goods) and the island can seem expensive, even exclusive, compared to its neighbours, but this shouldn't deter casual visitors from enjoying its stunning scenery.

Bryher

Each isle has its passionate supporters, but among the most fervent are those who back Bryher, including the 2003-2005 Children's Laureate, author Michael Morpurgo; the 1989 film *When the Whales*

Came, based on his novel, was both set and filmed here. Maybe this echoes the independent spirit of the residents themselves, but Bryher does feel like a place apart, even within Scilly. Just across from Tresco (until quite recently the two were connected and can still be reached on foot at very low tide), it takes its name from the Celtic for 'place of hills'; to the north are Shipman Head Down and Watch Hill; in the south Samson Hill.

It's a beautifully wild island, generally undeveloped and looking out on stunning rock fortresses such as Scilly Rock, Castle Bryher and Maiden Bower (Gweal Hill offers the best sunset vantage in the Scillies, while Samson Hill does the same for the whole archipelago). Also on the western shore lies Hell Bay, which delivers all that the name suggests when a storm's up. A little further south, the Hell Bay Hotel (*see p202*) is surely one of the most dramatically positioned in England, while artist Richard Pearce (01720 423665, www.rpearce.net) has a similarly startling outlook nearby from his Atlantic studio, a converted gig shed.

The considerably more sheltered east shore has fine beaches, such as Green Bay, and a friendly boat hire operation run by long-time islanders, the Bennetts (01720 422411). A circumambulation of Bryher takes little more than an hour but is wonderfully invigorating.

St Martin's

Flower growing is the main industry here, which accounts for the colourful fields, but the island has attracted a number of sensitive entrepreneurial operations, from the organic smallholding and café at Little Arthur Farm (*see p202*) to the award-winning St Martin's Bakery (Higher Town, 01720 423444, www.stmartinsbakery.co.uk), which also runs dedicated baking holidays. You'll find some stunning beaches and jaw-dropping views, in particular from St Martin's Head on the north-east coast. The island is sparsely inhabited and virtually pollution-free, making its waters among the best in the Scillies for scuba-diving. St Martin's Diving Services (Higher Town, St Martin's, 01720 422848, www.scilly diving.com) provides scuba and snorkelling equipment and tuition for all levels.

St Martin's main quay lies on Par Beach, a slice of pure white sand lapped by translucent waters. Just inland are Higher Town and St Martin's Vineyard (07712 295330, www.stmartinsvineyard.co.uk), where you can stock up on souvenir wine after one of the lively tours (Apr-Sept).

On St Martin's southern coast, Lawrence's Bay is a long, sandy beach that's a perfect spot for collecting shells or chilling out. Further west is Lower Town, from where you can enjoy terrific views across to the uninhabited islands of Teän and St Helen's (*see right*).

On the north coast, Great Bay and Little Bay are secluded spots worth seeking out. Climb across the boulders from the latter at low tide to wild White (pronounced 'Wit') Island to explore Underland Girt, a huge underground cave.

St Agnes

The craggy island of St Agnes is set apart from the trio of Bryher, Tresco and St Martin's, and is the most south-westerly community in the British Isles. The simple lifestyle is fully embraced here: bird- and butterfly-watching are about as energetic as it gets, and when the weather is fine most visitors are happy simply to admire the beautiful flowers and clear seas.

Boats land and leave from Porth Conger, on the north-west of the island, where you'll also find St Agnes's most attractive beach, Covean. When the tide is right you can walk across the sand bar from here to the tiny island of Gugh, where you'll find rocky outcrops and a Bronze Age standing stone and burial chamber.

Inland, St Agnes is dominated by the squat, white form of the Old Lighthouse, which dates from 1680, making it one of the oldest in England. Near to Periglis Cove on the western side of the island is a miniature stone maze, known as Troy Town Maze, which is said to have been laid out by the lighthouse keeper's bored son in 1729.

The wild heathland of the wonderfully named Wingletang Down takes up much of the south of St Agnes, edged on its western side by impressive coastal scenery and on its eastern side by Beady Pool. This inlet takes its name from a haul of beads from a wrecked 17th-century Venetian trader that was washed up on the shores. Above the cove, two enormous boulders indented with a three-foot deep basin form the Giant's Punchbowl, the most extraordinary rock formation on the Scillies.

The uninhabited islands

Samson, the largest uninhabited island, was populated until the 1850s, when poverty and the threat of eviction by Augustus Smith forced the islanders to resettle. A beautiful beach lies at the foot of North Hill, while significant prehistoric remains dot the slopes above. At low tide look out for the Samson Flats, the remains of ancient field systems that show up in the sands between Samson and Tresco. It was here that Prime Minister Harold Wilson, a lifelong devotee of the islands, once gave a shoreline press conference.

No trip to the Scillies is complete without a boat trip west to the extraordinary Bishop Rock lighthouse, perched on a rock base little wider than its own circumference. Now automated, it was a miracle of construction (after several late Victorian attempts) and surely saved many lives. The elaborate ball to celebrate its erection was held on the now desolate Rosevear to the east.

Island boat services regularly make half-day excursions out to Bishop Rock and the Western Rocks, as well as dropping passengers for picnics and walking on Samson, then collecting them after several hours. Boats can be hired privately for visits to the other islands mentioned.

Teän, just off St Martin's, has large, crescent-shaped sandy beaches, while, behind it, St Helen's has the ruins of a church that are worth exploring. On the other side of St Martin's, the milder Eastern Isles are home to puffins and grey seals, with fantastic beaches on Great Arthur and Great Ganilly. The best place to spot grey seals, puffins and shags is the Western Rocks beyond St Agnes, which bear the brunt of the Atlantic storms and have seen many shipwrecks.

WHERE TO STAY, EAT & DRINK

Due to the small supply of accommodation, it is essential to book in advance. Off-season (Nov-Feb), many visitor-oriented businesses close or reduce their provision. There are a number of decent, English Tourism Council-rated B&Bs on St Mary's, including Garrison House (01720 422972, www.garrisonhouse.co.uk, double £60-£76), in a Grade II-listed property. On St Agnes, the only option bar self-catering cottages and campsites is Covean Cottage (01720 422620, £104-£128 double), a lovely B&B a short walk through fields from the sea. For an extra £15 you get a great home-cooked dinner. Polreath Guesthouse & Tearoom on St Martin's (Higher Town, 01720 422046, www.polreath.com, £70-£100 double) offers two en suite bedrooms, both with sea views, in a pretty 19th-century farmhouse. Own-made cakes, filled baguettes and light lunches such as local crab salad or grilled Cornish goat's cheese on tapenade toast are served in the garden or conservatory.

Apart from St Mary's, which has a relatively wide range of places to eat and drink, dining options are restricted to the hotels, pubs and small cafés. On St Mary's a fab little licensed café and tea gardens can be found at Carn Vean (Pelistry, 01720 422462), while in Hugh Town, the Mermaid (01720 422701) is a popular drinking hole, ideal for soaking up the Scillonian atmosphere. The Vine Café (01720 423168) on Bryher is a wonderfully relaxed and welcoming place, serving great coffee, cakes and light lunches. A fixed-price, two-course evening meal (including a vegetarian option) is also available for £12, but you'll have to bring your own wine (no corkage). The Fraggle Rock (01720 422222) is Bryher's characterful waterside pub. It serves food at lunchtime and in the evening, including its renowned fish and chips, and – judging by the signed photos in the bar (Frank Bruno, George Cole and Bob Hoskins) – seems to have kept some celebs happy. Little Arthur Farm Café on St Martin's (01720 422457) offers excellent salads and filled rolls made with own-grown organic ingredients and freshly caught shellfish. During the tourist season, it opens two nights a week for its famous fish and chips – which earned the café a place in the finals of Radio 4's Food & Farming Awards 2004.

A fine spot to enjoy a beer and local pasties on St Agnes is the garden of the Turk's Head (01720 422434), overlooking the bay towards St Mary's. It's the most south-westerly pub in the British Isles.

The hotels listed below all have good restaurants; booking is essential for non-residents.

Hell Bay Hotel

Bryher, Isles of Scilly TR23 0PR (01720 422947/www.hellbay.co.uk). **Lunch served** noon-3pm, **dinner served** 6.30-9pm daily. **Main courses** (lunch) £9.50-£17. **Set dinner** £35 3 courses. **Rates** £260-£340 double (incl dinner). **Credit** MC, V.

In a spectacular position on the edge of the Atlantic, Hell Bay Hotel is a pioneer of contemporary (though not exactly cutting-edge) style in the Scillies. The relaxed, spacious suites, in soothing shades of blue and green, have a clean, New England feel, and most open on to private balconies or patios. All are equipped with VCRs and internet access. The hotel is dotted with works by locally connected artists such as Barbara Hepworth, Ivon Hitchens and Richard Pearce, whose studio is nearby. The menu in the restaurant is equally unfussy and makes liberal use of local resources: Hell Bay prawn cocktail, or seared scallops, new potato and bacon salad with chilli syrup, perhaps, followed by assiette of seafood, served with tagliatelle, tiger tail prawns and fish cream, or roast rack of lamb with mint jus, sage mash, roast parsnip and carrots. Desserts, such as chocolate truffle cake or meringue with strawberries and cream, tend towards the traditional. In the light, airy, wood-beamed bar, or the deck with its glorious views, you can feast on the likes of mussels or a local crab sandwich. Facilities include heated outdoor pool, gym, sauna and spa bath, and the hotel can set you up with water-sports hire. Bedrooms and restaurant are no-smoking.

Island Hotel

Old Grimsby, Tresco, Isles of Scilly TR24 0PU (01720 422883/www.tresco.co.uk). **Lunch served** noon-2.30pm, **dinner served** 7-9pm daily. **Main courses** (lunch) £6.50-£18. **Set menu** £37.50 3 courses. **Rates** £242-£428 double; £338-£582 suite double (incl dinner). **Credit** MC, V.

Situated right by the beach with breathtaking views, this swish, colonial-style hotel has a five-star location and excellent food. While its reception, bar and restaurant have all been given an airy, contemporary revamp, the accommodation could perhaps be a bit more deluxe given the hefty price tag. Having said that, the rooms are generously proportioned if somewhat dated in decor – some of the suites accommodating families of up to five – and many have balconies or terraces overlooking the sea. In the award-winning restaurant, sample chef Peter Hingston's light take on classical cuisine using seasonal, local ingredients. A typical menu includes seared Cornish scallops, black pudding and tarragon cream or Tresco and Bryher seafood mousse with a crab and caviar velouté to start, followed by steamed panache of seafood with saffron noodles and Thai nage, or pan-fried guinea fowl breast with Swiss rösti, confit vegetables and truffle sauce. Cornish burnt cream served with Viennese biscuits, or island fruit salad with Malibu granité rounds things off nicely. There is also a simpler menu of locally

The Isles of Scilly

Hell Bay Hotel
boasts
a stunning
location on
Bryher.

caught seafood, salads and sandwiches served on the bar's large decked terrace overlooking the sea. You can work off the meals on the tennis court, in the heated outdoor swimming pool, or on kayaks or windsurfers hired from the local sailing centre. Bedrooms and restaurant are no-smoking.

New Inn

New Grimsby, Tresco, Isles of Scilly TR24 0QQ (01720 422844/www.tresco.co.uk). **Lunch served** noon-2.30pm, **dinner served** 7-9pm daily. **Main courses** £7.95-£16. **Set dinner** £29 5 courses. **Rates** £144-£218 double (incl dinner). **Credit** MC, V.

Tresco's only pub is the 'cheaper' option for accommodation on the island. Rooms are upmarket (but stuck in a 1980s floral timewarp), and there's a heated outdoor pool. The evening menu in the restaurant features hearty dishes with an imaginative, contemporary bent. A typical meal might start with Cornish smoked salmon, moving on to oven-baked sea bass with flageolet bean cassoulet and basil butter sauce, or rack of lamb stuffed with aubergine caviar, wild mushroom and baby onions, and culminating in pistachio and strawberry crème brûlée or a selection of Cornish cheeses. In the bar – panelled with shipwreck-salvaged wood – and its attractive subtropical garden, a range of fresh fish dishes as well as traditional and more inventive pub meals is available. Bedrooms and restaurant are no-smoking.

St Martin's on the Isle Hotel

St Martin's, Isles of Scilly TR25 0QW (01720 422090/www.stmartinshotel.co.uk). **Lunch served** *Bar* phone for details. **Dinner served** *Restaurant* 7-9pm. **Dinner** approx £45 per person. **Rates** £260-£300 double (incl dinner); £320-£340 family room; £370-£410 suite. **Credit** MC, V.

The posh option on St Martin's was built in the late 1980s, overlooking gardens and, beyond, a quay and sandy beaches. Many of the rooms have enviable sea views, but they are otherwise pretty characterless. Several large rooms with extra beds are geared towards families. The hotel's main

Colonial-style accommodation and fab food at Island Hotel on Tresco.

draws are its indoor swimming pool and award-winning food in the restaurant. At time of writing, a new chef was poised to take the reins, so it remains to be seen whether there will be significant changes to a dinner menu including such dishes as ballotine of foie gras with caramelised apple and balsamic jelly (a starter) or honey-roast duck with pak choi and a spiced lemongrass jus (a main). Desserts, such as Calvados parfait with melon salad and lime coulis, have an appealingly light touch. Request the special shellfish menu, which makes the most of the local crab and lobster catch (orders 24 hours in advance, minimum two people). Sandwiches, soups and other lunch dishes are served in the bar, and there are also plans to open a bistro. It's worth noting that while many of the staff are charming, we encountered unnecessary rudeness from some quarters.

Star Castle Hotel

St Mary's, Isles of Scilly TR21 0JA (01720 422317/www.star-castle.co.uk). **Lunch served** noon-2pm, **dinner served** 6.30-8.30pm daily.

Main courses (lunch) £7-£10. **Set dinner** £32.50 5 courses. **Rates** £106-£278 double (incl dinner). **Credit** AmEx, MC, V.

This fortified, granite Elizabethan castle on Garrison Hill, built in the shape of an eight-cornered star, is an atmospheric place to stay – try to get a room in the main hotel rather than the modern annexes that make up the bulk of accommodation. The prevailing style is understated traditional; a couple of the eight castle rooms have two-poster beds. There are two on-site restaurants – one is in the original, stone-walled officers' mess room; the other, only open in summer and in a bright conservatory, specialises in seafood. A typical meal in the former might begin with such hearty fare as pan-fried pheasant breast with herbs and balsamic vinegar on a bed of winter leaves, or a lighter tomato, artichoke, roast pepper and pesto salad. Traditionally slanted mains suit the dining room's pedigree: oven-braised lamb shank on fondant potato with redcurrant sauce, perhaps, or poached supreme of salmon on a white wine, grape and saffron cream. There is also an indoor pool and grass tennis courts.

Orford to Southwold

An intriguing, very English coastline.

Suffolk has always retained its own distinct identity and a subtle sense of 'otherness'. Nowhere in the county is this more true than along the coast. An uneasy juxtaposition of the cosy and the bleak, the cultivated and the wild, the coast along the North Sea doesn't offer the sheltered sandy coves of the English Channel. The shoreline here is predominantly pebbly and the sea icy. Intrepid sunbathers huddle behind striped windbreaks, and walkers are buffeted by stiff offshore breezes.

It's perfect Barbara Vine territory and no wonder that Ruth Rendell's darker alter ego has set several of her claustrophobic crime novels in the county. The area's brooding, atmospheric side is probably least noticeable during the height of the summer, when crowds frolic on Southwold's shingle, and music lovers attend the Proms season at Snape Maltings. But if you ever happen to be in, say, Orford, on a biting winter's day, walking in the shadow of the commanding castle keep, past the fulminating fug of the blackened smokehouse and down to the quayside, as the mist rolls slowly and silently in from the River Alde, you'll know you're somewhere pretty special.

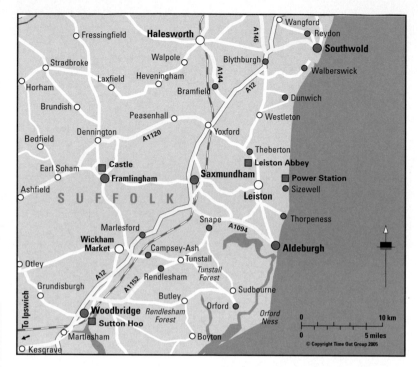

The map shows locations including: Fressingfield, Halesworth, Wangford, Reydon, Southwold, Stradbroke, Walpole, Blythburgh, Walberswick, Laxfield, Heveningham, Horham, Bramfield, Brundish, Peasenhall, Westleton, Dunwich, Bedfield, Dennington, Yoxford, Theberton, Earl Soham, Castle, Framlingham, Saxmundham, Leiston Abbey, Power Station, Sizewell, Ashfield, Leiston, SUFFOLK, Snape, Thorpeness, Marlesford, Wickham Market, Campsey-Ash, Aldeburgh, Otley, Tunstall, Tunstall Forest, Grundisburgh, Rendlesham, Sudbourne, Butley, Orford, Woodbridge, Rendlesham Forest, Sutton Hoo, Orford Ness, Martlesham, Boyton, Kesgrave, To Ipswich

© Copyright Time Out Group 2005

A shore thing

There's plenty to explore along the Suffolk coast. Woodbridge, a few miles north-east of Ipswich, may be inland now, but this lively one-time shipbuilding port makes an agreeable introduction to the area. Stretching back up a hill from the River Deben, you'll find a scattering of minor sights (Woodbridge Tide Mill, the Suffolk Horse Museum, Woodbridge Museum), plus antiques shops, pubs and restaurants. St Mary's Parish Church is home to the heaviest bells in Suffolk as well as the Deben Millennium Frieze – a 20-foot embroidered depiction of Woodbridge history over the past 2,000 years. Near Woodbridge, the 12th-century Framlingham Castle (Framlingham, 01728 724189, www.english-heritage.org.uk) has its walls but no keep. It also has 13 towers linked together by a walkway and overlooking an impressive moat.

On the opposite bank of the river from the town is the site of the most celebrated archaeological find made in Britain, Sutton Hoo (01394 389700, www.nationaltrust. org.uk/places/suttonhoo) – the fabulous treasure-stuffed ship of a seventh-century East Anglian king. The burial mounds were filled in and most of the treasure is now in the British Museum, but some pieces are on display in the exhibition centre.

Between Woodbridge and the coast, the wind-whipped Rendlesham and Tunstall forests provide a barrier that only adds to the invigorating feeling of isolation in little Orford. Overlooked by the keep of 12th-century Orford Castle (01394 450472, www.english-heritage.org.uk), the place offers walking, eating and drinking, and the opportunity to contemplate the immense expanse of Orford Ness (access information & ferry crossing 01394 450057, www. nationaltrust.org.uk/orfordness), the largest vegetated shingle spit in Europe and a unique habitat for plants and birds. In the 12th century the then-nascent shingle spit provided a sheltered harbour for Orford. Unfortunately, it wouldn't stop growing and it now all but cuts the village off from the sea. Boat trips run from the quay. Pick up picnic supplies from Richardson's Smokehouse (Bakers Lane, 01394 450103) or the shop attached to the Butley Orford Oysterage (Market Hill, 01394 450277, www.butleyorford oysterage.co.uk), and take a quick look at the Norman church of St Bartholomew – there's a fine font. Upstairs at the Orford Craft Shop (Front Street, 01394 450678, www. orford.org.uk) you'll find the intriguing 'Suffolk Underwater Studies'.

Accommodation	★★★
Food & drink	★★★
Nightlife	
Shopping	★
Culture	★★★
Sights	★★
Scenery	★★★★

Aldeburgh to Southwold

The next major settlement on the coast heading north is Aldeburgh. It's a classy place and big enough to retain a sense of its own identity regardless of the tourists who flock here on summer weekends. The carnival in August, which ends with a torchlit procession and fireworks on the beach, is a great occasion. The wide high street, which runs parallel to the sea, is an agreeable mix of the old-fashioned (there's a traditional butcher, fishmonger, greengrocer and baker) and the urbane. Two branches of Palmer & Burnett sell funky gifts and homeware at No.46 and No.138 and there are a couple of excellent delis: 152 – at No.152 (01728 454594, www.152aldeburgh.co.uk) – and the Aldeburgh Food Hall at No.183 (01728 454535). Two branches of Collen & Clare (25 Market Place and 33 High Street, 01502 724823, www.collenandclare.co.uk) stock a good range of clothing, lingerie and accessories from the likes of Johnny Loves Rosie and Pringle.

Constant erosion of the coastline means that the current seafront is something of a jumble – it was never meant to face the ocean. The oldest building in town is here – the 16th-century moot hall – as is a shiny modern lifeboat station and a popular boating pond. If you don't fancy eating at one of the town's number of excellent restaurants, then why not join the High Street queues at the excellent Aldeburgh Fish & Chip Shop (226 High Street, 01728 452250) or the Golden Galleon (see p218) and then take your booty on to the pebbly beach.

Heading back on to the A12 to Southwold, tiny Saxmundham seems to have more ironmongers than anything else, but is also home to Palmer & Burnett's third branch (30 High Street, 01728 603016) as well as the lovely Bell (31 High Street, 01728 602331), with rooms and food as well as Adnams ales. If you take the B1122 towards Southwold, you'll drive through the little village of Theberton (two miles north of Leiston). Its church, St Peter's, is worth a visit: it has a lovely round tower and thatched roof, and the entrance porch holds the remains of a Zeppelin airship that crashed nearby in 1917. Inside, the arches are beautifully decorated; they were painted during the Victorian age to emulate how a church would have looked before the Reformation. Thorpeness, a couple of miles north of Aldeburgh, is a surreal little place. With rows of black-boarded and half-timbered houses, it has the air of a Tudor theme village. The entire settlement was dreamed up as a fashionable resort by GS Ogilvie when he bought the Sizewell estate in 1910. Go for a row on the Meare, dug by hand by navvies, and sprinkled with 20 islands named after characters in *Peter Pan* in honour of Ogilvie's friend JM Barrie. Ogilvie also created a well and used a windmill to pump water to a tank on top of an 87-foot tower, which he disguised as an overgrown house, known as the 'House in the Clouds'. This extraordinary folly is inhabited so unfortunately cannot be visited, unlike the windmill (01394 384948, www.suffolkcoastandheaths.org). The Dolphin Inn (Peace Place, 01728 454994), which has rooms and a sizeable restaurant area, is good for refreshments.

A little further up the coast is the area's most controversial presence: Sizewell twin nuclear power stations. Apart from the legion of pylons striding across the coastal flats, the power stations are a low-key presence. The huge white dome of Sizewell B, the UK's only pressurised water reactor, is the most distinctive feature along this coast. There's a moderately popular beach by the power station for the truly blithe.

For whom the bell tolls

It seems hard to imagine that tiny Dunwich was once a thriving port. In the early Middle Ages up to 5,000 people lived within its walls, trading with the Baltic, Iceland, France and the Low Countries. Monasteries, more than a dozen churches, hospitals, palaces and even a mint reflected the town's role as a busy trading port and one of England's major shipbuilding towns. Continual coastal erosion, however, exacerbated by a three-day storm in 1286, meant that by the 16th century trade – along with the harbour – had dried up and medieval houses and churches dropped slowly but surely over the crumbling cliffs.

TOURIST INFORMATION

Aldeburgh
152 High Street, Aldeburgh, Suffolk IP15 5AQ (01728 453637/www. suffolkcoastal.gov.uk/leisure).
Southwold
69 High Street, Southwold, Suffolk IP18 6DS (01502 724729/www. visit-southwold.co.uk).
Woodbridge
Station Buildings, Woodbridge, Suffolk IP12 4AJ (01394 382240/ www.suffolkcoastal.gov.uk).

Snape, home to Snape Maltings Concert Hall, crafts and gift shops, a restaurant and tea room, and the starting point for several glorious walks.

On stormy nights it's said that you can hear the old church bells tolling beneath the waves. Little evidence of Dunwich's former glory now remains beyond the sparse ruins of Greyfriars Abbey and the salvaged remains of All Saints church and leper chapel in the churchyard of St James's. Don't miss the superb Dunwich Museum (St James Street, 01728 648796, closed Nov-Feb), which tells the story of this strange place and, together with a few cottages, a good pub (the Ship) and a seaside café, is all that remains of the town.

The northern extent of this area is marked by the cliff-top town of Southwold. It's the biggest 'resort' on this stretch of coast, and although during high season holidaymakers throng the pier (reopened in 2002 and housing a wonderfully retro amusement arcade) and picnic outside the brightly painted beach huts that stretch along the promenade, the picturesque Georgian town generally gets on with its own life. The most dominant force in Southwold is the estimable Adnams Brewery, which owns the town's best two hotels (the Crown and the Swan). There are

few greater Southwold pleasures than supping an Adnams brew.

Another must is the 20-minute walk along the seafront or cross-country to the ferry over the River Blyth to Walberswick. This somnolent little village was once home to painter Philip Wilson Steer and, in addition to the excellent Bell Inn, boasts a curious church-within-a-church. In the Middle Ages Walberswick was a sizeable port, and the original, 15th-century St Andrew's was to be a mighty church to reflect the status of the town. But its fortunes declined before the church was finished and much of it was dismantled to build the much smaller church that lies within the older building's ruins. Another notable church close by is at Blythburgh, a tiny village unfortunately bisected by the A12. The huge, light-suffused Holy Trinity is known as the 'Cathedral of the Marshes'. Its hammer-beam roof is decorated with 12 glorious painted angels, which probably escaped decapitation by iconoclastic puritans in the 17th century thanks to their inaccessibility. Carvings of the seven deadly sins adorn the pew ends.

The Trinity restaurant at the Crown & Castle – enthusiastic purveyors of local produce.

WHERE TO STAY

Demand for accommodation far outstrips supply on this part of the Suffolk coast, so book as far in advance as possible. Saxmundham's Bell Hotel (31 High Street, Saxmundham, IP17 1AF, 01728 602331), which dates back to the 17th century, has ten modest, reasonably priced rooms (£45-£65 including continental breakfast) and is well located for Aldeburgh's overspill during the festival at Snape Maltings.

The Randolph in Reydon (Wangford Road, Reydon, IP18 6PZ, 01502 723603/ www.therandolph.co.uk) currently has ten rooms, though at the time of writing it's undergoing refurbishment and more may be added (£55-£60 single, £65-£105 double including full English breakfast). Both places have a bar and decent restaurant attached. The Crown Hotel (Quay Street, The Thoroughfare, Woodbridge, IP12 1AD, 01394 384242/www.old english.co.uk) is right in the centre of Woodbridge and offers 21 well-furnished rooms (£75 single, from £95 double, including full English breakfast) as well as a cosy bar and restaurant (£12.95 for three courses).

Acton Lodge

18 South Green, Southwold, Suffolk IP18 6HB (01502 723217/www.southwold.ws/actonlodge). **Rates** £65-£80 double. **No credit cards.**
John and Brenda Smith have been running this popular B&B since 1991. It's a substantial villa on the edge of South Green with views over the sea or marshes towards Walberswick and Dunwich. Inside, many of the original features – marble fireplaces and stripped floors – have been carefully preserved, and rooms are spacious and well appointed. Breakfasts are notable, and include own-made fish cakes, bread and jams, locally caught and smoked haddock, kippers and bloaters, as well as fresh fruit and cereals.

Bell Inn

Ferry Road, Walberswick, Suffolk IP18 6TN (01502 723109/www.blythweb.co.uk/bellinn). **Rates** £75-£100 double; £100-£140 family room. **Credit** MC, V.
If you want to avoid the London crowds of nearby Southwold and Aldeburgh, then head for the tiny, waterside village of Walberswick and the 600-year-old Bell Inn. Charming and rambling, with brick exterior and beamed interior, the Bell has six rooms, sea views and above-average pub

Swan Hotel

grub. Rooms are plain but have en suite bathrooms and tea- and coffee-making facilities, and there's a family room for those who want to avoid the hurly-burly of the popular bar.

Crown & Castle
Orford, Woodbridge, Suffolk IP12 2LJ (01394 450205/www.crownandcastle.co.uk). **Rates** £320-£420 double; £450 family (prices cover obligatory 2-night stay). **Credit** MC, V.
It's well worth booking the two months in advance that are necessary to secure a place at this sophisticated and romantic inn, run by David and (food writer) Ruth Watson. Bedrooms on the first floor of the main building are kitted out in cool, light paints and fabrics, with big comfy beds, and power showers in the bathrooms. Those staying in the garden rooms miss the spectacular views of the castle and Orford Ness but have a little patio area that might suit guests with children and dogs better. For the Trinity Bistro, *see p219*.

Crown Hotel
90 High Street, Southwold, Suffolk IP18 6DP (01502 722275/www.adnams.co.uk). **Rates** £116-£128 double; £156-£238 suite; £161-£216 family room. **Credit** MC, V.
The excellent Crown is pub, wine bar, restaurant and small hotel in one. It started life as a humble posting inn called the Nag's Head. Now owned and restored in pastel hues by Adnams, it's a smaller and cheaper sibling to the Swan (*see below*). There are 14 simply decorated but fully equipped rooms, some with exposed beams. Midweek break offers include meals in the restaurant (phone for details).

Dunburgh
28 North Parade, Southwold, Suffolk IP18 6LT (01502 723253/www.southwold.ws/dunburgh). **Rates** £75-£90 double. **No credit cards.**
A friendly B&B, well located on a corner site overlooking the seafront and Southwold's newly renovated pier. All rooms have TV, CD player and hairdryer, and decoration has a Victorian theme. Go for the double room with four-poster and balcony overlooking the sea.

Ocean House
25 Crag Path, Aldeburgh, Suffolk IP15 5BS (01728 452094). **Rates** £70-£75 double. **No credit cards.**
Wonderfully situated overlooking the pebbly beach, Ocean House is a mid Victorian monolith that has been carefully restored to its original condition by the welcoming Phil and Juliet Brereton. Bedrooms have superb views out over the sea, and there's a games room in the basement. Ask for one of the first floor rooms at the front. You'll need to book months in advance to secure a spring or summer weekend, though. Four of the rooms are available for self-catering; phone for details.

Old Rectory
Station Road, Campsea Ashe, Suffolk IP13 0PU (01728 746524/www.theoldrectorysuffolk. com). **Rates** £85-£110 double. **Credit** MC, V.
An elegant Georgian house in the tiny inland village of Campsea Ashe near Woodbridge, the Old Rectory has just eight rooms but bags of character. Polished wood, pale furnishings and rugs all add to the tasteful impression. The excellent, no-choice dinner (three courses for £24) is particularly recommended (compulsory if staying on a Saturday night).

Swan Hotel
Market Place, Southwold, Suffolk IP18 6EG (01502 722186/www.adnams.co.uk). **Rates** £136-£176 double; £196-£206 suite. **Credit** MC, V.
A more expensive alternative to the Crown (*see above*), the self-assured Swan has long been the hub of Southwold social life. There are 26 bedrooms in the main hotel and a further 17 garden rooms, all decorated in an understated version of country house style. Bathrooms, though small, are modern and well equipped. We noticed the Swan was looking a little rougher around the edges on our last visit, but service remains great and the sea views (if you get a front bedroom) are superb. Continental breakfast is available in your room, or you can opt for the superior full English version served in the handsome dining room overlooking Southwold's market place.

Wentworth Hotel
Wentworth Road, Aldeburgh, Suffolk IP15 5BD (01728 452312/www.wentworth-aldeburgh.com). **Rates** £129-£188 double; £10 each additional child in parents' room. **Credit** AmEx, DC, MC, V.
The traditional and comfortable Wentworth faces the sea at the northern edge of town. A sizeable hotel with 30 well-appointed bedrooms (and an additional seven over the road in Darfield House) all cheerfully decorated, it also features a sunken terrace (good for drinks on sunny days), cosy lounges (one with a view of the sea), a restaurant and a bar.

WHERE TO EAT & DRINK
The best pubs in Southwold are those that allow alfresco spillover during fine weather. Try the Lord Nelson, between Market Hill and the sea (you can take your pint of Adnams to the seafront), or the Red Lion, where drinkers chill out on South Green. Southwold's Lighthouse restaurant (77 High Street, 01728 453377) offers reasonably priced food, with dishes such as crayfish and dolcelatte salad (£5.95).

In Woodbridge, the Old Bell & Steelyard on New Street serves up a decent pint and Peter's steak and ale pie (£7.50). The King's Head on Market Hill (01394

THE BATTLE OF BRITTEN

Few people are more associated with their native region than Benjamin Britten is with the Suffolk coast. Born in Lowestoft in 1913, he moved with the celebrated tenor (and his lifelong partner) Peter Pears to Aldeburgh in 1947. Many of his works are set in Suffolk, but his most famous legacy to the region is the Aldeburgh Festival (actually held in Snape), one of the world's leading classical music and opera festivals, founded by Britten, Pears and producer and librettist Eric Crozier.

But memorialising Suffolk's most famous son has proved a controversial business. Maggi Hambling's giant scallop sculpture (*see above*), dedicated to Britten, has been the talk of this quiet seaside town, and sadly the talk has been negative, to say the least. Displayed on Aldeburgh's beach, it has been criticised for blighting the serenity of the beach and vandalised twice, amid rumours that it is to be removed altogether.

One might expect this 'monstrous atrocity' to be centre stage on Aldeburgh's shingle beach. But there's no immediate sign of it. In fact, it's amazing that such an offensive object isn't easier to find. The beach's most outstanding features appear to be the large numbers of dog walkers, not to mention the wonderful sunsets that spread across an uninterrupted horizon.

The sculpture – four tonnes of burnished steel that has been cut and moulded into a giant open scallop – lies on the furthermost edge of the beach, but in spite of its position, it draws a steady stream of visitors who can't help but touch it, lie against it or clamber on top of it.

One local, asked why the scallop was so unloved, said simply: 'It would be better in Snape, even Thorpeness.' In fact, Hambling's shell appears to be as much an outsider as Britten himself was – his presence in the town is scarcely acknowledged despite the fact that he lies in the graveyard here. Hambling cut some words (from Britten's opera *Peter Grimes*) into the shell which – in the light of the sculpture's controversy – seem poignantly apt: 'I hear those voices that will not be drowned.'

Aldeburgh Festival
Snape Maltings Concert Hall, Snape, Suffolk IP17 1SP (box office 01728 687110/www.aldeburgh.co.uk). Tickets vary; phone to check.
Date June. **Credit** MC, V.

387750) offers pub grub in either the bar or the no-smoking dining room and serves a lovely pint of Suffolk cider.

In Snape, pubs that are worth a visit include the Crown Inn (Bridge Road, 01728 688324), which is good for food as well as accommodation, and the Golden Key (Priory Road, 01728 688510). In Aldeburgh the pick of the bunch is the tiny, friendly, locals-packed White Hart on the High Street. And don't miss out on a trip to the superb and well-positioned Bell Inn (*see p214*) in pretty Walberswick.

Butley-Orford Oysterage

Market Hill, Orford, Suffolk IP12 2LH (01394 450277/www.butleyorfordoysterage.co.uk). **Lunch served** noon-2.15pm daily. **Dinner served** *Apr-Oct* 6.30-9pm Mon-Fri, Sun; 6-9pm Sat. *Nov-Mar* 6.30-9pm Fri; 6-9pm Sat. **Main courses** £7-£14.50. **Credit** MC, V.
Feeling very much like a blast from seasides past, the Oysterage is not just a restaurant but also a shop, smoking house and HQ of a tiny fleet of fishing boats. From the freshest of local catches comes skate, sole, herring or sprats, and, of course, oysters from the creek, all of which made their way to the tables in the tiny, stripped-down dining room with the minimum of fuss or intervention. Most dishes from the blackboard menu are served simply, with bread and butter, new potatoes or a side salad.

Farmcafe

Main Road (A12), Marlesford, Suffolk IP13 0AG (01728 747717/www.farmcafe.co.uk). **Meals served** *Summer* 7am-5pm daily. *Winter* 7am-3pm Mon-Fri; 7am-4pm Sat, Sun. **Main courses** £5.40-£7.90. **Credit** MC, V.
Looks can be deceiving. Many driving past this unprepossessing cream-coloured building set beside the A12 at Marlesford would not give it a second glance. Step inside, though, and you find a simple, compact space that leads on to a terrace protected against the elements, Parisian-style, by plastic walls and heaters, with chunky tables, modern art, stone floors and lots of touristy leaflets and local events posters.

Flora Tearooms

The Beach, Dunwich, Suffolk IP17 3DR (01728 648433). **Meals served** *Mar-Nov* 11am-5pm daily. **Main courses** £5-£5.50. **Unlicensed**. **Corkage** no charge. **Credit** MC, V.
The black, weatherboarded, shed-like building looks straight on to the beach car park, and with its serried rows of plain tables inside and picnic sets outside, there is no denying that the Flora Tearooms is extremely basic. But it has been battering for day trippers and holiday makers for years, touting a no-frills fish and chips menu of lemon sole, cod, haddock and plaice, with a few modern offerings like whole grilled brill or skate.

Galley

21 Market Hill, Woodbridge, Suffolk IP12 4LX (01394 380055/www.galley.uk.com). **Lunch served** noon-2pm Tue-Sun. **Dinner served** 6-10pm Tue-Sat. **Main courses** £14.95-£21.95. **Credit** MC, V.
In the centre of Woodbridge the brightly painted (fuschia pink and turquoise) Galley serves modern food with the odd twist. Starters include the likes of crispy braised belly of pork with pickled carrot and ginger, and can be followed with grilled seabass fillets with flaked almonds and pomegranate. Light oak tables look out on to the square and service is charming.

Golden Galleon

137 High Street, Aldeburgh, Suffolk IP15 5AR (01728 454685). **Lunch served** noon-2pm Mon-Fri; noon-2.30pm Sat. **Dinner served** 5-8pm Mon-Wed; 4.30-8pm Fri, Sat. **Meals served** noon-6pm Sun. **Main courses** £5.50-£7.50. **No credit cards**.
If you prefer your fish and chips sitting at a table, then the upper-deck diner of the Golden Galleon is the place to go in Aldeburgh. Fresh local fish and chips with a good range of additional extras come from the fish shop downstairs and are served in a light and modern diner.

Harbour Inn

Black Shore, Southwold, Suffolk IP18 6TA (01502 722381). **Open** 11am-11pm Mon-Sat; noon-10.30pm Sun. **Lunch served** noon-2.30pm, **dinner served** 6-9pm daily. **Main courses** £8-£11. **Credit** MC, V.
After a long day crabbing or walking against the North Sea winds that whip along the beach, this comfortable pub with atmospheric clutter-filled rooms provides an opportunity to indulge in some comfort eating. Portions are large.

Lighthouse

77 High Street, Aldeburgh, Suffolk IP15 5AU (01728 453377/www.thelighthouse restaurant.co.uk). **Lunch served** noon-2pm Mon-Fri; noon-2.30pm Sat, Sun. **Dinner served** 6.30-10pm daily. **Main courses** £8.50-£14.75. **Credit** AmEx, MC, V.
Sara Fox and Peter Hill's culinary beacon opposite Aldeburgh's cinema is the lynchpin of the town's impressive foodie scene. Sara runs the local cookery school and the couple have recently opened the Munchies café further up the High Street (No.163, 01728 454566), serving tea, coffee and all-day snacks. So the Lighthouse can now concentrate on serving its daily-changing lunch, dinner and 'cinema' menus. Most of the food comes from the sea, and it is enticingly unpretentious: dressed Cromer crab with herb mayonnaise, say, or potted Norfolk shrimps with toast and lemon, followed by haddock fillet in beer batter with chips, crushed peas and tartare sauce, or perhaps a whole lobster with herb mayonnaise and chips.

Mark's Fish Shop

32 High Street, Southwold, Suffolk IP18 6AE (01502 723585). **Lunch served** 11.45am-1.30pm Tue-Fri; 11.45am-2pm Sat. **Dinner served** 5-7pm Tue-Thur; 5-8pm Fri, Sat. **Main courses** £3.50-£6.40. **No credit cards.**

An unpretentious fish and chip shop cum cosy licensed restaurant. Formica-topped tables and moulded seats are fixed in a small space that is bedecked with fishing nets, evocative black-and-white photos, paintings and toy fish. Despite sounding cheesy, they provide a certain charm.

152

152 High Street, Aldeburgh, Suffolk IP15 5AX (01728 454594/www.152aldeburgh.co.uk). **Lunch served** noon-3pm, **dinner served** 6-10pm daily. **Main courses** £10.50-£17. **Credit** AmEx, MC, V.

Under new ownership, 152 is still one of the best and most stylish places to eat in Aldeburgh. Tastefully refurbished in aubergine and cream, and close to the beach, the restaurant is a relaxing place. The emphasis is on high-quality local produce, especially fish and seafood (roast cod with water cress, saffron mash and red pepper pesto, £12.50).

Queen's Head

The Street, Bramfield, Suffolk IP19 9HT (01986 784214/www.queensheadbramfield. co.uk). **Lunch served** noon-2pm daily. **Dinner served** 6.30-10pm Mon-Sat; 7-9pm Sun. **Main courses** £5.95-£14.95. **Credit** AmEx, MC, V.

Overlooked by an unusual, circular, 12th-century flint church tower, this pub's garden has plenty of seating for alfresco dining, or you may prefer to sit in the large open hall with its massive brick fireplace or the cosy no-smoking snug. Adnams provides the ale and wines (£11.50-£20), and much is made of the use of organic local ingredients.

Ship

St James Street, Dunwich, Suffolk IP17 3DT (01728 648219). **Lunch served** noon-3pm, **dinner served** 6-9pm Mon-Fri. **Meals served** noon-10pm Sat, Sun. **Main courses** £7.95-£12. **Rates** £50-£68 double; £68-£98 family. **Credit** MC, V.

The attractions of modern-day Dunwich are bracing walks along gorse-and-heather-topped cliffs, a wide expanse of pebbly beach, the nearby RSPB reserve at Minsmere and fish and chips – it's the mainstay of menus both here at the Ship and at the Flora Tearooms on the beach (*see p218*).

Trinity Bistro

Crown & Castle Hotel, Orford, Suffolk IP12 2LJ (01394 450205/www.crownandcastle. co.uk). **Lunch served** noon-2pm daily. **Dinner served** *Apr-Oct* 7-9pm daily; *Nov-Mar* 7-9pm Mon-Sat. **Main courses** £9.50-£18. **Rates** £90-£145. **Credit** MC, V.

Combining a relaxed vibe with a huge dollop of urban chic, this restaurant glows with the attention to detail lavished on it. The menu, like the rest of the operation, is flexible and keen to please. The majority of the ingredients are locally produced, including fish from the local smokehouse. There's properly hung sirloin steak and chips, or a half pint of Orford-smoked prawns with spicy mayonnaise. The wine list is a model of its kind, with around 20 choices by the glass. Plus there's a new bar, a terrace for summer dining and a log fire in winter.

Southwold

Bury St Edmunds to Lavenham

A rural backwater that repays exploration.

It may be an unkind thing to say, but it's easy to understand why a lot of people pass inland Suffolk by, dismissing it as a backwater. To all intents and purposes, it's the bit that most holidaymakers drive through on the way to somewhere else. Look a little closer though, and you wonder whether this is a deliberate image created by those who prefer to keep the charms of this part of the country under tight wraps. It may not hold the obvious attractions of its neighbours – Constable country to the south, the Norfolk Broads to the north, Suffolk's rather wonderful windswept coastal towns to the east and Cambridge to the west – but the absence of attraction-seekers makes it all the more appealing to the discerning visitor.

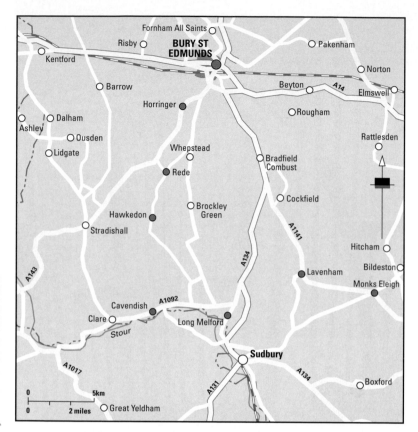

The area's very English rolling landscape is characterised by narrow, twisting roads, isolated farms, small hamlets and patches of woodland, which means you can go for hours without seeing anyone. There are signs of life – the occasional deer, a hare and plenty of pheasants – and the odd distant gunshot is a reminder that you're not entirely alone. It's perfect walking and cycling territory – especially for those not hugely enamoured of uphill slogs; even the laziest legs can cope with this landscape. You could compare it with the Cotswolds in some respects – but it's not as twee and it's more accessible from much of the country, especially London and the south.

Jigsaw country

The villages here are quiet, unassuming places: at the heart of many is a good pub; impressive 'wool churches', testament to Suffolk's medieval wool-trade wealth, are common too. A few are just extraordinarily pretty, with a handful of pert, primped cottages round a chocolate box village green. Away from Lavenham

and Bury St Edmunds, A-roads naturally draw you towards Cavendish and Long Melford, if not for their rich pickings in antiques shops, then certainly for their good restaurants.

Leaving the beaten track brings surprises in the shape of thatched cottages in bright pinks and yellows. The multicoloured village of Hartest, for example, is set in as big a valley as you're likely to find in this part of the world; Hawkedon, on the other hand, feels like it's on top of the world, but then its nearest neighbour is Rede, at 420 feet, the highest village in Suffolk.

TOURIST INFORMATION

Bury St Edmunds
6 Angel Hill, Bury St Edmunds,
Suffolk IP33 1UZ (01284 764667/
www.stedmundsbury.gov.uk).
Lavenham
Lady Street, Market Place, Lavenham,
Suffolk CO10 9RA (01787 248207/
www.lavenham.co.uk).

Accommodation	★★★
Food & drink	★★★
Nightlife	
Shopping	★
Culture	★
Sights	★
Scenery	★★★

These are places where history seems to ooze from soil and stone; even the place names have a historical resonance: Latin, Saxon, Scandinavian and Norman French tongues inform the names of whole clusters of villages. The Romans have left their mark in roads and numerous archaeological sites along the routes; the Saxon and, especially, Norman influence can be seen in ruined castles and churches. The Domesday Book recounts numerous manors and holdings in Suffolk and there is no question that it was a hugely rich and powerful area for centuries, right up until the Industrial Revolution. The wealth that was enjoyed here during the Middle Ages, when Suffolk was the centre of the woollen cloth-making trade, is manifest in churches such as those at Long Melford and Lavenham. The splendour of Elizabethan England is evident in such great manor houses as Melford Hall and Kentwell Hall, both at the northern edge of Long Melford and open to the public. Melford Hall (01787 880286, www.national trust.org.uk, open Easter-Oct) is a red-brick turreted manor house where Queen Elizabeth I herself once dined in 1578, soon after it was completed. Its neighbour Kentwell Hall (01787 310207, www.kent well.co.uk, off the A134 between Bury St Edmunds and Sudbury) is another red-brick Tudor mansion, bought in 1971 and restored from a state of dilapidation by the Phillips family, who now use it as their home. With its moats, maze and camera obscura, it's sometimes difficult to tell what's original and what's been introduced at the owner's whim, but who cares?

Bury St Edmunds

'A handsome little town of thriving and cleanly appearance.' This was how Dickens described Bury St Edmunds in *The Pickwick Papers*, and it's a succinct and accurate picture. In the early 19th century Bury made its money from textiles. Now sugar and beer are the dominant industries (sometimes there's a noticeable whiff in the air), but there's still a sense that the town resembles a Victorian burgher – solid, upright and intolerant of decadence and disorder. On market days it's busy with hawkers and shoppers from all around, bustling into and out of the pedestrianised grid of streets around Cornhill and the Butter Market. Prior to 1871, when the

market was disbanded due to complaints of 'rowdyism', Bury's market used to stretch as far as Angel Hill, the gentle slope that runs parallel to the Abbey Gardens. The modern market is the largest of its kind in East Anglia and takes place on Wednesdays and Saturdays. But when trading stops and the stalls have been dismantled, the streets are swept until they gleam, and an air of civic pride pervades.

It's a very welcoming town, with a helpful Tourist Information Centre (see p222) and a sedate, intelligent take on its past, which extends to the obvious efforts to keep monuments just so and stop modernity from encroaching in too brash and inappropriate a manner. Bury grew up around the Benedictine Abbey of Edmund – medieval England's patron saint – and was from the seventh century onwards a place of pilgrimage. Its motto is 'Shrine of a king, cradle of the law', a reference to the oath sworn in 1214 by the barons of England in the abbey to force King John to accept the demands later enshrined in the Magna Carta. Following the dissolution of the monasteries in 1539, much of the abbey disappeared, but its ruins can be seen in the well-groomed Abbey Gardens.

A town built on beer

Close by stands Suffolk's only cathedral St Edmundsbury Cathedral (01284 754933, www.stedscathedral.co.uk). Work commenced in 1510 and is only now reaching completion. The original building didn't include a tower because the adjacent abbey had several, but work began on a 150-foot lantern tower in 1999; the scaffolding is due to be dismantled some time in 2005. On 12 November 2004 the cathedral became the place of pilgrimage for thousands of musicians and listeners attending the funeral of DJ John Peel. (He is buried in the nearby village of Great Finborough, where he lived and from where he broadcast many of his programmes.)

The Abbey Gardens and cathedral are overlooked on one side by the ivy-festooned Angel Hotel, where Charles Dickens stayed, and at the far end by the Athenaeum assembly rooms, where Dickens gave public readings. A little further along the road, directly opposite the end of Churchgate Street, is the Norman Tower. Built between 1120 and 1148, it is the most complete surviving building of the original abbey complex.

The highly informative Greene King Brewery Museum (Westgate Street, 01284 714297) provides an amusing reminder that Bury's monastic past was not all piety and servitude; the monks played a vital part in the town's beer-brewing heritage. Find out about the 700-year history of Greene King and then sample some of its wares. Directly across the road from the museum is the Theatre Royal (01284 769505, www.theatreroyal.org) the third oldest surviving theatre in Britain. Owned by the National Trust, this Grade I-listed building, built in 1819, will be closed for restoration from spring 2005 until summer 2006. Subsequently, visitors will be able to appreciate its small and elegant Regency interior with improved facilities.

Bang in the town centre is Moyse's Hall Museum (The Cornhill, 01284 706183, www.stedmundsbury.gov.uk). Moyse's Hall dates from 1180 and claims to be the oldest surviving residential house in England. The truth about its origins are shrouded in mystery, but it has been a museum of archaeology and local history since 1899 and has an eclectic exhibition comprising local discoveries and donations. These include man traps, mummified cats and the relics of the notorious Red Barn murder committed by William Corder.

Also worth a browse is the sweet Bury St Edmunds Art Gallery (Cornhill, 01284 762081, www.burystedmundsart gallery.org), just round the corner from Moyse's Hall on the Market Cross and housed in Robert Adam's only public building in the area. In addition to its regularly changing exhibitions, the museum has a small shop with lovely one-off pieces by local artists who have exhibited here.

A short drive from the town, Ickworth House Park & Garden (Ickworth, Horringer, 01284 735270, www.nationaltrust.org.uk) is a totally outlandish property whose construction was begun in 1795 by Frederick Augustus Hervey, fourth Earl of Bristol, to house his collection of fine art. The building was not completed before his death. The government took it over in 1956 in lieu of death duties and then gave it to the National Trust. Set in Capability Brown parkland with a deer enclosure and a Georgian summerhouse, the main building houses paintings by Titian, Gainsborough and Velázquez among others. The house and its Italianate garden are open March to October; the park is open all year round.

Lavenham

The town of Lavenham is the jewel in Suffolk's crown. It first got a market charter in 1257 and for four centuries grew rich on the wool trade. In the 15th century Lavenham enjoyed a disproportionate share of the export market and by the time of the tax assessment of 1523-6 it was listed as the 14th wealthiest town in England, above more highly populated cities such as York and Lincoln. Wars in Europe in the first half of the 16th century saw a rapid decline in trade and when the Industrial Revolution of the 18th century took cloth-making away to the hill towns of the north, Lavenham was left architecturally frozen in time. Many of its timbered buildings and halls date from

the 14th and 15th centuries, when its wealthiest merchants were at their most confident and flamboyant.

The church, while lacking some of the charisma of the smaller village churches nearby, is a magnificent, imposing structure that rises up in black and grey flint and stone against the fields behind. As with many local wool churches, a browse inside yields clues to the identity of the town's wealthiest merchants, who were undoubtedly hoping to secure themselves a place in heaven through investment in God. Lavenham's most noteworthy include John de Vere, Earl of Oxford, and Thomas Spryng III. De Vere's emblems, the star and the boar, are visible not only in the wooden carvings of the porch he paid for, but in the stonework of the church tower and along the roof. Spryng was responsible for the magnificent wooden screen that creates a private family chapel inside the church.

It's possible to meander through the town, home to over 300 listed buildings, wondering at its remarkably untouched beams and crooked angles, but only the very observant will notice that telegraph lines have been hidden underground to preserve its character. The Tourist Information Centre on Lady Street (see p222) provides informative maps and pamphlets, or an Exploring Lavenham audio tour is available from Lavenham Pharmacy (99-100 High Street, 01787 247284). Head to the Market Place to look round the early 16th-century, timber-framed Guildhall of Corpus Christi (01787 247646, www.nationaltrust.org.uk), celebrated by architects as one of the finest medieval buildings in England. It houses exhibitions on local history and the woollen cloth trade

and has a walled garden with an interesting collection of dye plants. The neighbouring Little Hall (01787 247179, www.suffolk society.com) is an delightfully timbered building with gardens and offers further insight into the impact of wool money.

WHERE TO STAY

Ickworth Hotel & Restaurant

Horringer, Bury St Edmunds, Suffolk IP29 5QE (01284 735350/www.luxuryfamily hotels.com). **Rates** £180-£290 double; £360-£580 suite; £450-£825 1-bed apartment; £575-£1580 2-bed apartment. **Credit** AmEx, DC, MC, V.

If you're planning a break with children and can afford the rates at the Ickworth, look no further. Housed in the former east wing of Ickworth House (*see p224*) and set in 1,800 acres of National Trust parkland, the Ickworth is a rare beast. While its vast rooms are ornately furnished with a mix of stately home grandeur and contemporary largesse, the hotel is far from being stiff and stuffy. Staff are so helpful and friendly that it is a wonderfully relaxed environment to bring children to. In the basement (out of earshot of the rest of the hotel) there is an Ofsted-registered crèche where under-sevens can be left for up to two hours, and a chill-out room for over-sevens, complete with table tennis, PlayStations and table football. Less sedentary activities available include cycling (bikes, helmets, child seats and trailers are free to guests), swimming, tennis and horse-riding (lessons are also available in all three) or simply walking the grounds.

Adults can have a treatment at the Aquae Sulis spa or sit back with the papers and a coffee in the drawing room. It's not rocket science, but few family-friendly establishments manage to cater to the different needs of children and adults quite as well as Ickworth managers Peter and Jane Lord. The self-catering apartments in the Dower House offer more flexibility again, since they enjoy all the hotel facilities and more independence; they are ideal for groups – with or without children. Probably not the place for your romantic weekend *à deux*, however.

Lavenham Priory

Water Street, Lavenham, Sudbury, Suffolk CO10 9RW (01787 247404/www.lavenham priory.co.uk). **Rates** £95-£140 double; £135-£150 suite. **Credit** MC, V.

If you are seeking to impress someone romantically, bring them here; any of the six rooms will do the trick. It's a Grade I-listed, timber-framed merchant's house owned and run by Gilli and Tim Pitt, who pay painstaking, businesslike attention to every detail. The whole place has been thoughtfully restored to its Elizabethan period look with carefully sourced furniture and decoration. Each room offers a different bed or bath experience – four-posters, slipper, claw-foot – nothing kinky you understand, just exquisite and bespoke: from the Great Chamber, with its Napoleonic polonaise bed and en suite slipper bath; through the Painted Chamber, so-called because of the extant late medieval paintings on the walls and beams; to the Gallery Chamber with its locally made cherry-wood sleigh bed. The Priory Suite has its own staircase down to a private living room, where the floor has a small window revealing the underground stream running beneath.

Little details we particularly liked include the sliding panels that allow fresh air to blow in through the original timber-framed windows, and the fact that tea- and coffee-making facilities in each room include herbal teas and a cafétiere. At breakfast, guests can squeeze their own juice while they await the arrival of their full English, which comes with handmade Musk's Newmarket sausages. Need we go on? Perhaps just to add that you should book well ahead and beware of the 10.30am checkout.

The Manse

The Manse, The Green, Hartest, Suffolk IP29 4DH (01284 830226). **Rates** £60-£70 double. **No credit cards**.
From the comfort of their own home Bridget and Robin Oaten offer something quite special to weekend-breaking couples after the same degree of independence that you might get from self-catering, but with none of the chores. Only one couple at a time, though, since there's only one bedroom. It's pretty and enjoys a view over the village green, all the usual tea- and coffee-making facilities and an en suite bathroom. And it comes with fantastic touches: Penhaligon's toiletries; a decanter of sherry; a bowl of fresh fruit; a goose-down duvet, and even (no detail is overlooked) a torch to find your way home from the pub. In addition, guests are invited to relax in their own private drawing room, where a real fire could be burning in the hearth on arrival if the weather is chilly. Breakfast is served downstairs – again guests have the place to themselves – and includes own-made breads and – only in summer, when the chickens are performing – home-laid eggs.

Northgate House

8 Northgate Street, Bury St Edmunds, Suffolk IP33 1HQ (01284 760469/www.northgate house.com). **Rates** £100-£110 double. **Credit** AmEx, MC, V.
When owner Joy Fiennes and her late husband bought Northgate House it had been left empty for 15 years following the death of its owner, best-selling historical novelist Norah Lofts. It's hard to imagine that this Grade I-listed Queen Anne/Georgian townhouse houses a modestly self-styled B&B that's a good cut above the average. With original panelling in situ and decorated with chalky period hues and heavy, embroidered curtains, a light, airy and elegant atmosphere is achieved throughout, completely in keeping with the period of the building; you can almost hear the stiff silk dresses swishing down the hallway. It has only three bedrooms, but what rooms they are! Each is furnished with an en suite bathroom as big as the bedroom itself, with deep, roll-top, cast-iron baths and huge white bathrobes. Wooden shutters ensure that you won't be interrupted by early daylight, even on the brightest summer morning. The large, walled, classical garden boasts two huge London planes, the tallest trees in the borough. In fact, as you look out over the lawns while digesting a full English at the sizeable round breakfast table in an oak-panelled room, you could easily think you were in a remote country manor, not a stone's throw from a bustling market town centre.

Swan at Lavenham

High Street, Lavenham, Suffolk CO10 9QA (01787 247477/www.theswanat lavenham.co.uk). **Rates** £140-£220 double; £195-£260 suite. **Credit** AmEx, DC, MC, V.
Housed in a deceptively large and labyrinthine complex of half-timbered, 14th-century buildings, the Swan is stunning. Its magnificent Wool Hall, vast galleried dining room, oak panelling and stripped wood beams throughout mean that you're always aware of its heritage. But this is matched by whitewashed walls, Roman blinds and contemporary furniture that make the place swish and comfortable without being showy. The Old Bar is a bit of a corridor, but the walls of signatures and medals make it a neat homage to the American soldiers and pilots who were based near Lavenham during World War II. The Garden Bar is lighter and allows drinkers to experience the hotel's small private garden.
Upstairs, low overhead beams mean you have to keep your head down in the corridors, but you can safely straighten up once ensconced in your room. A welcome touch of humour came in the shape of a rubber duck in the bathroom, and we appreciated the CD player in addition to a TV. The downside? Much is made of 'rich fabrics and luxurious furnishings', but one feather pillow per person is mean and the blanket supply was stingy, especially for a high-ceilinged room in winter.

WHERE TO EAT & DRINK

When it comes to finding refreshment of the non-chain variety, Bury has a number of options. Go to the Grid (34 Abbeygate Street, 01284 706004) for a light tapas-style snack, with tables outdoors in summer, or enjoy the swish surroundings at the recently refurbished Cupola House (7 The Traverse, 01284 765808), housed in a listed building dating from 1693. The Abbeygate (first floor) or the Vaults (in the 12th-century undercroft) of the Angel Hotel (3 Angel Hill, 01284 714000, www.the angel.co.uk) offer the same lunch and dinner menus; prior booking is advisable, especially at the weekend. Being the home of Greene King, the town's pubs are very good on beer, but not so good on anything else. One worth visiting for a swifty is Britain's smallest pub, the Nutshell (The Traverse, 01284 764867).

Angel Hotel

Market Place, Lavenham, Suffolk CO10 9QZ (01787 247388/www.theangelhotel-lavenham.co.uk). **Lunch served** noon-2.15pm, **dinner served** 6.15-9.15pm daily. **Main courses** £8.95-£16. **Rates** £110 double. **Credit** AmEx, MC, V.
There has been a licensed premises on this site since 1420, and the current incarnation of the Angel Hotel has been in the same capable hands since 1990. The hotel is at the corner of the village

marketplace, and the restaurant has windows along two walls, making it a bright, airy place to watch the world by day and a cosy, softly lit place to dine, drink and soak up the atmosphere in the evening. The room has overhead beams, an open fire to one side and a 1930s oak bar at its hub; it's a happily modern mix of pub and restaurant. There's a traditional touch to the food. Starters could be duck, orange and chestnut terrine with Cumberland sauce and toast, or butternut squash and sweet potato soup, followed by a reliable local steak and ale pie, or a baked aubergine with curried chickpea and vegetable topping served with fresh veg or mixed leaf salad. Additional light meals and salads are on the lunch menu. It's popular, so do reserve a table.

Beehive

The Street, Horringer, Bury St Edmunds, Suffolk IP29 5SN (01284 735260). **Lunch served** noon-2pm daily **Dinner served** 7-9.30pm Mon-Sat. **Main courses** £8.95-£15.95. **Credit** MC, V.
Proprietor and barman Gary Kingshott offers an informal welcome at his gastropub; his warmth and lively chat pervade the whole place. The space is cosy, with low ceilings, but still feels light and airy, with several small anterooms for sitting and enjoying a pint. Starters, mains and snacks – nine of each – are chalked up on individual blackboards and tweaked regularly. Own-made sausages are a speciality of the house, in flavours such as venison and redcurrant, served with mash and gravy. Alternative mains might include sea bass with pesto and sunblush tomatoes. A snack of bread and mixed cheeses was several notches above most pubs' ploughman's, so you won't go far wrong, whatever your appetite.

Black Lion

Church Walk, The Green, Long Melford, Suffolk CO10 9DN (01787 312356/www.black lionhotel.net). **Wine bar Lunch served** noon-2pm, **dinner served** 7-9.30pm daily. *Restaurant* **Dinner served** 7-9.30pm daily. **Main courses** £7.95-£16.25. **Set lunch** (Sun) £18.95 3 courses. **Set dinner** £26.95 2 courses, £30.95 3 courses. **Rates** £120 double; £135-£165 suite. **Credit** AmEx, MC, V.
You might want to skip the restaurant at the Black Lion, with its pricier, fancier dishes, and make a beeline for the bar area, where there's an interesting blackboard menu and relaxed atmosphere. Some dishes are a blast from the past (lots of sunblushed tomatoes in evidence, along with strictly trad old favourites such as gammon steak with fried egg and chips); others are a bit more modish (red mullet fillet with stir-fried vegetables and basil and cashew pesto). But there's some talent in the kitchen, preparing red pepper and tomato soup, salmon wrapped in Parma ham with yoghurt, lentil and spinach sauce, and roast rib of beef with perfect Yorkshire pudding: all these dishes hit the mark.

Crown

The Green, Hartest, Suffolk IP29 4DH (01284 830250). **Lunch served** noon-2.30pm, **dinner served** 6-9pm Mon-Fri. **Meals served** noon-9pm Sat, Sun **Main courses** £5-£15. **Credit** AmEx, MC, V.
A Greene King pub right on the village green of a beautiful Suffolk village. All the signs show it must once have been an authentic local country boozer but over the years it's been transformed into a family-friendly place with laminated menus and a good adventure playground. Food is above the pre-prepared standard; choose dishes described as 'fresh' or from the chalkboard specials. If you're looking for a quiet drink, wait until the evening.

George

The Green, Cavendish, Suffolk CO10 8BA (01787 280248/www.georgecavendish.co.uk). **Lunch served** noon-3pm Tue-Sun. **Dinner served** 6.30-10pm Tue-Sat. **Main courses** £12-£14. **Set meal** (Mon-Sat) £10.95 2 courses. **Rates** £85-£110 double. **Credit** MC, V.
This yellow-painted inn overlooking the village green mixes the medieval (14th-century worm-eaten beams, timbered walls hiding daub and wattle, and an old stone fireplace) with contemporary chic (modern art, antique shop finds and neutral colours). It may have all the accoutrements of a smart country restaurant, but you can just call in for a pint. However, most are here for the food. And chef/proprietor Jonathan Nicholson delivers: his menu is as generous in scope as it is spare in tone: Parma ham and rabbit with waldorf salad and orange dressing; roast guinea fowl, petits pois à la francaise and roast artichokes. Nicholson was previously at Sir Terence Conran's Bluebird and Cantina del Ponte restaurants in London.

Great House

Market Place, Lavenham, Suffolk CO10 9QZ (01787 247431/www.greathouse.co.uk). **Lunch served** noon-2.30pm Tue-Sun. **Dinner served** 7-9.30pm Tue-Sat. **Main courses** £10.95-£18. **Set lunch** (Tue-Sat) £14.95 2 courses, £16.95 3 courses; (Sun) £23.95 3 courses. **Set dinner** (Tue-Fri) £23.95 3 courses. **Rates** £70-£150 double. **Credit** MC, V.
The pick of the bunch in Lavenham, the highly acclaimed Great House (previous occupants include Sir Stephen Spender) has been owned and run by Martine and Régis Crepy since 1985. (They also run the Maison Bleue in Bury St Edmunds, *see p228*) The main dining room is atmospheric, with a huge fireplace and original beams. As for the food, it's full-on French fare, while the wine list leans the same way, with prices starting at a very reasonable £2.10 for a glass of house wine. Not everything is spot on (a lukewarm starter, a soggy side order of veg), but minor niggles on a recent visit were more than made up for by beautiful calf's liver and bacon, moules poulette and tarte tatin with Calvados sauce. If all the

over-indulgence gets the better of you, you can stagger upstairs – it's a restaurant with rooms. Service is professional but not stuffy.

Harriets Tearooms

57 Cornhill Buildings, Cornhill, Bury St Edmunds, Suffolk IP33 1BT (01284 756256). **Open** 9.30am-5.30pm Mon-Fri; 9am-5.30pm Sat; 10.30am-5pm Sun. **Main courses** £7.45-£8.85. **Credit** MC, V.
Reminiscent of the tearooms that proliferate in Miss Marple mysteries, Harriets is a class act.

Standards and quality of service are impeccable. On arrival, regardless of how much you intend to spend or consume, you are guided to a clean table by a smartly aproned waitress and invited to peruse the list of speciality teas, coffees, sandwiches, pastries and cakes. Everything we tried was delicious. No smoking throughout.

Maison Bleue at Mortimer's

30-31 Churchgate Street, Bury St Edmunds, Suffolk IP33 1RG (01284 760623/www.maison bleue.co.uk). **Lunch served** noon-2.30pm Tue-

The stunning Northgate House is an architectural gem, as well as a fine B&B.

Fri; noon-2pm Sat. **Dinner served** 7-9.30pm Tue-Thur; 6.30-10pm Fri, Sat. **Main courses** £9.95-£27.95. **Set lunch** £13.95 2 courses, £15.95 3 courses. **Set dinner** £23.95 3 courses. **Credit** AmEx, MC, V.

Efficient and knowledgeable French staff, a wide choice of fresh fish and a stylish but unpretentious interior have helped make Maison Bleue a local institution. Although it bills itself as a seafood restaurant – oysters, prawns, scallops, tuna, monkfish and mackerel are all present and correct – the meat dishes are no slouch. Steak is cooked just so, and the rich lamb stew has meat that falls apart at the first appreciative sigh. Puddings tip a nod to British classics as well as French. Cooking, presentation, service: all exude a well-placed confidence. No smoking throughout. *See also* Great House, *p227*.

Old Cannon Brewery

86 Cannon Street, Bury St Edmunds, Suffolk IP33 1JR (01284 768769). **Lunch served** noon-2pm Mon-Fri; noon-2.30pm Sat, Sun. **Dinner served** 6.30-9pm Tue-Sat. **Main courses** £6.95-£11.95. **Credit** MC, V.

This stylish microbrewery also serves food and has built up a thriving business with younger locals – the atmosphere at weekends is positively humming, despite a slightly out-of-the-way location. Look up while you're standing at the bar and you'll see that the ceiling has been knocked out to show the beer still and pertaining pipework set in a wallpapered former chamber, complete with flying ducks; very droll.

Queens Head

Rede Road, Hawkedon, Suffolk IP29 4NN (01284 789218). **Lunch served** noon-3pm Sat, Sun. **Dinner served** 7-9.30pm Fri, Sat. **Main courses** £8.50-£15.95. **Credit** MC, V.

If you want a genuine country pub, and aren't going to get into a row with staunch supporters of the hunt, this is the place to come. It's not easy to find as it's barely signposted until you're almost upon it. The pub sign swinging outside has seen better days and the main bar, which has a foot in both Suffolk camps with Adnams and Greene King on draught, is pretty rough and ready, with old photographs hanging lopsidedly on the walls. At one end of the room is a vast fireplace, at the other end, the room extends far back and has been painted in rich red paint and furnished with heavy wood tables for dining (weekends only). Proprietor Scott Chapman clearly goes to great efforts to keep his clients happy: a London cigar merchant has been persuaded that a monthly visit to this out-of-the-way location is a worthwhile venture.

Tickle Manor Tearooms

17 High Street, Lavenham, Suffolk CO10 9PT (01787 248438). **Open/food served** 10.30am-5pm daily. **Main courses** £3-£5.95. **No credit cards.**

These spotless tearooms, with olde-worlde atmosphere and friendly service, pack in a steady stream of tourists and locals. The two-storey, 16th-century premises are small, but provide a decent choice of basics that make a welcome change from the rich, hearty food offered by more upmarket places in the area. Choose from a selection of sarnies, salads, soups and spuds. Own-made cakes include chocolate, apple, honey and carrot. If all that sightseeing has taken its toll, go the whole hog and enjoy a full cream tea. Varieties of tea include decaf and several herbal options. No smoking throughout.

Scutchers of Long Melford

Westgate Street, Long Melford, Suffolk CO10 9DP (01787 310200/www.scutchers.com). **Lunch served** noon-2pm, **dinner served** 7-9.30pm Tue-Sat. **Main courses** £12-£18. **Credit** AmEx, MC, V.

At Scutchers, ignore the bland (if inoffensive) decor and concentrate on the food. From basic to imaginative, with a nod to the Orient here and there, all dishes seem to work well. For starters, sesame prawn toasties with soy dip are ethereally light, while at the other end of the scale, sautéed foie gras on a rösti with haggis, mushy peas and a port jus sounds like it should be an ingredient too far, but manages to work brilliantly. Mains might be thinly sliced calf's liver with bacon (cooked to perfection), or grilled fillet of lemon sole with parmesan crust and a chive and vermouth sauce (ditto). Save room for dessert (bread and butter pudding with an apricot coulis, and other classics with a twist) and you won't be disappointed. Even with plenty of local competition, this place stands out from the crowd.

Swan

The Street, Monks Eleigh, Suffolk IP7 7AU (01449 741391). **Open** noon-3pm, 7-11pm Wed-Sun. **Lunch served** noon-2pm, **dinner served** 7-9.30pm Wed-Sun. **Main courses** £9-£15. **Credit** MC, V.

The exterior may be textbook 16th-century English country pub complete with impeccably maintained thatched roof, but the Swan's interior has been modernised on an open plan, and the polished wood floor, cool shades of sage and contemporary lighting are definitely more restaurant than hostelry. But there's still a strong sense of local identity with a dominant bar, log fire and excellently kept Adnams ales on tap. In the middle of all this, chef Nigel Ramsbottom cultivates a network of small producers to supply his religiously seasonal menus. From starter to pudding – creamy cauliflower soup and poached egg, to apple and ginger pudding with sticky toffee sauce – there is scarcely a misstep. This is straightforward cooking that throws into relief skill, technique and perfect timing, whether it's a classic braised lamb's knuckle with mash and red cabbage, or fresh fillet of plaice with creamy leeks and new potatoes.

North Norfolk coast

Windswept beaches, seabirds galore – and some gastronomic stars.

When Noel Coward wrote the famous line in Private Lives, 'Very flat, Norfolk', he was dismissing an area that, at 2,067 square miles, is England's fifth-largest county and ranges from the (admittedly hill-free) Fens in the west to the watery byways of the Broads in the east. Some of the wildest, most exhilarating scenery is to be found on the north Norfolk coast, much of which has been designated an Area of Outstanding Natural Beauty.

This stretch of salt marshes, creeks and windswept sandy beaches is renowned for its bird life, and draws spotters and walkers from across the UK and beyond. There's plenty here for the lover of history, too. From the Middle Ages until the Industrial Revolution (which largely bypassed it), Norfolk was one of the country's most prosperous and populous counties. Evidence can be found in the wealth of ecclesiastical architecture that remains: almost all of the county's many little villages boast a church that's worth a second look.

North Norfolk coast

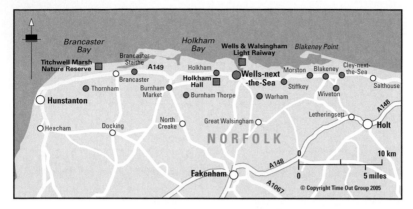

Map labels: Brancaster Bay · Holkham Bay · Wells & Walsingham Light Raiway · Blakeney Point · Titchwell Marsh Nature Reserve · Brancaster Staithe · A149 · Holkham · Morston · Blakeney · Cley-next-the-Sea · Brancaster · Holkham Hall · Wells-next-the-Sea · Stiffkey · Salthouse · Thornham · Burnham Market · Burnham Thorpe · Warham · Wiveton · Hunstanton · Heacham · Docking · North Creake · Great Walsingham · Letheringsett · Holt · NORFOLK · Fakenham · A148 · A1067 · 10 km · 5 miles · © Copyright Time Out Group 2005

Even if all you're after is a cosy retreat from urban life, the Norfolk coast has few equals. The area's isolation has meant that its hostelries have had to strive hard for custom. In the past decade the quality of both food and drink has soared – whether it be beer brewed from Norfolk barley (try Woodforde's prize-winning ales), Cromer crab with samphire freshly picked from the salt marshes, Brancaster mussels or locally smoked North Sea herring. In winter there's a wealth of game, with hare, pheasant and venison (perhaps from the Queen's herd at Sandringham) making frequent appearances.

The winding A149 between Thornham and Cley (little more than a lane in places, and slow-going in the August high season) goes through several attractive villages, though you'll find yet more enticements just off it – from picturesque fishermen's cottages and hidden-away harbours on the seaward side, to quiet hamlets and rolling countryside inland. Yes, including hills.

Thornham to Burnham Market

Head east along the A149 from the bucket-and-spade bustle of Hunstanton and you soon reach a wilder stretch of coastline. Thornham is a typical village of this stretch, hugging the main road. Small cottages of clunch, reddish-brown carstone and knapped flint can be seen on the High Street (the A149), but if you take the little road north, down Station Lane (which becomes Staithe Lane), you'll cross the Peddar's Way and Norfolk coastal path. This ancient route can be followed west for a two-and-a-half-mile hike along the salt marshes (with the sea visible in the distance) to the little village of Holme-next-the-Sea, but you can also pick up the coastal path at many villages east of here.

Continuing along the A149, you next encounter the village of Titchwell, home of the Titchwell Marsh Nature Reserve (01485 210779, www.rspb.org.uk/reserves), a

wetland reserve run by the Royal Society for the Protection of Birds. On the lagoons and foreshore winter visitors include dunlins and bar-tailed godwits, Brent geese, teals and widgeon, while avocets, sedge warblers and marsh harriers can be spotted in summer. The RSPB runs a visitor centre, shop (stocking birdwatching paraphernalia) and a café; there's a charge for parking.

Beach lovers should continue along the A149 to Brancaster. Turn north along Broad Lane until you reach a car park (charge payable). The beach – a huge expanse of sand past a hotel, beach kiosk and golf course – is one of Norfolk's best, and even in summer you don't have to walk far to have the place virtually to yourself. The currents, however, can be treacherous.

Brancaster is famous for its mussels, and during the season (when there's an 'r' in the month), bags of tender little bivalves are sold from fishermen's cottages in Brancaster Staithe. Small boats litter the silted-up inlets of the harbour; only at high tide can they make their way out to sea. The coastal path runs along the harbour, and you can walk across the marshes a mile to Burnham Deepdale. From Deepdale, it's worth making a detour a couple of miles inland (by car) to Burnham Market.

In the 13th century, the river Burn was navigable by seagoing boats as far as Burnham Thorpe, now almost three miles inland. Silting of the river led to a decrease in the commercial importance of the clutch of villages known as the Burnhams, but in the past 20 years there's been a curious and profound transformation in the fortunes of the largest of these villages, Burnham Market, a handsome old place with a long, tree-lined green at its centre. Perhaps encouraged by the success of the area's first gastropub, the Hoste Arms, affluent newcomers – many from London and the home counties – started buying up Burnham's beautiful old houses for use as second homes. The consequences have been mixed for the area. Here, more than

Accommodation	★★★
Food & drink	★★★★
Nightlife	
Shopping	★★
Culture	
Sights	★★
Scenery	★★★★

anywhere else in the county, locals have been priced out of the market and the Norfolk accent is rarely heard. Yet the newcomers' money has allowed some of the county's most interesting shops to flourish. High-quality food is a highlight. Gather the ingredients for a picnic at the first-class deli Humble Pie (Market Place, 01328 738581), the traditional baker's W Groom (Market Place, 01328 738289) and Satchells Wines (North Street, 01328 738272). Gurneys Fish Shop (Market Place, 01328 738967) is great for smoked fish, while non-food treats include two bookshops – Brazen Head (Market Place, 01328 730700) for second-hand books and White House (Market Place, 01328 730270) for new books and maps – plus various clothes, antiques and gift shops.

Burnham Market to Wells

Burnham Thorpe, a mile and a half inland from Burnham Market, is a tiny village most notable for being the birthplace of Horatio Nelson. Nelson held a farewell party at the pub (now called the Lord Nelson, *see p239*) before returning to sea in 1793. There are likely to be celebrations in the village in October 2005 to mark the bicentenary of the battle of Trafalgar.

From here, it's best to head for the B1155 to rejoin the coast road, which you reach just west of Holkham. The land for miles around here is owned by the Coke family, the Earls of Leicester. Holkham Hall, their stately pile (rebuilt in the Palladian style during the 18th century), is open on selected days in summer (01328 710227, www.holkham.co.uk), though the gardens (01328 711636) stay open longer. Holkham also has a beach, a pleasant sandy inlet reached on foot from the car park (pay and display) through pine woods. It's best to visit near high tide.

Less than two miles east of Holkham is the little town of Wells-next-the-Sea, which manages to cram in a beach resort, fishing port, picturesque shopping street and leafy green within its small circumference. The 'Burnham Market effect' has only recently had an impact here, so although there's fine dining at the Crown Hotel (*see p237*) and Italianate foodstuffs at the Wells Deli by the quay (15 The Quayside, 01328 711171, www.wellsdeli.co.uk), there are also old-fashioned independent shops – a butcher's, a baker's, a fishmonger's and a

hardware store – along the Staithe, a narrow high street that runs uphill from the quay. Crab fishing from the quay is a popular pastime; buy the wherewithal (line, bait and net cost around £2.50) from ML Walsingham & Son (78 Staithe Street, 01328 710438), about 100 yards up from the quay.

The sandy beach is a mile away from the town (there's a pay-and-display car park near the beach). Come at high tide or you'll have a long walk to the water. The other main local attraction is off the A149 just to the east of town. The Wells & Walsingham Light Railway (01328 711630, talking timetable 01328 710631, www.north norfolk.co.uk/walsinghamrail) operates a narrow-gauge steam locomotive to the beautiful village of Little Walsingham (30 minutes). Walsingham has been an important place of Christian pilgrimage for nigh-on 1,000 years; devout members of the Catholic and Orthodox churches are still drawn to the (rebuilt) shrine of Our Lady of Walsingham. Half-timbered medieval buildings are plentiful along the narrow streets, and there are enough tearooms, gift shops (religious souvenirs a speciality) and pubs to fill an afternoon before you catch the train back to Wells. The ruins and peaceful gardens of Walsingham Abbey are particularly popular in February for snowdrop walks (details from Walsingham Tourist Information Office, *see p234*).

Wells to Cley

The coast road gets narrower east of Wells as it goes through the little villages of Stiffkey (pronounced 'Stukey' by locals) and Morston. Look out for seasonal produce sold from roadside cottages: mussels, oysters, honeycomb and samphire. Trips to view the seals at Blakeney Point are run from Morston quay (contact Bean's Boats, 01263 740038, www.beansboat trips.co.uk; Seal Trips Temple, 01263 740791; or book at the Anchor Inn, *see p237*), though we'd recommend continuing on to the idyllic coastal village of Blakeney, which is peacefully sited well off the main road. The sea proper can be seen in the distance, but the creeks leading to the quay fill at high tide and motor boats (run by Bean's, *see above*) carry passengers out to the spit of land where a sizeable colony of seals can be viewed at surprisingly close quarters. Trips cost about £6. Hardy souls can take the two-and-a-half-mile hike from Blakeney along the coastal path and back inland to Cley.

Just to the east of the pay-and-display car park at the quay, there's a large duck pond that's home to many colourful species of wildfowl. Across the road are the vaulted cellars of the 14th-century Guildhall (free) which, in the 19th century, were used as a mortuary for drowned mariners.

Walsingham
Shire Hall Museum, Little Walsingham, Norfolk (01328 820510/ www.norfolkcoast.co.uk).
Wells
Staithe Street, Wells-next-the-Sea, Norfolk NR25 7RN (01328 710885). www.visitnorfolk.co.uk

Blakeney's two narrow streets down to the quay contain a handful of shops, pubs and restaurants, including a deli and Westons fishmonger's Fruits of the Sea Café (*see p237*), where you'll find such own-made enticements as potted shrimps and Basque-style crab. However, if you're after local delicacies to take home, continue along the A149 to Cley-next-the-Sea, home of the Cley Smoke House (High Street, 01263 740282, www.cleysmokehouse.com). This modest-sized shop is famous for turning North Sea herring into buckling, kippers, bloaters and red herring; it also smokes eel, cod's roe, trout and haddock and sells fresh-dressed crab. Cley's other foodie haven is Picnic Fayre (The Old Forge, 01263 740587, www.picnic-fayre.co.uk). Here such exotica as Tunisian orange and almond cake shares space with locally made chutneys, breads, cheeses and pies. Cley can also be used as a base for hikes. The energetic should take the lane east of the village down to the shingle beach (about half a mile; there's a paying car park) and from there it's possible to trek to Blakeney Point (four miles there and back). A more leisurely stroll takes Church Lane (off the A149 by Picnic Fayre) and runs past Cley's impressive church. It was built in the 13th century, when the village was a prosperous port; don't miss the stunning south porch, with its traceried battlements and fan-vaulted roof. Continue for half a mile along the serene Glaven valley to Wiveton and the welcoming Bell pub (*see p237*).

To keep abreast of Norfolk news, buy a copy of the *Eastern Daily Press* (known locally as the *EDP*). This publication outsells all the national dailies in Norfolk and is full of quirky nuggets about life in the county. Friday's issue contains the weekly Events guide, an excellent compendium of village fêtes, country and western dances, gigs, pantomimes, attractions and exhibitions taking place throughout Norfolk. Friday's issue also contains the property section – worth noting should you be smitten with life here.

WHERE TO STAY
Many of the pubs featured in Where to Eat & Drink (*see p237*) also have rooms.

George Hotel
High Street, Cley-next-the-Sea, Norfolk NR25 7RN (01263 740652/www.thegeorgehotel cley.com). **Lunch served** noon-2pm Mon-Fri; noon-2.30pm Sat, Sun. **Dinner served** 6.30-9pm Mon-Thur, Sun; 6.30-9.30pm Fri, Sat. **Main courses** £7.95-£14.95. **Rates** £50-£150 double; £175-£275 2-bed flat. **Credit** MC, V.
Tucked into one of the less overrun corners of the areas, the George Hotel has been quietly making a name for itself as a sanctuary from city life. The rambling inn has a variety of rooms with en suite facilities, including the Stiffkey suite with separate lounge, and the Mews cottage which can be self-catering or B&B. Each is different in character, but all share simple, clean furnishings with noticeably comfortable beds. The real lures are the entrancing views over the surrounding marshes. Downstairs, locals and visitors mingle in the airy, modern restaurant and bar. The food here is adventurous, taking full advantage of local ingredients, and prices are remarkably reasonable. Local art of varying success adorns the walls (stunning photos, questionable paintings, likeable pottery). The youngish staff are cheerful and helpful, coping amiably with children and dogs, and contributing to the relaxed ambience. The lane outside leads straight on to the long shingle spit of Blakeney Point, perfect for walking, bird-watching, seal-spotting or just mooching along the

Morston Hall

windswept dykes. Cley village itself has unexpected nooks for exploring, and Blakeney, Holkham and other beauty spots are a short drive away. An unassuming country pub that ticks a lot of boxes for a weekend escape.

Hoste Arms

The Green, Burnham Market, Norfolk PE31 8HD (01328 738777/www.hostearms.co.uk). **Lunch served** noon-2pm; **dinner served** 7-9pm daily. **Main courses** £8.95-£16.50. **Rates** £108-£168 double. **Credit** MC, V.
The Hoste Arms can lay claim to being the impetus behind Burnham Market's gentrification. Paul and Jeanne Whittome's 17th-century inn, winner of several prizes including the Norfolk Dining Pub of the Year three times (most recently in 2000), sits proud and much extended on the green. Inside, the bar and restaurant are dark, woody and stylish; there are leather armchairs in the pleasant conservatory and locally themed photographs and paintings on the walls. Outside are tables that are quickly taken in summer. The menu entices with dishes like roast cod and artichoke salad with truffle oil dressing, and locally reared oysters served in a variety of styles (tempura or grilled with parmesan topping). Execution is usually spot-on, typified by a succulent pot-roasted ham hock served with braised red cabbage and bitter orange compote, followed by an assiette of six desserts (good value for two at £7.95, given such delicacies as cardamom-spiced pineapple and papaya crumble). The local ales are good (try Woodforde's Great Eastern), and the wine list runs to 200 choices from all over the world. Pity about the uninspired children's menu.

The 43 bedrooms have been imaginatively designed by Jeanne. Choose between the exuberant English or French fabrics and antiques of the main hotel (some rooms have four-posters, fireplaces and large, luxurious bathrooms), the more modern Zulu wing inspired by Jeanne's homeland and decorated with African artefacts, or the small yet tastefully furnished rooms of the nearby Railway Inn (guests who don't fancy the five-minute walk to the Hoste Arms for breakfast can be collected by car in the morning).

Morston Hall

The Street, Morston, Norfolk NR25 7AA (01263 741041/www.morstonhall.com). **Lunch served** 12.30-1pm Sun. **Dinner served** 7.30-8pm daily. **Set lunch** £28 3 courses. **Set dinner** £42 4 courses. **Rates** £250 double. **Credit** AmEx, DC, MC, V.
Run by Galton Blackiston, who is also the chef, and his wife Tracy, this country-house hotel is very much a gastronomic destination. The porch is lined with awards – Morston Hall has been winning prizes since 1992, including a Michelin star in 1999. With that in mind, the room rate suddenly seems quite reasonable when you realise it includes a four-course dinner as well as breakfast. When you book, they'll ask if there's anything you

don't eat. Take this question seriously, since the menu is fixed. The food lives up to the acclaim. A small glass of celeriac soup and truffle oil was followed by a pyramid of lasagne in a creamy sauce layered with wild mushrooms, leeks, tomatoes and decorated with a topknot of fine onions. Scallops came as two circles separated by a ridge of guacamole resting on a terrine of peppers and courgettes. Chocolate in a mocha tart was perfectly offset by vanilla ice-cream; seven cheeses came with biscuits and olive and walnut bread, followed by coffee and petits fours.

The rooms, some of which have recently been refurbished, are in an unobtrusive traditional style, and all are equipped with VCRs and CD players, separate bath (some roll-top) and shower and fluffy bathrobes. Well-behaved (!) children and dogs are very welcome – the former for an extra charge of £25 a night for over-threes; the latter for £5 a night.

The Victoria

Park Road, Holkham, Norfolk NR23 1RG (01328 711008/www.victoriaatholkham.co.uk). **Lunch served** noon-2.30pm; **dinner served** 7-9.30pm daily. **Main courses** £11-£17. **Rates** £110-£140 double; £110-£200 1-bed lodge; £180-£300 2-bed lodge. **Credit** MC, V.
From the outside, it doesn't seem special – a mid 19th-century, flint-grey pub on an empty crossroads on the north Norfolk coast – but in the last four years the Earl of Leicester and his wife have turned their local into one of Britain's most appealing weekend haunts. There are only about a dozen rooms, but they've been decorated with individual style, dash and enthusiastic use of the furniture outfitters of Rajasthan. Colours are bold, baths are deep and claw-footed, some rooms have a soothing, seaside theme, while others are Victorian/colonial. Families are welcome and will be directed to the attic rooms, but at heart the Vic is a (sometimes smoky) pub/restaurant: guests are most likely to be youthful London couples lingering late in the deep sofas by the bar and birdwatchers supping the local ales (the coast and the vast, goose-infested expanse of Holkham beach is a ten-minute stroll from the front door). Most nights there are plenty of locals in the pub, but the restaurant is an even greater draw: a serious, meat-heavy menu, offering game and beef from his Lordship's estate, drop-dead fish and chips, local crab, oysters and pies, is complemented by an astute wine list. The English breakfast holds the line and can be followed by a brisk walk up to Holkham Hall (or a romp in the hotel's small playground). There's a little, book-lined residents' lounge and in the summer they fire up a barbecue in the courtyard – another reason to book well in advance at peak times.

WHERE TO EAT & DRINK

Bear in mind that all the hotels listed above have noteworthy restaurants, most notably Morston Hall.

Anchor Inn

*The Street, Morston, Norfolk NR25 7AA
(01263 741392).* **Open** *Bar* 11am-11pm
Mon-Sat; noon-10.30pm Sun. **Lunch served**
noon-2.30pm, **dinner served** 6-9pm Mon-Sat.
Meals served noon-8pm Sun. **Main courses**
£7.95-£14.50. **Credit** MC, V.
Several small rooms with wooden floors, open fires
and old furniture give this pleasant pub a relaxed
atmosphere, even if the quality of food can be
uneven. The long menu boasts classics like cod,
chips and mushy peas; crab salad and potatoes;
and beautifully fresh oysters. We enjoyed the steak
and kidney pudding, kept moist by its suet pastry.
Beers include Winton's and Old Speckled Hen and
many wines can be had by the glass or bottle.

The Bell

*Blakeney Road, Wiveton, Norfolk NR25 7TL
(01263 740101/www.wivetonbell.co.uk). Bar*
Open noon-2.30pm, 6.30-11pm Tue-Sat; noon-
2.30pm Sun. **Lunch served** noon-2pm Tue-
Sun. **Dinner served** 7-9pm Tue-Sat. **Main
courses** £7.95-£13.95. **Credit** MC, V.
Half a mile inland from Cley, the Bell is a friendly
old pub in the tiny village of Wiveton, across the
green from the church. Its one largish bar features
dark beams, bench seating, patterned carpets and
tasty ales from Adnams and Woodforde's.
Attached is a no-smoking conservatory where
hearty (and rather good) pub cooking is often
given a Danish twist, courtesy of landlord John
Olsen. Try the marinated herring with rye bread.
There are more tables in the grassy beer garden.

Crown

*The Buttlands, Wells-next-the-Sea, Norfolk
NR23 1EX (01328 710209/www.thecrownhotel
wells.co.uk). Brasserie* **Lunch served** noon-
2.30pm, **dinner served** 6.30-9.30pm daily.
Restaurant **Dinner served** 7-9pm daily. **Set
dinner** £24.95 2 courses, £29.95 3 courses incl
coffee. **Rates** £95-£105 double; £150 suite.
Credit AmEx, MC, V.
A handsome hotel, the Crown has a modern dining
room appealingly decorated with mustard-hued
walls and sea-themed artworks. The classy set-
price menu is global, yet highlights local ingredients. Canapés and a pre-starter might precede
smoked eel on blinis with celeriac remoulade, or a
bowl of soupy yet splendid watermelon curry.
Next: pan-fried sea bass on a pea and prawn risotto,
or perhaps char-grilled beef fillet with chicken
liver parfait. Don't miss the assiette of desserts.

Fishes

*Market Place, Burnham Market, Norfolk
PE31 8HE (01328 738588/www.fishes
restaurant.co.uk).* **Lunch served** noon-2pm
Tue-Sun. **Dinner served** 7 9.30pm Tue-Sat.
Set lunch £14.50 2 courses, £17.50 3 courses.
Set dinner £28.50 2 courses, £33.50 3 courses.
Credit MC, V.

Bay windows at this friendly fish restaurant give
a prime view across Burnham Market's green.
Pine tables, rattan chairs and cork-tile floors create a pleasant feel. The owner's enthusiasm for the
food is wholly justified. Fish soup comes laced
with red peppers, while smoked eel is subtle yet
intense. Roast halibut might arrive with
caramelised fennel and a subtle hollandaise.
Excellent rhubarb tart could figure among the
traditional puds. No smoking throughout.

Fruits of the Sea Café

*5A Westgate Street, Blakeney, Norfolk
NR25 7NQ (01263 741721/www.westonsof
blakeney.co.uk).* **Meals served** *Summer* 10am-
5.30pm daily. *Winter* 11am-5pm daily. **Main
courses** £3.95-£8.95. **Unlicensed. Corkage**
no charge. **Credit** MC, V.
Opened in August 2004, this unpretentious
seafood café is a real find. Owned by Westons fishmonger's, it occupies quaint premises next door,
with wooden flooring, beamed ceiling and whitewashed walls. The menu is a simple list of salads,
sandwiches, jacket potatoes and specials. Prices
are low, portions large and specials occasionally
adventurous: intense prawn, crayfish, red pepper
and tomato soup (£4.75); seafood gratin featuring
smoked haddock and salmon (£7.95). Follow up
with a cream tea or freshly ground coffee. Bring
your own wine. No smoking throughout.

Jolly Sailors

*Main Road (A149), Brancaster Staithe, Norfolk
PE31 8BJ (01485 210314/www.jollysailors.
co.uk).* **Open** *Bar* 11am-11pm Mon-Sat; noon
10.30pm Sun. **Meals served** noon-9pm daily.
Main courses £7.95-£13.95. **Credit** MC, V.
Walkers, yachting folk and, above all, beer
drinkers are lured into this pleasing old pub,
which now boasts its own brewery. The main bar
has tiled flooring, basic wooden benches and a
coal fire in winter. There's also a TV room with
comfy chairs, and a salmon-hued restaurant
where moderately priced food usually includes
locally reared mussels and oysters in season.
Morris troupes are wont to dance in the gardens
come summer. After a pint or two of Old Les, you
might join them.

King's Arms

*Westgate Street, Blakeney, Norfolk NR25 7NQ
(01263 740341).* **Meals served** noon-9.30pm
Mon-Sat; noon-9pm Sun. **Main courses** £5.95-
£14.95. **Rates** £60 double; £70 3-bed flat.
Credit MC, V.
Dangerously cosy (come here after a walk on the
salt marshes, not before, or you may never make
it), this white-painted flint hostelry consists of a
succession of tiny, low-ceilinged rooms that often
fill with outdoor types. Pub food is served all day,
children are welcome (especially in the new
garden room), and the well-kept real ales include
Old Speckled Hen, Marston's Pedigree and

Woodforde's Wherry. Such is the warmth of the place, you can even forgive the bizarre collection of black-and-white-minstrel posters.

Lifeboat Inn

Ship Lane, Thornham, Norfolk PE36 6LT (01485 512236/www.lifeboatinn.co.uk). **Lunch served** noon-2.30pm, **dinner served** 6.30-9.30pm daily. **Main courses** £8.50-£15.95. **Set dinner** £26 3 courses. **Rates** £78-£112 double. **Credit** MC, V.

At its kernel, the Lifeboat is a snug old pub with beams and nooks aplenty (along with beers from Adnams and Woodforde's, and cider from Aspall's). Popularity has been the impetus for various extensions, the best of which is the yellow-walled conservatory. Outside is a terrace, a

It shouldn't be too hard to guess what they serve at the lovely Fishes.

children's play area and, beyond the car park, outstanding views of the marshes. The Med-influenced menu features sound combinations of high-quality ingredients rendered with a light touch. Fish, especially, is cooked with delicacy, and they also do huge bowls of local mussels

Lord Nelson

Walsingham Road, Burnham Thorpe, Norfolk PE31 8HL (01328 738241/www.nelsons local.com). **Open** *Bar* 11am-3pm, 6-11pm Mon-Sat; 11am-3pm, 6.30-10.30pm Sun. **Lunch served** noon-2pm daily. **Dinner served** 7-9pm Mon-Sat. **Main courses** £9-£17.95. **Credit** MC, V.

This classic boozer in Horatio Nelson's home village is the absolute epitome of public house snugness. Settle down on an age-old high-backed wooden settle and your drink will be brought to table. Beer (including Woodforde's Nelson's Revenge) comes straight from the cask. Food, served in the no-smoking Ward room, helped win the new owners the *Eastern Daily Press* pub-restaurant of the year in 2004. You should arrive early in summer, or there might only be space in the (large) gardens, and you'll miss the plethora of Nelson memorabilia.

Red Lion

44 Wells Road, Stiffkey, Wells-next-the-Sea, Norfolk NR23 1AJ (01328 830552/www. stiffkey.com). **Open** *Bar* 11am-3pm, 6-11pm Mon-Sat; noon 3pm, 6-10.30pm Sun. **Lunch served** noon-2pm, **dinner served** 6-9pm daily. **Main courses** £6.50-£10.95. **Credit** MC, V.

A brick-and-flint cottage of a pub on the outskirts of the lovely village of Stiffkey, the Red Lion looks out across the A149 to a vista of pure rural loveliness. At the back (up a hill) is a dining patio; inside are pantiled floors, real fires in winter, a conservatory, dining area and three interconnecting bars. Local brewery Woodforde's provides a couple of the well-kept real ales, though you'll usually find something on tap from other Norfolk microbreweries. The menu is unpretentious and majors in seafood and fish.

Three Horseshoes

69 Bridge Street, Warham All Saints, Norfolk NR23 1NL (01328 710547). **Lunch served** noon-1.45pm, **dinner served** 6-8.30pm daily. **Main courses** £5.80-£8.20. **Rates** £48-£52 double. **No credit cards.**

Would that more pub food were like this: unfussy, fairly priced and cooked with genuine care and interest in ingredients. The Three Horseshoes is a lovely old place that boasts a restful setting within a quiet village. Outside is a garden and small courtyard; within, a clutch of rooms feature ancient stone or tiled floors, gas lighting and an abundance of knick-knacks for you to bang your head on as you wander round. Beer is local and sparklingly fresh. Soups and pies dominate the menu; artichoke soup might precede game and wine pie. Puds are admirable too.

White Horse

Main Road, Brancaster Staithe, Norfolk PE31 8BY (01485 210262/www.whitehorsebran caster.co.uk). **Lunch served** noon-2pm, **dinner served** 7-9pm daily. **Main courses** £13-£14. **Rates** £90-£170 double. **Credit** MC, V.

Although it is an ordinary-looking pub from the outside, inside the White Horse is a smart, urbane space delivering very polished food – the likes of dressed crab with celeriac remoulade and rocket salad, local lobster with garlic butter, and spring rump of lamb. Particularly impressive are the cockles, mussels and oysters that are harvested from the beds at the bottom of the garden. The conservatory dining room and terrace give fine views of the salt marshes and the distant sea. The pub also has 15 en suite bedrooms.

THE TIDE IS HIGH

The trick when visiting the north Norfolk coast is to know your tides. At low tide, the 'beaches' on the Wash (Snettisham, Heacham) are mere mud flats; from Hunstanton to Wells, you'll get vast expanses of sand and need binoculars to see any waves; yet at points east of Weybourne (including the resorts of Sheringham and Cromer), low tide is prime time, when, as well as pebbles, you'll get a couple of hundred yards of castle-builder's sand before the sea.

At high tide, the Wash becomes quenched, Wells beach dramatically reduces in size (sirens sound to warn

White Horse Hotel

4 High Street, Blakeney, Norfolk NR25 7AL (01263 740574/www.blakeneywhite horse.co.uk). Bar **Lunch served** noon-2pm, **dinner served** 6-9pm daily. *Restaurant* **Dinner served** 7-9pm daily. **Main courses** £10-£17. **Rates** £60-£120 double. **Credit** MC, V.

Just up the narrow High Street, this former coaching inn covers all bases. At heart it's a pub – charming bar and local ales – but there's a glassed-in courtyard and simple restaurant in the former stables (dinner only). Everything is judged nicely, modern yet conscious of the coastal setting and rural tastes. Fantastic cockle chowder is served in the bar, alongside perfect cod and chips, while the restaurant showcases more ambitious cooking.

bathers against being cut off on the dunes), while crabbing boats flood into the harbour to unload their snapping cargo. At high tide, too, the sand at Weybourne, Sheringham and Cromer is completely covered and only pebbles remain on view, though in winter you might enjoy an absolutely spectacular windswept walk scored to the crashing of waves against the sea defences.

A list of the month's high tides at King's Lynn can be found at www.lynnnews.co.uk. Times of high tides are also published every day in the *Eastern Daily Press* and, on Fridays and Tuesdays, in the *Lynn News*.

North Norfolk coast

The Brecon Beacons

Break for the border country to invigorate body and mind.

Head for mid Wales to the Black Mountains, which form the eastern half of the Brecon Beacons National Park, and you will at once be struck by the ethereal majesty of the landscape, fascinated by the rugged rural life and enchanted by the bohemian enclaves of society found here. Inspired by such superlative natural environs, artists, writers and craftsmen have flocked to the area since the early 1900s – especially during the '70s – and made the wild hills, bleak mountains and deep valleys their beloved home.

With a section of the Offa's Dyke Path running south from Hay Bluff along the ridge above the Olchon Valley and Vale of Ewyas until it meets the river Monnow, the Black Mountains (not to be confused with the Black Mountain in the western Brecon Beacons) straddle England and Wales: Powys is to the west; Herefordshire to the east. Life on the borders has been simply and honestly captured by Bruce Chatwin in *On the Black Hill.* First published in 1982, this tale of the inseparable Jones twins, Benjamin and Lewis, is set on the Vision, a farm resting in the Vale of Ewyas. The colourful characters that pepper the late author's celebrated novel can still be happened upon today, from the sheep farmer in the pub worrying about how much his yearlings will fetch at market to the hippies communing with nature, living in yurts down some dingly dell.

Accommodation	★★★
Food & drink	★★★
Nightlife	
Shopping	★★
Culture	★★
Sights	
Scenery	★★★★★

You'll find plenty of opportunity for cerebral activities here. Get lost among the miles of dusty bookshelves in Hay-on-Wye's specialist bookshops (the town is, purportedly, the world's largest second-hand book centre) or simply wander beside streams, through woods or on the hills with your head in the clouds. Yet, of course, there's a good deal to compel outdoor types to the Black Mountains too. Whether you're into walking, horse riding, mountain biking or boarding, climbing, canoeing, white-water rafting or even sailing, you'll find no end of high-energy pursuits.

Spring and summer are obviously the busiest times. Although there's no guarantee of good weather – this is Wales after all – the river banks are there for lazing between cool swims on hot days and the countryside is as green as can be. But do come off-season to experience the true spirit of the Black Mountains. In late autumn the emerald fronds of bracken turn russet-gold, setting the mountain escarpments on fire. During winter the dark silhouettes of frost-bitten ridges glimpsed through the branches of naked trees are a dramatic sight.

Town of books

Hay-on-Wye – rarely referred to locally by its Welsh name Y Gelli Gandryll – surrounds a crumbling castle, which is often eerily illuminated by green and purple lights at night. Behind its tumbledown walls lives the town's self-proclaimed king, Richard Booth. This is an eccentric town, to say the least. Bookworm Booth first launched his second-hand tome trade here in 1961 and declared Hay an independent state on 1 April 1977.

Hay is now a second-hand book empire, with 39 shops lining its narrow streets. The grand dames are Richard Booth's Bookshop (44 Lion Street, 01497 820322, www.richardbooth.demon.co.uk), with over 400,000 titles, and the Hay Cinema Bookshop (Castle Street, 01497 820071, www.haycinemabookshop.co.uk), covering everything from travel to religion to economics. Meanwhile, Boz Books (13A Castle Street, 01497 821277, www.bozbooks.co.uk) sells only works by Charles Dickens (aka Boz) and other 19th-century authors, while Rose's Books (14 Broad Street, 01497 820013, www.roses books.com) specialises in rare and out-of-print children's and illustrated books. Pick up the 'Hay-on-Wye Town of Books' leaflet from the tourist information centre (see below) for easy navigation. May heralds the prestigious Hay Literary Festival, when the literati, from young wordsmiths to wrinkly intellectuals, revel in ten days of full-on bibliophilia (see p256 **Booked up**).

Still, it's not all about books. The Rogue's Gallery (2 Broad Street, 01497 820914, www.cazclay.demon.co.uk) and the Haymakers (St Johns Place, 01497 820556, www.haymakers.co.uk) sell works by two different co-operatives of local artists and craftsmen and both are worth checking out. A not-to-be-missed shop is the Great English Outdoors (Mortimer House, Castle Street, 01497 821205, www.greatenglish.co.uk). Run by leather-worker Athene English, it stocks a covetable range of traditional Welsh blankets, wallets and cases made from 214-year-old reindeer hide and an array of quirky antique finds.

In warm weather, there's nothing better than packing a picnic – stock up with supplies of organic cider and freshly made goodies from Hay Wholefoods & Delicatessen (41 Lion Street, 01497 820708) – and following the path north from Hay Bridge along the Wye until you

TOURIST INFORMATION

Abergavenny
Monmouth Road, Abergavenny, Monmouthshire NP7 5HL (01873 857588/www.abergavenny.co.uk).
Brecon
Cattle Market Car Park, Brecon, Powys LD3 9DA (01874 622485/ www.visitbreconbeacons.com).
Crickhowell
Beaufort Chambers, Beaufort Street, Crickhowell, Powys NP8 1AA (01873 812105).
Hay-on-Wye
Craft Centre, Oxford Road, Hay-on-Wye, Herefordshire HE3 5EA (01497 820144/www.hay-on-wye.co.uk/craftcentre).
Knighton
Offa's Dyke Centre, West Street, Knighton, Powys LD7 1EN (01547 528753/www.offasdyke. demon.co.uk).
Libanus
Brecon Beacons Mountain Centre, Libanus, Powys LD3 8ER (01874 623366/www.breconbeacons.org).
www.brecon-beacons.net
www.gomidwales.co.uk
www.hay-on-wye.co.uk
www.tourism.powys.gov.uk
www.visitwyevalley.com

The Brecon Beacons

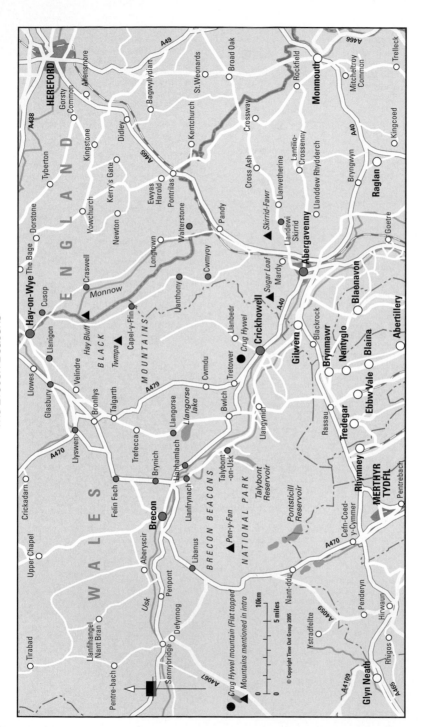

reach the Warren. Here you'll find meadows, a pebbly beach and a popular swimming spot. For canoeists, the Warren marks the final stretch of the three- to four-hour paddle downriver from Glasbury to Hay.

Hay Bluff to Llanthony Priory

Rising above Hay on Wye is Hay Bluff. You can pick up the Offa's Dyke Path from the bottom of the Hay school car park and follow it through Cusop Dingle and all the way up to the summit of Hay Bluff. Alternatively, drive to the stone circle car park on Hay Common and make your ascent from there. The relatively effortless climb to the top is, on a clear day, rewarded with magnificent views of the Wye Valley. Directly south-east of the Bluff rises the promontory of Twmpa, or Lord Hereford's Knob. Between the two mountains the Gospel Pass, a single-track road, cuts into the Vale of Ewyas. It passes through Capel-y-Ffin, a tiny hamlet with a white chapel, where the sculptor Eric Gill and a bunch of artist friends lived during the 1920s, and down on to Llanthony Priory. There are riding stables at both Capel-y-Ffin and Llanthony.

Half of the Priory (founded in 1107 by William de Lacy, brother of the Lord of Ewyas) still clings to the adjoining house; the remainder stands in ruins. Columns of old walls and great arches thrust skywards, backdropped by misty hills. Here you'll find the Priory Hotel (01873 890487, www.llanthonypriory.supanet.com), which is a romantic idea with its four-poster beds and dreamy location, but perhaps a little too basic in other respects to be truly comfortable. Do drop into the cosy cellar bar, though, for a swift half before or after climbing up and over the ridge above (Offa's Dyke Path again) and descending into the beautiful Olchon Valley below.

South of Llanthony is Cwmyoy (Vale of the Yoke). Here, built on a land slip, the higgledy-piggledy medieval church of St Martin has masterful stone lettering on its headstones, both inside and out. An engraving dated 1682 hangs on a wall near the altar and reads: 'Thomas Price he take his nap in our common mother lap waiting to heare the bridegroome say awake my dear and come away.' Look out also for the 13th-century crucifix.

Brecon to Abergavenny

The market town of Brecon (Aberhonddu) has all the hustle and bustle of Hay, but without the charm. However, it's a convenient base if you're planning to explore both the Central Brecon Beacons and the Black Mountains in the same trip. Brecon Cathedral (01874 625222, www.breconcathedral.org.uk) and Castle, parts of which date back to Norman times, perch on the hill. The River Usk flows through Brecon and pleasant strolls can

be had along the Promenade, a stretch of water north of the centre. Meanwhile, the Brecon and Monmouthshire Canal starts south of the centre. At the Canal Basin you'll find Brecon Theatre (Canal Wharf, 01874 611622, www.theatrbrycheiniog. co.uk), a lively regional performing arts venue. Brecon comes alive on the second Saturday of the month, when the Brecknockshire Farmers' Market is held in the covered Market Hall (High Street, 01874 610008, 10am-4pm). The main event in summer is the Brecon Jazz Festival (01874 611622, www.brecon jazz.co.uk), which attracts big names as well as new talent.

Just west of Brecon is Libanus and the Brecon Beacons Mountain Centre (01874 623366, www.breconbeacons.org). Here you can pick up a wide range of maps, leaflets, walking books and other information. There's also a tearoom and plenty of walks to choose from should you decide to make it your starting point for a day. The most popular hike in the Central Brecon Beacons is the ascent of Pen-y-Fan (pronounced 'Pen-ur-Van'), the highest mountain in south Wales at 2,907 feet. The traditional five-mile route starts from the Storey Arms on the A470 and should only be attempted in fine weather. A more adventurous alternative would be to start from Llanfrynach village and make your way up the 10½-mile route that approaches the summit of Pen-y-Fan via the lower peak of Fan-y-Big – a name Dylan Thomas would have surely approved of.

Heading south-east out of Brecon on the A40 towards Crickhowell and Abergavenny, you'll see a sign for Llangorse on your left and then a bit further along again, a sign to Talybont-on-Usk on your right. The waters of Llangorse Lake, the largest natural lake in south Wales, offer sailing and canoeing, while the village also acts as a hub for climbing and horse riding. At Talybont-on-Usk, have a canalside drink at the Star Inn (01874 676635), famed for its variety of real ales, before walking out to the Blaen-y-Glyn waterfalls at the head of the Talybont-on-Usk Valley above the reservoir. You can also pick up the Taff Trail here, a 55-mile cycle route that links Brecon with the Welsh capital, Cardiff, passing along disused tram lines and railroads on its course.

Once an important stop for stagecoaches, Crickhowell is one of the area's main places to eat, drink and stay. The pretty 16th-century bridge over the Usk here has 12 arches on one side and 13 on the other. Fill your knapsack with snacks from the baker and grocers on the High Street for the fairly gentle five-mile circular walk around Crug Hywel, its flat top earning it the nickname of Table Mountain. At the 1,481-foot summit you'll find an Iron Age fort that affords impressive views of the Usk Valley and the Central Brecon Beacons. The Crickhowell Adventure shop (1 High Street, 01873 810020) is a good source of local info, while the Cheese Press (18 High Street, 01873 811122) is a gift shop with a cosy, no-frills café at the back.

The market town of Abergavenny acts as the bottom left-hand corner of the triangle formed with Hay-on-Wye and Brecon, the Black Mountains lying within its bounds. Other than during the successful Abergavenny Food Festival (www.abergavennyfoodfestival.com), there's no real reason to linger except, perhaps, for a wander round the Norman castle (Castle Street, 01873 854282). Here, in 1175, the vengeful William de Braose slaughtered a score of local Welshmen after inviting them for a Christmas feast at his table. It's nearly as bloody a task to find a decent watering or dining hole in town, but if you're parched try the Hen and Chickens (01873 853613), a traditional pub on Flannel Street serving real ales. The Angel Hotel (see p254) is the other saving grace.

Abergavenny's main appeal is the surrounding peaks of the Sugar Loaf, Blorenge and Skirrid Fawr mountains. The annual Three Peaks Trial, held on the last Saturday of March (www.cardiffoutdoor group.org.uk), is an 18-mile endurance test that attempts each in succession. If you're not feeling quite so extreme, take your pick and tackle just one. The 3½-mile circuit of Skirrid Fawr (Holy Mountain) starts near the foodies' favourite, the Walnut Tree Inn – a factor that may aid your decision-making.

WHERE TO STAY

There's no shortage of friendly, family-run B&Bs in the Black Mountains and Central Brecon Beacons (tourist offices can supply you with lists of local ones), just beware the chintz. When it comes to hotels, especially those with a dash of style, choices are more limited. Plan well ahead for the Hay Literary Festival, which runs from late May to early June, and the Brecon Jazz Festival in August, as accommodation can get booked up as much as a year in advance. After a hard day's walking, guests tend to dine in; decent alternatives can be anything from a 15- to 45-minute drive away.

Allt yr Ynys Country House Hotel

Walterstone, nr Abergavenny, Herefordshire HR2 0DU (01873 890307/www.allthotel.co.uk). **Rates** £75-£130 double; £120-£160 suite/family room. **Credit** AmEx, MC, V.
Situated on a tongue of land between the Monnow and Honddu rivers, the Allt yr Ynys has a history stretching back to the eighth century. The restau-

rant (*see p254*) and three of the bedrooms are located in the wonderful 17th-century country house and there is every reason to book well in advance for one of these; wood-panelled and done out in elegant, traditional furnishings, room one has a Jacobean four-poster bed; two is more modern, with a lighter white, blue and pale green decor; three offers contemporary opulence with heavy, red-velvet window drapes. Outside, in the converted barns, you'll find 18 additional en suite rooms. Large, family rooms are available, with plenty of space for little feet to run around in, although they could do with updating. As well as 16 acres of garden, an indoor swimming pool, sauna and jacuzzi, Allt yr Ynys is ideally placed for exploring Abergavenny's three peaks or the wonderful Olchon Valley. Dogs are welcome at an additional charge of £10 per night. Breakfast, served until 10am, features smoked finnan haddock, freshly grilled kipper and a mix-and-match cooked breakfast.

Cantre Selyf

5 Lion Street, Brecon, Powys LD3 7AU (01874 622904/www.cantreselyf.co.uk). **Rates** £65-£70 double. **No credit cards.**
Although it is built on a medieval L-shaped plan, this fine townhouse dates from the 17th century, with mainly 18th-century interiors. In the twin and small double room you'll see such original and unusual features as pargeting on the ceilings, while the thick oak floorboards squeak and creak with age in the hallway. The large double room looks over the garden – which guests are welcome to use – and down to what remains of Brecon's old town walls. Unfortunately, none of the B&B's three rooms have baths, only showers, but all are en suite. Famed for her breakfasts, owner Helen Roberts serves up a choice of the full English, smoked salmon and scrambled eggs, vegetarian cheese-and-leek sausages, omelette of your choice or french toast, yoghurt and fruit. No mutts are allowed – the Robertses have cats and a dog of their own.

Felin Fach Griffin

Felin Fach, Brecon, Powys LD3 0UB (01874 620111/www.eatdrinksleep.ltd.uk). **Rates** £92.50-£115 double. **Credit** MC, V.
The Griffin's catch phrase, 'Eat, drink, sleep', sums it up: you will be doing plenty of each here. After dinner and fine wines in what is one of the country's leading gastropubs (*see p257*), seven comfortably chic rooms await in the rafters above. The decor is executed with the same panache as the cuisine. It is hard to believe that this building, located on the Hay-Brecon road, was derelict for seven years before chef-owner Charles Inkin got his hands on it and transformed it into the stylish yet thoroughly down-to-earth establishment it is today. Rooms are all neutral-toned floors and walls, swathes of light material, and bright, white linen complemented by thickly woven Welsh blankets. Bathrooms are capacious and unclut-

Relaxation
comes in many
forms in the
Brecon Beacons.

TAKE ACTION

BOATING

BEACON PARK BOATS
Llanfoist Wharf, Abergavenny, Monmouthshire NP7 9NG (01873 858277/www.beaconparkboats.com).

BRECON BOATS
The Travellers Rest Inn, Talybont-on-Usk, Brecon, Powys LD3 7YP (01874 676401).

CAMBRIAN CRUISERS
Ty Newydd, Pencelli, Brecon, Powys LD3 7LU (01874 665315/www.cambriancruisers.co.uk).

CASTLE NARROWBOATS
Church Road Wharf, Gilwern, Abergavenny, Monmouthshire NP7 0EP (01873 830001/www.castle narrowboats.co.uk).

DRAGONFLY CRUISES
Canal Road, Brecon, Powys LD3 7HL (07831 685222/www.dragonfly-cruises.co.uk).

RED LINE BOATS
Gotyre Wharf, Llanover, Abergavenny, Monmouthshire NP7 9EW (01873 880516/www.redlineboats.co.uk).

CANOEING & KAYAKING

PADDLES & PEDDLES
15 Castle Street, Hay-on-Wye, Herefordshire HR3 5DF (01497 820604/www.canoehire.co.uk).

WYE VALLEY CANOE CENTRE
The Boathouse, Glasbury-on-Wye, Herefordshire HR3 5NP (01497 847213/www.wyevalleycanoes.co.uk).

CLIMBING

CLIMB WHEN READY
Llangorse Rope Centre, Llangorse, Brecon, Powys LD3 7UH (01874 730700/www.climbwhenready.co.uk).

CYCLE HIRE

BIKES AND HIKES
The Struet, Brecon, Powys LD2 3PQ (01874 610071).

BI-PED CYCLES
Free Street, Brecon, Powys LD3 7EF (01874 622296/www.biped cycles.co.uk).

BRECON CYCLE CENTRE
10 Ship Street, Brecon, Powys LD3 9AF (01874 622651/www.breconcycles.com).

PEDALAWAY
Trereece Barn, Llangarron, Ross-on-Wye, Herefordshire HR9 6NH (01873 830219/www.pedalaway.com).

GLIDING, HANG-GLIDING & PARAGLIDING

BLACK MOUNTAINS GLIDING CLUB
The Airfield, Talgarth, Brecon, Powys LD3 0EJ (01874 711463/www.talgarthgc.co.uk).

PARAMANIA
Fforest Farm, Hundred House, Builth Wells, Powys LD1 5RT (01982 570406/www.paramania.co.uk).

PARAVENTURE SPORTS
12 Station Enterprises, Station
Road, Abergavenny, Monmouthshire
NP7 5HY (01873 856009/
www.paraventure.co.uk).

**WELSH PARAGLIDING AND
HANG GLIDING CENTRE**
Wilberton House, Frogmore Street,
Abergavenny, Monmouthshire NP7
5AL (01873 850910/
www.welshairsports.com).

HORSE RIDING

BLACK MOUNTAINS HOLIDAYS
*Castle Farm, Capel-y-Ffin, Abergavenny,
Monmouthshire NP7 7NP (01873
890961/www.hay-on-wye.co.uk/
bmholidays).*

**CANTREF RIDING CENTRE
& ADVENTURE FARM**
Upper Cantref Farm, Cantref, Brecon,
Powys LD3 8LR (01874 665223/
www.cantref.com).

ELLESMERE RIDING CENTRE
Llangorse, Brecon, Powys LD3 7UN
(01874 658252/www.trail-riding.co.uk).

FREE REIN
The Coach House, Clyro Court, Clyro,
Herefordshire HR3 5LE (01497
821356/www.free-rein.co.uk).

GOLDEN CASTLE RIDING STABLES
Llangattock, Crickhowell, Powys
NP8 1PY (01874 730987/
www.golden-castle.co.uk).

GRANGE TREKKING
The Grange, Capel-y-Ffin, Abergavenny,
Monmouthshire NP7 7NP (01873
890215/www.grangetrekking.co.uk).

LLANTHONY RIDING & TREKKING
Court Farm, Llanthony, Abergavenny,
Monmouthshire NP7 7NN (01873 890359/
www.llanthony.co.uk).

TREGOYD MOUNTAIN RIDERS
Tregoyd, Three Cocks, Brecon,
Powys LD3 0SP (01497 847351/
www.tregoydriding.co.uk).

TREVELOG TREKKING
Llanthony, Abergavenny, Monmouthshire
NP7 7NW (01873 890216/
www.pony-trekking.net).

HOT-AIR BALLOON FLIGHTS

FLYING COLOURS
8 St David's Crescent, Llanddewi
Rhydderch, Abergavenny NP7 9TR
(01873 840045/www.bailey
balloons.co.uk).

MOUNTAIN BOARDING

GREENMAN MOUNTAIN BOARD CENTRE
Penpont Estate, Brecon, Powys LD3 8EU
(01874 636202/www.penpont.com).

MULTI-ACTIVITY CENTRES

BLACK MOUNTAIN ACTIVITIES
Three Cocks, Brecon, Powys LD3 0SD
(01497 847897/www.black
mountain.co.uk).

MOUNTAIN & WATER
2 Upper Cwm Nant Gam, Llanelly Hill, nr
Abergavenny NP7 0RF (01873 831825/
www.mountainandwater.co.uk).

SKY TREK
Llangorse Rope and Riding Centre,
Llangorse, Brecon, Powys LD3 7UH
(01874 658272/www.activityuk.com).

Glorious
countryside and
award-winning
inns – Felin Fach
Griffin.

tered, with such quirky details as frog-shaped door handles and light pulls. The deep tubs and huge circular shower heads are a dream for sore muscles. Individual details include a carved wooden Rajasthani four-poster in room three and a brass four-poster in room six. Apart from having to provide your ETA, breakfast is a thoroughly relaxed affair around a long communal table, with favourite cereals, jugs of fresh milk, toast done on the Aga and thick bacon, bold bangers and eggs as-you-like, with just the perfect glint of grease. Four-legged friends can sleep in your room for £10 a night, and kids are OK too!

Gliffaes Country House Hotel

Crickhowell, Powys NP8 1RH (01874 730371/ www.gliffaes.com). **Rates** £80-£190 double. **Credit** AmEx, MC, V.

Locals may tell you that Gliffaes, which has been one of the best trad hotels in the area since it first opened its doors to guests in 1948, is looking a little shabby these days. But you'd better check when they last visited. Owners James and Susy Suitor are turning terrific tricks on their family inheritance, redecorating this splendid 19th-century Italianate pile with a hawk's eye for detail. Set in 32 acres of terraced grounds above the River Usk, it is affordable, too, with single rooms going from £65; prize rooms are still reasonable at £155-£190. Room six is the most coveted, with a balcony, river view and roll-top bath that looks out over the garden. Rooms three, which occupies the old library, and 17, with its Jacobean-style four-poster bed, are both equally splendid. When you're dining in the hushed restaurant you could hear a squirrel scratching its nose on a branch outside, while the drawing room and conservatory offer quietude and calm for those wanting to kick back with the daily paper. For the active, there's fishing and walking on the hotel's doorstep.

Old Post Office

Llanigon, Hay-on-Wye, Herefordshire HR3 5QA (01497 820008/www.oldpost-office.co.uk). **Rates** £40-£60 double. **No credit cards**.

Although parts of the building date back to the 1300s, this was only ever a post office for a few years in the 1980s. In fact, owners Linda Webb and James Moore would have called it by its earlier appellation, the Sun Inn, had they known more about the history of the place when they established it as a B&B some 14 years ago. Still, with word-of-mouth business continuing to come in thick and fast, they're not about to make any drastic changes to a formula that has worked so well for them. The Old Post Office is a relaxed vegetarian B&B with understated decor and no pretences. It's worth paying the £10 extra per person per night for the en suite attic room. Much more spacious than the double and twin rooms on the floor below, it has views across to the Beggins in the west and the Black Mountains in the east. Or opt for the spacious double in an adjoining converted barn, which has its own entrance.

Breakfast around the communal table, beautifully laid with blue crockery, will satiate with fried potato cakes, eggs, tomatoes, mushrooms, toast and home-made jams. Linda and James also run Oxford Cottage in Hay-on-Wye (Oxford Road, 01497 820008, www.oxfordcottage.co.uk), which sleeps up to six people and where you'll find all the ingredients you need to cook your own breakfast in the fridge. Book into an individual room or rent the whole cottage.

Peterstone Court Country House Hotel & Bistro

Llanhamlach, Brecon, Powys LD3 7YB (01874 665387/www.peterstone-court.com). **Lunch** served noon-2.30pm, **dinner served** 7-9.30pm daily. **Main courses** £12.50-£16.50. **Set lunch** (Sun) £14.95 2 courses, £17.50 3 courses. **Rates** £80-£150 double. **Credit** AmEx, MC, V.

Situated back off the Brecon Road between Brecon and Crickhowell, Peterstone Court is eager to shout about its celebrity endorsement – apparently it was a fave of Johnny Depp and John Malkovich when they were in Crickhowell to film *The Libertine*. However, the hotel may yet have a little way to go before it completely convinces as a premier destination. Opened in late 2003, it's the newest venture of owners Jess and Glyn Bridgeman and Sean Gerrard, who have turned the nearby Nantyffin Cider Mill Inn (*see p258*) into an award-winning restaurant. With the benefit of a grand shell to work with, they are slowly turning this Georgian manor house into a hotel that successfully combines the luxury of traditional furnishings and decor with such contemporary comforts as DVDs and flat-screen televisions in the bedrooms and modern art hanging in the stairwells. The hotel's terrace has views of the Central Brecon Beacons, the River Usk is at the bottom of the garden and there's a heated outdoor pool for the summer. A subterranean gym, which has a jacuzzi and sauna but is in need of a refit, is available for guests to use year-round.

Pwll-y-Faedda

Pwll-y-Faedda, Erwood, Builth Wells, Powys LD2 3YS (01982 560202/www.pwlly faedda.co.uk). **Dinner served** by prior arrangement. **Set dinner** £28 4 courses. **Rooms** £85-£93 double. **Credit** AmEx, MC, V.

If there's one place you stay this year, make it Pwll-y-Faedda. From the moment you open the door into the wood-panelled hallway of this 1920s fishing lodge, you know you have arrived somewhere rather special. Situated on the banks of the River Wye, with private fishing and surrounding walks, this B&B is lovingly run by Yolande and Jeremy Jaquet. Although the lodge can sleep up to 12, only three rooms are occupied at one time. That means that each evening no more than six guests sit down with their hosts in the chandelier-lit dining room. The three-course set menu typically features such dishes as Welsh goat's cheese with a black olive tapenade crust for starters and salmon in a lemon chive butter sauce served on a bed of spinach with crushed new potatoes for mains, followed by sticky toffee pudding. Coffee and chocolates are served in the elegant drawing room. A games room with a billiard table and a conservatory with river views are available for use at any time. When you finally retire, make sure you've booked into either the Cinnamon room (red, spicy decor with an oriental twist) or the Gold room (done up with brides in mind). All bedrooms, except the Blue twin room, look over the Wye.

The Start

Hay-on-Wye, Herefordshire HR3 5RS (01497 821391/www.the-start.net). **Rooms** £50 double. **No credit cards**.
If there is a more ebullient hostess than the Start's, we've yet to come across her. All smiles, with a wild crown of golden hair, Dawn Farnworth enthusiastically welcomes guests aboard her tightly run ship. Just across the bridge from Hay town centre, this convivial B&B has an enviable riverside location, despite its proximity to a small yet relatively busy B-road. A sizeable terrace looks over the garden, stomping ground of the hens that lay your breakfast eggs. The three en suite rooms (one with bath), all named after Hay streets, are immaculate. Delicate quilted bedspreads are handmade by Dawn's mother, while marmalades and jams on the breakfast table are Dawn's own creations – try the rhubarb and rose petal or gooseberry and elderflower flavours.

WHERE TO EAT & DRINK

Allt yr Ynys Country House Hotel

Walterstone, nr Abergavenny, Herefordshire HR2 0DU (01873 890307/www.allthotel.co.uk). **Lunch served** noon-2pm Mon-Fri, Sun. **Dinner served** 7-9.30pm Mon-Sat; 7-9pm Sun. **Main courses** £10-£19. **Set lunch** £17.50 3 courses. **Credit** AmEx, MC, V.
This Grade II-listed manor house has provided excellent dining for 14 years; eight under the current owners. The dining room is a masterpiece of understatement with good-quality glassware, cutlery and linen, and comfortable chairs. Ian Jackson uses underrated fish to great effect and his daily menus feature seasonal produce. Start with a risotto of creamed wild mushrooms with lightly poached egg and truffle-infused bubbles, or caramelised Cornish scallops on creamed celeriac and bacon with a chilli and coriander beurre blanc. Main courses include baked pavé of pollock with herb tapenade crust, puréed potatoes, braised celery, and tomato and basil vinaigrette. Even old standards like rack of Welsh lamb are given a new twist, served with garlic cream and a thyme and white wine sauce. Abergavenny is the meeting point for Welsh, Herefordshire and West Country cheesemakers, so the choice is tremendous. No smoking throughout.

Angel Hotel

15 Cross Street, Abergavenny, Monmouthshire NP7 5EN (01873 857121/www.angelhotel abergavenny.com). **Lunch served** noon-2.30pm, **dinner served** 7-10pm daily. **Main courses** £10.50-£16.40. **Set lunch** (Mon-Sat) £8.80 2 courses; (Sun) £14.80 3 courses. **Rates** £85-£120 double; £175 2-bed lodge. **Credit** AmEx, MC, V.
This Georgian coaching inn had gone to ruin, but since being bought and restored by Caradog Hotels in 2002, the bar and dining room have provided an excellent and – by local standards – opulent setting. Chef Mark Turton offers well-planned menus at staggeringly low prices. Starters of cream of mushroom soup and fan of melon with pink grapefruit sorbet are dramatically presented. Main courses include a generous plateful of the local staple, roast leg of Welsh lamb, complete with mint sauce and al dente veg. Puddings of chocolate fondant with rum ice-cream and caramelised lemon tart with vanilla mascarpone are hugely tempting. The wine list is short, well chosen and priced to sell.

Barn at Brynich

Brynich, Powys LD3 7SH (01874 623480/ www.brynich.co.uk). **Lunch served** noon-2.30pm daily. **Dinner served** 6-9.30pm Mon-Sat; 6-9pm Sun. **Main courses** £7-£13. **Rates** £145 1 bed cottage (3 nights, off-peak); £280 1 bed cottage (1 week, peak season). **Credit** MC, V.
This old farm has been renovated to a high standard. The restaurant, which takes up the whole of the central barn, has a dramatic feel: beams, a stone fireplace and whitewash mixed with local red mud create a rich, roseate glow. Outside, a children's play area makes it a godsend to families. Meals are rudimentary, using organic and local produce wherever possible. A starter of jardinière salad was glorious, with fresh rocket, salad burnet, sun-dried tomatoes, preserved artichoke hearts and asparagus finished with cilowen cheese. Excellent organic vegetable kebabs on tagliatelle come with a rich tomato sauce. 'Barn Favourites' include steak and ale pie or a trio of local sausages with mash and onion gravy. Timings and flavour combinations need to be watched on some dishes – a wonderful trout was marred by an unnecessary mushroom and red wine sauce. The wine list is short and predominantly New World. No smoking throughout.

The Bear Hotel

Crickhowell, Powys NP8 1BW (01873 810408/ www.bearhotel.co.uk). **Bar & bistro Open/ lunch served** noon-2pm daily. **Dinner served** 6-10pm Mon-Sat; 7-9pm Sun. **Main courses** £4.95-£15.95. *Restaurant* **Lunch served** noon-2pm Sun. **Dinner served** 7-9.30pm Tue-Sat. **Main courses** £12.50-£18.20. **Rooms** £75-£140 double. **Credit** AmEx, MC, V.
The food may win glowing reviews elsewhere, but we have yet to be impressed by the Bear's

Hay-on-Wye, king of the bookheap.

BOOKED UP

Where else in the world might you happen upon David Baddiel, ex-Catatonia frontwoman Cerys Matthews, Macy Gray, Louis de Bernières, David Lodge, Joseph Heller, Maya Angelou, Rory Bremner, Arthur Miller, Bill Clinton, John Le Carré (the list goes on and on and on...) while strolling around a small, rural town with a population of only 1,300? Well, you certainly can in Hay-on-Wye. Every year around 80,000 visitors descend on this tome town to hear politicians, comedians, playwrights, novelists, critics, academics and artists discuss ideas inside a tent in a primary school car park.

Launched in 1988 by Peter Florence with the proceeds of a poker game between young graduates, Hay Literary Festival has gone from a weekend-long pub-garden event to a ten-day frenzy of scholarly gymnastics in marquees and other venues across town. Nowadays there's plenty of music and partying thrown in too.

Despite the floods of national and international pilgrims to Hay Festival, the events – of which there is an archive of over 30,000 – are still an intimate experience. Venues are rarely larger than a small marquee and are filled with a hungry intellectual audience, whose passion for great words penned and read by favourite authors is palpable. Sadly, though, the festival has been a victim of new technology. Since ticket sales went online, you're far less likely to be able to stroll up to the box office on the day of an event and get your audience with, say, John Updike or Edna O'Brien. As with accommodation, festival-goers' mantra must now be: 'Book ahead, book ahead, book ahead.' Still, if you can't get tickets for the main festival, you'll be pleased to learn that December 2004 saw the first Hay Festival Weekender and there is now

a trilingual offshoot held in the village of Deià, Mallorca, which features Catalan-, Spanish- and English-speaking authors and commentators.
Hay Festival (information 0870 787 2848/box office 0870 990 1299/ www.hayfestival.com).

cholesterol-raising bar menu. Nevertheless, you can't fail to have an entertaining few hours over a drawn-out pint in this old coaching inn – the building dates back to 1432 and a 19th-century coaching timetable is displayed in the low-beamed bar. This is prime people-watching and eaves-dropping territory, with folk from Crickhowell and the surrounding hills congregating for ani-mated conversation and plenty of 'he said, she said, he said'.

The Beaufort

Beaufort Street, Crickhowell, Powys NP8 1AD (01873 810402). **Lunch served** noon-2.30pm Wed-Sat; noon-3pm Sun. **Dinner served** 7-9.30pm Tue-Sat; 7-9pm Sun. **Main courses** £12.50-£16. **Set dinner** (Tue-Thur) £18.95 3 courses. **Credit** MC, V.
Since late 2003, the Beaufort has offered well-planned, seasonal menus and a short but attrac-tive wine list. Chef Heather Matthews cut her teeth at the Daneswood House Hotel in Shipham and seems to enjoy using the abundant local produce. Crickhowell is a town full of rock stars, so if you're lucky you might spot somebody from Oasis down-ing a sherry or two in this flash, newly modernised lounge bar. Starters include own-cured gravadlax, watercress salad and crème fraîche, or warm duck confit salad. Main courses are tried and trusted combinations that rarely disappoint – say, thyme-roasted poussin with parmesan mash and roast vegetables, medallions of local beef with truffled creamed potatoes, wild mushrooms and Madeira jus, or fried skate wing with pommes anna, spinach purée and beurre noisette. To finish, try white and dark chocolate terrine or the hazelnut parfait. Most items on the wine list are under £20 and there's a good choice of half-bottles.

Blue Boar

Castle Street, Hay-on-Wye, Herefordshire HR3 5DF (01497 820884). **Breakfast served** 10.30am-noon, **lunch served** noon-3pm, **dinner served** 6-9pm daily. **Main courses** £7.95-£13.95. **Credit** MC, V.
A local institution, the Blue Boar is snug for cosy chats around an open fire. Local gossip reverber-ates among the curios that hang from the rafters and nestle on old chests. Wriggle on to one of the dark wooden pews, polished by ample bottoms (which may owe their size to the hearty food from the extensive bar menu). Dishes can be a bit hit-and-miss, so go for reliable choices such as the steak and chips or Welsh rarebit. Good for a pint or a glass of wine at any time, the Blue Boar has a late licence during Hay Literary Festival.

The Bull's Head

Craswell, Herefordshire HR2 0PN (01981 510616). **Open** *Bar* 11am-11pm daily. **Meals served** noon-8pm Mon-Sat; noon-5pm Sun. **Main courses** £7.95-£12.95. **Rates** £45-£55 double. **Credit** MC, V.

The Bull's Head, located on the eastern side of the Black Hill, is loved by everyone in the area and exalted for its generous menu; locally reared and grown meat and vegetables are combined with ales brewed at the Wye Valley Brewery (also served at the bar) to create traditional dishes with a twist. The pork-stuffed, bacon-wrapped fillet of venison with a stilton and port sauce, or Craswell's 'crassie' pie with beef, bacon and Butty Bach ale gravy are prime examples. If there's one thing the Bull's Head is famous for, however, it's the enor-mous 'huffer' sandwiches from the slim but satis-fying bar menu. Try the Atkins dieter's nemesis, the chips and cheddar huffer. The bar, unchanged from when it was a single-room farmers' pub, has peeling wallpaper, high-backed wooden pews and a wood burner. There's a huge garden for sunny days. Note that the Bull's Head is for sale – so there may be changes afoot,

The Café

39 High Street, Brecon, Powys LD3 7AP (01874 611191). **Meals served** 10am-4pm daily. **Main courses** £3-£4.75. **No credit cards.**
If you're in Brecon for the farmers' market, then the Café, down the High Street from the Market Hall, is the best place in town for an own-made cake or pudding with a Fair Trade/organic frothy cappuccino or hot chocolate. Whitewashed floor-boards, shocking-pink chairs and a brushed-steel counter offer a rare slice of shabby chic. If there's a group of you, make your way down to the basement with its acid decor, leather sofas and big communal table. You can refuel at lunchtime with the likes of a cheese toastie, lasagne, or chilli and jacket potato.

Felin Fach Griffin

Felin Fach, nr Brecon, Powys LD3 0UB (01874 620111/www.eatdrinksleep.ltd.uk). **Lunch served** 12.30-2.30pm Tue-Sun. **Dinner served** 7-9.30pm daily. **Main courses** £13.50-£17. **Credit** DC, MC, V.
The Griffin is an award-winning gastropub, voted Local Food Pub of the Year 2004 at the Les Routiers Awards and Best Restaurant of 2004/5 at the Wales Food and Drink Awards. A sprawl-ing interior with subdued lighting and well-chosen background music puts customers at their ease. Appetisers like butternut squash soup with hazelnut oil are wonderful. Starters include roast scallops with baby gems, peas and lemon butter, or salad of seared tuna, baby artichoke, tapenade and gazpacho. Lobster, wood pigeon and spring vegetable salad was not only original but satisfy-ing – the bitter taste of the pigeon offset by the lobster's sweetness. Main course oak-smoked salmon was brimming with flavour, served on a bed of crushed new potatoes and spinach sur-rounded by a moat of chive butter. Unusual desserts like yoghurt mousse with figs marinated in sangria were light and appealing – just as you'd expect of this local star.

Gliffaes Country House Hotel

Crickhowell, Powys NP8 1RH (01874 730371/ www.gliffaes.com). **Lunch served** noon-2.30pm, **dinner served** 7.30-9.15pm daily. **Main courses** £12-£17. **Set dinner** £24.50 2 courses, £29.50 3 courses. **Credit** AmEx, MC, V.

An understated approach to country-house interiors makes this one of the most relaxing hotels we've seen. Menus retain conservative classics, giving them an attractive modern twist. French onion soup was lighter than the norm, while a rich ham hock and foie gras terrine was balanced with nicely sharp pear chutney. Fried calf's liver came on a bed of mash and topped with crispy bacon and shallots. Also on the menu was seared tuna with a warm salad of tomato, green bean and olives garnished with hard-boiled egg. A supporter of the admirable Slow Food Movement, Gliffaes has a policy of sourcing three-quarters of its fresh produce from within 25 miles of the hotel. The wine list includes house wines at £12.50.

Kilvert's Hotel

The Bullring, Hay-on-Wye, Herefordshire HR3 5AG (01497 821042/www.kilverts.co.uk). **Lunch served** noon-2pm, **dinner served** 7-9pm daily. **Main courses** £8.95-£14.50. **Set dinner** £17.50 2 courses, £21.95 3 courses. **Rates** £70-£90 double. **Credit** AmEx, MC, V.

With a roomy bar and decent pub food, Kilvert's is popular year-round. But it's best during the Hay Literary Festival and in summer when you can sit by the pond with a poetry book in one hand and a pint in the other. Children will love the rambling lawns. Alternatively, take a table on the front terrace and watch the doolally literati and locals pass by. Kilvert's also has 11 en suite guest rooms and a reasonable restaurant.

Llangoed Hall

Llyswen, Brecon, Powys LD3 0YP (01874 754525/www.llangoedhall.com). **Lunch served** 12.30-2.30pm, **dinner served** 7-9.30pm daily. **Set lunch** £25 3 courses. **Set dinner** £43 3 courses. **Rates** £195-£340 double; £350-£385 suite. **Credit** AmEx, DC, MC, V.

Sir Bernard Ashley bought Llangoed Hall in 1987 and launched this luxurious country-house hotel on unsuspecting Powys. Renovated as a showcase for Laura Ashley's interior designs, and latterly fabrics and furnishings from Sir Bernard's textile company Elanbach, it has an enviable position overlooking the River Wye. The well-lit, yellow-walled dining room is a lively place with personable, international staff. A lounge menu includes sandwiches, salads and grills, while the dinner menu features cenarth blue cheese soufflé on a rocket and walnut salad and potted shrimps with crab mayonnaise and quails' eggs. Mains might include Breconshire venison loin on a leek and puy lentil stew or crisply presented red mullet on a warm niçoise salad. The wine list is voluminous, with plenty of vintage champagnes.

Llanwenarth Hotel

Brecon Road, Abergavenny, Monmouthshire NP8 1EP (01873 810550/www.llanwenarth hotel.com). **Lunch served** noon-2pm Mon-Sat; noon-3pm Sun. **Dinner served** 5.30-9.30pm Mon-Sat; 6-9pm Sun. **Main courses** £9.45-£13.95. **Set lunch** £9.95 2 courses, £12.25 3 courses. **Set dinner** (5.30-7pm) £14.25 3 courses. **Rates** £85 double; £105 family room. **Credit** MC, V.

Once known as the Pantriwlgoch, this roadside hotel is under new ownership and has reverted to its original name. The interior now boasts cheerful colours and comfortable furniture. The menu has also improved. Starters of black pudding and boudin blanc on mash with red wine reduction, baked filo pastry parcels of goat's cheese with rocket salad or moules marinière are well prepared. Thoughtful vegetarian options include oyster mushroom fettuccine with truffle oil and parmesan, or baked pepper, tomato and onion tartlet with smoked cheese and spinach. There's also local beef, lamb and fish. A short but user-friendly wine list offers a good house wine and some attractive half-bottles.

Nantyffin Cider Mill Inn

Brecon Road, Crickhowell, Powys NP8 1SG (01873 810775/www.cidermill.co.uk). **Lunch served** noon-2.30pm Tue-Sun. **Dinner served** 7-9.30pm Tue-Sat. **Main courses** £10.95-£14.95. **Set lunch** (Tue-Fri) £10 2 courses, £13 3 courses. **Credit** AmEx, MC, V.

Chef Sean Gerrard has built up something of a local dining empire with his business partners Glyn and Jessica Bridgeman. The flagship enterprise is probably Nantyffin Cider Mill, its vivid pink-washed frontage unmissable in a bold roadside position. The menus have an attractive Mediterranean character, enhanced by outside tables in summer. Starters of seared scallops on a richly dressed caesar salad can be followed by slow-cooked shoulder of lamb or fresh fish from the blackboard. The group also owns the neighbouring Manor Hotel (Brecon Road, Crickhowell, Powys NP8 1SE; 01873 810212) and the wonderfully located Peterstone Court (*see p253*), a relaxed hotel and bistro in Brecon Beacons National Park. All three restaurants serve organic duck, chicken and lamb from their own farm in Llangynidr.

Shepherd's Ice Cream Parlour & Coffee Shop

9 High Town, Hay-on-Wye, Herefordshire HR3 5AE (01497 821898). **Open** 9.30am-5.30pm Mon-Sat; 10.30am-5.30pm Sun. **No credit cards.**

Once sold from a hole in the wall on nearby Lion Street, Shepherd's Ice Cream now has its own Edwardian-style ice-cream parlour on the main high street. The delicious sheep's milk ice-cream was initially produced on Shepherd's sheep farm in 1986 and the business has gone from strength to strength ever since. Sheep's milk (a naturally homogenised milk high in solids) is rich and creamy enough to eliminate the need for cream, butter or eggs. That means you can lick away at such flavours as damson, hazelnut or ginger without doing too much damage to your waistline. Try the fresh fruit sorbets and ice-cream cakes too.

Tipple 'n' Tiffin

Theatr Brycheiniog, Canal Wharf, Brecon, Powys LD3 7EW (01874 611866/www. brycheiniog.co.uk). **Lunch served** noon-2.30pm, **dinner served** 7-9pm Mon-Sat. **Main courses** £6-£8. **Credit** AmEx, DC, MC, V.
Richard and Louise Gudsell's restaurant is located on the ground-floor corner of the Theatr Brycheiniog that overlooks Brecon's tiny canal basin. The setting is unconventional; so is the menu. All dishes are somewhere between starter and main course in size, and designed to be shared. What started as a good idea for theatre-goers (pre-show dinners are available) has become a great venue for everybody. Penclawdd cockles served with crispy bacon, salad and salsa vie for attention with Menai mussels flavoured with white wine, cream and roast garlic. Appealing dishes are pepper and goat's cheese terrine or a substantial chorizo, feta, sun-blush tomato and olive salad. Or try Tamworth pork marinated in hoisin, or rabbit cooked with leeks and served with a root vegetable mash. Most dishes have a homely, fresh-from-the-oven feel that adds to the enjoyment. The short wine list is predominantly New World; half of the selection is available by the glass. No smoking throughout.

Walnut Tree Inn

Llandewi Skirrid, Monmouthshire NP7 8AW (01873 852797/www.thewalnuttreeinn.com). **Lunch served** noon-2.30pm Tue-Sun. **Dinner served** 7-10pm Tue-Sat. **Main courses** £12.75-£21.50. **Credit** MC, V.

The opening-up of the old dining room has given this excellent restaurant a more airy feel. The food is still Welsh/Italian – a strange hybrid virtually invented by ex-owner Franco Taruschio. For starters, expect fresh asparagus with poached egg. Pasta includes taglione with sweet, fresh scallops in tomato and basil sauce. Apart from the fresh sewin, pollock, swordfish and turbot, there is a magnificent brodetto of fish served with bruschetta. There's also a well-prepared poached ham hock with baby vegetables in savoury broth. To follow: warm figs with Welsh honey, balsamic and mascarpone. Good wines and delightful service round off a great experience – but be warned, there's no longer a good-value, fixed-priced lunch and prices on the à la carte have increased noticeably.

White Swan

Llanfrynach, Powys LD3 7BZ (01874 665276/ www.the-white-swan.com). **Lunch served** noon-2pm Wed-Sat; noon-2.30pm Sun. **Dinner served** 7-9.30pm Wed-Sat; 7-9pm Sun. **Main courses** £10.95-£14.95. **Credit** MC, V.
Relaunched as a gastropub five years ago, the White Swan provides a fine setting. The dining room facing the village church looks great – all ancient wood and stone surfaces – but is only open during the evening. Lunch is served in the bar overlooking a cute terrace. Meat and veg are local and there's an excellent selection of fish delivered every other day from Swansea. Starters included a massive bruschetta of buffalo mozzarella, rather pale tomatoes and basil with balsamic and pesto. (Salads of black pudding and dry-cured local bacon with tomato jam are served at dinner only.) Mains included an overdone cod fillet with creamed leeks and parsley sauce, honey-glazed lamb shank or organic chicken in parma ham with a lemon and herb risotto. The wine list features good-value New World bottles among Old World stars.

Upper Hepste valley

Ludlow

Quiet charms and fine food.

Where exactly is Ludlow? That's a common question when you say you're visiting this medieval market town in Shropshire. And it's just as well. For, in contrast to England's more famous holiday destinations – Stratford, say, or the Cotswolds – Ludlow's charm doesn't come with crowds. Call it a dark horse, a late bloomer, a well-kept secret: Ludlow is only now beginning to appear on the tourist map. This is largely due to its burgeoning status as a foodie favourite, but its physical beauty is also a big draw, from Shropshire's buxom hills and fecund valleys to the town's splendid Georgian and Tudor architecture.

So what took people so long to discover Ludlow? After all, the great and the good have been singing Ludlow's praises for aeons: Housman immortalised its 'blue remembered hills' in *A Shropshire Lad*; John Betjeman dubbed it 'the loveliest town in England'; and Pevsner raved about the architecture (there are 500 listed buildings). Tourists, however, remained oblivious. This was largely down to one thing: location. Tucked away in the hills near the borders of Wales and Herefordshire, Ludlow is an hour away from the nearest motorway – literally on the road to nowhere. But its isolation has also been its saving grace. The high street is largely free of chain stores. Local farmers still peddle their foodstuffs in local shops. And the pace of life is so unhurried that Ludlow has officially been recognised by the international Slow Movement as Britain's first official 'Slow City' (www.cittaslow.org).

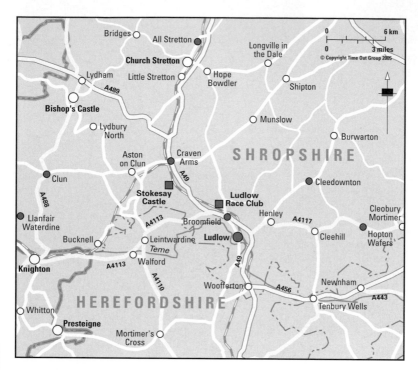

Ironically, what threatened to kill Ludlow has only made it stronger. In the early 1990s Tesco announced it was opening a superstore in town. Locals were horrified: could local shops – butchers, grocers, bakers – survive the corporate onslaught? Determined to keep the town alive, the townspeople played to their strengths: in 1994 they threw the town's first annual Food Festival, a three-day showcase for local producers. It was a smash hit. That same year, top chef Shaun Hill arrived from London and opened the Merchant House restaurant (now closed) – Ludlow's first Michelin-starred eaterie. Other chefs followed, lured by the abundance of excellent local produce. Tesco eventually came, but the town survived. Thrived even. Now Ludlow is a happy marriage of something old and something new – a role model for towns in 21st-century Britain.

Grand designs

There's more to Ludlow than Michelin stars and farmers' markets. For a start, the architecture is as spectacular as the food. Ludlow Castle (01584 873355, www.ludlowcastle.com), built in the 11th century to protect England from attacks by the Welsh, is one of England's most romantic ruins. The roof is gone, but its proud limestone walls still stand, turning various shades of pink and purple in the

evening sun. It's architecturally significant – it combines Norman, medieval and Tudor styles – and historically important too: this was once the home of Roger Mortimer, who toppled Edward II in 1326 and put Ludlow on the political map; later it played an important part in the Wars of the Roses; and Prince Arthur died here on his honeymoon with Catherine of Aragon, allowing Henry VIII to become king.

Across the square, Castle Lodge (Castle Square, 01584 878098), a privately owned Tudor house, is open to the public every day. Considered to be one of England's 1,000 best buildings by Simon Jenkins, its empty, oak-panelled rooms – complete with creaky stairs and lopsided floors – are pure faded glory.

St Laurence's Church, the burial place of poet AE Housman, dates back to 1199. The magnificent building, a combination of Norman and early English architecture, is often assumed to be a cathedral. Certainly its cream-coloured tower dominates the skyline; if you climb to the top, brace yourself for the best views in Ludlow. No wonder Jenkins christened it one of England's 18 finest churches.

The Feathers Hotel (Bull Ring, 01584 875261, www.feathersatludlow.co.uk), a Grade I-listed, half-timbered extravaganza, is considered one of the finest examples

Accommodation	★★
Food & drink	★★★★
Nightlife	
Shopping	★★
Culture	★★
Sights	★★
Scenery	★★★★

of Tudor architecture in England (it's certainly among the most photographed). Nearby Broad Street, a sloping avenue of Georgian and Tudor buildings, is an architectural showpiece.

Shopping in Shropshire

Its ancient architecture is impressive, but Ludlow is not a living museum: on the contrary, it's a thriving market town. Regular street markets are held on Castle Square on Monday, Friday and Saturday, and, from April to September, on Wednesday too. Antique and flea markets are occasionally held here (first and third Sundays of the month) as are local produce markets (second Thursday of the month).

For shopping, Ludlow's forte is food and antiques. On the food front, there are four butchers. Carters (6 King Street, 01584 874665) won the best sausage award in Ludlow at the 2004 Food Festival, while DW Walls (14 High Street, 01584 872060) won best pork pie. Also worth seeking out are AH Griffiths (11 Bull Ring, 01584 872141) and Reg Martin & Sons (1 Market Street, 01584 872008). For bakers, try the famous SC Price & Son (7 Castle Street, 01584 872815). Bread is prepared the old-fashioned way: staff come into work before midnight to prepare the dough and return at dawn to bake it, without using any chemical agents. Other bakers include R Walton (7-8 Market Street, 01584 872088), De Grey's (see p269) and Richard C Swift (5 Parkway, off Corve Street, 01584 874767). For all-round epicurean delights, visit the Deli on the Square (4 Church Street, 01584 877353); chocaholics should head for the Chocolate Gourmet (Castle Square, 01584 879332); cheese connoisseurs swear by Mousetrap Cheese (6 Church Street, 01584 879556). In addition to the market, a good place to buy fresh fruit and veg is the Farmers' Produce Market (1 Mill Street, 01584 873532).

Antique shops are ten a penny in Ludlow. The best hunting ground is on Corve Street. For old furniture, porcelain and glass, Corve Street Antiques (141A Corve Street, 01584 879100) is good value; G&D Ginger (5 Corve Street, 01584 876939), at the other end of the price scale, specialises in high-quality, antique oak and country furniture. The quirkiest street in the town, Quality Square, yields one of the quirkiest shops, the Silk Top Hat Gallery (4 Quality Square,

01584 875363), which sells unusual gifts and contemporary art. But the most striking shop is Dinham House (Dinham Road, below the castle, 01584 878100). The largest Georgian house in Ludlow, it was once occupied by Lucien Bonaparte, Napoleon's brother, who lived here for six months in 1811. Today, it is a showroom for wood-burning stoves by Clearview and handcrafted furniture, but it manages to retain a grand period feel.

Get outside

Ludlow is small and easy to navigate, but guided walks, run by the Ludlow Historical Research Group, put everything into perspective. They start by the cannon at the Castle entrance every Saturday and Sunday at 2.30pm (plus bank holidays from April to October). Charges are £2 for adults, £1 children. For details phone 01584 874205.

For a romantic stroll along the River Teme, walk downhill from the Castle towards Dinham Bridge, but, instead of crossing the bridge, follow the road to the right. You'll soon come to the lovely Linney Riverside Park, where you can rent a rowing boat in season.

For a country walk, head downhill from the castle, past Dinham House, and cross over Dinham Bridge. For a short walk, turn left along the river. The path soon rises and takes you on to Whitcliffe Common, which boasts fine views of Ludlow. The path eventually takes you downhill again to Ludford Bridge Road. Turn left, cross over the bridge, and you're back in town. The whole walk takes about 20 minutes. For something more ambitious, start again at Dinham Bridge. After you cross it, instead of turning left towards Whitcliffe Common, go right and follow the path along the edge of the hill. The Mortimer Trail, a 30-mile walk, takes in Mortimer Forest – prime wildlife-watching territory – and ends up in the village of Kington. For more information on walks in the Ludlow area, see the Secret Hills Discovery Centre (see p264) or visit the Tourist Information Centre (see below).

Beyond Ludlow

The rolling countryside surrounding Ludlow – windswept hills, lush valleys, gurgling streams – is an attraction in its own right, but there are a couple of bona fide tourist attractions too. The Ludlow Races is where Ludlow picks up speed. Located a couple of miles north of town on the A49 to

Ludlow

TOURIST INFORMATION
Ludlow
Castle Street, Ludlow SY8 1AS
(01584 875053/www.ludlow.org.uk).

Shrewsbury, the Ludlow Race Club (Bromfield, Ludlow, 01584 856221, www.ludlow-racecourse.co.uk) hosts 15 National Hunt races a year.

Stokesay Castle (between Ludlow and Craven Arms on the A49, 01588 672544, www.english-heritage.org.uk) is considered to be England's finest 13th-century manor house. Technically, it's not a castle, but it resembles one: back in 1291 Edward I granted its owner a 'licence to crenellate' the tower for defence purposes. It's notable for its grand hall, ornate, panelled living room and the tower with fine views.

Secret Hills, the Shropshire Hills Discovery Centre (Ludlow Road, Craven Arms, 01588 676000/www.secrethills. com), traces the evolution of the Shropshire landscape. Its museum, devoted to the study of nature, ecology and archaeology, is notable for its amazing grass roof and an exhibition on the Shropshire mammoth. It also offers visitors several classic countryside walks: Onny Meadows, the Riverside Ramble, the Hill & Dales Hike and the Three Woods Walk.

The nearby village of Clun, hidden in a green valley, was immortalised by Housman for being 'the quietest under the sun' – a description that still applies today. Bishops Castle, a village north-west of Clun, is famous for its beer: real ale drinkers sup in droves at its independent, pub-based breweries. Church Stretton, 30 minutes north of Ludlow along the A49, has a dramatic backdrop: the town and its surrounding communities and countryside have been dubbed Little Switzerland and the Highlands of England on account of the hilly terrain.

Ironbridge, an hour's drive north-east of Ludlow, is famous as the 'birthplace of the Industrial Revolution'. Ten museums are strewn along the densely forested, mineral-rich Severn Gorge, where, in 1709, ironmaster Abraham Darby first used coke as a fuel for smelting iron. His experiments revolutionised transport, engineering and construction. Today, you can walk across the eponymous Iron Bridge, built in 1777, learn about the role of iron in industrialisation at the Museum of Iron or stroll through a replica Victorian town. For full information on all of the museums, call 01952 884391/www.ironbridge.org.uk.

Festive fun

The Food Festival (01584 873957/ www.foodfestival.co.uk), Ludlow's most famous event, attracts foodies from across Britain. Held every September, it features events such as the Ludlow Sausage Trail (eat your way around the town's butchers), the Real Ale Trail (drink your way around its pubs) and the Festival Loaf Trail (forget your Atkins diet). The grounds of Ludlow Castle, which host displays from chefs and

farmers, become the setting for an all-day picnic. The Slow Food Movement (www.slow foodludlow.org.uk), big in these parts, is also out in full – albeit laid-back – force.

The Ludlow Medieval Christmas Fayre (www.ludlowcraftevents.co.uk), a craft show held near the end of November, is another stellar event. The Ludlow Arts Festival (late June-early July, www.ludlowfestival.co.uk) features open-air Shakespeare in the grounds of the castle, plus opera, dance, music and a fireworks display.

The Assembly Rooms (1 Mill Street, 01584 878141/www.ludlowassembly rooms.co.uk) is Ludlow's year-round cultural hotspot. It shows indie films and stages theatre, dance and music concerts. Local arty types hang out at the café.

WHERE TO STAY

Birches Mill

Clun, nr Craven Arms, Shropshire SY7 8NL (01588 640409/www.virtual-shropshire.co.uk/ birchesmill). **Rates** £68-£76 double; £250-£415 1-bed cottage; £300-£490 2-bed cottage. **No credit cards.**
In a lush valley amid the Shropshire hills, Birches Mill is 30 minutes' drive from Ludlow – and galaxies away from modern life. There are no TVs in the rooms and no mobile phone signals – just idyllic walking country. The stone mill house, built in 1640 on the banks of the River Unk, is rustic but luxurious: antique furniture and stone fireplaces meet terry-cloth bathrobes and Body Shop products. At breakfast, the owners serve organic jam made with fruit from their garden. Evening meals for groups can be cooked by arrangement; there are also two self-catering cottages with wood-burning stoves. No children under eight.

Bromley Court

Broadgate Mews, 73-74 Lower Broad Street, Ludlow, Shropshire SY8 1PH (01584 876996/www.ludlowhotels.com). **Rates** £105 1-bed cottage; £120 1-bed family cottage. **Credit** MC, V.
Welcome to the Tudor age. Comprised of three 17th-century cottages, Bromley Court is the epitome of quaint. Each cottage has low, beamed ceilings, creaky stairs and sloping floors. Antique beds, patchwork quilts and William Morris fabrics add to the cosiness. The cottages, located on a quiet street near the town centre, each have sitting rooms, electric fires and kitchenettes; all open on to a shared garden. Guests have the option of a cooked breakfast at the house of Phil and Patricia Ross, the B&B's charming owners.

The Clive Restaurant with Rooms

Bromfield, Shropshire SY8 2JR (01584 856565/www.theclive.co.uk). **Lunch served** noon-2.30pm, **dinner served** 6.30-9.30pm

A spectacular setting for Mr Underhill's hotel and restaurant.

Mon-Thur. **Meals served** noon-9.30pm Sat; noon-9pm Sun. **Main courses** £13-£16. **Set meal** (Mon-Sat) £25 3 courses. **Rates** £70-£90 double. **Credit** AmEx, MC, V.

Jumping on the fashionable 'restaurant with rooms' bandwagon, the Clive – which can be found just a five-minute drive from the centre of Ludlow – does the job with real panache. The bedrooms, housed in converted barns and stables, are simple, spacious and stylish. The rustic element of each building – stone exterior, wooden beams – is carefully combined with a more modern sensibility, revealed in blond wood floors and halogen lights. Bathrooms, with slate grey tiles, are similarly slick.

The Crown at Hopton

Hopton Wafers, Cleobury Mortimer, Shropshire DY14 ONB (01299 270372/www.crown athopton.co.uk). **Rates** £85 double. **Credit** AmEx, MC, V.

The Crown, an ivy-covered, 16th-century coaching inn, is a real sight for travellers' sore eyes. Not only does it have a glorious setting – in the heart of Shropshire's rolling hills, 20 minutes' drive from Ludlow – but, on a dark night, its glowing, firelit windows make a cheerful prospect indeed. The pub, with its oak beams, log fires and red brickwork, is similarly comforting. So too is the classic country cooking that is served here.

Ludlow

Upstairs, the decent bedrooms are decorated with period panache – brass beds, floral curtains, more oak beams – but, for such an ancient building, they are surprisingly spacious and comfortable. Classy touches, such as chocolates left on the pillow, and quirky ones, such as the female mannequin in the corridor, add to the overall character of the place.

Dinham Hall

By the Castle, Ludlow, Shropshire SY8 1EJ (01584 876464/www.dinhamhall.co.uk). **Rates** £140-£190 double; £240 suite. **Credit** AmEx, DC, MC, V.

This elegant Georgian hotel attracts a well-heeled clientele, from the local gentry who dine at the restaurant to the shooting parties who descend en masse during season. The handsome bedrooms are done up in an opulent style: think chandeliers, oak or brass beds and sumptuous drapes. Decanters of sherry add to the classy vibe. Downstairs, the public rooms are country-house posh; to complement the gardens, an atrium is in the works for 2006. For a view, ask for a room overlooking Ludlow Castle or the river.

Jinlye Guest House

Castle Hill, All Stretton, Church Stretton, Shropshire SY6 6JP (01694 723243/ www.jinlye.co.uk). **Rates** £60-£76 double. **Credit** (over £100) MC, V.

Located at the summit of Longmynd, 1,400ft above sea level, this excellent B&B lies in the heart of Little Switzerland, so named because of its supposed resemblance to the Alps. As you'd expect, it's a walker's fantasy, with a staggering view at every turn. The guesthouse is beautiful too. A stone crofter's cottage, it boasts beamed ceilings, inglenook fireplaces and sturdy oak furniture; an atrium overlooks the colourful gardens; bedrooms are decorated in a pleasingly feminine style, with pink and green shades, Tiffany-style lamps and damask fabrics. Bathrooms are large. Pets are not allowed, though you can bring your horse (boarding is available at a nearby stable). Jinlye doesn't do dinner, but Ludlow is 30 minutes' drive away and there are several pubs and restaurants close at hand.

Mr Underhill's

Dinham, Ludlow, Shropshire SY8 1EH (01584 874431/www.mr-underhills.co.uk). **Rates** £110-£160 double; £185-£230 suite. **Credit** MC, V.

Perched on the edge of the rushing River Teme, Mr Underhill's boasts one of the most bucolic settings in all of Ludlow. Like its famed attached restaurant (*see p270*), the bedrooms are understated but luxurious. Most are decorated in neutral shades, with crisp white bedding and blond wood furnishings. Some come equipped with flatscreen TVs and power showers; all have comfortable beds and river views. The Mill House suites are particularly stylish; the Shed, another sumptuous suite, is spectacularly located by the water's edge; the river soundtrack soothes the soul. No smoking throughout.

The Moor Hall

Cleedownton, near Ludlow, Shropshire SY8 3EG (01584 823209/www.moorhall.co.uk). **Rates** £50-£56 double. **No credit cards**.

This Georgian country pile, four miles from Ludlow, is the stuff of romance novels. The view from every ivy-framed window – rolling moors, lush farmland, fecund valleys – resembles a landscape painting. And the public rooms – two sitting rooms, dining room and library bar – are pure *Country Life*, with ticking grandfather clocks, velvet curtains and paintings of nautical scenes. The grand central staircase, and the cupola above it, are further talking points. The bedrooms themselves are comfortable but plain: the real romance is in curling up with a book by the fire or walking by the lake or gardens. No children under ten.

Mulberry House

10 Corve Street, Ludlow, Shropshire SY8 1DA (01584 876765/www.tencorvestreet.co.uk). **Rates** £80-£90 double. **Credit** MC, V.

Mulberry House is the height of good taste. Located in the heart of Ludlow, this discreet Georgian B&B has no sign outside. Inside, owners Anna and Robert Reed have decorated in an elegant style. Rooms are painted in eye-catching Georgian shades – Chinese blue, crimson and orchard green – with beds covered in plain white linen. Antique furniture and *toile de joie* fabrics add to the period feel. Breakfast is cooked with food from local butchers and bakers. No children.

Overton Grange

Old Hereford Road, Ludlow, Shropshire SY8 4AD (01584 873500/www.overtongrange hotel.com). **Rates** £130-£160 double. **Credit** MC, V.

The stately Overton Grange has long been famous for its restaurant, Les Marches (*see p270*). Now the bedrooms of this Edwardian house, once fusty and traditional, should turn a few heads. As part of a makeover, the chintz and china dolls are gradually being replaced by a luxurious glam look: white bedding offset by rich plums and silvery greys; tactile suedes, satins and velvets; and retro touches such as art deco lamps. The rest of the house, from the oak-panelled breakfast room to the plush library, retains a pleasingly old world feel. Outside, the outlook remains the same: handsome gardens and fine views of the Shropshire countryside.

Stretton Hall Hotel

Shrewsbury Road, All Stretton, Church Stretton, Shropshire SY6 6HG (01694 723224/www.strettonhall.co.uk). **Rates** £80-£130 double. **Credit** AmEx, DC, MC, V.

TEA AND CINEMA

How do you take your tea? At the Bird on the Rock tearoom, it is served with heaps of nostalgia – and a splash of Hollywood glamour. Set in the sleepy hamlet of Clungunford, east of Ludlow, the Bird on the Rock is far from the madding crowd. And yet the people come here in droves for a cuppa – and a taste of yesteryear.

A shrine to the 1930s, the tearoom resembles an old movie set, with period-costumed waiters, old Bovril ads and faded newspaper cuttings. There's a touch of showbiz glitter too: Madonna's sunglasses from *Evita* hang on the wall next to an autographed still of Tom Cruise from *Far and Away*; there's Stephen Fry's bowler hat from *Jeeves & Wooster* and the collar worn by David Suchet in *Poirot*. And, from the Golden Age of Hollywood, there are framed photographs of Rita Hayworth and Margaret Lockwood. The cinematic touch is down to the owners, Doug and Annabel Hawkes, who in another life were period costume designers for Hollywood films. Back in 1999 they decided to get out of the rat race and open a tea room. Decorating it was no problem: they already had shedloads of memorabilia.

The question was location. Shropshire, which hasn't changed much since the 1930s, seemed the perfect place for a nostalgia kick. But Ludlow's foodie reputation was another big draw. At the Bird on the Rock, they take tea very seriously. The shop stocks 80 varieties from around the globe, and even has its own estate in Sri Lanka. Doug Hawkes talks about tea as if it were wine: the best vintages, the importance of growing conditions, the complex flavours of the Shropshire blend. The gourmet teas go down even better with the own-made cakes and pastries, and light lunches are also served. The pace is leisurely – it is recommended you book a table in advance – and the atmosphere civilised; mobile phones must be switched off. Just as well too. Ring tones would clash with the crackling fire, hushed conversation and Noël Coward soundtrack. Whoever said nostalgia ain't what it used to be hadn't been to the Bird on the Rock.

Bird on the Rock, Clungunford, nr Craven Arms, B4367 Knighton Road, SY7 0PX (01588 660631/www.birdon therock.com). **Open** *Winter* 10.30am-5pm Wed-Sun; *Summer* 10am-6pm Wed-Sun. **No credit cards**.

In Church Stretton, the heart of Shropshire's 'Little Switzerland', and boasting fine views of the landscape, is this handsome Georgian hotel. The typically period interior includes a handsome oak fireplace in the bar. Some of the rooms are plain, but the superior doubles at the front of the building are striking, particularly the four-poster bedroom, with its views of the Long Mynd. The gardens feature more idyllic vistas, and a tree house for kids. The hotel is also noted for its acclaimed Lemon Tree restaurant (*see p270*).

WHERE TO EAT & DRINK

Ludlow's foodie reputation is wholly justified. What with the excellent butchers, bakers and farmers' markets, chefs are spoiled for fresh ingredients. If the restaurants below are full – and some get booked up months in advance – there are a few low-key options: the **Courtyard Restaurant** (2 Quality Square, 01584 878080) is a simple, stylish café with a blackboard menu and decent, imaginative cooking. It's open for lunch all year; dinner is served at weekends and all week during the busier months.

Next door, **Ego** (Quality Square, 01584 878000) is a fashionable bar and café with a light, trendy snack menu and an array of tempting desserts. Outside Ludlow, a couple of country pubs do grub that's a cut above the norm: the **Crown Country Inn** (Munslow, nr Craven Arms, 01584 841205) and the **Crown at Hopton** (Hopton Wafers, Cleobury Mortimer, 01299 270372). Taxi fares to both are around £10 each way. In addition to the watering holes listed below, the **Bull Hotel** (14 Bull Ring, 01584 873611) – the oldest pub in Ludlow – and the cosy **Wheatsheaf Inn** (Lower Broad Street, 01584 87298) are decent drinking spots.

The Ludlow food scene has recently suffered one loss – the closure of Merchant House at the end of February 2005. At the time of writing chef/proprietor Shaun Hill – who ran the restaurant with his wife Anja – is looking for new premises.

Church Inn

Buttercross, Ludlow, Shropshire SY8 1AW (01584 872174/www.thechurchinn.com). **Lunch served** noon-2pm daily. **Dinner served** 6.30-9pm Mon-Sat; 6.30-8.30pm Sun. **Main courses** £6.25-£9.95. **Rates** £70-£80 double. **Credit** MC, V.

Attention all you lovers of real ale: the Church Inn is the real deal. This homely 14th-century pub keeps eight different casks of the stuff. Each brew comes with a connoisseurs' description written on the blackboard menu ('an elegant, straw-coloured bitter with a subtle hop flavour and dry finish', is their take on one fine-sounding ale). What's more, punters can taste before they purchase. If you don't drink beer, just soak up the atmosphere: the church-themed decor includes a wooden pulpit (where staff work the till) and a church bell that is rung to signify last orders. A full menu of pub grub and puddings is served; the pub also rents out comfortable rooms, three of which have glorious views of the church.

The Cookhouse

Bromfield, Shropshire SY8 2JR (01584 856565/ www.thecookhouse.org.uk). **Lunch served** noon-2.30pm, **dinner served** 6.30-9.30pm daily. *Brasserie* **Main courses** £12.95-£15.95. **Set lunch** £12.50 2 courses. *Restaurant* **Main courses** £13.95-£15.95. **Set dinner** £25 3 courses. **Rates** £70-£90 double. **Credit** AmEx, DC, MC, V.

A roadside halt of superior credentials, this large, slightly severe-looking building (it boasts a plain Georgian brick frontage, though the main structure is almost certainly older) provides wayfarers with 15 rooms (*see p264*), an accomplished restaurant, a bar with two distinct areas and a modern brasserie. The restaurant, the Clive, serves sophisticated meals that might start with chicken and chorizo terrine and continue with roast fillet of Shropshire beef in a wild mushroom sauce, or decent vegetarian options like fennel and sundried tomato risotto. A recent casserole of venison with a thyme and juniper sauce made a satisfying and hearty winter meal. Less formal, the Cookhouse brasserie is relaxingly low-lit, with brown paper tablecloths (you're encouraged to draw on them) and sleek modern furniture. Prices are good and the food several notches above most rest-stop fare. The bar has some good traditional ales (Hobson's) and local ciders.

De Grey's

5-6 Broad Street, Ludlow, Shropshire SY8 1NG (01584 872764/www.degreys.co.uk). **Lunch served** 9am-4.30pm Mon-Sat; noon-2.30pm Sun. **Dinner served** 7-8.30pm Fri, Sat. **Main courses** £5-£12. **Set breakfast** £6.10 continental. **Credit** MC, V.

Beamed ceilings, copper pots and aproned waitresses provide a pleasingly old-fashioned ambience at Ludlow's famous tea room. The place is bustling by day – afternoon tea is De Grey's raison d'être, but it's also a hugely popular spot for lunch. The menu includes tempting home-made soups, freshly made sandwiches and jacket potatoes; the medley of cakes and pastries will break even the most hardened Atkins devotee. On weekend evenings, De Grey's is also open for dinner, specialising in fish and local Herefordshire beef.

Dinham Hall Hotel

By the Castle, Ludlow, Shropshire SY8 1EJ (01584 876464/www.dinhamhall.co.uk). **Lunch served** 12.30-1.45pm Tue-Sun. **Dinner served** 7-8.45pm daily. **Main courses** (lunch) £13.50. **Set dinner** £35 3 courses; £42.50 4 courses. **Rates** £140-£190 double; £240 suite. **Credit** AmEx, DC, MC, V.

Dinham Hall, a favourite with the local blue bloods, is a classy country house hotel (*see p267*). The restaurant too, is a cut above the norm: the setting is elegant, the wine list sophisticated and the service exemplary. Happily, the food lives up to the surroundings. Roast quail with red onion potato cake and a green peppercorn sauce feature on the list of starters. Main courses on a recent visit included a succulent grilled breast of duck, served with braised red cabbage, baked fig, confit potato and a flavourful port and thyme jus. For pudding, vanilla crème brûlée with almond tuiles went down a treat. Coffee and chocolates are served by the fire in a homely lounge. If you can't get a booking at a Michelin, dine here.

Hibiscus

17 Corve Street, Ludlow, Shropshire SY8 1DA (01584 872325/www.hibiscusrestaurant.co.uk). **Lunch served** noon-1.30pm Wed-Sat. **Dinner served** 7-9.30pm Tue-Sat. **Set lunch** £25 3 courses. **Set dinner** £42.50 3 courses. **Credit** MC, V.

With its award-winning French double act – Claude Bosi in the kitchen and his wife Claire at front of house – Hibiscus has been steered into exalted company; it's regularly spoken of as one of the best restaurants in the country. The decor is simple but classy – bare stone, wood panels, mellow lighting and a constantly changing selection of contemporary artworks – and the mood pleasantly relaxed. Fresh local ingredients go without saying, and the seasonal food is sophisticated and impressively executed; in summer, exquisite ravioli of white onion and lime, whole roast lobster with baby plum tomato confit; in the colder months, tartare of langoustine and saddle

Ludlow

of Mortimer Forest venison. By way of dessert, three mini crème brûlées – pea and marjoram, elderflower and peach, cherry tomato and brown sugar – gave the perfect measure of the kitchen's imagination and talent.

Koo

127 Old Street, Ludlow, Shropshire SY8 1NU (01584 878462/www.koo-ook.com). **Lunch served** noon-2pm, **dinner served** 7-10pm Tue-Sat. **Set lunch** £12.50 2 courses. **Set dinner** (Tue, Wed) £18.95 3 courses; (Thur-Sat) £22.95 4 courses. **Credit** MC, V.
'Authentic', proclaims the menu. That's pushing it a bit. For sure, we're glad there's a Japanese restaurant in Ludlow (every town should have one), but a liberal scattering of sesame seeds over nearly every dish in sight does not textbook nihon no ryori make. And the soundtrack was Latino! Overlook the eccentricities, though, and you'll find much to like. The aquamarine walls and ceiling set an unpretentious note, the staff – especially the mama-san – are lovely, and the ingredients are grade A. OK, so we'd never seen maki sliced so thin, and gyoza turned out, without prior warning from the menu, to be a veggie variety; but all in all, our meal – agedashi tofu, gyudon – was tasty and nicely presented. The dessert plate, in a move that was by then familiar, included a sesame biscuit. Sesame overdose notwithstanding, this is good value; they also do bento boxes to take away.

The Lemon Tree

Shrewsbury Road, All Stretton, Church Stretton, Shropshire SY6 6HG (01694 723224/www.strettonhall.co.uk). **Lunch served** 12.30-2pm, **dinner served** 7-9pm daily. **Main courses** £10.95- £16.95. **Credit** AmEx, DC, MC, V.
The Lemon Tree is the local gourmands' dining spot of choice – and a scenic 30-minute drive from Ludlow. Though it's housed in Stretton Hall, a traditional period hotel, the restaurant has a bright, contemporary feel, with acid-yellow walls and a nouvelle menu. On our visit, the food, from a starter of wild mushroom risotto, to a local duck breast served with kirsch cherry compote and crispy parsnips, was elegantly presented and capably cooked. The pudding, however, was a disappointment: a frozen espresso and orange mousse, while flavourful, was rock hard. No smoking throughout.

Les Marches

Overton Grange Hotel, Old Hereford Road, Ludlow, Shropshire SY8 4AD (01584 873500/ www.overtongrangehotel.co.uk). **Lunch served** noon-2pm, **dinner served** 7-9pm daily. **Set meal** £39.50 3 courses, £49.50 7-course tasting menu. **Credit** MC, V.
A gourmet grandee in a luxury country hotel (*see p267*). Where most restaurants around these parts plough a furrow that could broadly be described

as English country cooking, head chef Olivier Bossut and his underlings produce food in unabashed French haute cuisine tradition. Dining options run from à la carte to a three-course set menu and a push-the-boat-out tasting menu, and whatever course you take, the presentation of the food will be of the kind that's so painstaking you almost feel bad about disturbing the artful dabs of sauce and the delicate arrangment of leaves. So, for starters, chocolate raviolis of game in a fresh girolle mushroom veloute. Then, as a main, paupiette of wild sea bass with a red mullet farcé. And, to conclude, pear tart bourdaloue with cinnamon ice-cream. All delicous, and all prepared with a masterful hand. No smoking throughout.

Mr Underhill's

Dinham, Ludlow, Shropshire SY8 1EH (01584 874431/www.mr-underhills.co.uk). **Dinner served** 7.15-8.15pm Wed-Sun; also occasional Mon, call for details. **Set dinner** £40 5 courses incl coffee. **Credit** MC, V.
For location, this place certainly trumps its local rivals; down by the babbling weir just a short lob from the castle walls. The long dining room, decked out with linen-draped tables and wicker-backed chairs, has subdued, attractive lighting, and food is more than satisfactory: asparagus cream with parmesan crisp to start, perhaps, and a roasted rack and slow-cooked shoulder of Marches lamb with garden sorrel and mint to follow. A daily tasting menu is also served. The place is a hotel too, and parking is at something of a premium. No smoking throughout.

The Unicorn Inn

66 Corve Street, Ludlow, Shropshire SY8 1DU (01584 873555/www.theunicorninn.com). **Lunch served** noon-2.15pm, **dinner served** 6-9.15pm Mon-Sat; 6.30-9pm Sun. **Main courses** £10.95-£16.95. **Credit** MC, V.
The Unicorn, generally considered to serve the best pub grub in Ludlow, is an archetypally cosy English inn. Dating back to 1654, it features a stone fireplace, oak panelling and beamed ceilings. The blackboard menu veers between traditional English comfort food and more ambitious fusion fare. Stick to the comfort food: our Hereford rump steak, served with herbed butter, red onion tempura and roasted root veg, hit the spot; for dessert, a lemon ginger cheesecake was superb. A full vegetarian menu is also available.

The Waterdine

Llanfair Waterdine, nr Knighton, Shropshire LD7 1TU (01547 528214/www.water dine.com). **Lunch served** noon-2pm Tue-Sun. **Dinner served** 7-9.30pm Tue-Sat. **Main courses** £10.50-£16.50. **Set lunch** (Sun) £17.50 3 courses. **Set dinner** (Sat) £27.50 3 courses. **Rates** £90 double. **Credit** MC, V.
For the vista alone, it would be hard to beat the rear dining room at this 16th-century drover's inn:

Ludlow

from nearest to furthest, a flowery garden, green fields, the River Teme doing duty as the England-Wales border, and a steep hill from which, meteorological conditions permitting, mist rises in an Arthurian fashion. We got a faultless welcome, even though we were late. Head chef Ken Adams used to run a restaurant (now Hibiscus) in Ludlow, and his short, seasonal three-course menu is formed from local ingredients (some very local – herbs, vegetables and fruit come from the garden) and imaginative twists on traditional fare. Fillet of brill wrapped in smoked salmon was perfectly done, as was herb risotto with balsamic roast vegetables. Desserts might include strawberry and elderflower mousse or – our choice – ginger pudding with lemongrass cream, a scrummy nursery treat. There are rooms here too, and an attractive church to explore across the road.

Manchester

A no-nonsense, good-time city.

Social-reforming judge and writer Edward Parry got Manchester just right around a century ago: 'Manchester is the place where people do things. Don't talk about what you are going to do – do it. That is the Manchester habit.'

The habit stuck. Today's Manchester is as determined, forward-thinking and hard working as ever. The Manchester habit is one of invention and innovation – the city has more award-winning new buildings than anywhere in Britain outside London. Look up and you'll see a forest of cranes busy shaping this ever-restless city.

Despite the frenetic building activity, Manchester remains a compact, human-sized city – with lots to appease the 21st-century cityphile. New urban pleasure zones mingle with grand merchants' houses (remants of the days when Manchester was HQ for the world cotton industry), sexy department stores adjoin half-timbered pubs and, everywhere, there's a sense that there are bigger and better things to come.

Take the city's once neglected Northern Quarter: ten years ago this was a hinterland of adult shops and empty warehouses. Now the area, with its fabulous Craft and Design Centre, American delis and hip boutiques, is so trendy that it often doubles for New York as a film location. The gay scene is bouncing back, too, after a few years of its venues featuring unwillingly on the hellish hen-party trail. And food lovers are well catered for – 2004 saw an explosion of exciting new restaurants offering ever more elaborate creations in ever more dramatic settings.

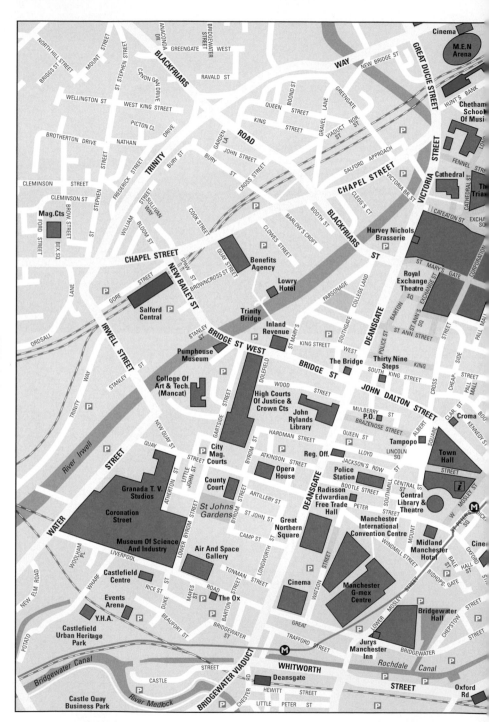

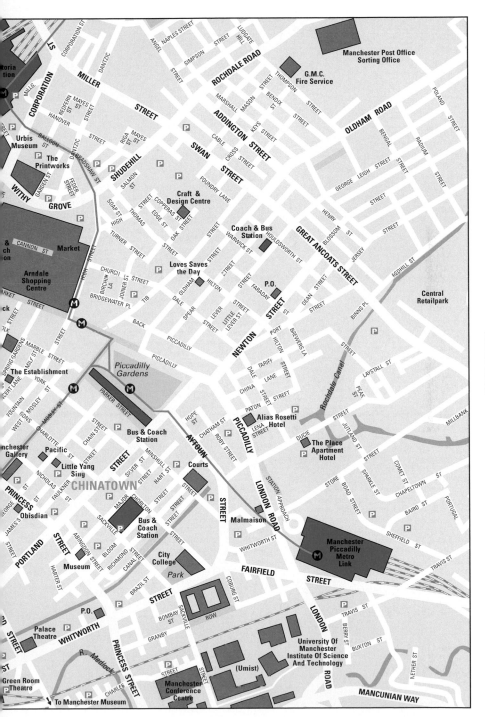

Accommodation	★★★★
Food & drink	★★★★
Nightlife	★★★★
Shopping	★★★★★
Culture	★★★
Sights	★★
Scenery	★

its share of warm sunny days. New urban squares, canal-side bars and outdoor festivals in the spruced-up Castlefield basin give the city a much-needed blast of fresh air from May to September. And when the sun goes down? Well, that's when the fun really begins...

WHERE TO STAY

Shopping

While many cities have bulldozed their heritage to make way for bland new malls and chain stores, Manchester has cleverly made room for both – resulting in a city centre that offers a rich stew of local designers, top-flight department stores and quirky collectibles stores all within a good Saturday afternoon's stroll from each other.

Great department stores include Kendals (Deansgate, 0161 832 3414), which has had more facelifts than Cher, but still offers an old-school vibe over six floors – with a good cosmetics department and menswear section in the basement. Selfridges (Exchange Square, 08708 377377, www.selfridges.com) is worth a visit for the basement food hall alone – but its funky fashions shouldn't be missed either. Opposite, Harvey Nichols (New Cathedral Street, 0161 828 8888, www.harvey nichols.com) tries a little too hard and is undoubtedly pricey, but is still worth a look.

The fashion conscious should head for King Street – you'll find Vivienne Westwood (0161 835 2121, www.hervia.com) in a suitably decadent salon, Armani Collezioni/ Emporio Armani (0161 839 8789, www. emporioarmani.com), purveyors of crisp Italian tailoring, and DKNY (0161 819 1948), offering brisk, wearable NYC fashions.

Funkier fashions can be found in the Northern Quarter. Oi Polloi (70 Tib Street, 0161 831 7870, www.oipolloi.com) sells clothes sourced from New York, and labels you'll not see anywhere else. Affleck's Palace (52 Church Street, 0161 834 2039, www.afflecks-palace.co.uk) is a wonderland of gothic and weird clothes, collectibles and jewellery, while the Manchester Craft and Design Centre (17 Oak Street, 0161 832 4274, www.craftanddesign.com) is a calm cloister of exciting city-made sculptures, jewellery and ceramics.

Manchester and music are inseparable, and there are plenty of great record shops in town. Try Piccadilly Records (Oldham Street, 0161 834 8789), offering an unsurpassed mix of new and rare vinyl, or Fat City (Oldham Street, 0161 237 1181, www.fatcity.co.uk) for independent and import releases.

So much to do...

These days, Manchester feels far more cosmopolitan than provincial, especially in summertime. And, yes, the city does have

Alias Rosetti

107 Piccadilly, M1 2DB (0161 247 7744/ www.aliashotels.com). **Rates** £110-£155 double; £265 suite. **Credit** AmEx, MC, V.
An urban and individual take on the hotel as all-in, all-night entertainment provider, with a very sceney bar and restaurant, the Rosetti had a far more serious past as the grandiose headquarters of a Victorian cotton magnate. Its Grade I-listed status protects both interior and exterior, so the rooms are great slices of the original office, with high, girdered ceilings, huge, arched windows and, sometimes, decorative wall tiling. Furnishings are of low-key 1960s office/retro variety – funky to some, somewhat incongruous to others. All mod cons are present and correct – Roberts radio, television set, DVD player, bathrobes, room service from the Italian restaurant in the lobby – but the effect is aesthetic rather than sybaritic. The starkness of the rooms is offset by notably warm staff and communal self-serve snack bars on each floor. There are great weekend packages for party folk who'll appreciate the club nights in the louche bar (which makes for noisy nights on the lower floors).

Jurys Manchester Inn

56 Great Bridgewater Street, M1 5LE (0161 953 8888/www.jurysdoyle.com). **Rates** £59-£115 double. **Credit** AmEx, DC, MC, V.
Ireland's solid, dependable chain doubtless won't win many prizes for the Scandinavian-inspired bedroom furnishings, or fusion Pacific Rim cooking in its restaurants, but if you're looking for excellent value, decent-sized rooms in the heart of the city (and can't bear another soulless Travel Lodge) there are shockingly few options in Manchester. That's why Jurys is such a delight. The comfortable rooms can accommodate up to two adults and two children and feature satellite TV. There's a restaurant and the Inn Bar, a passable pub, with good-value bar meals. Well placed for Gmex and Bridgewater Hall.

Manchester

Lowry Hotel

50 Dearmans Place, Chapel Wharf, Salford, M3 5LH (0161 827 4000/www.thelowry.com). **Rates** £230-£260 double; £595 suite. **Credit** AmEx, DC, MC, V.

Ian Brown once said Manchester had everything apart from a beach. Well, this stunning five-star hotel has everything apart from a pool (although one is on the way). Spacious, elegant rooms feature two telephone lines, voice messaging, high-speed internet access, satellite TV, CD players, fax connection, minibar and safe. Italian marble en suite bathrooms are sumptuously stocked and many rooms have views over the river. Marco Pierre White's River Room restaurant and bar is rightly praised as one of the best in the city, while the Espa beauty salon offers a seriously seductive range of treatments from hot stone therapy to stress-busting massage. Well placed for Selfridges, Harvey Nichols and the MEN arena.

Malmaison

London Road, Piccadilly, M1 3AQ (0161 278 1000/www.malmaison.com). **Rates** £135-£165 double; £195-£220 suite. **Credit** AmEx, DC, MC, V.

Bold, if slightly small, rooms feature CD players, CD libraries, satellite TV, free internet access and fully stocked mini-bars. Bathrooms have power showers and deep comfortable baths. Suites, obviously, offer more space. Malmaison likes to think of itself as the funky alternative to four-star sterility – and largely succeeds. The richly swagged and moodily lit bar is great for a pre-dinner cocktail, while the equally opulent brasserie offers quirky, memorable meals at a decent price. After all the indulgences, unwind in the Petit Spa or burn off a few calories in the compact gym. Well placed for the Gay Village and Piccadilly Station.

Midland Manchester

Peter Street, City Centre, M60 2DS (0161 236 3333/www.quintessential-hotels.co.uk). **Rates** £165-£185 double; £250-£600 suite. **Credit** AmEx, DC, MC, V.

For over a hundred years, the Midland set the standard other hotels in Manchester aspired to. Recently, though, the arrival of hip and stylish new kids in town has left the Midland looking a little over-dressed. A thorough refurbishment programme, due to be completed next year, should bring this wonderful palace back to prominence. If you're after drama, elegance and old-fashioned trimmings, though, this is still the place. Rooms verge on stately, with oversized beds, dining tables and solid furnishings. The French restaurant is a hushed shrine to Gallic cooking, and the basement leisure suite is suitably decadent.

The Ox

71 Liverpool Road, Castlefield, M3 4NQ (0161 839 7740/www.theox.co.uk). **Open** *pub* 11am-11pm Mon-Sat; noon-10.30pm Sun.

Meals served noon-9.45pm Mon-sat; 12.30-6.30pm Sun. **Rates** £44.95 double. **Credit** AmEx, MC, V.

This is a great gastropub with just nine en suite rooms – and a great, buzzy bar/restaurant attracting a friendly crowd of business and media types. There are simply not enough decently priced rooms in the city and the Ox cleverly offers everything a budget-conscious weekend-breaker needs (even passes to a nearby leisure club). Rooms are simple, but feature TV, tea- and coffee-making facilities, and are spotlessly clean.

The Place Apartment Hotel

Ducie Street, Piccadilly, M1 2TP (0161 778 7500/www.theplacehotel.com). **Rates** £119-£179 double; £209 deluxe apartment; £319 penthouse. **Credit** AmEx, DC, MC, V.

Individually designed loft-style apartments give the Place its distinctive edge – and make a night here feel like you're staying in a friend's pad (albeit a friend with far too much money). All apartments have shiny new kitchens, separate bedrooms, Sky TV, DVDs and CD players. Deluxe apartments have even higher levels of luxury, exposed brick walls and great views of the city. Bathrooms are suitably stunning. The new Cotton House restaurant is quickly gaining a reputation as one of the best, and most atmospheric, in this part of the city. Its dazzling design and huge scale miraculously don't overpower what is a decadently enjoyable eating experience. Best to book a table.

Radisson Edwardian

Free Trade Hall, Peter Street, M2 5GP (0161 835 9929/www.radissonedwardian.com). **Rates** £115-£241 double; £380-£1,500 suite. **Credit** AmEx, DC, JCB, MC, V.

The Radisson Edwardian is the city's latest luxury retreat, and is housed in one of the best and most sympathetic conversion projects the city has seen: the famous Free Trade Hall, where the trade union movement held its first meetings, a building with almost biblical significance to the city. (It's also where a fan once famously shouted 'Judas!' to a newly electrified Bob Dylan in 1966, a recording of which was mislabelled for years as the Royal Albert Hall bootleg.) The Italianate façade and much of the interior still stand. The Opus One and Alto Terrace restaurants offer competent dining – the former a seductive, black and red bordello. The 263 luxurious rooms have high-speed and wireless internet access, Bang and Olufsen entertainment systems and advanced telephone systems with voicemail. A luxurious health spa features swimming pool, saunas and Elemis treatments. Well placed for theatreland.

WHERE TO EAT & DRINK

Only those living in the past will have failed to notice that the land of black pudding and Boddies now provides excellent, world-class (and globe-spanning) cuisine. Its Food and

Drink Festival is one of the city's most exciting events. And Manchester's renowned bar scene continues to be as exciting and eclectic as ever; few major cities can boast as many unreconstituted old ale houses sitting next to sleek new cocktail joints and grill bars – it's this diversity that makes a pub crawl around town so rewarding.

Bluu (Smithfield Building, off Thomas Street, 0161 839 7195, www.bluu.co.uk) is a cool perma-popular restaurant/bar in what's fast becoming the cuisine crossroads of the Northern Quarter. Menus cleverly set local produce against Asian and Mediterranean flavours, usually successfully. DJs provide a funky backdrop in the separate bar area. In Castlefield,

Choice (Castle Quay, Castlefield, 0161 833 3400, www.choicebarandrestaurant.co.uk) has many passionate fans and is one of the city's quieter success stories. Modern British food, contemporary yet understated surroundings, a canalside location and hip piano bar combine to make this place a success.

Current drinking hot spots include One Central Street (1 Central Street, 0161 211 9000). Perhaps the best of the venues occupying that fuzzy area between bar and club culture, OCS is a dark, underground space with a great, funky music policy. The Label bar (78 Deansgate, 0161 833 1878) is friendlier than many style bars along this stretch; it has a Mediterranean menu, a good range of premium beers and chilled

An abundance of luxury at the Lowry.

beats until 2am. If you're just after a coffee, over the road you'll find Suburb (63 Deansgate, 0161 832 3642) serving the best coffee, paninis and fruit teas in the city centre. Deansgate Locks (Whitworth Street West), a stretch of railway arches converted into showy bars and clubs along the Rochdale Canal, is worth a look if you like dressing up and drinking imported Peruvian beer. Try Loaf (3A-5 Deansgate Locks, 0161 819 5858, www.loaf-manchester.co.uk) – its doormen are friendlier than the rest, and not everyone looks like a footballer (or his wife).

The Northern Quarter's range of bars continues to reflect the healthy economy in this once-neglected zone: Socio Rehab (Edge Street) is a suitably exclusive

cocktail bar. You'll have to have your wits about you to spot it, as there's only a tiny plaque on the wall revealing its location. Dry Bar (28-30 Oldham Street, 0161 236 9840, www.drybar.co.uk), once owned by Factory Records, was the first style bar in the city and still attracts a loyal following. For an even better range of (real) beer, try Bar Fringe (8 Swan Street, 0161 835 3815) with a less posey crowd and great local brews.

The Printworks (Exchange Square, www.theprintworks.com) features an IMAX cinema, a multiplex and plenty of drinking dens. Waxy O'Connors (0161 835 1210) is a subterranean Irish lair that's actually better than it sounds, serving excellent bar food. Paparazzi (0161 832 1234) is a

Manchester

newly opened bar/club that gets rammed at the weekends, playing a floor-friendly mix of indie dance.

The Gay Village is in rude health, with a clutch of shiny new bars to tempt you over to the wild side of Canal Street. Queer (4 Canal Street, 0161 228 1360, www.queer-manchester.co.uk) offers free internet access from your drinking stool, while Taurus (1 Canal Street, 0161 236 4593, www.taurus-bar.co.uk) is a smart, likeable place serving good food and a bewildering range of spirits to a dressy, mixed crowd. Spirit (63 Richmond Street, 0161 237 9725) is one of the street's smarter venues attracting a slightly less preeny crowd, in a venue that opts for subtle rather than kitsch. Bravely.

If you're after a more traditional drinking experience, Manchester won't disappoint. The Briton's Protection (50 Great Bridgewater Street, 0161 236 5895) is a fabulous, dark, tiled and wood-panelled gem. Its whisky menu has to be the most complete this side of the Trossachs. The Knott Bar (374 Deansgate, 0161 839 9229) proves that real ale isn't the preserve of the CAMRA set. You can't miss Peveril of the Peak (127 Great Bridgewater Street, 0161 236 6364): its emerald green tiled exterior makes this ancient watering hole stand out like an exotic bush in a desert of steel office blocks. Mr Thomas's Chop House (52 Cross Street, 0161 832 2245) is a genuine Victorian boozer with a wonderful carved and tiled interior. Food is excellent, too.

The Bridge

58 Bridge Street, Deansgate, M3 3WB (0161 834 0242/www.thebridgemanchester.co.uk). **Lunch served** noon-3pm, **dinner served** 5.30-9.30pm Mon-Sat. **Meals served** noon-6pm Sun. **Main courses** £8.50-£12.95. **Credit** AmEx, MC, V.

SIGHTSEEING

John Rylands Library

150 Deansgate, (0161 275 3751/www.rylib web.man.ac.uk). **Open** closed to summer 2006. **Admission** free.
The collections span back to the third millennium BC and are written on most kinds of materials, from clay to papyrus, wood to bone. The oldest fragment of the New Testament, the first edition of Shakespeare's sonnets and wonderfully illustrated Aramaic manuscripts are just some of the treasures.

Manchester Art Gallery

Mosely Street, M2 3JL (0161 235 8888/ www.manchestergalleries.org). **Open** 10am-5pm Tue-Fri. **Admission** free.
A bold new extension has added space and light to this once stuffy city-centre gallery. The collection is world ranking, featuring works by Stubbs, Gainsborough, Turner and Constable. Temporary exhibitions are more new wave.

Manchester Museum

Oxford Road, M13 9PL (0161 275 2634/ www.museum.man.ac.uk). **Open** 10am-5pm Mon-Sat; 11am-4pm Sun. **Admission** free. Recently spruced up, the museum has a new inhabitant, and it's worth a visit to see him alone. The 30ft T-Rex skeleton hardly fits in the foyer of this excellent museum. There are excellent exhibits on holograms, fossils and Egyptology – and a child-friendly vivarium with all manner of wriggly wonders.

Museum of Science and Industry

Liverpool Road, Castlefield, M3 4FP (0161 832 2244/www.msim.org.uk). **Open** 10am-5pm daily. **Admission** free.
A no-nonsense look at the innovations and innovators that fuelled Britain's rise to industrial glory. Xperiment! offers the requisite hands-on experience for kids, but, this aside, the space is devoted to explaining the forces that have shaped the modern world. And what a space. At over 20 acres, it's one of the largest museums of its kind in the world.

Urbis

Cathedral Gardens, M4 3BG (0161 605 8200/www.urbis.org.uk). **Open** 10am-6pm Tue-Sun. **Admission** free.
You can't fail to notice this huge, glass-clad ski-slope of a building. The transparent wedge is home to Urbis – the museum of the modern city. It had a shaky start but, thanks to a new curator, things are on the up. Through exhibitions covering street art, graphic design and club culture, cities as far apart as Sao Paulo and Tokyo are dissected.

Love Saves the Day

This ebullient gastropub is hard to leave. Come for a lunchtime pint and you'll still be here in the evening if you're not careful. That said, there are worse ways to spend the day. Food is unashamedly traditional, despite the recent gentrification. Spam fritters never tasted this good at school.

Croma

1 Clarence Street, M2 4DE (0161 237 9799/ www.cromamanchester.co.uk). **Meals served** noon-11pm Mon-Sat; noon-10.30pm Sun. **Main courses** £5.50-£7. **Credit** AmEx, MC, V.
In a city that is practically paved with modern Italian-leaning menus, Croma consistently comes out on top. It does so because, even when it's super busy (which is 95% of the time), its standards never seem to drop. From a riotous salad niçoise to a meaty fillet of Dover sole with capers, this exciting restaurant never disappoints. Not least when you get the bill.

The Establishment

43-45 Spring Gardens, M2 2BG (0161 839 6300/www.establishmentrestaurant.com). **Lunch served** noon-2.30pm Mon-Fri. **Dinner served** 7-10pm Mon-Sat. **Main courses** £18-£25. **Set lunch** £17.50 2 courses, £19.95 3 courses. **Credit** AmEx, MC, V.
Modern and classical British and French food served in a stunning, Gothic bank hall complete with a stark, purple inner womb. The Establishment is a showy flagship for the new, bullish breed of Manchester restaurant. Arriving with a bang last year, things have settled down nicely, as have the flavours. Strong, confident and passionate cooking – with prices to match.

Greens

43 Lapwing Lane, West Didsbury, M20 2NT (0161 434 4259). **Lunch served** noon-2pm Tue-Fri; 12.30-3.30pm Sun. **Dinner served** 5.30-10.30pm daily. **Main courses** £10.50. **Set dinner** (5.30-10.30pm Mon, 5.30-7pm Tue-Fri, all day Sun) £12.50 3 courses. **Credit** MC, V.

Constantly surprising and always busy, Greens challenges your perceptions of what vegetarian cooking can offer. And Chef Simon Rimmer isn't even a vegetarian. Dishes like crispy mushrooms taste so good, why kill the duck? Similarly, the filo pastry strudel filled with leeks, mushrooms, tomato and cream cheese served with port wine sauce leaves no room (or need) for flesh.

Harvey Nichols Brasserie

2nd Floor, 21 New Cathedral Street, M1 1AD (0161 828 8898/www.harveynichols.com). **Meals served** noon-7pm Mon; noon-10.30pm Tue-Sat; noon-6pm Sun. **Main courses** £9.50-£12.50. **Credit** AmEx, DC, MC, V.
Often busier than the store itself, this excellent venture offers some of the best modern British cooking in town. Service is efficient – so it's a good choice if you don't want to hang around. Fish is delicately cooked and meats are grilled to perfection. Wines are top notch and the design is as you'd expect from Harvey Nic's.

Little Yang Sing

17 George Street, M1 4HE (0161 228 7722/ www.littleyangsing.co.uk). **Meals served** noon-midnight Mon-Thur; noon-12.30am Fri; noon-1am Sat; noon-11pm Sun. **Main courses** £8-£13. **Set meal** (noon-5pm daily) £8.50 2 courses, £10.50 3 courses. **Credit** MC, V.
Arguments rage over whether Yang Sing (34 Princess Street, 0161 236 2200) or this, its little brother, is the best Chinese in town. We chose here because it's less formal – with fresh modern furnishings, attentive staff and a buzzy crowd. Food is never less than superb – especially the sui mai dumplings and the excellent banquet options.

Love Saves the Day

46-50 Oldham Street, M4 1LE (0161 832 0777/www.lovesavestheday.com). **Lunch served** 9am-6pm Mon-Sat, 10.30am-4pm Sun. **Main courses** £5.50-£6.95. **Credit** AmEx, DC, MC, V.

This is one of the city's best delis, serving wonderful cooked meats, lovely fresh breads, excellent, aromatic coffee and a judiciously selected range of wines. Love Saves The Day is great for breakfast, brunch or just hanging out with a good book for an hour or so.

Obsidian

18 Princess Street, M1 4LY (0161 238 4348/ www.obsidianmanchester.co.uk). **Lunch served** noon-2.30pm, **dinner served** 6-10pm daily. **Main courses** £13.50-£19.50. **Set meal** (lunch, 6-7pm) £12 2 courses, £16 3 courses. **Credit** AmEx, MC, V.

This super stylish restaurant sits below the equally handsome new hotel, the Arora, and is an eclectic experience, boldly mixing flavours from around the globe. Take, for example, a starter of poached and deep-fried egg, with wild mushrooms and white truffle oil, or a main course Tandoori monkfish with spiced chickpeas, grilled lime and coriander butter. The interior's palette of rich wood, polished marble and even a petrified tree is surprisingly enticing.

Pacific

58-60 George Street, M1 4HF (0161 228 6668). **Meals served** noon-midnight daily. **Dim Sum** noon-6pm daily. **Main courses** £8-£12. **Set menu** £20.50 3 courses (minimum 2 people). **Credit** AmEx, DC, MC, V.

Two restaurants in one, Pacific offers a totally new dining experience in Manchester's Chinatown district. The innovation doesn't stop with the funky, fresh decor either. Whether you choose Thai (upper floor) or Chinese (ground) you'll not be disappointed – each cuisine has its own kitchen and chef; this is definitely no theme restaurant, as its popularity testifies.

Punjab Tandoori

177 Wilmslow Road, Rusholme, M14 5AP (0161 225 2960). **Lunch served** noon-midnight Mon-Thur, Sun; noon-1am Fri, Sat. **Main courses** £5.50-£8.50. **Set meal** £16-£21 3 courses (minimum 2). **Credit** AmEx, MC, V.

There's lots of competition on Wilmslow Road's famous 'Curry Mile' and, to be honest, most are worth a visit. But we love the Punjab's exciting adventures with the subcontinent's favourite flavours. Try the dosas – rolled pancakes filled with wonderfully spicy ingredients. Vegetarians are well catered for here.

Stock

4 Norfolk Street, M2 1BW (0161 839 6644/ www.stockrestaurant.co.uk). **Lunch served** noon-2.30pm, **dinner served** 6-10pm Mon-Sat. **Main courses** £16-£40. **Set lunch** £12.95 2 courses, £15.95 3 courses. **Credit** AmEx, MC, V.

In the grand setting of Manchester's former Stock Exchange, this is an upmarket Italian with class and clout. Wonderfully fresh seafood, unusual regional Italian specialities and a great wine list make Stock a memorable night out in sumptuous surroundings.

Tampopo

16 Albert Square, M2 5PF (0161 819 1966/ www.tampopo.co.uk). **Lunch served** noon-11pm Mon-Sat; noon-10pm Sun. **Main courses** £6.75-£9.25. **Set meal** (noon-7pm) £6.95 2 courses. **Credit** AmEx, DC, MC, V.

A Manchester favourite, Tampopo brings the flavours of south-east Asia to the city with a style and authenticity that's hard to beat. Within the stripped-down, communal interior, super fresh ingredients are prepared in a flash to a crowd of devotees. Try gyozo dumplings and Penang curry, both signature dishes and a good introduction to the flavours on offer.

Thirty Nine Steps

39 South King Street, M2 6DE (0161 834 9155/www.39stepsrest.co.uk). **Lunch served** noon-2.30pm, **dinner served** 6.30-10.30pm Mon-Sat. **Main courses** £9.95-£16.95. **Set lunch** (Sat) £15.95 2 courses incl glass of wine. **Credit** AmEx, MC, V.

New restaurants come, new restaurants close. But this place quietly keeps cooking up brilliant French-inspired dishes for a hungry crowd of disciples. Scallops with black pudding are truly wonderful here, as are most of the seafood dishes. Advance booking is recommended at weekends.

NIGHTLIFE

Clubnights come and go. As do venues – recent losses include the excellent Band on the Wall, one of the city's best places to hear bands. That said, rumours of the death of clubbing are greatly exaggerated.

Essential (8 Minshull Street, 0161 835 1300, www.essentialmanchester.com) is a big gay playground pumping out house and other anthemic tunes, but for a more exciting night in the Village look out for Homiesexual (at Mutz Nutz, 105 Princess Street, 0161 236 9266, www.mutznutz-nightclub.co.uk) – playing a wicked mix of urban, hip hop and soul every Thursday.

Matt and Phred's (64 Tib Street, 0161 831 7003, www.mattandphreds.com) offers cool jazz to a warm crowd – it gets busy at weekends, while Night and Day (26 Oldham Street, 0161 236 4597, www.nightnday.org) has an excellent programme of music featuring up-and-coming national and local bands.

Tangled (at the Phoenix, Oxford Road, 07989 704362, www.tangled.co.uk) is as legendary for its breaks and beats as it is for its genuinely friendly crowd, while

the big daddy of them all, Sankey's Soap (Jersey Street, 0161 661 9668, www.tribalgathering.co.uk) is as healthy as ever, attracting superstar DJs and the awesome Tribal Sessions. Get a ticket or be prepared to queue. Friends and Family (The Roadhouse, Newton Street, 0161 237 9789, www.theroadhouselive.co.uk) is an intimate hip hop venue, and the Music Box (Oxford Road, 0161 236 9971, www.jillys.co.uk) hosts Mr Scruff's legendary – and legendarily eclectic – Keep it Unreal nights. But if you just want a no-nonsense dance to a great mix of tunes you've heard of, you can't beat Fab Café (111 Portland Street, 0161 236 2019,

www.fabcafe.co.uk), playing kitsch, electronica and funk to a happy crowd and a Dalek.

If music's not your bag, Manchester's comedy circuit is particularly healthy. The Comedy Store (Whitworth Street West, 0870 593 2932, www.thecomedy store.co.uk) has a consistently rib-tickling programme of home-grown and US talent.

To keep up to date with Manchester's ever-changing menu of nocturnal activities you could pick up a copy of the city's listings magazine, *City Life*, or log on to www.manchesteronline.co.uk, the website for the city's paper, the *Manchester Evening News*.

Harrogate

Take the waters and smell the flowers – this old spa town is blooming again.

There isn't a town in the North-east that can compete with Harrogate for pleasure and indulgence. When it comes to art, food, shopping and all-round consumption, Harrogate – at its best – is a treat, a spa town that has emerged from the doldrums as a highly desirable destination.

Its attractions are immediately apparent: the peerless Stray, 215 acres of formal common which are practically hallucinatory in spring with four million crocuses and daffodils; the handsome stock of stone mansions that reinforces the impression of comfortable wealth; the seductive shops dotted through its elegant heart.

This has long been the habitat of North Yorkshire gentry, the crusty colonels and intrepid dowagers who came to define a highly conservative town. They can still be found, like endangered game, at their favourite watering holes, but otherwise Harrogate has moved on – indeed, has returned a Lib Dem MP since 1997 – and smart modern now sits comfortably alongside well-starched traditional. Restaurants such as the Courtyard and Sasso (for both see p295) define its new-wave cooking; there are as many galleries selling contemporary art as those dealing in Dales landscapes; and with careful navigation you can dodge the mustier, heavyweight hotels in favour of boutique numbers and stylish self-catering apartments.

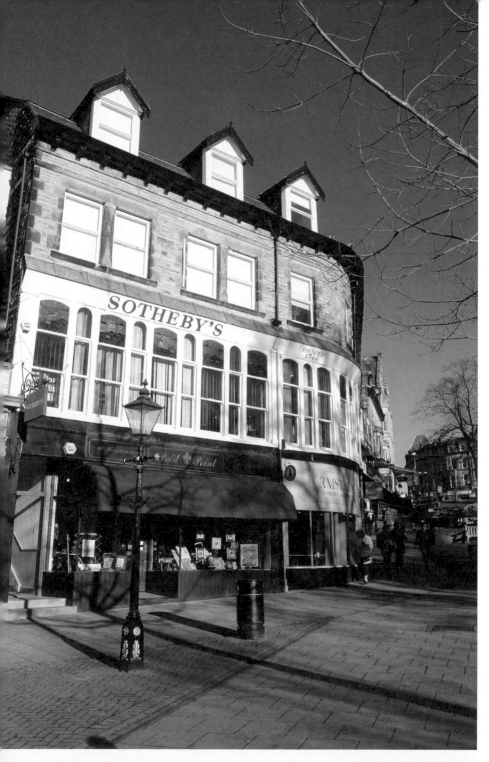

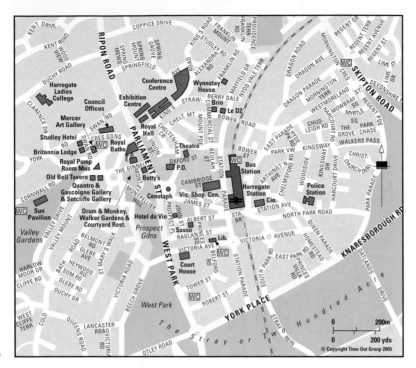

Mixing the best of the new with the best of the old is the way to get the most out of Harrogate. Pop into the Royal Pump Room (Crown Place, 01423 556188, www.harrogate.gov.uk/museums) for the story of the town and its 88 different mineral springs that supposedly cured everything from gout to psoriasis. The sulphur spring beneath the Pump Room still works; drink a shot for free or take home a bottle for 99p. Everyone agrees the taste is vile, giving rise to crafty claims it can only be dispelled by sucking on Farrah's Harrogate Toffee, still sold in its distinctive blue and silver tins from Farrah's shop around the corner on Montpellier Parade (01423 883000, www.farrahs.com).

For the full spa experience, chill out at the fabulously restored Turkish Baths (see p294 **Turkish delights**), followed by a massage or facial at the adjoining Health Spa, or book into the Treatment Rooms (8 Royal Parade, 01423 875678, www.beauty-thetreatmentrooms.co.uk) for more serious pampering.

The revamped showcase gardens at Harlow Carr are another stellar attraction (see p288 **Horticulture shock**). Indeed, Harrogate is a town of parks and flowers, famous for its spring and autumn flower shows, glorious bedding displays and frequent Floral Town prizes. Even the most

cynical sneerer at municipal flower beds would be softened by the timeless, gentle pleasure of the Elgar Walk through the Valley Gardens, supposedly the route taken by Sir Edward during his stay at the Majestic Hotel. Watch the model boats on Sunday mornings, or buy an ice-cream from the Magnesia Well Café (01423 525149) and enjoy it on the greensward beneath the bandstand, accompanied by a Yorkshire brass band.

Cultural Harrogate is marked by theatre, conference centre and the Harrogate International Festival (www.harrogate-festival.org.uk), a week-long festival of classical, jazz and world music held in July. It runs in tandem with the Harrogate Crime Writing Festival; participants in 2005 include Ruth Rendell, Frances Fyfield, Alexander McCall Smith and Val McDermid. Harrogate, after all, is where Agatha Christie was found after a nationwide search when she mysteriously went missing for 11 days in 1926. She ended up at the Old Swan Hotel, known then as the Harrogate Hydropathic. Alan Bennett once made a beguiling BBC documentary, Dinner at Noon, about this famous retreat, but the magic has sadly gone.

What never go away here are art and antiques. The Mercer Municipal Art Gallery (Swan Road, 01423 556188,

Accommodation	★★★
Food & drink	★★★
Nightlife	★
Shopping	★★★
Culture	★
Sights	★★
Scenery	★★★

www.harrogate.gov.uk/museums), housed in the town's oldest spa building – the Promenade Rooms – belies its age with a challenging modern edge to many of its exhibitions. Elsewhere, the commercial scene is a permanent showcase of polished work and, with a couple of snooty exceptions, browsing is welcome. The Sutcliffe Gallery (5 Royal Parade, 01423 562976, www.sutcliffegalleries.co.uk) and Walker Gallery (6 Montpellier Gardens, 01423 567933, www.walkerfineart.co.uk) both deal in pricey, 19th-century paintings. McTague of Harrogate (17-19 Cheltenham Mount, 01423 567086, www.mctague.co.uk) does a strong line in Yorkshire locations. Contemporary work can be found in the Pumphouse Gallery (1 Crown Place, 01423 520599), the Gascoigne Gallery (Royal Parade, 01423 525000), and Walker Contemporary Gallery (13 Montpellier Parade, 01423 526366, www.walkerfine art.co.uk). Godfrey & Watt (7 Westminster Arcade, 01423 525300, www.godfreyand watt.co.uk) sells paintings, ceramics, Lucy Casson's tin sculptures and a fine selection of modern jewellery. If you're lucky, your visit will coincide with one of Sarah Cox and Jo Caswell's contemporary art exhibition-sales (every two months). The event is quite literally an open-house weekend, as the works of around 20 to 30 artists are displayed in a domestic setting (The Picture House, 88 West End Avenue, 07916 159235).

Harrogate's hinterland boasts a wealth of impressive places to visit; it's also a natural launching pad for outings to Nidderdale and the Yorkshire Dales National Park. Fountains Abbey with the adjoining deer park and ornamental lakes of Studley Royal is a World Heritage site; Harewood House is a royal stately home with a lake, a vast, landscaped chunk of Yorkshire and bird garden; Ripley Castle is a popular destination with a pretty estate village.

At Knaresborough, ten minutes away by road or rail, you can hire wooden rowing boats on the River Nidd from Blenkhorns Boats (01423 862105), or walk along Nidd Gorge, a densely wooded valley with bridges, footpaths and boardwalks maintained by the Woodland Trust (www.wt-woods.org.uk/niddgorge). Another delightful short walk is among the almost secret rocks and lake of Plumpton Rocks

(www.plumptonrocks.co.uk), a privately owned estate at Spofforth, five miles east of Harrogate. Ten miles north-west, the National Trust site at Brimham Rocks (01423 780688, www.nationaltrust.org.uk) has more weird and wonderful rock formations to explore.

WHERE TO STAY

In Harrogate's 19th-century heyday as a fashionable spa, grand hotels sprouted up all over town, and doctors in top hats and frock coats would dash from one to another on their rounds. The birth of the NHS in the 1940s led to Harrogate's decline as a spa. Hotels closed or became hospitals or apartments. Of the old relics, the Cairn, the Crown, the Old Swan and the mighty, 156-bedroom Majestic remain, primarily serving the conference trade. Instead of staying in one of these, choose from our selection of the best in town, or head for an inn or a country-house hotel.

Boar's Head Hotel

Ripley Castle Estate, Ripley, North Yorkshire HG3 3AY (01423 771888/www.boarshead ripley.co.uk). **Rates** £105-£125 single; £125-£150 double. **Credit** AmEx, MC, V.
Four miles north of Harrogate and set in a cobbled market square complete with stocks, this upmarket pub-cum-hotel is part of the Ripley Castle estate. As well as a capable bistro and restaurant (*see p293*), it offers 25 elegant and comfortable bedrooms – plus the benefits of a lovely castle, gardens and deer park on the doorstep.

Britannia Lodge

16 Swan Road, Harrogate, North Yorkshire HG1 2SA (01423 508482/www.britlodge. co.uk). **Rates** £80 double. **Credit** MC, V.
A happy exception to the prevailing pink-Dralon design doldrums that for too long have beset the standard British guesthouse, Britannia Lodge features some elegantly furnished public rooms, contemporary-country bedrooms and good breakfasts. It's close to the Pump Room and the Valley Gardens, and a two-bedroom self-catering apartment is also available.

General Tarleton

Boroughbridge Road, Ferrensby, North Yorkshire HG5 0PZ (01423 340284/ www.generaltarleton.co.uk). **Rates** £85 single; £97-£120 double. **Credit** AmEx, MC, V.

TOURIST INFORMATION
Royal Baths, Crescent Road, Harrogate, North Yorkshire HG1 2RR (01423 537300/ www.enjoyharrogate.com).

Another out-of-town option is this substantially expanded roadhouse at Ferrensby, six miles north-east of Harrogate in the Vale of York. The General Tarleton boasts comfortable rooms, all of them en suite, a cosy bar/dining area, a more formal dining room and above-average food and wine. Eating options run from open sandwiches through to three course meals – *see p295.*

Hotel du Vin

Prospect Place, Harrogate, North Yorkshire HG1 1LB (01423 856800/www.hoteldu vin.com). **Rates** £95-£140 double; £145-£275 suite. **Credit** AmEx, MC, V.

A small wall plaque on the face of this Georgian terrace overlooking the Stray is the only indication that the address is a hotel at all. But then, with

HORTICULTURE SHOCK

(sidebar: Harrogate)

Under dynamic curator Matthew Wilson, the beautiful gardens at Harlow Carr have been transformed from the pleasant retreat where Percy Thrower first launched TV gardening – in black and white – into a hot modern attraction. Spread across 68 acres of natural valley and sloping lawns just south of Harrogate, it provides a rewarding afternoon for expert botanists and dilettantes.

The dense woodland has been criss-crossed by all-weather pathways that lead to a lovely wildflower meadow of cowslips, primroses, snake's head fritillaries, common spotted orchids and ragged robins. Gently curving screens created by the resident willow weaver open on to a revamped scented garden featuring jasmine, honeysuckle and wisteria combined with contemporary planting of chocolate cosmos, nigella and alliums.

But the starriest of the new turns is the Gardens Through Time (as seen on BBC2 in 2004). They are at the end of the newly planted herbaceous border: seven historical gardens showing the changes in style and fashion from the Regency period through Lutyens and Jekyll to the Festival of Britain garden, and concluding with Diarmuid Gavin's 21st-century layout.

Harlow Carr has its own rich history, too. A valuable sulphur spring first attracted Henry Wright to the site in 1840. To entice visitors to take a dip in his odorous pool, he built a hotel, bathhouse and ornamental garden.

Gardeners today occasionally hit one of the old brass pipes that took the sulphur water into Harrogate. In 1946, long after the hotel had closed down, Colonel Charles Grey founded the Northern Horticultural Society and developed Harlow Carr as a northern counterpart to the Royal Horticultural Society gardens at Wisley. It has been under the wing of the RHS since the two societies merged in 2001.

'If it grows here, it will grow anywhere,' say gardeners, because high rainfall, heavy clay and acid soil with damaging frost pockets make Harlow Carr one of the most challenging horticultural sites in the country. You wouldn't know it as you follow the much-loved Streamside Garden. One of the longest in the country, it's especially magical in spring when it explodes with primulas, blue Himalyan poppies, astilbes, hostas and ferns.

For added value, there's a full programme of courses and workshops that cover such topics as garden design, willow weaving, pruning and flower painting. There's a well-stocked plant centre, a library of 4,000 horticultural volumes and an excellent bookshop. Not least, this year Harrogate's premier tearoom Betty's opened a café and shop at Harlow Carr – its first new branch for 32 years. Something is definitely stirring in the woods.

Harlow Carr Gardens
Crag Lane, Beckwithshaw, Harrogate, North Yorkshire HG3 1QB (01423 565418/www.rhs.org.uk/shop and plant centre 01423 501809).

Fountains Abbey

this chain of boutique hotels – recently taken over by the Malmaison group – discretion is a watchword. The decor is modern, open-plan and consciously quirky: a stainless-steel staircase, a purple billiard table, worn leather chairs, a realist mural painted on forbiddingly dark walls, distressed wood floors. Rooms are stylish with white cotton sheets, plasma screens, DVD players and roll-top baths. But the peaceful retreat switches to a different circuit at weekends, when the bar and bistro are jumping.

Studley Hotel

28 Swan Road, Harrogate, North Yorkshire HG1 2SE (01423 560425/www.studleyhotel. co.uk). **Rates** £70 single; £94-£104 double/twin; £130 suite. **Credit** AmEx, MC, V.
At first glance, this solid, stone-walled establishment near the Valley Gardens looks like the quintessential Harrogate hotel of swirly carpets and Anaglypta walls. But the double rooms have been revamped with pleasant contemporary furnishings in neutral colours and the single ones are set to follow suit. Added value comes from the basement Orchid Restaurant, serving superior oriental dishes; just don't expect to be the solitary hotel diner. The locals have caught on to this place, so book ahead for dinner. There's a swimming pool available at the nearby Swallow St George hotel.

Wynnstay House

60 Franklin Road, Harrogate, North Yorkshire HG1 5EE (01423 560476/ www.wynnstayhouse.com). **Rates** £45-£70 single; £60-£75 double/twin. **Credit** MC, V.
Wynnstay House occupies one of the substantial Victorian terraces that underpin Harrogate's bed and breakfast trade. The establishment is a simply furnished and comfortable B&B with six rooms, all of which have en suite showers. No smoking throughout.

Yorke Arms at Ramsgill

Ramsgill-in-Nidderdale, North Yorkshire HG3 5RL (01423 755243/www.yorke- arms.co.uk). **Rates** £120-£170 single (incl dinner); £240-£380 (incl dinner). **Credit** AmEx, DC, MC, V.
The most luxurious retreat in the district is a 20-mile drive up Nidderdale. This former shooting lodge serves stunning food, prepared by owner Frances Atkins (*see p295*), and boasts newly furnished bedrooms with minibars, tea and coffee facilities, LCD TVs and – more absorbing than any gogglebox – lovely Dales views. The common rooms, all squashy sofas, classic chintz, polished oak and roaring fires, have a soothing, country-house feel.

A SHOPPING GEM

Fine art and antiques fairs are a steady feature of the Harrogate year and the Montpellier Quarter is stuffed with antiques shops. For top-end 18th-century English furniture, Georgian silver or antique glass, browse Armstrongs (10-11 Montpellier Parade, 01423 5068430), Paul Wetherell (30-31 Montpellier Parade, 01423 5078100) or Charles Lumb (2 Montpellier Gardens, 01423 503776). More affordable are the stalls within the Montpellier Mews Antique Market (Montpellier Street, 01423 530484) and the Ginnel Antiques Centre (The Ginnel, off Parliament Street, 01423 567182). The pick of Cheltenham Crescent shopping is the top-quality selection of second-hand books at Richard Axe Books (12 Cheltenham Crescent, 01423 561867) and French antiques and shabby chic at Kate Marshall's (35-37 Cheltenham Crescent, 01423 523817). Nearby is cutting-edge interior design at Domane Interiors (32 Commercial Street, 01423 851515, www.domaneinteriors.co.uk).

The most amazing shop in Harrogate, however, is its most modest. It never advertises and it never opens on Saturdays, so you'll have to extend your weekend for it. Woods (65-67 Station Parade, 01423 530111, www.woodsofharrogate.com) is a sumptuously covetable linen shop on three floors, serviced by an old and beautifully maintained lift. The quality here is incomparable, whether it's a pure linen dish cloth for £8.50 or an Egyptian cotton sheet at £259. Woods' interior design service is used by a long list of Britain's rich, from Debrett's finest to lottery winners. No names, of course.

Hoopers (28-32 James Street, 01423 504091, www.hoopers.ltd.uk) is an independent department store whose satellite Hoopers for Men (7-11 Princes Street, 01423 564514) has Armani, Boss, Paul Smith and more. Another stylish men's shop is Lynx (12 West Park, 01423 521486). For women, British and European designers are found at Morgan Clare's (3 Montpellier Gardens, 01423 565709). Julie Fitzmaurice (40-42 Parliament Street, 01423 562932) has couture as well as names like Paul Costelloe and Original Blues. Designer babies and toddlers are dressed by Juniper (Bower House, Station Parade, 01423 526020) and Nucleus (2 Parliament Street, 01423 505907) and shod by Bootiful (39 Cheltenham Crescent, 01423 725827).

Food lovers will appreciate Harrogate more for its gourmet shopping than for its mere handful of noteworthy restaurants. Here you should have no trouble finding suitably scrumptious gifts, the ingredients for a superior picnic hamper or the makings of a lavish feast in your weekend retreat.

Start at Betty's (*see p292*), whose first tearoom opened in 1919. For years, Betty's and its rival, Taylor's Café Imperial, eyed each other from across the street until they merged and moved to the beautiful Edwardian building that bears Betty's name today. There are six branches of this exquisite tearoom and cake shop, but this is the flagship where the string quartet first struck up and where pinafores are still starched to imperial standards.

For all the history and tradition, there's nothing dated about its superb baking. The window displays a dozen different breads every day: wholegrain, Turkestan, Parmesan and herb, sun-dried tomato, Yorkshire cobble. Inside there are more temptations: crumpets, pikelets, fruit tarts, gingerbread, fruit loaf, Betty's famous Fat Rascals and delectable handmade chocolates in ever-changing animal shapes. The Taylor's pedigree brings some of the world's most exotic teas and coffees to the party: single estate Darjeeling or a wine-flavoured Yemeni Mocha – superior products at superior prices.

Betty's also has its own superbly equipped cookery school (01423 814016, www.bettyscookeryschool. co.uk). It holds weekend courses on bread, pastry, chocolate and more, including children's courses; prices start from £55. Book well in advance.

The Cheeseboard (1 Commercial Street, 01423 508837) is a cool, dark outlet for a strong selection of domestic and European cheeses. Go Yorkshire with a Richard III wensleydale or one of Judy Bell's excellent blues from her farm near Thirsk – Yorkshire blue, Byland blue or a creamy buffalo blue from a Yorkshire water buffalo herd.

Theobroma (5 Westminster Arcade, 01423 506507, www.theobroma.co.uk) is Greek for 'food of the gods', an apt name for Michelle Woods's gorgeous, chandeliered, little chocolate shop. She stocks top-of-the-range chocolate such as Prestat, Valrhona, Charbonnel et Walker and Rococo. A box of Debauve et Gallais truffles will set you back an eye-popping £52, but an individual Mary chocolate from Belgium costs just 40p.

For a short parade that packs in four terrific gourmet shops, head for King's Road, beyond the Conference Centre. Ramus Seafoods (Nos.132-136, 01423 563271) is a comprehensive purveyor of wet fish and seafood, from east coast crab and Morcambe Bay shrimps to Canadian lobster. Ramus will put together a platter of any size to take back to your lodgings, brimming with lobster, oysters, shrimp and smoked salmon. Regal Fruiterers (No.142, 01423 509609) supply both ordinary and exotic fruit and veg. Then there's Arcimboldo's (No.146, 01423 508760),

a smart independent deli whose house cooks make delicious pies, pastries and quality takeaway dishes. Next door again, Thierry Dumouchel's (No.146A, 01423 502534) has gorgeous baguettes and French pâtisserie, including fruit tarts and sublime almond croissants.

At the other end of town (but worth the trek) is one of the few specialist food bookshops outside London, Allison Wagstaff's Cook Book Shop (Spring Cottage, Cold Bath Place, 01423 536537).

WHERE TO EAT & DRINK

For a town as well groomed as Harrogate, eating and drinking can be disappointing, with too many chains and formulaic joints competing for the conference trade. Choose carefully from a handful of central restaurants, or head to one of three superior gastropubs in the countryside.

For drinking in Harrogate, the Old Bell Tavern (6 Royal Parade, 01423 507930), housed in Farrah's old toffee shop opposite the Pump Room, serves eight real ales and Belgium and German beers with a serviceable upstairs restaurant. There's usually a lively weekend scene at the **Hotel du Vin** (*see p288*).

Betty's

1 Parliament Street, Harrogate, North Yorkshire HG1 2QU (01423 877300/ www.bettysandtaylors.co.uk). **Meals served** 9am-9pm daily. **Main courses** £7-£10. **Credit** MC, V.

This place can do a proper meal as well as morning coffee or afternoon high tea. Old reliables are

The Hotel du Vin
– opened here in
September 2003
– feels like it has
always been part
of Harrogate.

Harrogate

Swiss rösti served with bacon and raclette cheese or Masham sausage and mash, before a corrupting selection of cakes and pastries. Alcohol is served too. Children are welcomed with a Little Rascals menu of old-fashioned favourites such as cinnamon toast and Marmite fingers. Early evening is the best time to beat the queues (no bookings are taken). *See also p287.*

Boar's Head

Ripley Castle Estate, Ripley, North Yorkshire HG3 3AY (01423 771888/www.boarshead ripley.co.uk). **Bistro** **Lunch served** noon-2pm, **dinner served** 7-9pm daily. **Main courses** £10.95-£16. *Restaurant* **Lunch served** noon-2pm, 7-9pm daily. **Set lunch** £13 2 courses, £17 3 courses. **Set dinner** £25-£34.95 3 courses. *Both* **Credit** AmEx, DC, MC, V.

Meander through this picture-postcard estate village, do the castle and gardens, then lunch on solid dishes of ham hock and parsnip terrine, salmon on creamed leeks and duck breast with chorizo. For more sophistication, the hotel dining room sparkles with silver and glass set against classic deep red walls hung with gilded portraits of the ancestors. The menu at the Boar's Head offers dishes like crab and scallop with mango and chilli salsa, spring lamb with stuffed figs and, for pudding, Jaffa Cake soufflé.

Brio

44 Commercial Street, Harrogate, North Yorkshire HG1 1TZ (01423 529933/ www.brios.co.uk). **Lunch served** noon-2pm Tue-Sun. **Dinner served** 6-10.15pm Tue-Fri; 6-11pm Sat; 6-10pm Sun. **Main courses** £11.50-£15.95. **Credit** AmEx, DC, MC, V.

The contemporary interior of etched glass and bold colours belies Brio's former life as a car showroom. Now this place is a bright, vibrant, family-friendly Italian trattoria with fully switched-on charm offensives for women of all ages. Good tapenade to start sets up expectation of (excellent) pasta dishes such as linguine with bottarga (dried tuna roe) or farfalline with fagioli beans and pancetta.

TURKISH DELIGHTS

In the 18th and 19th centuries, visitors flocked to Harrogate to drink and bathe in the mineral springs for their supposed healing properties. The Promenade Rooms (now the Mercer Art Gallery), Pump Room and the Royal Bath Assembly Rooms were lavishly built for visitors 'taking the cure'.

When the Royal Baths opened in 1897, it was judged the most advanced hydrotherapy centre in the world. Here the affluent classes, even royalty, took electric-shock baths, Vichy massages and peat baths. Grand ladies held bath-chair races down Parliament Street, and so many ministers visited it was said they could have held a cabinet meeting. Harrogate was a medicinal spa equal to anywhere in Europe.

Today the Royal Baths house a branch of JD Wetherspoon, the Med Bar and the Tourist Information Bureau, but Harrogate Council has kept control of one particular gem: the Turkish Baths, one of only three Victorian Turkish Baths in England (the others are in Carlisle and Swindon, and neither are as complete as these). The Islamic arches, glazed brick-work, mosaics, painted ceilings and terrazzo floors have been restored at a cost of £1 million. The whole suite of rooms has been brought back to dazzling life.

Set aside two and a half hours for the full hamman experience. There are single-sex and mixed sessions throughout the day and evening (swimsuits required for all sessions), while Wednesday morning is open for tours before the heat is on. There's a no-booking policy, so turn up early. Change in oak and mahogany cubicles, shower, then enter the steam room where eucalyptus vapours clear the airways. The cold-water plunge pool is a bracing preparation for a series of interconnecting heat rooms, all elaborately decorated in Moorish style. Progress through the warm tepidarium, the hot calidarium and the even hotter laconium. Repeat as often as required, taking showers or plunges in between. A half-hour cool-down in the frigidarium (actually pleasantly warm), wrapped in soft white towels on comfortable beds, is compulsory to reacclimatise you to the outside world.

Each session costs £12. The adjoining Health Spa offers a whole range of treatments that must be booked in advance (01423 556746). Combine a Turkish bath with a full body massage (£36.80), a facial (£34.70) and a manicure (£16.80) or take a half-day pampering package (£68.30), perhaps with a light lunch in the lovely glass-roofed Winter Garden Lounge. It may not cure your lumbago, but you will stride out feeling clean, relaxed and exhilarated.

Royal Baths
Parliament Street, Harrogate, North Yorkshire HG1 2WH (01423 556746, www.harrogate.gov.uk/turkishbaths).

Courtyard Restaurant

1 Montpellier Mews, Harrogate, North Yorkshire HG1 2TQ (01423 530708). **Lunch served** 12.30-2.30pm, **dinner served** 6.30-9.30pm Mon-Sat. **Main courses** £13.95-£17.50. **Credit** AmEx, MC, V.
This is the best of the bistros and wine bars in the sharply priced antiques quarter. Bright, modern dishes complement a fresh, smart interior. Lunch offers Whitby crab and salmon fish cake, with a leek and blue cheese fondue, flavoured with truffle oil, followed by confit of duck leg. Desserts might include dark and white chocolate cheesecake with orange sorbet and lemon anglaise. Dinner, more expansively and expensively, deals in the likes of Nidderdale beef, poached sea bass, and asparagus and wild mushroom torte.

Drum & Monkey

5 Montpellier Gardens, Harrogate, North Yorkshire HG1 2TF (01423 502650). **Open Bar** 11am-4.30pm, 6-11pm Mon-Sat. **Lunch served** noon-2.30pm, **dinner served** 6.30-10.15pm Mon-Sat. **Main courses** £9.25-£23.95. **Credit** MC, V.
The Drum & Monkey is a Harrogate legend. Impervious to changing fashion, it serves mussels, oysters, smoked salmon and fresh crab and lobster to the county set. Upstairs or downstairs, the lobster thermidor, plaice with prawn and brandy sauce, fish pie and any number of tried-and-trusted English ways with seafood and shellfish march out to the same institutional beat. Timewarp or treasure? Either way, the place looks indestructible. Arrive early for a seat at the slate-topped bar and a glass of steely white wine.

Le D2

7 Bower Road, Harrogate, North Yorkshire HG1 1BB (01423 502700). **Lunch served** noon-2pm Tue-Sat. **Dinner served** 6-9.30pm Tue-Thur; 6-10pm Fri, Sat. **Main courses** £8.95-£15.95. **Credit** MC, V.
This sparky little brasserie serves appealing modern fare – a fine pumpkin risotto with spring onions and blue cheese, for example, or steak, kidney and mushroom pie from a fairly priced three-course lunch menu at £9.95 (the three-course set dinner is also good value at £16.50). Own-made bread rolls, fresh, crisp salads and a dozen or so wines by the glass support an à la carte selection that includes roast duck and calf's liver. Lemon walls and blue-and-white spotted tablecloths bring a bright, fresh touch to a sturdy stone terrace.

General Tarleton Inn

Boroughbridge Road, Ferrensby, North Yorkshire HG5 0PZ (01423 340284/ www.generaltarleton.co.uk). **Bar Open** noon-3pm, 6-11pm daily, *Restaurant* **Lunch served** noon-1.45pm Sun. **Dinner served** 6-9.15pm Mon-Sat. **Set dinner** £29.50 3 courses. *Both* **Credit** AmEx, MC, V.

The long marriage to the Angel at Hetton – one of Britain's most influential gastropubs – may be over, but John Topham is still supplying dependable quality control at the Tarleton. Cosy up to the fire in the traditional bar, or settle more formally in the dining room for king scallops with black pudding, cullen skink and Thai crab cakes. The Provençal fish soup with croûtons, gruyère and rouille is a fabulous filler. Meat-eaters can have Goosnargh duck breast, slow-roast saddleback pork or new-season Yorkshire lamb; the children's menu offers proper sausage and mash, own-made goujons or pasta; and all ages will love the treacle tart or sticky toffee pud.

Quantro

3 Royal Parade, Harrogate, North Yorkshire HG1 2SZ (01423 503034/www.quantro.co.uk). **Lunch served** noon-2pm Mon-Sat. **Dinner served** 6-10pm Mon-Fri; 6-10.30pm Sat. **Main courses** £10.80-£16.50. **Credit** AmEx, MC, V.
Quantro is a contemporary restaurant of pleasing simplicity in a light, airy space with dark wood furnishings and lime-green walls. The menu is equally contemporary: lemon chicken papardelle with preserved ginger and coriander, or rump of lamb with tabouleh and fondant potatoes. Children under eight aren't admitted.

Sasso

8-10 Princes Square, Harrogate, North Yorkshire HG1 1LX (01423 508838). **Lunch served** noon-2pm Tue-Sat. **Dinner served** 6.30-10pm Mon-Thur; 6.30-10.30pm Fri, Sat. **Main courses** £7.95-£16.95. **Credit** MC, V.
Sasso is an unpretentious basement trattoria of real quality. Stefano Lancelotti makes his own pasta and the difference really shows in his cannelloni filled with parsley and ricotta, topped with gorgonzola and walnuts. He also does pork fillet wrapped in prosciutto, duck breast with dried plums, then proper panna cotta and tiramisu for afters. The food is top value, too – check out the £7.25 set lunch menu.

Yorke Arms at Ramsgill

Ramsgill-in-Nidderdale, North Yorkshire HG3 5RL (01423 755243/www.yorke-arms.co.uk). **Lunch served** noon-2pm daily. **Dinner served** 7-9pm Mon-Sat. **Main courses** £17.50-£24. **Credit** AmEx, DC, MC, V.
Drive out to Upper Nidderdale in prime Dales countryside, where Frances Atkins has transformed the Yorke Arms on Ramsgill's village green into a destination hotel and restaurant. She sources local produce to present a tasting menu and confident carte of modern British dishes that have earned her a Michelin star. Superior game dishes might include saddle of hare with wild mushrooms, or roast partridge with ceps. When dessert time comes, look out for her beautifully matched assembly of lemon jelly with floating islands and honey madeleines.

Helmsley & Harome

Country (town) pleasures.

To the north and east of Helmsley rises the limestone platform of the Yorkshire Moors, windswept and appealingly barren. That's an adjective nobody could apply to the handsome market town of Helmsley and its hinterland, an area so comfortably off that the economic scale doesn't go quite far enough down to accommodate the likes of taxi drivers. (Which, in combination with a dearth of weekend public transport, means that you really can't do without a car here.)

What it does have is a great location: ringed by the pretty Hambledon Hills, Cleveland Hills and the aforementioned moors, and less than an hour's drive from the coast via the scenic route, it offers easy access to a variety of inspiring terrain. More prosaically, its proximity to York, Leeds and the M1 provides a deep reservoir of affluent urban visitors. Still, this is very much the country – fertile agricultural country too – even if local businesses have reacted to the laws of supply and demand by creating a microclimate of fine contemporary cooking with indulgent accommodation to match, best exemplified by the Michelin-acclaimed Star Inn in Harome.

Helmsley & Harcme

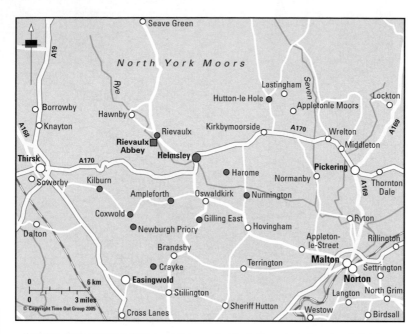

If you're after a family holiday near the Yorkshire Moors, don't come here. This one's for grown-ups, the main ways of filling time between enormous breakfasts, fish and chip lunches and formal dinners being village explorations, pottering around historic buildings and gardens, and country pursuits ranging from drives to hikes to hunting and shooting. (Gun rooms are a standard hotel facility.)

Helmsley itself is a small but perfectly formed town, with a fast-flowing river (the Rye) and an attractive market square surrounded by well-kept greystone buildings occupied by a mix of hotels and hostelries and some interesting independent shops. Market day is Friday, but the shopping is good all week, with a mix of art galleries, bookshops, antiques and decent gift stores, along with an improbably small but appealing department store, Browns (22 Market Place, 01439 770247). It is virtually impossible to escape without making a purchase at Hunters (13 Market Place, 01439 771876, www.huntersof helmsey.com), a huge but homely deli/ grocer on the square peddling a vast amount of local wares, many of them pies.

The town has several sights worth a look. Helmsley Castle (01439 770442, www.english-heritage.org.uk) comprises an impressive 12th-century keep, a Tudor pile and a new visitors' centre where excavated artefacts are on display for the first time. Duncombe Park (01439 770213, www.dun combepark.com), the family home of Lord

and Lady Feversham, is a grand stately home dating from 1713; its grounds are a rare and fine example of relatively untouched garden design from the period. There's a stalwartly British weekend events programme: steam fairs, dog shows, band music, falconry and antiques fairs. Helmsley Walled Garden (Cleveland Way, 01439 771427, www.helmsleywalled garden.co.uk, closed Nov-Mar) is as it sounds, except perhaps cuter: once the kitchen garden for the Duncombe Estate, it's now a calming and charming spot containing unusual varieties such as Yorkshire apples and clematis.

Hard by Helmsley is one of Britain's finest monastic sites, Rievaulx ('Rye-Vallis') Abbey (01439 798228, www.english-heritage.org.uk/rievaulxabbey). There's a capacious car park, but the best way to approach is along the Cleveland Way (which starts in Helmsley). It's an easy three-mile walk, which insinuates you gradually and atmospherically into the timeless Rye Valley setting. The 13th-century abbey is unquestionably significant both historically and architecturally (the Cistercian monks dominated not only the spiritual but also the economic life of the area for centuries, and the refectory is a significant construction), but what makes it special today is the particular beauty of a particular ruin seen in a particular light, its clerestory windows grasping for the sky.

Nearby Rievaulx Terrace & Temples (01439 748283, www.nationaltrust.org.uk,

Accommodation	★★★
Food & drink	★★★
Nightlife	
Shopping	★★
Culture	
Sights	★★
Scenery	★★★★

closed Nov-Apr) is nothing to do with the abbey, except that it offers views thereof, but it does have architecturally impressive 18th-century gardens.

Still to the west of Helmsley, the rolling country south of the A170 is worth a look, continuing the theme of ecclesiastical ruins and historic homes. Just south of the partly be-thatched village of Harome – with a pond, a cricket obsession and a great food shop courtesy of the Star Inn (see p303) – is Nunnington Hall (01439 748283, www.nationaltrust.org.uk, closed Sept-mid Mar), a 17th-century manor house with a haunted maid's room. To the east, past Ampleforth with its huge Catholic school (church services at Ampleforth Abbey are accompanied by a boys' choir of notable quality), Byland Abbey is an open-all-hours ruin (pretty, but pales against Rievaulx) and

Newburgh Priory (01347 868435, open certain days during May and June only, call for times) is a Tudor mansion with some public access (though they let former resident Oliver Cromwell in).

In the same village, Coxwold is the 15th- to 17th-century home of the innovative novelist Laurence Sterne (he called it Shandy Hall after his landmark character, Tristram). It's now a fascinating museum of his life, open to the public (01347 868465, closed Nov-Easter). The area from here towards Thirsk is known for its cabinet-making, and the next village, Kilburn, is home to the Mouseman Visitor Centre & Gallery (01347 869102, www.robertthompsons.co.uk), which interprets the works of Robert Thompson, the furniture maker known for his rodent trademark, and sells those of his descendants. You can also see his work in the local church. The massive Kilburn White Horse carved into the nearby hillside is a curiosity dating from an ambitious school project of 1857.

Into the nearer reaches of the North York National Park – rather undersold as 'the largest single expanse of heather in the world' – there are rewarding drives and bike rides upnearby deep-cut dales. Farndale is particularly pretty, notably the path from

Harome

Low Mill to Church House. Hutton-Le-Hole is the archetypal moorland village, with little becks and village greens, where the enjoyable, open-air Ryedale Folk Museum (01751 417367, www.ryedalefolkmuseum.co.uk) comprises 17 fully accessorised old buildings, including a remarkable Edwardian photographic studio. Check for opening times.

WHERE TO STAY

In addition to the places below, several of the venues in Where to Eat & Drink (*see p301*) also offer attractive accommodation, notably the Abbey Inn and Durham Ox. Worth checking out in Helmsley is the Black Swan, part of a chain (01439 770466, www.macdonaldhotels.co.uk) but with a smart and individual appearance. Worth mentioning as a curio, though a little out of the area, is Crab Manor in Asenby (01845 577286, www.crabandlobster.co.uk), a Georgian house whose rooms are each modelled after a different luxury hotel.

Feversham Arms

Helmsley, North Yorkshire YO62 5AG (01439 770766/www.fevershamarms.com). **Rates** £190-£260 double (incl dinner, breakfast). **Credit** AmEx, MC, V.

From the front: a mellow, bow-windowed town house that looks far too much like a cherished private residence to be a hotel. From the back: an outdoor pool pulls in the other direction, seeming inappropriate and corporate. In the middle, a happy fusion of the two: somehow 17 rooms and generous public areas fit in without complaint, and the pool is a real asset – a well-landscaped terrace perfect for warm afternoons. The Feversham Arms's ethos is one of contemporary country comforts, with a homely feel (in a good way). Rooms are done out in an agreeable, nonconfrontational style, courtesy of the likes of Designers Guild and Fired Earth, with the odd quirk: local watercolours, teddy bears and sweet filing-drawer boxes for CDs. Downstairs, two bar/lounges with real fires are cosy at any time of day, and the restaurant is formal but not dauntingly so,. You can get casual room-service meals, but dinner is meant to be an occasion, with most people dressing up a notch from the outdoor gear that's the norm at daytime. The food is also dressy: showy stuff like oysters and lobster rubs shoulders with (local) English vernacular – ham knuckle and foie gras terrine with pease pudding, for example – on a modern European menu presented with attention and style. It can be a little expensive so look out for the many special deals.

No.54

54 Bondgate, Helmsley, North Yorkshire YO62 5EZ (01439 771533/www.no54.co.uk). **Rates** £74 double. **No credit cards**.

TOURIST INFORMATION

Helmsley
Town Hall, Market Place, Helmsley, North Yorkshire YO62 5BL (01439 770173/www.ryedale.gov.uk/tourism).

No.54 looks just like all the other flat-fronted stone houses in its terrace, but its past as a veterinary surgery suits it well for B&B-dom, with the reception rooms transforming into breakfast room and lounge, and the treatment rooms around a pretty courtyard perfect for conversion into secluded, corridor-free bedrooms. Not that you'd guess at its past if you weren't told: it feels like a cheerful private home run with pride and care. Rooms are small but nicely proportioned, done in pale neutrals with well-dressed beds, simple antique and contemporary furniture, Roberts radios and robes in the well-specced modern bathrooms. Personal touches include a glass of bright boiled sweets and well-chosen books. Breakfast is taken communally around a polished table (or a continental version is delivered to your room), and usually features home-baked muffins and locally sourced fry-ups. A charming, non-institutional B&B.

Star Inn

*Harome, near Helmsley, North Yorkshire
YO62 5JE (01439
770397/www.thestaratharome.co.uk).* **Rates**
£130-£210 double. **Credit** MC, V.
Harome has become a destination because of the
Star Inn, and staying the night is the only way to
properly appreciate the food and wine (*see p303*)
without enduring a winding car journey afterwards. Accommodation is divided between the
Cross House Lodge (rooms just across the road
from the pub) and Black Eagle Cottages (self-
catering suites that are ten minutes' walk from the
pub). Although it's very comfortable – snug even
– attractively decorated and comprehensively
stocked (everything from sewing kits to magazines), the accommodation is not on a par with the
exemplary cooking. One tip – if you stay in the
cottages, ask when you book to have any perish-
ables in your welcome basket put in the fridge. We
arrived on a cold evening to discover the fire on
and the contents of the goodie basket (which
included yoghurt) fizzing away. Overall, though,
a classy but friendly, well-run operation. Stock up
on yet more food (much of it local, some of it produced in the restaurant kitchen) from the Star
Inn's shop (next to the pub; 01439 770082).

WHERE TO EAT & DRINK

First, note that most hotels do decent
packed lunches for days out, as does
Hunters (*see p298*), also an excellent
source of picnic materials. Second, bear
in mind that the Feversham Arms hotel
(*see p300*) also operates as a fine-dining
restaurant at dinner and offers a gastropub-
style menu at lunch (and hot drinks with
Wensleydale and fruit cake at any time).

The Hare Inn at Scawton (01845
597289, www.hareinn.co.uk), near Rievaulx
Abbey, recently changed ownership, but
we've heard good reports of its modern
British food and a Sunday lunch for around
£8. If you're visiting Hutton-le-Hole or pretty
Farndale, the Plough at Fadmoor is rated
locally for its food. For a novelty, you could
try driving east to Pickering or Grosmont to
pick up one of the Pullman dining services
on the scenic North Yorkshire Moors
Railway (01751 472508, www.nymr.
demon.co.uk) – there's even a murder
mystery package.

Beer-drinkers have a slightly lean time,
with the pubs that serve the best beer
falling short on atmosphere. Still, the
Wombwell Arms in Wass (01347 868280,
www.thewombwellarms.co.uk) is under
new ownership: the beer is still good and
changes are planned. The New Inn at
Cropton (01751 417330, www.cropton
brewery.co.uk), a proper local, brews nine
of its own beers (brewery tours year-round,
by appointment out of season).

Helmsley doesn't have any unmissable
pubs, but we recommend the Feathers
(Market Place, 01439 770275,
www.feathershotelhelmsley.co.uk) for a
decent glass of wine and the Royal Oak
(Market Place, no phone) if you'd like to
seek out the locals' local.

Abbey Inn

*Byland Abbey, Coxwold, North Yorkshire
YO61 4BD (01347 868204/www.bylandabbey
inn.co.uk).* **Lunch served** noon-2pm Tue-Sat;
noon-3pm Sun. **Dinner served** 6.30-9pm Mon-
Sat. **Main courses** £8.50-£16. **Credit** MC, V.
Byland Abbey is marked as a village on the map
but in fact it comprises just two edifices, both
handsome and historic: the ruins of a 12th-century
Cistercian abbey and, facing it across a tiny country road, the Abbey Inn, dating from the early
17th. A broad, beautiful, ivy-enrobed building, it
lives comfortably with its past. Country kitchen
tables mingle easily with tapestry-backed chairs
and a multitude of rugs in the unusually capacious
interior that sits halfway between pub and restaurant. The feeling is one of an enterprise that's on
top of its game, with tables full right through to
closing time and professional yet familial staff.
The menu is restaurant rather than gastropub, in
modern British/European vernacular. The warming main courses during our winter visit were

There's good food and drink at the Star Inn, plus bedrooms to sleep it off in afterwards.

hearty and classically conceived – salmon and beetroot with horseradish crème fraîche, venison haunch with redcurrant glaze and onion compôte – with starters venturing a little more creativity: baby leek and cheese bread and butter pudding, warm crab and goat's cheese tart with saffron and chive sauce, and smoked trout with an aubergine salsa. The wine list is a considered one, with lots by the glass; cask ales include Black Sheep.

Crown

Market Place, Helmsley, North Yorkshire YO62 5BJ (01439 770297). **Lunch served** noon-1.45pm Mon-Sat; noon-1.30pm Sun. **High tea served** 3.30-5.45pm daily. **Dinner served** 6-8pm Mon-Thur; 6-8.30pm Fri, Sat. **Main courses** (lunch only) £6.95-£7.25. **Set dinner** £10.90 1 course; £14 2 courses, £16.75 3 courses. **Credit** MC, V.
This family-owned, 16th-century coaching house is perhaps a little too traditional in its accommodation (read velour headboards) for our taste, but tradition be praised when it comes to its high teas – fish and chips, bread and butter, and own-made cakes, buns, scones and pies. The enjoyably unreconstructed facilities also include two cosy pub-style bars, done out with early 20th-century sporting memorabilia – the refreshments tariff from Arsenal's Highbury stadium (tea 3d) – probably contemporary to the last redecoration, and a nice pint of Comptons. Proudly kept and a necessary balance to the influx of the contemporary.

Durham Ox

Westway, Crayke, North Yorkshire YO61 4TE (01347 821506/www.thedurhamox.com). **Lunch served** noon-2.30pm Mon-Sat; noon-3pm Sun. **Dinner served** 6-9.30pm Mon-Fri; 6-10pm Sat; 6-8.30pm Sun. **Main courses** £8.95-£18.95. **Rates** £80 double. **Credit** AmEx, MC, V.
The lovely whitewashed country inn looks timeless, but there's a refreshing restlessness within, as the carte changes monthly and the blackboard daily. Jason Plevey's assured British cooking works with the seasons and region. You could find asparagus with poached egg and spring onion mash, rack of new season lamb, pigeon salad on toasted brioche, or smoked haddock with poached egg and black pudding. Eat in a mezzanine bar amid inglenook and leather, outside on the deck or in the vivid blue, more formal restaurant. After one of the fruity desserts, emulate the Grand Old Duke of York's men who reputedly marched up and down the hill outside.

Fairfax Arms

Main Street, Gilling East, North Yorkshire YO62 4JH (01439 788212). **Lunch served** noon-2pm Tue-Sun. **Dinner served** 6.30-9.30pm Tue-Sat; 6.30-8pm Sun. **Main courses** £7.95-£14.95. **Rates** £70 double; £100 family. **Credit** AmEx, DC, MC, V.

The Fairfax Arms pleases both locals and visitors, the former with its good, unpretentious food and real ales (it's a freehouse), the latter with the above plus a beer garden with duck-populated stream, pleasant accommodation and its setting in a village complete with castle, church and miniature railway, with passenger days on summer Sundays. Daily specials might include rack of lamb, scampi or a balti, with more formal dishes and some wicked desserts appearing on the main menu. Despite its beams and fireplaces, the Fairfax doesn't play on its 17th-century origins, and has a fairly smart living room-feel in its warren of rooms. Don't be surprised to encounter golf groups; this the unofficial HQ of the Gilling Golf Club, and you can pay green fees for the lovely course in the grounds of Gilling Castle (an Ampleforth College property).

Ryeburn of Helmsley

Ryeburn Ice-cream & Tearooms, Cleveland Way, North Yorkshire YO62 5AT (01439 770331). **Open** Mar-Oct 10am-5pm daily. Nov-Feb 10am-4.30pm daily (call to confirm times during winter). **Snacks** 65p-£5. **No credit cards.**
A local institution – and recent National Ice Cream Champion – conveniently parked right at the start of the Cleveland Way. Ryeburn's 45 or so toothsome ice-creams and sorbets (made on the premises from cream from local herds) come in a seductive array of flavours from tiramisu to bilberry yoghurt and in presentations from the unadorned cone to the wastrel sundae. The cake menu is no less tempting, with eight or so sliceable beauties flaunting themselves shamelessly in the display cabinet. And there are own-made chocolates too, in every shade of indulgence. All this decadence is served up in the briskest, brightest, most wholesome environment you could imagine, all pine chairs, aprons and easy-wipe tables. If you prefer something plain, there are toasties and teacakes, or just a good cup of coffee – though be warned, a chocolate will shimmy its way on to the saucer.

Star Inn

Harome, near Helmsley, North Yorkshire YO62 5JE (01439 770397/www.thestarat harome.co.uk). **Lunch served** 11.30am-2pm, **dinner served** 6.30-9.15pm Tue-Sat. **Meals served** noon-6pm Sun. **Main courses** £9.95-£18.95. **Credit** MC, V.
If you want to eat in the Michelin-starred dining room and then stay in the luxury accommodation, you'll need to save up and book early. But if you turn up on spec at pub opening time you can eat in the lovely old polished-oak bar, the best room on the premises. Either way it's a treat. Feast on Ryedale roe deer, Whitby crab, Fadmoor beetroot with Ragstone goat's cheese, or beef fillet reared on a village farm. For pudding, order Andrew Pern's signature dish of baked ginger parkin with rhubarb ripple ice-cream and hot spiced treacle. Throughout, the commitment to local, regional and seasonal ingredients is for real.

Seaham & the Durham coast

A beguiling combination of luxury hotel and rugged countryside.

The main focus of any break in this area is Seaham Hall (*see p308* **Serenity in Seaham**) – there's nothing of its calibre for many miles. But don't let that put you off; Durham and the surrounding countryside merit attention – if you can prise yourself away from the spa, that is.

The closest attraction to the hotel is the Durham Coastal Footpath. A major feature of the Durham Heritage Coast, it's an 11-mile route running between Seaham and Crimdon (there are sandy beaches at both). The cliff path passes through an important National Nature Reserve featuring spectacular Durham denes – dramatic, wooded ravines hollowed out of the magnesian limestone by glaciers. Because of the local coal industry, this was once a highly polluted coastline, but since pit closures a decade ago and a major regeneration project, it has reverted to its pristine beauty. Rare grasses and plants nurture, among other scarce creatures, the Durham argus butterfly. Several miles of coastline are owned by the National Trust, including – just south of Seaham – Warren House Gill (a Site of Special Scientific Interest) and Foxholes Dene, as well as Beacon Hill, the highest point on the Durham coast. Seaham also has a mile-long 'time line' of historical plaques from the harbour – built for coal export by the Londonderry family in 1828 – to Seaham Hall, where the poet Byron was married.

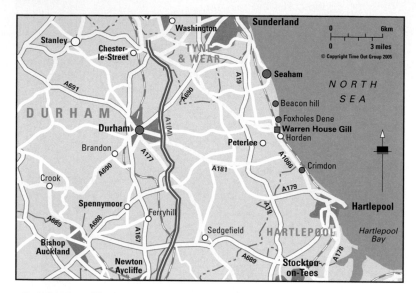

Durham, about 20 minutes' drive away, is the obvious day trip. The castle (0191 334 3800, www.durhamcastle.com) is one of the largest Norman castles and one of the grandest Romanesque palaces to survive in England. This and the cathedral (0191 386 4266, www.durhamcathedral.co.uk) – founded in 1093 – form a World Heritage Site. Durham is a small but beautiful city, offering plenty of wonderful vistas and it is ideal for wandering around: apart from the sights, there's a decent array of shops in a pedestrian-friendly set of streets. Finally, there's also the river – not only is it extremely scenic, but there are rowing boats for hire.

WHERE TO EAT & DRINK

Almshouses Café

Palace Green, Durham, County Durham DH1 3RL (0191 386 1054). **Meals served** *Sept-May* 9am-5pm daily. *June-Aug* 9am-8pm daily. **Main courses** £4.95-£6.20. **Credit** MC, V.
Though facing the cathedral and housed in a terrace of ancient stone buildings, the restaurant has a cheerfully bright and modern interior. Blackboards list daily-changing dishes. The selection usually includes a couple of soups, a salad bowl with various dressings, a pâté or two, a vegetarian and a meat dish, as well as an array of delicious puddings and cakes. All (apart from the bread) are prepared on the premises. A full-flavoured yellow pea, roast tomato and rosemary soup preceded a slice of moist cotherstone cheese, watercress and red pepper quiche. The lemon and almond polenta cake to finish was superb. No smoking throughout.

Bistro 21

Aykley Heads House, Aykley Heads, Durham, County Durham DH1 5TS (0191 384 4354). **Lunch served** noon-2pm Mon-Sat. **Dinner served** 7-10.30pm Mon-Fri; 6-10.30pm Sat. **Main courses** £10.50-£16.50. **Set lunch** £13 2 courses, £15.50 3 courses. **Credit** AmEx, DC, MC, V.
Housed in part of a converted farmhouse, Terry Laybourne's landmark bistro has a minimalist yet cosily rustic decor, and a menu of simple dishes that punch above their weight for flavour. The good-value set-lunch menu includes ham knuckle and parsley terrine with plum chutney, a superb signature dish that also appears on the carte. Char-grilled pork chop with black pudding mash and apple sauce is another favourite. There's a short but varied wine list, with plenty of bottles under £20.

Hide Café Bar & Grill

39 Saddler Street, Durham, County Durham DH1 3NU (0191 384 1999/www.hidebar.com). **Open** 9.30am-11pm Mon-Sat; 10am-10.30pm Sun. **Meals served** 9.30am-3pm, 6-10pm Mon-Fri; 9.30am-4pm, 6-10.30pm Sat; 10am-4pm Sun. **Main courses** £7.95-£16.95. **Credit** MC, V.
A stylish café-bar with cool music and smart decor. The food is eclectic, and runs from tradi-

Accommodation	★★★★
Food & drink	★★★
Nightlife	
Shopping	★★
Culture	★★
Sights	★★★
Scenery	★★★

Bistro 21

tional breakfasts and an all-day café menu of pizzas, salads and stir-fries, through to a three-course affair in the grill, where advance bookings are required. It's a cut above average: bruschetta with rocket, goat's cheese and vine tomatoes followed by roast, line-caught cod with crushed potatoes and beurre blanc. The drinks list encompasses shooters, cocktails, champagnes and wines. There are branches in Yarm and Newcastle.

TOURIST INFORMATION

Durham
Millennium Place, Durham, County Durham DH1 1WA (0191 384 3720/www.durhamtourism.co.uk).

SERENITY IN SEAHAM

If you catch a taxi to Seaham Hall, chances are the cabbie will be only too eager to rattle off a list of celebs he's driven here. Hotel staff, however, are far more discreet. This Georgian mansion has been given a sophisticated 21st-century makeover, right down to a handy helipad. Perched on the edge of the North Sea, it's surrounded by wild countryside, and the atmosphere is luxurious without being stuffy. When the weather is bad, the area can look bleak – but as it's hard to prise yourself away from the combined attractions of the hotel and spa, that doesn't really matter.

There's nothing frilly about Seaham Hall. No two bedroom suites are alike, but all are decorated in similar muted shades (mushroom, sand, taupe) and equipped with electronic equipment and deluxe bathrooms. Big, very comfortable beds are made with wonderfully soft linen. Many rooms have limestone fireplaces; most have views of the sea.

Staff are extremely welcoming and not at all snooty, which means it's easy to overlook the odd glitch (in our experience, lukewarm afternoon tea and hesitant service in the restaurant). On arrival, you're greeted with a smile, and this friendliness continues in the spa.

The Serenity Spa is a knockout. It's reached by a glamorous underground walkway from the hotel, which makes you feel as though you're in a James Bond movie. The spa has a decent-sized swimming pool, numerous hot tubs (including two outdoor ones – very exhilarating in winter), plunge pools, a steam room, sauna and sanarium, fitness suite – the list goes on. And then there are the treatments – for the full range, see the website, but they run from manicures and facials to an impressive choice of massages. One tip: take your own reading material, as what appears to be a pile of magazines turns out to be endless copies of the same glossy.

The hotel restaurant (the White Room) has a modern European menu (the Ozone in the spa offers oriental dishes, and there's also a juice bar). Typical mains might be roast monkfish with tagliatelle, mussels and saffron, or Gressingham duck breast with chicory, foie gras and duck jus. On the whole, the cooking is a lot more assured than the service, which can be a bit nervous. Visit the vaulted cellars before dinner if your wallet can cope with the temptation.

Seaham Hall is expensive for where it is, but not for what you get. For sister establishment the Samling, *see p316*. **Seaham Hall & Serenity Spa** Lord Byron's Walk, Seaham, County Durham SR7 7AG (0191 516 1400/ www.seaham-hall.com). **Lunch served** noon-2pm, **dinner served** 7-10pm daily. **Main courses** £25-£30. **Set lunch** £22.50 3 courses. **Rates** £195-£565 double. **Credit** AmEx, DC, MC, V.

Seaham & the Durham coast

Windermere & Ambleside

Ideal country for eating, walking, and contemplating the view.

The Lake District sends mixed messages. On the one hand its image is of an overpacked tourist trap. On the other, it's an area of remote beauty, with some of England's wildest, most striking scenery. The truth is, the Lake District is both. Immortalised by the Romantics, the area has become iconic: Wordsworth and Coleridge tramped it and sailed it and wrote about it, stamping its image in the mind of future generations. But what Wordsworth would have made of his poetry being emblazoned on tea towels and boxes of fudge is anyone's guess.

The area around Windermere, Bowness and Ambleside attracts more than 12 million visitors a year, so it's a busy place. But veer off the beaten track and you can quickly be plunged into peace and quiet. Among those seeking the sanctuary of the Lakes are nature-lovers, environmentalists, compass-wielding, serious walkers, and those who just want a break. To accommodate them, the area has more than its fair share of sumptuous country-house hotels and rustic inns hidden away in the hills.

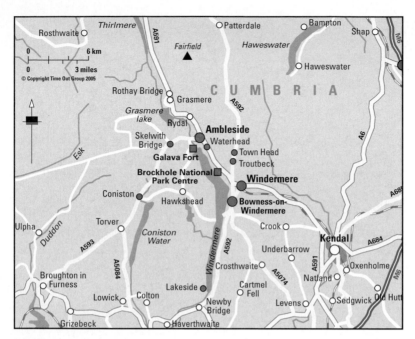

Windermere and Bowness

These days, Windermere is whistling distance from the M6 and in summer its picture-postcard perfection must contend with snaking traffic, gift shops and ice-cream kiosks, and crowds. But if you take a walk, in less than an hour you can be on a deserted hilltop looking down to the lake below. Public transport is good. If walking isn't for you, hop on a bus to nearby Coniston for the scenic route across the fells. Windermere is England's largest lake, about ten and a half miles long and 200 feet deep. It's the Lake District's centre for watersports, but the days of power boats zipping across the water have come to an end with the recent enforcement of a ten-mile-an-hour speed limit. The Windermere Outdoor Adventure Activities Centre (01539 447183, www.woa.co.uk) is worth checking out for its water sports classes, including canoeing and windsurfing. Take a deep breath before plunging in, though – even in summer, the water can be pretty chilly.

Windermere town, a mile inland from the lake, has virtually merged with its twin, Bowness-on-Windermere. Bowness, with its lakefront location and small bay, attracts the lion's share of visitors.

It was the arrival of the railway in the 1840s that transformed a remote, rural outpost into a tourist attraction, bringing people from the rapidly-industrialising cities to enjoy fresh air and views. The Victorian heritage is still much in evidence today in the form of stoic-looking stone guesthouses and B&Bs, plus some fine country houses. Many of these elegantly appointed buildings, former residences of wealthy industrialists and landed families, are now upmarket hotels – Storrs Hall, Gilpin Lodge and Miller Howe are typical of those that still retain a silver service and bone china kind of appeal. They often also sport stunning views from lakeside lounges and conservatories, ideal locations for afternoon tea. These teas are a lakeland speciality: if you book a day ahead, many hotels will lay on a mid-afternoon feast, complete with Dundee cake, Darjeeling tea, finger sandwiches, scones, tray bakes and stacks of hot buttered toast. Evening meals can pale in comparison – there's a tendency for them to be a bit formal, with rather dated French-based cooking styles.

If you're not a seasoned walker or water sports enthusiast, there's another way to enjoy the area. A trip on an old-fashioned Windermere lake steamer reveals mountain views, secluded bays and wooded islands (01539 531188, www.windermere-lake cruises.co.uk). The southern end of the lake boasts some strikingly unspoiled scenery and is noticeably more peaceful than the north. Boats and steamers make regular stops at Bowness, Brockhole, Ambleside and Lakeside – all great spots for pottering and ambling.

Accommodation	★★★★
Food & drink	★★★★
Nightlife	
Shopping	★
Culture	
Sights	★
Scenery	★★★★★

The Lake District Visitor Centre (01539 724555, www.lake-district.gov.uk) is the best place to check out what's going on. Get off the ferry at Brockhole and drop in. There's plenty for kids to do: supervised outdoor workshops, treasure trails and entertaining talks; indoor exhibitions and the café save the day when the heavens open. The centre is surrounded by 30 acres of gardens and grounds, including a wild flower meadow and kitchen garden.

Blackwell Arts & Crafts House (01539 446139, www.blackwell.org.uk), just south of Bowness, has a dramatic hillside presence looking over Windermere. Built at the turn of the 20th century, its quirky design, clever use of natural light and artistic flourishes are an ideal backdrop for its gallery. Run by the Lakeland Arts Trust, Blackwell has a wide range of exhibits, from 17th-century craftwork collections to contemporary art displays – and, of course, Arts and Crafts pieces.

On the main road from Bowness to Ambleside, the Windermere Steamboat Museum (01539 445565, www.steamboat. co.uk) is home to one of the world's finest collections of historical steamboats. It's a gem; check out the Arthur Ransome exhibition and the boats used in the BBC's version of *Swallows and Amazons*.

Ambleside

Between three scenic fells – Loughrigg, Fairfield and Wansfell – Ambleside has been a centre of local trade for centuries. Today, its main trade is tourism, while the surrounding area is big on sheep farming. Beatrix Potter's story-telling prowess may have spawned a whole industry of souvenir shops and guided tours in these parts, but she is also admired locally for breeding Herdwick sheep.

2,000 years ago, the Romans set up base in Fort Galava, near present-day Waterhead (a stopping point for the Windermere ferry). After the Romans moved on to higher ground, Waterhead was pretty much left alone until the development of the tourist industry in the 1850s, when steamboats began to chug up and down the lake, off-loading fashionable, well-hoeled visitors. There's an elegant, orderly appeal to the neat rows of Victorian guesthouses and hotels in Waterhead, and on nearby Ambleside's Compton Road, Lake Road and Church Street.

A refuelling stop and base for exploring the nearby hills, Ambleside is also where walkers and climbers can pick up the latest in the way of waterproofs, sturdy boots and hats. Delis and organic food shops have also made their mark, but old-school cafés and shops are still holding their own. The Apple Pie Eating House (Rydal Road, 01539 433679) bakes the best tray bakes for miles, and for a few pennies you can bag a currant slice, a square of chewy Grasmere gingerbread and a deliciously syrupy flapjack. The café serves cheerful, great-value meals too – hearty Cumberland sausage and cider pies are good choices.

A Taste of Lakeland (Rydal Road, 01539 432319, www.atasteoflakeland.co.uk) lives up to its name, rounding up a fine selection of foods from the area's farms and cottage industries. Besides outstanding preserves, the shop stocks bottled beers from local breweries such as Barngates, Coniston, Dent and Tirril.

Fronting the main car park on Ambleside's Bridge Street in the oldest part of the town, and precariously balanced over a tiny bridge across Stock Beck, is Bridge House (01539 432617, www.national trust.org.uk). Built in the 17th century, it's probably the most photographed building in the Lake District. While you're in the area, pop into the nearby Adrian Sankey's Workshop (Rydal Road, 01539 433039, www.glassmakers.co.uk) for a display of glass-blowing using medieval techniques.

Walks

There is a wealth of scenic tracks hugging the lake or meandering through woodland in the Windermere and Ambleside areas. Orrest Head is only a 20-minute walk from Windermere town centre and its crowds. The walk here is more of a leisurely amble than a full-on challenge. You'll be rewarded with panoramic views of Windermere below and rolling fells south of the lake.

Troutbeck and Troutbeck Bridge, sited close to Windermere and Ambleside, are as famed for the low-level surrounding

TOURIST INFORMATION

Ambleside
Central Buildings, Market Cross, Ambleside, Cumbria LA22 9BS (015394 32582/ www.amblesideonline.co.uk).
Bowness
Glebe Road, Bowness, Cumbria LA23 3HJ (015394 42895/ www.lake-district.gov.uk).
Windermere
Victoria Street, Windermere, Cumbria LA23 1AD (015394 46499/www.lakelandgateway info).

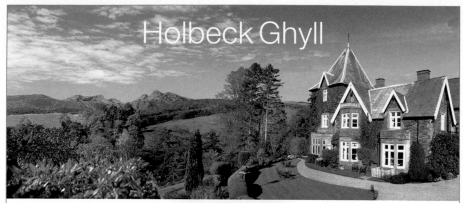

walks as for their stone-fronted, 17th-century inns. The Queens Head Hotel (01539 432174, www.queensheadhotel.com) and Mortal Man (01539 433193, www.landmark-inns.co.uk) are both handily located on the walkers' circuit – a great spot to tank up with top-quality local beer.

For respite from summer crowds, a gentle walk from Stock Ghyll Lane, behind the Salutation Hotel in the centre of Ambleside, leads to a myriad of waterfalls, the best known of which is 70-foot-high Stockgyll Force. Visit in spring and, yes, there will also be a host of golden daffodils.

For more serious walkers, there are steeper fells such as Wansfell and Loughrigg. As walkers know, it's a good idea to check the weather forecast before setting out, and to be prepared for fluctuating temperatures.

WHERE TO STAY

See also the Drunken Duck (*see p318*), Gilpin Lodge (*see p318*) and the Queen's Head (*see p321*).

Holbeck Ghyll

Holbeck Lane, Windermere, Cumbria LA23 1LU (01539 432375/www.holbeckghyll.com). **Lunch served** 12.30-2pm, **dinner served** 7-9.30pm daily. **Set lunch** £22.50 2 courses, £27.50 3 courses. **Set dinner** £45 4 courses incl coffee. **Rates** £200-£320 double; £350 suite (incl dinner) **Credit** AmEx, DC, MC, V.
Surrounded by acres of woodland, and sited on a hill overlooking the lake, this former hunting lodge is as memorable for its furnishings as for its majestic setting. Oak panelling, polished dark wood tables in the dining room, and intricate stained-glass windows lend a lived-in elegance. Chef David McLaughlin's modern British and French menus are perfectly executed, focusing on simplicity rather than fussy flourishes. You might try best end of lamb with shallot purée and rosemary jus, or roasted scallops with celeriac and balsamic dressing. The extensive grounds include a jogging trail and tennis court, and there's an on-site spa too. Luxury like this doesn't come cheap, but it's worth splashing out for.

Linthwaite House

Crook Road, Bowness-on-Windermere, Cumbria LA23 3JA (01539 488600/www.linthwaite.com). **Lunch served** 12.30-1.30pm, **dinner served** 7.15-9pm daily. **Main courses** (lunch) £6.95-£14.95. **Set lunch** (Mon-Sat) £15.95 3 courses; (Sun) £18.95 3 courses. **Set dinner** £44 4 courses incl coffee. **Rates** £140-£280 double; £250-£310 suite. **Credit** AmEx, DC, MC, V.
This Edwardian country house with striking, black-timbered frontage is surrounded by 14 acres of grounds and looks on to the Langdale fells and

Windermere. There's even a nearby tarn (small lake), great for a stroll or a spot of fly-fishing. Professionally run, without being pompous or pretentious, Linthwaite House is a great retreat, with its log fires and afternoon teas are legendary. Gracefully appointed dining rooms are formal, but there isn't a strict dress code. Highly polished mahogany tables set the tone for refined dining in the evenings, but at lunchtime, if it's warm, you can sit outdoors on the terrace and tuck into a chicken club sandwich or even Cumbrian-style bangers and mash. All bedrooms are no smoking.

Miller Howe

Rayrigg Road, Windermere, Cumbria LA23 1EY (01539 442536/www.millerhowe.com). **Lunch served** 12.30-2pm daily. **Dinner served** 6.45-7.45pm Mon-Fri, Sun; 8pm Sat. **Set lunch** (Mon-Sat) £19.50 3 courses; (Sun) £21.50 4 courses. **Set dinner** £42.50 6 courses. **Rates** £180-£280 double (incl dinner); £240-£350 1-bed cottage. **Credit** AmEx, MC, V.
Miller Howe may have lost some of its sheen in recent years, but this famous country-house hotel is still as popular as ever. Furnishings are flamboyant: a profusion of drapes, flounces and tassels, cherubic figurines and porcelain collections. Besides the split-level dining room, there are three elegant lounges, plus an appealing, colonial-style conservatory and garden terrace with magnificent views across the lake. Bedrooms are equally opulent; we're talking floral prints, cushions, chandeliers – the works. The cooking isn't quite as memorable; there's a dated, formal-French feel to much of the menu. The cook's a dab hand with British puddings though (the sticky toffee pudding is scrumptious), and the cream teas are out of this world.

Rothay Manor

Rothay Bridge, Ambleside, Cumbria LA22 0EH (01539 433605/www.rothaymanor.co.uk). **Lunch served** 12.30-1.45pm, **dinner served** 7.30-9pm daily. **Main courses** (lunch) £10. **Set lunch** (Mon-Sat) £17.50 3 courses; (Sun) £19.50 3 courses. **Set dinner** £33 3 courses, £37 4 courses. **Rates** £145-£165 double; £190 suite. **Credit** AmEx, DC, MC, V.
Set in secluded grounds, this family-run Regency country-house hotel keeps up the revered traditions of croquet games on the lawn, roasts on Sundays and occasional afternoon bridge sessions. The long-standing clientele swears by the afternoon teas, cream cakes and freshly baked scones. Decor is of the dark wood, sweeping drapes and country-style printed fabrics school. The hotel welcomes families and puts on an early evening tea for children. As one might guess, the menu throws no new-wave punches – you're likely to find comfortable, '70s-style choices such as melon wedges and Cumberland ham, cream of mushroom soup, and medallions of beef in creamy peppercorn sauce. Despite the stupendous setting, the prices are surprisingly reasonable.

Samling

*Ambleside Road, Windermere, Cumbria LA23
1LR (01539 431922/www.thesamling.com).*
Lunch served *by appointment* 1pm Sun.
Dinner served *by appointment* 7-9.30pm
daily. **Set lunch** £45 4 courses. **Set dinner**
£45 4 courses, £60 9-course tasting menu.
Rates £195-£265 double; £315-£415 suite.
Credit AmEx, MC, V.
Perched on the top of a steep hill and set in 67
acres of private land, the Samling boasts a splendid view of the lake below and is noted for its discreet contemporary elegance (recently refurbished
to boot). Indulgent treats include breakfast in bed,
lovely deep bathtubs and warming sitting room
fires. Despite a well-to-do clientele, the atmosphere
is pretty relaxed and unstuffy. Expect lavish, yet
light meals. There are nine-course tasting menus
as well as a carte, and the restaurant has just been
awarded a Michelin star. Choice morsels might
include braised Herdwick lamb with vegetables
from the hotel's organic garden, and ginger cream
with lychee sorbet. *See p307* for sister establishment Seaham Hotel.

Storrs Hall

*Bowness, Windermere, Cumbria LA23 3LG
(01539 447111/www.elh.co.uk/hotels/storrs
hall).* **Rates** £150-£185 double; £295 suite;
£189-£247 1-bed lodge (per night, 3-night stay
required Fri-Sun). **Credit** AmEx, MC, V.
A Grade II-listed, recently refurbished Georgian
manor, Storrs Hall has recreated its opulent heritage with formal splendour. Despite the exalted
setting, the atmosphere is surprisingly relaxed,
and staff are professional without being austere.
Fabulous lake views framed by huge windows are
complemented by two elegant lounges. The
restaurant's menu is mainly French, but tucked
in among the warm quail salad, seafood bouill-
abaisse and foie gras is a homely sounding
custard-ripple ice-cream and a selection of British
cheeses. You're expected to get into the swing of
things and dress for dinner. Bedrooms maintain
the grandeur level, decked out with lush trimmings, canopied beds, and sparkling chandeliers.
For a more laid-back setting, check out the self-
catering pine lodges by the lakefront – they're set
in wooded grounds, tastefully furnished, and
make a great starting point for exploring the lake.

Waterhead Hotel

*Lake Road, Ambleside, Cumbria LA22 0ER
(01539 432566/www.thewaterhead.co.uk).*
Lunch served noon-2.30pm, **dinner served**
7-9.30pm daily. **Main courses** (lunch) £5-£15.
Set dinner £30 3 courses. **Rates** £160-£200
double; £220 suite. **Credit** AmEx, DC, MC, V.
Recently reopened after a major refit, the
Waterhead is Windermere and Ambleside's
smartest contemporary hotel – its enviable location right by the lakeside is a major asset. Inside,
the lobby is an impressive and refreshing blend
of light wood flooring with lush floral arrange-

ments and plenty of natural light. Spacious bedrooms have white walls, high ceilings and expansive windows, plus all the trimmings you'd expect
of an upmarket hotel: flat-screen TV, DVD (and a
range of movies available) and, best of all, under-
floor heating in the bathroom. Guests also get to
use the facilities at Low Wood's leisure club, a
short drive away.
   The glass-fronted Bay restaurant and bar has an
almost Mediterranean feel – an open kitchen on
one side, the lake on the other, lending a smart,
almost city vibe, especially in the evenings. Staff
are on the ball and cheerful. The hotel and restaurant are a hit with a well-heeled, youthful clientele
looking for more informal surroundings – something outside the confines of the traditional
country house hotel genre. Food is a mix of modern British and classic French. On a recent visit,

Holbeck Ghyll –
old school, and all
the better for it.

chicken feuillete scored points for crisp, puff pastry, tender chicken filling and an appealing citrusy tang of buttery orange hollandaise sauce. A meaty beef medallion, cloaked in a brown jus, flavoured with blue cheese, was accompanied with a pile of thickly cut chips. Breakfast is a magnificent spread. Grab a table by the window and enjoy the view – it's fabulous.

WHERE TO EAT & DRINK

Note that all the hotels listed in Where to Stay (*see p315*) are also great places for a meal, with many of them serving afternoon tea.

Chester's Café by the River

Skelwith Bridge, nr Ambleside, Cumbria LA22 9NJ (01539 432553/www.chesters-cafebytheriver.co.uk). **Open** 10am-5pm daily. **Lunch served** noon-3.30pm daily. **Main courses** £8.95-£14.95. **Credit** MC, V.
Handily located, just off the main road from Ambleside, this stone- and slate-fronted café sits by the River Brathay at an ideal spot for a leisurely stroll. The café caters for breakfasts, snacks and lunches. Choices could include a hot-pot of locally smoked haddock or braised Cumbrian Galloway beef. We're sold on the own-baked lemon meringue pies, tea breads and pastries.

Drunken Duck

Barngates, Ambleside, Cumbria LA22 0NG (01539 436347/www.drunkenduckinn.co.uk). **Lunch served** noon-2.30pm, **dinner served** 6-8.45pm daily. **Main courses** £14.95-£22.95. **Rates** £95-£210 double. **Credit** AmEx, MC, V.
This 400-year-old landmark, set in the middle of unspoiled fells, is one of the Lake District's real treasures. Well weathered, the Drunken Duck's picturesque setting attracts a healthy mix of seasoned walkers, nature-loving visitors and locals out for a few pints. A seamless combination of award-winning own-brews, rustic pub decor and fine, modern British cooking is underpinned by friendly, down-to-earth and professional staff. As a watering hole, you'd be hard pressed to find better – dark wood furniture, locally sourced prints and artefacts, and a decent wine list add to the experience, but what really scores are award-winning beers from the on-site Barngates microbrewery. Chester's Strong and Ugly, and Tag Lag are just two top-notch choices, as distinctive in character as in name.

Meals are a sight more pricey than the homely surroundings suggest. The Duck's big on using local suppliers and our Cartmel Valley smoked salmon, served with a tangle of niçoise salad was sublime – delicate wafers of salmon complementing a sharpish balsamic salad dressing. Portions are huge, so it's best to work up an appetite beforehand. A main course of juicy, meaty pork loin slices, served with sautéed mushrooms, buttery leaf spinach and a moat of velvety-smooth foie

gras sauce, won our gold star for quality. Puds are just a touch aspirational – if you can, go for the steamed sponges and pies rather than the overly fussy French-style creations. Breakfasts are memorable – take your pick from notables such as softly set poached eggs cloaked in hollandaise sauce, classic Cumberland sausage fry-ups, and posh eggy bread. 16 rooms, housed behind the inn, are light and airy, well appointed and spacious. Large windows, the odd antique and a lovely, leafy garden add to their appeal. This is one of Cumbria's best-loved inns – it's no surprise that rooms are booked months in advance.

Gilpin Lodge

Crook Road, Windermere, Cumbria LA23 3NE (01539 488818/www.gilpinlodge.com). **Coffee served** 9am-noon, **lunch served** noon-2pm, **tea served** 3.30-5.30pm, **dinner served** 6.45-9.15pm daily. **Set lunch** £18 2 courses, £22 3 courses. **Set dinner** £42.50 5 courses. **Rates** £160-£310 double incl dinner. **Credit** AmEx, DC, JCB, MC, V.
More like a family home than a hotel and restaurant, Gilpin Lodge combines friendly warmth with understated elegance. Four cosy dining rooms include a bright and airy conservatory, and a Garden Room that opens out on to the terrace. Meals are sophisticated and modern without

going down the fusion route. In autumn, you could sit down to a confit of pheasant with casseroled root vegetables, followed by auburn-hued saffron ice-cream. Breakfasts, in winter, are a fireside feast – of anything from slow-cooked porridge to strawberry and champagne sorbet. Whatever you do, don't pass over the finger sandwiches and drop scones for afternoon tea – they're delicious. Its 14 rooms are spacious – subtle touches such as fresh flowers and own-made biscuits add to the charm.

Glass House

Rydal Road, Ambleside, Cumbria LA22 9AN (01539 432137/www.theglasshouserestaurant. co.uk). **Lunch served** noon-5pm daily. **Dinner served** 6.30-9.30pm Mon-Fri, Sun; 6.30-10pm Sat. **Main courses** £11.25-£18.50. **Set dinner** £12.50 2 courses, £15 3 courses. **Credit** MC, V.

After achieving a degree of notoriety on makeover show *Ramsay's Kitchen Nightmares*, the Glass House continues to pull in curious punters. Housed in a 15th-century mill conversion, interesting features include weighty oak beams and a striking display of old iron artefacts. The impressive glass frontage lends an upbeat vibe, which works well with the modern European menu. At lunchtime open sandwiches, chunky soups and hearty hot-pots cater to all tastes and appetites.

There's also an early supper laid on for cinema-goers and early diners. A varied dinner menu ups the tone, with dishes such as risotto, maple-glazed pancetta, and liquorice ice-cream.

Jerichos

Birch Street, Windermere, Cumbria LA23 1EG (01539 442522). **Dinner served** 6.45-9.30pm Tue-Sun. **Main courses** £13.50-£17.50. **Credit** MC, V.

This former chippy in Windermere town centre has been reinvented as a modern European restaurant. Run by Chris Blaydes (former head chef at Miller Howe) and wife Jo, the simple and concise menu shows off local produce, and boasts clean flavours and imaginative combinations. Typical dishes might be pan-fried fillet of sea bream with black bean noodles, or pesto risotto and lavender crème brûlée. The wine list is commendable and reasonably priced, with many choices available by the glass. No smoking throughout.

Lucy's on a Plate

1 Church Street, Ambleside, Cumbria LA22 0BU (01539 431191/www.lucysofambleside. co.uk). **Open/meals served** 10am-9pm daily. **Main courses** £6-£19. **Credit** MC, V.

Waterhead Hotel

Lucy's fancy deli leads you to a friendly rustic café, catering to customers with cosmopolitan tastes. An extensive menu embraces such curiosities as Spanish-style breakfasts made with Cumberland sausages, filled focaccias and Middle Eastern dips. Cooking tends to be hearty rather than awe-inspiring – big on portions, but of variable quality. Nursery school staples such as crunchy macaroni cheese are passable, but for a more flavoursome experience, plump for a ciaburger – meaty, garlicky burgers (or veggie variations) tucked inside a warm ciabatta bun. Lucy 4, the branch across the road (2 St Mary's Lane), has a fine choice of wines and tapas.

Porthole Eating House

3 Ash Street, Bowness-on-Windermere, Cumbria LA23 3EB (01539 442793/www.porthole.fsworld.co.uk). **Dinner served** 6-10.30pm Mon, Wed-Sun. **Main courses** £11.50-£25. **Credit** AmEx, DC, MC, V.

For over 30 years, this charming restaurant, set in a 17th-century cottage, has served a loyal fan club of customers who come here for Anglo Italian dishes along with a couple of '70s-style French classics. Expect such retro gems as spaghetti bolognese, pan-fried veal escalopes in creamy

sauce and tiramisu. It's not all nostalgic cooking though – for those with more adventurous tastes, there are the likes of Thai-style fish cakes with coconut mash. In summer, sit out on the back patio and relax over a bottle of fine German wine.

Queen's Head

Townhead, Troutbeck, Cumbria LA23 1PW (01539 432174/www.queensheadhotel.com). **Lunch served** noon-2.30pm, **dinner served** 6.30-9pm daily. **Main courses** £7.25-£14.25. **Set meal** £15.50 3 courses. **Rates** £85-£105 double. **Credit** MC, V.

This sturdy, 17th-century coaching inn is home to a Pandora's Box of fascinating and quirky historical features. How an Elizabethan four-poster bed frame came to be embedded in the dark-wood bar is anyone's guess – but it does look at home. In keeping with Troutbeck Valley's rural setting, the inn's winter-warming fires, stone-flagged floor and weighty oak beams reflect a country feel. Even off-season, expect to find hardy walkers and casual visitors by the fireside, unwinding with a pint of excellent local beer – Coniston Brewing Company's Bluebird Bitter or Tirril Brewery's Old Faithful. Cooking styles aren't quite as simple as the inn's wholesome atmosphere. Alongside stylised and somewhat out-of-place hazelnut dressings, feta cheese salads and beetroot-cured salmon are the real winners – the comfort dishes. Hearty and satisfying, a steak, ale and mushroom cobbler – a meaty stew crowned with a rustic scone-like topping – won our approval for its tender meat and gravy-soaked crust. Equally good was grilled salmon, accompanied by roughly-crushed potatoes and a warm olive oil and yellow pepper dressing. A generous wedge of moist banana sponge topped with coconut ice-cream scored for nostalgic nursery-pud appeal. Rooms are clean and well maintained – their uneven flooring and rough-finished walls are a reminder of the building's considerable age.

Zeffirellis

Compston Road, Ambleside, Cumbria LA22 9AD (01539 433845/www.zeffirellis.co.uk). **Lunch served** 10am-4.30pm, **dinner served** 6-9.30pm daily. **Main courses** £2.95-£8. **Set meal** (incl cinema ticket) £14 2 courses. **Credit** MC, V.

Not just another pizza joint attached to a cinema, Zefferellis is a star attraction for nearby residents – and it's easy to see why. During the day, a friendly modern café welcomes young families and casual visitors. There's a vegetarian menu with an Italian accent – ingredients are fresh, and pizzas, jacket potatoes and pastas are tasty, wholesome and reasonably priced. After a day's walking with the kids, this is a great spot to unwind. In-house baking is spot-on too – we loved the freshly baked scones. Next time we'll choose the lemon tarts. In the evenings, more formal seating arrangements in the lower level dining area offer smart dinner options.

Edinburgh

There's life beyond the frenzied festival.

For some people, Edinburgh's history and cultural attractions alone would compel them to book a trip. Others might pose a few questions: 'Yeah, yeah, castles and all that, but what about the restaurants? Theatres? Clubs? Never mind the old stuff, where's the fun?' Of course, if it hadn't been for the history – and the development of a capital with a certain self-conceit – then the fun would have never started.

In terms of its status as an official world heritage centre, this city does exactly what it says on the tin. Even if you scoot through pre-history, the Romans and the Dark Ages, you're still left with around 1,000 years of events starting with Malcolm III's establishment of a castle in the 11th century, consolidated by David I, who founded Holyrood Abbey in the 12th. Castle and abbey were a handy mile apart, providing an east–west axis around which the medieval Old Town developed. Today that axis is known as the Royal Mile, encompassing the Lawnmarket, High Street and Canongate.

Edinburgh

Scottish National Gallery of Modern Art

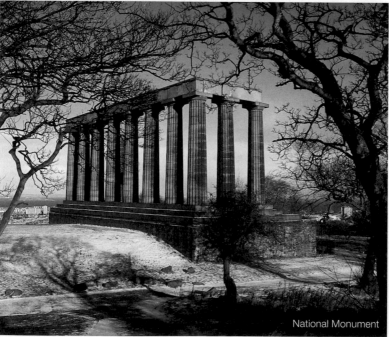

National Monument

Accommodation	★★★★
Food & drink	★★★★
Nightlife	★★★
Shopping	★★★
Culture	★★★★
Sights	★★★
Scenery	★★★

Then there are later associations with the Stewarts (James IV built the Palace of Holyroodhouse in the late 15th century), personalities from the 16th century like John Knox and Mary Queen of Scots, the brutal 17th-century 'killing times' with Covenanters striving for freedom of worship, the Enlightenment (virtually invented in Scotland according to author Arthur Herman) and the creation of an elegant New Town from the late 18th century. As a summary this hardly scratches the surface – but all of it can still be investigated around the city today.

Edinburgh has been the capital of Scotland for over 500 years and was the first-choice site for the re-establishment of a Scottish Parliament in 1999. It has also been a centre for the courts, civil service, academics, bankers and actuaries for quite some time. Put this all together and you get a certain demeanour: a traditional aversion to vulgarity, a lack of brashness, a bourgeois assurance, in fact, not entirely excised by the new psychological brutalism of the 21st century. Edinburgh takes its pleasures in a particular manner...

Yes, there may be streets with cheap pubs and clubs and students' bars, and areas like Leith where new money mixes with an ingrained saltiness – but the city is far better defined by the biggest event of its year, when visitor numbers hit a phenomenal peak. August is the month of 'the Festival', a handy catch-all term that actually encompasses the official International Festival as well as the Fringe, Film, Book, and Jazz and Blues Festivals, plus the Military Tattoo – all administratively separate. If you're looking for a quiet romantic weekend, pick another month. For unparalleled vibrancy, walk this way.

At the more wintry end of things, the recently invented Capital Christmas is a mix of family attractions and city centre funfair throughout December, largely for locals, while Edinburgh's Hogmanay is a four-day extravaganza that builds to a massive street party on 31 December and into the small hours of the new year, attracting visitors from all over the world.

Entertainments that last all year round include dedicated comedy clubs, art-house cinema, the National Galleries of Scotland, as well as a commendable collection of smaller, independent art galleries, regular classical concerts and a host of contemporary music venues. These cater for everything from the occasional blockbuster gig (U2 or the Red Hot Chili Peppers at Murrayfield, the national rugby stadium, for example), to more intimate indie music at venues like the Liquid Rooms, as well as a decent choice of clubs playing a wide range of dance music. Theatre-goers enjoy a variety of venues doing everything from the classics to new experimental work, and there are expansive green spaces like the Royal Botanic Garden, or Holyrood Park with the 823-foot volcanic peak, Arthur's Seat, at its centre. Then, of course, there are excellent places to eat (more on those below), bars with more varieties of whisky than you knew existed, a small but well established gay scene, and much more besides.

WHERE TO STAY

Balmoral

1 Princes Street, EH2 2EQ (0131 556 2414/ www.thebalmoralhotel.com). **Rates** £240-£290 double; £990 suite. **Credit** AmEx, DC, MC, V. Certainly the most imposing hotel in the city, the Balmoral sits at the east end of Princes Street, its clock tower a landmark since 1902. Originally a railway hotel, it's now owned by Rocco Forte and was substantially refurbished in 2003-04. While it retains many classic elements, some rooms and public spaces have been given an elegant, contemporary makeover. Its popular spa offers the usual array of treatments (reiki and aromatherapy among them) and there is also a small pool and gym. The flagship restaurant, Number One, under the control of chef Jeff Bland, has a Michelin star. Big-end luxury.

Caledonian Hilton

Princes Street, EH1 2AB (0131 222 8888/ www.hilton.com). **Rates** £155-£235 double; £320-£900 suite. **Credit** AmEx, DC, MC, V. Another Edwardian railway hotel – dating from 1903 – this red sandstone pile at the west end of Princes Street retains some sense of individuality despite being owned by the Hilton chain. The rooms are either contemporary or 'grand house rococo', this latter theme spilling over into the elaborate and mannered restaurant, the Pompadour, serving French-influenced cuisine. A rolling

Edinburgh

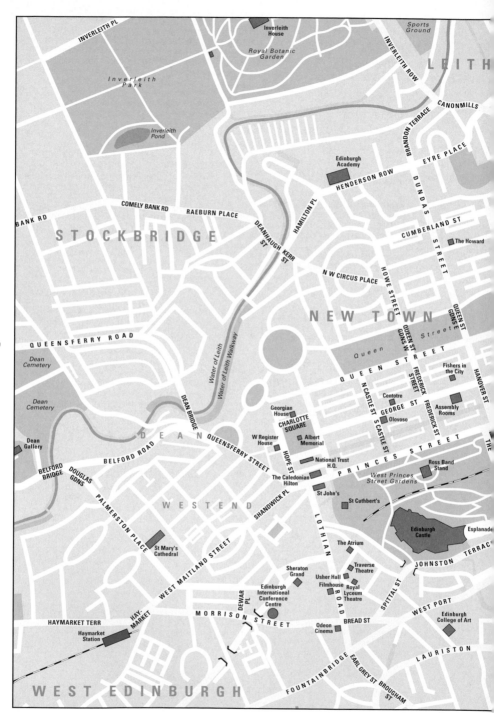

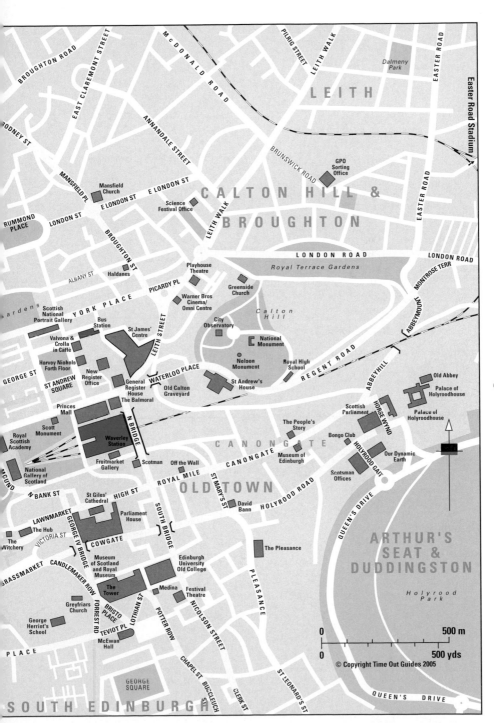

BROUGHTON ROAD
EAST CLAREMONT STREET
McDONALD ROAD
PILRIG STREET
LEITH WALK
EASTER ROAD
Dalmeny Park
Easter Road Stadium

RODNEY ST
MANSFIELD PL
ANNANDALE STREET
BRUNSWICK ROAD

LEITH

GPO Sorting Office
EASTER ROAD

RUMMOND PLACE
Mansfield Church
E LONDON ST
E LONDON ST
Science Festival Office

CALTON HILL &
BROUGHTON

LONDON ST
Haldanes
ALBANY ST
BROUGHTON ST
PICARDY PL
LEITH WALK
LONDON ROAD
LONDON ROAD
Royal Terrace Gardens
MONTROSE TERR

Gardens
Scottish National Portrait Gallery
YORK PLACE
Playhouse Theatre
Greenside Church
Calton Hill
ABBEYMOUNT

Bus Station
St James' Centre
Warner Bros Cinema/ Omni Centre
City Observatory
National Monument

Valvona & Crolla in Caffè
LEITH STREET
Nelson Monument
Royal High School
REGENT ROAD
ABBEYHILL

Harvey Nichols Forth Floor
New Register Office
WATERLOO PLACE
St Andrew's House
ST ANDREW SQUARE

GEORGE ST
General Register House
Old Calton Graveyard
Scottish Parliament
HORSE WYND
Old Abbey
Palace of Holyroodhouse

Princes Mall
The Balmoral
N BRIDGE
The People's Story
Palace of Holyroodhouse

Scott Monument
Waverley Station
CANONGATE
Bongo Club
HOLYROOD GAIT

Royal Scottish Academy
Fruitmarket Gallery
Scotman
Off the Wall
CANONGATE
Museum of Edinburgh
Our Dynamic Earth

National Gallery of Scotland
Scotsman
ROYAL MILE
Scotsman Offices
QUEEN'S DRIVE

N BANK ST
St Giles' Cathedral
HIGH ST
OLD TOWN
ST MARY'S ST
HOLYROOD ROAD

LAWNMARKET
GEORGE IV BRIDGE
Parliament House
SOUTH BRIDGE
David Bann
ARTHUR'S SEAT & DUDDINGSTON

The Hub
VICTORIA ST
COWGATE
The Pleasance
PLEASANCE

The Witchery
BRASSMARKET
CANDLEMAKER ROW
Museum of Scotland and Royal Museum
Edinburgh University Old College
Holyrood Park

Greyfriars Church
The Tower
BRISTO PLACE
Medina
Festival Theatre
NICOLSON STREET

George Herriot's School
FORREST RD
LOTHIAN ST
POTTER ROW
ST LEONARD'S ST

McEwan Hall
TEVIOT PL
CHAPEL ST
BUCCLEUCH ST
CLERK ST

PLACE
GEORGE SQUARE

SOUTH EDINBURGH
QUEEN'S DRIVE

0 ————— 500 m
0 ————— 500 yds
© Copyright Time Out Guides 2005

Edinburgh

refurbishment over the winter of 2004/05 has seen the old place spruced up, and it also has a small health club with gym, pool, sauna and steam room. Because it's a Hilton, it makes sense to look out for special offers (check the website), and aim for a castle view.

Howard

34 Great King Street, EH3 6QH (0131 557 3500/www.thehoward.com). **Rates** £210-£265 double; £250-£365 suite. **Credit** AmEx, DC, MC, V.
The New Town is a tribute to post-Enlightenment urban planning when 'the quality' abandoned old Edinburgh and fled north to elegant terraces laid out in the final decades of the 18th century and into the 19th. The buildings that now form the Howard date from the 1820s, while the interior plays on the historical theme; elegance is the key word and guests even have a dedicated butler. The idea is that you're in a luxurious, private Georgian house rather than 'a hotel'. The Atholl dining room is good, while the themed breaks (whisky and theatre among others) help give a visit to the city some focus.

Malmaison

1 Tower Place, Leith, EH6 7DB (0131 468 5000/www.malmaison.com). **Rates** £99-£135 double; £165-£195 suite. **Credit** AmEx, DC, MC, V.
Malmaison may have planted its flag in seven other locations, but this was the original. It's housed in a baronial-style former seamen's mission dating from 1833 (in the docks area, of course) and overlooks the Water of Leith, Edinburgh's 'city river'. There's a small gym, while rooms have the comfortable and classy decor typical of the chain. There are nice touches: CD player, decent shower, in-room wine and nibbles. Malmaison can't be accused of resting on its laurels; since the hotel opened in 1994, its café-bar and brasserie have both undergone substantial refurbishment. Also handy for Leith's pubs and restaurants.

Prestonfield

Priestfield Road, EH16 5UT (0131 668 3346/ www.prestonfield.com). **Rates** £195-£225 double; £275 suite. **Credit** AmEx, DC, MC, V.
James Thomson is Edinburgh's star restaurateur with eateries like the Witchery and the Tower (*see p334*). But in 2003, he expanded into the hotel business with the opening of Prestonfield. This is a late 17th-century mansion in the shadow of Arthur's Seat, which has been completely made over. It's not often that the word 'sumptuous' can be accurately applied, but it certainly can to this mix of late-period Stewart style and 21st-century sensibility. That means flat-screen TVs, DVD players, expensive sound systems and modern fabrics among the silk brocades and antiques. The hotel features in a lot of 'best of' lists, and its restaurant (Rhubarb) is pretty good too.

Scotsman

20 North Bridge, EH1 1YT (0131 556 5565/ www.thescotsmanhotel.co.uk). **Rates** £295-£395 double; £500-£1,500 suite. **Credit** AmEx, DC, MC, V.
This establishment really shook up the luxury hotel scene in Edinburgh when it arrived in 2001. Housed in the former offices of *the Scotsman* newspaper, it offers rooms with a thoughtful, contemporary design, DVD and CD players, internet access, wide-screen televisions and more. There's a buzzing brasserie (North Bridge), a reverential fine dining room (Vermilion), a health club with a stainless-steel swimming pool straight out of James Bond, and spa treatments that are far from po-faced (they include the 'Stressed Cow' massage and the 'Mucky Cow' mud wrap). It also manages to pull off the trick of feeling like a real refuge from the city-centre bustle outside.

Sheraton Grand

1 Festival Square, EH3 9SR (0131 229 9131/ www.sheraton.com). **Rates** £105-£290 double; £400-£450 suite **Credit** AmEx, DC, MC, V.
The Sheraton arrived on the Edinburgh scene in the mid 1980s with its bland façade and aspirational decor, then got largely ignored as 'just another big corporate hotel' (despite its perfectly decent if unsexy fine dining room, the Grill). But all that changed with the opening of its Sir Terry Farrell-designed extension in 2001. It houses not only one of the city's best Italian restaurants, Santini, but also a truly world-class spa, One. This offers every type of pampering you can imagine (including ayurvedic treatments) as well as the expected gym, swimming pool, and even an outdoor hydropool with a view (although a hat is advisable in winter).

WHERE TO EAT & DRINK

Before getting down to the food, let's think whisky. You're in Scotland, after all, and Edinburgh boasts some excellent venues where drinkers can sample the rarest of single malts. The Scotch Malt Whisky Society bottles whisky from individual casks whose output only runs into a few hundred bottles. Membership is required but it's not overly expensive and there is a choice of two members' rooms to sit and sip in (the Vaults, 87 Giles Street, Leith, 0131 554 3451, or 28 Queen Street, New Town, 0131 220 2044, www.smws.com). The best pubs for whisky include the Bow Bar (80 West Bow, 0131 226 7667), Kays (39 Jamaica Street, 0131 225 1858), the Canny Man's (239 Morningside Road, 0131 447 1484), and Bennet's (8 Leven Street, 0131 229 5143).
Edinburgh also has a good selection of café-bars where you can snack and drink. The enduring example of robust hipsterdom is the City Café (19 Blair Street, 0131 220 0125), then there are more upmarket

varieties like Rick's (55A Frederick Street, 0131 622 7800) and the Opal Lounge (51A George Street, 0131 226 2275), while the Blue Moon is the city's homely gay café-bar (36 Broughton Street, 0131 556 2788). Debate rages over the best café in Edinburgh, but Glass and Thompson (2 Dundas Street, 0131 557 0909) edges it with excellent food.

For a city of its size, Edinburgh does very well for restaurants. Some of the best modern European eateries are in the big hotels, but are happy to welcome non-residents: Number One at the Balmoral, for example (0131 557 6727, see p325), or Vermilion at the Scotsman (see p328).

The city is also blessed with a variety of seafood venues, particularly in Leith. These include Fisher's (1 The Shore, 0131 554 5666), Skippers (1A Dock Place, 0131 554 1018) and the Waterfront (1C Dock Place, 0131 554 7427). The latter two came under common ownership in 2004.

Meanwhile, the pick of the Indian restaurants would include Suruchi (14A Nicolson Street, 0131 556 6583), the vegetarian Kalpna (2-3 St Patrick's Square, 0131 667 9890) and the rugged, frontier-themed Namaste (15 Bristo Place, 0131 466 7061). Other Asian notables are Dusit, one of the best Thai eateries in the city (49A Thistle Street, 0131 220 6846); the extravagantly appointed Chinese Dragon Way (74-78 South Clerk Street, 0131 668 1328); and the rather decent Izzi, which serves both Chinese and Japanese dishes (119 Lothian Road, 0131 466 9888).

Chinese and Indian aside, the most popular cuisine in the city is Italian. Santini behind the Sheraton Grand is very contemporary and high-quality (8 Conference Square, 0131 221 7788), while Cosmo is old-school posh (58A North Castle Street, 0131 226 6743). The most celebrated Italian name in these parts, however, is Valvona and Crolla, a delicatessen dating to 1934. At the back of the shop (19 Elm Row, Leith Walk, 0131 556 6066) is its Caffè Bar. There's nothing over-elaborate here, just good food made from great ingredients, served during the day. In 2004, Edinburgh benefited from two spin-off ventures: Centotre (see right) and the Valvona and Crolla VinCaffè (see p334).

Finally, when talking about food in Edinburgh there's a name that can't be left out: James Thomson. He opened the Witchery (see p334) in 1979, added the Secret Garden in 1989, created the Tower (see p334) in 1998, then introduced Rhubarb at Prestonfield in 2003 (see p328). It's all destination dining and he is the city's undisputed star restaurateur. And given the bargain post-theatre supper at the Witchery, you don't even need to be minted to eat there.

Atrium

10 Cambridge Street, EH1 2ED (0131 228 8882). **Lunch served** noon-2pm Mon-Fri. **Dinner served** 6-10pm Mon-Sat. **Main courses** £19-£22. **Set lunch** £9.50 1 course, £13.50 2 courses, £17.50 3 courses. **Set dinner** £25 3 courses. **Credit** AmEx, MC, V.

Top-end dining is often characterised by linen as crisp as the waiter's manner and a table so cluttered with crystal that you're scared to look sideways. Not here. When Andrew Radford opened the Atrium back in 1993, he set a new benchmark for fine dining in the Scottish capital. The enduring modern design still looks good after more than a decade; combined with low lighting, a skilled kitchen and professional but approachable staff, it adds up to Edinburgh's most relaxed destination restaurant. A typical lunch might start with duck breast, beetroot and celeriac purée, followed by fillet of halibut with glazed vegetables and vanilla sauce, topped off with custard tart with blueberries soaked in Grand Marnier for dessert. Dinner is in a similar modern European vein, and there's an award winning wine list.

Centotre

103 George Street, EH2 3ES (0131 225 1550/ www.centotre.com). **Meals served** noon-10pm Mon-Thur; noon-10.30pm Fri, Sat; 11am-5pm Sun. **Main courses** £7.95-£24.95. **Credit** AmEx, MC, V.

Victor and Carina Contini are part of the Valvona and Crolla dynasty (see p334), but after years with the family business, they wanted to try something different – hence Centotre's arrival in spring 2004. It's an all-day Italian eaterie in a former bank, bringing modern energy and enthusiasm to a grand space with pillars and stately cornicing. The ethos is to serve simple food based on good-quality ingredients, from breakfast through to dinner. Typical pasta dishes include rigatoni with a rich tomato meatball sugo, or spaghettini with cherry tomatoes, garlic, extra virgin olive oil and basil. There are also dishes involving veal, free-range chicken, and even a char-grilled steak with chilli, rocket and chips. Pizza is a real forte, however, and truly excellent (mozzarella di bufala, tomato, prosciutto di Parma, basil and parmigiano reggiano, perhaps). The dessert choice may include classics like crema cotta, ice-creams that actually taste Italian, and a couple of very good cheeses. The wine list is compact but exceptional, the grappa list truly educational.

David Bann

56-58 St Mary's Street, EH1 1SX (0131 556 5888/www.davidbann.com). **Meals served** 11am-10pm Mon-Thur; 11am-10.30pm Fri, Sat. **Main courses** £6.90-£10.90. **Credit** AmEx, DC, MC, V.

Simply put, David Bann's eponymous eaterie is the best vegetarian option in Edinburgh. He set up shop here towards the end of 2002 after building his reputation at the now-defunct Bann UK in

Edinburgh

Edinburgh Castle

Castlehill, (0131 225 9846/www.historic-scotland.gov.uk). **Open** Winter 9.30am-5pm daily. Summer 9.30am-6pm daily. **Admission** £9.80; £7.50 concessions; £3.50 5-15s; free under-5s.**Credit** AmEx, MC, V.

Everyone goes to Edinburgh Castle and you should too. It has incomparable views from its battlements, it houses the oldest surviving structure in the city (St Margaret's Chapel, early 12th-century), it's home to the Scottish crown jewels, and generally has more history in its stones than you could shake a sceptre at. Some of the most interesting buildings date from the 15th century (the great hall and a particularly sturdy palace), but one of the most affecting is the Scottish National War Memorial (www.snwm.org). Once a simple barracks, it was completely refurbished in the 1920s as a shrine and hall of honour for the many service personnel who died in World War I. (Now it also commemorates those from conflicts since 1918.) If you only associate castle tours with the draughty boredom of school trips, you could be pleasantly surprised.

Museum of Scotland

Chambers Street, EH1 1JF (0131 247 4422/www.nms.ac.uk). **Open** 10am-5pm Mon, Wed-Sat; 10am-8pm Tue; noon-5pm Sun. **Admission** free. **Credit** (shop) MC, V.

Everything you ever wanted to know about Scotland is here, from its geological origins and early inhabitants, through the start of recorded history and all the way to the impact of the Industrial Revolution, the British Empire and beyond. Many of the artefacts are first class, the narrative flow as you work through the various galleries is considered and coherent, and it's all housed in an award-winning building that opened at the end of 1998. Whether you're looking at a 4,000-year-old torc from Dumfriesshire, Roman silver dating from AD 400 found in East Lothian, or Jacobite bits and bobs from the 18th century, this museum confers a real sense of Scotland through time. The Tower restaurant is on the top floor (see p334). The Museum of Scotland adjoins the Royal Museum, a Victorian establishment originally intended as a showpiece for industry but with space these days for natural history, geology, applied arts, science and technology. Its spectacular atrium houses Café Delos, a cut above usual museum fare in terms of eats and drinks.

The Royal Mile

Not so much a single venue as the street that forms the backbone of the Old Town. It runs downhill from the castle in the west to the late 15th-century Palace of Holyroodhouse in the east (and the adjacent ruins of Holyrood Abbey). En route it takes in attractions like the Camera Obscura; Gladstone's Land (a preserved, 17th-century merchant's house); Lady Stair's House (a museum dedicated to Scottish writers Burns, Scott and Stevenson); St Giles, the High Kirk of Edinburgh (a cathedral in pre-Reformation times with its 15th-century tower intact); the Tron Kirk; John Knox's House; the Museum of Childhood; the People's Story (a social history museum housed in a late 16th-century building called the Canongate

Tollbooth); and more. Before the monied classes moved out to the New Town, the Royal Mile and its surrounds *were* Edinburgh – so it's definitely worth a walk browsing the various distractions as the mood takes you.

Scottish Parliament

Horse Wynd, EH99 1SP (0131 348 5000/ www.scottish.parliament.uk). **Open** daily (visiting times vary, call or check website). **Admission** free. Tours (call or check website for times) £3.50; £1.75 concessions. **Credit** MC, V.

The most important, ambitious and expensive public building in Scotland in living memory. Depending on which person is carping the loudest, it went over budget by a factor of anything up to ten – so everyone you meet will have an opinion. What's more, it was three years late, and the two principal drivers behind the project died during its construction (architect Enric Miralles and Scotland's first minister Donald Dewar). The whole mess finally spawned an official inquiry, but in October 2004 the Queen declared the £431 million edifice officially open. If you're a UK taxpayer, you might want to check it out for value. Visitors from elsewhere could look at the design and wonder: a waste of money or an absolute functional marvel of contemporary architecture? There are daily guided tours when parliament is not in session; Fridays to Mondays only when it is. Take one and make up your own mind.

Scottish National Gallery of Modern Art

75 Belford Road, EH4 3DR (0131 624 6200/ www.nationalgalleries.org). **Open** 10am-5pm Mon-Wed, Fri-Sun; 10am-7pm Thur. **Admission** free. **Credit** (shop) MC, V.

About a mile from the west end of Princes Street, this gallery offers a real contrast to city-centre bustle. It's housed in a classical-style building dating from the 1820s, while the grounds are home to sculptures by the likes of Moore, Hepworth and Whiteread, as well as a major environmental installation by Charles Jencks called *Landform*. *Indoors* on two floors there is space for a permanent collection featuring big names like Magritte and Pollock, but also temporary exhibitions, which in recent years have included Frank Auerbach, local hero John Bellany, Cindy Sherman, Lucien Freud and Andy Warhol. Many Edinburghers treat this as a perfect Sunday afternoon's outing and the basement café isn't bad either. Across the road at No.73, the Dean Gallery acts as an overspill space, but with a particular emphasis on Sir Eduardo Paolozzi.

Edinburgh

Museum of Scotland

The Royal Mile

nearby Hunter Square. It's not solely a restaurant, though, and takes a flexible approach. If you want a quick coffee (from 11am) or a light meal, that's fine, but you could also plump for a pretty good three-course lunch or dinner (nori timbale to start; a rich walnut, mushroom and haggis wellington for main; then apple and Calvados tartlet for dessert). The influences are obviously international, the slick decor is more contemporary bar than rustic wholefood café, the wine list is short and affordable, and there are good beers and a great weekend brunch. An excellent place to have dinner, then linger over wine or cocktails.

Fishers in the City

58 Thistle Street, EH2 1EN (0131 225 5109/ www.fishersbistros.co.uk). **Meals** noon-10.30pm daily. **Main courses** £8.50-£27.95. **Credit** AmEx, MC, V.

The original Fishers down in Leith (*see p329*) opened in 1991 and is well established as one of the city's best seafood bistros. It made absolute sense, therefore, to open this city-centre version in 2001. It's a smart eaterie that blends a seafood theme with a modern touch – the maritime decor steers well clear of kitsch. The menu is ever-changing, apart from a short list of hardy perennials like half-a-dozen Loch Fyne oysters, or the brilliant fish soup. There are specials depending on what's been pulled out of the sea lately, while a more general three courses could involve grilled queenie scallops on the half shell, glazed with dill and gherkin hollandaise to start; Finnan haddie topped with sea bass taramasalata and prawn guacamole as a main; then chocolate truffle cake for pudding. Lively atmosphere, decent wine list.

Haldane's

39A Albany Street, EH1 3QY (0131 556 8407/www.haldanesrestaurant.com). **Lunch served** noon-1.45pm Mon-Fri. **Dinner served** 6-9pm Mon-Thur, Sun; 6-9.30pm Fri, Sat. **Main courses** £16.95-£28. **Set lunch** £17.50 2 courses. **Credit** AmEx, DC, MC, V.

Arguably the best Scottish restaurant in the city, albeit one that doesn't wear its nationality on its (tartan) sleeve. Haldane's has been around since the mid 1990s when George and Michelle Kelso decided to up sticks from the hotel they ran near Glencoe and establish their own country house-flavoured restaurant in the capital. Occupying a basement on the eastern fringes of the New Town, it has a traditional drawing-room feel; some tables overlook a small garden, while others face an open fire. George is the chef and his menu focuses on high-quality Scottish ingredients in a Franco-Caledonian style. So three courses might encompass roasted tomato and butternut squash soup, and a saddle of Highland venison with black pudding, pear compote and port wine sauce, rounded off with white chocolate pudding with black cherries and a lime syrup. The wine list is as serious as the food and diners should dress smart but casual.

Harvey Nichols Forth Floor

Harvey Nichols, 30-34 St Andrew's Square, EH2 2AD (0131 524 8350/www.harvey nichols.com). *Brasserie* **Meals served** 10am-6pm Mon; 10am-10pm Tue-Sat; noon-6pm Sun. **Main courses** £8-£11.50. **Set lunch** £14.50 2 courses. **Set dinner** £10.50 2 courses, £14 3 courses. *Restaurant* **Lunch served** noon-3pm Mon; noon-3pm Tue-Sat; noon-3.30pm Sun. **Dinner served** 6-10pm Tue-Sat. **Main courses** £14.50-£22.50. **Set lunch** £18.50 2 courses, £22.50 3 courses. *Both* **Credit** AmEx, DC, MC, V.

Since the Edinburgh outpost of the department store opened in 2002, even anti-fashion sceptics have admitted that Harvey Nichols' fourth floor restaurant and bar-brasserie are pretty good. The views are tremendous (including the Firth of Forth, hence the punning name) while the decor is funky. During the day, it's a snack stop for shoppers, but at night there's a real buzz under the red, recessed lights. The restaurant has a more elaborate menu than the bar-brasserie, and better sightlines – but it's effectively all one space, discreetly divided by a glass partition. In the restaurant, three courses could involve roast saddle of rabbit with Puy lentils, Toulouse sausage and smoked bacon to start, lamb chump with roast sweet potatoes and confit shallots as a main, coffee and walnut bombe with white chocolate sauce for dessert. Forth Floor offers special events (Valentine's Day dinner, jazz on Sundays, Edinburgh International Festival Fireworks dinner with a great view of the pyrotechnics), so phone for details.

Off the Wall

105 High Street, Royal Mile, EH1 1SG (0131 558 1497/www.off-the-wall.co.uk). **Lunch served** noon-2pm, **dinner served** 7-10pm Mon-Sat. **Main courses** £19.95-£21.95. **Set lunch** £19.95 3 courses. **Credit** AmEx, MC, V.

There's a theory that if you're going to hide, it's best to do it somewhere obvious – and this understated, contemporary restaurant, up a flight of stairs on the main tourist street, is an ideal retreat. In among the tartan shops and backpacker hostels of the Royal Mile, where compact cameras flash and 90% of pedestrians in August are 'doing the Festival', the blessed counterpoint is Off the Wall. It has been here since 2000, and chef David Anderson has built a solid reputation. All meat, game and seafood come from Scottish sources, but the style leans towards France. That means supreme of squab pigeon, braised duck leg, creamed leeks and juniper jus to start; fillet of beef with roasted root vegetables as a main; then mango and almond tart with black cherries and vanilla ice-cream to finish. A great restaurant – and wonderfully discreet despite the location.

Oloroso

33 Castle Street, EH2 3DN (0131 226 7614/ www.oloroso.co.uk). **Lunch served** noon-2.30pm, **dinner served** 7-10.30pm daily.

Main courses £17-£23. **Set lunch** (Sun) £15.95 2 courses, £19.50 3 courses incl glass of wine. **Credit** AmEx, MC, V.

Since its much-lauded opening in 2001, Oloroso – under chef/founder Tony Singh – has consolidated its position as cosmopolitan bar and food hub for the beautiful people. Atop a city-centre office building (lift to the third, then stairs to the fourth-floor restaurant), it has a roof terrace with excellent views. The bar area buzzes with atmosphere and many come just to drink, although there are excellent bar meals and snacks to be had (devilled lambs' kidneys with mash and sauce diablé, for example). In the adjacent dining room, the grill menu is a big feature with all beef steak from Highland cattle – seafood and veal are also available. Meanwhile, the à la carte could bring smoked haddock and chive risotto with poached egg and parmesan oil to start; breast of corn-fed chicken with saffron potatoes, carrot purée, pepper stew and pesto as a main; then champagne and watermelon jelly with marmalade and rosewater ice-cream for dessert. Sharp, contemporary decor and a lengthy international wine list.

Restaurant Martin Wishart

54 The Shore, Leith, EH6 6RA (0131 553 3557/www.martin-wishart.co.uk). **Lunch served** noon-2pm Tue-Fri. **Dinner served** 6.45-9.30pm Tue-Sat. **Main courses** £21.50-£26. **Set lunch** £18.50 3 courses. **Credit** AmEx, MC, V.

You've pondered a wine list with more than 300 bins and start off with a lobster and smoked haddock soufflé; your main is veal fillet with foie gras mousse, sweetbreads, pomme mousseline, and truffle jus; dessert is chocolate fondant with pistachio sauce and vanilla ice-cream. It's all excellent. This is happening in a simple, neat room near Edinburgh's docks, separated from the Water of Leith by the width of a cobbled street. The exemplary front of house service is supervised by Cecile (Mrs Wishart), while Mr Wishart is in the kitchen, drawing on his experience from working with Michel Roux and Marco Pierre White in London, and Albert Roux in Amsterdam. He came back to Edinburgh to set up his eponymous eaterie in 1999 and won a Michelin star within a couple of years (retained). One of the best restaurants in Scotland, and it has a separate vegetarian menu as well.

Tower

Museum of Scotland, Chambers Street, EH1 1JF (0131 225 3003/www.tower-restaurant.com). **Lunch served** noon-4.30pm, **dinner served** 5-11pm daily. **Main courses** £14.50-£27. **Set lunch** £9.95 2 courses. **Pre-theatre** (5-6.30pm) £12.50 2 courses. **Credit** AmEx, DC, MC, V.

It's contemporary, cosmopolitan, sits atop Scotland's premier museum, the Old Town views are incomparable, and the food's not half bad. Since James Thomson opened the Tower in late 1998, it's been on everyone's list of best Edinburgh eateries. Access is via the main museum entrance. Once inside you take a lift to the top floor – security staff are on hand to make sure you don't get lost. There's a light lunch menu and a pre-theatre, but à la carte offers all kind of choices including crustacea (oysters or langoustines perhaps), a char-grill list (Aberdeen Angus rib-eye steak served with a tattie scone, tomato, mushroom and garlic butter) while three courses for dinner could bring cured, air-dried beef with truffle oil and rocket to start; suckling pig, roasted roots and blue cheese dumplings for a main; then chilled raspberry and ginger soup with vanilla custard for dessert. There's a good international wine list and a terrace for Scotland's brief summer.

Valvona and Crolla VinCaffè

Multrees Walk, off St Andrew's Square, EH1 3DQ (0131 557 0088/www.valvonacrolla.com). **Meals served** 8am-11pm Mon-Wed; 8am-midnight Thur-Sat; 11am-6pm Sun. **Main courses** £9-£18. **Credit** AmEx, DC, MC, V.

While one branch of the Contini family opened Centotre, independent of Valvona and Crolla branding earlier in 2004 (*see p329*), in the autumn the full weight of the name was swung behind the VinCaffè, in the posh pedestrian shopping precinct next to Harvey Nichols. This has a ground-floor bar for drinks and snacks and an upstairs restaurant (modern and minimal, dark wood and leather banquettes) serving some highly acclaimed, although far from inexpensive, Italian food. As in the original Valvona and Crolla on Elm Row, and in Centotre, it's about high-quality ingredients put together well. You could have a pasta dish as simple as taglierini with courgette, parmigiano reggiano and cream sauce; a deft pizza with mushrooms, mozzarella di bufala, tomatoes, griddled radicchio, chilli and garlic; or a more full-on stufato di cervo (Italian stew made with venison, potatoes, peppers, tomatoes, red wine and thyme); polish it off with pistachio cake for pudding, perhaps. A palpable hit.

Witchery by the Castle

Castlehill, EH1 2NF (0131 225 5613/ www.thewitchery.com). **Lunch served** noon-4pm, **dinner served** 5.30-11.30pm daily. **Main courses** £15-£50. **Set meal** (noon-4pm, 5.30-6.30pm, 10.30-11.30pm) £11.95 2 courses. **Credit** AmEx, DC, MC, V.

So it's just turned 10.30pm, the cobbles on the Royal Mile are glistening, you turn to your other half, look deep into his/her eyes and say, 'Fancy a late supper in a 16th-century building up by the castle then?' Works every time. The Witchery is a well-established operation and over the years has developed a reputation as a destination restaurant in world terms, let alone Scottish ones. The original Witchery dining room is rich and atmospheric (wood panelling, red leather, tapestries, candlelight), while a second called the Secret Garden is even more so. The menu is the same in both, and a typical three courses at dinner could

Edinburgh

Harvey Nichols Forth Floor

start with salad of salted duck with oven-dried figs, progressing to spiced rib of Aberdeen Angus beef with roast roots and polenta fries as a main, finishing with the highly recommended dessert selection (chocolate torte, rum panna cotta, blueberry brûlée or mango parfait, to name a few). The wine list is huge and distinguished.

NIGHTLIFE

The local licensing laws mean Edinburgh has a range of venues that stay open late. Café-bars like Assembly (41 Lothian Street, 0131 220 4288), the Basement (10A-12A Broughton Street, 0131 557 0097) or Beluga (30A Chambers Street, 0131 624 4545) all keep going until 1am. Others like Favorit (19-20 Teviot Place, 0131 220 6880) and Negociants (45 Lothian Street, 0131 225 6313) stay open until 3am, as does the legendary live music pub Whistle Binkies (7 Niddry Street, 0131 557 5114).

Nightclubs also generally keep going until 3am. Politely put, the general areas of Lothian Road and the Cowgate attract the younger, up-for-it element. Listed here are some of the more interesting places.

Bongo Club

37 Holyrood Road, EH8 8BA (0131 558 7604/ www.thebongoclub.co.uk). **Open** 11am-3am daily. **Admission** free-£7. **No credit cards.**
A venue that forms the clubbing arm of arts organisation Out of the Blue, the Bongo hosts various nights including live theatre, music, film and dance classes as well as DJs. The club nights embrace everything from roots reggae to more eclectic mixes of hip hop, house and funk. Rough round the edges but a blessed escape from teenies and handbag house.

Medina

45-47 Lothian Street, EH1 1HB (0131 225 6313/www.medinaedinburgh.co.uk). **Open** 10am-3am daily. **Admission** £3 after 10pm Wed-Sun. **Credit** MC, V.
Underneath Negociants café-bar, this is a North African-themed bar-cum-club with a fairly relaxed ambience. Some people dance, some people just slump on the cushions and listen, others come for salsa classes on Mondays. It's near the university, so it attracts students, but can be fairly chilled if you catch it on the right night.

Vegas

Various venues throughout Scotland (booking line 0131 220 3234/0131 558 3824/ www.vegasscotland.co.uk). **Open** 10pm-3am Sat. **Credit** (advance booking only) AmEx, MC, V.
This is a classic Edinburgh club night that invites people to dress up Rat Pack style and take part in an orgy of general fabulousness. The dress code is interpreted quite loosely, and the club features showgirls, jazz funk and swing bands, Sinatra-style crooners, the occasional burlesque act and plenty more. You can catch it at Ego (14 Picardy Place, EH1 3JT, 0131 478 7434), or even occasionally at Ocean Terminal shopping mall in Leith, as well as at various other venues in Scotland. Check the website for details.

Glasgow

A city made for fun.

It's the biggest city in Scotland, it has easily the best nightlife, grand Victorian architecture, more than enough culture to keep art and museum junkies happy, some swish hotels, some good restaurants and it's such a shopping destination that visitors have been known to fly in from Reykjavik – or even get the train from Edinburgh – for a spot of retail therapy. It was all quite different 1,500 years ago though.

The city's origin myth features St Ninian dedicating a burial ground on or near the site of what is now Glasgow Cathedral some time in the early sixth century, then St Mungo founding a monastic community there in the early seventh century – these are very rough dates of course. With a raised position, but quite near to a fordable stretch of the Clyde, the cathedral site makes geographic sense, although some modern scholarship suggests that Govan (three miles west and on the south bank) was a more likely starting point for today's city. However, there's harder evidence of Glasgow's growing status as a trading town from the 12th century onwards and it really started to hit the mercantilism big time in the 18th century, particularly with tobacco. This laid a commercial substructure for the city's massive expansion in the 19th century. The industrial revolution saw Glasgow and its satellites along the Clyde become a world centre for heavy industry and shipbuilding. The population exploded and in its Victorian heyday Glasgow was known as 'the second city of the Empire', but this status didn't last.

THE WORLD'S YOUR OYSTER

Accommodation	★★★★
Food & drink	★★★★
Nightlife	★★★★★
Shopping	★★★★★
Culture	★★★★
Sights	★★★★
Scenery	★★

Street and Sauchiehall Street themselves are stuffed with retail outlets, and the Argyle Arcade is the city's specialist jewellery mall, while Ingram Street has the likes of Ralph Lauren, Versace and Emporio Armani, the latter in the Italian Centre mini-mall. So there are more than enough places to pick up some cool togs in anticipation of dinner followed by clubbing.

After World War II, the inexorable closures of engineering works and shipyards took their toll and by the 1970s the city's reputation was based more around urban dereliction, endemic poverty and a tough street culture than commercial prowess. So a reinvention process began.

In the last couple of decades Glasgow has picked itself up by the bootstraps. It was European City of Culture in 1990, then UK City of Architecture and Design in 1999. A wave of new hotels and restaurants has opened, as have important facilities such as the Burrell Collection (1983), the Scottish Exhibition and Conference Centre (1985), the Royal Concert Hall (1990), the Gallery of Modern Art (1996), the Clyde Auditorium (1997).

The city has also made more of a fuss of famous son Charles Rennie Mackintosh: architect, designer, and artist. In 1996, the beautiful House for an Art Lover opened in Bellahouston Park, inspired by a set of his drawings from 1901 (www.housefor anartlover.co.uk). Fans can also see a reconstruction of interiors from where he lived from 1906 to 1914 at the Mackintosh House in the Hunterian Art Gallery at Hillhead Street (www.hunterian.gla.ac.uk) as well as displays of his drawings, designs and watercolours. His biggest architectural work meanwhile, Glasgow School of Art in Renfrew Street (www.gsa.ac.uk), does guided tours. The website of the Charles Rennie Mackintosh Society (www.crm society.com) is useful for finding out what there is and when you can go to see it.

Despite all this effort, poverty and its associated problems have not been eradicated, particularly in peripheral housing estates, but there is prosperity. In fact, the city centre has been transformed into a real hotspot for general good times whether you want to eat, drink, go to a concert or nightclub, or simply shop. Glasgow truly is a shopping mecca. Buchanan Galleries, at the north end of Buchanan Street (www.buchanan galleries.co.uk), has all the household names from Austin Reed to the Warner Bros Studios Store and is the biggest mall in Scotland. Princes Square, also on Buchanan Street, is smaller but more self-consciously upmarket with names such as Reiss and Calvin Klein (www.princes square.co.uk). Argyle Street, Buchanan

WHERE TO STAY

ArtHouse

129 Bath Street, G2 2SY (0141 221 6789/ www.arthousehotel.com). **Rates** £115 double; £155 suite. **Credit** AmEx, DC, MC, V.
In Glasgow's city centre grid, it takes a little effort to disentangle yourself from the bustle, stand back and look at the architecture – much of which is actually handsome and elaborate. This certainly goes for the ArtHouse. It's a listed building dating to 1911 but was completely refurbished for the hotel's opening in 1999. The establishment bills itself with some justification as a centre of 'urban glamour'. All the rooms are individually designed in a modern style with rich colours and artworks throughout, while original fixtures and fittings around the public areas underpin a carefully nurtured image of classiness. There are lots of great restaurants literally on its doorstep, although the hotel's main dining room (the ArtHouse Grill) is a decent option.

City Inn

Finnieston Quay, G3 8HN (0141 240 1002/ www.cityinn.com). **Rates** £59-£119 double. **Credit** AmEx, DC, MC, V.
City Inns is a small chain of modern hotels with a clean, contemporary look. There are five across the UK, one of which stands happily on the banks of the Clyde just west of Glasgow city centre. In the same stretch of river you'll find the landmark Finnieston Crane, and the Scottish Exhibition (SECC) and Conference Centre and Clyde Auditorium – all within a few yards of each other. The facilities are decent (CD players in the rooms, a small gym, a restaurant with riverside terrace) and what it might lack in soul it makes up for in location. Get a south-facing room with floor-to-ceiling window, order up something from 24-hour room service, and watch the river flow.

Langs

2 Port Dundas Place, G2 3LD (0141 333 1500/www.langshotels.co.uk). **Rates** £110-£140 double; £110-£148 family; £140-£173 suite. **Credit** AmEx, DC, MC, V.

TOURIST INFORMATION
11 George Square, G2 1DY (0141 204 4480/www.seeglasgow.com).

Glasgow

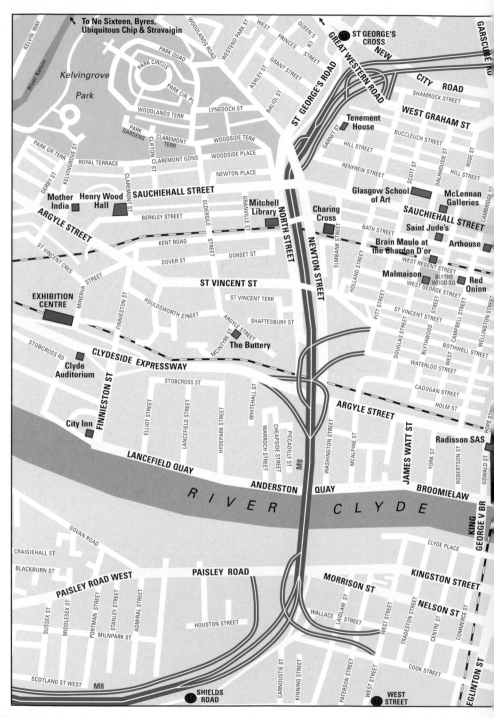

To No Sixteen, Byres,
Ubiquitous Chip & Stravaigin

Kelvingrove
Park

River Kelvin

KELVIN WAY

WOODLANDS ROAD

WESTEND PARK ST
WEST PRINCES STREET
QUEEN'S CR
GREAT WESTERN ROAD
NEW
ST GEORGE'S CROSS
GARSCUBE RD

PARK QUAD
PARK CIRCUS
PARK CIR. PL
ASHLEY ST
GRANT STREET
BALIOL ST
ST GEORGE'S ROAD
CITY ROAD
SHAMROCK STREET
WEST GRAHAM ST

WOODLANDS TERR
LYNEDOCH ST
Tenement House
GARNET ST
BUCCLEUCH STREET
SCOTT ST
DALHOUSIE ST
HILL STREET
ROSE ST

PARK GARDENS
CLAREMONT TERR
WOODSIDE TERR
HILL STREET
RENFREW STREET

PARK GR TERR
ROYAL TERRACE
CLIFTON ST
CLAREMONT GDNS
WOODSIDE PLACE
NEWTON PLACE
CLAREMONT ST

DERBY ST
KELVINGROVE ST
Mother India
Henry Wood Hall
SAUCHIEHALL STREET
Glasgow School of Art
McLennan Galleries
SAUCHIEHALL STREET

ARGYLE STREET
BERKLEY STREET
Mitchell Library
GRANVILLE ST
Charing Cross
BATH STREET
Saint Jude's
CAMBRIDGE ST

ST VINCENT CRES
KENT ROAD
ELDERSLIE STREET
NORTH STREET
NEWTON STREET
Brain Maule at the Chardon D'or
Arthouse
ELMBANK STREET

DOVER ST
DORSET ST
WEST REGENT STREET
Malmaison
BLYTHS WOOD SQ.
Red Onion

ST VINCENT ST
ST VINCENT TERR
HOLLAND STREET
WEST GEORGE STREET

EXHIBITION CENTRE
MINERVA STREET
HOULDSWORTH STREET
SHAFTESBURY ST
PITT STREET
ST VINCENT STREET
DOUGLAS STREET
BLYTHWOOD
WEST CAMPBELL STREET
WELLINGTON STREET

FINNIESTON ST
ARGYLE STREET
McINTYRE ST
The Buttery
BOTHWELL STREET
WATERLOO STREET

Clyde Auditorium
CLYDESIDE EXPRESSWAY
STOBCROSS ST
WHITEHALL ST
CADOGAN STREET
HOLM ST

STOBCROSS RD
ELLIOT STREET
LANCEFIELD STREET
HYDEPARK STREET
WARROCH STREET
CHEAPSIDE STREET
PICCADILLY ST
ARGYLE STREET
JAMES WATT ST
HOPE STREET

City Inn
FINNIESTON STREET
M8
WASHINGTON STREET
McALPINE ST
Radisson SAS
YORK ST
ROBERTSON ST
OSWALD ST

LANCEFIELD QUAY
ANDERSTON QUAY
BROOMIELAW

R I V E R   C L Y D E

KING GEORGE V BR

GOVAN ROAD
CLYDE PLACE

CRAIGIEHALL ST
BLACKBURN ST
PAISLEY ROAD WEST
PAISLEY ROAD
MORRISON ST
KINGSTON STREET

SUSSEX ST
MIDDLESEX ST
PORTMAN STREET
STANLEY STREET
ADMIRAL STREET
HOUSTON STREET
MILNPARK ST
WALLACE ST
LAIDLAW ST
WEST STREET
NELSON ST
TRADESTON STREET
CENTRE ST
COMMERCE ST
EGLINTON ST

SCOTLAND ST WEST
M8
SHIELDS ROAD
CARNOUSTIE ST
KINNING STREET
PATERSON STREET
WEST STREET
WEST STREET
COOK STREET

Glasgow

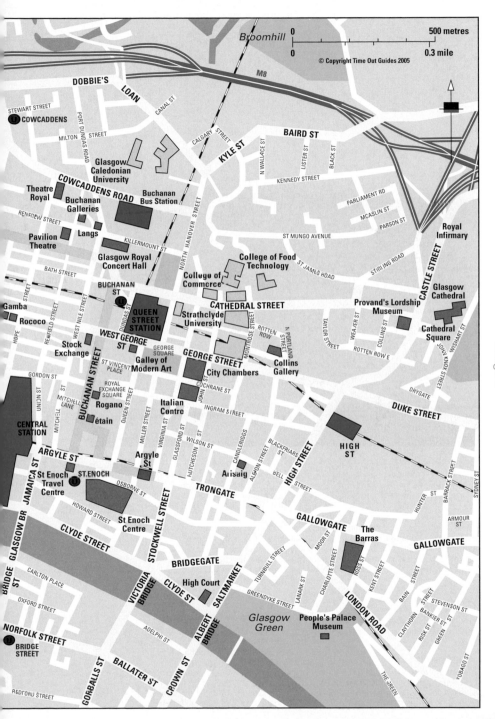

Broomhill

0   500 metres

0   0.3 mile

© Copyright Time Out Guides 2005

M8

DOBBIE'S LOAN

STEWART STREET
COWCADDENS

MILTON STREET

PORT DUNDAS ROAD

CANAL ST

CALGARY STREET

KYLE ST

BAIRD ST

N WALLACE ST

LISTER ST

BLACK ST

KENNEDY STREET

Glasgow
Caledonian
University

Buchanan
Bus Station

Theatre
Royal

COWCADDENS ROAD

Buchanan
Galleries

RENFREW STREET

NORTH HANOVER STREET

PARLIAMENT RD

MCASLIN ST

PARSON ST

Royal
Infirmary

Pavilion
Theatre

Langs

KILLERMOUNT ST

ST MUNGO AVENUE

Glasgow Royal
Concert Hall

BATH STREET

BUCHANAN
ST

College of Food
Technology

ST JAMES ROAD

STIRLING ROAD

CASTLE STREET

Glasgow
Cathedral

Gamba

Rococo

HOPE STREET

RENFIELD STREET

WEST NILE STREET

DUNDAS ST

QUEEN
STREET
STATION

College of
Commerce

Strathclyde
University

CATHEDRAL STREET

ROTTEN STREET

MONTROSE STREET

N PORTLAND STREET

TAYLOR STREET

WEAVER ST

COLLINS ST

Provand's Lordship
Museum

Cathedral
Square

JOHN KNOX STREET

WISHART ST

Stock
Exchange

WEST GEORGE
ST

BUCHANAN STREET

ST VINCENT
PLACE

GEORGE
SQUARE

GEORGE STREET

ROTTEN ROW

ROTTEN ROW E

Collins
Gallery

DRYGATE

Galley of
Modern Art

ROYAL
EXCHANGE
SQUARE

City Chambers

COCHRANE ST

JOHN ST

INGRAM STREET

DUKE STREET

GORDON ST

UNION ST

MITCHELL ST

MITCHELL
LANE

Rogano

étain

QUEEN STREET

MILLER STREET

Italian
Centre

VIRGINIA ST

GLASSFORD ST

WILSON ST

HUTCHESON ST

CANDLERIGGS

ALBION STREET

BLACKFRIARS
ST

HIGH STREET

HIGH
ST

HUNTER ST

BARRACK STREET

SYDNEY ST

CENTRAL
STATION

ARGYLE ST

JAMAICA ST

St Enoch
Travel
Centre

ST.ENOCH

Argyle
St

OSBORNE ST

Arisaig

BELL STREET

TRONGATE

GALLOWGATE

MOOR ST

ARMOUR
ST

GALLOWGATE

GLASGOW BR

BRIDGE
ST

CLYDE STREET

HOWARD STREET

St Enoch
Centre

STOCKWELL STREET

BRIDGEGATE

The
Barras

ROSS ST

KENT STREET

BAIN STREET

CLAYTHORN STREET

STEVENSON ST

BANKIER ST

RISK ST

GREEN ST

NORFOLK STREET

BRIDGE
STREET

CARLTON PLACE

OXFORD STREET

VICTORIA
BRIDGE

CLYDE ST

High Court

SALTMARKET

ALBERT
BRIDGE

ADELPHI ST

Glasgow
Green

People's Palace
Museum

GREENDYKE STREET

TURNBULL STREET

LANARK ST

CHARLOTTE STREET

LONDON ROAD

THE GREEN

TOBAGO ST

GORBALLS ST

BALLATER ST

CROWN ST

REDFORD STREET

Glasgow

Necropolis

Next to the Royal Concert Hall and no distance at all from the celebrated Theatre Royal, the populist Pavilion Theatre and a frighteningly large UGC cinema complex, Langs appeared on the scene in late 2000. It gained few plaudits for the modern, boxy exterior but the inside was something else entirely, aiming at international traveller grooviness. Even a standard room will have a Playstation, CD player and contemporary design flourishes, while there are also duplexes, themed suites and more. There are two restaurants (the Asian-fusion Oshi and the modern European Las Brisas), a sociable bar and a spa with a good range of treatments (also called Oshi). The hotel offers various special packages including 'glamour sensual', 'pyjama party' or more predictably, given the location, 'theatre'.

Malmaison

278 West George Street, G2 4LL (0141 572 1000/www.malmaison.com). **Rates** £135 double; £165-£195 suite. **Credit** AmEx, DC, MC, V.

Another city, another Malmaison, but this time in a converted 19th-century Greek Orthodox church to the west of Glasgow central. The beds are all a decent size, the design and colour schemes are confident in that classic contemporary manner – as you would expect of the chain – and if your budget can run to a suite, then a few are attractively split-level. Some rooms are on the small side (as is the gym) but the CD players in each room, CD libraries, decent toiletries and all the rest compensate. If you want to eat or drink in, the basement has a smart French-flavoured brasserie as well as a champagne bar with a soupçon of atmosphere.

One Devonshire Gardens

1 Devonshire Gardens, G12 0UX (0141 339 2001/www.onedevonshiregardens.com). **Rates** £150-£235 double; £295-£495 suite; £365-£495 family. **Credit** AmEx, DC, MC, V.
Very simply the best hotel in Glasgow and according to some the best city hotel in the entire UK. It's around two miles north-west of the centre, along the Great Western Road, in polite, terraced

surroundings. Service is unobtrusive and first-class, the decor looks modern but with a deep-seated classical loveliness, all the rooms have their own style, there's a small gym and a garden that is ideal for those rare Glaswegian occasions when alfresco drinks are a good idea. Gordon Ramsay once ran the prestigious dining room here, and the hotel still has a posh restaurant called No.5 (foie gras parfait, then seared fillets of John Dory for dinner perhaps) but from autumn 2004 a concept diner replaced the former Ramsay effort. This is Room, sister venture to the establishment in Leeds and also run by John Pallagi and Simon Wright. The idea of a modern take on Scotch eggs followed by lamb goulash raised a few eyebrows at first, but now the locals love it.

Radisson SAS

301 Argyle Street, G2 8DL (0141 204 3333/ www.radisson.com). **Rates** £129-£190 double; £220-£260 suite. **Credit** AmEx, DC, MC, V.
This hefty, international chain hotel landed on Argyle Street at the end of 2002, near Glasgow Central railway station. Nonetheless, it's not bad – big, bold and audacious. The colourful, exterior design gives you the impression it would be more at home in the Low Countries for some reason, while there are an assortment of rooms and suites, all fairly swish if a tad corporate-contemporary. Facilities include a reasonable gym, a pool, sauna, a couple of bars and two restaurants (one is Spanish themed; the other modern Mediterranean and more formal). The Radisson SAS is hardly low-key, but great for anyone who wants to be in the heart of the city.

Saint Jude's

190 Bath Street, G2 4HG (0141 352 8800). **Rates** £95 double; £150 suite. **Credit** AmEx, DC, MC, V.
In a nutshell, this is Glasgow's original boutique hotel (since 1999). The building is an early Victorian townhouse and while there may not be many rooms (five plus one suite), they are all done out rather splendidly, in modern style, with DVD and CD players, internet access and comfortable, big beds. The basement bar is pretty good at cocktails, does reasonable food and has weekend DJs. Meanwhile, the ground-floor restaurant, with its minimalist decor, is worth patronising whether you're staying here or not. Saint Jude's isn't a place for in-house swimming pools or obscure body wraps, but it is a very grown-up place to crash.

WHERE TO EAT & DRINK

Glaswegians love their modern café-bars, old-school boozers, designer restaurants, and curry houses. But what they don't love is a surplus of mannered formality – what they'd consider an excess bullshit in other words. So an affable, big bloke from Pakistan bringing a steaming dish of lamb bhuna to the table is fine; a delicate young woman from Thailand politely offering a prawn wrapped in almost translucent pastry is less popular (Glasgow has few Thai restaurants but loads of Indian-style ones). This also means that the city currently has no fine-dining restaurants considered chi-chi enough for Michelin stars, probably because the locals can't be bothered with the sheer fuss that surrounds eating in them. This certainly doesn't mean that it lacks fine restaurants, but even the very best tend to have an accessibility that their equivalents elsewhere might not.

Aside from the selection reviewed below, there are quite a few worth a trip: the modern European Saint Jude's (*see p343*) is the main dining room of the eponymous boutique hotel, and has its fans. So does Room (1 Devonshire Gardens, 0141 341 0000), a new venture in Glasgow's top hotel from the creators of the original Room in Leeds. It's modern, minimalist and classy, and its menu leans heavily towards retro irony (prawn cocktail to start, mixed grill as a main, all poshed up). It has been a big hit since its autumn 2004 opening, so seems to be working in a space where Gordon Ramsay famously failed.

Fish lovers will want to try Two Fat Ladies (88 Dumbarton Road, 0141 339 1944, www.twofatladies.5pm.co.uk) or Gamba (*see p346*). The people behind Gamba also have another couple of places: Café Ostra (The Italian Centre, 15 John Street, 0141 552 4433, www.cafeostra.com), a more informal seafood café; also Papingo (104 Bath Street, 0141 332 6678), a well-established, modern French venue. The pick of the Italians would be the upmarket La Parmigiana (447 Great Western Road, 0141 334 0686) and Fratelli Sarti (133 Wellington Street, 0141 204 0440, www.fratellisarti.com). This is appealing, little, traditional and trattoria-style but only one part of the burgeoning Fratelli Sarti empire (there's another restaurant round the corner at 121 Bath Street, and several more in the city centre). Glasgow's designer-ish Chinese restaurant is Dragon-i (311-313 Hope Street, 0141 332 7728), handy for the Theatre Royal, while for an enormous and genuine Cantonese menu you should head for Chinatown (42 New City Road, 0141 353 0037).

And so to curry. The Wee Curry Shops provide a very informal and down-home experience (7 Buccleuch Street, 0141 353 0777; 25 Ashton Lane, 0141 357 5280), while the Ashoka (108 Elderslie Street, 0141 221 1761) heads the other direction in decor terms, its basement space a deep, rich red. This restaurant is not to be confused with the unrelated chain of Ashokas in Glasgow owned by the Harlequin Group (the very decent original is at 1284 Argyle Street, 0141 339 3371).

Finally, the Shish Mahal has been a comfort to locals for decades (66-68 Park Road, 0141 334 7899).

The best gastropubs include Stravaigin Café Bar (*see p351*), Bar Gandolfi (64 Albion Street, 0141 552 4462) with the more restaurant-like Café Gandolfi downstairs, and the Liquid Ship (171 Great Western Road, 0141 331 1901). Honourable mentions also to the Babbity Bowster (16-18 Blackfriars Street, 0141 552 5055) and the roomy, laid-back Firebird (1321 Argyle Street, 0141 334 0594), which has arguably the best pizzas in the city.

For more of that eats-drinks crossover, Glasgow has a vast number of modern café-bars that transform into pre-club haunts and drinking dens as the evening progresses. There is a fair turnover among these venues as proprietors aim for 'the next big trend', but some of the more interesting and durable include Bar 10 (10 Mitchell Lane, 0141 572 1448), a relaxed, central venue that seems to have been around forever; the Lite Bar at the Corinthian (191 Ingram Street, 0141 552 1101) where the decor vaults exuberantly over the top; and the cavernous Bargo (80 Albion Street, 0141 553 4771) where you can people-watch from the balcony.

Traditional pubs include the Horseshoe (17 Drury Street, 0141 229 5711), the Clutha Vaults (167-169 Stockwell Street, 0141 552 7520), the Scotia (112 Stockwell Street, 0141 552 8681), or the Griffin (266 Bath Street, 0141 331 5171). The Bon Accord (153 North Street, 0141 248 4427, www.thebonaccord.freeserve. co.uk) is acclaimed for the quality of its real ales (good selection of whiskies too).

Finally, the scrumptiously decorated Polo Lounge is the pick of the gay bars (84 Wilson Street, 0141 553 1221, www.pololounge.co.uk).

Arisaig

24 Candleriggs, G1 1LD (0141 552 4251/ www.arisaig.com). **Dinner served** 5-10pm Mon-Thur, Sun. **Meals served** noon-10pm Fri, Sat. **Main courses** £9.95-£17.95. **Set meal** (Mon-Thur, Sun 5-7pm) £12.95 2 courses. **Credit** AmEx, MC, V.
Named after that little coastal chunk of the country south of Mallaig, this fine restaurant has a woody-bistro look and comes with an interesting Scottish menu and very good service. The excellent house fish cakes are not the potato-heavy nightmares you get elsewhere. What's more, care is taken with the sourcing of raw materials (Aultbea smoked salmon, Orkney mussels) and it has even picked up an award from the

Vegetarian Society for the quality of its veggie menu choices. Good whiskies feature in some of the sauces (Cragganmore with venison sausages; Lagavulin alongside the fillet of Scotch beef), and the fruit dumpling dessert is nearly as good as Gran used to make. Due to the numbers coming through the door, the proprietors have opened a larger branch at 140 St Vincent Street, G2 5TF (0141 204 5399).

Brian Maule at the Chardon d'Or

176 West Regent Street, G2 4RL (0141 248 3801/www.brianmaule.com). **Lunch served** noon-2pm Mon-Fri. **Dinner served** 6-9.30pm Mon-Sat. **Main courses** £12-£17.50. **Credit** AmEx, MC, V.

The life of Brian: Ayrshire lad trains in France, then becomes head chef at Le Gavroche in London. Returns to Scotland to open this place (in translation, the Golden Thistle) in 2002 where his name features to such an extent on the signage that you're never in doubt who's in charge. But given the standards, Glaswegians (and the wider Scottish foodie public) can forgive the branding. The interior is quietly tasteful and modern, if not a cutting-edge design statement, while the French-style cooking is confident enough not to over-elaborate. Three courses could start with something as simple as a ragoût of scallops with pasta and fennel in a light cream sauce; then pork medallions with ceps, flavoured with parsley, shallots and garlic as a main; vanilla crème brûlée for dessert. Affordable lunch and pre-theatre menus are a good alternative to a full-blown dinner.

The Buttery

652 Argyle Street, G3 8UF (0141 221 8188). **Lunch served** noon-2pm Tue-Fri. **Dinner served** 6.30-9.30pm Tue-Sat. **Main courses** (lunch only) £13-£15. **Set lunch** £16 2 courses. **Set dinner** £34 2 courses, £38 3 courses. **Credit** AmEx, MC, V.

The Buttery has been trading in one form or another on the ground floor of this traditional tenement since 1869 (save for a short hiatus in 2002). It was such a haunt for the city's great and good, goes the story, that when Glasgow was redeveloped in the 1960s and 1970s, the tenement was left alone while the surrounding area was devastated. Now its neighbours include grotesque blocks of flats and a motorway flyover; even the tenement looks anomalous in situ, let alone an award-winning restaurant. But once inside there's a classy, old-school feel – with dark wood panelling – and an elaborate three courses could involve risotto of artichokes to start; a cassoulet of west coast fish and shellfish with tomato and lemongrass, and saffron and coriander couscous as a main; cherry-centred chocolate pudding with kumquat confit and Kirsch ice to finish. Excellent cooking, lots of Scottish ingredients, and a great attention to detail in an unlikely urban setting.

Glasgow

House for an Art Lover

étain

*Princes Square, Buchanan Street, G1 3JX
(0141 225 5630/www.conran.com).* **Lunch
served** noon-2.30pm Mon-Fri; noon-3pm Sun.
Dinner served 7-10pm Mon-Thur; 6.30-10pm
Fri, Sat. **Set meal** £32 3 courses. **Credit**
AmEx, DC, MC, V.

This is one of Sir Terence Conran's most prestigious restaurants outside London, but it's not the easiest to locate. Go the top floor of Princes Square shopping mall and you'll find another Conran creation: Zinc Bar & Grill (same address and phone number). Ask staff and they'll lead you through the back saying something about 'Glasgow's best kept secret'. So étain does actually exist; it even has a separate, if obscure, entrance at the rear of the mall (between Buchanan and Queen streets) where a glass lift will whisk you straight up to the dining room. While Zinc has warm wooden fittings, colours and furnishings, étain looks light, minimal, even stark. Both restaurants operate from a single kitchen, but at the much more formal étain three courses could bring warm dunsyre blue cheese tart with pear and walnut salad to start; roast Scottish partridge with potato purée, stuffed cabbage and bacon as a main; then iced prune and Armagnac parfait with hazelnut mousse for dessert. An impressive, discreet space – but beware the 12.5% 'discretionary' service charge that will be added to your bill; this practice is not common in Scotland.

Gamba

*225A West George Street, G2 2ND (0141 572
0899/www.gamba.co.uk).* **Lunch served** noon-2.30pm, **dinner served** 5-10.30pm Mon-Sat.
Main courses £11.50-£21.95. **Set lunch**
£15.95 2 courses, £18.95 3 courses. **Pre-theatre**
(5-6.15pm) £15 2 courses, £18 3 courses incl
glass of wine. **Credit** AmEx, MC, V.

This is an upmarket seafood restaurant – perhaps the very best in Glasgow – co-owned by Alan Tomkins and head chef Derek Marshall. Since they also run Café Ostra, and Tomkins has Papingo, there's a lot of experience of the local scene at work here, particularly at the quality end. Established in 1998, Gamba itself is a basement affair with an ornamental fountain by the door, and an understated, modern interior. Three courses at dinner might feature a nice and simple half-dozen oysters to start; roast fillet of cod on shiitake mushroom fish cream, with peas and crayfish tails as a main; then valrhona chocolate tart with maple syrup and sesame ice-cream for dessert. There are good choices here: you can eat unadorned dishes or others that give more than a passing nod to modern European and Asian mores.

Mother India

*28 Westminster Terrace, G3 7RU (0141 221
1663).* **Lunch served** noon-2pm Wed-Fri.
Dinner served 5.30-10.30pm Mon-Thur; 4.30-10pm Sun. **Meals served** 1-11pm Sat. **Main
courses** £6.50-£12.95. **Credit** AmEx, MC, V.

It's not unusual for people to eat here then declare it's the best Indian meal they've ever had. From the outset you know you're not dealing with sub-continental cliché, as the downstairs dining space looks more like an upmarket Scottish bistro than a typical curry house: stone walls in places, fleur-de-lys wallpaper in others, photographs of old Glasgow and a chequered, stone-tiled floor. Upstairs is a little more opulent – the premises once housed a very polite tearoom. The menu isn't huge, everything is made to order, and generic sauces are not just thrown on top of separately cooked meats, so even the most familiar dish (patina gosht say) has the opportunity to shine. There are good house specials and vegetarian options, and the spiced haddock starter works well. In 2004, after a decade of success, the owners opened a sister venue nearby: same standards but with a small-dish tapas approach: Mother India Café, 1355 Argyle Street G3 (0141 339 9145).

No. Sixteen

16 Byres Road, G11 5JY (0141 339 2544).
Lunch served noon-2.30pm Mon-Sat; 12.30-3pm Sun. **Dinner served** 5.30pm-last orders 9.30pm daily. **Main courses** £10.90-£15.80.
Credit MC, V.

With its vaguely distressed, light grey frontage and driftwood-style installation in the window, No. Sixteen could almost pass for a relaxed little seaside bistro. Given that there are very few tables on its two floors, relaxation is not always guaranteed; fortunately, good cooking comes as standard. The reputation of this place has been growing steadily for years. It keeps edging up that fantasy list of 'best eats in Glasgow', gathering accolades on the way for its creative approach – even the most demanding critics have been fairly generous with their praise. Three typical courses could bring pan-fried calf's liver on a flatbread croûton with red onion marmalade to start; herb-crusted rib-eye steak on cauliflower purée with haricots verts and confit tomatoes as a main; deconstructed lemon and white chocolate cheesecake for dessert. And they're pretty good with their wines too.

Red Onion

*257 West Campbell Street G2 4TT (0141 221
6000/www.red-onion.co.uk).* **Meals served**
noon-11pm daily. **Main courses** £6-£15.
Credit AmEx, MC, V.

In these parts, John Quigley has a reputation as a celebrity chef. Once upon a time he was an actual world-travelling, rock 'n' roll cook for the likes of Bryan Adams and Tina Turner, but then he came home to Glasgow in 1996. He had an eponymous restaurant on Bath Street for several years, then set up Red Onion in autumn 2004, which he runs with his wife Gillian. This gives full vent to a 'contemporary casual dining' approach including sandwiches, salads and a children's menu. A typical dinner in its modern surroundings could entail grilled asparagus with hollandaise; coq au vin or

shepherd's pie as a main; then lemon cheesecake with strawberries. But it's not all retro – if you want sea bass fillet with hot and sour vegetable noodles, or five-spiced duck, you can get those too.

Rococo

202 West George Street, G2 2NR (0141 221 5004/www.rococoglasgow.com). **Lunch served** noon-2.30pm Mon-Sat. **Dinner served** 5-9pm Mon-Thur; 5-9.30pm Fri, Sat. **Set meals** £29 2 courses, £36.50 3 courses. **Credit** AmEx, MC, V.

This is one of Glasgow's more self-consciously chic restaurants; head chef Mark Tamburrini runs a classy operation. Its basement premises are plush, modern, restrained and even the fairy lights on the ceiling manage to appear low-key. The wine list runs to around 400 choices (these include some top-end examples from Bordeaux, Burgundy and Champagne), while a three-course dinner could bring black pudding from the Isle of Lewis with poached egg, confit potatoes and sauce soubise; pot-roasted supreme of corn-fed chicken with creamed Brussels sprouts, rosemary fondant, air-dried bacon and pea velouté; then pear and almond tart with praline anglaise. When on its game, Rococo is among Glasgow's very best.

ArtHouse

Glasgow

Most visits to the city would include the splendid Kelvingrove Art Gallery and Museum (Argyle Street, G3 8AG, 0141 287 2699, www.glasgowmuseums.com) but this has been closed since summer 2003 for a major refurbishment. The scheduled date for reopening is spring 2006. Meanwhile, here are some alternatives.

THE CATHEDRAL PRECINCT

The prosperous merchants of 18th-century Glasgow and the industrialists of the 19th century preserved virtually nothing of the medieval town – almost the entire city is Victorian or later. Fortunately there is one corner that gives some sense of a deeper history. Glasgow Cathedral (Cathedral Square, www.glasgowcathedral.org.uk) is largely a 13th-century structure, allegedly on a site that has featured a religious building of some kind for more than 1,400 years. The adjacent cemetery (the Necropolis) is Victorian-Gothic but weathered enough to add to the sense of timelessness. Nearby is St Mungo's Museum of Religious Life and Art (2 Castle Street, G4 0RH, 0141 553 2557, www.glasgow museums.com), a faux-medieval building but with some interesting artefacts and displays (including Dali's *Christ of St John on the Cross*), while the Provand's Lordship next door (3 Castle Street, G4 0RB, 0141 552 8819, www.glasgowmuseums.com) is the city's oldest house (1471), now serving as a museum of 15th-century life.

THE BURRELL COLLECTION

Pollok Country Park, 2060 Pollokshaws Road, G43 1AT (0141 287 2550/www.glasgow museums.com). **Open** 10am-5pm Mon-Thur, Sat; 11am-5pm Fri, Sun. **Admission** free. **Credit** *Shop* AmEx, MC, V.

This was regarded as the jewel in the crown of local attractions when it opened in 1983, and it's still going strong. Sir William Burrell was a rich shipping owner with a penchant for collecting art from all over the world. He gifted his rather tremendous collection to the City of Glasgow in 1944 but for years no decent home could be found for it (Sir William died in 1958). The grounds of Pollok Country Park

became available in 1967, but it still took another 16 years to get the purpose-built gallery up and running. It now houses over 8,000 works ranging from medieval tapestries to paintings by Rembrandt, oriental ceramics to Rodin sculptures. You could easily spend an entire day exploring.

GLASGOW CITY CHAMBERS

George Square, G2 1DU (0141 287 4018/ www.glasgow.gov.uk). **Open** 9am-5pm Mon-Fri. **Admission** free.

This is the home of local government and testament to Glasgow's 'second city of the Empire' status when Britain had an empire – the sheer Italianate cockiness of the City Chambers is quite something to behold. Queen Victoria opened the building in 1888. Architect William Young based the entrance on the Arch of Constantine in Rome, there's an amazing marble staircase and you really feel you should be bumping into Lucretia Borgia here rather than the convener of the policy and resources committee. Council business permitting, there are free guided tours twice a day, Monday to Friday (10.30am and 2.30pm), except on weekends or public holidays.

GALLERY OF MODERN ART

Royal Exchange Square, G1 3AH (0141 229 1996/www.glasgowmuseums.com). **Open** *Gallery* 10am-8pm Mon, Tue, Thur; 10am-5pm Wed, Sat; 11am-5pm Fri, Sun. *Library* 5-8pm Mon, Tue; 10am-5pm Wed, Sat; 10am-8pm Thur; 11am-5pm Fri, Sun. **Admission** free. **Credit** *Shop* MC, V.

This has a very handy central location for one of the most popular modern art galleries in the UK. It's housed in a building, parts of which date to 1778 (a merchant's mansion), others to 1827 (the former Royal Exchange), although it didn't actually open as a gallery until 1996. The surrounding square is full of shops and cafés, many with outside tables, and on sunny summer weekends the whole area buzzes with people doing coffee, wine or lunch. As for the art, it has a definite local slant from established Scottish names like Peter Howson or Stephen Campbell to recent acquisitions from the likes of Turner nominee

Christine Borland. It's far from parochial though, with a changing programme of exhibitions and other examples of artworks from across the globe.

SHARMANKA KINETIC GALLERY & THEATRE

14 King Street (second floor), G1 5HD (0141 552 7080/www.sharmanka.com). **Performances** 7pm Thur; 3pm, 7pm Sun. **Admission** £4; £3 concessions; free under 16s. **No credit cards**.
Glasgow's best-kept secret? Quite possibly. This is an absolute gem of a place that puts on a fabulously Slavic interpretation of life,

the universe and everything in a kinetic art show using carved wooden puppets, bits of scrap, lighting and music. It was orginally founded in St Petersburg in 1989 by the sculptor Eduard Bersudsky and theatre director Tatyana Jakovskaya, and it then moved to Glasgow with its creators in the mid 1990s. (Bersudsky is also known for his collaborative work on the Millennium Clock that now stands in Edinburgh's Royal Museum.) There are usually three full performances of the show each week (Thursdays and Sundays at 7pm and a Sunday matinee at 3pm) but Sharmanka are happy to do an attenuated version by appointment.

Glasgow Cathedral.

Housed in a former Sheriff's Court, the Corinthian restaurant's Lite Bar is a criminally flash place.

Rogano

*11 Exchange Place, off Buchanan Street,
G1 3AN (0141 248 4055/www.rogano.com).*
Lunch served noon-2.30pm, **dinner served**
6.30-10.30pm daily. **Main courses** £18.50-
£35. **Credit** AmEx, DC, MC, V.
In the summertime, Rogano has a terrace on the
pedestrianised thoroughfare outside. Despite the
fact this is subject to the visual intrusion of
teenie-goths as they pass to congregate in nearby
Royal Exchange Square, the establishment still
exudes old-style class. Even an espresso on that
terrace will bring a couple of petits fours on the
side for example. Indoors, there's that famous 1935
art deco interior and a bar, seafood restaurant and
downstairs café. You get snacks at the bar (including oysters) and good meals in the café space,
which has a late menu for the post-theatre crowd
(daily except Saturday). The restaurant is beautiful and more formal: a classic moules marinière to
start, followed by grilled sea bass with squid ink
linguini and pimento coulis and lime and coconut
tart with mascarpone ice-cream. There are alternatives to seafood, though also vegetarian options);
the wine list leans to French whites.

Stravaigin/Stravaigin Café-Bar

*28 Gibson Street, G12 8NX (0141 334 2665/
www.stravaigin.com). Café* **Meals served**
11am-10.30pm daily. **Main courses** £7.95-
£16.95. *Restaurant* **Lunch served** noon-
2.30pm Fri Sun. **Dinner served** 5-11pm
Tue-Sun. **Main courses** £15.45-£22.50.
Both **Credit** AmEx, DC, MC, V.
Stravaigin opened in Gibson Street in the mid
1990s and fast became a Glasgow favourite. It's a
basement with simple modern decor, red brick
walls and a food philosophy of 'think global, eat
local'. Rated by many among the city's top five
restaurants, a Sunday lunch might offer asparagus and rosemary egg tartlets on orange-dressed
herb salad, drizzled with gremolata, to kick off;
roast loin of Knoydart venison on pancetta and
syboe mash with shallot and rich thyme gravy as
a main; rhubarb and ginger soup with sour cream
and black pepper ice-cream for dessert. Gibson
Street also has the ground-floor Stravaigin Café-
Bar, a more informal space featuring home-grown
items (steak, fish and chips, haggis) but also dishes
with an international influence. The millennium
addition to the empire was Stravaigin 2 (8
Ruthven Lane, off Byres Road, G12 9BG, 0141 334
7165), a converted townhouse with decorative
greenery outside and a contemporary bistro interior. The global approach takes full effect here
with extravagant flavour combinations – it's also
famed for its burgers: chicken, beef or ostrich.

The Ubiquitous Chip

*12 Ashton Lane G12 8SJ (0141 334 5007/
www.ubiquitouschip.co.uk). Brasserie* **Meals
served** noon-11pm Mon-Sat; 12.30-11pm Sun.
Main courses £6.15-£15.45. *Restaurant*
Lunch served noon-2.30pm; 12.30-3pm Sun.
Dinner served 5.30-11pm Mon-Sat; 6.30-
11pm Sun. **Set lunch** £22.80 2 courses, £28.65
3 courses incl coffee, (Sun) £17.95 3 courses incl
appetiser and glass of sparkling wine. **Set
dinner** £33.80 2 courses, £38.95 3 courses incl
coffee. *Both* **Credit** AmEx, DC, MC, V.
This is a complex of adjoining venues including
an upstairs bistro, bars, a formal ground-floor dining room and – perhaps the most celebrated – a
cobbled courtyard with tables. The courtyard is
covered and has a water feature, and what the decorative plantlife lacks in youth it makes up for in
biomass. The Chip has been around since 1971;
Alasdair Gray murals aid the sense of something
special. The cooking is ambitious and lunch can
involve west coast scallops with crispy squid,
sautéed duck livers, french toast and Madeira
sauce, then roast quail stuffed with beef and ham
sausage, roast crushed paprika potatoes, wilted
spinach and wine sauce. Raw materials are high-
standard but can run out on busy nights; impro-
vised alternative dishes may occasionally
disappoint – but you are eating in an institution.

NIGHTLIFE

If you're looking for things to do at night,
you've come to the right city. There are
more gig venues, pre-club bars and clubs
than anywhere else in Scotland. In fact,
Glasgow definitely rates as a European-
class destination for clubbing and music,
let alone a UK one.

If you want to see a band, then
Barrowlands is the classic choice (242
Gallowgate, 0141 552 4601, www.glasgow-
barrowland.com). It's a former dancehall
and everyone from Alien Ant Farm to the
Yeah Yeah Yeahs have graced the stage.
The Carling Academy (121 Eglinton
Street, 0905 020 3999, www.glasgow-
academy.co.uk) is a former cinema that
fulfils a similar role. Meanwhile the
Scottish Exhibition and Conference
Centre at Finnieston (www.secc.co.uk)
is a cavernous, riverside venue with a hall
that can hold thousands, and also has the
armadillo-like Clyde Auditorium adjacent
for more polite, sit-down moments. Another
celebrated venue is King Tut's Wah Wah
Hut (272a St Vincent Street, 0141 221
5279, www.kingtuts.co.uk).

As for clubs themselves, the most
popular include the Arches (253 Argyle
Street, 0870 240 7528, www.the
arches.co.uk), which does theatre and
live music as well as regular big-name
DJs; also Archaos (25-37 Queen Street,
0141 204 3189, www.archaosnightclub.
co.uk), the city's largest with a fairly
mainstream crowd; the Tunnel (84 Mitchell
Street, 0141 204 1000, www.tunnel
glasgow.co.uk), another attraction for
big-name DJs; and the Sub Club (22
Jamaica Street, 0141 248 4600), a
basement with history and attitude.

Mid Argyll & Bute

Go west, life is peaceful there.

A big part of the reason for visiting Mid Argyll and Bute is the sense of getting away from it all, a feeling of space and detachment in hills and sea lochs that seem wonderfully wild and remote – even though much of the area is within 50 miles of Glasgow as the crow flies (the distance between London and Brighton). Of course, this does mean investing a little time getting there, but the roadside scenery and short ferry crossings add to the experience rather than detract from it.

Most visitors will approach Mid Argyll via Glasgow and there are two main routes. The north-west option out of the city, the A82, is fairly urban for the first nine miles but then views of the Clyde open up and it doesn't take long to reach Loch Lomond, such a popular tourist area that it's almost a Scottish national icon. The road hugs the west bank of the loch as far as Tarbet (not to be confused with Tarbert) then the A83 goes around the head of Loch Long before climbing steeply up Glen Croe to the wonderfully named viewpoint, Rest and Be Thankful. It also skirts an area of mountains known as the Arrochar Alps – these are particularly craggy on top (Gandalf country), and the biggest, Beinn Ime, rises to 3,317 feet. From the Rest and Be Thankful it's all downhill through Glen Kinglas to the head of Loch Fyne – a fun drive.

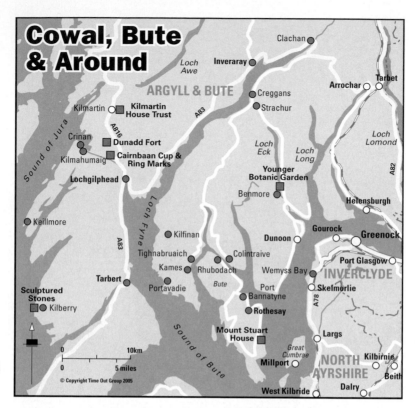

Cowal, Bute & Around

Clachan

Loch Awe

Inveraray

ARGYLL & BUTE

Creggans

Strachur

Arrochar

Tarbet

Kilmartin

Kilmartin House Trust

A83

Crinan

A816

Dunadd Fort

Kilmahumaig

Cairnbaan Cup & Ring Marks

Lochgilphead

Loch Eck

Loch Long

Younger Botanic Garden

Benmore

Loch Lomond

A82

Helensburgh

Keillmore

Loch Fyne

Kilfinan

A83

Tighnabruaich

Kames

Rhubodach

Tarbert

Portavadie

Bute

Colintraive

Dunoon

Wemyss Bay

Port Bannatyne

Gourock

Greenock

Port Glasgow

INVERCLYDE

Skelmorlie

A78

Rothesay

Sculptured Stones

Kilberry

Mount Stuart House

Sound of Bute

Largs

Great Cumbrae

Millport

NORTH AYRSHIRE

Kilbirnie

Beith

West Kilbride

Dalry

Sound of Jura

0   10km

0   5 miles

© Copyright Time Out Group 2005

Sound of Bute

Alternatively, if you leave Glasgow on the M8 westbound and follow the signs, you'll reach Gourock (26 miles, via the A8 and A770). Once you're properly out of the clutches of the city, the views along the south bank of the Clyde are expansive; going through Port Glasgow and Greenock you also get a glimpse of the area's industrial past.

The peninsulas and islands of Argyll have profound historical significance for modern Scotland. Looking at the sea as a conduit rather than a barrier, it dawns that the people from these parts and those of the north-east of Ireland have had connections for millennia. Kilmartin Valley in particular (*see p360* **Rocks of ages**) is littered with prehistoric monuments and is also home to the hill fort of Dunadd, where the Dark Ages Irish settlers, the Scotti, anchored their kingdom. At Kilmartin's southern end is evidence of a more recent history, however: the Crinan Canal, still carrying vessels from Loch Fyne to the western seaways after more than 200 years.

Further south is Knapdale, the hinterland off the main road down to Campbeltown. Either side of the remote Loch Sween on

its west coast are reminders that this wasn't always such a backwater. The ruins of Castle Sween date from the 12th century, while the early 13th-century Keills Chapel, almost at the very end of nowhere on a small spit of land at the far side of the loch, has an incredible collection of Celtic cross slabs as well as the seventh-century cross that once stood outside.

North-west of Knapdale, via the small town of Lochgilphead, are the upper reaches of Loch Fyne. This loch has scenic qualities of its own, but around 25 miles from Lochgilphead on the western shore, you'll find the area's traditional tourist destination: Inveraray. This is a 'planned town', commissioned by the third Duke of Argyll in the mid 18th century and completed in the 1770s. The architectural style and whitewashed buildings give it a definite atmosphere, while it's also home to attractions like Inveraray Jail, a 19th-century courthouse and prison, now an interactive museum (01499 302381, www.inverarayjail.co.uk). Then there's the 18th-century Inveraray Castle (01499 302203, www.inveraray-castle.com), also initiated by the third Duke, which took over

Accommodation	★★★
Food & drink	★★★
Nightlife	
Shopping	
Culture	★★
Sights	★
Scenery	★★★★★

40 years to complete. The Tapestry and Armoury rooms are particularly impressive, but there is a sense of unease about the castle – perhaps because it was constructed in the years immediately after Culloden and speaks of the hubris of pro-Hanoverian aristocrats at a time when life for Highland Jacobite sympathisers was brutal.

Round the head of Loch Fyne from Inveraray is the Cowal peninsula. It's divided from the rest of the mainland by the loch on one side, the Firth of Clyde and Loch Long on the other, so it's almost an island itself. Caledonian MacBrayne operates the 25-minute ferry service between Gourock and Cowal's main town, Dunoon (08705 650000, www.calmac.co.uk). This runs virtually every hour, with around a dozen sailings a day even in winter, but check the website for precise times and ticket details. Western Ferries operates a similar service from McInroy's Point around two miles west of Gourock on the A770 (www.western-ferries.co.uk), also to Dunoon. On the other side of Cowal, if you don't want to do the drive around Loch Fyne to get to Knapdale or up to Kilmartin, Caledonian MacBrayne also runs a 25-minute ferry service from Portavadie on the south-west tip of the peninsula over to Tarbert. This village, at the junction of Knapdale and the Mull of Kintyre, is in a truly beautiful setting and approaching it from seaward is a rare experience.

Cowal has a reputation for peace and quiet, although that reputation takes a buffeting once a year when the Cowal Highland Gathering (01369 703206, www.cowalgathering.com) hits Dunoon towards the end of August. This is the world's biggest Highland games, dating from 1893. It lasts for three days and includes all the shinty, athletics, bagpiping, and Highland dancing you would expect, but in addition takes on the atmosphere of an enormous village fête with events and stalls. Cowal is also home to the Botanic Garden at Benmore (0131 552 7171, www.rbge.org.uk), 11 kilometres north of Dunoon. This is an outpost of the Royal Botanic Garden in Edinburgh and was gifted to the nation in 1925 by HG Younger of the old Edinburgh brewing family. Its avenue of giant redwoods, planted in 1863,

is simply awesome and you could easily spend a day just wandering. It's typical Cowal, in fact: placid countryside and the smell of the outdoors. Unless you take up the activities offered via some local hotels (fishing, sailing, shooting) there isn't really much to do around here – and that's just how people like it.

South of Cowal, across two strips of water known as the Kyles of Bute, lies the Isle of Bute itself. It was once a prime holiday destination for the Glaswegian working classes, and the main town of Rothesay (population 5,000) still has that atmosphere of walks on the esplanade and candy floss. From the 1970s, of course, holiday habits changed, Glaswegians headed for the Spanish costas, and in recent decades the island has been searching for a new identity. All the same, Bute is home to one of the most amazing stately homes anywhere in the UK – the Victorian Gothic fantasy of Mount Stuart (*see p.358* **Gothica**), which makes a visit more than worthwhile. Caledonian MacBrayne (*see above*) operates the 35-minute service from Wemyss Bay (west via the M8, A8 and A78) to Rothesay, as well as the regular, five-minute crossing from Colintraive on Cowal to Rhubodach on the north of Bute.

A weekend here is the exact opposite of a shopping, clubbing, designer café-bar break. The area is scenic and contemplative, and there are some very good restaurants serving seafood straight from the water. Also, if you know where to look, you can find historical sites that trace human settlement in these parts from prehistory through to the British dynastic spats of the 18th century and infrastructural developments of the 19th. It's quite a mix.

(*see p.358* **Gothica**)

TOURIST INFORMATION

Dunoon
7 Alexandra Parade, Dunoon, Argyll PA23 8AB (0870 720 0629).
Inveraray
Front Street, Inveraray, Argyll PA32 8UY (0870 720 0616).
Lochgilphead
Lochnell Street, Lochgilphead, Argyll PA31 8JL (0870 720 0618)
Isle of Bute
Victoria Street, Rothesay, Isle of Bute PA20 0AH (0870 720 0619/ www.isle-of-bute.com).
Tarbert
Harbour Street, Tarbert, Argyll PA29 6UD (0870 720 0624).
www.visitscotland.com
www.visitscottishheartlands.com

Mid Argyll & Bute

Royal Hotel

WHERE TO STAY

This area isn't populous or teeming with Travelodges – and that's precisely why people visit. All the things that make for dependable if predictable travelling in other parts of the UK simply ain't here. (Look at a map of Knapdale, for example, and you'll only find three roads worth mentioning; two of those are single-track.) Because there is a limited number of decent places to stay, it's essential to book ahead, especially at the height of the summer season.

Columba Hotel

East Pier Road, Tarbert, Loch Fyne, Argyll PA29 6UF (01880 820808/www.columbahotel.com). **Rates** £76-£92 double. **Credit** MC, V.
It's been a long drive, albeit a beautiful one, and you've probably come across the south end of Loch Fyne on the ferry from Portavadie as a finale. Now all you really want to do is get into a hotel room, have a shower, then collect yourself for some serious eating later. Thankfully you can get from the ferry off-ramp at Tarbert to the Columba in all of two minutes. This Victorian establishment, right on the waterfront, is ably run by the Butler family and provides comfortable rooms that manage to be homely rather than ostentatious, and marvellous breakfasts. Its restaurant also does an ambitious dinner menu, and there's superior bar food too. Like many other establishments on the Argyll coast, the seafood is particularly fresh.

Creggans Inn

Strachur, Argyll PA27 8BX (01369 860279/ www.creggans-inn.co.uk). **Rates** £100-£120 double; £140-£190 suite. **Credit** AmEx, MC, V.

This is a lochside establishment with a little bit of history. Not only has there been an inn on the site for around 400 years, but in 1957 these very premises were bought by Sir Fitzroy MacLean. This remarkable man was a diplomat, soldier, traveller and writer. One of his best-loved books is *Eastern Approaches*, an account of his career from 1937 to 1945, spanning travels in the USSR, service with the SAS in North Africa, and his role as Churchill's military representative to Tito in Yugoslavia. Sir Fitzroy died in 1996 and the Creggans first passed to his son Sir Charles, then in 2000 to Alex Robertson, who runs it today. The rooms are well maintained and serviceable, some with great views of Loch Fyne, but, above all, this is just the place to sit in the bar, order up some good, simple bar food (fish and chips perhaps), sip your pint, and read something by the man himself. Bedrooms are no-smoking.

George Hotel

Main Street East, Inveraray, Argyll PA32 8TT (01499 302111/www.thegeorgehotel.co.uk). **Rates** £60-£120 double. **Credit** MC, V.
The last battle on British soil was at Culloden, near Inverness, in 1746. This was not a Scotland versus England thing. It was about the right of succession to the British throne: the Catholic Charles Edward Stuart on the one hand, the Protestant House of Hanover on the other in the shape of King George II. The Dukes of Argyll were pro-Hanover and Inveraray is their turf. No surprise then that this hotel, which has been going since 1777, is called the George (it was hardly going to be called the Bonnie Prince Charlie). The bedrooms have all been refurbished in recent years, in sympathy with the building's history. The very traditional-style bar has an open fire, good atmosphere, a great

CRINAN HOTEL

If you're looking for the clean lines and modern design flourishes of a cosmopolitan boutique hotel, you won't find them here. The decor, in rooms and public spaces at Crinan, is better described as post-1970s polite. However, in no way be deterred. Let us consider the setting: the very west end of the Crinan Canal in a tiny hamlet of barely 60 souls, looking north across the pocket-sized Loch Crinan to Duntrune Castle, and north-west over the Sound of Jura. The hotel itself is a white, four-storey edifice that looks slightly out of place on the far-flung coast of Argyll (more 'English Riviera' perhaps?), while the voluble hosts are Nick Ryan and his wife Frances Macdonald. Nick is a former *Caterer & Hotelkeeper* hotelier of the year; Frances is a working artist whose paintings can be seen around the premises. They've run the place for over 30 years, and in 2004 even opened a health and beauty room. And the food? So fresh it's still moving. Chef Ben Tish has access to raw materials landed on the doorstep and can turn his hand to simple dishes or more elaborate Franco-Caledonian productions in the Westward dining room (*see p359*). The hotel bar also does a very good menu, and that's where you can rub shoulders with passing pleasure-boat people and local fishermen. Utterly fabulous setting, experienced proprietors, wonderful seafood, interesting wines – who needs a PlayStation or a funny-shaped headboard?
Crinan by Lochgilphead, Argyll PA31 8SR (01546 830261/www.crinanhotel.com). **Lunch served** noon-3pm, **dinner served** 7-8.30pm daily. **Main courses** (lunch) £9.95-£16.95. **Set dinner** £42.50 4 courses incl coffee & chocolates. **Rates** £170-£310 double (incl dinner). **Credit** MC, V.

choice of whiskies and decent food. A commendable venue for sinking into the mindset of 18th-century Scotland, dram in hand.

Kilberry Inn
Kilberry, nr Tarbert, Argyll PA29 6YD (01880 770223/www.kilberryinn.com). **Rates** £79-£85 double. **Credit** MC, V.
This inn sits on the far side of Knapdale, on the single-track coast road (B8024) that looks across to Islay and Jura. To call it 'out of the way' would be quite an understatement. It's also a very small and homely establishment (three simple bedrooms) and only opens from April to October – so booking ahead is obviously vital. Despite these caveats, it is fantastic. The owners, the Primroses, are nice people, they seem to have won more pub food awards than they've sold hot dinners, and if you've spent a long day touring and want nothing more than to kick back in an unfussy, friendly environment, be very well fed (*see p360*), have a decent beer, then toddle off to bed, this is the place. No smoking throughout.

Kilfinan Hotel
Kilfinan, nr Tighnabruaich, Argyll PA21 2EP (01700 821201/www.kilfinan.com). **Rates** £74-£104 double. **Credit** MC, V.
Sitting on the road that runs up the south-west side of the Cowal peninsula, a little way inland from Loch Fyne (B8000), the Kilfinan Hotel is an 18th-century coaching inn that grew into something a little more extensive over the years. The hotel's proprietors, the Cressdees, are hard-working folk and during the summer season the venue can host the odd music festival, ceilidh or even clan gathering (far from every night, though). They also have a special machine in the garden to deal with the dreaded Scottish midge. The bedrooms have that classic look that is pleasing to the mum of a metropolitan design git rather than the git himself, but they're comfortable and well looked after. The hotel is next to Kilfinan Parish Church; the church burial vault houses ninth-century grave slabs and cross slabs. Worth a look after breakfast.

Port Royal Hotel
37 Marine Road, Port Bannatyne, Isle of Bute PA20 0LW (01700 505073/www.butehotel.com). **Rates** £44-£52 double. **Credit** MC, V.
Bute is celebrated for various things, including Mount Stuart (*see p358*), the island's history as a holiday spot for working-class Glaswegians, even for the quite astounding Victorian toilets on the pier in Rothesay. But interesting places to stay weren't among its notable features – until Dag and Olga Crawford took over the Port Royal in 2001. He's Norwegian and once worked for the BBC presenting *Farming Today*; she's a Russian palaeobiologist; Port Bannatyne, meanwhile, is a sleepy little village with a small harbour, around two miles north of Rothesay. The result is a

GOTHICA

Mid Argyll & Bute

The Stuarts are an old, aristocratic family who can not only date their heritage to 11th-century Anglo-Normans, but have held the Lordship of Bute since around 1200. Although they had grand houses on the island before, it wasn't until an early 18th-century pile burned down in 1877 that John Crichton-Stuart, the third Marquess, in collaboration with celebrated architect Robert Rowand Anderson, went for broke to construct what would become today's Mount Stuart – set in extensive grounds five miles south of Rothesay. The third Marquess and Rowand Anderson never actually completed their very ambitious project, but fortunately the sixth Marquess started an ongoing programme of restoration in the 1980s, which has made a huge difference to what visitors can see today: an absolutely thrilling paradigm of Victorian Gothic. It opened to the public in 1995, and an award-winning visitor centre, straight from the pages of a Scandinavian design magazine, was added nearby in 2001. This houses a restaurant, shop and small art gallery.

In Mount Stuart itself, the Italian-marble Grand Hall is reminiscent of the atrium at Edinburgh's Scottish National Portrait Gallery (also by Rowand Anderson) but much more opulent, with astrological and astronomical design themes. The Dining Room houses paintings by Reynolds and Gainsborough,

among others, while the ceiling of the Horoscope Room is decorated with the positions of the stars and planets when the third Marquess was born. As if that wasn't enough, the Henry VIII Room has a four-poster bed bought by the fourth Marquess from Citizen Kane himself, William Randolph Hearst. The celebrity associations keep coming: Mount Stuart was the venue for Stella McCartney's wedding in 2003.

Outside, 300 acres of gardens were first laid out in 1717 by James Stuart, the second Earl of Bute, but developed and extended by the third Earl and others. They include a homage to the Via Dolorosa, Christ's route to crucifixion.

Mount Stuart
Isle of Bute, PA20 9LR (01700 503877/ www.mountstuart.com). **Open** (Easter weekend, May-Sept) *House* 11am-5pm Mon-Fri, Sun; 10am-6pm Sat. *Gardens* 10am-6pm daily. **Admission** £7; £5.50 OAP; £3 5-16s; free under-5s. **Credit** MC, V.

fascinating collision of cultures. Over the last few years, the Crawfords have refurbished the old harbour-side inn (it dates from the early 19th century), and the five bedrooms were completed in winter 2003/04. It's relaxed, informal, and has a growing reputation for real ales and Russian food (*see p361*). No smoking throughout.

Royal Hotel
Tighnabruaich, Argyll PA21 2BE (01700 811239, www.royalhotel.org.uk). **Rates** £110-£160 double. **Credit** MC, V.
Once upon a time, the Royal looked like any other fading Argyll hotel, bypassed by modern holiday habits and apparently doomed to run down into coach-party decrepitude. Thankfully the McKie family had other ideas. They took over the show in 1997, completely transformed the place, and now preside over a very well-established haven of good taste (and cuisine). Fishing village Tighnabruaich and its neighbouring hamlet of Kames are strung out along the coast overlooking the Kyles of Bute, and the hotel commands expansive views. There are two dining options on the ground floor, the bistro-like Deck and the more formal Crustacean, while the McKies retained the attached public bar round the back of the hotel, still patronised by locals. The rooms are all very neatly and quite simply done with attractive colour schemes; they don't all face over the water though, so ask for a sea-view room when booking. Splendid fact: all the fresh game on the hotel menu comes from a man called Winston Churchill. For more about the food, *see p361*.

Stonefield Castle
Tarbert, Loch Fyne, Argyll PA29 6YJ (01880 820836/www.stonefieldcastle.co.uk). **Rates** £100-£250 double (incl dinner). **Credit** MC, V.
Since you're in Scotland, it might cross your mind to stay in a castle, and Stonefield is a castle in the true sense of dear old Caledonia's constructed national identity: it's a baronial-style mansion that was completed in the year Victoria came to the throne, rather than a medieval fortress. That said, it has a grandeur to it and the setting is splendid: around two miles north of Tarbert in gardens to please a botanist (astounding rhododendrons) and with views of Loch Fyne that would please anyone. The decor may be far from award-winning, but this establishment is all about the exterior (views, gardens, location) rather than the interior. There is a good choice of single malt whiskies in the bar, though.

WHERE TO EAT
Although the dining options in Mid Argyll and Bute are limited, visitors can eat very well indeed. The availability of fresh seafood (jumbo prawns or scallops, for example) is high, and it's no accident that the original Loch Fyne Oyster Bar, progenitor of a chain of restaurants in England, still sits happily on the shore of its namesake in the heart of Mid Argyll. Some of the best restaurants come with rooms attached, which is testament to the difficulty of earning a living from a stand-alone eatery in these parts.

Anchorage Seafood Restaurant
Harbour Street, Tarbert, Loch Fyne, Argyll PA29 6UD (01880 820881). **Lunch served** *May-Sept* 12.30-2.30pm daily. **Dinner served** *Feb-Oct* 6-9.30pm daily. **Main courses** £13.50-£17.95. **Credit** MC, V.
It's not often that you find actual restaurants (as opposed to pubs, inns and hotel dining rooms) around here, but the Anchorage is one of the few. Mind you, Tarbert is a teeming metropolis of 1,000 people. The kitchen is ably run by Clare Johnson while David Wilson deals with front of house. In the small, neat dining room, the blackboard menu changes from day to day, but a typical three courses could see queenie scallops toasted with ginger and lemongrass as a starter; cod roasted with white bean and parsley purée as a main; then molten chocolate babycake and vanilla ice-cream for dessert. There's Scotch beef, lamb and venison on the menu too, and don't miss the mermaid in the Gents. No smoking throughout.

Crinan Hotel
Crinan by Lochgilphead, Argyll PA31 8SR (01546 830261/www.crinanhotel.com). **Lunch served** noon-3pm, **dinner served** 7-8.30pm daily. **Main courses** (lunch) £9.95-£16.95. **Set dinner** £42.50 4 courses incl coffee & handmade chocolates. **Credit** MC, V.
This upmarket hotel offers a choice of good bar food or excellent fine dining. A typical Crinan pub-grub main course is grilled fillet of mackerel with parsley mash. Meanwhile, in the Westward restaurant, the polite decor is in tune with the rest of the hotel and chef Ben Tish certainly has great judgement. He's been in charge for several years now and the critics still rave. Three courses at dinner could entail a complex terrine of Argyll rabbit and foie gras, gewürztraminer jelly and toasted brioche to start; but then a simple plate of Loch Crinan jumbo prawns landed in the afternoon as a main; vanilla parfait with slow-roasted figs and plums, and raspberry ice-cream for dessert. Highly accomplished cooking.

Inver Cottage
Strathlachlan, Strachur, Argyll PA27 8BU (01369 860537/www.invercottage.co.uk). **Lunch served** *Apr-June, Sept* noon-2pm Tue-Sun. *July, Aug* noon-2pm daily. *Oct* noon-2pm Thur-Sun. **Dinner served** *Apr-June, Sept, Oct* 6-9pm Thur-Sat. *July, Aug* 6-9pm daily. **Main courses** £7-£16. **Credit** MC, V.
A very smart coffee house and restaurant with craft shop. Once a croft, it overlooks the ruins of the medieval Castle Lachlan on the east side of

Mid Argyll & Bute

Loch Fyne around six miles south of Strachur. ('New' Castle Lachlan, dating from the 18th century, is about half a mile back up the strath.) Inver Cottage does snacks and light meals during the day, more elaborate cooking in the evening. Local ingredients include Loch Fyne scallops or venison; a comfort food option might be steak and Guinness pie. Then there are some deft desserts (good sticky toffee pud, for example). It's the kind of place you stumble across by accident, then rave about to your friends afterwards for the unexpected quality of the cooking out in the wilds.

Kilberry Inn

Kilberry, nr Tarbert, Argyll PA29 6YD (01880 770223/www.kilberryinn.com). **Open** 11am-3pm, 6.30-10.30pm Tue-Sat; noon-3pm Sun. **Lunch served** 12.30-2pm Tue-Sun. **Dinner served** 7-8.30pm Tue-Sat. **Main courses** £11-£16. **Credit** MC, V.
In these times of diet faddism and endemic eating disorders, it might seem unfashionable to mention an inn where guests who stay for more than a day or two gain a few pounds. The food here exists in a state of nostalgic grace – this is what you wish your mother used to make. At lunch, it could mean salmon mousse and oatcakes to start; sausage pie as a main; then own-made Bakewell tart. In the evenings it can get a little more elaborate (pork medallions in prune and Armagnac sauce, for example). Comfort food with class. No smoking.

Loch Fyne Oyster Bar

Clachan, Cairndow, Argyll PA26 8BL (01499 600264/www.lochfyne.com). **Meals served** *Winter* 9am-6.30pm daily (times vary; booking advisable). *Summer* 9am-8.30pm daily. **Main courses** £4.95-£25. **Credit** AmEx, MC, V.
Described as a 'sister business' to the namesake chain of Loch Fyne restaurants in England (not part of the limited company that operates them though), this was the original that spawned the whole enterprise. It's also the closest to the raw materials, eco-conscious, and is actually owned and run by staff. The premises are simple (whitewashed walls, wooden booths and tables) and although it may be too bright and busy for a romantic encounter, it's an ideal stopover for seafood-lovers. The menu breaks down into starters and light dishes (local kippers for example), mains (skewered king scallops in bacon), specialities (Loch Fyne oysters in chilli and coriander), or the daily specials (chargrilled halibut with parsley butter, perhaps). The seafood platter is spectacular and there's an adjacent shop if you want to take anything home.

Pinto's

1 Argyll Street, Lochgilphead, Argyll PA31 8LZ (01546 602547). *Summer* **Lunch served** 11.30am-3pm Mon-Sat. **Dinner served** 7-10pm Tue-Sat. **Main courses** £9.25-£10.75. *Rest of year* reduced hours – phone for details. **Credit** MC, V.

ROCKS OF AGES

Scotland is not short on history, yet nowhere else has quite the atmosphere or sense of immanence as Kilmartin. In a short stretch of countryside just north of Lochgilphead, you can find up to 150 prehistoric monuments, plus another couple of hundred from later periods. The sheer concentration of the past here really does give you pause. Fortunately, there is an excellent visitor centre to help make sense of it all, with a decent and attractive café (Kilmartin House, 01546 510278, www.kilmartin.org).

One of the best places to start is from the top of Dunadd, at Kilmartin's south end. It's an outcrop all of 177 feet high, so takes no time to climb, and gives all-round views of the valley – a spookily flat and enclosed space of about a square mile. Although people have probably been here since the last Ice Age, it's said that the Scotti from Ireland settled and created a kingdom – Dalriada – around the sixth century. Dunadd was their hill fort. Today, it's a much etiolated pile with little surviving to show what it would have been like at its peak, but the carving of a footprint on one of the summit rocks, used in coronation ceremonies for the Dalriadan kings, can still be seen. Dare you try it?

From Dunadd, the visitor centre at Kilmartin House is just four miles north, and parking spots by the main road en route – adjacent to standing stones and other features – are fairly obvious. All the same, Kilmartin House is the best place to pick up a comprehensive guide to the valley's beaten and unbeaten tracks. There are henges, barrows, chambered cairns and much more around here but, ultimately, it's all about people – wherever you're from, Kilmartin provides a sense of human endeavour through time: early settlement, prehistory, ancient links between what we now call Argyll and Antrim, early Christianity, Dark Ages kingdoms, the legacy of that Scotti name, plus a haunting sense of attention having shifted. For thousands of years, Kilmartin was an important centre. Now it's quiet, peripheral and you could easily pass through it in five minutes by car. Stop a while.

Loch Fyne Oyster Bar

Although Lochgilphead is a reasonably bustling little town of 6,000 at the junction of Kilmartin, Knapdale and Loch Fyne (technically on an inlet called Loch Gilp), the idea of a vegetarian diner there seemed terribly improbable to city sceptics. Since it lacks the setting of Tarbert or the 18th-century aesthetics of Inveraray, visitors will see why. Pinto's is a slightly spartan little place, run with enthusiasm since 2002 by Linda and Ian Ward. During the day, you could get a plate of pasta, or maybe veggie sausages in a Yorkshire pudding with red wine sauce. In the evenings, it's candlelit and more elaborate and the themed banquet nights are very popular. Wines are organic. The Wards also have a vegetarian B&B, ten miles up the road towards Inveraray (Cruachan, Inverae Farm Road, Minard, 01546 886378).

Royal Hotel

Tighnabruaich, Argyll PA21 2BE (01700 811239/www.royalhotel.org.uk). **Lunch served** noon-2.30pm daily. **Dinner served** 6-8.30pm Mon-Thur, Sun; 6-9pm Fri, Sat. **Main courses** £9.95-£18.95. **Credit** MC, V.
Although you can have very good bar food here, the more serious eating options are at the front of the premises with views over to the Isle of Bute; well-sourced ingredients are paramount in both. The Deck is a more informal bistro space (dishes like jumbo langoustine with creamed, smoked garlic, rib-eye steak with big chips, or fillet of venison) while the more formal fine dining area, the Crustacean, sits on the other side of the entrance foyer. Here, chef Claire McKie offers a menu that could bring Jerusalem artichoke soup with truffle oil to start; then a tian of scallops and salmon; some carrot sherbet; a main like local venison, rosemary barley risotto, kale, and cocoa reduction;

then Valrhona chocolate tart for dessert. Wines (around 60) are listed by grape variety. Very civilised indeed.

Russian Tavern

Port Royal Hotel, 37 Marine Road, Port Bannatyne, Isle of Bute PA20 0LW (01700 505073/www.butehotel.com). **Meals served** noon-10pm daily. **Main courses** £12-£18. **Credit** MC, V.
The catering wing of the friendly and offbeat Port Royal Hotel (*see p357*), the Russian Tavern is on a mission to bring authentic Russian dishes, and top-class Scottish ingredients to Bute. But before mentioning the food, it's important to note that the Port Royal was named in CAMRA's *Good Beer Guide 2005* as being among the top 16 pubs in the entire UK, as well as being the very best in Scotland and Northern Ireland (we're talking beer poured straight from casks on the bar, proper cider, a brilliant range of vodkas and more besides). As for dinner in the tavern's informal surroundings, you could try some locally landed langoustine to start, follow them with Highland ox steak with latkas, red cabbage and sauerkraut for mains – or the legendary stroganoff – then a Pavlova for dessert. A gem. No smoking throughout.

West End Café

3 Gallowgate, Rothesay, Isle of Bute PA20 0HR (01700 503596). **Meals served** noon-2pm, 4-11pm Mon-Sat; 4-11pm Sun. **Main courses** £3.75-£5.95. **No credit cards.**
This award-winning chippy is the place to go for fish and chips when you're on Bute; no more, no less. Take them away and eat as you walk along the seafront.

Speyside

Big country, gorgeous birds, and whisky a go go.

If you're interested in Scotch whisky then Speyside will have a very special draw. It also scores high for nature and all the attractions and activities that can be filed under 'the great outdoors': scenery, walking, skiing and even water sports. If you're desperate for shops and nightclubs, you should go elsewhere. But if you want a weekend where you might wake up and glance out of your hotel window to see a young deer foraging in the garden, then Speyside could be for you. The River Spey rises from Loch Spey, a small body of water deep in the Monadhliath Mountains. From its source it heads roughly east through the hills to Newtonmore, then north-east via Kingussie and Aviemore towards Grantown on Spey. Around this stretch of the river, the two serious draws are wildlife and countryside. For more on wildlife, *see p366* **Call of the Wild**. Scenery ranges from wide-sky river valley to epic mountains, and the area is also host to some of the country's most extensive pine forests. The Abernethy Forest Nature Reserve, for example, north-east of Aviemore, is the biggest stretch of native pinewood left in Britain. Woodland aficionados also have the option of the Queen's Forest, Glenmore Forest Park and Rothiemurchus, all around Loch Morlich, east and south-east of Aviemore; Rothiemurchus, in particular, is drop-dead gorgeous. Those who only want a short stroll with the smell of the pines could try a circumnavigation of scenic Loch an Eilean (two and a half miles south of Aviemore via Inverdruie).

Take me higher

South of Loch Morlich you're into the big
country – good for experienced walkers
who want to get above the tree line. The
Cairngorm plateau is a subarctic wilderness
lording it over Speyside with lots of land
more than 3,000 feet above sea level.
It includes four of the five highest peaks
in Britain (Ben Macdui, Braeriach, Cairn
Toul and Cairn Gorm itself), as well as the
commercial ski area on the mountain that
gives its name to the district. There is a
road up to the ski centre (01479 861261,
www.cairngormmountain.com) and then
a funicular railway to carry you from the
centre's car park right up to the Ptarmigan
Station (01479 861 341), a shop and
café not far from the summit. It's an
entertaining excursion for both walkers
and non-walkers, in winter or summer, but
let's be clear: inexperienced people who
wander around at this altitude face serious
risks. Anyone can enjoy a coffee in the
Ptarmigan café, but don't strike out across
the tops unless you're properly equipped
and know what you're doing. One of the
best places to learn the relevant skills is
Glenmore Lodge down at Loch Morlich,
Scotland's main national outdoors training
centre. Instructors teach everything from
winter mountain safety to first aid, and
rock climbing to kayaking (01479 861256,
www.glenmorelodge.org.uk).

Continuing in a general outdoorsy spirit,
there are also assorted water sports and
activities such as sailing and windsurfing
at Loch Insh, south of Aviemore by Kincraig
(01540 651272, www.lochinsh.com).

Not only, but also

Other attractions in this southern reach
of Speyside include the ruins of Ruthven
Barracks, just outside Kingussie (www.
historic-scotland.gov.uk). The barracks was
built by the British army a few years after
the first Jacobite rebellion of 1715, and
was caught up in the more celebrated
rebellion of 1745-6 featuring Bonnie Prince
Charlie. It's a fine place to wander and
muse on the brutal political realities of
18th-century Britain. The Highland Folk
Museum at Newtonmore and Kingussie
offers more of a social history, however.
Laid out over a large area, the Newtonmore
site gives a taste of rural life in the

Accommodation	★★★
Food & drink	★★
Nightlife	
Shopping	
Culture	★
Sights	★
Scenery	★★★★★

Highlands and includes a recreation of a 300-year-old farming township; Kingussie is big on displays of farming artefacts, but also has an outdoors section with old buildings (both sites 01540 661307, www.highlandfolk.com).

The Strathspey Steam Railway is a much more Harry Potter-esque experience, (01479 810725, www.strathspeyrailway.co.uk). It chugs its way from Aviemore up to Boat of Garten, then on to the stop at Broomhill (possibly familiar to fans of BBC's *Monarch of the Glen* as home to Glenbogle Station). The railway's peak season is June to September, and aside from a few special trips around Christmas the trains tend to go into cold storage from November to February: more details from the website.

Whisky galore

Follow the Spey even further north-east, past Grantown on Spey, to Ballindalloch to discover an attraction best appreciated from a glass: Scotch whisky. From Ballindalloch up to Rothes via Charlestown of Aberlour, around Glenlivet and Dufftown, and on the roads towards the nearby towns of Keith and Elgin, lies the biggest concentration of distilleries on the planet.

Although most Scotch is still sold in the shape of popular blends (like Bell's, Famous Grouse or Teacher's), since the 1970s there has been a well-documented upsurge in sales of single malts: whiskies of a certain age from individual distilleries. These tend to be categorised by area and, in industry terms, the designation 'Speyside' extends beyond the banks of the Spey into adjacent glens and tributaries, even taking in relatively distant distilleries on rivers like the Findhorn in the west and the Deveron in the east. But you don't have to go that far to find famous names: Glenfarclas and Cragganmore are both made at Ballindalloch; Macallan at Craigellachie; Glenfiddich just outside Dufftown; and Glenlivet at Glenlivet, of course. There are literally dozens of distilleries on and around this stretch of the Spey, and each has its own approach to visitors. Some will have a dedicated visitors' centre and offer tours all year; others are only open by appointment; some charge an entry fee; some don't. The one venue that has surely made the most of its public profile is Glenfiddich (*see p370* **The Valley of the deer**). If you want to see

several distilleries, the Malt Whisky Trail (www.maltwhiskytrail.com) is a tourist-friendly itinerary that includes Glenfiddich, Glenlivet, Cardow and Glen Grant (all in the immediate locale), as well as Bendromach and Dallas Dhu up by Forres and Strathisla over at Keith.

Most distilleries with visitors' centres give guests every opportunity to buy their product. Otherwise, there is a great choice at the Whisky Shop in Dufftown (1 Fife Street, 01340 821097, www.dufftown.co.uk/ whkyshp.htm). It stocks all the popular varieties as well as some fine rare bottlings, and staff will even organise tastings. The best place to drink whisky on this part of Speyside – or virtually anywhere – is probably the Quaich Bar at the Craigellachie Hotel (*see p367*).

Walk on

The Speyside Way is one of Scotland's four official, long-distance footpaths. It runs from Aviemore all the way to Spey Bay on the Moray Firth coast, then a few kilometres east to the fishing port of Buckie. There are spurs to Dufftown and Tomintoul, but the core distance from Aviemore to Buckie is a shade over 60 miles. It's a good route for people who like to muddle along doing short, fairly flat meanders each day with the prospect of a decent-sized village at the end. For more details about the path, see www.moray.gov.uk.

While whisky may be Speyside's signature product, it does have another comestible to its name: soup. Back in 1868 a man called George Baxter borrowed £100 and opened a small grocery in Fochabers. This was the start of a success story that eventually became the Baxters Food Group, which still has a big, upmarket retail centre called the Highland Village, at Mosstodloch on the Spey just outside Fochabers (01343 820666, www.highland-village.co.uk).

Speyside

WHERE TO STAY

When it comes to accommodation on Speyside, it's best to think small. Aside from the complex of Macdonald hotels in Aviemore and a Hilton just outside the ski resort, big names and big establishments are absent. The average hardy walker in Aviemore and the Cairngorms is more likely to kip in a tent or a bunkhouse than a four-star hotel. Meanwhile, up in whisky country, distilleries are hardly labour intensive; the main villages (Dufftown, Charlestown of Aberlour, Rothes) are far from populous, and life tends to be fairly quiet. Accommodation reflects this: there are B&Bs everywhere and also a sprinkling of highly individual, small hotels that have managed to carve niches for themselves.

Archiestown Hotel

Archiestown, by Aberlour, Moray AB38 7QL (01340 810218/www.archiestownhotel.co.uk). **Lunch served** noon-2pm, **dinner served** 7-9pm daily. **Main courses** £14.50-£19.50. **Rates** £72-£100 double. **Credit** MC, V.

A small establishment that's fairly out of the way, the Archiestown sits in the tiny village of the same name on the B9102 back road that runs up the west side of the Spey from Grantown on Spey. A solid, red granite building in the main square, it's hard to miss. There's a huntin', shootin', fishin' atmosphere to the hotel, but you don't have to be a sportsman to stay here. Many guests just appreciate the peace and quiet, and the cooking in the hotel's bistro. It's not contemporary but it is comfortable, and if you can get a room with a view south towards Ben Rinnes, on the other side of Strathspey, you'll be a happy guest.

Auchendean Lodge

Dulnain Bridge, by Grantown on Spey, Inverness-shire PH26 3LU (01479 851347/ www.auchendean.com). **Dinner served** 7.30-9pm. **Set menu** £31 4 courses. **Rates** £142-£198 double incl dinner. **Credit** MC, V.

An Edwardian lodge sitting on a small rise just a short distance from the Spey, where the River Dulnain joins its big brother. The setting is both peaceful and panoramic, looking over the valley

CALL OF THE WILD

Bison roaming the hillside, huge birds of prey diving from the sky: Speyside boasts a biomass that you'd need a heart of stone not to appreciate.

The Highland Wildlife Park at Kincraig (between Kingussie and Aviemore on the B9152, 01540 651270, www.highland wildlifepark.org) provides a habitat for species that used to live in the wild, or still do. It is home not only to rare European bison but also to wolves, lynx and wild boar, pine martens, red deer and capercaillie.

The focus is on just one animal at the Cairngorm Reindeer Centre at Glenmore (around seven miles east of Aviemore on the minor road for Loch Morlich, Glenmore Lodge and the Cairngorm ski area, 01479 861228, www.reindeer-company.demon.co.uk). Here you can get up close and personal with Santa's little helpers as well as taking a short trip up the slopes of Cairngorm mountain to see them in the wild. The sight of a herd gradually looming into view out of the mist is quite something – especially across snow.

Ospreys were persecuted out of existence in Scotland around the time of World War I, but in 1959 a pair reappeared at Loch Garten. Their presence was protected and encouraged, and now the ospreys' toehold in these islands is much improved, although still fragile. Run by the RSPB, the Loch Garten Osprey Centre (two and a half miles east of Boat of Garten village, 01479 821409, www.rspb.org.uk) is dedicated to the birds, and its visitors' centre is the best place to find out about them. During the season (spring to late summer) a closed-circuit television camera is trained on the nest so people can view adult birds and their young. Ospreys are huge, with a wingspan of up to five and a half feet, and seeing one pull a fish from the loch is unforgettable. Hard-core birdwatchers will also be interested in the RSPB site at Insh Marshes, just outside Kingussie on the B970 (01540 661518, www.rspb.org.uk), which is home to lapwings in the spring, and whooper swans and greylag geese in winter.

Speyside

A shrine to whisky – the Craigellachie Hotel.

to the mountains. Decor of bedrooms and public spaces is very much in keeping with the building's origins; sitting in the lounge, it's easy to imagine yourself at a pre-World War I house party. The garden is a real feature – decorative but also for the growing of herbs, salad leaves, fruits and vegetables; free-range chickens provide eggs for breakfast. Given that Auchendean is so small, there's rarely room at dinner for non-residents, but that's more of an incentive to stay over. This is a gay-friendly hotel – certainly a rarity in these parts outside the metropolises of Edinburgh and Glasgow. Co-proprietors Ian Kirk and Eric Hart have created something special here.

The Boat

Boat of Garten, Inverness-shire PH24 3BH (01479 831258/www.boathotel.co.uk). **Rates** £119-£129 double; £160-£170 suite. **Credit** MC, V.

There's not a lot to Boat of Garten, a tiny village on the west bank of the Spey a few miles northeast of Aviemore. But it does have a small railway station where the steam trains stop; it's handy for Loch Garten and its ospreys – a short drive on the other side of the river; and it's home to the Boat Hotel. It's a fairly ambitious establishment, granite-built, Victorian, which served as the station hotel when the village was connected to the main railway network. The dining room is among the best places to eat on Speyside (*see p.369*), while the bedrooms are comfortable and cared-for, even if the decor errs on the side of that classic feminine look shared by so many hotels; don't men ever select bedroom fabrics? Staff are friendly, though, and if you arrive on the steam train, it's very romantic indeed.

Corrour House

Rothiemurchus, near Aviemore, Inverness-shire PH22 1QH (01479 810220/www.corrour househotel.co.uk). **Rates** £80-£100 double. **Credit** MC, V.

If Aviemore can be described as bustling – and sometimes it really can – then it's useful to find a peaceful haven of country-house respectability just a mile from the village centre. Head along the B970 towards Coylumbridge and before long you'll get to Corrour (signposted on the south side of the road before Inverdruie). A granite-built Victorian dower house with its own large gardens and woodland, Corrour House sits on the Rothiemurchus Estate and looks over to a dramatic cleft in the Cairngorms, the hill pass called the Lairig Ghru. Inside, decor is terribly neat and polite; with only eight rooms it really feels like you have wandered into the private – if commodious – home of a Highland lady. But a walk in the garden to soak up the view late on a summer evening, then a good Speyside whisky to take up to bed? Damn fine. And yes, this might be where you'll catch sight of a deer in the garden.

Craigellachie Hotel

Craigellachie, Speyside, Banffshire AB38 9SR (01340 881204/www.craigellachie.com). **Rates** £140-£160 double; £180 suite. **Credit** MC, V.

The big white one on the hill. The Craigellachie Hotel is slap bang on the Speyside Way, and close to both the Macallan distillery (on the other side of the river) and the Speyside Cooperage Centre. It's the whisky country hotel par excellence and has the bar to prove it: the Quaich is not big, but it is very, very clever. The man in charge is Tatsuya Minagawa and around the walls of this

Speyside

neatly appointed whisky nirvana are more than 600 varieties, including Japanese brands as well as rare Scotch single malts. The more exclusive of these can set you back from £49 to £175 per dram (fortunately, the majority are much more affordable). The Quaich will even cater to waifs and strays from the Speyside Way looking for an hour of bar lunch luxury – rucksacks can be left in the vestibule. In fact, walkers could be sorely tempted to brandish their credit cards and slump comfortably for the rest of the day. The Craigellachie also boasts a decent restaurant (*see p369*). The general atmosphere is in keeping with its status as a late Victorian hotel (library, games room, old-fashioned look), although transformed by modern materials and fabrics. Altogether quite a treat.

The Cross

Tweed Mill Brae, Ardbroilach Road, Kingussie, Inverness-shire PH21 1LB (01540 661166/ www.thecross.co.uk). **Rates** £110-£160. **Credit** MC, V.
Advertising itself as a 'restaurant with rooms' rather than a hotel, the Cross has been one of the brighter stars in the Speyside hospitality firmament for years – under previous owners and the current ones. Housed in a converted 19th-century tweed mill, the interior has a modern-but-rustic chalet look. Small but important touches are noticeable everywhere (good books and magazines to read, decent-sized beds, non-kitsch Scottish music), while the cooking just keeps gathering accolades (*see p371*). The small River Gynack burbling by outside completes an almost perfect picture.

Heatherbrae

Dell Road, Nethy Bridge, Inverness-shire PH25 3DG (01479 821345). **Rates** £57-£66 double; £70 family room (sleeps 4). **Credit** MC, V.
Red squirrels gambol in the trees outside and the happy clink of pool balls emanates from the convivial bar at the Heatherbrae. It's a basic but deeply lovable small hotel a short hike up Dell Road from the centre of the village, on the south side of the River Nethy. Housed in a sturdy old granite villa, it serves hearty food, there's usually some decent beer, and it's very handy for anyone who wants to head off just a few hundred yards further up the road and get lost (figuratively) on the tracks and paths of Abernethy Forest Nature Reserve with its native Scots pine.

Macdonald Highlands Hotel

Aviemore Highland Resort, Aviemore, Inverness-shire PH22 1PN (08451 255455/ www.macdonald-hotels.co.uk). **Rates** £110-£170 double; £160-£200 suite. **Credit** AmEx, DC, MC, V.
Bang in the middle of Aviemore you'll find the 'Centre'. This was formerly a misbegotten monstrosity of 1960s development with hotels, ice rink, cinema and other facilities designed to cater to vis-

iting skiers (winter) and climbers (summer) and thus boost the area's economy. Aiming for Alpine sophistication, the reality was more concrete shopping mall. The Centre may have been useful in some respects but it was never long on aesthetics, or European jet-set cachet. In the late 1990s, various parties got together to try again, including Macdonald Hotels.The much improved result includes four of its establishments cheek-by-jowl: the Four Seasons, the Highlands, the Academy (for families) and the Aviemore Inn. They didn't quite go as far as flattening the old complex (despite the fact that the cheers would have been heard as far afield as Inverness and Blair Atholl), so it's hard to say that any of the hotels are terribly cutting edge on the outside. The inside is a different matter, however. All four have that chain dependability (there are over 60 Macdonald hotels across the UK), but the biggest one here, and the pick of the quartet, is the Macdonald Highlands. It has been done out contemporary-style, with smart rooms, a restaurant-with-a-view and a swanky whisky-cocktail bar called the Laggan. Around Aviemore Highland Resort there is also the Leisure Arena with swimming pool, gym and the Vital Spa, accessible to hotel guests.

Muckrach Lodge

Dulnain Bridge, by Grantown on Spey, Inverness-shire PH26 3LY (01479 851257/ www.muckrach.co.uk). **Rates** £140-£160 double. **Credit** AmEx, MC, V.
A mid 19th-century sporting lodge that was transformed into a hotel in the 1960s, Muckrach is just outside Dulnain Bridge on the A938 towards Carrbridge (it's also just a couple of miles from where the River Dulnain meets the Spey). With its Victorian exterior and the mounted stag horns and tartan carpet in reception, visitors would be forgiven for thinking they were in for a full blast of Caledonian cliché, but this is not actually the case. Although the rooms are hardly Anouska Hempel, they're not overly fussy either – polite and restrained with traditional flourishes. They take their food seriously here (*see p371*) and the owners (the Macfarlanes) are a hospitable pair. Staff are very clued up about distillery visits.

WHERE TO EAT & DRINK

The Speyside area is not crammed with major population centres. Newtonmore and Kingussie are pleasant villages, while Aviemore and Grantown on Spey are more bustling, with pubs and restaurants. Most hotels are unable to fill their dining rooms every evening with residents – exceptions include Auchendean Lodge by Dulnain Bridge (*see p366*) and the Cross in Kingussie (*see above*) – so have to balance the needs of tourists and locals to remain in business during the year. That's even more the case with stand-alone restaurants. In the heaving metropolis of Aviemore, if you're running a café-bar on the main street (Café

The Boat

Mambo) or a good, old Highland pub (the Old Bridge Inn), then there's no problem. But any business that tries to combine local tastes with visitors' expectations will inevitably have to compromise – whether in terms of food or decor. There are some fine places to eat along Speyside, but they tend to be quite traditional.

The Boat

Boat of Garten, Inverness-shire PH24 3BH (01479 831258/www.boathotel.co.uk). Bar **Lunch served** 12.30-2pm, **dinner served** 6.30-9pm daily. *Restaurant* **Dinner served** 7-9pm daily. **Main courses** £8-£14. **Set dinner** £32.50 3 courses. **Credit** MC, V.

One word sums up the dining room at the Boat: 'blue'. The walls are blue and so is the carpet. It is more peaceful than overwhelming, though, and art prints break up the effect. In any case, it makes a welcome change from the usual Highlands habit of overemphasising the Scottishness of every-thing. Food is well-presented, with mains such as saddle of venison on pear and baby leek confit, with orange brandy glaze. You could top and tail this with scallops to start and fruits in choux pastry for dessert, say. The Boat makes the best of good local ingredients (beef, lamb, venison, trout) and chef Tony Alcott smokes and cures his own poultry, game and salmon at the hotel using wood chippings from whisky barrels. Very civilised.

Boathouse

Loch Insh Watersports Centre, by Kincraig, Inverness-shire PH21 1NU (01540 651272/ www.lochinsh.com). **Meals served** 11am-5.30pm Mon-Thur, Sun; 11am-7.30pm Fri, Sat. **Main courses** £5.25-£12.50. **Rates** £44 double; £246-£1,382 chalets. **Credit** AmEx, MC, V.

Loch Insh, around halfway between Kingussie and Aviemore, is better known for sailing, canoe-ing and windsurfing than for haute cuisine. But all this outdoor activity can build up an appetite, and cunningly the water sports centre includes a well-appointed canteen that serves warming chilli, filling burgers or good soup during the day (coffee and cakes too). It gets a little more serious in the evenings, with steak, salmon or vegetarian dishes like pasta with pesto and sun-dried tomatoes. Catch it on a sunny day and you can sit on the balcony overlooking the loch.

Café Mambo

Units 12-13, Grampian Road, Aviemore, Inverness-shire PH22 1RB (01479 811670). **Open** noon-12.30am Mon-Sat; 12.30pm-12.30am Sun. **Meals served** noon-8.30pm Mon-Sat; 12.30-7.30pm Sun. **Main courses** £7.50-£13.95. **Credit** MC, V.

For decades, Aviemore was famed for being the Highland resort with a tacky approach to tourism – although it couldn't be faulted when it came to easy access to fabulous countryside. Then, in 1998, a style bar appeared. Not only did the vil-lage suddenly acquire a venue where daytime passers-by could get a latte or a glass of wine, but it also introduced Tex-Mex dishes, decent tunes, shooters and cocktails. If you want to take a break in a relaxed café-bar environment where you can pick away at a plate of nachos, and then return for a lively evening later, Café Mambo is your only point of call.

Craigellachie Hotel

Craigellachie, Banffshire AB38 9SR (01340 881204/www.craigellachie.com) **Lunch served** noon-2pm, **dinner served** 6-9pm daily. **Set menu** £33.25 3 courses. **Credit** AmEx, DC, MC, V.

Speyside

THE VALLEY OF THE DEER

There is something rather heart-warming about the fact that while many whisky producers are owned by international conglomerates, Glenfiddich (which means 'valley of the deer') is still in the hands of the Grant family. The distillery was founded by William Grant in 1886; the distinctive triangular-shaped bottle first saw the light of day in 1957. The company was the first to market single malt Scotch in England (1963), the first to set up a visitors' centre (1969), and it created the prestigious Glenfiddich Food and Drink Awards in 1970. These days, 12-year-old Glenfiddich Special Reserve is the world's biggest-selling single malt Scotch, while one of the company's blends (William Grant's 21-year-old) featured in a recent edition of Jim Murray's *Whisky Bible* as blended Scotch of the year. This is serious stuff.

A basic distillery visit is free. It kicks off with a film about the company's history, followed by a tour following the whisky-making process from start to bottling, and is rounded off with a wee dram. If you've only ever sampled the ubiquitous 12-year-old drowned in ice, the intensity of a fresh sample in its natal surroundings will have the impact of a totally different drink.

In addition, the distillery runs more in-depth 'connoisseurs' tours (£12 per person), which include a tutored tasting session at the end; these are best booked in advance.

The Glenfiddich company also encourages contemporary art with its series of artist-in-residence exhibitions. Since 2002 invited artists have been able to live and work on site for three months during the summer; their work then goes on show in a specially created gallery. Past artists – from a wide range of disciplines – have come from all over Europe as well as close to home (graduates of Gray's School of Art in Aberdeen, for example).

Those more interested in exploring the hands-on business of whisky production in all its many aspects will enjoy a visit to the Speyside Cooperage Centre (01340 871108, www.speyside cooperage.co.uk), around three miles from Glenfiddich up by Craigellachie. Around 100,000 whisky barrels are made or repaired here every year and its visitors' centre will tell you all about it.

Glenfiddich Distillery
Dufftown, Banffshire AB55 4AH (01340 820373/www.glenfiddich.com). **Open** Nov-Easter 9.30am-4.30pm Mon-Fri. Easter-Oct 9.30am-4.30pm Mon-Sat; noon-4.30pm Sun.

The dining room at Craigellachie could be accused of going overboard on the plaid and antlers, but it is very cosy – a word that could equally be applied to the service. Three typical courses could be carpaccio of local venison with parmesan shavings and red pesto to start; braised shank of local lamb in a sage and red wine reduction for a main; then blackcurrant bavarois with Earl Grey tea sorbet for dessert. Afterwards? Back upstairs to the Quaich Bar for another whisky, of course (*see p367*).

The Cross

Tweed Mill Brae, Ardbroilach Road, Kingussie, Inverness-shire PH21 1LB (01540 661166/ www.thecross.co.uk). **Dinner served** 7-8.30pm Tue-Sat. **Set menu** £35 3 courses. **Credit** AmEx, MC, V.

The dining room here is in keeping with the modern rustic chalet look of the rest of the premises (*see p368*), and although it might not sound it, that's a compliment. Patio doors open from the restaurant on to the terrace overlooking the Gynack, a tributary of the Spey: perfect for a summer aperitif. The menu is seasonal, and ingredients come from local sources or from the country's finest vendors. A typical three courses might involve confit of duck with red cabbage to start; fillet of Highland beef with red onion marmalade and chips as a main; and lemon tart to finish. The Cross also boasts one of the most impressive wine lists on Speyside.

La Faisanderie

2 Balvenie Street, Dufftown, Banffshire AB55 4AD (01340 821273/www.dufftown.co.uk/ lafaisanderie.htm. **Lunch served** noon-1.30pm Fri-Sun. **Dinner served** 6-8.30pm Mon, Thur, Sun; 7-9pm Fri, Sat. **Main courses** £14.90-£16.70. **Set lunch** £12.20 2 courses, £15.10 3 courses. **Set dinner** £24 3 courses. **Credit** MC, V.

A genuine French restaurant run by a genuine Frenchman (Eric Obry) in the heart of whisky country – so there are no points for concluding that this establishment concentrates on Scottish ingredients presented in a French style. It's a small, simple space with no frills, bang in the middle of the village; it's the care taken with the food that grabs the attention. Dishes can range from the fairly simple (watercress soup to start) to the fairly ambitious (halibut in Noilly Prat sauce as a main, or a kind of frangipane orange samosa for dessert). An ideal place to stop if you've been visiting the nearby Glenfiddich distillery. No smoking throughout.

Muckrach Lodge

Dulnain Bridge, by Grantown on Spey, Moray PH26 3LY (01479 851257/www.muckrach. co.uk). **Lunch served** 12.30-2pm, **dinner served** 7-9pm daily (closed Mon, Tue in Jan & Feb). **Main courses** *Bistro* £10.95-£16.95. **Set menu** *Restaurant* £35 5 courses. **Rates** £140-160 double. **Credit** MC, V.

Muckrach Lodge offers a choice when it comes to food. There's the fine-dining room, the Finlarig, all white linen, gleaming glassware and ruched curtains. Or there's an airy and informal bistro in the conservatory, serving simpler fare of the steak and pasta variety. Overseeing both is Stephen Robertson, who has worked at acclaimed Scottish country-house piles in Perthshire. In the Finlarig, three courses might involve an Asian-style confit of duck with stir-fried vegetables, soy and ginger sauce to start, followed by pan-fried venison with braised red cabbage and peppercorn sauce as a main, and Belgian chocolate mousse with raspberry coulis for dessert. If peat-smoked haddock is on the menu, go for it – it's excellent. Not a bad range of wines either.

Old Bridge Inn

2 Dalfaber Road, Aviemore, Inverness-shire PH22 1PU (01479 811137/www.oldbridge inn.co.uk). **Open** 11am-midnight daily. **Lunch served** noon-2pm Mon-Sat; 12.30-2pm Sun. **Dinner served** 6-9pm daily. **Main courses** £7.50-£14. **Rates** £30 double. **Credit** MC, V.

The Old Bridge Inn is a decent, old-school Highland bar with space for eats (plus seats outside for the summer). It does good beer, a fine range of whiskies, has a basic à la carte and serves char-grills and blackboard specials. You won't find anything over-elaborate but you will get an excellent venison steak to go with your pint of cask ale. The inn's guest beers tend to come from the Cairngorm Brewery on the Dalfaber Industrial Estate at the north end of Aviemore (01479 812222, www.cairngormbrewery.com).

Old Monastery

Drybridge, near Buckie, Moray AB56 5JB (01542 832660/www.oldmonastery.com). **Lunch served** *May-Oct* noon-3pm Tue-Sat. **Dinner served** 7-11pm Tue-Sat. **Set dinner** £13.95 2 courses, £17.95 3 courses. **Credit** MC, V.

This is either the first or last restaurant on Speyside, depending on your outlook. It's way up north, around seven miles outside Fochabers, on the hillside outside Buckie (the small port that marks one end of the Speyside Way). Its situation means it has great views over the Moray Firth coast. It's housed in an old monastery, but the building has served as a restaurant under various owners for some years now. Leaded, arched windows and other original features remind you of its former function, but otherwise decor is 'country-house polite'. A typical dinner might bring a simple smoked salmon with asparagus and horseradish cream to start; lamb chops with mint mash and rosemary jus as a main; whisky chocolate pudding (made with Macallan whisky) for dessert. Musicians entertain diners on some Saturday evenings. Note that at the time of writing, the place had just acquired new owners, so some changes are bound to occur.

Strangford Lough

Take a map and wellies to explore this beautiful landscape.

A pristine, peaceful playground for yachts and pleasure craft, Strangford Lough is probably one of the most important marine sites in Europe – and it's also one of the most beautiful places in the world. Characterised by its unique drumlins – soft, roly-poly, fertile hills and islands, created by Ice-Age glaciers – it is a large, shallow, intertidal sea lough. Mature woodland, sheep-strewn fields, organic farms, large stone-walled estates, pretty villages and yacht clubs define its shores. At low tide the shallow waters of the north end recede, exposing vast, shimmering sand flats and the feeding grounds for massive flocks of birds that migrate here in the winter months, turning the population into twitchers.

Its southern entrance, or 'Narrows', is a deep channel with some of the fastest, strongest currents in Europe. These give rise to its Viking name, literally 'strong fjord', and make for dramatic ferry crossings and stunning scenery. Because of the area's subsequent raiders and settlers, there is no shortage of Viking forts, Anglo-Norman tower houses, early Christian monasteries, 18th-century stately homes, 19th-century linen mills and spine-tingling, head-clearing, ancient landscapes.

The exceptionally mild and sunny microclimate allows palm trees to grow in even the most exposed areas, so you can enjoy a long season of outdoor activities. Don't forget an Ordnance Survey map, wellies, a pair of binoculars and swimming togs.

Strangford Lough

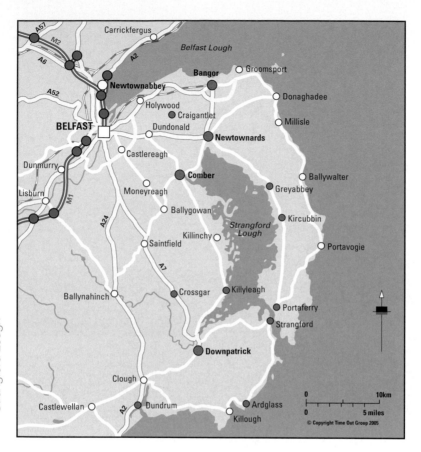

Newtownards to Grey Abbey

While the town centre of Newtownards, at the northern tip of the lough, holds no great draw, the prominent scraggy hill (a volcanic crag) locally known as Scrabo, affords stupendous views. The panorama stretches the full 19 miles of the lough and beyond to the Mourne Mountains, the Isle of Man and, on a good day, Scotland. Turn to the north and you'll see Belfast. (Scrabo Country Park 028 9181 1491, www.ehsni.gov.uk.)

Home to Stone Age and pre-Christian settlers, Triassic dinosaurs and great Irish deer over a period of 5,000 years, the hillside is a higgledy-piggledy network of pathways through gorse, whitethorn and dramatic disused quarries. It also boasts a golf course, albeit a rather wild and comical one, and a solid sandstone monument that was erected in 1859 to Charles William Vane-Stewart, third Marquess of Londonderry. It commemorates his efforts to relieve the plight of tenant families during the famine.

When Scrabo Tower is open (Apr-late Sept, 10.30am-6pm Mon-Thur, Sat, Sun), you can check out the exhibition of pottery, flint arrows and stone axe heads. Sadly, the legendary Irish teas once provided by the Miss Millins, granddaughters of the tower's first caretaker and a local quarryman, are history too. However, Scrabo and the beech and hazel woods of Killynether provide lovely picnic spots and opportunities to stretch your legs. In the spring, the hillside bursts into flower and Killynether is carpeted with bluebells.

Here also is the reclaimed land of Ards Airport (028 9181 3327, www.ulsterflying club.com), home to the Ulster Flying Club and venue of a sporadic airshow. If Scrabo Hill has given you a taste for aerial views, then consider a surprisingly affordable 'air experience flight' (£70 for 40 minutes). This will take you 'anywhere you want to go' in a four-seater plane at 2,500 feet. You can even take the controls, although the breathtaking views should satisfy the most

Accommodation	★★★
Food & drink	★★★
Nightlife	
Shopping	
Culture	★
Sights	★★
Scenery	★★★★★

demanding thrill seekers. This is also the spot for microlight flights (£70/60mins, Gerry Snodden 028 9087 3244, www.g.l.craig.btinternet.co.uk/umc.html).

Sandstone quarried from Scrabo was shipped as far as Dublin and New York in the 18th century. It was also used for the original façade of Newtownards town hall, a fine, listed Georgian market house which now provides gallery space and craft studios. Rather tatty exhibitions can disappoint, and it is best to visit the profusion of artists and craftspeople in their home studios. Ards man Mark Hanvey, for example, turns exquisite, paper-thin wooden bowls (49 Scrabo Road, 028 9181 5317, www.markhanvey.co.uk). Others are listed in a beautifully illustrated publication, *The Creative Peninsula*, available from Ards Tourist Information Centre (*see p376*).

Here you'll also find an extremely impressive set of brochures from the Kingdoms of Down regional tourist group (028 9182 2881, www.kingdomsof down.com). If you're after active pursuits, the owners of Mike the Bike (53 Frances Street, 028 9181 1311), who fly, windsurf, kayak, sail and, unsurprisingly, cycle their way round the lough, are also a fantastic source of information on where best to do any of these activities. They also provide 'unsinkable' equipment, which they will deliver 'anywhere you like'.

Newtownards is a good place to stock up on picnic food (Homegrown, 66B East Street, 028 9181 8318), and if you really want to shop, Wardens, next to Knotts bakery (*see p382*), is a nice old family-run department store complete with hardware and haberdashery sections (45-47 High Street, 028 9181 2147).

If you leave Newtownards, following signs to Portaferry, you will soon find yourself winding your way along the coastal road, right beside the lough. If the tide is out and the sparkling sand flats are exposed, horse riders, dog walkers, cockle pickers and a mass of migrant birds populate the beach. (Stop off at one of the many view and picnic points for a closer look.) When the tide is lapping the stony shores, year-round wind- and kite-surfers zip at exhilarating speed back and forth between islands across the shallow waters, best witnessed when the sea is whipped up to a white-edged, muddy froth (Belfast-based C2Sky

Kite Adventures, 028 9033 1921, run courses). Where the lough deepens, sailing is available at the friendly and unpretentious Newtownards Sailing Club (161 Portaferry Road, 028 9181 3426, www.newtownardssailingclub.co.uk).

However, if dry land is your preference, then the neo-classical stately home Mount Stewart (Portaferry Road, 028 4278 8387, www.ntni.org.uk) is worth a visit. Don't miss out on its heavenly World Heritage Site gardens, five-acre lake and the hill-top banqueting house, Temple of the Winds. In the summer regular jazz weekends bring credible musicians and provide an excuse for civilised, wine-fuelled picnicking among the stunning, exotic plants and trees.

Fringed by impressive miles of old stone walls and wind-pruned deciduous woodland, the estate stops just short of Grey Abbey, a village of good antique shops, tearooms and the enchanting ruins of Cistercian monastery Grey Abbey (028 9054 3037, www.ehsni.gov.uk). The first fully Gothic-style building in Ireland, it was founded in 1193 by Affreca, daughter of Godred, Viking king of the Isle of Man, and wife to Anglo-Norman conqueror John de Courcy. Tradition has it that the abbey was built as a gesture of thanksgiving for safe landing after a storm at sea. She is buried there and her stone effigy can still be seen.

The abbey survied until the dissolution of the monasteries in 1541, and the ruins are now set in very attractive parkland with the backdrop of Grey Abbey House, a fine 18th-century mansion (private views for groups by appointment only, 028 4278 8666) – it's an intriguing place for a wander.

If you really want to stretch your legs, put on your wellies and head out from the car park just beyond Grey Abbey in the direction of the islands. These provided sanctuary for the United Irishmen hunted by Lord Castlereagh during the 1798 rebellion, including local hero Rev James Porter who was sent to the gallows in Grey Abbey. Nowadays, the beach is a magnet for sun-worshippers. You have to walk a fair distance into the surf to get any kind of depth, making it ideal for kids and paddlers.

Grey Abbey to Strangford

There's another sailing club (Lough Road, 028 4273 8422) and a couple of excellent places to eat in Kircubbin, a significant harbour for the transport of kelp, brown (unbleached) linen and coal in the 19th century. Otherwise you'd be best advised to make tracks to Lisbane church, the tiny white 18th-century chapel which featured in the 1990 film of Sam Hanna Bell's *December Bride*.

The bird-filled estuary and Mourne Mountain backdrop are breathtakingly beautiful. So too are the views of Strangford from Castle Hill at Ardkeen.

Named after the castle built by the knight William Baron Savage, this land was a reward for his part in the bloody Anglo-Norman conquest undertaken by John de Courcy. The hilly promontory is now marked with church ruins and crooked gravestones.

It's particularly jaw-dropping at sunset, but so are the views all the way to Portaferry. Take the Abbacy Road on the way out of Ardkeen Park – a ribbon of houses – and follow the winding road through drumlins, salt marshes and low-lying, flood-prone fields until you meet the coast again.

This will give you a particularly stunning approach to Portaferry, past shipwrecks of wartime vessels, which mistook Strangford Lough for Belfast Lough, and the limpid, kelp-filled waters of boat moorings. This area is popular with divers (DV Diving, 138 Mountstewart Road, 028 9146 4671, www.dvdiving.co.uk). The town, once down at heel, is now a magnet for holiday homes with a mini-marina and harbour. It's here you can take the open-decked Carferry (028 4488 1637) across the swirling whirlpools and spitting currents of Europe's fastest tides, at the Narrows, to the calm and very quaint village of Strangford.

Before you go, Strangford village and the natural beauty of the lough are best seen from the top of Portaferry's Windmill Hill. You should also have a look at the unusual L-shaped, 16th-century tower house built for the Savage family, or take a boat trip to see the seals, or fish offshore. Ards Tourist Information Centre (*see p376*) arranges summer boat trips, or you can go with local men for bespoke jaunts (Des Rogers 028 4272 8297 or John Murray 028 4272 8414). Dress for the elements at the Port, an excellent shop for all-weather walking and sailing gear (Ferry Street, 028 4272 9666, summer season only).

Landlubbers may prefer to visit the aquarium and seal sanctuary (Exploris, Castle Street, 028 4272 8062, www.exploris.org.uk), just beside the castle. The flat country roads are good for cycling and walking as far as Quintin Castle. Wind-whipped, castellated and partially hidden by woodland on the exposed south shores of the peninsula, this is perfect Famous Five territory, with lighthouses, stories of ghosts and a rumour that Sean Connery is moving in.

Evenings should be spent at Fiddlers, (10-12 Church Street, Portaferry 028 4272 8393, www.fiddlersgreenportaferry.com), the hub for raucous music sessions and the centre of operations for the Portaferry Gala week float parade (www.portaferry gala.com). Thousands line the streets to applaud the huge and spectacular creations fashioned from farm machinery by fiercely competitive local teams.

Thought to have been founded by the Vikings, Strangford, with its sheltered harbour, was once a thriving port town. However, the absence of a rail link and the advent of steamships, which required deeper water, led to its decline. Nowadays many of its pretty properties belong to wealthy Belfast commuters.

Take a detour along the coastal road to see the seals at Cloughy Rocks, the earliest datable tower house at Kilclief, the dramatic scenery at St John's Point lighthouse, or the picturesque harbour at Ardglass, the 19th-century headquarters of the herring trade, which employed more than 3,000 fishermen at its peak.

Alternatively, visit the calmer lough shores where the gardens and mature woodland of Castle Ward slope down to the sea (Strangford, 028 4488 1204, www.nitni.org.uk). With a Gothic west front and classical east front (both inside and out) this beguiling 18th-century mansion and pristinely preserved 19th-century farmyard is a charming setting for the opera that takes place every summer (028 9066 1090, www.castlewardopera.com).

Strangford to Killyleah

Next take the road to Downpatrick. Down Cathedral (028 4461 4922, www.down cathedral.org), a stunningly elegant and unostentatious cathedral, is poised among a cluster of trees and ancient graves, facing the Mourne Mountains on the Hill of Down. A place of Christian worship for an unbroken 1,500 years, it is said to be the resting place for St Patrick. His unmarked grave was commemorated with a stone laid by John de Courcy.

You can take in other local sites on board vintage passenger trains (028 4461 5779, www.downpatricksteamrailway.co.uk) on the original railway line that supported the linen trade between Belfast and Newcastle: Viking king Magnus Barefoot's grave, the limpid waters of the Quoile Pondage (a 450-acre freshwater bird sanctuary) and the 12th-century Cistercian monastery, Inch Abbey (028 9054 3034, www.ehsni.gov.uk), built with money donated by John de Courcy, in atonement for his murderous conquest of Downpatrick.

Refreshments are best found, locals say, at the Daily Grind Coffee Shop (28 St Patrick's Avenue, 028 4461 7173) or Denvirs (14-16 English Street, 028 4461 2012), a 1642 coaching house and handy pit stop for the county gaol and museum. The Saint Patrick Centre (www.saintpatrick centre.com, 028 4461 9000) allows you to immerse yourself in an interactive history of Ireland's patron saint. However, you may prefer the natural beauty of nearby churches (Raholp and Saul) and numerous holy wells (including Struell Wells), which mark the progress of Christianity since St Patrick arrived on the shores of Strangford Lough in AD 461.

Next take the road over the Quoile Bridge, through the lovely drumlins to Killyleagh, a pretty village of multicoloured houses and a privately owned fairy-tale castle, where Van Morrison holds the odd outdoor concert. A significant maritime port exporting cotton from the town mill and linen from Ireland's largest flax mill at Shrigley, the harbour is now the site for a sympathetic development of chi-chi second homes.

The focal point is a replica statue, erected by Prince Andrew, baron of Killyleagh, to physician and naturalist Sir Hans Sloane, former pupil of the 17th-century Killyleagh School of Philosophy and founder of the British Museum; Sloane Square, Sloane Street and Hans Place in London are all named after him. Not only do we have him to thank for the development of the smallpox vaccine, he also invented drinking chocolate; you can buy blocks of it, based on his original concoction, at Picnic (*see p383*). For beverages of a more intoxicating kind, take a quick detour to Crossgar to the excellent wine merchant, James Nicholson (Killyleagh Street, 028 4483 0091, www.jnwine.com).

Killyleagh to Comber

Give yourself plenty of time and make sure you have a map to navigate the next leg of your journey, a breathtakingly beautiful stretch of the lough, densely dotted with islands. The sailing club at Ringhaddy (c/o 028 9145 4937, www.ringhaddy.co.uk) has the air of a gated community, but if you're interested in boats you should be welcome here and at Whiterock (Strangford Lough Yacht Club, Whiterock Bay, 028 9754 1883, www.strangford-lough-yacht-club.com), two of the centres for Strangford Race Week (www.slrw.org.uk, 028 4461 2233).

Even if you're not a sailor, it's still worth walking, cycling or driving along the causeway and country roads as they twist

Castle Ward

through and around seaweedy inlets, bird-filled salt marshes, Scots pine-covered islands and a manicured patchwork of hilly fields. Enjoy particularly panoramic views from hill tops on the Ballymorran Road and Ringhaddy Road, facing south.

To absorb the mystical, timeless quality of the landscape, visit Mahee Island and the ruins of Nendrum, a Benedictine settlement sacked and plundered repeatedly in Viking and Anglo-Norman raids. The lush, grassy knoll, topped with wind-gnarled trees and lichen-bleached ruins, is a spellbinding summer picnic spot with terrific all-round views of the lough. It's also worth visiting in the autumn when

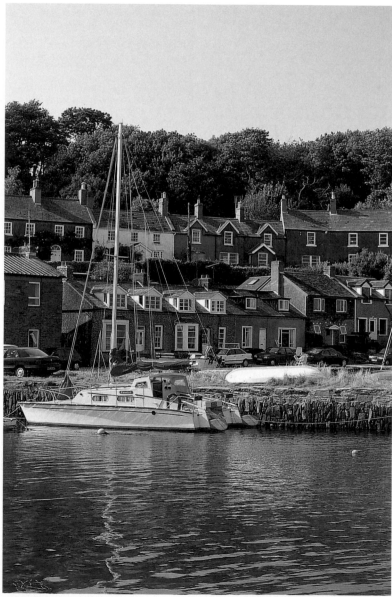

Tranquil Portaferry harbour.

the shore is saturated by the sea aster's blue, daisy-like flowers and displays of silver seed heads.

It's fascinating to see the profusion of wildlife and migrating birds in their natural habitat, but if you want to learn more, take the road to Comber to the stunningly situated and hugely informative Castle Espie (Ballydrain Road, Comber, 028 9187 4146, www.wwt.org.uk), a wildfowl and wetlands centre that hosts an equally laid-back and friendly Green Living Fair in September.

In Comber you should stop off briefly at Andrews Mill, a linen-spinning mill, which closed in 1997. Then continue to Clatteringford, an unashamedly unfashionable linen outlet and mail-order company run by the Andrews' descendants on a very pretty family farm (51 Old Ballygowan Road, 028 9187 4545, www.clatteringford.com).

While the mill provided work for women, farms like this were created to employ the men of the parish, grow flax for the mill and food for the community. The Andrews family has an illustrious history, producing a prime minister, a lord chief justice and the designer of the Belfast-built Titanic. You can buy commemorative damask table linen with the same design and quality as that supplied to the doomed White Star liner.

Much of the town square in Comber has been demolished, but it's worth a trip to Pheasant's Hill (Unit 3, 10-12 Bridge Street, 028 9187 8470). A shop selling rare-breed meat and organic produce, it's an important outlet for the many hobby farmers in County Down. This includes Pheasant's Hill Farm, near Downpatrick (37 Killyleagh Road, 028 4461 7246), where you can go watch the pretty Tamworths enjoy a happy, outdoor life before they are turned into rather delicious sausages – an ideal present to take home.

WHERE TO STAY

Anna's House

35 Lisbarnett Road, Comber, County Down BT23 6AW (028 9754 1566/www.annas house.com). **Rates** £60 double. **Credit** MC, V.
If Anna knows you are coming, you will be greeted at the door of your car and welcomed straight into the kitchen of this cosy, low-ceilinged County Down farmhouse for a reviving cup of tea or pre-dinner drink. You will probably also meet her loquacious husband Ken, a keen member of the Down Cathedral choir and the mastermind behind an ambitious new project to extend their home and provide a large lake-view sitting room for guests. In the meantime you will share the comfortable, eccentric family space – stuffed with books, local art and records – and the carefully laid dining

table with your hosts, unless of course you request some privacy. What makes Anna's House unique is her emphasis on good, mostly organic, food and home baking. The smell of fresh bread and espresso curls through the house in the morning, while a breakfast of shiny, just-picked blackberries, sweet-stewed damsons and fluffy herb omelette is typical. Rooms are small but comfortable with linen sheets, wild flowers and a shared fridge for fresh organic milk. Don't miss Anna's whimsical secret garden, or the breathtakingly beautiful church and 17th-century manor courthouse over the next hill on the Kilmood Church Road. No smoking throughout.

Ballymote House

Killough Road, Downpatrick, County Down BT30 8BJ (028 4461 5500/www.ballymote house.com). **Rates** £70 double. **Credit** MC, V.
Set in sweeping gardens of mature trees and rhododendrons at the end of a bumpy lane, Ballymote is a well-worn family home, stuffed full of fine hand-me-down antiques, fading silk curtains and pure-bred dogs. Blissful beds in well-proportioned and tastefully decorated rooms are turned down at night, while adjoining bathrooms with huge bathtubs are stocked with everything from Floris powder puffs to Alka Seltzer. Enjoy a G&T in the drawing room by the roar of a log fire, watch telly in the snug or use the office for emails. Nicola, a passionate and well-practised cook with a penchant for traditional, blue-blooded food will cook (with notice) for parties of up to ten in the formal dining room – we enjoyed an earthy Jerusalem artichoke soup followed by local pheasant with a Marsala and grape cream, and cheeses. Or you can sit round the large kitchen table for Ardglass prawns and a bottle of Chablis. The serious breakfast, which comes on a help-yourself platter and changes every day for long-stay guests, will set you up for stunning local walks – don't miss the enchanting stone circle nearby – or horsey pursuits, should you want to bring a four legged friend with you. No smoking throughout.

Beech Hill Country House

23 Ballymoney Road, Craigantlet, Newtownards, County Down BT23 4TG (028 9042 5892/www.beech-hill.net). **Rates** £70 double. **Credit** MC, V.
Nestled in the green and pleasant land of the Craigantlet Hills, BeechHill Country House is near Belfast City Airport, and also Fontana (*see p382*) and Shanks (*see p383*), where you will find some excellent eating. The quiet, tailored comfort of Victoria Brann's home and her discreet, reserved style will appeal to those who enjoy a sense of privacy. The modern Georgian-style house is immaculately tidy and furnished with polished antiques. On dark winter nights, interlined chintz curtains are drawn, beds with weighty winter duvets are thoughtfully preheated and an extra radiator is provided to ensure a sense of cosy, personal welcome, despite the lino bathroom floors and

pump-action soap-dispensers. Breakfast is served in the light-filled, orchid- and print-decorated dining room. Help yourself to a selection of cereals, breads and fresh fruits, while Victoria cooks whatever takes your fancy on the Aga. Bedrooms are no-smoking.

Carriage House

71 Main Street, Dundrum, County Down BT33 0LU (028 4375 1635/www.carriagehoused undrum.com). **Rates** £60 double. **No credit cards**.

Located in the village of Dundrum between Downpatrick and the Mourne Mountains, the Carriage House is the distinctive purple-blue building with the profusion of window-box flowers beside the Buck's Head restaurant. Bright and uncluttered, the interior sympathetically juxtaposes delicate antiques with authentic retro or modern furnishings and displays a discerning selection of art. Bedrooms are homely and indulgent, with tasteful, treat-filled trays, powerful showers, decent soaps and plump beds piled with soft pillows. Breakfast, served in the conservatory with views of the courtyard, is also a treat, with fresh fruit salads, star-anise-spiced plums, herby sausages and local breads. Afterwards take a stroll to the top of the walled garden for a chance encounter with Humphrey the hedgehog, into the village, or up to Dundrum Castle for panoramic views of the bay. No-smoking bedrooms.

Edenvale House

130 Portaferry Road, Newtownards, County Down BT22 2AH (028 9181 4881/www.eden valehouse.com). **Rates** £65 double; £75 3-bed family room. **Credit** MC, V.

Jolly, well-groomed and chatty ex-Pony Club mum, Diane Whyte, provides a warm and homely welcome at this Georgian farmhouse. Her bedrooms are feminine, flowery and just on the right side of fussy with draped headboards, embroidered linen, attractive antique furniture and collections of china. Waffle bathrobes, towelling slippers and electric blankets are provided, as are copies of *Hello!*. In the morning you will enjoy glimpses of the sea, and as much effort is made for one guest at breakfast as for a full house, starting with hot stewed fruit and crème fraîche. Many of the ingredients are from Marks & Spencer, but Diane cooks with flair and takes great care with her dining table. No smoking throughout.

Portaferry Hotel

The Strand, Portaferry, County Down BT22 1PE (028 4272 8231/www.portaferryhotel.com). **Rates** £100 double; additional £10 for extra bed in room. **Credit** AmEx, DC, MC, V.

With over 30 years in business, John and Marie Herlihy provide one of the few opportunities in Northern Ireland to experience a traditional, family-run hotel – in this case, a two-storey Georgian building with fabulous views of Strangford Lough. It lost some character during a 1980s makeover, which replaced a turf fire in the bar with gas, and old furnishings with some bland floral designs. However, the wind-whipped, sea-lashed front porch gives way to a warm, calm, comfortable interior of antique display cabinets, some well-chosen local art and a pleasant team of long-serving, loyal staff in waistcoats and black ties. John Herlihy makes no apologies for discouraging young families or rowdy folk, but others will experience deferential service and a wry sense of humour. The quality of food in the dining room depends on the ebb and flow of staff, but the seafood-focused menu can be extremely good and you can rely on a tasty breakfast and high tea. Curtains are drawn when it's dark, but before then you can enjoy mesmerising sunsets and the gliding of the ferry back and forth across the lough.

WHERE TO EAT & DRINK

Bay Tree

118 High Street, Holywood, County Down BT18 9HW (028 9042 1419/www.baytreeholy wood.com). **Lunch served** noon-2.30pm Mon-Sat. **Dinner served** 7-9.30pm Fri. **Main courses** £2.75-£7. **Set dinner** £19.50 2 courses, £22.50 3 courses. **Credit** MC, V.

The wait in the queue that forms punctually at noon is a small sacrifice for the outstandingly good food served in this café, which attracts the lion's share of the grey pound in Holywood as well as an appreciative following of young mothers. The delicious simplicity of savoury dishes such as pan-fried plaice with champ and pure parsley butter, or grilled goat's cheese with dressed puy lentils and toasted walnuts may make you want to linger. Be careful not to miss the coffee-tinged banoffi, strawberry and rhubarb crumble or the mountainous caramelised meringues: the Bay Tree's owner, Sue Farmer, has to be one of the best pastry cooks in the land. Open late for three-course menus on Friday nights. No smoking throughout.

Buck's Head

77 Main Street, Dundrum, County Down BT33 0LU (028 4375 1868). **Bar Open** noon-12.30am Mon-Sat; noon-10.30pm Sun. **Lunch served** *Winter* noon-2.30pm Tue-Sun. *Summer* noon-2.30pm daily. **Dinner served** *Winter* 7-9pm Tue-Sun. *Summer* 7-9pm daily. **Main courses** £7.50-£10.95. **Set dinner** £19.50 2 courses, £24.50 3 courses. **Credit** MC, V.

Once just a small pub with cosy horseshoe seating, the Buck's Head now fills its stunning dining room extension seven days a week. The set evening menu, which combines traditional favourites with global store-cupboard ingredients, isn't always as daring as the funky new design, but seafood from nearby Dundrum Bay makes for spankingly fresh tempura oysters with chilli, soy and sesame-oil dip. Mains, such as pan-fried lemon chicken with tagliatelle, fennel purée and basil oil, are carefully cooked and tasty. Giant, berry-strewn meringues or slabs of warmed brownie with a trail of thickened cream appeal to the sweet-toothed, but even better than dessert is the Buck's Head satin-smooth chocolate fudge with whole roasted hazelnuts, which comes with coffee. A hand-picked selection of wines from local merchants makes this a special place for dinner, but it's also great for pub lunches and high teas.

Curran's Bar

83 Strangford Road, Chapeltown, Ardglass, County Down BT30 7SP (028 4484 1332/ www.curransbar.net). Bar **Open** 11am-11pm Mon-Fri, Sun; 11am-1am Sat. **Meals served** 12.30-9pm daily. **Main courses** £9.95-£14.95. **Credit** MC, V.

On the road from Strangford to Ardglass, in the tiny settlement of Chapeltown, you'll find Curran's Bar. Originally built in 1791, it provided shelter and succour for the local community celebrating weddings or commiserating the loss of family to the church graveyard opposite or to boats taking emigrants from Sheepland harbour to America. In 1886 the snug became the Bishop's Room, set aside for Patrick McAlister, then Bishop of Down and Connor, and in the 1920s Edward Curran had his own porter-bottling room, but both have been replaced in the renovation, which created the current cosy conglomeration of firelit bars and opulent restaurant. An ambitiously lengthy menu serves typical pub fare from battered chicken strips to Thai prawn curry. Fresh seafood from Ardglass and dry-hung steaks are the specialities, though.

Strangford Lough

Dufferin Arms

35 High Street, Killyleagh, County Down BT30 9QF (028 4482 1182). **Lunch served** noon-2.30pm, **dinner served** 5.30-8.30pm Mon-Thur. **Meals served** noon-8.30pm Fri; noon-9.30pm Sat, Sun. **Main courses** £9.95-£12.75. **Credit** MC, V.

Originally a coaching inn, the Dufferin has been serving beers since 1803, and is now one of the best places for a pint of the black stuff, thanks to Jarvis, a 'gentleman's barman' who started in the trade at 14. Once a man's bar with 'no spitting or singing', as the memorabilia reminds us, the Dufferin now welcomes all and sundry. On Saturday afternoons, there are traditional folk and bluegrass sessions, when musicians can outnumber customers even though the small rooms and booth seating are packed. People travel for a bowl of the legendary chowder, Guinness and oysters, or specials such as pheasant casserole with chestnuts and mushrooms. You can also eat quite well in the basement restaurant, where an impressive effort is made to source local ingredients such as Finnebrogue venison and seafood from the lough.

Finnegan's Bar

1 Cook Brae, Kircubbin, County Down BT22 2SQ (028 4273 8282). Bar **Open** 11am-11pm Mon-Thur; 11am-1am Fri, Sat; 11am-midnight Sun. **Lunch served** noon-2pm Mon, Wed-Sat; noon-4pm Sun. **Dinner served** 6.30-8.30pm Fri, Sat. **Main courses** £12-£23. **Credit** MC, V.

Finnegan's may not look very inviting, but don't judge this place on appearances. The current owners have cleaned up the bar with a gentle tartan makeover, while maintaining the fringed light, burgundy velvet and glowing fire character of the rickety lounge. This spruce, modest dining room provides some of the best vernacular food you will find. Go for the gorgeously simple seafood – a pretty crab salad with scallions and lemony mayo, followed by seared sweet scallops with mustard butter, or – if you're very hungry – half a roast duck. It comes with a fluffy sage and thyme stuffing and crispy skin, sticky with Grand Marnier – not to mention the very typical complementary selection of three kinds of potatoes, and veg such as shredded leeks, squeaking in butter. Steamed lemon pudding is also gob-smackingly good. It's not cheap, but worth every penny.

Fontana

61A High Street, Holywood, County Down BT18 9AE (028 9080 9908). **Lunch served** noon-2.30pm Tue-Fri. **Dinner served** 5-9.30pm Tue-Fri; 6.30-10pm Sat. **Brunch served** 11am-3pm Sun. **Main courses** £13.50-£18.50. **Set meal** (lunch, 5-7pm Tue-Fri) £14.75 2 courses, £17.75 3 courses. **Credit** MC, V.

Fontana has a capable and inspired chef at the helm – Canadian Colleen Bennett, who followed celebrity schoolmate Jeanne Rankin to Northern Ireland to work at Roscoffs, and later Shanks. Bright and breezy, she runs a relaxed but enthu-siastic team from an open kitchen. The recently updated restaurant is gorgeous – modern flock wallpaper, bold purple orchids, Paul Smith-esque stripes and shimmering silks make for a smart, cool room that suits the easygoing sophistication of the menu and wine list. Fish cakes are petite patties of chunky seafood held together with a crisp, barely noticeable batter, and served with a crème fraîche tartare. Pink and tender haunch of venison comes with divine, rosemary-flecked polenta and meaty, slow-roasted tomatoes. Finish with coffee and cardamom crème brûlée or lemon panna cotta.

Hoops Coffee Shop

7 Main Street, Grey Abbey, County Down BT22 2NE (028 4278 8091). **Lunch served** 11am-5pm Wed-Sat. **Main courses** £2-£3.75. **No credit cards.**

Based in a courtyard of antique shops, Hoops is the place to garner strength over a good cup of tea and excellent own-baked cakes (try the orange drizzle) before you haggle. Decked out with antique pine chairs, blue gingham tablecloths and collections of copper pots, jelly moulds and blue-and-white crockery, it's a homely café with wood-burning stoves and a whiff of peat. Lunches such as the gratifying smoked salmon quiche, leek and potato pie, or baked ham salad are simple, but hit the spot.

Knotts Cake & Coffee Shop

49 High Street, Newtownards, County Down BT23 7HS (028 9181 9098). **Open/food served** 9am-5.30pm Mon-Sat. **Main courses** £5-£6.95. **Credit** MC, V.

Knotts is a successful and efficient coffee shop, and a good example of Northern Ireland's thriving bakeries. Here you'll find a sea of silver-haired, comfy-anoraked push-chair drivers, for Newtownards is the kind of place where grandparents mind the children. Once you pass the bakery queues for unique griddle breads, sickly sweet 'wee buns' and fresh cream swiss rolls, you'll join another fast-moving line for a self-service counter of country cooking. Squidgy sandwiches, stonking pies and lots of home-style savoury stuff – beef olives, Irish stew – are served alongside local renditions of fashionable salads and cliff-like chunks of sweet tarts and desserts. Tea is generally stronger than coffee, but cappucinos are competently made, and the vaulted glass-and-wood ceiling makes for a light and airy café. No smoking throughout.

Old Post Office

191 Killinchy Road, Lisbane, Comber, County Down BT23 6AA (028 9754 3335). **Open/food served** 9.30am-5pm Mon-Sat. **Main courses** £3.75-£6.25. **No credit cards.** Once a dwelling on the Londonderry estate and dating from the mid 19th century, the Old Post Office is a partially thatched warren of tearooms

Strangford Lough

with exposed tree-trunk beams, creamy rough-cast plaster and flagstone floors. Every room, mantelpiece and the old shop counter provide display space for local art and craft – including Eden spongeware pottery and a discreet number of potpourri packages. Stoves and open fires burning peat make it a cosy spot for winter months, while picnic benches and a garden provide a pleasant fair-weather setting. Cakes and desserts have an industrial appearance, but all food is fresh and made daily by the owners, who are also the village bakers. You can enjoy homely lunches of lasagne and salad or Irish stew. Decent cappuccinos accompany warm cinnamon swirls.

Paul Arthurs

66 Main Street, Kircubbin, County Down BT22 2SP (028 4273 8192/www.paul arthurs.com). Restaurant **Lunch served** noon-2.30pm Sun. **Dinner served** 5-9pm Tue-Thur; 5-9.30pm Fri, Sat. **Main courses** £12.95-£16.50. **Credit** AmEx, DC, MC, V.

In his determination to brighten streets and enlighten palates, Paul Arthurs has single-handedly created one of County Down's showcase restaurants. While he earns his bread and butter with a first-rate chippy on the ground floor, the upstairs restaurant in this flower-adorned, terracotta terrace offers sophisticated but simple bistro dining. With great connections to local creel fisherman, and through his butcher background, Arthurs sources fabulous raw materials, which he handles with energy, honesty and flair. Sautéed crab claws with garlic, chilli and coriander butter top the concise menu of dishes such as fresh gnocchi with saffron cream and tomato salsa, summer vegetable risotto with creamy gorgonzola or chargrilled rib-eye with chips and Café de Paris butter. Luxuries such as foie gras and lobster make the odd appearance, and food is laced with cream and butter, but try to keep room for gorgeously simple desserts. Accommodation is being added to the list of attractions: six en suite rooms will be available or nearing completion as this guide is published (June 2005), but there were no rates available at the time of writing.

Pebbles

12 Main Street, Grey Abbey, County Down BT22 2NE (028 4278 8031). **Lunch served** noon-2.30pm daily. **Dinner served** 7-9.30pm alternate Fri (phone for details). **Main courses** £9.50-£15. **Unlicensed. Corkage** £1.50. **Credit** MC, V.

Pebbles, a pretty but twee craft shop, also has a surprisingly good café and bistro on alternate Friday nights (call to check dates; reservations essential). The cakes and 'tray bakes' displayed on its marble slab are hefty and cloyingly sweet, and a daytime savoury menu veers from humongous mixed grills of steak, chicken, sausage and bacon, or burgers with wedges and dips to wild mushroom risotto with rocket. However, the deliciously smoky, oniony, creamy broth of a shellfish-packed chowder restores our faith and encourages us to return for a much more sophisticated evening choice, including warm parsley salad with haricot beans and tongue, baked hake with courgettes, lemon and thyme, and brown sugar meringues with sugared figs. Decent espresso coffees are also served. Bring your own wine. No smoking throughout.

Picnic

47 High Street, Killyleagh, County Down BT30 9QF (028 4482 8525). **Open/food served** *June-Sept* 7am-7pm Mon-Fri; 10am-4pm Sat, Sun. *Oct-May* 7am-7pm Mon-Fri; 10am-4pm Sat. **Main courses** £3.25-£7.50. **No credit cards**.

'I came here for a pint and stayed,' says deli owner John Dougherty of his adoptive home town, Killyleagh. Now, together with his Australian wife, Katherine – an ex-Melbourne restaurateur – and her cousins, he runs Picnic, a bustling all-day spot opposite the gates to Killyleagh Castle. In summer, a club of 30 cyclists visits every weekend for coffee and cakes on the outdoor benches, and all day, every day, locals pop into the cute shop, whose generously packed shelves, sturdy baskets, tiered cake stands and swinging blackboards lure customers with an irresistible choice of food. John is a passionate chef, making specials like the delicious, herby drop scones, served with mascarpone and roast red pepper, or the layered chilli beef and chickpea polenta pie. Baklava, Turkish delight and flourless chocolate cakes accompany fab coffees or own-made berrylicious smoothies. No smoking throughout.

Shanks

The Blackwood, Clandeboye Estate, Crawfordsburn Road, Bangor, County Down BT19 1GB (028 9185 3313/www.shanks restaurant.com). **Lunch served** 12.30-2.30pm Tue-Fri. **Dinner served** 7-10pm Tue-Sat. **Set meal** (lunch; dinner Tue-Thur) £21 2 courses, £25 3 courses. **Set dinner** £45 3 courses. **Credit** AmEx, MC, V.

For many, the Michelin-starred Shanks is the ultimate night out. Set in a golf club in beautiful woodland at Clandeboye Estate, its seriously smart, Conran-designed dining room enjoys lovely views. In the evening, with a twinkly piano in the upstairs bar and the animated chatter of enthusiastic diners, it's even more romantic. An A-list team of chefs led by the charismatic Robbie Millar produces painterly displays of delicious and rich food. Gratin of local scallops comes with an intense shallot purée, spinach, gruyère and chives. Turbot is paired with morels, pommes fondant, braised lettuce and tarragon velouté. The three-course menu (£45) ends with inspired desserts such as amaretti-stuffed pear with mascarpone, crème anglaise and chestnut honey. While an extensive, steeply priced wine list makes Shanks an extravagant experience, you can enjoy simpler set lunch and early supper menus midweek. Cool but flawless service. No smoking throughout.

Mid Kerry

Magnificent scenery, indulgent spas and the lord of the ring roads.

If you look at a map of Ireland, down at the bottom left you'll see fingers of land stretching into the Atlantic. The largest of these is County Kerry's Iveragh Peninsula, anchored at its landward side by the town of Killarney and bordered on the north by Dingle Bay, on the south by the estuary of the Kenmare River.

Killarney celebrated 250 years of tourism in 2004, and the reason people come here is simple: for the beautiful countryside and seascapes. Needless to say, it gets very busy in the summer season. Just to the south of Killarney is Kenmare, a village with a reputation for food and drink out of all proportion to its size.

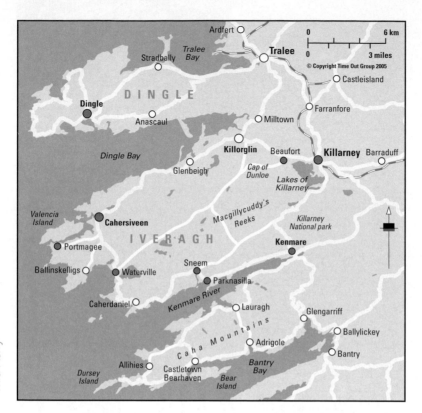

The peninsula is home to the highest range of hills in Ireland – Macgillycuddy's Reeks, topped out by the 3,414-foot Carrantuohill – and, adjacent to Killarney, the lakes and mountains of Killarney National Park (http://homepage.eircom. net/~knp). Here you'll find some of the most magnificent and rugged land in Ireland. At its core is the former Muckross Estate, which was gifted to the fledgling nation in 1932 by its American owners; this comprises Muckross House and 10,700 acres of land including the 'lake district' of Lough Leane, Muckross Lake (with the 1,655-foot Torc Mountain sitting directly above) and the Upper Lake. To the west behind Lough Leane are Tomies Mountain (2,411 feet) and Purple Mountain (2,730 feet). The combination of broken land, small islands in the lakes, varied waterscape and discrete high peaks is the kind of aesthetic package that you can look at all day. Hill tops aside, one of the best vantage points to take it all in is the Ladies' View on the N71 towards Kenmare (part of the Ring of Kerry). The road climbs up and away from the Upper Lake, heading south, until you come to a lay-by with the

inevitable café and shop, and a sign explaining that Queen Victoria's ladies-in-waiting were so impressed by the vista when they stopped here in 1861, it has been called the Ladies' View ever since. But keep going a few hundred yards up the road and there's another space to pull over, this time with no shop, café or sign.

The park proper is home to a wild herd of indigenous red deer, remnants of ancient oakwood and much else. There's a visitor centre at Muckross House (064 31440, www.muckross-house.ie), which sits on the shores of Muckross Lake. Completed in 1843 for MP Henry Arthur Herbert, the pile is also worth visiting for its well-preserved Victorian interior, including a grand, stag head-studded hall, a working kitchen and a library housing an eclectic collection of tomes. There is also an on-site restaurant, a garden centre and craft workshops. The ruins of the 15th-century Muckross Abbey are a short walk away.

Another historic structure graces the shore of Lough Leane: Ross Castle is a 15th-century tower with later additions. From here, you can take a boat trip to Innisfallen Island on the lough, thought

Accommodation	★★★★
Food & drink	★★★
Nightlife	
Shopping	
Culture	
Sights	★
Scenery	★★★★★

to be an important religious settlement from the seventh century, although the remains to be seen today date from the tenth at the earliest.

While the Killarney–Kenmare axis is engrossing in itself, most people venture further – around the Ring of Kerry. The name can be misleading in a country with so many prehistoric sites. Is it a huge stone circle? An ancient fort? No, it's actually the route round the Iveragh Peninsula, but it's a gorgeous tour. The entire journey is over 100 miles if you go on the main roads and much more if you opt for the fun version, exploring the interior on minor ones. There are mountains, bays, beaches, rivers, wide panoramas and the big old North Atlantic running uninterrupted all the way to Newfoundland. At the western extent, Valentia Island – peppered with megalithic tombs and standing stones – is definitely worth a visit. Take the summer ferry from Reenard Point near Cahersiveen (€1.50 or €5 with car, 8.15am-10pm daily April to end September, 066 9476141) or the bridge from Portmagee.

One thing about the Ring of Kerry, though: out of season, you can drive for ages and encounter very little that a city dweller would describe as 'traffic', so it doesn't matter if you do the route clockwise or anticlockwise. Summer is a different story. Organised coach tours set off in the morning and follow an anticlockwise route that makes life very hard for the contrarian motorist. It's much better to have a leisurely breakfast, give the coaches a decent head start, then set off at lunchtime. Doing the Ring that way, starting and finishing at Killarney, the last stretch of road is from Kenmare back to the main town. You climb up over the hill pass between the two, via the Ladies' View, then wind back past the Killarney lakes in an amazing finale to the day.

The Ring notwithstanding, the absolutely unmissable stretch of countryside around here is the Gap of Dunloe. This is a fabulously steep and dramatic hill pass between the massif of Macgillycuddy's Reeks to the west and the Purple and Tomies Mountains to the east. The numerous exposed outcrops, water tumbling off the rocks and small loughs give the impression that the glaciation

that formed the Gap only finished a couple of weeks ago. In winter it makes for the most spectacular drive, but in summer it's a haunt of the area's jaunting-car industry (pony-and-trap rides for tourists), so park at the northern 'entrance' to the Gap (by Kate Kearney's Cottage, a shop-café on the minor road up from Beaufort off the N72) and explore it on foot.

WHERE TO STAY
There are some utterly fabulous places to stay in Mid Kerry, but many of them close in the winter. The tourist business is so seasonal that even fairly major hotels can shut up shop for four to five months. We concentrate on establishments that open all year round, or if they do close, do so only for a few weeks after Christmas for an annual wash and brush-up. Fortunately that still leaves quite a choice. Around Killarney, in particular, the number of new hotels that have sprung up in recent years (with spas attached) shows that the area's visitor-magnet status endures, while Kenmare hosts two of the very best hotels in the whole of Ireland. The spa phenomenon is particularly handy if you've been doing the great outdoors and need a massage or the ministering jets of a hydrotherapy pool.

Meanwhile, if you do visit in summer and want some more accommodation options, you could try Caragh Lodge, a small country house overlooking the achingly lovely Caragh Lake (066 9769115, www.caraghlodge.com, €195-€350 double), or Coolclogher House, a very pukka manor just outside Killarney (064 35996, www.coolclogherhouse.com, €75-€95 B&B). Otherwise, Killarney is stuffed with hotels, while Kenmare is more a centre for guesthouses, with some notable exceptions (see p390). Finally, on a further-flung part of the Ring of Kerry, the Derrynane Hotel by Caherdaniel (066 9475136, www.derrynane.com, €99-€159 double) has an unprepossessing 1960s-motel look, but it's right on the shoreline with an outdoor pool, and the proprietors are grand people. The Butlers Arms at Waterville (066 9474144, www.manorhousehotels.com, €140-€200) is the more upmarket option out that way.

TOURIST INFORMATION
Dialling code from the UK: 00 353

Killarney
Beech Road, Killarney (064 31633/ www.corkkerry.ie).

Seasonal offices in **Cahersiveen** (066 9472589), **Kenmare** (064 41233) and **Waterville** (066 9474646).
www.killarney.ie

Mid Kerry

Aghadoe Heights Hotel & Spa

Lakes of Killarney, Kerry (064 31766/www. aghadoeheights.com). Bar **Meals served** 11am-9pm daily. **Main courses** €15-€20. *Restaurant* **Lunch served** 12.30-2pm Sun. **Dinner served** 6.30-9.30pm daily. **Set buffet** (Sun) €45. **Set menu** €60 5 courses. **Rates** €230-€350 double; €450-€650 suite; €950-€2,000 penthouse. **Credit** AmEx, DC, MC, V.
This hotel is just north-west of Killarney, off the N22 and overlooking Lough Leane and the mountains. On the minor road that takes you there, you pass thatched cottages, the old Aghadoe burial ground and vistas that make you go 'ooh' – then suddenly the hotel's new Scandinavian-chic façade hoves into view (exterior and interior have been substantially refurbished quite recently). It's a contemporary and opulent pile, with marbled entrance hall, light, airy restaurant (Fredericks) with white seating, and plush, modern rooms. Even the swimming pool has a view, while the hotel makes a big deal of its Aveda Concept Resort Spa. This offers all the usual facials and massages but also veers off into Himalayan rejuvenation therapy and precious stone therapy, to name but a couple.

The Brehon

Killarney (064 30700/www.thebrehon.com). **Dinner served** 6.30-9.30pm daily. **Main courses** €20-€27. **Rates** €170-€260 double; €320-€410 suites. **Credit** AmEx, MC, V.
As you drive south out of Killarney with Lough Leane and the mountains on your right, there are any number of hotels – but this brash 2004 addition to the club is the stand-out. Critics might say its frontage is more suited to an economic development area somewhere on the coast of the South China Sea rather than opposite Killarney National Park, but other establishments along this strip are hardly traditional, just less bulky and obvious. From the exposed stone behind reception to the creamy beige colour scheme in the dining room, via the modern bar and the dotty signature fabric used on seating, bolsters and bed covers, everything about the Brehon shouts, 'We're new and trendy and international.' The Thai-flavoured spa, Angsana, fits in nicely with the general theme. As you emerge from the lift to its basement home, it smells like the Asian spice section of your local wholefood shop. Specials here include the Ayurvedic Rainshower treatment and the Arabic-influenced Rasul Special, involving a mud application in a steam room. There's no swimming pool but the spa does have a 'vitality pool' for hydrotherapy. (Note: the Brehon is a conference venue, so you could be having a quiet drink in the bar and suddenly be surrounded by 150 travel agents.)

Great Southern Hotel

East Avenue Road, Killarney, Kerry (064 31262/www.greatsouthernhotels.com). **Dinner served** 6.30-9pm daily. **Set menu** €38 4 courses. **Rates** €150-€280 double; €350-€500 suite. **Credit** AmEx, DC, MC, V.

Great Southern Hotels started off as a Victorian railway hotel group and still has nine properties around Ireland. As you walk up to the entrance of its Killarney establishment with classical columns and plaque unveiled by Taoiseach Bertie Ahern in 2004 (celebrating the hotel's 150th anniversary), you know this is going to be a very traditional stop-over. It stands as an old-school riposte to the contemporary styling of more recent arrivals on the local hotel scene, although they have fitted in a very swish fine-dining room called Peppers (caesar salad then dover sole, perhaps, but served up in a chic space), a swimming pool and basic spa. This latter facility does facials and body treatments, although none of the more exotic offerings that characterise some other hotel spas in the area. To sum up: a refuge from modernist overkill.

VILLAGE FARE

Although Kenmare is famed for its restaurant complement, a number of them are fairly informal places – more like pubs that have evolved into eateries thanks to the forces of tourist-driven natural selection. PF McCarthy (14 Main Street, 064 41516) is the modern example: a small and tidy blond-wood affair with the bar area at the front and seating behind, where you could start with seafood chowder or broccoli and blue cheese soup, then try a simple baked lemon sole or salmon fritters with cider and apple sauce for mains. The Purple Heather (Henry Street, 064 41016), meanwhile, has been run by the same family, the O'Connells, since 1964. It's a lot more traditional, nicely cared for, and has a long-standing reputation for the quality of its dishes. There's good seafood soup, pâtés (salmon or chicken liver with Cumberland sauce), crabmeat comes with assorted salads, open sandwiches and even Guinness fruit cake to round off. The Purple Heather has a sister establishment a few doors along (Packie's, Henry Street, 064 41508) that's more restaurant-like. Finally, the Horseshoe (3 Main Street, 064 41553) is another traditional-style venue with a friendly, rustic vibe; it's where you go for a good honest beef and Guinness stew (although it does close for a couple of months after Christmas). Crowley's (26 Henry Street, 064 41472) is a must-visit Kenmare drinking pub; order a Guinness and get a taste of the true Kerry.

Great Southern Hotel

Parknasilla, nr Sneem, Kerry (064 45122/ www.greatsouthernhotels.com) **Lunch served** noon-5pm, **dinner served** 7-9pm daily. **Set menu** €45 3 courses. **Rates** €240-€400 double; €400-€450 suite. **Credit** AmEx, DC, MC, V.

Sister establishment to the Killarney incarnation, this Great Southern outpost is about 12 miles west of Kenmare on the Kenmare River estuary; the nearest village of any size is Sneem, on the Ring of Kerry. Like its Killarney sibling, this hotel gives a real flavour of what holidays hereabouts were like for the more genteel visitor back when it opened in 1895. George Bernard Shaw even had nice things to say about it, which is doubtless why its humongous, traditional-style dining room is called the Pygmalion. The odd piece of contemporary art around the place is a nice touch, and there are extensive subtropical grounds, things to do (tennis, golf, archery), an indoor pool plus an outdoor Canadian hot tub overlooking the fractal and scenic stretch of coast where the hotel sits. Location, location, location.

Killarney Park Hotel

Town Centre, Killarney, Kerry (064 35555/ www.killarneyparkhotel.ie). **Dinner served** 7-9pm daily. **Set menu** €57.50 4 courses. **Rates** €260-€385 double; €360-€750 suite. **Credit** AmEx, MC, V.

Easily spotted, this is the big yellow thing in the town centre; the multiple-prize-winning hotel is

Macgillycuddy's Reeks

Mid Kerry

more contemporary on the inside than might be expected, even though the building only dates from the early 1990s. The log fire in the lounge and the restrained bar with its muted lighting ooze relaxation. Indeed, the most ostentatious public area is probably the main dining room, the Park, and even then not in an overwhelming way. Without getting too Californian about it, the Killarney Park has a great vibe. The rooms are contemporary but somehow also lush, while the spa extends beyond mere facials and massages to the likes of healing bath or stone ceremonies and indulgent 'spa ritual' packages tailored to men, pregnant women and jet-lagged travellers, among others. At 20m, the pool is a decent size if you just want to swim.

Killarney Plaza

Kenmare Place, Killarney, Kerry (064 21100/ www.killarneyplaza.com). **Lunch served** 12.30-2pm, **dinner served** 6-9.30pm daily. **Main courses** (lunch) €6-€15. **Set dinner** €35 4 courses. **Rates** €240-€500 double; €600 suite. **Credit** AmEx, DC, MC, V.

Marble in the foyer? Check. Stained glass artwork thing on the landing a little way up the main staircase? Check. Mosaic monogram decorating the reception desk? Check. Molton Brown spa? Check. If there was ever a modern hotel (2002) that pours on the ostentation, it's this one. Ditto the rooms, which have an aspirational, modern take on traditional luxury. It's either vulgar or lush – there is no middle opinion. Housed in a big white building in the centre of town, the Plaza offers three eating options (the Café du Parc bar, Petrus fine-dining room and Mentons bistro), while the Molton Brown spa, which opened in 2004, received rave reviews for treatments from the Equabalance facial with Egyptian jasmine oil to full-on, signature 'Earth, Fire and Water' therapy, incorporating mud, dry heat and steam. In the off-season, there are some decent bed-and-fed deals for visitors who stay two or three nights.

Park Hotel Kenmare

Kenmare, Kerry (064 41200/www.park kenmare.com). **Lunch served** 11am-6pm, **dinner served** 7-9pm daily. **Main courses** (lunch) €7.50-€18. **Set dinner** €69 4 courses. **Rates** €316-€434 double; €392-€526 suite. **Credit** AmEx, DC, MC, V.

This grand hotel once belonged to the Great Southern group, which sold it on in the 1970s. It was eventually bought by Francis Brennan, who redeveloped the premises in sympathetic style; his brother John is general manager. Over the last couple of decades, the Park Hotel Kenmare has been known – simply – as one of the very best in Ireland. The decor is in keeping with its late Victorian origins, although some of the furniture and antique pieces added in recent years are lovely, even to a non-expert. Service is affable, the fine-dining room is absolutely top class, quite possibly the best in the South-west, and the place

certainly has enough going for it to make for a memorable stay. But in 2004, a feature was added that stands out as a jewel in the crown: Sàmas spa, acclaimed as one of the top facilities of its kind in Europe. In a separate building (accessed through the basement by guests), it's a modern departure from the rest of the hotel. Treatments aside, just spending an hour in the sauna, steam room and outdoor hydrotherapy pool (overlooking the Kenmare River) is an experience you'll surely want to repeat.

Sheen Falls Lodge

Kenmare, Kerry (064 41600/www.sheen fallslodge.ie). Bistro **Dinner served** (Easter-Nov) 6.30-10pm daily. **Main courses** €15-€23. *Restaurant* **Dinner served** 7-9.30pm daily. **Set menu** €65 3 courses. **Main courses** €33-€38. **Rates** €280-€425 double; €495-€1,835 suite. **Closed** Jan. **Credit** AmEx, DC, MC, V.

Sitting on the south side of the Kenmare River, just a few minutes from Kenmare itself, this country pile has quite a history. Apart from its local associations with Sir William Petty and his acquisition of Irish estates in the 17th century (he was Cromwell's physician-general), there has been a fishing lodge here since the 18th century, which was eventually incorporated into the current building. Given the state of the luxury tourist industry in south-west Ireland in the 1980s, what prompted Danish shipping millionaire Bent Høyer to buy the place and transform it into a top-end hotel is anyone's guess. But the establishment has subsequently developed an international reputation, and many are grateful that Mr Høyer made the effort.

The river's white-water falls are right outside (the hotel has fishing rights). There are stables on site and a large estate to explore; there's an indoor pool and a spa that steers away from more outlandish therapies; the hotel even has its own helicopter pad (and it gets used). The posh restaurant is La Cascade, which operates at an elevated standard, while Oscar's Bistro is where you go for moules marinière, pasta or a steak. Rooms are generally classic with some minimalist Danish furniture and marble bathrooms. You can even tour the wine cellar with its 13,000-plus bottles or participate in a tasting. But the best thing about the place is sitting in the bar, perfectly relaxed with a whisky in hand, and watching the water fall down the Sheen.

WHERE TO EAT & DRINK

Some of the best places to eat in Mid Kerry are in top hotels – notably the Park Hotel Kenmare (*see above*), the Sheen Falls Lodge (*see above*), the Aghadoe Heights (*see p388*) and the Killarney Park (*see p389*) – but as these have already been touched on, the listings below concentrate on interesting places outside a hotel environment. Bustling

Killarney offers quite a few year-round options. Kenmare, meanwhile, is famously said to have more restaurants than pubs, but since the village only comprises three streets (with eateries on all of them), it's not quite the boast it appears to be. On the Ring of Kerry, good restaurants are, understandably, more spread out and some places curtail their hours in the winter or hibernate altogether. One such gem worth seeking out in the high season is the Lime Tree in Kenmare's Shelbourne Street (064 41225, www.limetreerestaurant.com, open Easter-Nov). Set back from the road in a 19th-century townhouse, and with an art gallery attached, it's one of the village's destination dining spots with a modern European approach. Out on the western reaches of the Ring of Kerry, Paddyfrogs in Waterville (066 9478766, opposite the Waterville Craft Market) is open March to October, give or take a week or two. Launched in 2004, it's a Franco-Irish venture in a new building with a modern stone interior. It has outdoor seating at the

back for those long summer evenings, and if you're wondering about the name, the couple who run it are local woman Sandra Foster and chef Max Legeuet from France.

Bistro Blue

Derreensillagh, Castle Cove, Kerry (064 45588). **Dinner served** *July-Sept* 7-9pm Tue-Sun. *Oct-June* 7-9pm Fri, Sat. **Main courses** €15.50-€19.50. **Rates** €80-€100 double. **Credit** MC, V.

Alyson Liles moved to this south-west stretch of the Iveragh Peninsula in 2003 to open a bed and breakfast, then added a small bistro later the same year. It's a very small and homely establishment in a whitewashed farmhouse cottage (20 people will pack it out), with stone walls, blue-and-white 'oilskin' tablecloths and a generally welcoming atmosphere. Three typical courses would be Thai fish and prawn soup with coconut to start; organic venison casserole with cranberries, vegetables and champ as a main; spicy apple crumble for dessert. The home-style cooking is of a good standard and Alyson's enthusiasm runs to specials – often seafood, given the location – such as fillet of

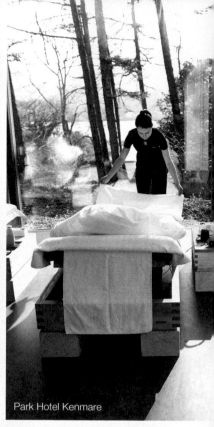

Park Hotel Kenmare

plaice with black butter on spinach. Chocolate fans will appreciate her special dessert of chocolate meringue with chocolate and vanilla ice-cream, topped with chocolate sauce and almonds. Given the size of this operation, the opening times do tend to be seasonal and pretty flexible depending on just how many tourists are around, but it serves dinner on Friday and Saturday evenings in the winter.

The Club

Market Square, Kenmare, Kerry (064 42958/ www.theclubrestaurant.com). **Dinner served** *mid Feb-mid Mar* 6-10pm Fri-Sun; *mid Mar-May, Sept-mid Dec* 6-10pm Wed-Sun; *June-Aug, mid Dec-mid Jan* 6-10pm daily. **Closed** mid Jan-mid Feb. **Main courses** €13.95-€20. **Set dinner** (6-7.30pm) €20 4 courses (not available Sat in June-Aug). **Credit** MC, V.

Sister establishment to the Cooperage in Killarney, the Club is a relatively recent addition to Kenmare's main square (late 2003). The look is very current with clean lines, leather seating and blond-wood partitions. While the kitchen offers some modern takes on traditional Irish dishes (starters like smoked haddock cooked in milk with onion and potato, topped with cheese), its international leanings are dominant, whether reflected in a starter of frogs' legs in batter with mixed herb mayonnaise, or mains from Hungary, Italy and elsewhere. A Spanish-style main course might involve roasted saddle of boar with prunes,

oranges, onions, fresh rosemary, cognac glaze and game jus; a French example would be slow-roasted pheasant in red wine stuffed with sage and leek. The seafood specials are always worth considering too (pan-fried monkfish, butterfish or sea bass).

The Cooperage

Old Market Lane, Killarney, Kerry (064 37716/www.thecooperagerestaurant.com). **Lunch served** 12.30-2.30pm Wed-Sat. **Dinner served** 6-9.30pm Mon-Fri, Sun; 6-10pm Sat. **Main courses** €18-€22. **Set dinner** (6-7.30pm) €20 3 courses incl coffee. **Credit** MC, V.

The Cooperage opened in 1998 and has established itself as one of the town's favourite contemporary eateries. It's a modern bistro with stone-tiled floor, black seating and tables, and art, including some large photo installations of 'chef at work'. The bar area is very much in the style-bar mould. Starters include chunky, country-style seafood bisque, and steamed, shelled, local mussels, tossed in white wine and cream and served in a filo basket. For mains there is grilled sirloin with mushroom, chive and crispy bacon sauce, or perhaps poached fillet of salmon with a light muscadet sauce, chives and sweet pimientos. And given the twinkling blue lights in the window, it's surely appropriate to go for blueberry ice-cream with blueberry compote in puff pastry for dessert? The Cooperage's sister restaurant is the Club in Kenmare.

Gaby's Seafood Restaurant

27 High Street, Killarney, Kerry (064 32519). **Dinner served** 6-10pm Mon-Sat. **Closed** mid Feb-Mar. **Main courses** €24-€44. **Credit** AmEx, DC, MC, V.

It's warm, it's woody, and it's the kind of establishment you'll probably take an instant shine to. But it's not all seafood so you can feel free to visit with a fish-averse friend or partner (there are vegetarian and meat options – rack of Kerry lamb, for example). But as for the wet stuff, you could start with half a dozen Atlantic rock oysters or a cassoulette of prawns and monkfish. Mains might include black sole meunière or grilled lobster, while there are also seafood platters including the Kerry shellfish option, which comprises five oysters, crab claws, half a lobster and assorted other crustacea as available. Gaby's Seafood also has a decent choice of wines and a much-loved crème brûlée for dessert.

Jam

77 High Street, Killarney, Kerry (064 31441). **Food served** 8am-5pm Mon-Sat. **Snacks** €5-€7. **Credit** DC, MC, V.

Nothing highfalutin or fancy here, Jam is simply a modern bakery-café where you can grab a decent coffee and some top-standard snack food like scones, brilliant quiche, filled pastries, sand-

wiches and even some gluten-free items for those who want them. A welcome alternative to the fuss of a restaurant at lunchtime. There's also a branch at 6 Henry Street, Kenmare (064 41591).

Mulcahy's

16 Henry Street, Kenmare, Kerry (064 42383). **Dinner served** *Nov-Apr* 6-10pm Mon, Thur-Sun. *May-Oct* 6-10pm daily. **Main courses** €18-€28. **Credit** MC, V.
A modern, designery restaurant where chef Bruce Mulcahy takes his cooking very seriously and shows a definite international flair. That means a starter like spring roll of duck confit with Asian noodle salad and chilli jam; pan-fried black sole on the bone, warm potato salad, mascarpone and tomato and brown butter sauce as a main; then caramelised cashew nut crème brûlée for dessert. The two luxury hotels notwithstanding (Sheen Falls Lodge and the Park Hotel Kenmare), this is among the best two or three stand-alone establishments in the village. Mulcahy's restaurant is also attached to a very good bed and breakfast outfit (Virginia's, 064 41021, www.virginias-kenmare.com).

Old Presbytery

Cathedral Place, Killarney, Kerry (064 30555/ www.oldpresbytery.com). **Dinner served** *Apr-Oct* 6.30-10pm Mon, Wed-Sun. *Nov-Mar* 6.30-10pm Wed-Sun. **Main courses** €18.50-€25.90. **Set menu** (6.30-7pm) €23 2 courses incl coffee. **Closed** Jan. **Credit** AmEx, DC, MC, V.
This sits opposite the Pugin-designed St Mary's cathedral in a four-square and proper Georgian townhouse. Inside, the dining room is sympathetically contemporary without making too much of a fuss, while the food is modern European with the odd genuflection to Asia. Three courses could entail chicken liver pâté with toasted brioche and red onion marmalade to start; pan-fried John Dory with braised fennel and Japanese dressing as a main; banana parfait with mango sorbet for dessert. The proprietors, Gerry Browne and Mary Rose Hickey, only tend to close for a few weeks in the winter for annual holidays.

O'Neill's – the Point Bar

Reenard Point, nr Cahersiveen, Kerry (066 9472165). **Dinner served** *Dec-Apr* 6.30-9.30pm Fri-Sun. *May-Nov* 5.30-10pm daily. **Main courses** €19-€23. **No credit cards**.
Around a mile south of the centre of Cahersiveen village on the N70, at the north-western extent of the Ring of Kerry, there's a turning to Reenard Point where the (seasonal) ferry chugs across to Valentia Island. Follow that minor road down its 1½-mile length to the end and there isn't anything here except a fantastic view (where the mainland meets the sea with Valentia Island and Beginish Island very close by), a seafood business and a

pub: the Point Bar. This latter establishment is a light seaweed green and slate on the outside, wooden and neat on the inside, and gets very busy indeed in peak season when tourists head this way to make the ferry hop. Catch it when it's quieter though, and it's a splendid place for a pint or some pub grub involving seafood.

QC's Seafood Bar & Restaurant

3 Main Street, Cahersiveen, Kerry (066 947 2244/www.qcbar.com). **Lunch served** *Easter-Oct* 12.30-2.30pm Mon-Sat. **Dinner served** *Easter-Oct* 6.30-9.30pm daily. *Nov-Easter* 6.30-9.30pm Fri-Sun. **Main courses** €12-€25. **Credit** (€25 minimum) MC, V.
Bang in the centre of Cahersiveen village and much recommended by just about everyone, QC's is a woody, stone-walled, seafood bistro affair run by Andrew and Kate Cooke. You can eat in the bar, the restaurant area or (new since 2004) an outdoor space at the rear of the premises. Dishes such as crab, a baby squid with citrus dressing, or some lightly battered hake with melted butter are much raved about, but the establishment has a Spanish-style charcoal grill that produces rather fantastic signature offerings like char-grilled crab claws, prawns and more. (The wine list leans towards Spain as well.) If you fancy a starter as a main course, they'll do you a bigger portion. It's important to watch out for the specials, and although fishophobes can be catered for (lamb, steak), if you're going to come here you really should make the most of the stuff from that ocean on the doorstep.

Treyvaud's

62 High Street, Killarney, Kerry (064 33062 /www.treyvaudsrestaurant.com). **Meals served** *Mar-Sept* noon-10pm daily. *Oct-Nov* noon-10pm Wed-Sun. *Dec-Feb* noon-10pm Thur-Sun. **Main courses** €15.95-€24.95. **Set lunch** (Sun) €19.95 3 courses incl coffee. **Credit** MC, V.
A relatively recent addition to the Killarney scene, Treyvaud's is easily identifiable by its predominantly yellow-and-red frontage on the busy High Street. The colour scheme continues in the modern interior with yellow walls and red seating offset against dark wood tables. The restaurant runs to salads and light meals at lunchtime (fish cakes, a simple omelette) as well as full-on dinners in the evening when its sense of adventure becomes more apparent. That might mean shredded duck confit with Irish cream cheese and beetroot carpaccio to start, then pan-fried fillet of ostrich with caramelised shallots and red wine jus as a main. The place is run by brothers Paul and Mark Treyvaud, whose dad Michel enjoyed quite a career as a chef – he still helps out at their annual 'game night' in November. If you're in the area and don't get enough wild boar or roast rabbit in your diet, this is the evening for you.

Index

Index

Numbers in **bold** indicate the key entry for the topic; numbers in *italics* indicate illustrations.

C

FIVE STAR RATINGS

★★★★★

Index

Index

H

I

J

K

L

Index

M

N

Index

Index

W

Y

Z

ACCOMMODATION

RESTAURANTS, PUBS & CAFÉS

Advertisers' Index

Please refer to relevant sections for addresses / telephone numbers

Festivals & Events

Dates are given where available; for the latest information, see the relevant website.

JANUARY

London

New Year's Day Parade (1 January)
If you like a good parade, the capital's New Year effort is a tough act to beat. Regally called a 'celebration of nations', it features more than 10,000 performers from 20 different countries strutting their stuff around central London.
www.londonparade.co.uk

Glasgow

Celtic Connections
The UK's top Celtic music festival, featuring well-known acts and the best new talent in a mix of concerts, ceilidhs, workshops, club nights and talks.
www.celticconnections.com

FEBRUARY

London

Chinese New Year Celebrations (Sunday after Chinese New Year)
A bright spectacle of dances, martial arts, music and costume fills the West End, centred around Leicester Square and Trafalgar Square.
www.chinatownchinese.com

London Fashion WeekEnd (Weekend after London Fashion Week)
Here is the ordinary mortal's chance to crash the glamour of Fashion Week as retailers and fashionistas set up shop at the Duke of York's Headquarters on the King's Road.
www.londonfashionweek.co.uk

Manchester

Manchester International Short Film Festival
With 300 films on show, this is Britain's largest independent film festival, known for its cutting-edge spirit.
www.kinofilm.org.uk

MARCH

London (Barbican)

Australian Film Festival
The only European festival devoted solely to Australian cinema.
www.barbican.org.uk/australianfilm

Glasgow

Glasgow Comedy Festival
Glasgow is very proud of its new comedy festival, which hosts almost 200 events throughout the city, including big-shot stand-up, sketch shows, film, drama and workshops.
www.glasgowcomedyfestival.com

Exeter

Exeter Festival of South West Food & Drink
Clotted cream is just the beginning of Devon's gastronomic delights. This festival aims to teach the younger generation the importance of sourcing meat and produce, as students and kids are encouraged to talk to farmers and chefs.
www.tasteofthewest.co.uk

APRIL

Bury St Edmunds

East Anglian Beer Festival (starts fourth Wednesday in April)
With 80 different ales, this festival aims to provide beer from every brewery in East Anglia. Takes places in the Corn Exchange.
www.camra.org.uk

London

Chelsea Art Fair

For a few days, Chelsea Old Town Hall becomes home to one of the best collections of contemporary and 20th-century art in Europe. Roughly 40 well-known galleries show off paintings, ceramics, drawings and prints. *www.rbkc.gov.uk*

Bute, Scotland

Isle of Bute Jazz Festival

Jazz sessions from morning till night (Thur-Mon). Saturday there are also marching bands, a street parade and jazz cruises. *www.butejazz.com*

Speyside

Speyside Whisky Festival

The festival brings out a quarter of a million drams of malt and single-malt whisky, plus a merry selection of entertainment. *www.spiritofspeyside.com*

MAY

Cumbria

Cumbria & Lake District Food & Drink Festival

One of the best food and drink festivals around. *www.cumbriafoodfestival.net*

Bury St Edmunds

Bury St Edmunds Festival

A major East Anglia event, with top classical, jazz, comedy and dance performers. There are theatre, walks, workshops and exhibitions too. *www.buryfestival.co.uk*

Exeter

Devon County Show

This is a major agriculture event showcasing livestock and horticulture, but it's also got Roman chariot racing, parachute displays, axe-racing and chainsaw-sculpting. *www.devoncountyshow.co.uk*

Brecon Beacons

Guardian Hay Festival

The pinnacle of British literary festivals, the Hay Festival is crammed with celebrity authors, influential critics, fine wines, storytelling and comedy. Hay is an idyllic market town with 39 bookshops for its population of 1,500. Tickets for the festival go on sale the preceding spring – check in winter 2005 for the 2006 dates. *www.hayfestival.com*

Tetbury

Annual Woolsack Races & Traditional Street Fair (Bank Holiday Monday)

Something you'd only ever find in the country – watch competitors race up and down Gumstool Hill carrying 60lb woolsacks. *www.tetburyonline.co.uk*

London

London Comedy Festival

Ten days of Britain's biggest, most diverse and star-studded comedy festival. Check the website for 2006 dates. *www.londoncomedyfestival.com*

Chelsea Flower Show

Held on the 11-acre grounds of the Royal Hospital in Chelsea, this is the mother of all flower shows. *www.rhs.org.uk*

Regent's Park Open Air Theatre

Sitting outdoors in Regent's Park watching Shakespeare and sipping wine is a gorgeous way to spend a summer evening in London. In 2005 the plays are *Twelfth Night* and *Cymbeline*. *www.londontheatre.co.uk*

JUNE

Manchester

X.Trax Showcase

A vibrant, large-scale meeting of Britain's Caribbean, Asian and African artists. They show off their work in a broad range of indoor and outdoor shows, installations, music and street performance. *www.xtrax.org.uk*

Isle of Wight

Old Gaffers Classic Boat Festival

The island is a boaties' paradise in the summer. Old Gaffers is a unique chance to inspect and delight in 100 old gaff-rigged boats. *www.yarmoutholdgaffersfestival.co.uk*

Isle of Wight Music Festival

An excellent non-nautical reason to come
to the island in summer. The IOW festival
always scores several rock heavyweights.
www.isleofwightfestival.org

Isle of Wight's Round the Island Yacht Race (fourth Saturday in June)

This yacht race is one of the biggest of its kind
in the world. Almost 2,000 yachts and 12,000
sailors set sail on a 50-nautical-mile chase
west from Cowes.
www.roundtheisland.org.uk

Woodstock, Oxfordshire

Blenheim Palace Flower Show

Blemheim Palace gardens are resplendent
with gorgeous and ornate flower arrangements
for the duration of this show.
*http://blenheimpalaceflowershow.co.uk/
front.htm*

Aldeburgh, Suffolk

Aldeburgh Festival

Music combines the best of old and new
classical, played by top musicians in a
gorgeous setting.
www.aldeburgh.co.uk

Devon

Gold Coast Oceanfest

Saunton Sands, Croyde Bay and Woolacombe
Sands are taken over by dudes and dudettes
in trunks and bikinis riding the waves.
www.goldcoastoceanfest.co.uk

Exeter

Exeter Summer Festival

Classical, jazz, swing, folk, opera, blues and
pop are on tap at the Exeter summer bash, and
there is also the usual summer array of visual
art and drama.
www.exeter.gov.uk

London

Meltdown, South Bank

A celebrity artist curates the festival each
year, choosing his or her own line-up. In
2004, Morrissey ran the show, which
included the Libertines and the Ordinary
Boys. Check website nearer the time for
2006 dates.
www.rfh.org.uk/meltdown

Wimbledon (26 June-9 July 2006)

The grand slam to end all grand slams,
as long as the rain stays away. From
Henman Hill to Centre Court, the excitement
is intense – and the crowds are immense,
so join the public ticket ballot or be prepared
to queue.
www.wimbledon.org

Glastonbury, Somerset

Glastonbury Festival

The UK's most famous festival is taking a year
off in 2006, but the musical mudbath is due to
return in 2007.
www.glastonburyfestivals.co.uk

JULY

Ludlow

Ludlow Festival (25 June-10 July 2005)

Open-air Shakespeare in the grounds of the
castle, plus opera, dance, poetry, music and
a fireworks display.
www.ludlowfestival.co.uk

Chichester

Chichester Festivities (27 June-11 July 2005)

The festival, based around the city's
Norman cathedral, features talks, walks,
candelit concerts, sculpture, classical
music, jazz, comedy, street arts, fireworks
and more.
www.chifest.org.uk

Burford, Oxfordshire

Cornbury Music Festival (9-10 July 2005)

A brave contribution to the hectic summer
music scene, Cornbury is still in its infancy
but hopes to attract around 14,000 people this
year. The 2005 line-up includes Elvis Costello
& the Imposters, Jools Holland, Will Young
and Amy Winehouse.
www.cornburyfestival.com

Cirencester

Cotswold Show & Country Fair (9-10 July 2005)

The Cotswolds' homespun charm is put on jolly (and large-scale) display – livestock, arts and crafts, gastronomic delights and much more. Be warned: the event attracts upwards of 30,000 people each summer.
www.cotswoldshow.co.uk

Harrogate

Harrogate International Festival (21 July-5 August 2005)
A week of classical, jazz and world music performed by contemporary stars – 2005 will include performances by BBC Young Musician of the Year Nicola Benedetti and the Classical Brit Award Winner Freddy Kempf.
www.harrogate-festival.org.uk

Harrogate Crime Writing Festival (21-24 July 2005)
Runs in tandem with the International Festival. The 2005 speakers include Ruth Rendell, Michael Connelly and Alexander McCall Smith.
www.harrogate-festival.org.uk/crime

Plymouth

World Powerboat Championship (15-17 July 2005)
The brightest stars of the powerboating world race each other for the title of World Powerboat Champion – at speeds nearing 160mph.
www.chrisparsonageracing.com

Sandringham, North Norfolk Coast

Sandringham Flower Show (28-29 July 2005)
The Queen's Norfolk retreat is even more splendid than normal when it's ablaze with flowers. Check the website for other events on at Sandringham.
www.sandringhamestate.co.uk

London

95.8 Capital FM Party in the Park (around 11 July 2005)
Summer in the city is all about partying in parks. Here you can see the likes of Lenny Kravitz, Sugababes and Anastacia belting out tunes in Hyde Park. Book well in advance and check the website for exact dates.
www.capitalfm.com/pitp

Westonbirt, Tetbury

July concert/fireworks (30 July 2005)
Westonbirt Arboretum hosts various events and festivals throughout the year. This is one of the finest.
www.forestry.gov.uk

AUGUST

Torbay, South Devon

Kick Up the Arts (first Thursday in August)
Crammed with arty goodies and events, the Kick Up the Arts festival gains extra points for its stunning location at Paignton Green, overlooking the bay.
www.englishrivierafestivals.co.uk

Isle of Wight

Cowes Week (30 July-6 August 2005)
August on the Isle of Wight is heralded by the longest-running, most prestigious and largest sailing regatta in the world.
www.skandiacowesweek.co.uk

Sidmouth, Devon

Sidmouth International Festival (30 July-6 August 2005)
Europe's largest celebration of international folk music sweeps into town for a week every summer, with around 600 concerts, dances and exhibitions.
www.sidmouthfestival.com

Eastnor Castle, Herefordshire

Big Chill (5-7 August 2005)
Held at Eastnor Castle in the Malvern Hills, the Big Chill is a rather grown-up festival featuring music, art, dance and film. It always sells out.
www.bigchill.net

Brecon Beacons

Brecon Jazz Festival (12-14 August 2005)
The Welsh market town swings every summer with big names and fresh talent, showing off their scat-and-sax skills at various venues. Last year's event featured

the likes of Amy Winehouse, Claire Martin, Kenny Wheeler and Dennis Rollins.
www.breconjazz.co.uk

Manchester

Manchester Gay Pride
(19-29 August 2005)
One of Europe's most splendid – you'd be hard pressed not to get caught up in the ten-day spate of parties and parades.
www.manchesterpride.com

Chichester

The Rox Festival
Rox is writ increasingly large on the alternative music scene. Saturday is rock- and punk-based; Sunday sees blues, soul, reggae and hip hop.
www.the-rox.com

Woodstock

Performing Arts Classic Proms
(Friday in August)
The Performing Arts Symphony fills Blenheim Palace with its Classic Proms night, culminating in a fireworks finale set to Tchaikovsky.

Dunoon, Cowal

Cowal Highland Gathering
(last weekend in August)
These spectacular highland games have been going since 1894, and now boast 3,000 competitors and a crowd of 20,000 that flocks to see men in tartan grunt as they hurl shot-puts, hammers and cabers.
www.cowalgathering.com

Edinburgh

Edinburgh International Festival
(14 August-4 September 2005)
Edinburgh Fringe Festival
(7-29 August 2005)
Edinburgh Film Festival
(17-28 August 2005)
Edinburgh becomes the envy of the world every August with its famous International Festival, of which one of its offshoots, the Fringe Festival, is the shining glory. Every possible type of theatre is on constant tap around town, with around 1,500 different shows.
www.edinburghfestivals.co.uk

London

Notting Hill Carnival
(28-29 August 2005)
A vibrant highlight of the London summer, but be prepared for crowds.
www.rbkc.gov.uk/NottingHill

SEPTEMBER

Brighton

National Speed Trials
(1-15 September 2005)
Car enthusiasts should check out this traditional spectacle as vehicles old and new pack out Madeira Drive.

Beamish, near Durham

Prize Leek Show & Harvest Festival
(first weekend in September)
The fattest leeks and marrows of the harvest season on display at the Beamish Museum.
www.beamish.org.uk

Bristol

International Festival of Kites
& Air Creations
(3-4 September 2005)
Up to 100,000 enthusiasts convene to see traditional, Chinese and funny-shaped kites let loose on the skies over the 850-acre Ashton Court Estate.
www.kite-festival.org

Soil Association's Organic
Food Festival
(3-4 September 2005)
Britain's largest celebration of organic food and drink sees the birth this year of the festival's fringe, which will include the Vienna Vegetable Orchestra: after the musicians have finished playing their vegetables, they cook the 'instruments' and feed them to the crowd.
www.organicfoodfairs.co.uk

London

Regent Street Festival
(4 September 2005)
A BBC music stage, food stalls, street performers, a 600-metre lawn and a Mad Hatter's tea party for the kids fill what is

normally one of London's most traffic-congested areas, between Oxford Circus and Piccadilly Circus. Proceeds go to the BBC Children in Need Campaign.
www.regentstreetonline.com

Ludlow
Ludlow Marches Food & Drink Festival (9-11 September 2005)
Food-centric Ludlow's festival is not to be missed. There will be middle white pig and Longhorn Beef, local handmade cheese, game, cider, perry, ale and much more.
www.foodfestival.co.uk

Woodstock
Great British Cheese Festival (24-25 September 2005)
Britain's largest cheese festival, with over 450 different cheeses laid out for your delectation in the grounds of Blenheim Palace.
www.cotswold.gov.uk

Durham
Durham Literature Festival (around 26 September-23 October 2005)
A wide range of readings, performances and lectures – last year's line-up included Ian Rankin, Iain Banks and performances of the *Vagina Monologues*. Check the website for exact dates.
www.literaturefestival.co.uk

OCTOBER

Manchester
Manchester Food & Drink Festival (1-11 October 2005)
Manchester's food scene has more and more to celebrate each year.
www.foodanddrinkfestival.com

Manchester Poetry Festival (around 7-16 October 2005)
Dotted with luminaries – last year included Carol Ann Duffy and Simon Armitage – the poetry festival offers readings, talks, workshops and so on.
www.manchesterpoetryfestival.co.uk

Brighton
Early Music Festival (1-16 October 2005)
One of the best opportunities in the UK to hear medieval music.
www.bremf.org.uk

Argyll, Scotland
Cowalfest (7-16 October 2005)
Ramblers will be in heaven during this ten-day event of 70 walks around the Cowal/Bute peninsula. Art installations and exhibitions are dotted about the area too.
www.cowalwalking.org

Windermere
Powerboat Record Attempts (11-15 October 2005)
The world's best powerboat racers zoom across the lovely Lake Windermere. They set off from the Low Wood Hotel and you can watch from various lakeside outposts.

NOVEMBER

Ludlow
Ludlow Medieval Christmas Fayre (last weekend in November)
Vendors in medieval garb set up shop outside Ludlow Castle. The Fayre aims to reconstruct a traditional Shropshire Christmas.
www.ludlowcraftevents.co.uk

Ottery St Mary, Devon
5th November celebrations
Every town has something to offer on Guy Fawkes Night, but few have this. Embracing a 17th-century tradition to ward off evil spirits, children, women and men hurtle through the streets clutching flaming, tar-soaked barrels.
www.tarbarrels.co.uk

DECEMBER

Durham
Christmas Festival (first weekend in December)